D1279045

Criminal Procedure

Criminal Procedure
A Worldwide Study

Edited by

Craig M. Bradley

Carolina Academic Press
Durham, North Carolina

Library of Congress Cataloging-in-Publication Data

Criminal procedure : a worldwide study / edited by Craig M. Bradley.
p. cm.
Includes bibliographical references and index.
ISBN 0-89089-670-4
1. Criminal procedure. 2. Comparative law. I. Bradley, Craig M.
K5401.C66 1999
345'.05—dc21 99-21670
CIP

Carolina Academic Press
700 Kent Street
Durham, North Carolina 27701
Telephone (919) 489-7486
Facsimile (919) 493-5668
E-mail: cap@cap-press.com
www.cap-press.com

Printed in the United States of America

Contents

Overview

Craig M. Bradley[1]

There have long been two main approaches to criminal procedure in most of the world: the inquisitorial (or civil law) system which originated and prevails on the European continent and the accusatorial (or common law) system, which prevails in Great Britain and its former colonies. Countries as diverse as Argentina, South Africa, Egypt, Russia, Japan and China all have criminal procedure systems derived from one of, or increasingly, a combination of, these models. In the traditional inquisitorial model, a theoretically neutral judicial officer conducts the criminal investigation and a judge (or a panel of judges), who has full access to the investigation file (dossier), determines guilt or innocence. The trial is a relatively brief and informal affair conducted by a presiding judge without a jury; the accused does not necessarily have a right not to testify and neither counsel has much of a role, if the defendant even has counsel. It is not necessarily continuous, may not require the attendance of all witnesses and can last in excess of a year. Both the behavior of the police and the conduct of judicial proceedings are governed by a more or less detailed code of criminal procedure.

The accusatorial model, by contrast, starts with a police investigation that is openly not neutral but rather, at least after it has focused on a suspect, is aimed at collecting evidence that will prove his guilt. Then an adversarial trial is held before a neutral decision maker, judge or jury, with no prior knowledge of the case, and no dossier. The defendant has a right to a jury. The attorneys conduct the trial, with each side attempting to convince the decision maker of the rectitude of her position. The trial is continuous and subject to the principle of orality (i.e. evidence against the defendant must be presented by live witnesses in court, subject to cross-examination). This common law system prevails in Britain and its former colonies, including Australia, Canada, and the United States. Traditionally, the common law system, as the name implies, was governed not by a code but by court-made law that developed incrementally over time.

Each system has certain advantages and disadvantages. The continental model has the distinct advantage of being much more efficient than the common law approach. The pretrial investigation is, at least in theory, more neutral, with the examining magistrate using the resources of the state to uncover all the evidence, wherever it may lead, in his search for truth. A jury need not be selected and the

---

1. I would like to thank Profs. Damaska and Frase as well as Judge Lensing for their comments on earlier drafts of this chapter.

trial is conducted expeditiously by a judge or judges, rather than by the opposing parties. The trial need not be continuous and may proceed sporadically over a year or more. Since the state is theoretically neutral, acting in the best interests of both parties, there is no need for a defense attorney (though defense attorneys are now required in most countries). Nor is live testimony necessarily required—witness' statements are contained in the dossier. Because the system works so efficiently, plea bargaining is not necessary to reduce the caseload, and is circumscribed.[2] That is, in the usual case, the prosecution must establish the defendant's guilt through the presentation of evidence, most of which is already in the dossier, even though, following that presentation, the defendant may choose to confess. Similarly, witnesses at trial, including experts, are witnesses of the court, not of the parties, and are questioned by the presiding judge in a way that is designed to produce balanced, rather than biased, testimony.

But these very advantages contain inherent weaknesses. If a defendant does not have a vigorous advocate who is prepared to examine the evidence solely from the defendant's point of view, then there is a greater chance that an innocent person may be convicted simply because, on the most obvious view of the evidence, he appeared to be the likeliest suspect. There is something too cozy, to one raised in the adversarial tradition, about an examining magistrate passing along a file, which sets forth a detailed case for the defendant's guilt, to her judicial colleague at the trial court.[3] The lack of a principle of orality and, possibly, even of a defense attorney, is further troubling. We are not comfortable, especially in the United States, where distrust of government is mother's milk, with a system in which government officials determine guilt with little input from the defendant's advocate, and none from ordinary citizens on a jury.[4]

The adversarial approach, with its trial by combat aura, seems more fair to us. According to adversarial theory, each side is represented by a committed advocate, fighting to the rhetorical death for his cause, with the final decision rendered, not by "faceless bureaucrats," but by a commonsense consensus of the defendant's peers. Every piece of the government's case, which is vigorously presented by the prosecuting attorney, is with equal vigor contested by the defendant's lawyer, with only the fittest evidence surviving. The inherent hostility that every government official feels toward those accused of crime is displayed openly and challenged, rather than operating *sub silente* against the defendant. Since this system mistrusts the government, the defendant is endowed with an entire quiver of rights that he may launch against the government at various stages of the proceeding, including rights against unreasonable searches, to silence, to counsel, and to confront witnesses against him. Breaches of these rights may cause a conviction to be reversed.

But this combative approach also contains inherent weaknesses. For one thing, the prosecution typically has greater resources than the defense, including a pro-

2. However, plea bargaining, as the chapters on Germany and Italy illustrate, has sprung up as a direct response to the more elaborate, and time consuming, rights structure that has developed in these countries.

3. "Americans tend to equate inquisitorial systems with coercive interrogation, unbridled search, and unduly efficient crime-control." Abraham Goldstein, *Reflections on Two Models: Inquisitorial Themes in American Criminal Procedure*, 26 Stan. L. Rev. 1009,1018 (1974).

4. However, juries are available in Spain, and in some parts of Russia, and most other civil law countries use "lay" judges—citizens who hear the evidence, have access to the dossier, and vote along with the professional judges. See §III in each chapter.

fessional police force to carry out investigations and a whole legal department of well-paid prosecutors who are generally skilled and enthusiastic. The defendant, by contrast, is likely to be represented by a court-appointed attorney or public defender, who will have few investigative resources, who may be overworked and underpaid, and who will probably believe that his client is guilty. (Obviously, belief in the defendant's guilt may affect the performance of a privately retained attorney but, one suspects, to a lesser extent.) Thus, despite defense counsel's stance of vigorous resistance to the prosecution's case, he may, for various reasons, not have his heart in it or have inadequate resources to properly defend the case.

Even more troubling, in their efforts to advance only the view of the case most favorable to their side, the attorneys may skew the truth-finding process. The attorney who is most skilled at choosing a favorable jury, at arguing to the jury, at locating witnesses, and at examining and cross-examining them is more likely to prevail, regardless of the defendant's actual guilt or innocence.

Finally, and most disturbing, this system, with its jurors, who must be laboriously picked , argued to, and instructed, and its detailed procedural rules (to ensure fair play), is extremely cumbersome. Given the limited resources available to the criminal justice system and the high cost of jury trials,[5] the majority of cases must be resolved *without*[6] a trial. Instead, a plea bargaining system induces defendants to give up their rights and plead guilty, frequently by offering to convict them of lesser crimes than they apparently committed, thus disadvantaging both the defendant and society.

In fact, the plea bargaining system is even worse than it appears on its face, because the weaker the prosecution's case, the more likely it is that a favorable bargain will be offered to the defendant. But "weakness" in the prosecution's case also correlates with innocence of the defendant. Thus, innocent defendants will, on average, be offered more attractive plea bargains than will the guilty. Of course, if the prosecutor believes the defendant to be innocent, he must dismiss the case. But there is undoubtedly a group of defendants whom the prosecutor believes to be guilty but who are not, to whom highly favorable plea bargains may be offered.

For example, in my experience as a prosecutor, it seemed that the most common non-drug felony in Washington, D.C. was armed robbery of a convenience store or of a person walking alone on the street. Frequently, the only witness was the victim. If the victim made a positive identification of the defendant, either after the crime or from a photo spread and lineup, the prosecutor would, absent any reason to mistrust the identification, prosecute the case. However, prosecutors are aware that eyewitness identifications are notoriously unreliable and that juries may mistrust them. Accordingly, favorable plea bargains in single witness armed robberies are almost always offered. A typical bargain in case where the victim was not harmed was a plea to unarmed robbery with no recommendation as to sentence. The judge would give such a defendant a much lighter sentence than if he

5. *But see* Albert Alschuler, *Implementing the Criminal Defendant's Right to Trial: Alternatives to the Plea Bargaining System*, 50 U. Chi. L. Rev. 931 (1983) (arguing that for about $850 million more than was then being spent on the criminal justice system, every defendant could be given a 3-day jury trial).

6. The National Center for State Courts found that in 13 jurisdictions surveyed, the percentage of felony cases resolved by jury trial ranged from a low of 2.1 in Texas to a high of 6.9 in Alaska. Jeffrey Abramson, *We, The Jury* 298 (1994).

had been convicted of armed robbery after a trial. Defense attorneys, who know from experience that their clients are likely to lie to them, will generally urge their client to accept a bargain even though the client denies the crime, unless the client can offer a convincing defense.[7] No doubt, some defendants who are innocent end up pleading guilty.

To a large extent, the differences in criminal procedure reflect the different fundamental assumptions underlying the inquisitorial and the common law system, as discussed in the book *Criminal Justice in Europe*.[8] In inquisitorial systems, "the state is the benevolent and most powerful protector and guarantor of public interest and can, moreover, be trusted to 'police' itself as long as its authority is organized in a way that will allow it to do so."[9] In accusatorial systems, by contrast, there is "a negative image of the state and a minimalist view of its functions."[10] Thus, the accusatorial approach to criminal justice emphasizes separation of powers and the resolution of a conflict between equal parties.[11] These traditions mean that, in the Netherlands, for example, with its inquisitorial approach, the "most salient" feature of pretrial process is the degree to which all parties co-operate in arriving at a pre-prepared version of [the truth] that is subsequently recorded in a case file or dossier as the basis for the coming trial. Professional investigators employed by the state—police, forensic psychiatrists, and scientists—are expected not only to do most of the work, but to do it in a detached and impartial way, an assumption that allows the defense to leave most matters of investigation to [state officials][12]…. Prosecutors see themselves as "magistrates…engaged in an impartial weighing of the different interests involved."[13]

Although it is not spelled out this explicitly, a similar philosophy underlies the approach to criminal justice in the countries presented in this book, such as Israel and France, that are the closest to the pure inquisitorial model.

In England and the other common law states, by contrast:

> Each party is responsible for developing evidence to support its arguments. Investigation is motivated by self-interest rather than public interest. There is no investigating judge to seek out "truth" and, despite official rhetoric about impartiality in prosecution, the concrete legal duties of police and prosecution lawyers do not extend to seeking out exculpatory evidence.[14] Indeed, what constitutes truth is subject to negotiation by the parties. Extensive plea bargaining simply produces an agreed approximation of events.… It is rare for any judicial authority to challenge these agreed assertions.[15]

---

7. In the United States, it is not necessary that the defendant admit his guilt to plead guilty, though the prosecutor must satisfy the court that there is an adequate factual basis for the plea. *North Carolina v. Alford*, 400 U.S. 25 (1970).

8. Christopher Harding, *et al.*, editors (1995).

9. Nico Jörg et al., *Are Inquisitorial and Adversarial Systems Converging? in Criminal Justice in Europe*, supra, n. 8 at pp. 41, 44.

10. *Id.* at 45.

11. *Id.*

12. *Id.* at 47.

13. Stewart Field, et al., *Prosecutors, Examining Judges, and Control of Police Investigations in Criminal Justice in Europe*, supra n. 8 at p. 236.

14. They do extend to turning over exculpatory evidence if it is found, however. *United States v. Bagley*, 473 U.S. 667 (1985).

15. *Id.* at 48.

Karl Llewellyn aptly described these two approaches as "parental" and "arm's length" systems of criminal procedure.[16]

Of course, in the diverse law of different countries, these differing approaches have never been as clear as the presentation of these archetypes would suggest-a point emphasized by Prof. Damaska 25 years ago.[17] In recent years, however, it would seem that the closure of the gap between the two models has been accelerating[18] Defense lawyers now play a more prominent role in civil law trials, and suspects have more rights for those lawyers to protect.[19] Though jury trials remain in disfavor on the continent, they are newly available in Spain and parts of Russia.[20] A right against self-incrimination at trial, and against involuntary confessions, is now generally enforced, and the use of an exclusionary rule to force police to obey rules governing searches and interrogations is increasingly being used in most of the countries discussed in this book.[21] *Miranda-type* warnings[22] are also widely required. [23]In short, defendants are entitled to more "rights" than they used to be, as well as to an advocate whose job it is to vindicate those rights.

By contrast, while inquisitorial systems have become more adversarial, many of the examples of movement in the English (and the U.S.) system toward the continental model are more in the realm of proposal than of fact.[24] However, one striking example is that, with the exception of the United States, all of the countries presented in the book, and most other countries, have a nationally applicable code of criminal procedure rather than relying on judicial precedents as the means of governing the criminal process.[25] The use of a code is in the civil law tradition. How-

---

16. K. Llewellyn, Jurisprudence at p. 444–450 (1962).

17. See, Mirjan Damaska, *Evidentiary Barriers to Conviction and Two Models of Criminal Procedure*, 121 U. of Pa. L.R. 506, 569 (1973).

18. On convergence between the United States and Germany, see Richard Frase & Thomas Weigend, *German Criminal Justice as a Guide to American Law Reform: Similar Problems, Better Solutions?*, 18 B.C. Int'l & Comp. L. Rev. 317 (1995); *see also* Craig Bradley, *The Failure of the Criminal Procedure Revolution* 95–143 (1993) (discussing how various common law and civil law countries are moving toward a U.S.-style, rights-oriented approach to rules governing criminal investigation).

19. See, e.g. the sections on Interrogations (§II C 1) and the role of defense lawyers (§III B 3) for each country discussed in this book. See also, Stewart Field & Andrew West, *A Tale of Two Reforms: French Defense Rights and Police Powers in Transition*, 6 Crim. L.F. 473 (1995).

20. Jury trials were used in Germany between 1890 and 1920 and in the Netherlands from 1811 to 1813. Stewart Field, et al., *Prosecutors, Examining Judges, and Control of Police Investigations, in Criminal Justice in Europe* 227, 229 (Phil Fennell et al. eds., 1995). Jury trials have also been abandoned in Japan and India, and are used increasingly rarely in England. Stephen J. Adler, *The Jury* at xv–xvi (1994). France has nine "jurors" in Assize Court whose function is similar to that of lay judges in Germany. France §III B. German, *Id.*

21. Nico Jörg et al., *Are Inquisitorial and Adversarial Systems Converging?*, in *Criminal Justice in Europe*, supra note 8, at 48, 54. See §II A 5 of each chapter.

22. A practice imported from England. *Miranda v. Arizona*, 384 U.S. 436, 486–88 (1966).

23. See §II C 1 of each chapter.

24. "Worries about the partisan nature of policing have led to calls for the introduction of a pretrial truth-finder such as the investigating judge (in England)." Jörg et al., *supra* note 8, at 49. Other "proposals include greater judicial involvement in indicating sentences and regulating deals." *Id.* at 52.

25. Another exception is Australia, where police are governed primarily by state, rather than federal, codes. Craig Bradley, *The Emerging International Consensus in Criminal Procedure*, 14 Mich. Jour. of Int'l Law 171, 191–95 (1993).

ever, the exposition of defendant's rights, and the limitation of police powers found in those codes reflect the common law's mistrust of government.

Until recently, the narrow attitude in the United States, encouraged by the Supreme Court, was that the inquisitorial system depended upon the use of terror and torture suggested by its namesake, the Spanish Inquisition. In a famous passage from *Murphy v. Waterfront Commission of New York Harbor,*[26] the Supreme Court described the Anglo-American privilege against self-incrimination as follows:

> It reflects many of our fundamental values and most noble aspirations: our unwillingness to subject those suspected of crime to the cruel trilemma of self-accusation, perjury or contempt; our preference for an accusatorial rather than an inquisitorial system of criminal justice; our fear that self-incriminating statements will be elicited by inhumane treatment and abuses....[27]

The notion that an "inquisitorial" system of justice was inextricably linked to torture and unreliable results, combined with Americans' traditional ignorance of other languages and cultures, and the elimination of states as "laboratories" due to the national uniformity of criminal procedure rules enforced by the U.S. Supreme Court, meant that Americans really had no sense of alternatives to the classic common law system. The U.S. adversarial/jury system, while often criticised, is nevertheless generally thought by American lawyers to be the only fair way to proceed.

For example, I and, I'm sure, most of my contemporaries managed to pass through three years of law school without ever finding out that jury trials do not generally occur in criminal cases on the European continent. One's attitude toward such Supreme Court cases as *Williams v. Florida*[28] and *Apodaca v. Oregon,*[29] in which the Court held that twelve-person juries and unanimous verdicts were not constitutionally required, (each of which might be considered a move in the inquisitorial direction) might well be influenced by the knowledge that perfectly civilized countries dispense with juries altogether.

In the 1970s, however, this insular attitude began to change, as scholars like Abraham Goldstein, John Langbein, Lloyd Weinreb, and Mirjan Damaska began to publish comparative articles in leading U.S. law journals.[30] Still, as noted, there is little in the case law to indicate that U.S. judges, and particularly the Supreme Court, have been influenced by the comparative material found in the legal literature. *Williams* and *Apodaca,* for example, while containing extensive discussions of the English roots of the American jury system, make no mention of continental

---

26. 378 U.S. 52 (1964).

27. *Id.* at 55; *accord Culombe v. Connecticut*, 367 U.S. 568, 581 (1961) (emphasis added): "This principle [against self-incrimination], branded into the consciousness of our civilization by the memory of the secret inquisitions, sometimes practiced with torture, *which were borrowed briefly from the continent*, during the era of the Star Chamber, was well known to those who established the American governments."

28. 399 U.S. 78 (1970).

29. 406 U.S. 404 (1972).

30. Abraham Goldstein & Martin Marcus, *The Myth of Judicial Supervision in Three "Inquisitorial" Systems: France, Italy, and Germany*, 87 Yale L.J. 240 (1977); John Langbein & Lloyd Weinreb, *Continental Criminal Procedure: "Myth" and Reality*, 87 Yale L.J. 1549 (1977); John Langbein, *Comparative Criminal Procedure* (1977); Mirjan Damaska, *supra*, n. 15. However, nearly four decades ago, Jerome Hall discussed the importance of the comparative approach in *The Fundamental Aspects of Criminal Law*, in *Essays in Criminal Science* 159 (Gerhard O.W. Mueller ed., 1961). *See also*, Karl Llewellyn, *supra* n. 14.

procedure.[31] Other developments in the United States, such as the requirement that exculpatory evidence be handed over to the defense[32] and, in some states, extensive mutual discovery obligations, have a decidedly continental tone, but do not appear to be based on knowledge of the continental system.[33]

Still, because of developments in the civil law world, it does seem that movement toward, though not full adoption of, the adversarial model, characterized by conviction-oriented police and prosecutors checked by aggressive assertion of rights by suspects and their attorneys, is the wave of the future. As societies become more diverse, the notion that government can be trusted to do right by minority groups is being considered increasingly anachronistic by reformers in civil law countries.[34] The more informal approach of the continental system may be well suited to a society in which everyone is of the same or similar background. But it is not suitable where minority groups are mistrusted by, and mistrust, the majority and its police forces.

In the absence of shared norms, formal delineation of rights by courts or legislatures, and their enforcement by counsel, are essential. It is impossible to claim, at this remove, that such concerns *actually motivated* reformers in these countries to move toward the adversarial approach. The availability of information about certain rights in other countries may also have led the ordinary citizen to demand similar consideration from his government. But, whatever the motivations of the decision-makers, the development of Spanish, Italian, Russian,[35] Dutch and even to some extent English[36] law governing police procedures in recent years has been in an adversarial, rights-oriented direction at the same time that the trend in most societies has been toward greater ethnic diversity. The movement of Europe toward political unity has also contributed, through the actions of the European Courts of Human Rights and of Justice, to increasing similarity among European systems.

---

31. *Williams,* 399 U.S. at 87–98; *Apodaca,* 406 U.S. at 407–10. Even in the 1980's Supreme Court Chief Justice Burger, Judge Malcolm Wilkey of the U.S. Court of Appeals for the D.C. Circuit, and others thought that "no other civilized nation in the world" had an exclusionary rule. Craig Bradley, *The Exclusionary Rule in Germany* 96 Harv. L. R. 1032 (1983).

32. *United States v. Bagley, supra,* n. 14. In the United States, at least, this obligation extends to impeachment evidence. *Id.* at 678. However, in neither the United States nor the Netherlands, are the police expected to search out all possibly exculpatory material nor necessarily even to hand over such material absent a request by the defense attorney. *Id.* at 681–82; *see also* Jörg et al., *supra* note 9, at 49.

33. Older features of the Anglo-American system such as "an organized police force and overt acceptance of police power to detain and interrogate in order to generate evidence against the suspect" originated with inquisitorial systems. Jörg et al., *supra* note 9, at 48; *see also* Goldstein, *supra* note 3, at 1018.

34. Kelk, in *Criminal Justice in Europe, supra* n. 8, at p. 6–7, points to "diminishing tolerance" in the Netherlands, which can "be seen in our attitude toward ethnic minorities," and concludes that this trend has contributed to "juridification" (the establishment of formal rules) "not because of any deep-seated interest in the classical values of liberty, equality and fraternity" but to establish "social control in the sense of supervision and one person watching another." Kelk makes it clear that he is opposed to this trend and objects to "lawyers who are guilty of unacceptable practice in attempting to use the rules of criminal procedure(for example with regard to procedural mistakes) for the benefit of their clients." *Id.* at 15. To an American lawyer, this is a very strange declaration.

35. As the authors of the Chapters on Spain, Italy and Russia all point out, recent reforms have moved toward the adversarial approach. This is also true in the Netherlands. Jorg et al., *supra* n. 8 at p. 53.

36. Bradley, *supra* note 18, at pp. 96–108.

This alone does not explain the trend toward the adversarial approach. However, when it recognized that, in an increasingly unified Europe, *every* ethnic and linguistic group—Germans, French and Belgians alike—will be a minority, it is not surprising that the trend is toward more formal and detailed declarations of rights.

By contrast, in still-insular China, relatively non-diverse Japan,[37] and in Israel, where there is a minority whose rights are not considered important by the majority, (albeit a minority who, from the Israeli point of view, is prone to criminal and terrorist acts) we continue to see more abbreviated, and frequently discontinuous, trials conducted by courts without juries or lay assessors, where the rights of defendants are not a major focus of the proceedings.[38] Argentina, by contrast, a country with a deplorable history of civil rights abuses, now has an absolute right to counsel[39] and adopted the principles of concentrated and oral trials in 1993,[40] though in other respects (no juries or lay assessors, trial conducted by presiding judge) it resembles the more traditional inquisitorial model.

In the end, the reader of this book will realize that the two model system has broken down. Most of the civil law countries discussed have moved away from the traditional inquisitorial model and toward the adversarial, though to different degrees and in different respects. A trend can be found, however, as to three of the most significant and controversial aspects of the Warren Court criminal procedure "revolution" in the United States. First, an exclusionary rule is increasingly employed to bar the prosecution's use of evidence obtained through police misconduct.[41] Second, police are generally required to give warnings as to rights to suspects prior to interrogation.[42] Third, defendants in criminal cases, at least where imprisonment is possible, are entitled to be represented by counsel and to have counsel appointed if they cannot afford to hire one.[43]

There are also two important trends which have not yet been adopted by the United States, in addition to the lack of a national code discussed above. The first is that, although exclusionary remedies are increasingly available in other countries, they are not mandatory, (except as to coerced confessions). Rather, they are in the discretion of the trial court,[44] based on various criteria such as whether use

---

37. Japan does have a small indigenous minority, the Ainu, plus a small number of ethnic Koreans neither of whom have any political power.

38. In Israel, there is not an absolute right to appointed counsel except in capital cases and in cases "punishable by a prison sentence of no less than ten years," no principle of orality, and discontinuous trials. Israel, §III B 3. In Japan, though counsel is generally provided, there is no jury or lay assessors, there is no principle of orality, the trials are discontinuous and may last for years. The conduct of the trial itself, however, is deemed "adversarial" by authors in both countries, in the sense that the lawyers, assuming the defendant has one, conduct direct and cross-examination themselves rather than the presiding judge assuming primary responsibility. For a discussion of Japanese criminal procedure, see, Hiroshi Oda, *Japanese Law* (1992) p. 398–403.

39. *Argentina*, §III B 3.

40. *Argentina*, §III B 1.

41. See §§II A 5 and II B 3 of each chapter. The precise rationale for evidentiary exclusion differs from country to country, however, and only the United States has a rule that is usually mandatory.

42. See §§ II B 1 and 2 of each chapter. As to this requirement, the United States Supreme Court was influenced by the British "Judges Rules" which have long required warnings as to the right to silence and that statements may be used against the declarant.

43. See §§ III B 1 and 3 of each chapter.

44. See §§II A 5 and II C 3 in each chapter. Italy purports to have a mandatory rule, but, "in practice this provision has limited effect." *Id.* The United States gets around the seeming harsh-

of the evidence would "bring the administration of justice into disrepute" (Canada) or "make the proceedings unfair." (England), and are used more sparingly. The second is that detailed rules for the length and conduct of interrogations are spelled out in many countries' codes.[45] In the United States, by contrast, after the *Miranda* requirements have been met, the Supreme Court has not further set rules governing interrogations, such as length and whether certain types of deceit may be employed, beyond the prohibition of coercive methods.(There is, however, a relatively recently imposed requirement that an accused must, "absent extraordinary circumstances" be brought before a judicial officer for a "probable cause hearing" within 48 hours of his arrest. It remains unclear how much of that 48 hours can be devoted to interrogation.)[46]

As for trials, it is interesting to see that jury trials are considered vehicles for reform in Spain and Russia despite their general disfavor elsewhere, including, to some extent, their mother country England, where only about a quarter of contested trials (not counting guilty pleas) were held before juries in 1996.[47] The "mixed" system, as used in Germany, Italy and other continental jurisdictions has much to recommend it. In the United States, the process of choosing, instructing, and arguing to a jury is very cumbersome. Moreover, the search for truth is impeded as extensive, and time consuming, evidence rules have been developed to decide what juries may and may not hear. Not surprisingly, countries that use juries also tend to step up plea bargaining because the system cannot afford to have too many of these extended proceedings. The more efficient mixed system, with lay people participating as "judges," is much less cumbersome and thus creates less pressure for guilty pleas, while maintaining citizen participation.[48] Moreover, juries are extremely malleable, thus placing too much weight on the skill, and resources, of lawyers in manipulating them, and too little weight on the actual guilt or innocence of the accused. The United States, most notably in the acquittals of O.J. Simpson, and the Los Angeles police who participated in the Rodney King beatings, is frequently plagued by what are widely considered unjust and incorrect jury verdicts.

A note on the theory and organization of this book.

This book is designed to serve as both a reference and a teaching tool. It is organized in outline form so that the reader/researcher can readily compare each aspect of one country's system with the same aspect of other countries'. All of the chapters use the same numbering system at least through the first Arabic number.

---

ness of rules excluding evidence whenever the police violate the rules by declaring that certain police conduct, such as searching an open field, does not fall within the Fourth Amendment at all, and consequently is not subject to court regulation. There is also an exception to the exclusionary rule for evidence seized pursuant to a defective judicial warrant. See § II A 4. Still evidentiary exclusion due to police rule-breaking seems to be a considerably more common phenomenon in the U.S. than in the other countries discussed in the book.

45. See §§ II C 1 and 2.

46. *County of Riverside v. McLaughlin*, 500 U.S. 44 (1991). Since the accused will normally (but not necessarily) receive counsel at this hearing, that will usually put an end to interrogation.

47. See *England* §III.

48. This view has previously been suggested in, Craig Bradley and Joseph Hoffmann, *Public Perception, Justice, and the "Search for Truth" in Criminal Cases*, 69 So. Cal. L. R. 1267, 1284, 1288–89, 1292 (1996).

Thus, for example, §II A1, "Stops" will be the same in each chapter, but not all chapters will have a subsection II A1a. This form will make comparison easier. It will also create some awkwardness since the outline is based on the American system and may have terms and concepts that cannot readily be applied to all of the other countries discussed. However, even though both terminology and practices will vary from country to country, the basic aspects of bringing a criminal case from investigation through prosecution are the same. That is, to follow the example, all police have occasion to stop and question suspects, whether or not that activity is subject to legal controls and regardless of what it is called. It thus seemed worth the price in awkwardness to require each chapter to proceed on the same chronological outline of the criminal process.

As to the countries chosen, the original criteria for including countries in the book were three: to achieve a global representation; to use countries where the law on the books could be thought to reasonably reflect the law in action; and to use authors who had previously published in English. However, as the book developed, it became apparent that there were not major differences in the approaches of all of the countries considered since, in addition to the countries discussed in this book, such diverse places as Japan, Australia, Egypt and Poland, all had systems that were based on the two European models. The Egyptian system, for example, is based on the French, and the Japanese represents a combination of German, American and French approaches.[49] While it would certainly be interesting to see how Egypt, for example, a former British colony and current Muslim state, or Japan, differ from the other countries, such chapters would likely, on the whole, have been rather similar to the others.

Accordingly, it seemed desirable to include two major countries—China and Russia—which are of great geo-political importance, but whose systems are not yet well developed, in terms of both exposition and provision of rights to criminal defendants. Those chapters serve as a counterpoint to the other, more advanced countries as well as providing information about two important countries as to which little material concerning criminal justice is available.

49. "Despite the overwhelming influence of American law on the Code, in practice, the influence of German law can still be seen in the implementation of the Code. This is particularly evident in the process of investigation as well as the reliance at the trial on written documents—dossiers prepared by the police and the public prosecutors." Oda, *supra*, n. 38 at p. 398. Indeed, the American influences are few, and the Japanese system also does not embrace recent German developments either. (ed.)

Criminal Procedure

Chapter 1

Argentina

Alejandro D. Carrió
Alejandro M. Garro

I. Introduction

The sources of law regulating the conduct of the police, prosecutors, judges, and other actors of the criminal justice system of Argentina are mostly found in the rules of criminal procedure, as embodied in codes adopted by each of its twenty-three provinces and those of the National (federal) Code of Criminal Procedure which came into force in 1993 (hereinafter also referred to as "CcrP"). Other areas of judicial and police activity are covered by rules of practice adopted by the criminal courts, and the regulations and customary practices of the different security forces.[1] Due to obvious limitations of space and time, the following discussion will focus on the federal rules of criminal procedure as embodied in the CcrP of 1993, with occasional references to any significant variations in state codes of criminal procedure. The CcrP is applied by the national criminal courts sitting in the City of Buenos Aires (the federal capital) in the prosecution of ordinary crimes, as well as by federal district courts sitting throughout the country in the prosecution of federal offenses.[2] In the rest of the country, state courts have the final word on the interpretation of state codes of criminal procedure.

The CcrP retains the basic features of criminal procedure shared by most Continental legal systems influenced by French law. Thus, the preliminary or pre-trial investigation is in the hands of a judge (*juez de instrucción*, hereinafter "investigative magistrate," "magistrate" or "judge"), though the public prosecutor may take over the investigation at any time if authorized to do so by the judge.[3] Since 1993, the adjudicatory function for a majority of crimes has been in the hands of panels

1. CcrP art. 4.
2. Most criminal offenses are tried by the regular state courts, or those national criminal courts sitting in the federal capital of Buenos Aires, or the place where the relevant events took place. Federal jurisdiction is limited to the prosecution of offenses involving the interests of the federal government or those dealing with specific acts of Congress to which exclusive federal jurisdiction is attached (e.g., drug-related offenses, infringement of copyright, trade-mark, patent of trade-mark and patent laws) CcrP art. 34.
3. CcrP art. 196.

of three professional judges in charge of determining both the facts and the law in a concentrated and oral trial.[4] Judgments rendered by the trial courts must include both a reasoned finding of facts leading to a verdict, as well as reasoned determination of the applicable law. Appeals against these judgments can be taken only on the alleged misapplication of the law and before the National Criminal Court of Cassation. This is a court of last resort on criminal matters that was established in 1993 when the CcrP entered into force.[5] Federal courts of appeal entertain challenges against the most significant interlocutory decisions rendered by investigative magistrates (e.g., whether the accused should stand trial, pre-trial detention decrees).

Although the Argentine legal system does not recognize the doctrine of *stare decisis*, the rules and practices followed in the criminal process are shaped, to a certain extent, by interpretative standards issued from time to time by state and federal courts. The Argentine constitutional system has placed in the hands of all judges, both at the federal and state level and regardless of their rank, the responsibility of passing judgment on the constitutionality of legislative and executive (police) action.[6] The rights guaranteed by the National Constitution protect individuals from the actions of both the federal and provincial governments.[7] State courts, applying their own constitutions, are entitled to grant criminal defendants more rights than those conferred by the federal Constitution, but this rarely happens. By and large, constitutional standards constraining police and prosecutorial activity throughout the country are formulated by the federal Supreme Court of Argentina ("Supreme Court"), whose decisions, while not formally binding except in the case at hand, enjoy a significant degree of persuasive authority. Although the power of judicial review is dispersed, in the sense that every judge in the country has the power to review the constitutionality of statutes and executive action, most of the constitutional jurisprudence shaping Argentine criminal procedure comes from the Supreme Court in its interpretation of Article 18 of the National Constitution ("CN"), which is the functional counterpart of the Fourth, Fifth, and Sixth Amendments to the Constitution of the United States. The pertinent part of Article 18 of the CN, reads thus:

No inhabitant may be punished without previous trial held in accordance with a law enacted before the trial, nor tried before special commissions or removed from the jurisdiction of the judges appointed by law before the commission of the crime. No one shall be required to provide evidence against himself or arrested except upon a written order issued by a competent authority. Defense in court of the

---

4. Crimes carrying a maximum penalty not exceeding three years of imprisonment are tried by single-judge courts. Law No. 24050, 7 Jan. 1992, *Organización y Competencia Penal* (Law on the Organization and Jurisdiction of Criminal Courts, hereinafter "OCP"), art. 2(c). See also Law No. 24121, 8 Sept. 1992, *Implementación y Organización del Proceso Penal Oral (Law on the Implementation and Organization of Oral Criminal Trials*, 51-D ADLA 3913, hereinafter ("IOPPO"), art. 8.

5. Law No. 23984, *Código Procesal Penal de la Nación* ("CcrP"), 51-C ADLA 2904.

6. *Ex Parte Sojo*, 32 Fallos 120 (1887); *Municipalidad de la Capital v. Elortondo*, 33 Fallos 162, 194-95 (1888); *Calvette*, 1 Fallos 340, 348 (1868).

7. *Constitución de la Nación Argentina* ("CN"), as amended and enacted on 23 Aug. 1994, replacing the text of the first National Constitution of 1853. The doctrine that all the rights and liberties set forth in the first chapter of the Constitution apply equally to the federal and provincial governments was affirmed early by the Supreme Court. *Hileret y Rodríguez v. Provincia del Tucumán*, 98 Fallos 20 (1903); *Pereyra Iraola v. Buenos Aires*, 138 Fallos 161 (1923).

person and of his rights shall not be violated. Dwellings, written communications and private papers shall not be violated or trespassed, and a statute shall determine in which cases and for what cause their search and occupation may take place. . .

References to Supreme Court cases in this report intend to illustrate the main jurisprudential trends followed by the Court during a certain period of time. Whereas this case-law serves as a guidance regarding the Court's willingness to implement constitutional principles, decisional law in Argentina, even if coming from the highest court, should not be construed, as an Anglo-American observer may casually assume, as a representation of the "good law" to be followed by the Court itself and other lower courts. The non-binding nature of judicial decisions and successive changes in the composition of the Supreme Court has shown that this is not necessarily the case. Thus the occasional need to indicate different judicial approaches that have been taken on the same point by Supreme Court and other appellate courts. The Supreme Court lacks the power to render advisory opinions and must await a ripe "case or controversy" involving a party who has suffered an injury in order to review the constitutionality of statutes or presidential decrees.[8] Decisions rendered by state and federal courts involving individual rights reach the Supreme Court only by way of an extraordinary writ of error (*recurso extraordinario*). This writ is available as of right and not as a matter of discretion; only against judgments of the highest provincial or federal courts that qualify as "final" and implicate the interpretation of a constitutional or federal question;[9] and as long as the decision on appeal allegedly infringes, or refuses to recognize, a constitutional right of the appellant.[10] Numerous obstacles of an institutional nature have prevented a more active intervention of the Supreme Court in the shaping of minimum constitutional standards for the preliminary stage of the criminal process.

As anticipated, the Argentine criminal process distinguishes between a pre-trial investigatory stage conducted by an investigative magistrate, and a trial properly speaking, which is conducted by a different court. Unfortunately, many rulings handed down by investigative magistrates during the course of a pre-trial criminal investigation do not constitute "final" judgments, the Supreme Court of Argentina has refused to review the constitutionality of many steps taken by the police during a criminal investigation until after conviction.[11] Thus, the Court has held that

---

8. *Montes de Oca v. Fisco Nacional*, 1 Fallos 455 (1865) (On the need for an actual and ripe controversy for the exercise of judicial review.)

9. The appellate jurisdiction of the Supreme Court of Argentina is regulated in Article 14 of Law 48 of 1863, [1852-1880] ADLA 363, which was modeled in turn after Section 25 of the 1789 Judiciary Act of the United States.

10. It follows that the Supreme Court lacks jurisdiction to review a decision affirming constitutional rights. *Bartra Rojas*, CSJN, 305 Fallos 913; *Spangemberg*, 256 Fallos 54. For cases in which the Supreme Court has inexplicably accepted cases for review despite the fact that the decision on appeal actually affirmed the constitutional rights of criminal defendants, see *Todres*, 280 Fallos 297 (1971). See also, 252 Fallos 195; 253 Fallos 31; 304 Fallos 152-S; 307 Fallos 2483.

11. *Ordoñez*, CSJN, 223 Fallos 128 (1952); *Petre*, CSJN, 234 Fallos 450 (1956); Martínez, CSJN, 245 Fallos 384 (1959); 305 Fallos 1022; 306 Fallos 1783; 307 Fallos 1186-S, 1615, and 2348 (refusing to examine the constitutionality of pre-trial detention decrees); *Banco Provincia v. Dickin Neville*, 259 Fallos 26 (1963) (refusing to examine the constitutionality of court rulings extending the secrecy of the investigative steps taken by the examining magistrate during the early steps of the investigation); *Gomez*, 118 LL 164 (1964) (the finality requirement is not met when the challenged court ruling summoned a suspect to appear before the court for interrogation); *Balestra*, CSJN, 311 Fallos 565 (refusing to review a decision that turned down a recusal).

the constitutional validity of a decision of the investigative magistrate denying the defendant the right to confront witnesses, or providing for some evidentiary measures during the investigation, are beyond the appellate jurisdiction of the Supreme Court.[12] Only recently, and by way of exception, the Supreme Court has accepted for review early constitutional challenges against an assertion of jurisdiction by a court[13] and a pre-trial detention decree (*auto de prisión preventiva*). In those exceptional instances, the Court held that such interlocutory decision, though not formally "final," may be treated as such due to the irreparable nature of the damage suffered by the detainee.[14]

Moreover, the mere fact that a constitutional issue implicates the interpretation of a rule of criminal procedure has lead the Supreme Court, more often than not, to dismiss an appeal on the ground that the challenged decision involves a mere procedural issue, rather than a substantive federal (constitutional) question suitable of extraordinary review by the Supreme Court.[15] After many years of military government, when Argentina returned to constitutional rule in 1983, the Supreme Court became more receptive to review constitutional standards in the criminal process. However, a long-standing tradition of non-review explains the relative paucity and analytical shortcomings of Argentine constitutional jurisprudence over significant areas of due process.

Under the American Convention on Human Rights, ratified by Argentina in 1984,[16] the jurisprudence elaborated by the Inter-American Commission on Human Rights ("Inter-American Commission") and the Inter-American Court of Human Rights ("Inter-American Court") is becoming increasingly influential in establishing minimum standards of due process.[17] According to the 1994 amendments introduced to the Argentine Constitution, the American Convention, as well

---

But see, *Ojeda*, CSJN, 300 Fallos 857 (holding that the forceful removal of a defense counsel and his replacement for a public defender, on the alleged incompetency of the former, results "in an undue restriction to the right to counsel leading to irreparable damage, especially in criminal proceedings").

12. *Arnold*, CSJN, 256 Fallos 28; *Suárez*, CSJN, 280 Fallos 121; *Escobar*, CSJN, 247 Fallos 86.

13. *Videla*, CSJN, 306 Fallos 2101; *Tiscornia*, CSJN, 310 Fallos 1623. For a similar rationale supporting review of decisions dismissing the prosecution of a case on the ground that the alleged facts do not constitute a criminal offense, see *Paskavan*, CSJN, 107 ED 784; *Arisnavarreta*, CSJN, 306 Fallos 344; *Zadoff*, CSJN, 307 Fallos 784.

14. *Gundín*, CSJN, JA, 1991-III-518; *Chanfreau*, CSJN, 310 Fallos 2246; *Kacoliris*, CSJN, 11 May 1993, LL, 18 Nov. 1993; *Martínez de Hoz*, LL, 1993-C-194.

15. *CAEME*, CSJN, 250 Fallos 108; *Trisi de Aldecoa*, CSJN, 258 Fallos 62 (refusing to review constitutional challenges against pre-trial detention decrees on the ground that they implicate procedural issues beyond the appellate jurisdiction of the Court). But see, *Santamaría*, 237 CSJN 60; *Iriart*, CSJN, 307 Fallos 1039, in which the Court saw fit to admit review despite the fact that the issues involved the proper application of procedural rules.

16. Law No. 23054, ALJA, 1984-A-11.

17. Thus, Article 8 of the American Convention provides minimum standards that are critical to the fairness of criminal procedure (e.g., the defendant's right to a hearing, to be presumed innocent, and to be assisted by legal counsel of his own choosing). Whereas the Inter-American-court has had few opportunities to elaborate on the types of procedural protections that the American Convention accords criminal defendants, the Inter-American Commission has applied Article 8 to find member states in violation of the Convention. See, e.g., IACHR, Resolution 74/90 (Héctor Gerónimo López Aurelli, Argentina), 4 October 1990, 1990-91 *Annual Report of the Inter- American Commission of Human Rights*. See also *Giroldi*, CSJN, 318 Fallos 514 (1995).

as other human rights treaties, enjoy constitutional rank.[18] Moreover, Argentina accepted the compulsory jurisdiction of the Inter-American Court of Human Rights ("Inter-American Court"), whose judgments are final and enforceable as those rendered by domestic courts.[19] Thus, the discussion in this chapter will make occasional references to the limits on the police and prosecutorial powers of the members states to the American Convention on Human Rights.

II. Police Procedures

A. Arrest, Search and Seizure Law

1. Stops and 2. Frisks

Article 18 of the CN provides that "no one. . . shall be arrested except upon a written order issued by a competent authority." This seems to provide constitutional protection against all kinds of arbitrary "arrests." Yet, the rules of criminal procedure and the courts have failed to draw fine distinctions and connections between the different levels of intrusion involved in every imaginable situation of police-citizen contact and the constitutional protection that such intrusion may deserve. Thus, the rules of criminal procedure give the police the power to stop, detain, or arrest any one in a public place without a written order issued by a competent authority, as long as there are strong indications of guilt (*indicios vehementes de culpabilidad*) and other exigent circumstances defined by statute.[20] Stopping a person in a public place and putting a few questions to him or her is not required to be justified by any level of suspicion under Argentine law.

Moreover, statutes providing for the organization of the police and security forces authorize transitory restrictions of personal freedom for the alleged purpose of allowing routine identity checks (*averiguación de antecedentes*). Although the constitutionality of this statute has been controversial,[21] police officers retain the authority to detain any person for as long as ten hours, whenever there are "well-grounded reasons to presume that a person has committed or may commit a criminal offense or minor infraction and such person fails to establish her personal

---

18. CN, art. 75.22.

19. American Convention, art. 63.

20. CcrP art. 284: "Police officers and personnel have the duty to detain, even without a judicial order: 1) Those who attempt to commit a crime subject to compulsory prosecution which is punished with imprisonment, at the moment they are ready to commit it; 2) those who flee, being legally detained; 3) by way of exception, those against whom there are strong indications of guilt, whenever there is imminent danger of escape or a serious hindering of the investigation, and for the sole purpose of carrying the suspect before the judge who will decide on the detention; and 4) those who are caught committing a crime subject to compulsory prosecution punished with imprisonment." The term "crime subject to public prosecution" (*delitos de acción pública*) refers to those offenses which the prosecutor has the duty to investigate on its own motion, as opposed to those in which the dignity or reputation of the victim are involved (e.g., rape, sexual assault, slander), requiring the complaint of the aggrieved party for the prosecution to go forward. Argentine Criminal Code, arts. 71-76.

21. Bidart Campos & D. Herrendorf, *Detener personas en averiguación de antecedentes por orden policial es inconstitucional*, ED, 1 March 1990; *La Nación*, 10 June 199, *La detención de personas por la policía* (editorial); *La Prensa*, 12 June 1990, *La detención de personas* (editorial).

identity."[22] Even if a stop or a brief detention is devoid of any justification, any judicial challenge is likely to become moot by the time a court is ready to rule on the question. The potential exclusion of the evidence gathered or statements taken as a result of an illegal stop or arrest will be discussed further below.

Outside the realm of routine identity checks, a restriction of personal freedom in a public place requires a showing of "strong indications of guilt," an expression that may indicate something more than a mere suspicion of involvement in the commission of a crime but that has not been subject to judicial articulation.

Stops of vehicles. The police may stop vehicles randomly and at any time; no particular level of suspicion seems to be required. This issue is not covered by the rules of criminal procedure and there is a dearth of case law on the subject. In *Daray*, three members of the Supreme Court noted in passing and without much discussion that "it is beyond dispute that security officers, as part of their functions, have the power check routinely the vehicle's identification and the driver's license."[23] Presumably this dictum does not go as far as to authorize the police to search a car without some showing that criminal activity is afoot, but the courts are yet to establish clear limits in this regard.

The absence of a clear standard on searches and seizures is reflected in a decision rendered by the Supreme Court right before this chapter went to press. In *Fernández Prieto*, decided by the Supreme Court on November 12, 1998 (Docket No. F. 140. XXXIII, still unpublished), police officers had stopped a vehicle driven by the defendant and two youngsters in the downtown area of a populated city at around 7 p.m. The vehicle was stopped, according to the officers, due to the "suspicious attitude" of the occupants, without further elaboration. The occupants were ordered out of the car and a search of the vehicle and the trunk revealed the presence of a weapon, bullets and marijuana. The Supreme Court affirmed the conviction of the occupants of the car on charges of possession of drugs, holding that the warrantless search of the vehicle was justified on grounds of "urgency" and the difficulties in obtaining a warrant before stopping a moving vehicle. Five out of the nine justices (Justices Nazareno, Moliné O'Connor, Belluscio, López y Vázquez) made no effort to question the reasons advanced by the police for qualifying as

22. Organic Law of the Federal Police (*Ley Orgánica de la Policía Federal*), art. 5.1: "Aside from the circumstances set forth in the Code of Criminal Procedure, [the federal police] shall have no authority to detain persons without an order issued by a competent judicial authority. However, whenever there are duly grounded reasons to presume that a person has committed or may commit a criminal offense or a minor infraction and such person fails to establish her personal identity, such person may be taken into custody to the pertinent police station. Notice shall be given to the competent correctional court, and the detainee may be held for the minimum amount of time required to establish her identity, which in no case shall exceed ten hours. The detainee shall be allowed to establish immediate communication with a family member or a person of his trust, for the purpose of making that person know of the situation. Those who are kept for identification purposes may not be placed together with, or in places kept for, those who have been detained for crimes or minor infractions" ((as amended by Law 23950, 11 Sept. 1991, 1991-B ALJA- 1610). Before the adoption of this amendment in 1991, the maximum period of detention for routine identity checks had been established in twenty-four hours. The original bill reducing the maximum period to ten hours had been subject to a partial presidential veto (Decree 1203/91), which increased the period to sixteen hours. Congress finally prevailed by insisting with a two-third vote of both houses that the period of detention should not exceed ten hours. *Ambito Financiero*, 15 Aug. 1991, at 26, *El Congreso rechazó el veto de Menem a la ley de detención.*

23. *Daray*, CSJN, LL, 1995-B-349 (JJ. Nazareno, Moliné O'Connor, and Levene, concurring).

"suspicious" the driving of a car in a populated area at rush hour. The dissenters (Justices Petracchi, Bossert and Fayt) harshly rebuked the majority opinion, which failed to provide any explanation for the Court's failure to consider the statutory requirement of "strong indications of guilt," or the constitutional standard set forth in *Daray* to the effect that Article 18 of the Constitution calls for a showing of probable cause or some reasonable ground justifying arrests, searches and seizures.

3. *Arrests*

Neither the courts or the rules of criminal procedure define the term arrest or elaborate on the meaning of "strong indications of guilt" (*indicios vehementes de culpabilidad*),[24] the line between "strong indications" and other levels of suspicion falling short of that standard never having been drawn. There is no case-law specifying the extent of intrusion or restraint into a person's freedom that qualifies as an "arrest." The absence of an elaborate standard is due to the lack of effective procedural remedies to review the constitutionality of any deprivation of freedom that extends for less than 10 hours (in the case of routine identity checks) and the inability of the writ of habeas corpus to redress the arbitrariness of an arrest as long as it has been ordered by any "competent authority." Moreover, statements or objects obtained as a result of an illegal arrest, unlike those obtained as a result of an illegal search, have not been excluded from evidence.

a. *Arrest warrants.* Article 18 of the CN provides that "dwellings, personal correspondence and private documents shall not be violated or trespassed, and a statute shall determine in which cases and under what circumstances their search and occupation may take place." The rules of criminal procedure adopted by the provinces and the federal district are meant to implement Congress' intent as to which searches and seizures are lawful. Under the federal rules of criminal procedure, the issuance of a judicial order in the form of a search warrant (*autorización de registro domiciliario*) is required only for arrests conducted in the home or private dwelling of the detainee or in someone else's home.[25] The law does not require the issuance of an arrest warrant, but rather of a search warrant, even if the sole purpose of the warrant is to detain an individual to be found in a private dwelling. The officer carrying out the arrest must secure a search warrant indicating the place and time of the search. The search warrant should also refer to the "strong indications of guilt" supporting the arrest and why the arrest is vital to the success of the investigation. However, the lack of an effective mechanism of enforcement has not allowed a strict observance of the warrant requirements.

4. *Searches*

Article 18 of the CN provides that "dwellings, personal correspondence and private documents shall not be violated or trespassed, and a statute is to determine

24. CcrP art. 284.3.

25. CcrP art. 224: "Whenever there are grounds to presume that the elements of the crime may be found at a certain place, or that the accused (*imputado*) or a person suspected of having committed a crime may be found therein, the judge shall order in writing, the search of that place. . ."

in what cases and under what circumstances their search and occupation shall be permitted." Noticeably, this constitutional provision does not set a standard of "reasonableness" or any other similar formula aimed at validating some searches and excluding others. The "statute" setting forth the cases in which searches and seizures are to be lawfully conducted is found in the rules of criminal procedure adopted by each state and by the federal district, as embodied in their codes of criminal procedure. However, neither these rules nor court decisions have elaborated on the type of action that qualifies as a "search" nor on whether the protection granted to a private dwelling is to be extended to other areas where individuals place a similar expectation of privacy. Some decisions of the criminal court of appeals sitting in the city of Buenos Aires have shown some willingness to extend the constitutional protection to areas which are not expressly mentioned in Article 18 of the CN. Thus, it has been held that a locker assigned to the defendant by his employer for him to keep his personal belongings is entitled to a protection analogous to that conferred to a private dwelling, because "the concept of 'dwelling' and the requirement of a judicial warrant permitting entrance by the authorities should not be construed narrowly to the extent that they purport to implement constitutional guarantees (art. 18, CN)."[26] However, the constitutional protection against illegal or arbitrary searches, to the extent that it has been granted by the Supreme Court and by the Criminal Court of Cassation, has been confined to searches of homes or private dwellings, personal written communications, and private documents, these being the items expressly mentioned in Article 18 of the CN.

In *Fabro* the Supreme Court dealt with the constitutionality of the search of an automobile from which the police seized a forged certificate of title.[27] It was disputed whether such document had been voluntarily given to the police or was found as the result of a forceful search by the police. In any event, the Supreme Court upheld that the seizure of the certificate of title on the ground that such a document "cannot be considered as one of the private documents referred to in Article 18 of the Constitution, because it is a public instrument that must be exhibited upon request of a competent authority."[28] The Court also stated that assuming the document had not been voluntarily delivered to the police, in any event the defendants had failed to establish that the interior of an automobile deserves the same constitutional protection as the home.[29] A similar question was brought before the Court in *Aguirre et al.*, although the main issue in this case focused on a warrantless search conducted in a car parked in a parking lot close to the hotel where the defendant was staying as a guest.[30] The Court upheld the validity of the search, noting that the petitioner "failed to establish that a garage located in a parking lot used by all the guests, the access to which was subject to the consent of the hotel

---

26. See *Ayala*, CNCrimCorr.-IV, LL, 1990-E-543. On a related issue of the extension of the right to privacy, *see Pierro*, Supreme Court of the Province of Mendoza, JA, 1992-I-443 (holding that personal letters seized by the police may be read only by the investigative magistrate in charge of the case).

27. *Fabro*, CSJN, 26 Feb. 1991, LL, 1191-E-351 (with note by Nemesio González).

28. Ibidem, paragraph 7.

29. Ibidem, paragraph 8 ("Petitioner failed to establish that the procedural rules, national or provincial, applicable to the search of a private dwelling and to searches of a person should also apply to the search of an automobile. . .").

30. *Aguirre et al.*, CSJN, 23 Feb. 1992, Writ of Error (R.E.) No. A-643, XXIII.

owner, were to be included within the notion of 'dwelling' referred to in Article 18 of the Constitution."[31] A more recent decision of the Criminal Court of Cassation sweepingly held that the search of a car lacks the protection that the Constitution only provides to a private dwelling.[32]

a. *Search Warrants.* Searches in private dwellings must be conducted in daylight hours, except in cases where delay may result in the loss of the evidence, or when the affected party consents to an entrance during the night.[33] The requirement of a judicial warrant for entering into a private dwelling may be obviated only in the presence of exigent circumstances, such as the police being in hot pursuit, or the hearing of voices asking for help from inside the house.[34] The search warrant must be in writing, specifying the time and place of the search and the officers authorized to carry it out.[35] Such officers are required to produce a report of the events, listing the evidence gathered during the search.[36] The requisition and seizure (*secuestro*) of a person's effects or possessions also calls for the issuance of a written and reasoned judicial warrant, which must be based in turn on "sufficient reasons to believe that [the suspect] hides in his body objects related to the crime."[37]

---

31. The Court took pains to distinguish this case from one in which the incriminating evidence would have been seized from a private garage guarded by a key and which was functionally attached to the hotel room.

32. *Kolek*, CNCP-III, 25 April 1994, LL, 1994-E-129 (with note by Hernán Gullco).

33. CcrP art. 225: "When the search is to be carried out in a private dwelling, it must be conducted between sunrise and sunset. However, the search may be conducted at any time if the interested party or her representative consents thereto, or in cases of extreme gravity and urgency, or when the pubic order is endangered."

34. CcrP art. 227: "Notwithstanding the foregoing rules, the police may search a private dwelling without a judicial warrant when: 1) A fire, explosion, flooding or any other catastrophe threatens the life of its occupants. 2) It is reported that suspicious persons were seen entering the dwelling with the outward motive of perpetrating a crime. 3) A person who is chased and accused of having committed a crime enters into the dwelling. 4) Voices are heard from inside the dwelling crying for help or announcing that a crime is being committed therein."

35. CcrP art. 224, second paragraph: "The judge may avail herself of the public force and proceed personally with the search, or delegate this function to police officers. In such a case the search order shall be issued in writing, indicating the place, date and time at which it shall be carried out, and the name of those commissioned to perform it. A transcript shall be prepared pursuant to articles 138 and 139."

36. CcrP art. 228: "The search warrant shall be notified to the occupant or possessor of the dwelling where the search is to be performed. If this person is not found, the search shall be notified to the person in charge of the dwelling, or to any person of legal age who is found in the place, preferably to members of the occupant's family. The person who has been thus notified shall be invited to be present while the search is being conducted. If no person is found, this circumstance shall be noted in the transcript. Once the search has been completed, the results of the search shall be noted in the transcript, indicating those events that are useful to the investigation. The transcript shall be signed by all those present. If someone refuses to sign it, the reasons therefore shall be noted in the transcript."

37. CcrP art. 230: "The judge shall order the requisition of a person by virtue of a reasoned ruling, as long as there are sufficient reasons to believe that he hides in his body objects related to the crime. The person may be invited to exhibit those objects before the requisition is carried out. Requisitions shall be carried out separately, paying respect to people's dignity. If a woman is the subject of a requisition, it shall be carried out by another woman. A transcript of the proceedings of requisition shall be signed by the person who is subject to the requisition, and if he refuses to sign it, the reasons should be noted thereon. In the absence of justified reasons, the refusal to submit to the requisition shall not impede the same to be carried out."

(i) Article 224 of the CcrP indicates that a written and reasoned decision (*auto fundado*) by the investigative magistrate is required for all searches, but the articles that follow provide that a search warrant signed by a judge is required only for searches of homes or enclosed structures intended to be used as a private residence (*morada*).[38] The same provision vaguely defines what is needed to support the issuance of a search warrant, that is, "reasons to believe" that objects pertaining to a crime or a person suspected of having committed a crime may be found in such a place. The rules fail to provide any further indication as to the reasonableness of those motives or the credibility of the sources of information on which the warrant is based. As a matter of practice, investigative magistrates simply fill out a form with broad statements conferring wide discretion to the police officers in charge of the search.

(ii) The federal rules of criminal procedure call for an indication of the place and time at which the search is to be conducted, but they fail to require a particularized description of the person or objects to be seized. The absence of a wealth of judicial decisions on the legal sufficiency of a search warrant suggests that the propriety of the information on which such warrant is based rests entirely at the discretion of the issuing magistrate. This approach was confirmed in *Torres*, in which a state judge from the city of Rosario with jurisdiction over petty crimes (*faltas*) issued a warrant authorizing the search of Torres' home, whom the warrant identified as "a well-known offender for illegal possession of drugs."[39] The warrant stated that "as per information that has been received. . .[Torres] carries with him objects of dubious origin." The warrant was issued despite the state court's evident lack of jurisdiction, since drug-related offenses are under the exclusive jurisdiction of the federal courts.[40] Once the police searched for and found in Torres' home the drugs they were looking after, the search was suspended and a new warrant was obtained from a federal court with proper jurisdiction. Torres was tried and convicted for illegal possession of drugs. He challenged the constitutionality of the original search on the ground that it was issued by a court without jurisdiction and that the warrant failed to indicate the facts and circumstances pointing to any serious level of certainty as to Torres' connection with a criminal activity. The Supreme Court affirmed Torres' conviction without examining the sufficiency of the information on which the warrant was based. As to the lack of jurisdiction of the state court to issue the warrant, the Supreme Court held that the state court had the power to order the search of any dwelling where criminal activity was presumably

38. In *Bredeston*, CSJN, 311 Fallos 2790, the Supreme Court held that a search conducted in the facilities of a club is a search "conducted in a public place which, by its very nature, is not protected by the constitutional guarantee of inviolability of a private dwelling."

39. *Torres*, CSJN, 19 May 1992 (J. Petracchi dissenting), 148 ED 720, JA, 1992-IV-99 (with note by Alberto Garay).

40. As of many years ago, drug offenses are regulated by federal law, and drug charges confer exclusive subject matter jurisdiction to the federal courts. The state court that issued the warrant (*Juzgado de Faltas de 2a Nominación de Rosario*) has jurisdiction to deal, inter alia, with violations of a provincial law punishing with a fine "any person who by acquiring or receiving, without verifying their legitimate origin, objects whose quality, price, or the circumstances in which they are being offered, give rise to suspicions that they are the product of a criminal offense." Law No. 3743 (Santa Fe), art. 89(b). The search was carried out, however, by the police unit in charge of investigating drug offenses (*Sección Estupefacientes de la Unidad Regional II de Rosario*). In addition to the drugs found in Torres' home, police officers also seized a cassette recording, which was returned to Torres once it was established that it was his.

afoot. The Court added that if the search turns up with evidence pointing to the perpetration of a criminal offense that is beyond the jurisdiction of the issuing court, this should not necessarily lead to the suppression of such evidence.[41] A dissenting opinion noted the absence of data in the warrant that would allow the Court to assess the credibility of the information received by the issuing court. In the absence of such information, added the dissent, there can be no meaningful judicial review of the constitutionality of the search.[42] The majority opinion in *Torres* leads to the conclusion that there is no effective way to secure judicial review of the weight or credibility of the information upon which a search warrant is based. By way of exception, a more recent decision handed down by the Court of Appeals on Criminal and Economic matters (*Cámara de Apelaciones en lo Penal Económico*) held null and void a search warrant based on information from the police officers which the issuing magistrate had found "sufficiently persuasive." The court of appeals noted that the federal rules of criminal procedure requires the issuance of a search warrant to be based on "reasons to believe that criminal elements could be found in such a place." The level of justification called for by that provision, according to the Court of Appeals, requires the warrant to include some indicia of reliability beyond the subjective perception of the issuing court.[43]

(iii) *Execution of warrants.* As noted, searches of dwellings must be conducted in daylight hours, except in "most serious and urgent" cases (e.g., whenever delay may result in the loss of evidence and the police do not have the time to obtain a warrant) or if the affected party consents to an entrance during the night.[44] It has been also noted that the rules of criminal procedure do not elaborate on the conduct that the police must observe while carrying out a search nor on the particularities of the place or persons to be searched or things to be seized. Accordingly, there is no limit as to what the police can look at and gather once they are inside the dwelling, except those set at the discretion of the issuing magistrate. Police officers in Argentina, as previously noted, have always assumed the authority to conduct searches incidental to an arrest, and there are no judicial decisions disputing those powers.

The occupants of the house must be given notice of the search,[45] though this has not been interpreted as a requirement to knock and announce the presence of the police before entering a dwelling. There are, however, contrary and isolated opinions on this matter. A concurring opinion in *Fiorentino* stated that if consent to the search is to be found, such a consent must be "verifiably given before the representatives of the public authority enter into the dwelling."[46] More specifically, the Federal Court of Appeals of La Plata held that if a search is conducted at night under exigent circumstances, the validity of the search requires the police to knock

41. *Torres*, supra, paragraph 8 of the majority opinion.

42. Ibidem, J. Petracchi, paragraph 13 of his dissenting opinion ("If judges were exempted from the duty to examine the reasons and background supporting a warrant request by the administrative authorities, and if they were authorized to issue search warrants without expressing the reasons for it, then any judicial intervention would be meaningless, because it would fail to provide any guarantee to secure the inviolability of a home.").

43. *Helzer*, CNPenal Economico-A, 17 Oct. 1996, JA, No. 6032, 9 April 1997, at 64 (Judge Romero dissenting).

44. CcrP art. 225.

45. CcrP art. 228.

46. *Fiorentino*, 307 Fallos 1752, 1766 (J. Petracchi, concurring).

and announce themselves as such.[47] Although the suspect or occupants of the house must be invited to attend the search, the validity of the search is not made to depend on such attendance. If the affected party cannot be found, the police will conduct the search in the presence of witnesses. A report of what transpired at the search and of the evidence seized must be submitted by the officer in charge of the search, who need not be the prosecutor or a judicial officer.

(iv) *Wiretaps.* Article 18 of the CN guarantees the inviolability of the "dwelling,"

"personal correspondence," and "private documents." In turn, the rules of criminal procedure authorize a court to intercept and seize any written communication sent by or addressed to the accused, as long as the court deems such interception "useful for the determination whether a crime has been committed."[48] Similar grounds would entitle an investigative magistrate to authorize the interception of telephone communications.[49] However, letters or documents sent or delivered to defense counsel and which are related to his or professional role in the case are clearly and expressly excluded from the court's interference.[50]

Article 19 of the CN provides the right to privacy with express constitutional support:

"Private actions of persons which in no way offend the public order and morality and which do not harm a third party are reserved solely to the judgment of God and are exempted from the jurisdiction of the judges. No inhabitant of the nation shall be required to do what the law does not command, nor barred from doing what the law does not prohibit."

In *Fiorentino*, the Supreme Court made reference in one passage to the connection between the constitutional protection against warrantless searches of private dwellings and the right to privacy.[51] However, the courts have not developed a constitutional jurisprudence aimed at extending the protection expressly granted to private dwellings and private documents to other spaces or communications surrounded by a reasonable expectation of privacy.[52]

b. *Warrantless Searches.* As noted, a search warrant is required only to conduct a search in a private dwelling.[53] This requirement may be obviated only in the pres-

---

47. *Iurato*, CfedLa Plata-III, 26 April 1994, JA, 1994-IV-3 (with note by Alejandro Carrió).

48. CcrP art. 234.

49. CcrP art. 236. Divulging the contents of a telephone conversation without the consent of the parties is impermissible. But see *L.F.*, CNCrimCorr, JA, 1981-II-333 (revealing what has transpired in a .

50. CcrP art. 237.

51. *Fiorentino*, CSJN, 306 Fallos 1752, paragraph 9 (referring to the individual right to the privacy of the home of every inhabitant, correlated to the general principle of Article 19 [of the Argentine Constitution].

52. In a case in which notice of the existence of a crime was obtained through a warrantless surveillance of a telephone conversation maintained by the defendant, a dissenting opinion to the judgment on appeal that affirmed the conviction found support in articles 18 and 33 of the CN for the constitutional protection due to a person's "expectation of privacy." *Guzmán*, CNCrimCorr.-II, 16 May 1989, Docket No. 35.688 (dissenting opinion of Judge Vázquez Acuña, referring to international human rights treaties and case-law from the United States Supreme Court).

53. CcrP art. 226, first paragraph (providing that the requirement of conducting searches during daylight hours does not apply to searches to be carried out in "public buildings, administrative offices, meeting or recreational establishments, associations, and any other enclosed place unless it is destined to be used for lodging or private residence.").

ence of exigent circumstances, such as the police being in hot pursuit of persons entering into the dwelling or hearing voices asking for help from inside a house.[54]

c. *Consent Searches.* The rules of criminal procedure fail to indicate whether consent may be used as a waiver of the judicial warrant required by law. As noted, the rules of criminal procedure refer to the consent of the affected party only as a means to circumvent the requirement that searches of private dwellings be conducted in daylight hours.[55] Court opinions are divided as to whether the "consent" of the occupant of a dwelling, as manifested by his failure to raise objections to the police's entry, may validate an otherwise warrantless search.

The compelling circumstances surrounding the occupant's failure to object to the entrance of the police raise serious doubts as to its voluntariness. Whereas some courts have taken the position that such "consent" can never circumvent the need for a judicial warrant for a valid search,[56] the Supreme Court is yet to adopt clear stance on this point. The issue came up in *Fiorentino*, a leading case in the development of the exclusionary rule. Fiorentino was a nineteen-year old who was accosted by four police officers in the hall next to the apartment in which he lived with his parents. Police officers seized his keys to his apartment, to which they gained access accompanied by Fiorentino. The officers encountered Fiorentino's parents in the kitchen, identified themselves, and asked them to stay in the kitchen while they proceeded with a search. Fiorentino was charged and found guilty for illegal possession of five cigarettes of marijuana recovered from his bedroom. The intermediate court of appeals dismissed Fiorentino's claim that the evidence should be excluded as resulting from a warrantless search. According to the appellate court, Fiorentino's parents had consented to the search by failing to raise an objection to the police entrance, and Fiorentino's consent was inferred from his failure to object to the police's presence. In this case, the Supreme Court decided to depart from its traditional doctrine that issues dealing with the manner in which the evidence was obtained fails to raise a "substantial federal question" warranting review, accepting to hear the case extraordinary writ of error filed against the judgment of the appellate court. Thus the court held that the application of Article 18 of the CN on the inviolability of private dwellings was at stake. According to the Court, the circumstances under which Fiorentino's consent were given—i.e., under arrest and escorted by four police officers—defied any inference of consent.[57] The Court also dismissed the allegation that Fiorentino's parents gave tacit "consent" to the search. Even assuming that such consent had been actually given, said the Court, it was given too late, for the police had already entered the dwelling before Fiorentino's parents could raise any objection. In the absence of any exigent cir-

54. CcrP art. 227.

55. CcrP art. 225.

56. *Barboza*, 24 Oct. 1984.

57. *Fiorentino*, CSJN, JA, 1985-II-108, noting the absence "of a valid consent that would have allowed the entrance of the police into the defendant's home"). In paragraph 6, the Court also noted that it was unreasonable to expect a youth such as Fiorentino to refuse entrance to the police. The concurring opinion of J. Petracchi suggested that a valid consent presupposes that the defendant had been warned that he may refuse to give such consent, though it also noted that it is for the legislature to provide that consent may be resorted to as an exception to the requirement of a judicial warrant. *See also*, *Hansen*, CSJN, 308 Fallos 2447. In this case, the Solicitor General (Procurador General) had suggested that nowhere in the Code of Criminal Procedure consent by the occupant of a dwelling is mentioned as a way to circumvent the mandatory requirement of obtaining a judicial warrant.

cumstances that could dispense the need to procure a judicial warrant, the Court concluded that the seizure of the drugs had to be excluded.[58]

Shortly thereafter the Supreme Court decided another case involving the seizure of drugs resulting from a warrantless search, insisting that the occupant's mere failure to object does not raise an inference of consent nor dispenses with the need to obtain a judicial warrant. Thus, in a case in which a search had been conducted late at night by five police officers, the Court stated that expecting the defendant to resist the entrance of the police under those circumstances is to "demand a standard of behavior inconsistent with that followed by ordinary people."[59] However, the Court has failed to keep a workable and consistent standard identifying the circumstances according to which consent may circumvent the need for a search warrant. In *Romero*, the Supreme Court that the mere fact that the accused was under custody at the time he gave his consent to a search does not automatically invalidate the search,[60] especially if the defendant subsequently acknowledged to the judge that he was willing to cooperate with the police.[61] In contrast, the Court stated in *Rayford* that failure to object may amount to a valid consent only if the circumstances of the case show "beyond any doubt" that the individual was free to raise objections.[62] Other than these seemingly contradictory guidelines, the Supreme Court has not provided any other standards to ascertain the circumstances that would allow an inference of defendant's willingness to authorize the entrance by the police.

In *Fiscal v. Fernández,* consent was inferred from the mere failure to raise objections to the entrance of a police officer dressed in civilian clothes who failed to identify himself as a policeman. The officer had entered into the defendant's house in the company of a friend of the defendant.[63] Once inside the house, the defendant handed out a significant amount of cocaine to his friend and accomplice, at which point the police officer proceeded to identify himself and arrest them. According to a majority of the members of the Court, the mere fact that the occupant of the house was deceived as to the identity of the police officer did not necessarily point to a fraudulent misrepresentation by the latter. The Supreme Court upheld the warrantless entrance of the police to the defendant's home and the evidence seized therein.[64] The fact that the defendant did not even bother to inquire about the identity of the person who was accompanying his friend, proceeding to deliver the drug in his presence, may have prompted the Court to find

58. *Fiorentino*, ibidem ("Once the illegality of the search is established, the ensuing seizure is also illegal, because it is no more than the fruit of a proceeding condemned by law. The use of such evidence to base a conviction would amount to accept that the judicial process may benefit from the use of illegal means and from evidence secured in violation of defendant's constitutional rights. Such a use is not only inconsistent with the rule of law, but it is also an impairment of the regular administration of justice..." See also *Monticelli de Prozillo*, CNCrim.Corr-I, LL-1984-373.

59. *Cichero*, CSJN, 307 Fallos 440 (paragraph 6). See also *Barbieri*, CSJN, 308 Fallos 853; *Capurro*, CSJN, 11 Dec. 1986, Docket No. C-437-XX.

60. *Romero*, CSJN, 306 Fallos 752, with note by Francisco D'Albora.

61. *Ferrer*, CSJN, 1991-A-3, with note by Carlos Borinsky.

62. *Rayford*, CSJN, 308 Fallos 733. *See also, Pierro*, Supreme Court of Mendoza, JA, 1992-I-443 (opinion of J. Salvini).

63. *Fiscal v. Fernández,* CSJN, LL, 1991-B-190.

64. Ibidem, paragraph 8 (noting the absence of any "machination, misrepresentation or fraud in order to enter into the dwelling").

that his expectation of privacy was less pronounced than in other cases.[65] A more puzzling rationale was provided in *Fato,* where the Supreme Court, following an argument submitted by the Solicitor General (*Procurador General*), stated that the search of a dwelling (*allanamiento de domicilio*) entails an activity aimed at breaking the resistance of the person who has the right to oppose the entrance of the police. From this premise the Court disturbingly concluded that there is no "search," properly speaking, once consent to the entrance is furnished up-front, in which case the rules and exceptions applicable to searches and seizures are not applicable.[66]

If the decisions rendered by the Supreme Court fail to provide clear guidelines as to the circumstances under which consent to a search may be validly inferred, the Court's jurisprudence is not more illuminating as to who is entitled to give such consent, other than the suspect against whom the search is addressed. Thus, in *Hansen*, the Supreme Court refused to uphold the search of the defendant's home when his mother consented to the entrance,[67] while in *Martinez* the consent provided by a woman who was staying in a hotel room with the defendant was held sufficient to validate the search of the room.[68] Despite this wide spectrum of uncertainty, since the 1980's the courts have shown increasing willingness to scrutinize the degree of "voluntariness" surrounding the consent allegedly granted by the occupants of a dwelling subject to a search.

5. *Enforcing the Rules*

The rule that wrongfully obtained evidence may not be used at trial has had a torturous path in the jurisprudence developed by the Supreme Court. It was affirmed early by the Supreme Court in *Charles Hermanos*, a case decided in 1891, but it was subsequently abandoned for almost a century. In *Charles Hermanos*, custom officials had conducted a warrantless search at the defendants' commercial establishment, seizing documents, books and files. The defendants were convicted for contraband and forgery on the basis of that evidence. Efforts to exclude such evidence on the ground that custom officials lacked the authority to conduct the search were dismissed by the lower courts. The Supreme Court reversed the conviction on the ground that Article 18 of the CN required the exclusion of evidence illegally seized for the sake of preserving values such as morality, security, and privacy.[69]

---

65. Ibidem, paragraph 8 (concluding that "[u]nder the circumstances, the Court does not perceive an illegitimate interference on part of the government in a place such as a dwelling, where a person may have a heightened expectancy of intimacy and privacy.").

66. *Fato*, CSJN, 24 March 1988, 311 Fallos 836.

67. *Hansen*, CSJN, 308 Fallos 2447.

68. *Martínez*, CSJN, 311 Fallos 962. See also, *Dalmao Montiel*, CSJN, 311 Fallos 2171 (holding that the consent provided by the captain of a boat sufficed to validate the search of the defendant's cabin).

69. Ibidem ("Whether the documents and files seized are authentic or not, they cannot be introduced in evidence. . .[Those documents and files] are the result of an illegal search, even if carried out with the purpose of investigating a crime. . .[T]he law, in the name of morality, security and privacy. . .compels the inadmissibility of such evidence against the defendants."). See also, *Siganevich*, 177 Fallos 390 (a case in which the Supreme Court also recognized that the seizure of a pack of unopened envelopes that appeared to indicate a violation to the law of bets and games also raised a constitutional issue subject to review by the Court).

Subsequent cases in which the Supreme Court was called to make a pronouncement about the exclusion of wrongfully obtained evidence were dismissed on the questionable ground that the legality of a search was not an issue involving constitutional application, but rather the proper interpretation of local procedural statutes that do not warrant Supreme Court review. Thus, the Court held in *Colombres Garmendia* that questions regarding whether the evidence had or had not been properly obtained involved mere questions of fact, evidence, and the interpretation of the local rules of criminal procedure on which state courts have a final say.[70] During this period, lower courts, confident that the legality of a search did not involve a constitutional matter, regularly upheld warantless searches of private dwellings. The occupant's consent was inferred from what police reports routinely referred to as failure to object to the entrance of the police. Not much effort of analysis was devoted to a determination whether the "consent" of the occupant had been freely given.

This jurisprudential trend began to change in the early 1980s, when several panels of the Court of Appeals of the City of Buenos Aires started to deviate from the "hands-off" approach to warrantless searches adopted by the Supreme Court.[71] It was not until *Montenegro*,[72] a case decided in 1981, almost a century after *Charles Hermanos*, that the Supreme Court returned to the doctrine that police misconduct may vitiate the proceedings to such an extent as to compel the exclusion of evidence. The *Montenegro* case, however, did not involve an illegal search but a conviction supported on the evidence of stolen effects which the po-

70. *Colombres Garmendia*, CSJN, 275 Fallos 454 (1969), LL, 138-376 (with note by Germán Bidart Campos). In this case, the Internal Revenue Service (*Dirección General Impositiva*) sought and obtained a warrant to search the office of an attorney. The warrant failed to specify the type of objects which were sought by the tax authorities in connection with tax fraud allegedly perpetrated by the attorney. Police officers conducted a sweeping search, which the Criminal Court of Appeals nullified on the ground that the search warrant should have identified, at the very least, the purpose of the search. Although the appellate decision was not one which had allegedly infringed the constitutional rights of the defendant, the Supreme Court was seized of the matter but dismissed the writ of error on the ground that "the circumstances under which a search warrant is to be issued" implicates a procedural question not subject to review by the Supreme Court. *See also,Gullo*, 301 Fallos 676 (1979); *Ibarguren*, CSJN, 305 Fallos 1727; *Monzón*, 98 ED 284 (1982); *Fiscal v.Nacif*, 303 Fallos 2029 (1981); and other cases reported in 277 Fallos 467 and 303 Fallos 1593-S.

71. See, e.g., *Avila*, LL, 1983-B-115; *Palacio*, 101 ED 252 (1982); *Alori*, LL, 1983-B-119. *See also*, *Fernández*, CamFedLa Plata, 2 Nov. 1983, JA, 1983-I-523. The earliest and probably most comprehensive articulation of the exclusionary rule within this line of decisions was made in *Monticelli de Prozillo*, CfedCrimCorr-I, LL, 1984-D-373. In this case, police officers proceeded to search the home of a woman, who had "spontaneously" confessed under custody that a weapon which had been used in a robbery was hidden in her home. The weapon was found and seized by the police, who entered the home of the defendant "without any objections" having been raised by her mother. The trial court dismissed the challenge to the legality of the search, but the Court of Appeals held that it was null and void on the ground that it violated not only the constitutional clause protecting the inviolability of the home, but also the privilege against self-incrimation. The Court of Appeals refuse to find the alleged "consent" given by the mother of the accused as a ground for dispensing with the requirement for the warrant. More importantly, as noted in the opinion of Judge Gil Lavedra, the defendant's mother was not the proper person to grant such consent, and "there was no indication that the police were prevented from requesting the pertinent search warrant" (paragraph 6).

72. *Montenegro*, CSJN, 303 Fallos 1938 (1981)

lice were able to locate thanks to Montenegro's confession extracted under torture. The admissibility of evidence obtained by virtue of a warrantless search was not taken up by the Supreme Court until *Fiorentino*, which was decided at the end of the 1984 term.[73] In that case, discussed earlier, having found no valid consent from the defendant's (and his parents') failure to object to the search, the Court suppressed the incriminating evidence despite the absence of threats or violance to obtain entry.

The rationale for excluding wrongfully obtained evidence has been found in a variety of factors, mostly grounded on formal (normative) or ethical grounds, rather than on the purpose to deter police misconduct. The remedy of exclusion has been supported in Article 172 of the CcrP, providing that "[t]he nullity of an act, once it has been declared, shall result in the nullity of all other acts deriving therefrom. . ." On the basis of this provision it has been reasoned that if the search is invalid, the resulting evidence cannot be used at trial.[74] In an effort to rest the remedy of exclusion in the wording of the Constitution, other courts have held that the exclusion of wrongfully obtained evidence is compelled under Article 18 of the CN, to the effect that "no one may be punished without previous trial held in accordance with a law passed before the commission of the crime."According to this view, the constitutional mandate to support a conviction in a previous law, generally construed as a prohibition against statutes adopted *ex post facto*, is also meant to include other elements of due process, precluding the use of wrongfully obtained evidence.[75] Discouraging police misconduct, while occasionally referred to as a major benefit of the exclusionary rule,[76] has not been found its dominant rationale. In *Montenegro*, the Supreme Court intimated that the remedy of exclusion is to be found in the Constitution, although without articulating which were the words of the Constitution granting that power to the judges.[77]

The exclusionary rule has been applied often enough by intermediate appellate courts, especially in cases concerning illegal possession of drugs, so as to have an impact on how trial courts handle these cases.[78] Whether these decisions have had

---

73. *Fiorentino*, CSJN, JA-II-108 (1985); on remand, see JA-III-549 (1985); 306 Fallos 1752. It is noteworthy that in October of 1983 a constitutional government took office in Argentina after many years of military rule, which had been characterized by gross and systematic violations of human rights. The composition of the Supreme Court had been changed by the new constitutional government pursuant to the constitutional mechanism of presidential nomination followed by Senatorial consent.

74. *But see, P., H.A.*, CNCrimCorr.-III, 26 May 1983, 107 ED 430 (to the effect that the nullity of the proceedings is not the proper remedy to question the legality of the evidence gathered by the police during the pre-trial investigation).

75. *G.E.*, CNCrim.Corr.-III, 6 July 1982, 101 ED 252 (opinion of Judge Arslanian, stating that the admission of wrongfully obtained evidence has an impact on the "essential elements" of due process).

76. *C., J.A.*, Cfed.LaPlata, 7 Aug. 1984, 110 ED 649 (opinion of Judge Garro).

77. See *Montenegro*, supra, paragraph 5, to the effect that "compliance with the constitutional mandate by the judges cannot be limited to the prosecution and eventual punishment of those responsible for the violations."

78. During the early 1980's the exclusionary rule has been consistently applied to crimes such as illegal possession of weapons (*Monticelli de Prozillo*, CNFedCrim.Corr-I, 10 Aug. 1984, LL-1984-D-373; *Rojas*, ibidem, 24 Aug. 1984, 57 JPBA 99; *Piumato*, ibidem, Division II, 9 Aug. 1984, LL-1984-D- 235; *González, Jorge*, CNCrim-VII, 28 June 1985, 57 JPBA 82); infringement to copyright protection (*Alori*, CNCrim-III, JA, 1983-III-588); and possession of illegal instru-

a noticeable impact on every day police practices is difficult to ascertain in the absence of meaningful field surveys which are yet to be conducted.

Standing. In principle, only a defendant whose constitutional rights were violated has standing to contest the validity of a search. However, the connection between an illegal search of someone else's home and subsequent incriminating evidence against a defendant may be so close that the evidence may be supressed at the request of some one other than the owner or occupant of the home. In a split decision, the Supreme Court decided in *Rayford* that a co-defendant may be allowed to suppress evidence obtained in violation of the constitutional rights of another co-defendant.[79] Police officers had seized drugs at the home of Reginald Rayford, a U.S. citizen who was in transit in Argentina. No warrant had been obtained for the search, allegedly conducted without objections on the part of Rayford. On his way to the police station, Rayford told the escorting officers that "B" had provided the drugs to him. "B" was immediately arrested and his statements led in turn to the arrest of "C," who allegedly furnished the drugs to to "B." Although the three codefendants ultimately confessed their participation in the illegal possession of drugs with which they were charged, they were acquitted by the trial court on the ground that the whole proceeding had been tainted by the warrantless search conducted in Rayford's home. The Court of Appeals reversed on the ground that Rayford's consent to the police entrance had validated an otherwise invalid search. Only one of the three co-defendants, "B," sought a reversal of his conviction by the Supreme Court on account of the illegal search practiced in Rayford's home.The Supreme Court reversed the conviction against the three on the ground that the incriminating statements made by the codefendants were the sole and proximate cause of the warantless and illegal search conducted in Rayford's home and of the wrongful seizure of the drugs found therein. The Court ruled that "B," whose constitutional rights were not directly implicated by the illegality of the search, was nevertheless entitled to seek its suppression. The Court found that the evidence against "B" was so "intimately connected" to the illegal search as to deprive "B" and "C" of the due process rights to which they are entitled under Article 18 of the CN. After ruling that "B" had standing to contest the legality of the search, the Court found that Rayford, who could barely understand or speak Spanish, could not have "consented" to the search.[80]

Francomano was a subsequent case in which a codefendant was convicted on the basis of a coerced confession extracted from another codefendant. The Supreme Court held that one of the codefendants has standing to contest the violation of the other's constitutional right against self-incrimination.[81] In *Daray*, a

---

ments of forgery (*Tapia Aguilera*, CNFedCrimCorr-I, LL, 1985-D-391). All the other reported cases ruling the exclusion of wrongfully obtained evidence (13 out of a total of 19 cases) dealt with the illegal possession of drugs. See Carrió, *Garantías constitucionales* 158, n. 20.

79. *Rayford*, CSJN, 13 May 1985, 308 Fallos 733.

80. *Rayford*, ibidem (J. Caballero dissented on the ground that the writ of error was not technically admissible, and J. Belluscio dissented on the ground that even admitting the illegality of the search, the judicial confessions of the co-defendants provided independent grounds to the convictions).

81. *Francomano*, CSJN, 310 Fallos 2402. In this case, Francomano's incriminating statements against his codefendant Vilas had been obtained under duress. Those statements lead to Vilas' arrest and seizure of incriminating evidence. Vilas' conviction was overturned by the Supreme Court on the basis of the exclusionary rule sustained in *Charles Hermanos*, *Montenegro*, *Fiorentino*, and *Rayford*. In the fourth paragraph of the decision, the Court confirmed "an in-

more recent case, the Supreme Court affirmed that a defendant has standing to challenge the violation of the constitutional rights of a third party, as long as the defendant's situation appears "intimately connected" to the constitutional wrongdoing suffered by that third party. Three of the Justices explained that to hold otherwise would result in a systematic violation of constitutional rights by the police in order to secure evidence against persons other than those directly affected by police misconduct.[82]

Fruit of the Poisonous Tree. In *Montenegro* and *Fiorentino,* the application of the exclusionary rule by the Supreme Court of Argentina lead to the inadmissiblity of evidence that was the immediate and direct result of illegal police behaviour (i.e., the exclusion of the incriminating statements resulting from Montenegro's coerced confession and of the drugs seized from Fiorentino's apartment). After the Supreme Court remanded the *Montenegro* case to the intermediate appellate court for further proceedings (without passing judgment as to the admissiblity of the incriminating evidence subsequently found in Montenegro's home), the court of appeals acquitted Montenegro on the ground that not only the coerced confession, but also the search and seizure conducted in Montenegro's home warranted exclusion.[83]

In a subsequent case decided by another division of the same court of appeals, the court decided to exclude not only the evidence seized by virtue of a warrantless search, but also the incriminating statements made by a witness who was present at the scene. The statements of another witness who declared immediately thereafter were also excluded.[84] Most courts of appeals have also maintained that the nullity of a search and seizure entails the invaldity of the testimonial evidence gathered at the search, as well as any expert testimony regarding the objects of the seizure.[85] As noted, the Supreme Court in *Rayford* found that the illegality of the search of Rayford's home resulted in the inadmissiblity of all of the defendants' incriminating statements. *Daray* has further supported the exclusion of both illegally obtained evidence and its fruits, ordering the suppression not only the defendant's statements obtained after an illegal arrest, but also the products of a search and seizure conducted pursuant to a warrant and incriminating statements given by the defendants'neighbours as well. The Court held that this broad exclusion was compelled because all the steps taken during the investigation had been tainted by the illegal arrest.[86] Doubts on the consistency with which the Supreme Court is willing

---

valid string of evidence starting with Francomano's statements and followed by an uninterrupted causal chain ending with petitioner's arrest." The Supreme Court added that "the exclusion should extend to evidence incriminating a third party whenever. . .such evidence orginates in a flawed investigatory lead." The Court noted the absence of "an independent source of knowledge that would corroborate a finding of defendant's guilt without relying on evidence that was wrongfully obtained." *Francomano et al.*, supra, ibidem.

82. *Daray*, CSJN, LL, 1995-B-349 (Justices Nazareno, Moliné O'Connor, and Levene, concurring.).

83. *Montenegro*, CNCrim.Corr.-III, 9 March 1982, LL, 1982-D-256 (opinion of Judge Gómez).

84. *G.E., J.M.*, CNCrim.Corr.-VI, 4 Aug. 1983, 107 ED 347 (Opinion of Judge Andereggen: "Having held that the seizure of the drugs resulted from an illegal search, testimony that originated from such flawed proceedings is also inadmissible").

85. *P.G.*, CNCrim.Corr.-III, 6 July 1982, 101 ED 252; *Villanueva*, CámFedLa Plata- II, 27 Dec. 1984, LL, 1985-B-270 (*contra*, *Losada*, CámFedLa Plata-II, 16 Feb. 1984, LL, 1984-C- 47); *Tapia Aguilera*, CNFedCrimCorr.-II, 2 July 1985, LL, 1985-D-391; *Vitar*, P., CNCrimCorr.-IV, 25 Sept. 1984, 57 JPBA 83.

86. *Daray*, CSJN, LL, 1995-B-349, with note by Alejandro Carrió.

to exclude evidence resulting indirectly from illegal police behaviour were cast by way of a *dictum* in *Fiscal v. Fernández,*[87] but the more recent holding in *Daray* suggests a consolidated trend toward the "fruit of the poisonous tree" exclusion.

Exceptions. The Supreme Court carved an exception to the application of the exclusionary rule whenever it was found that evidence that had been wrongfully obtained "may" have been obtained through a different, autonomous, and independent source. In *Ruiz,* a case involving the robbery of several taxi cabs, Ruiz's allegedly coerced confession under custody led to the driver's identification of Ruiz as the culprit and and to the testimony of a car dealer to whom Ruiz had sold some of the stolen cabs.[88] Ruiz was convicted of three different counts of robbery on the basis of his alleged coerced confession. When the case reached the Supreme Court, the Court saw it fit to distinguish between the evidence that resulted exclusively from Ruiz's coerced confession (which was held inadmissible) and the one deriving from independent sources of incriminating evidence (which was held sufficient to support his conviction). Thus, the Court reversed one of the counts of robbery against Ruiz on the ground that the only way to obtain the testimony of the victim and the car dealer was through Ruiz's invalid confession. With regard to the other two counts of robbery, the Supreme Court found that the incriminating evidence originated from the robbery of a drug store with one of the stolen cabs, and also from the seizure of an identification document belonging to one of the taxi drivers, all of which had taken place before Ruiz had been arrested. Accordingly, the Court distinguished between "the possibility of obtaining evidence from sources other than those deemed to be illegitimate" and evidence obtained "only through one investigatory path, which was flawed from its inception and contaminated the ensuing proceeding."[89]

In addition to the exception based on the finding of a potential "independent source," the Supreme Court stated in *Martínez* that the mere fact that some of the evidence had been wrongfully obtained need not result in the dismissal of the charges against the defendant, for it is necessary to determine that said evidence

---

87. Fiscal v. Fernández, LL, 1991-B-190. In this case, a police officer, who never identified himself as such, entered into the Bolivian Consultate in the City of Mendoza, accompanied by a friend of the Consul. In the presence of the disguised police officer, the friend delivered a significant amount of cocaine to the Consul, who was charged and convicted on the basis of such evidence. The Supreme Court refused to categorize as a deception the mere failure of the officer to identify himself. It also refused to consider a "search" what in the Court's eyes appeared as a regular entry into one's home which had been consented to by the Consul. On that basis, the Court held that the evidence had been obtained through legal means (Judges ought to safeguard, within a strict constitutional framework, the principle of justice demanding that crime does not pay. . .In matters of criminal procedure, the duty to ascertain the objective truth only allows the exclusion of wrongfully obtained evidence only when such evidence, "per se," had been obtained through illegal or unconstitutional means). Ibidem, paragr. 14. This language, as noted by a legal commentator, in addition to being unnecesary to decide the case before the Court, raised at that time serious doubts on the application of the doctrine leading to the exclusion of the so-called "fruit of the poisonous tree," as expanded in Rayford and Ruiz. See Alejandro D. Carrió, note in LL, 1191-C-857.1

88. *Ruiz,* 310 Fallos 1847; LL, 1988-B-444.

89. *Ruiz,* ibidem, paragraphs 13 and 14. *See also, Villanueva et al.*, CámFedLa Plata-II, 27 Dec. 1984, LL, 1985-B-270 (opinion of Judge Garro, reversing a conviction based on evidence held to have been wrongfully obtained and the absence "of any other independent source of evidence that could be used against the defendant").

was actually relevant to the conviction.[90] In this regard, it appears sensible to place on the defendant the burden of establishing a relevant link between the finding of guilt and the illegally obtained evidence, a determination ultimately left to the trier of facts. However, rather than overturning the judgment and remanding the case to the lower court to determine the weight of the remaining evidence, the Supreme Court in *Martínez* affirmed the conviction on the ground that the defendant was unable to meet the burden of proof at the time of bringing the writ before the Supreme Court.[91]

Collateral Use. The question of whether wrongfully obtained evidence which has been held inadmissible at trial may be nevertheless used in other proceedings or for other purposes can not be answered in light of a specific case. To our knowledge, there is no reported case in which this issue came up. Because the classical remedy invoked by the courts is one leading to the nullification of such evidence, it is implausible to suggest that the courts would be entitled to rely upon such evidence for any purpose whatsoever. Also noticeable is the sweeping condemnation of the use of wrongfully obtained evidence made by the Court in *Fiorentino,* where the Supreme Court stated that "[s]uch a use is not only inconsistent with the rule of law, but it is also an impairment to the regular administration of justice. . ."[92] According to this statement, it is difficult to conceive the acceptance of wrongfully obtained evidence for purposes other than the prosecution's case-in-chief while mantaining the consistency with the reasons for the exclusion.

B. Lineups and Other Identification Procedures

The rules of criminal procedure provide judges with a broad authorization to pursue investigative techniques aimed at the "recognition" of persons and objects.[93] Identification procedures may range from those relying entirely on the perception and recall of eyewitnesses, to those comparing a person's fingerprints, hair, blood, or handwriting to samples found at the scene of the crime or through other means of investigation. Thus, Article 270 of the CcrP reads:

"The judge may order the recognition of a person for the purpose of identifying her, or to establish that whoever mentions or alludes to that person actually knows her or has seen her. The recognition shall be carried out by technical means,

90. *Martínez*, CSJN, 311 Fallos 962. The defendant challenged his conviction arguing that the evidence against him had been obtained through illegal searches, to which the Court responded: ". . .[E]ven assuming the irregularity of some of the searches of private dwellings in which incriminating evidence turned up, it has not been established in the writ of error that the suppression of such evidence would have resulted in a different outcome than the one actually reached by the lower court, or to put in other words, that the remaining evidence was not sufficient to support a finding of guilt."

91. In contrast, the Supreme Court in *Montenegro* overturned a conviction based on a coerced confession and remanded the case to the lower court with the order of supressing Montenegro's statements as evidence. The lower court, in turn, decided to extend the supression to the remaining evidence flowing from such invalid confession. See *Montenegro*, CNCrim.Corr.-III, 9 March 1982, LL, 1982-D-256.

92. *Fiorentino*, supra.

93. CcrP arts. 270 and 275.

by witnesses or in any other way, if possible right away, under penalty of sanctions against the judicial organ that fails to comply with this rule."

1. *Lineups*

Lineups (*reconocimiento en rueda de personas*) and photographic displays (*reconocimiento por fotografía*) are within the realm of investigatory measures governed by the rules of criminal procedure.[94] In *Cincotta*, the Supreme Court held that forcing a suspect to stand in a line-up does not violate the privilege against self-incrimiantion embodied in Article 18 of the CN.[95] The Supreme Court has also been reluctant to find due process limitations in the manner in which lineups are conducted, holding that this issue concerns issues of fact, evidence, and procedure which are beyond the scope of the appellate jurisdiction of the Supreme Court.[96] Before proceeding to the identification, the witness shall be asked to describe the person who is to be identified, so that it may be ascertained whether the witness had known or seen that person before the lineup.[97] The rules of criminal procedure also seek to guard a line-up from identification methods that are unnecessarily suggestive.[98] However, the Supreme Court has refused to review a conviction in which the defendant complained of a suggestive lineup conducted at the police station, in the absence of the investigative magistrate and his defense counsel. In *Sánchez*, the Court held that identification procedures conducted at the police station may be reproduced after adversarial proceedings have been initiated by formal charges or an indictment, thus dismissing the writ brought before the Supreme Court.[99]

2. *Other Identification Procedures*

The Supreme Court held in *Cincotta* that the privilege against self-incrimination only applies to "verbal communications" of the defendant, to the exclusion of blood, urine, or hair samples demanded for identification purposes.[100] Accordingly, in *H.G.S.*, a case involving the misappropriation of a child, the Supreme Court has held that it is constitutionally permissible to compel the defendant to submit to a blood test.[101]

---

94. CcrP arts. 277 and 274.
95. *Cincotta*, CSJN, 255 Fallos 18. See also *Schuster*, CSJN, 300 Fallos 894-S.
96. *Castro Roberts*, CSJN, 311 Fallos 2337-S.
97. CcrP art. 271.
98. CcrP art. 272, paragraph 1: "The recognition [of persons] shall be carried out immediately after the interrogation [referred to in the previous article 271]. The person to be identified or recognized shall be placed before the witness, together with two or more persons of similar exterior appearance, leaving up to her the place where to be placed within the lineup."
99. *Sanchez*, CSJN, 311 Fallos 325.
100. *Cincotta*, supra. Other cases, not related to identification procedures, have thrown more light on the limits (or absence thereof) of compelling an individual to cooperate with the courts. Thus, in *Bacqué*, the defendant objected to a court's order to furnish documents related to charges of fraud filed against him. The objection rested on the privilege against self-incrimination, cited in support of the defendant's refusal to provide incriminating evidence against himself. The Court dismissed the challenge on the ground that the court's order did not amount to a final judgment susceptible of review. *Bacqué*, CSJN, 249 Fallos 530. Also, a court of appeals held that an individual can be compelled to provide blood samples for the purpose of determining the content of alcohol because in such a case the suspect plays a mere passive role in the production of evidence, and that only compelling him to perform an "active" role would be protected by the privilege against self-incrimination. *Aranguren*, CNCrimCorr.-I, JA, 1992-III-23.
101. *H.G.S.*, CSJN, 4 December 1995, LL, 30 May 1997, p14.

C. Interrogation

Returning to Article 18 of the CN, it reads in part that "nobody shall be compelled to testify against himself." This constitutional guarantee operates differently depending on whether it is framed within a police or judicial context. Thus, the privilege against self-incrimination is relatively weak when the police seek statements, admissions or confessions from a suspect. It is more widely and generously applied once the suspect or accused makes his initial appearance in court and charges are formally brought against him.

1. Before Formal Charge in Court

Before and after the adoption of the CcrP in 1993, the legislative scheme has been one in which the police are not supposed to conduct the interrogation of those whom they suspect of being involved in criminal activity. This function has always been meant to be discharged by the investigative magistrate at the time the detainee makes his initial appearance. However, it has also been an inveterate practice in Argentina for the police to subject to interrogation those whom they encounter.[102] The suspect's statements ellicited by the police are generally labelled as "spontaneous" declarations (*declaraciones espontáneas*) in the police reports, and the probative value of these statements has been controversial. Courts have been reluctant to examine closely whether those statements had been actually volunteered by a person under custody, though acknowledging that an extrajudicial confession does not enjoy the same weight as one given before a court. Thus, in *Quezada*, a case in which the defendant was convicted on the basis of his uncorroborated extrajudicial confession, the Supreme Court reversed and noted:

"Even accepting that the police were to have the power to question suspects while pursuing a criminal investigation, any admission of guilt by the defendant would not qualify as a confession, because the rules of criminal procedure only validate judicial confessions. Incriminating statements received by the police may be accepted as circumstancial evidence, as long as they are corroborated by other pieces of evidence."

Other cases discussing the probative value of incriminating statements given under police custody, and subsequently recanted before the investigative magistrate, went as far as to confer on those extrajudicial statements the value of a "presumption,"[103] or even a "strong presumption"[104] of truth. Also, In *Cohan de Broge,* a court of appeals held that while the defendant's extrajudicial confession cannot be used at trial, the testimony of the police officer who overheard those incriminating statements from the defendant could be validly used against him.[105] Because custodial interrogations generally take place in the "privacy" of a police station, there is no way to verify in any effective manner whether the suspect had been

102. On Argentine practices regarding police questioning, see J. Vázquez Rossi, *La defensa penal* 115 (1978).

103. *Solís de Chaves*, CSJN, JA, 1933-41-551; *Fiscal c. Torres*, CSJN, 215 Fallos 41; *Paul*, CSJN, 275 Fallos 423.

104. *Diaz*, CSJN, JA, 1935-51-6.

105. *Cohan de Broger*, CNCrim-IV, 26 May 1987, LL, 1987-D-403 (with note by Alejandro D. Carrió).

actually warned of his rights. Therefore, the judge-made-rule that it is for the defendant to prove that his confession was extracted under physical coerecion or duress defies reality.

In order to deprive the so-called "spontaneous" statements of any evidentiary value, an amendment introduced to the rules of criminal procedure in 1984 expressly provided that a confession "must be given before the competent court," and that any confession given before the police "shall lack evidentiary force and shall not be used at trial."[106]There is no question that the motivating force of this amendment was to do away with police interrogations,[107] yet a suspect's "spontaneous" statements at the police station continued to be included in the dossier routinely sent by the police to the investigative magistrate. In more than one occasion those statements, allegedly volunteered by the defendant, were accepted as "presumptive" evidence. Thus, in *Cabral,*[108] the defendant was getting out of a taxi-cab with computer equipment at the very moment he was confronted by the police. Cabral's evasive responses to questions regarding the origin of the equipment prompted the officers to "invite" him to accompany them to the police station, as police reports customarily recite. On his way to the police station, Cabral allegedly "manifested spontaneously" where and from whom he had obtained the computer equipment. He also confessed that part of the equipment was stored in his apartment and was about to sell the equipment to a computer company at the time he was detained. Cabral was convicted for covering up a smuggling operation. According to the Supreme Court, while Cabral's statements could not be used at trial, it could still be used as a lead to find other evidence.[109]

According to the rules of criminal procedure, as they stood before 1993, it was customary for a few days to elapse between the custodial interrogation and the date of the appearance of the detainee before the judge for interrogation. At that point, medical reports were unlikely to evidence the marks of any physical coercion the detainee may have been subjected to while being interrogated under custody, hence the threat to the integrity of the criminal process posed by incriminating statements under custodial interrogation. Those rules have changed under the CcrP of 1993, to the effect that the police enjoy less time (a maximum of six hours) to keep the defendant under custody before presenting him to the investigative magistrate,[110] and the police are expressly barred from questioning the suspect.[111] The only questions that the police can address to a detainee are those concerning his identity, and even those questions must be preceded by the warnings regarding his

106. Law No. 23465, 47 ADLA-A-100 (amending Article 316 of the former Code of Criminal Procedure).

107. See note by Alejandro D. Carrió in LL, 1987-D-403.

108. *Cabral, Agustín*, 14 Dec. 1992, LL, 1993-B-257.

109. Ibidem, paragraph 4 ("The mere communication of such datum, as long as it was not given under coercion, should not be discarded by the investigation; [O]therwise. . .the aforementioned procedural restriction would preclude the police to investigate the leads resulting from such communication. . .").

110. According to Article 286 of the CcrP, if an individual has been detained by the police without a judicial warrant, he or she must be brought "immediately before the competent judicial authority within a period of time not exceeding six hours."

111. Paragraph 9 of Article 184 provides in turn that police forces may "resort to public force as needed." Immediately thereafter, this article adds that "police officers. . .can not elicit any statement from the accused. They are entitled to interrogate him only for the purpose of verifying his identity, after reading aloud to him the rights and guarantees. . . ."

right to remain silent, to consult with a lawyer and have him present at the interrogation, etc.[112] Because extrajudicial statements are theoretically inadmissible, the courts have developed guidelines as to when and under which circumstances a suspect may waive his rights and the extent to which jailhouse informants and police deceptive practices may be resorted to for the purposes of obtaining incriminating statements.

Exceptions and Qualifications. The Supreme Court of Argentina is yet to design a set of clear constitutional guidelines aimed at distinguishing between incriminating statements given to the police that ought to be excluded and those which, having been preceded by the proper warnings, may be used at the trial. The only clear standard developed to this day is that extrajudicial confessions are devoid of any value if the defendant is able to establish that they were extracted under coercion.[113] Not surprisingly, in most situations defendants are unable to meet this burden of proof. In cases in which such burden was met, such as in *Montenegro*, the Supreme Court held that involuntary confessions ought to be excluded, regardless of their reliability. In *Francomano*, decided in 1988, the Supreme Court unsuccessfully sought to develop a constitutional test for custodial interrogations short of demanding a showing from the defendant that his statements where given under physical coercion.[114] The various concurring opinions failed to provide a standard shared by a full majority of the Court. According to two of its members, incriminating statements given before the police may be admitted in evidence only if made in the presence of defense counsel, or if the prosecution is able to establish that the accused freely waived his right to be assisted by counsel. A third member of the Court was of the opinion that extrajudicial confessions should be completely disregarded once recanted before the investigative magistrate. The remaining two members of the Court opted for reversing the conviction of Francomano on the ground that the decision of the court of appeals, which entails a *de novo* review on the facts and the law, failed to provide the bare essentials of supporting reasoning required for a judicial decision to be constitutionally valid.[115]

112. CcrP art. 184, referring to the "rights and guarantees" set forth in articles 104 (appoint counsel of his choice), 295 (to be informed of the right to consult with a lawyer and have counsel present at the interrogation), 296 (to remain silent and not to be required to declare under oath or promise to tell the truth), and 298 (to be informed of the charges and evidence against him and warned of his right to remain silent, without an inference of guilt to be drawn from such silence).

113. *Mansilla*, CSJN, 271 Fallos 1143. *But see*, *Colman*, CSJN, 181 Fallos 182. In this case the Supreme Court did not hesitate to order an extrajudicial confession to be entirely stricken from the record, without demanding the defendant to establish that it had been extracted under coercion. However, the defedant in *Colman* was a foreigner who could hardly speak or understand the Spanish language and he had not been even offered the assistance of an interpreter. The Supreme Court failed to highlight how crucial were these facts to the outcome of this case, but the fact that the Court did not elaborate on any exception to the rule that extrajudicial confessions have a presumptive evidentiary value appears to indicate that the Court had no intention to depart from that rule.

114. *Francomano*, CSJN, 310 Fallos 2384, LL, 1988-B-454. The case is commented by Alejandro D. Carrió in LL, 1988-C-966.

115. *Francomano*, CSJN, 310 Fallos 2402. Francomano's incriminating statements against his co-defendant Vilas had been obtained under duress. Those statements lead to Vilas' arrest and seizure of incriminating evidence. Vilas' conviction was overturned by the Supreme Court on the basis of the exclusionary rule sustained in *Charles Hermanos*, *Montenegro*, *Fiorentino*, and *Rayford*. In the fourth paragraph of the decision, the Court found "an invalid string of evidence start-

Not surprisingly, lower courts have continued to rely on extrajudicial confessions unless the defendant is able to establish they were extracted under coercion. Thus, in *De la Fuente*, the defendant was caught red-handed holding forged checks.[116] The police officer who was in charge of his custody testified having heard the defendant confess other crimes committed through the use of forged checks. The trial court invalidated those statements pursuant to the exclusionary rule developed in *Montenegro* and *Francomano*. The appellate court reversed on the ground that the evidence obtained was not based on the defendant's extrajudicial confession, but rather on the testimony of the police officer who received "communications" furnished by the defendant, which amounted to valid evidence in the absence of any indication that they had been given under coercion.[117]

2. *After Defendant is Formally Charged*

Once a defendant is taken before the investigative magistrate for judicial questioning (*indagatoria*), he must be fully advised of his rights. The panoply of the defendant's rights surrounding his judicial interrogation includes the right to remain silent and to have an attorney present.[118] If the defendant fails to retain an attorney of her choice or decides to waive her right to appoint one, a public defender will be appointed as a matter of law.[119] Experience shows that defendants rarely choose to stand mute at this stage, probably because they have little to lose and much to gain by presenting their side of the story. If innocent, this may lead to an early dismissal of the charges. And if the accused is guilty, it may appear unwise, by a stubborn refusal to collaborate in clearing up the facts, to incur the displeasure of the same investigative magistrate who will rule on whether the accused should remain detained pending trial. Thus, the unavailability of silence as a viable strategy would prompt most defendants to provide an explanation to avoid his responsibility, mitigate his eventual punishment, or provide some indication of sincere repentance. Defendants cannot be required to speak under oath, nor exhorted to tell the truth, and any refusal to speak cannot be commented upon at any stage of the proceedings, though the defendant need not be informed of this fact.[120] Thus, even if the defendant is willing to take the stand, swearing him in and making him liable for perjury amounts to a violation of the privilege against self-incrimination.[121] Actu-

---

ing with Francomano's statements and followed by an uninterrupted causal chain ending with petitioner's arrest."

116. *De la Fuente*, CNCrim-VI, 27 March 1990, LL, 1991-D-338.

117. *See also*, *Patterson*, CNCrimCorr.-I, 20 Nov. 1991, JA, 1992-II-556; *Cabral, Héctor*, CNCrimCorr.-VI, 26 Nov. 1991, JA, 1992-II-286.

118. CcrP art. 295: "Only the defense counsel and the prosecutor may be present at the act of interrogation of the accused. This right shall be made known to the defendant before he starts to speak."

119. CcrP art. 107.

120. CcrP art. 184: "The accused may remain silent. In no case he shall be required to speak under oath or promise to tell the truth, nor it may be used any coercion, threat, or any other means to compel, induce or lead him to declare against his will, nor charges or promises may be used to obtain his confession. Failure to comply with this provision shall render the act null and void, without prejudice to the criminal or disciplinary sanctions that may apply." *Mendoza*, 1 Fallos 350 (1864) (requesting the defendant to speak under oath amounts to a violation of the privilege against self-incrimination).

121. *Diario El Atlántico*, CSJN, 281 Fallos 177 (1971) (stating that the oath requirement carries with it such moral coercion as to amount to a form of compulsion).

ally, while it is true that the defendant may not be prosecuted for perjury, any inconsistency in his statements, though tolerated under the circumstances, are likely to affect his general credibility and that may be commented upon in the final decision.

The privilege against self-incrimination has also been understood as protecting any third-party witness, as long as the questions addressed to him refer to his involvement in a crime under investigation.[122] Although Argentine law does not allow the granting of immunity to a witness, a witness who fails to speak the truth under oath in order to avoid incriminating himself cannot be prosecuted for perjury.[123]

3. *Enforcing the Rules*

For a long time, the Supreme Court refused to scrutinize the voluntariness with which extrajudicial confessions had been given. Every time that such an issue was brought up for review under a writ of error, the Supreme Court dismissed the writ on the ground that it failed to pose a substantive federal question, merely involving the examination of questions of fact, evidence, and the interpretation of local procedural rules.[124] At times, the Supreme Court refused to examine a challenge against the voluntariness of an extrajudicial confession on the ground that other incriminating evidence sufficed to support a conviction.[125]

Supreme Court review of involuntary confessions became available with the *Montenegro* case, decided in 1981.[126] In that case, the defendant's conviction for robbery was based on his admittance before the police that he had kept the stolen goods in his home, where the police subsequently recovered them. Medical reports, however, established that the defendant had been beaten while in police custody. This time, the Court found that the issue of involuntary confessions raised a constitutional issue warranting review, thus enhancing the relevance of police interrogations to the privilege against self-incrimination. Irrespective of its reliability in a particular case, held the Court, any confession extracted under coercion violated Article 18 of the CN and had to be excluded. To be held otherwise, concluded the Court, would turn the criminal justice system into an accomplice to the illegal methods used by the police.[127]

Exceptions or Qualifications. While coerced statements made by the accused are inadmissible, it is the accused, rather than the prosecution, who bears the burden of proving that the confession was coerced. Moreover, even though the police are prohibited from interrogating the defendant, and any statements made to the police are in principle null and void,[128] as a matter of practice those statements are relied upon as evidentiary leads to uncover additional incriminating evidence

122. *Rodríguez Pamías*, CSJN, 227 Fallos 63 (1953).

123. *Montero*, CSJN, 123 LL 628 (1966); *Tomljenovic*, 140 LL 700 (1970).

124. *Romano*, CSJN, 259 Fallos 69 (1964); *Lafuente*, CSJN, 302 Fallos 571 (1980); *Fiscal c. Nacif*, 303 Fallos 2029 (1981). *See also*, *Asensio*, CSJN, 295 Fallos 538.

125. *Pichumil*, CSJN, 302 Fallos 574-S; *Guzzeti*, CSJN, 269 Fallos 43; *A.J.C.*, 99 ED 337.

126. *Montenegro*, CSJN, 303 Fallos 1938 (1981).

127. Ibidem. *See also, Ruiz, Roque*, CSJN, 17 Sept. 1987, 310 Fallos 1847; LL, 1988-B-444 (with note by Alejandro D. Carrió). Referring to *Montenegro* and *Fiorentino* (dealing with the exclusion of wrongfully obtained evidence from an invalid search), the Court held that any evidence obtained as a result of a coerced extrajudicial confession had to be excluded, unless such evidence could also be obtained through an "autonomous or independent" source.

128. CcrP art. 184.

which the police subsequently turn over to the investigative magistrate. Thus, judges are able to take the "fruits" of police misconduct into consideration and use this evidence to construct a criminal case against the declarant.[129]

III. Court Procedures

Argentine law does not draw formal distinctions between major and minor crimes, felonies and misdemeanors. The jurisdiction of the criminal courts vary from province to province, but at the national (federal) level, the great majority of criminal offenses are tried by criminal courts of general jurisdiction (*tribunales en lo criminal*).[130] Crimes that are punished with a prison term not exceeding three years (e.g., assault, intentional damage of property) are subject to the jurisdiction of correctional courts (*tribunales en lo correccional*). A special tribunal for minors (*tribunal de menores*) tries cases in which the accused had not reached eighteen years of age at the time the offense was committed and the punishment does not involve deprivation of freedom, or if the prison term does not exceed three years.[131] Minor infractions (*faltas*) punished with a fine or less than thirty days of imprisonment are not typified in the Criminal Code they are rather vaguely defined (e.g., vagrancy, drunkness, disorderly conduct) in police ordinances (*edictos policiales*). Those police ordinances, some of which were adopted more than half a century ago, define the different infractions and provide for summary proceedings conducted before the Chief of the Federal Police.[132] Sentences imposed by the Chief of Police may be appealed within twenty-four hours before the pertinent correctional court.[133]

A. Pretrial

This preliminary stage (*sumario*) may be triggered by a request (*notitia criminis*) from the police, public prosecutor, or any individual,[134] and it is aimed at de-

129. See *Americas Watch, Police Violence in Argentina: Torture and Police Killings in Buenos Aires* 21 (1991).

130. CcrP art. 25.

131. CcrP arts. 28-29.

132. CcrP art. 538 (keeping in force arts. 585-590 of the former Code of Criminal Procedure, Law No. 2372). Under some of these police ordinances, a person may be arrested and held up to thirty days if convicted for infractions punishing "habitual loafers," "known criminals wandering with no specific motive around docks, railway stations, bus stops, hotels or theaters." The Supreme Court has upheld the constitutionality of these police ordinances. CSJN, 240 Fallos 235; 241 Fallos 99; 301 Fallos 1217.

133. Article 587 of the former Code of Criminal Procedure, as re-enacted by CcrP art. 538. It has been held that fines or limited prison terms imposed by the Chief of Police and municipal appellate tribunals for minor infractions, as well as fines imposed by other administrative agencies, are unconstitutional unless subject to effective judicial control. *Madala*, CSJN, 305 Fallos 129; *Di Salvo*, CSJN, 311 Fallos 334; *Ahumada v. Aduana*, CSJN, 272 Fallos 30.

134. CcrP arts. 186, 188, and 195.

termining whether there is a *prima facie* case against the defendant.[135] In theory, the pretrial phase is meant to be a swift stage and is not supposed to take longer than four months from the time the judicial interrogation takes place;[136] in practice, it takes much longer. Despite the absence of preliminary motions during the pretrial stage and the limitations imposed by procedural rules on the intervention of the parties, counsel for the victim and the defense counsel seek to take every conceivable opportunity at this early stage to engage in an adversarial battle of arguments. Every procedural motion, as well as their judicial responses in the form of written resolutions (*autos*), are transcribed into a record or dossier (*expediente*), whose volume increases day by day. Thus what in theory is meant to be a swift and mostly inquisitorial step becomes in practice a lengthy and adversarial stage in which the most relevant evidence that would play at the trial is submitted and produced by the parties.

The investigation of any type of criminal offense, with the exception of minor infractions governed by police ordinances, is in the hands of the investigative magistrate, who may at her discretion delegate this function in the public prosecutor.[137] The public prosecutor takes over the investigation in those cases in which the suspect is caught red-handed (*in fraganti*) and the magistrate is of the opinion that the detention of the suspect during the trial is not warranted.[138] The judge or magistrate is supposed to act as an impartial finder of facts, rather than as an agent to fight crimes, monitoring compliance with the procedural rules while safeguarding the rights of the accused. By and large, the investigative magistrate can be expected to be reasonably impartial. However, with the exception of complex or highly publicized cases in which the investigative magistrate appears as the dominant figure, police and low-ranking court officials tend to play a towering role during the investigation. In principle, the police are assigned the role of mere "auxiliaries" to the investigative magistrate,[139] whom they are bound to report all their investigatory activities.[140] They are authorized to undertake all urgent steps necessary to clear the crime and prevent the destruction of evidence. In the process of preparing a report at the police station, the police are authorized to interrogate witnesses and to order medical, ballistic, and handwriting tests.[141] If the gathered evidence offers "strong indications" that a suspect is involved in the perpetration of the offense, the police are also authorized to make an arrest, provide for the incommunication

135. CcrP art. 193.

136. CcrP art. 207: "The pretrial investigation (*instrucción*) shall take place within four months as of the judicial interrogation. If this period were insufficient, the judge may request an extension from the Court of Appeals, which may grant such an extension for an additional period of up to two months, depending on the reasons for the delay and the nature of the investigation. However, the extension may exceed this term in exceptional circumstances, in cases of extreme seriousness and difficulties in the investigation."

137. CcrP art. 196.

138. CcrP art. 353 (as introduced by Law No. 24826 of 11 June 1997): "When a person is caught *in fraganti* in the commission of a crime subject to public prosecution (*delito de acción pública*), and the judge considers *prima facie* that his pretrial detention is not appropriate, the investigation shall be conducted by the public prosecutor. . . . The investigation conducted by the public prosecutor shall not exceed a period of fifteen days. . . ."

139. CcrP art. 186.

140. CcrP art. 184.

141. CcrP art. 184.

of the detainee for as long as six hours,[142] and bring him before the investigative magistrate.

In theory police inquiries should proceed only to the point necessary to avoid the disappearance of evidence, yet in practice the police usually conduct extensive inquiries prior to forwarding the findings to the investigative magistrate. Overworked judges tend to delegate to the police and lower-ranking court officers many of the tasks that are meant to be personally performed by the investigative magistrate, without investing much efforts in ensuring adherence by the police to the rules circumscribing their investigatory powers. The requirement of placing the suspect "at the disposal" of the investigative magistrate is generally deemed to be met if the police simply notifies the judge that a person has been arrested and that they are acting on the investigation of a crime. At times, the investigation undertaken by the police permits the release of the suspect a few hours after the arrest, without booking him, when the evidence gathered is deemed insufficient to implicate him further in the investigation. At other times, the investigation that the police undertake on their own leads to further steps reflected in a more complete police report, to the advantage of investigating magistrates. Thus, this expanded police activity, well beyond the limits intended by the legislator, is said to operate as a filter which contributes to the early dropping of investigations mistakenly commenced against innocent suspects and speeding investigatory steps that can not be undertaken by an understaffed judicial machinery.

1. *Initial Court Appearance*

The arraignment is prompted by the detention of the suspect and the need to request his version of the events through a judicial interrogation (*declaración indagatoria*). The questioning of the suspect takes place whenever the investigative magistrate finds "sufficient grounds" to believe that the suspect is involved in the commission of the crime."[143] If the suspect was arrested the interrogation will take place immediately after the arrest. Otherwise the magistrate may summons the suspect's court appearance at any other time during the course of an existing investigation, whenever the "sufficient grounds" are deemed to exist. Once the suspect is brought in his presence, within twenty-four hours as of the moment of the arrest, the investigative magistrate must proceed with the interrogation.[144] It is at this point when the judicial inquiry, properly speaking, begins.

The investigative magistrate must call upon the suspect or "accused" (*imputado*) to give his name, occupation, and to provide information on his general background. The defendant must be advised of his constitutional guarantees, in-

142. CcrP art. 184.8 and 205 (providing that the investigative magistrate may decide to extend the incommunication for a maximum period of seventy-two hours). If the arrest needs to be undertaken in a private dwelling, the police need to obtain a judicial warrant pursuant to Articles 224 and 225 of the CcrP and the constitutional jurisprudence discussed above in connection with arrests and searches and seizures.

143. CcrP art. 294.

144. CcrP art. 294: "Whenever there are sufficient grounds to suspect that a person has participated in the commission of a crime, the magistrate shall proceed to interrogate him. If the person has been detained, the interrogation shall take place immediately, or within twenty-four hours of the arrest, at the latest. This period may be extended for another twenty-four hours whenever the magistrate has been unable to receive the declaration, or when requested by the accused in order to appoint defense counsel."

cluding the right to refuse to be questioned or to answer any particular question, as well as the right to retain counsel of his choice[145] or to have counsel appointed by the court.[146] After a warning that he has the right, at his option, to remain silent, the accused will be asked what (if anything) he wishes to say about the charges.[147] At this point, the suspect, who is not put under oath, formally becomes a "defendant." Only the public prosecutor and defense counsel may be present at the hearing in which the interrogation takes place. If the defendant chooses to talk, and he usually does talk, he is likely to avail himself of the opportunity to tell his side of the story. Most of the questioning is done by the investigating magistrate. Neither the prosecutor or defense counsel is allowed to object to the questions posed by the magistrate, and they cannot pose questions to the defendant without the judge's authorization,[148] which is generally granted.

No physical compulsion may be used to make the defendant talk;[149] no adverse inference may be drawn from his silence; and no comments are allowed by the prosecutor or the judge upon his failure to testify. Moreover, he is not required to announce his refusal to talk in any formal way. Yet, the defendant has little to lose and much to gain by presenting his side of the story, and experience shows that a large number of defendants do not stand mute. From the standpoint of the defendant, it may appear unwise to stubbornly refuse to cooperate in clearing up the facts, especially when the power to decide whether he should remain detained pending trial is in the hands of the same investigative magistrate who conducts the interrogation. Moreover, whatever the defendant says in his defense is not under oath, and he is induced to at least attempt to provide an explanation of the facts, which coupled with references to his personal circumstances (e.g., poverty, lack of education) and

---

145. CcrP art. 104: "The accused shall have the right to be represented by an attorney of his trust licenced to practice law or by the public defender; he may also assume his own defense, provided that such a choice does not affect the efficacy of the defense and does not hinder the proceedings. In this case, the court shall summon the accused to appoint defense counsel within three days, or otherwise be represented by a public defender appointed by the court. In no case the accused may be represented by an agent (*apoderado*). The appointment of defense counsel shall imply, unless express manifestation to the contrary, the granting of a power to be represented for the civil action. This power of attorney shall subsist until it is revoked. The accused may appoint defense counsel by any means, even if he is incommunicado."

146. CcrP art. 107: "Aside from what is provided in Article 104, at the first opportunity, and in any event before the judicial declaration (*indagatoria*) takes place, the judge shall invite the accused to appoint defense counsel among the lawyers licenced to practice. If the accused has failed to make such appointment at the time the judicial declaration is to be taken, the judge shall appoint on his motion a public defender, unless the accused is authorized to assume his own defense."

147. CcrP arts. 297 and 298.

148. CcrP art. 295: "Only the public prosecutor and counsel for the accused may be present at his declaration. The accused shall be informed of this right before the declaration begins." On what the public prosecutor and defense counsel can and cannot do at this stage, see CcrP arts. 198 and 203.

149. CcrP art. 299: "Unless the accused refuses to declare, the judge shall invite him to manifest anything that he may deem convenient to discharge him or clarify the facts, and to indicate the evidence he considers appropriate. The declaration shall be recorded verbatim, in the own words employed by the accused, unless he chooses to dictate it. Afterwards, the judge shall pose the questions he deems convenient, in a clear and accurate, and never suggestive or misleading, manner. The declarant may dictate his answers, which shall not be elicited peremptorily. The public prosecutor and defense counsels shall have the duties and powers set forth in Articles 198 and 203. If, due to the length of the act, signs of fatigue or the absence of calm were to be observed in the accused, the declaration shall be stayed until those signs disappear."

statements indicative of sincere repentance may have a mitigating effect at the time of sentencing. The rules of criminal procedure adopted in 1993 expressly provide, in a language that was not present in the former code,[150] that the warning addressed to the defendant to the effect that he is entitled to appoint counsel of his choice must take place before the interrogation begins.[151] It follows that it is possible for the defendant to be guided by counsel's advice when called upon to exercise the option to talk or to stand mute. This constitutional right to counsel also plays a role in the case of *incommunicado* detentions.

Incommunicado Detentions. The investigative magistrate, and the police officer who opened the investigation as well, may decide to keep a suspect *incommunicado* whenever "there are reasonable grounds to fear that the defendant may concoct an agreement with others or otherwise hinder the investigation."[152] If this measure is taken by the police, it cannot be extended for more than six hours, at the end of which the *incommunicado* defendant must be submitted to a medical examination.[153] If the incommunication is decreed by an investigative magistrate the defendant may be so held for as long as forty-eight hours, with a possibility of an extension for a twenty-four hour period.[154]

Although intended for exceptional circumstances, *incommunicado* detentions have been routinely decreed.[155] Under the rules of criminal procedure predating the adoption of the 1993 CcrP, *incommunicado* defendants were not entitled to talk to a lawyer or to anybody else until the lifting of the incommunication, generally immediately after the defendant's judicial interrogation.[156] This was held to constitute a violation of the right to counsel guaranteed by the American Convention on

150. In the past, the Supreme Court casted doubts as to whether the right of the accused to be informed of his right to be assisted by a counsel of his choice was required to take place before the hearing. Several Supreme Court decisions found of no constitutional consequence that the accused was not advised of his right to counsel until a later point of the judicial interrogation *Romano*, CSJN, 259 Fallos 69 (1964); *Mauri*, CSJN, 298 Fallos 498 (1977).

151. CcrP art. 197: "At the first opportunity, even during the police investigation and in any event before the judicial declaration, the judge shall invite the accused to appoint defense counsel; if the accused fails to make the appointment or the attorney refuses to accept the appointment immediately, the judge shall proceed pursuant to Article 107. Defense counsel may confer with his client immediately before the acts referred to in Article 184, last paragraph [i.e., whenever the accused expresses the urgent need to declare], and Article 294 [i.e., at the moment of the judicial declaration], on pain of nullity of those acts."

152. CcrP art. 205.

153. CcrP art. 184.8. According to Article 205 of the CcrP, the judge may, by virtue of a "reasoned opinion" (*auto fundado*), extend the six-hour *incommunicado* detention for sixty-six hours, to complete a total period of seventy-two hours.

154. CcrP art. 205: "The judge may decree the incommunication of the detainee for no longer than forty-eight hours, which may be extended for another twenty-four hours by a reasoned opinion, whenever there are reasonable grounds to fear that the defendant may concoct an agreement with others or otherwise hinder the investigation. When the police has exercised the authority granted by Article 184.8, the judge may extend the incommunication until completing a maximum period of seventy-two hours. In no case the incommunication shall prevent the detainee to communicate with his defense counsel immediately before his judicial declaration or before undertaken any other act requiring the detainee's personal intervention. The *incommunicado* detainee shall be allowed to use books and other objects that he requests, provided that they may not be used to avoid the incommunication or to threaten his life or that of others. Also, he shall be allowed to undertake civil acts that cannot be postponed, as long as they do not decrease his solvency or hinder the goals of the investigation."

155. Caferata Nores, *El imputado* 94-97 (1982).

156. Edwards, *El defensor técnico en la prevención policial* 118-135 (1992).

Human Rights[157] and the regulation of *incommunicado* detentions was changed in 1993.[158] In several cases that were decided immediately after the new code had come into force, investigative magistrates decided to proceed with the questioning of the defendants after they had expressed their wish to be assisted by the public defenders appointed to represent them. It was not disputed, however, that none of the defendants had made an express request to confer with their counsel prior to the beginning of the interrogation. The public defenders, who were notified of their appointment after the conclusion of the interrogation, sought to suppress the incriminating statements offered by the defendants. The suppression was granted by the courts on the ground that the public defenders had not been notified of their appointment before the commencement of the interrogation, thus depriving the defendants of their constitutional right to an "effective defense" (*derecho a contar con una defensa eficiente*), which included the chance for attorney and client to confer with each other before the judicial interrogation begins.[159]

Right to Bail. Once arrested, the suspect's release depends on whether he is entitled to be released on bail or, to put it in the terms of the rules of criminal procedure, to be "exempted from imprisonment" (*exención de prisión*). Although the suspect is deemed to be "at the disposition" of the investigative magistrate as of the very moment of his arrest, defense counsel is unlikely to file a request for bail until the judge has an opportunity to receive the police report and to interrogate the defendant. Only then defense counsel may become aware of the charges brought against his client; pressing the court to rule before that time risks an early denial of bail.

Release on bail is likely to be granted if the maximum sentence contemplated for the crime with which the suspect is charged does not exceed eight years of imprisonment,[160] or if in light of the nature of the criminal offense with which the defendant is charged, the defendant's personality and his criminal record (*condenación condicional*), the court estimates *prima facie* that he will receive a suspended sentence, rather than actually be sent to jail.[161] The weight of the evidence against the accused (or the existence of "probable cause" of his involvement) is irrelevant to the decision whether to release him pending adjudication.[162] The

157. *M.M.L. y otro*, CNFedRosario-B, 6 Oct. 1989, cited by Edwards, idem, at 122 (holding art. 680 of the previous CcrP in violation of art. 8.2(d) of the American Convention on Human Rights.) See American Convention on Human Rights, art. 8.2(d), providing for the right of every person accused of a criminal offense "to defend himself personally or to be assisted by legal counsel of his own choosing, and to communicate freely and privately with his counsel".

158. CcrP arts. 197, 205, and 294.

159. *Navarrete*, Criminal Court of First Instance (*Tribunal Oral*, hereinafter "Criminal Court") No. 9, 20 April 1993; *Píriz*, Criminal Court No. 2, 31 March 1993, LL, 24 Sept. 1993. Neither court referred to the defendant's privilege against self-incrimination, probably in order to avoid placing on the defendant the burden of establishing coercion in order to nullify the judicial interrogation. Also, the court deemed irrelevant whether a defendant deprived of the opportunity to confer with his lawyer before the interrogation actually made any incriminating statements while declaring before the magistrate. See also, *A.G.A.*, Criminal Court No. 7, 27 April 1993, ED, 9 Sept. 1993; *Colina Vega*, Criminal Court No. 2, 20 May 1993, LL, 2 Sept. 1993.

160. CcrP art. 316.

161. CcrP arts. arts. 316-19.

162. *Alurralde*, CSJN, 54 Fallos 264 (1893), to the effect that a determination as to whether the defendant should be released on bail rests on the penalty established for the charged crime, irrespective of the allegations or defenses raised by the defendant.

need to ensure the defendant's presence at trial, or to prevent him from carrying on criminal activities, has been cited as the most common constitutional rationale for keeping in jail some one who has not yet been tried. Even if the judge initially refuses to release the defendant, his "exemption from incarceration" (*excarcelación*) may come at a later point if the judge finds, for example, that the time the defendant spent in jail, compared with that he his likely to serve if convicted, would make him eligible for parole.[163]

The Supreme Court has not shown a consistent approach toward the admission of a constitutional right to bail. An early line of decisions affirmed a constitutional right to bail in favor of those charged with crimes not punishable by imprisonment.[164] More recent decisions refused to review denials of bail by lower courts on the ground that those decisions are interlocutory rather than final, involving the interpretation of local procedural rules.[165] Only in exceptional cases the Court has accepted denials of bail for review. Those decisions were based on the ground that a refusal to free a suspect who has not yet been tried entails irreparable harm for those whose trials will not end in a conviction.[166] In these exceptional cases, the request for review has been generally accompanied by an additional constitutional grievance, such as a challenge to the constitutionality of the statute on the basis of which bail was denied.[167] The federal rules of criminal procedure, as well as those adopted in some Argentine provinces, provide that defendants charged with certain types of crimes cannot be released on bail. Despite wide criticisms voiced against such blank refusal to the right to bail, the Supreme Court has refused to invalidate any of those rules on constitutional grounds. According to the weight of scholarly authority, depriving a person of his freedom when he has not yet been convicted violates Article 18 of the CN, providing that "no inhabitant shall be punished without a previous trial." While admitting that this right is not absolute, most legal commentators are of the opinion that bail may be refused only if the court finds strong reasons for believing that the suspect has committed the crime and the evi-

---

163. CcrP art. 317(5).

164. *Fiscal v. Martínez*, CSJN, 7 Fallos 371 (1869); *Aguirre*, CSJN, 16 Fallos 88 (1875); *Alurralde et al.*, CSJN, 54 Fallos 264 (1893); *Amoretti*, CSJN, 64 Fallos 352 (1895); *Llanos*, CSJN, 102 Fallos 219 (1905). The cases arose in connection with early criminal statutes adopted before the enactment of the Criminal Code of 1921, providing for expulsion from the country of those convicted of rebellion. In those decisions, the Supreme Court held the unconstitutionality of procedural statutes denying a right to bail to persons accused of crimes subject to banishment. Relying on the final clause of Article 18 of the CN, to the effect that "jails must be kept clean and healthy for the security and not for the punishment of the prisoners confined therein," the Court reasoned that keeping in custody persons who could not actually be sent to jail even if convicted deprived the pretrial detention of any constitutional foundation.

165. *Szpitalny*, CSJN, 287 Fallos 343 (1973); *Muroquio*, CSJN, 297 Fallos 495 (1977).

166. *Massera*, CSJN, 109 ED 127 (1984). Occasionally, the Supreme Court made reference to a "constitutional right" to be free pending the final adjudication of the case. See, e.g., *C.M.P.*, CSJN, 111 ED 465 (1984) (stating that a particular construction of a statutory provision concerning bail was consistent with "the constitutional right to remain free during the intermediate stages of a criminal process"); *Instituto Nacional de Reaseguros*, CSJN, 301 Fallos 664 (1979); *Todres*, CSJN, 280 Fallos 297 (1971).

167. *Aguilera*, CSJN, 300 Fallos 321 (1981); *Machicote*, CSJN, 300 Fallos 642 (1978) (Upholding a statutory provision making defendants charged with five or more separate crimes ineligible for bail, for it was reasonable to assume that those charges made it unlikely that the defendants would attend the trial if released on bail.)

dence before the court points to a specific, rational grounds to believe that the defendant will flee, thereby preventing the trial to take place.[168]

2. *Charging Instrument*

Once the judicial interrogation is completed, the investigative magistrate must decide within ten days, and on the basis of the evidence presented so far, whether there are "sufficient elements of persuasion" (*elementos de convicción suficientes*) to believe that a criminal offense has been committed and of the defendant's participation in it.[169] If the evidence is insufficient to implicate him, the defendant must be unconditionally released for lack of cause (*falta de mérito*), without prejudice to the continuation of the criminal inquiry.[170] If, on the other hand, the magistrate finds "sufficient elements of persuasion," he must issue issue a charging decision or indictment (*auto de procesamiento*) within ten days after the judicial interrogation. The indictment is issued by the investigative magistrate, without the participation of a grand jury or court, and it must specify the charges, the evidence against the defendant, and the criminal statute that has been allegedly infringed.[171]

The indictment may or may not be accompanied by a pre-trial detention decree, but in any event the judge must decide at that point in time whether the defendant is to remain in custody or released. Even if the charging decision provides that the defendant is to remain in custody, the magistrate retains the power to dismiss the case (*sobreseimiento*) and release the defendant if at any time during the course of the investigation she were to find that the offense actually never took place or that the defendant had nothing to do with it.[172] Public prosecutors have no discretion to decide whether to bring charges and, if so, which charges to bring. They are required to bring a prosecutorial request (*requerimiento de instrucción*) if all the elements of the commission of a criminal offense subject to public prosecution have been met.[173]

3. *Preliminary Hearing*

The granting of bail and the decision as to whether the defendant should be kept in custody pending the trial does not depend on the evidence that can be produced against him at a preliminary hearing, nor on a determination of "probable cause," but rather on the seriousness of the crime, the defendant's criminal record

168. See, e.g., Julio Maier, *Cuestiones fundamentales sobre la libertad del imputado* 29- 33 (1981); J. Cafferata Nores, *El imputado no procesado*, JA, No. 5209, 7 July 1981; J. Virgolini, *El derecho a la libertad en el proceso penal* 40 (1984); 1 Vélez Mariconde, *Derecho Procesal Penal Argentino* 321 (3rd ed. 1982).

169. CcrP art. 306.

170. CcrP art. 309. The decision to release a defendant for lack of cause need not be based on reasons, but it may be appealed by the prosecutor and the victim (*querellante particular*). CcrP art. 311.

171. CcrP art. 308.

172. CcrP art. 336: "A dismissal shall proceed when: (1) the criminal action is extinguished; (2) the acts under investigation did not take place; (3) the act under investigation does not fit within the statute; (4) the crime was not committed by the accused; (5) there is a cause for justification, inimputability, inculpability, or a defense. In the case of paragraphs (2), (3), (4), and (5), the judge shall state that the proceedings do not affect the reputation and honor enjoyed by the accused."

173. CcrP art. 188.

and other personal circumstances. If, on the one hand, the investigative magistrate finds "sufficient elements of persuasion" to the effect that the defendant is more likely than not to have committed a crime, but the requirements for keeping him incarcerated pending trial have not been met,[174] the judge may issue an indictment while ordering the defendant's release under certain conditions. It is beyond dispute that the evidence against the defendant need not be conclusive to warrant an indictment,[175] but the kind and quantity of evidence that would amount to the level of probability of guilt warranting a finding of "sufficient elements of persuasion" has never been fully articulated by the courts. The fact that the defendant has been granted a "provisional release" (*libertad provisoria*) does not impede the continuation of the investigation and a subsequent determination as to whether the defendant should stand trial for the alleged crime.

On the other hand, if "sufficient elements of persuasion" pointing to the defendant's guilt are found to exist, the investigative magistrate must order a pre-trial detention decree, provided that the charges are serious enough as to merit a penalty exceeding eight years of imprisonment and that, *prima facie*, the defendant will be actually sent to jail rather than enjoy the benefit of a suspended sentence.[176] The defendant may also be kept in detention while the trial is pending if his or her personal traits and the nature of the crime provides to the court well-founded reasons to believe that he or she will flee or hinder the investigation.[177] Pretrial release may be conditioned upon the posting of a personal or real security, or upon the defendant's own recognizance and agreement to appear in court whenever required.[178] The court's decision allowing or refusing bail may be appealed within

---

174. CcrP art. 310, first paragraph: "Whenever the requirements set forth in Article 312 have not been met and an indictment is issued without a pre-trial decree, the accused shall be provisionally released and the judge may order him to remain in or not to go to a given place, or to present himself to a given authority pursuant to a schedule to be determined. If the crime with which he has been charged provide for disqualification (*inhabilitación*) for a certain activity, the defendant may be also ordered to abstain from such activity. . ."

175. *Horiansky*, 82 ED 595 (1978).

176. CcrP art. 312: "Unless the judge confirms the provisional release previously granted to the defendant, the judge shall order that he be kept in pretrial detention (*prisión preventiva*) whenever: (1) The criminal offense or offenses attributed to him are punished with imprisonment and the judge believes, *prima facie*, that the benefit of a suspended sentence (*condenación condicional*) is not available. (2) Even if a sentence of imprisonment with the benefit of a suspended sentence is available, there can be no provisional release pursuant to Article 319." Release on bail does not proceed, according to Article 319 of the CcrP, whenever "an objective assessment of the facts" the criminal record of the defendant, and other circumstances of the case lead the magistrate to believe that the defendant "will try to flee or hinder the investigation." The benefit of a suspended sentence may be granted only to first-time offenders whose sentence does not exceed three years of imprisonment. Under Article 26 of the Criminal Code, the decision rests at the discretion of the sentencing court, which must take into account, among other elements, "the moral character of the defendant, his behavior after the offense, the motives prompting him to commit it, and any other circumstances advising against the effective deprivation of freedom."

177. CcrP art. 319: "With due respect for the principle of innocence and pursuant to Article 2 of this Code, bail may be denied whenever [the judge] has well-grounded reasons to believe that the defendant will try to flee or hinder the investigation, as per a neutral and interim assessment of the facts, the likelihood of recidivism, his personal conditions and past record if previously released on bail."

178. CcrP arts. 320-24, distinguishing between a release conditioned upon the defendant's own recognizance (*caución juratoria*), the posting of a personal surety (*caución personal*), and posting a real security (*caución real*).

twenty-four hours by the prosecutor or by the defense counsel.[179] Any decision granting bail must be carried out immediately, even if the prosecutor has filed an appeal.[180]

4. *Pretrial Motions*

The rules of criminal procedure do not provide much room for litigating issues or raising collateral questions unrelated to the determination of guilt. The only defenses (*excepciones*) that may be set up at the trial are those related to the court's lack of jurisdiction of the court, double jeopardy claims, the running of the statute of limitations, and a few other instances impeding the prosecution to go forward.[181] In the case of exceptional and gross deviations from the procedural rules (e.g., an investigative magistrate compelling a defendant to testify under oath), any of the parties to the proceedings may request that the tainted act be held null and void and stricken from the record. Thus, if a defendant wants to suppress evidence on the ground that it has been obtained in violation of rules that are expressly sanctioned with nullity,[182] he may file a motion to declare that such an act, and all proceedings undertaken thereafter, be declared void and stricken from the record.[183]

A motion seeking the nullity of any procedural act is not available unless and until such an act rests on a judicial decision susceptible of appeal. In addition, a motion to suppress must be filed within the stage of the proceeding in which the allegedly void act took place.[184] Accordingly, the procedural opportunity to request the suppression of evidence wrongfully obtained during the pre-trial stage is not available unless it is raised prior to the trial by way of a challenge to a judicial decision affirming such evidence. This means that an illegal seizure made by the police, from which a thorough investigation ensues, can not be challenged immediately after its occurrence, but only after the rendering of an appealable judicial decision such as a pre-trial detention decree. If the defendant remains free on bail during the course of the investigation, and a motion for the suppression of evidence is brought at the end of the judicial inquiry, courts of appeal have shown some reluctance to grant such a sweeping remedy, which entails not only the exclusion of the wrongfully obtained evidence but also of all subsequent investigatory steps. More often than not, appellate courts are inclined to consider the evidence subject to challenge as "harmless error," thus allowing the case to move forward. By way of exception, if the evidence has been allegedly obtained in violation of the defendant's constitutional rights, motions for its suppression have been more generously accepted by some appellate courts at any time, on the ground that a procedural flaw of this magnitude is not susceptible of being subsequently "cured."[185]

---

179. CcrP art. 332.

180. Ibidem (providing that the judicial decision on bail may be appealed but that such an appeal shall not have "suspensive effects," i.e., it shall not entail a stay of the decision appealed from).

181. CcrP art. 339.

182. CcrP art. 166: "Procedural acts shall be null and void whenever they fail to observe the provisions expressly prescribed on penalty of nullity."

183. CcrP art. 172: "An act that has been declared void shall render null and void all the acts subsequently undertaken whose validity depends on the void act."

184. CcrP art. 170.

185. 1 D'Albora, *Curso de Derecho Procesal Penal* 158-59.

5. *Discovery*

In principle, any of the parties to the proceeding (i.e., the public prosecutor, the victim, and the defendant) acquire access to the dossier or written report prepared by the police as soon as the judicial interrogation has been completed. The right of the defendant to a timely inspection of the dossier is not without limits. The investigative magistrate may decree by a written and reasoned decision that the pretrial proceedings shall remain secret during the first ten days of the investigation if "publicity is likely to endanger the discovery of the truth."[186] The judicial decree providing for the "secrecy of the investigation" (*secreto del sumario*) may be extended for another ten-day period if "the seriousness of the crime or the complexity of the investigation so demand."[187] During this period of confidentiality, the defendant and his defense counsel are prevented from attending the examination of witnesses, monitoring the seizure of evidence, examining laboratory tests and expert reports, etc. The public prosecutor, however, may examine the record in spite of its secrecy.[188] The authority of the investigative magistrate to decree the confidentiality of the pretrial investigations has never been successfully challenged. In those instances where the issue came up for review, the Supreme Court held that the defendant's constitutional right to be heard, confront witnesses and present evidence on his behalf is satisfied as long as this opportunity is given at a later stage in the proceedings.[189]

As noted, even if the defendant is given access to the statements of accusing witnesses, documents that may be used against him and expert reports ordered by the police or the investigative magistrate, the role of the prosecutor, the victim, and defense counsel is very limited at this point. They are allowed to suggest that some investigatory steps be taken, but the investigative magistrate has almost unbridled discretion to accept or reject such proposals.[190] At the time of the judicial interrogation, the defense counsel is not permitted to object to any question put to the defendant by the judge or to pose any question to his client without the authorization of the judge. The role of counsel during this pretrial stage is mostly limited to ensure that her client's answers are transcribed accurately in the dossier and that the examination is conducted in a regula way.

B. Trial

At the conclusion of the pretrial investigation, the investigative magistrate must decide whether in her judgment the evidence is strong enough to warrant a decision for the opening of the trial stage (*auto de elevación a juicio*). Thus, the judge is due to request, first to the public prosecutor, and then to the victim-prosecutor, to conduct a thorough examination of the record during six days to determine whether further investigatory steps should be taken, or whether the defendant

186. CcrP art. 204.

187. CcrP art. 204.

188. The rules of criminal procedure in some Argentine provinces (e.g., Córdoba, Mendoza, Catamarca, Salta, La Rioja) allow the defendant and counsel to examine the record in spite of the secret and to control some investigatory steps.

189. *Ordoñez*, CSJN, 223 Fallos 128 (1952); *Escobar*, 247 Fallos 86 (1960).

190. *Beltrame*, CNCrimCorr-VI, 6 Nov. 1977; *Garber*, CNCrimCorr-V, 12 ED 733.

should stand trial or be exonerated.[191] Counsel for the defense also has the right to inspect the whole dossier, suggest the taking of additional evidence, and to submit arguments within six days to respond to the accusation that may be brought by the public prosecutor or the victim.[192] If additional evidence is requested by any of the parties, it is within the discretion of the investigative magistrate to determine whether those additional investigatory steps are "pertinent and useful."[193]

If the prosecutor believes that the evidence gathered during the pretrial stage does not warrant a trial, he is bound to request the defendant's exoneration and the dismissal (*sobreseimiento*) of the case, providing reasons supporting this conclusion. The investigative magistrate may or may not agree with public prosecutor. On the one hand, if the investigative magistrate sides with the prosecutor's request for exoneration, a decision will be issued dismissing the case against the defendant. However, this decision of the investigative magistrate exonerating the defendant may be appealed within three days by counsel for the victim,[194] because under Argentine law the victim is not only entitled to appear in the criminal proceeding for the purpose of seeking monetary compensation, but it may also seek an order for the defendant to stand trial and his eventual conviction and punishment, thus asserting procedural rights similar to those given to the public prosecutor.[195] If the victim appeals the dismissal ordered by the investigative magistrate, the dossier goes to a three-judge panel (on a higher level of the judicial hierarchy) which, having studied the dossier and having given defense counsel an opportunity to submit arguments and to suggest the taking of additional evidence, determines whether or not the accused should stand trial. On the other hand, if the investigative magistrate disagrees with the public prosecutor's request for a dismissal, because in his opinion the evidence is strong enough to warrant the bringing of formal charges against the defendant, the dossier will also be transmitted to a three-judge panel. If , after studying the dossier and hearing the defense counsel, that panel decides that the defendant should stand trial, the prosecutor who originally refused to accuse must be replaced by another prosecutor who will appear at the trial and for whom the three-judge panel's order to bring charges is binding.[196]

If the prosecutor finds that the evidence against the defendant is strong enough to warrant the bringing of formal charges, he has the duty to submit a written accusation and a request for a judicial decree ordering the opening of the trial stage. This formal presentation by the prosecutor must specify the facts constituting the crime charged and the criminal statute allegedly violated by the defendant.[197] The accusation brought by the public prosecutor automatically triggers the trial process. Moreover, the judicial decree ordering the defendant to stand trial is not subject to appeal.[198] As noted below in connection with guilty pleas, the defendant's admission of guilt is not binding on the investigative magistrate or on the trial court. Whether the defendant should stand trial and, if so, whether he is guilty or not, is to be taken independently of whether he decides to contest his guilt, un-

191. CcrP art. 346.
192. CcrP art. 349.
193. CcrP art. 348, paragraph 1.
194. CcrP art. 352.
195. CcrP arts. 82 and 87.
196. CcrP art. 348, paragraph 2.
197. CcrP art. 347.
198. CcrP art. 352.

less the nature of the changes warrant the application of an "abbreviated trial," as explained below.

1. Nature of the Trial

Until the reforms were introduced in 1993, criminal proceedings at the federal level consisted of a succession of written motions and intermittent interlocutory decisions. Probably the most radical of those reforms was the adoption of a concentrated and oral trial conducted by a panel of three judges.[199] The dossier, reflecting the evidence gathered during the pretrial stage, plays a role during the trial as well. In principle, only the evidence received in open court (as distinguished from the contents of the dossier) may be considered in reaching a decision. However, the most relevant evidence is likely to have been collected before the trial. Although the prosecutor, the victim, and the defense may request the re-examination of any witness or the reproduction of any evidence, the witnesses are likely to be the same as those whose testimony is recorded in the dossier. The trial court retains the power to request the production of additional evidence if in its discretion such evidence will be conducive to clarify the facts. There is a limit, of course, as to how far can the court go in requesting "measures to improve the decision of the case" (*medidas para mejor proveer*) without infringing on the parties' right to be heard. Thus, in *Saulo*, defense counsel noted during his closing argument that the weakness of the prosecution's case had been confirmed by the prosecutor's failure to summon a key witness. Immediately thereafter, the the trial court summoned on its own motion that particular witness, whose testimony proved to be crucial in the conviction of the defendant. The court of appeals reversed on the ground that despite the authority given to the court by the rules of criminal procedure, encouraging the production of evidence not adduced by the parties when necessary to clarify the facts, in this particular case the trial court had improperly assumed an inquisitorial posture, when calling *sua sponte* for the declaration of a witness whose testimony the prosecutor purposedly intended to exclude.[200]

Once the evidence has been produced, the parties are allowed to present a summation (*alegatos*) in their closing arguments (*discusión final*).[201] Immediately thereafter the trial court takes an opportunity to deliberate and renders a judgment passing on issues of law as well as fact, determinining guilt or innocence of the defendant and the appropriate sentence.[202] The weight of the evidence is governed by a standard of "free evaluation" (*sana crítica*), but both the finding of facts and the determination of the sentence must be supported by reasons. The mere assertion of a trial court, without more elaboration, that "the witnesses' declarations have established the defendant's guilt" has been held plainly insufficient to support a conviction.[203] The trial court is not bound to adopt the prosecutor's legal characterization of the defendant's conduct. As long

199. Law No. 24050, 7 Jan. 1992, on the Organization and Jurisdiction of Criminal Courts (*Ley de Organización y Competencia Penal*), art. 2(c); Law No. 24121, 8 Sept. 1992, on the Implementationand Organization of Criminal Trials (*Ley de Implementación y Organización del Proceso Penal Oral*), art. 8, 51-D ADLA 3913.

200. *Saulo*, CNCrimCorr., JA-1957-III-433

201. CcrP art. 393.

202. CcrP arts. 398-399.

203. CNCrimCorr-II, II Fallos 209.

as the judgment rests on the facts or acts which were the focus of the investigation and the defendant was given ample opportunity to present her case, the application of a criminal statute different from the one invoked by the prosecutor has been held constitutionally permissible.[204]

Guilty Pleas. Even if the defendant admitted his guilt during the pretrial investigation, or if he decides to confess in response to the questioning by the judge presiding at the trial, the trial proceedings must go on.[205] In other words, the defendant cannot waive his right to trial by "pleading guilty" (or *nolo contendere*). It is true that, by fully confessing, the defendant can contribute to the shortening of his trial. But agreements between the prosecution and the defense, granting sentencing and other concessions have been traditionally regarded as repugnant to public policy.

However, in the face of mounting criminal caseloads, an amendment allowing for the prompt consensual disposition of criminal cases was introduced in 1997. This amendment provides for an "abbreviated trial" (*juicio abreviado*) in those cases where the charges brought by the prosecutor do not require a deprivation of his freedom or do not exceed six years of imprisonment.[206] According to this scheme, the defendant may agree to a summary adjudication of the case in exchange for a reduced sentence should he be found guilty. The trial court may either accept the terms of the agreement or rule in favor of the continuation of the trial to ascertain the facts. In case the stipulation is accepted, the trial court must pronounce the sentence within ten days, which can not be harsher than the one agreed upon by the prosecutor and the defendant. If the trial court does not approve the agreement, the case is transmitted to another trial court to proceed with the trial, in which the defendant's admission of guilt and the prosecutor's request for a penalty is to be disregarded.[207]

2. *Defendant*

As noted, at the judicial interrogation during the pretrial stage the defendant is not required to speak under oath and his refusal to speak may not be commented upon at any stage of the proceedings.[208] The same safeguards surround his declaration during the trial.[209] Yet the defendant is entitled to assert his right to make an unsworn statement and to communicate with his defense counsel at any time during the trial, except during the course of the interrogation or before responding to any of the questions posed to him.[210] It is also part of the defendant's right of due process to compel the attendance of witnesses in his favor and to cross-examine witnesses against him. It is noteworthy that while a defendant who lies may not be prosecuted for perjury, any inconsistency in his statements is likely to affect his general credibility and may be commented upon in the final judgment.[211]

204. CcrP art. 401, *Panzer*, CSJN, 302 Fallos 328 (1980).

205. If the defendant flees or is declared mentally incompetent to stand trial, the proceedings must be stayed until he reappears or regains his sanity. *Lanvin*, CNFedCorr, JA, 1972-205.

206. CcrP art. 431bis, as introduced by Law No. 24825, 11 June 1997.

207. CcrP art. 431bis, paragraph 4.

208. CcrP art. 296.

209. CcrP art. 296.

210. CcrP art. 380.

211. CcrP art. 378.

3. *Lawyers*

Any defendant who fails to retain an attorney of her choice is entitled to be represented by a public defender (*defensor oficial*) remunerated by the State.[212] The right to be represented by a public defender is not subject to the defendant's proof of lack of financial resources. Moreover, the constitutional right to counsel has been held to attach to any type of offense, no matter how petty is the case.[213] The defendant may waive his right to be represented by counsel, but such a waiver may not be inferred or tacitly assumed as a result of the defendant's failure to make an express request.[214] Moreover, it has been held that an express waiver to be assisted by counsel at the time of the judicial interrogation shall not be construed as a waiver to avail himself of counsel's advice at a later stage of the proceedings.[215]

The right to counsel has been understood as encompassing a right to appear *pro se*, but this right of self-representation is accepted only if the defendant shows that he is capable of presenting an "effective" defense. In those cases in which it was found that an appearance *pro se* posed an obstacle to the regular development of the proceedings, the Supreme Court upheld the court's duty to appoint a public defender against the defendant's wishes.[216] However, in one case in which a court inexplicably forced the appointment of a public defender despite defendant's appointment of a counsel of his choice, the Supreme Court held that the constitutional right to counsel was violated by failing to inform the defendant of the "grave decision" to appoint a public defender to represent him.[217]

The office of the public prosecutor belongs to a larger hierarchical organization known as the "Public Ministry." A public prosecutor in Argentina cuts a figure more akin to members of the judiciary than to the the partisan advocate that characterizes the role of the district attorney in the United States. It is not uncommon for a judge to have served as a prosecutor previously to being appointed to the bench. As a practical matter, the office of the public prosecutor lacks the financial resources and the legal powers to conduct a criminal investigation, which is in the hands of the investigative magistrate and the police. Although prosecutors are allowed to receive and process a criminal complaint (*denuncia*), this is rare.[218] During the pretrial investigation, the role of the prosecutor is to assist the investigative magistrate in ascertaining the truth and finding the culprits. The prosecutor may, though she is not bound to, attend the judicial interrogation of the accused and advise the magistrate on steps to be taken during the course of the investigation.[219] She lacks the authority to question the defendant without the authorization of the

212. CcrP art. 107.

213. *Moyano*, CSJN, 296 Fallos 65 (1976).

214. *Sueldo*, CSJN, 110 ED 789 (1984).

215. *Rojas Molina*, CSJN, 189 Fallos 34 (1941).

216. *Valle*, CSJN, 269 Fallos 405 (1967). Although the grounds for the investigating magistrate's findings that the defendant's self-representation hindered the proceedings cannot be easily ascertained from this opinion, the Supreme Court held that the judge acted within his powers in imposing a public defender to represent him.

217. *Paz*, CSJN, 279 Fallos 91 (1977).

218. CcrP art. 188. In some Argentine provinces, prosecutors are empowered to decide whether the facts reported in the complaint implicate the violation of a criminal statute or not, thus retaining some kind of power, though not discretion, to decide whether the complaint merits the opening of a judicial inquiry.

219. CcrP arts. 65-71.

judge and is not allowed to order that a particular step be taken. During the trial, both in theory and in practice, the actions of the prosecutor are not characterized by an adversarial zeal, but rather as those of a neutral decision maker.

4. *Expert Witnesses*

During the pretrial phase and at trial, expert witnesses (*peritos*) are chosen by the court from a permanent list of official experts, who bear the status of auxiliary officers of the court.[220] Although listed in the official roster of experts, the bulk of their income comes from their own private business or profession, since official experts are likely to obtain judicial appointments only occasionally. The public prosecutor, the victim, or the defendant are entitled to offer the testimony of their own expert, in addition to that of the official expert.[221] Party-appointed experts are paid by the appointing party or by the party who must ultimately bear the costs of the proceedings.[222] As a practical matter, however, courts are likely to follow the opinion of the official expert.

5. *Judges*

The trial court is composed by judges who are not the same as the investigative magistrates in charge of the preliminary investigation, though all of them are judges subject to the same appointment mechanisms. Both at the federal and state levels, Argentine judges are non-elected officials, appointed for life by the executive branch with consent by the Senate at the federal level and a state legislature at the state level.

At the trial, the bench consists of a panel of three professional judges, who decide both on the facts and the law, without the assistance of a jury (as in common law countries) or lay assessors (as in many countries of Continental Europe). The Constitution of Argentina has proclaimed for more than a century the establishment of trials by jury, and that intention has been reaffirmed with the adoption of the 1994 amendment.[223] However, Congress has failed to this date to comply with this constitutional mandate, which has been the subject of perennial debate.

6. *Victims*

The victim of a crime may retain an attorney to act on his behalf in order to participate in the prosecution of the criminal proceeding as a "victim-prosecutor" (*querellante particular*). The victim's participation in this legal capacity starts from the very beginning of the investigation: suggesting means of evidence to the investigative magistrate, seeking a judicial decree forcing the defendant to stand trial, his criminal conviction and punishment. The procedural rights of the victim prosecu-

---

220. CcrP arts. 253 and 258.

221. CcrP art. 259.

222. CcrP art. 267.

223. CN art. 24 ("Congress shall promote the reform of all branches of the legislation in force and the establishment of trial by jury"); art. 118 ("All ordinary criminal trials, except cases of impeachment originating in the Chamber of Deputies, shall be resolved by a trial by jury, after this institution is established in the Republic."); art. 75.12 ("Congress shall have the power:. . .12. To issue . . whatever laws are required to establish trial by jury.").

tor to submit and monitor the evidence against the defendant and to file motions and appeals are substantially similar (although not in every detail) to those of the public prosecutor. Thus, the victim prosecutor may submit a written accusation in addition to the charges brought by the public prosecutor. In this case, while the prosecutor will remain technically responsible for the prosecution of the case, in practice the victim prosecutor is the party who leads the prosecution. If the public prosecutor were to request a dismissal of the case or refuses to go forward with the investigation, the victim prosecutor may nevertheless file an accusation,[224] in which case the investigative magistrate shall transfer the dossier to the intermediate appellate court, which may order another prosecutor to bring charges.[225]

The legal capacity of the victim, which may be a physical person or a legal entity,[226] to intervene as a victim prosecutor has a significant impact on the development of the case. In most cases, it prevents the routine and premature dismissal of cases, proposing new lines of inquiry and checking on the investigatory steps taken by the judge. If the case goes to trial, the defendant will face two accusing parties, both allowed to present evidence, cross-examine witnesses, present closing arguments, recover attorney's fees from a convicted defendant, and eventually appeal his acquittal.[227] In most cases, the victim's decision to become a party to the criminal proceedings is aimed at forcing a deal with the defendant. By reaching a settlement and compensating the victim, the defendant greatly improves his chances to obtain an early dismissal of the case, especially in complex cases where the defendant is likely to face the counsel for the victim continuously challenging his defenses or submitting evidence to the court.[228] Whereas the defendant is able to mitigate this problem by setting the claim for compensation and removing counsel for the victim from the proceedings, the settlement does not ensure the victim an exoneration or a more lenient treatment.

In addition to her eventual participation in the prosecution, the victim may also seek a determination of civil liability and an award for compensatory damages, thus becoming a "civil party" (*actor civil*)[229] to the criminal proceedings.[230] If the victim appears as a civil party in the criminal proceeding, then the criminal

---

224. It is noteworthy, however, that Article 245 of the Criminal Code makes the filing of unsupported criminal charges a criminal offense.

225. CcrP art. 348.

226. *Díaz Urbano*, CNCrimCorr, JA, 1977-V-261.

227. CcrP art. 435.

228. Under Argentine law, the victim's settlement of her claim for compensation or the victim's waiver of the civil action automatically compels the withdraw of his status as a party to the criminal proceedings. Article 1097 of the Civil Code reads: "A civil action shall not be deemed waived by the fact that the aggrieved persons failed to bring a criminal complaint or for having desisted therefrom during their lifetime; nor shall it be understood that the victims waive the criminal action on account of having brought a civil action or having desisted therefrom. But if they waived the civil action or made an agreement as to the payment of damages, the criminal action shall be deemed waived."

229. CcrP art. 87.

230. Criminal Code, arts. 29-33. Article 29 of the Criminal Code reads: "The sentence may provide for: 1. Compensation for actual harm and pain and suffering caused to the victim and his family or to a third party. In the absence of full evidence, the court may determine the amount within its discretion. 2. The restitution of the object obtained by the crime, and if restitution is impossible, the payment by the convict of the regular price of the object, as well as its sentimental value if it has such. 3. The procedural costs. 4. When the civil compensation has not been satisfied while the convict is serving the sentence, or if a judgment of compensation has been ren-

judgment and the decision involving the civil claim will be handed down by the same court. Alternatively, the victim may pursue his claim for damages by way of an independent civil action. According to this scenario, the criminal proceeding is likely to end before the civil one, and in any event the conclusion of the criminal proceeding becomes a "prejudicial" question to be settled before a determination of civil liability by the civil court.[231] Thus, the fact-finding process involved in the determination of civil liability is strengthened, because no evidentiary obstacles stand in the way for the use of the criminal dossier - including the pretrial investigation, the evidence introduced at the trial, and the decision of the court - as evidence in the civil action. As a matter of fact, plaintiffs tend to regard the civil courts as more generous, or less conservative, than criminal courts in awarding monetary damages. It is therefore common for the injured party to appear as a victim prosecutor to press the criminal charges, while opting for bringing an independent civil action after the conclusion of the criminal proceedings.[232] A criminal conviction is deemed conclusive as to the defendant's civil liability, but an exoneration or acquittal in the criminal proceeding does not have a collateral estoppel effect in the subsequent civil action. By limiting the res judicata effect of an acquittal to the Court's precise finding of facts, the dismissal of the case or the defendant's acquittal of a criminal charge does not prevent another court from imposing civil liability on the bases of a lighter standard of weighing the evidence as to the defendant's negligence or rules of strict liability.[233]

C. Appeals

An appeal against a ruling of the investigative magistrate is on the law and the facts, but it is available only against those decisions expressly indicated by law (e.g., rulings of dismissals, those ordering the detention of the accused during the trial, and those deciding that the accused is to stand trial) or against interlocutory rulings "causing irreparable harm."[234] In contrast, a judgment rendered by a trial court is subject to an appeal only on points of law.[235] Whereas appeals against decisions of investigative magistrates must be brought within three days before an intermediate court of appeals,[236] challenges against the judgment (which, as noted, includes the verdict and the sentence) rendered by the trial courts must be brought within ten days by way of a writ of cassation (*recurso de casación*) before the

---

dered in favor of the victim and his family, the court, before paroling the convict, shall determine the portion of his salary which shall be applied to the payment of such debt."

231. See Argentine Civil Code, Article 1101: "When the criminal action has preceded the civil action or is brought while the latter is pending, no judgment shall be rendered in the civil action before the rendering of the judgment in the criminal action, except in the following cases: (1) When the defendant has died before the rendering of the criminal judgment, in which case the civil action may be brought or continued against the defendant's heirs. (2) In the event of the absence of the defendant, when the criminal action cannot be brought or continued."

232. See John R. Gerber, *Joinder of Civil and Criminal Relief: A Comparative Analysis*, 22 Syracuse L. Rev. 669, 672 (1971).

233. Civil Code, arts. 1102-1103; *Urueña, Victor c. Celestino, Omar*, CNCiv-G, 13 Aug. 1991, LL, 3 Feb. 1993, p. 6; *M. De P., c. Herrera de Noble, Ernestina*, CNCiv-A, 23 May 1989, LL, 9 Oct. 1989, p. 4.

234. CcrP art. 449.

235. CcrP art. 456.

236. CcrP art. 449.

Criminal Court of Cassation.[237] If the aggrieved party challenges the constitutionality of a statute, decree, ordinance, or administrative ruling applied by the trial court, he or she may also bring a writ of unconstitutionality (*recurso de inconstitucionalidad*) before the Criminal Court of Cassation,[238] which decision on this point may ultimately be reviewed by the Supreme Court through an extraordinary writ of error (*recurso extraordinario*). In any event, all challenges (regardless of the form they take and the higher court in charge of ultimately deciding on its availability) are taken as of right, rather than by permission or leave of the court or upon a grant of certiorari. In exercising the powers of review, Argentine courts, regardless of their hierarchy, lack the power to select the cases they consider worthy of review.

Review by way of appeal or cassation must be sought before the same judge or tribunal that rendered the challenged decision. If that court finds that the legal requirements to challenge its decision have been met, it shall transmit the dossier to the higher court for a disposition of the case.[239] If the appeal or the writ of cassation is dismissed on the ground that, in the view of the lower court, the decision is not susceptible to challenge , the aggrieved party may bring a complaint (*queja*) directly before the higher court, which may disagree with the lower court and decide that challenge should be heard.[240] If the trial court judgment is reversed on the ground of having misapplied the law, the higher court will render a new decision, instead of remanding the case for a new trial.[241]

Under Argentine law, an appeal against the judgment and sentence given by the trial court is perceived as a continuation of the one and only criminal proceeding, rather than as an exceptional mechanism to reconsider an erroneous "final" decision. One of the corollaries to this perception is that the right to appeal is given not only to the defendant but to the prosecutor as well, in case of an acquittal or a sentence the prosecutor regards as too mild. The Supreme Court has held that to permit the appeal of an acquittal by the prosecution does not violate due process nor constitutes a double jeopardy violation.[242] The victim prosecutor is allowed to avail himself of the same recourses which are made available to the public prosecutor.[243] According to the rules of criminal procedures the defendant is entitled to appeal a conviction only if the sentence is beyond three years of imprisonment, or a security measure for an indefinite period of time, or a suspension to practice a certain profession for longer than five years, or a fine or the payment of damages exceeding a certain amount.[244] Arguing that the extraordinary writ of error before the Supreme Court provided sufficient judicial review, the Criminal Court of Cassation in *Giroldi* upheld this limitation on the defendant's right to appeal against a challenge that it violates his right to appeal a criminal conviction to a higher court, guaran-

237. CcrP art. 463.

238. CcrP arts. 474-475.

239. CcrP arts. 450 and 464.

240. CcrP arts. 476-478.

241. CcrP art. 470. However, if an intermediate court of appeals find that a ruling of the investigative magistrate is null and void on procedural grounds, in such a case the appellate court shall reverse and remand the case back to the investigative magistrate for further proceedings.

242. *Gómez*, CSJN, 299 Fallos 19 (1977).

243. CcrP art. 460.

244. CcrP art. 459.

teed in Article 8.2(h) of the American Convention on Human Rights.[245] The ruling was subsequently reversed by the Supreme Court, which held CcrP art 459 unconstitutional for violating the defendant's right of due process under Article 8.2(h) of the American Convention. See Giroldi, CSJN, 318 Fallos 514; JA-1995-III-571; LL-1995-D-461; 163 ED161 (1995).

The defendant's right to appoint a counsel of his choice, or to be assisted by a government-paid public defender, attaches until the completion of the appellate process. The right to be assisted by counsel on appeal was affirmed in *Rojas Molina*.[246] While holding that a waiver of the right to counsel at the appellate stage is not to be presumed, the Court stated in *Arnaiz* that it is the duty of the appellate courts to ensure that every defendant is assisted by counsel retained by the defendant or appointed by the court. [247]

1. *Ineffective Assistance of Counsel*

Some court decisions have traced a constitutional right to an "effective defense" to Article 18 of the CN.[248] The violation of this constitutional guarantee was accepted as a ground for review in *Rojas Molina*, where the defendant had protested his innocence before the investigative magistrate, but the public defender appointed by the court to represent him had failed to submit a defense, present closing arguments, and to appeal a seventeen-year jail sentence imposed by the court. The Supreme Court reversed on the ground that the right to counsel guaranteed by Article 18 of the CN is not satisfied with the formal appointment of an attorney to represent the defendant, but rather it calls for "the need of an effective defense' (*necesidad de una defensa efectiva*).[249] In *Magui Agüero* the Supreme Court resorted to the right to an "effective defense" to reverse a conviction in which a public defender failed to communicate with the defendant in order to contest an appeal filed by the public prosecutor.[250] In *G.M.* the Court made a similar finding in a case where the defense counsel had not been notified of a writ originally filed *in forma pauperis,* thus depriving counsel of the opportunity to file a brief in support of the writ.[251] The Supreme Court held in several cases that the negligence of the defense counsel in representing the defendant, such as counsel's failure to file an appeal in time, amounts to an ineffective assistance of counsel warranting a reversal of the defendant's conviction.[252] However, the Supreme Court failed in *Fratz* to find a violation of the right to an effective defense in a case in which the public defender appointed to represent the defendant at the trial conceded to the defendant's guilt, despite the fact that such guilt had been emphatically denied by the defendant himself at the time of judicial interrogation.The Court refused to find any constitutional wrong in the alleged lack of diligence of the public

245. *Giroldi*, CNCP-I, 22 Sept. 1993, JA, No. 5885, 15 June 1993, with note by Alberto Garay.

246. *Rojas Molina*, CSJN, 189 Fallos 34 (1941).

247. *Arnaiz*, 237 Fallos 158 (1957).

248. *Toral*, CNCrimCorr., LL, 1979-B-209; *Giuliani*, CNCrimCorr., LL, 1976-D- 380.

249. *Rojas Molina*, CSJN, 189 Fallos 34.

250. *Magui Aguero*, CSJN, 311 Fallos 2502.

251. *G.M.*, CSJN, ED, 146-209.

252. *Cardullo*, CSJN, 302 Fallos 1669; *Ojer González*, CSJN, LL, 1993-B-285; *Vallín*, CSJN, ED, 147-101.

defender, holding that the right to an effective defense is not affected as long as the defendant availed himself of the assistance of a counsel of his choice during the appellate process.[253] Moreover, in those cases in which the defendant himself (rather than his defense counsel) consented to his conviction, thus foregoing the opportunity to file an appeal, the Court upheld the convictions on the ground that the right to an effective defense is not infringed as long as the defendant was able to avail himself of legal advise before consenting to his conviction.[254]

2. *Other Grounds for Appeal*

Cases reversed on appeal can be counted by the thousands, since the opportunities for appeal abound and in favor of all the parties to the proceedings.[255] Statistics made available by the Ministry of Justice in the early 1980's indicate that the rate of convictions is rather low. In 1982, of the total number of crimes reported to the police only 5.82% resulted in convictions, and statistics for previous years range between 8% and 10%.[256] There are no statistics available as to the percentage of cases reaching the trial stage that actually end in convictions. However, the principle of compulsory prosecution, the loose standards for sending the cases for trial compared with the more stringent ones for a finding of guilt, contribute to a low conviction rate. We have been unable to find statistics as to the number of cases reversed on appeal annually, yet almost all convictions are appealed and such vulnerability to attack leads to a traditional high rate of reversal. This rate is likely to have decreased since the adoption of the 1993 rules of criminal procedure. The 1993 code replaced a traditional *de novo* standard of review with a writ of cassation before the Criminal Court of Cassation, which only admits appeals for errors of law. Yet, the following legal mechanisms encourage a relatively high rate of appeals and reversals.

When an appeal is taken by the defendant, the appellate court may not convict him of a more serious crime or increase the penalty imposed that trial. Thus, in *Basseler*, a case in which an appeal had been taken by a convicted defendant, the Supreme Court held that the scope of review by the appellate court is limited to entertaining the defendant's claim that his conviction be overturned or his sentence reduced.[257] The principle that the defendant's position can not be worsened on appeal (*reformatio in pejus*) has received statutory recognition but does not enjoy constitutional rank, and it applies only in cases in which a conviction has been appealed by the defendant alone with the alleged purpose of not discouraging defendants to exercise their right to appeal. If the defendant challenges his conviction but the prosecutor also appeals seeking a harsher penalty, the appellate court re-

253. *Fratz*, CSJN, 301 Fallos 557 (1979). For other cases in which the Supreme Court refused to review a conviction in which the performance of the defense counsel was alleged to be manifestly incompetent, see *Claus*, CSJN, 298 Fallos 364; *Ponteprimo*, CSJN, 229 Fallos 7.

254. *Mac Leod*, CSJN, 217 Fallos 1022; *López*, CSJN, 310 Fallos 1797, LL, 1988-B-252 (with note by Néstor P. Sagüés).

255. CcrP arts. 432-473.

256. According to the 1982 Criminal Statistics Report issued by the Ministry of Justice, in a population of approximately thirty million, the number of criminal cases involving the police increased from 227,578 in 1980 to 255,336 in 1981, and to 313,315 in 1982.

257. *Basseler*, CSJN, 284 Fallos 125 (1960).

mains free to side with the prosecution and increase the penalty.[258] Thus, the exercise of the right to appeal not only involves no risk for the defendant but also ensures that if neither the victim or public prosecutor appeals, the appellate court may not convict her of a more serious crime or increase the punishment already imposed.

Successive Appeals/Collateral Attack. Under Argentine law, a defendant who is convicted in state court must exhaust the means of appeal available in the state court system before finally turning to the Supreme Court. The Supreme Court exercises its appellate jurisdiction only by way of an extraordinary writ of error (*recurso extraordinario)* on the ground that the state court decision has denied to the defendant a right guaranteed by the Federal Constitution. Aside from this extraordinary remedy available against final judgments, once a case has been commenced in a court of competent jurisdiction, the proceedings must continue and terminate before the state court. It is not possible to bring a "collateral" attack against such proceedings before a federal court claiming that the proceedings before that court were unconstitutional. Accordingly, in *Pucci*, a civilian defendant had been tried and convicted to a two-year prison term by a court martial. After the sentence of the military tribunal had been consented by both the defendant and his defense counsel, and the time period to appeal had expired, the defendant brought a writ of habeas corpus before a federal court challenging the constitutionality of the exercise of military jurisdiction over civilians. The Supreme Court refused to review the conviction on the ground that the writ of habeas corpus may not be used to attack final decisions of other courts which have become res judicata.[259]

Endnotes

Abbreviations

ADLA	=	Anuario de Legislación Argentina
ALJA	=	Anuario de Legislación de Jurisprudencia Argentina
CfedCrimCorr.–II	=	Federal Court of Appeals on Criminal and Correctional Matters
CfedLa Plata	=	Federal Court of Appeals of La Plata
CNCass	=	National Criminal Court of Cassation
CNCrim–VI	=	National Criminal Court, Division VI

258. CcrP art. 445: "A recourse against a judgment shall confer on the higher court the power to review it only as to those grievances referred to by the appellant. Recourses brought by the public prosecutor allow the higher court to modify or revoke the judgment, even if favorable to the defendant. The appellate decision may not worsen the position of the defendant if only he brought the appeal."

259. *Pucci*, CSJN, 243 Fallos 306 (J. Alfredo Orgaz, dissenting); *Cormack y Fuentes*, CSJN, 311 Fallos 2048-S; *Pucheta*, CSJN, 311 Fallos 133, LL, 1988-D-233 (J. E. Bacqué dissenting) (with note by Néstor P. Sagüés) and other Supreme Court decisions reported in 281 Fallos 377, 303 Fallos 1354; and 303 Fallos 517.

CNCrim.Corr.–I	=	National Criminal and Correctional Court, Division I
CNCiv-A	=	National Civil Court of Appeals, Division A
CNCP-III	=	National Court of Criminal Cassation, Division III
CNPenal Económico-A	=	National Court of Appeals on Criminal and Economic Matters, Division A
CSJN	=	Supreme Court of Justice of the Nation
JA	=	Revista de Jurisprudencia Argentina
JPBA	=	Jurisprudencia Penal de Buenos Aires
LL	=	Revista Jurídica La Ley
ED	=	Revista El Derecho
Fallos	=	Fallos de la Corte Suprema de Justicia de la Nación

* * *

Chapter 2

Canada

Kent W. Roach

I. Introduction

Criminal procedure is a matter of federal or national jurisdiction reserved to the Parliament of Canada. Since 1892, Canada has had a *Criminal Code*[1] which contains both substantive criminal law and criminal procedure. This *Code* has never been comprehensive especially with respect to criminal procedure. Gaps in statutory criminal procedure are filled by decisions of the courts interpreting the *Canadian Charter of Rights and Freedoms*[2] (henceforth the Charter) and the common law which now reflects Charter values. For example, police powers concerning stops, interrogations and searches of the person generally depend on judge made common and constitutional law. The Law Reform Commission of Canada has proposed that Parliament enact a comprehensive code of criminal procedure,[3] but this has not been a priority. Most recent criminal procedure legislation has been piece-meal reaction to the constitutional jurisprudence of the Supreme Court of Canada.

The Charter affects police powers by providing rights against unreasonable searches and seizures, arbitrary detention and the right to counsel upon arrest or detention. It also guarantees fair trials and the right not to be denied reasonable bail. Any law that is inconsistent with Charter rights is of no force and effect to the extent of its inconsistency.[4] Nevertheless, section1 of the Charter allows governments to justify restrictions on all Charter rights provided that they are reasonable limits, prescribed by law, that can be demonstrably justified in a free and democratic society.[5] Under section 24 of the Charter, criminal courts can award any remedy within their jurisdiction that is appropriate and just for the violation of the Charter. They are required to exclude unconstitutionally obtained evidence under sec-

1. RSC 1985 c.C-34 (as amended).
2. Part I of the *Canada Act, 1982* U.K. c.11 (henceforth "the Charter").
3. Law Reform Commission of Canada *Recodifying Criminal Procedure* (1991).
4. *Constitution Act, 1982* section 52(1).
5. Parliament may also enact criminal laws notwithstanding the legal rights in the Charter for a renewable five year period. *Constitution Act, 1982* section 33. This opting out power has not yet been exercised with respect to any law concerning criminal proceedings.

tion 24(2) of the Charter if, in all the circumstances, its admission would bring the administration of justice into disrepute.

II. Police Procedures

A. Arrest, Search, and Seizure Law

1. Stops

Section 9 of the Charter addresses pre-trial detention by providing that "everyone has the right not to be arbitrarily detained or imprisoned." The *Criminal Code of Canada* does not give the police any general statutory powers to stop and detain individuals or vehicles. The Supreme Court of Canada has held that police constables have a common law power to stop motor vehicles in order to detect drunk driving. The Court recognized that:

The objectionable nature of a random stop is chiefly that it is made on a purely arbitrary basis, without any grounds for suspicion or belief that the particular driver has committed or is committing an offence. It is this aspect of the random stop that makes it capable of producing unpleasant psychological effects for the innocent driver.[6]

The Court held, however, that such effects were justified because of the short duration of a stop and because it was part of a well-publicized programme designed to deter drunk driving. Some provinces have enacted motor vehicle legislation which empowers the police to stop cars for reasons related to motor vehicle safety. Such legislation is an "arbitrary detention" under section 9 of the Charter because it authorizes stops on a random and arbitrary basis with no criteria to govern the exercise of police discretion. Nevertheless, the violation has been held to be justified under section 1 of the Charter because drivers are engaged in a licensed activity; highway safety is an important objective and the duration of the stop would be brief.[7]

The Supreme Court has condemned the use of these motor vehicle stops for purposes other than highway safety. For example, a police officer flagrantly violated a driver's rights against unreasonable search and seizure when the police officer inquired into the contents of a gym bag on the front seat of a car that was stopped. The Court held that a random traffic stop "does not and cannot constitute a general search warrant for searching every vehicle, driver and passenger that is pulled over. Unless there are reasonable and probable grounds for conducting the search, or drugs, alcohol or weapons are in plain view in the interior of the vehicle, the evidence flowing from such a search should not be admitted."[8]

There are no statutory rules governing the detention or questioning of witnesses. The general common law rule is that a police officer may ask questions and request identification, but that people not under arrest have no obligation to co-op-

6. *Dedman* (1985) 20 C.C.C.(3d) 97 at 122 (S.C.C.).
7. *Hufsky* (1988) 40 C.C.C.(3d) 398 (S.C.C.); *Ladouceur* (1990) 56 C.C.C.(3d) 22 (S.C.C.).
8. *Mellenthin* (1992) 76 C.C.C.(3d) 481 at 491 (S.C.C.).

erate. Police sometimes exercise their infrequently reviewed discretion to make investigative stops in an unjustified and discriminatory manner.[9]

In an innovative decision, not yet followed in other provinces, the Ontario Court of Appeal has held that police have a common law power to stop and detain a person where there is no reasonable and probable cause for an arrest if they can demonstrate an objectively determined articulable cause or reasonable suspicion of a crime. This requires more than a subjective hunch based on the officer's experience or intuition because "such subjectively based assessments can too easily mask discriminatory conduct based on such irrelevant factors as the detainee's sex, colour, age, ethnic origin or sexual orientation."[10] Articulable cause and the length of a justified detention depends on the totality of the circumstances. In the case, there was no articulable cause when the police stopped an individual seen emerging from a dwelling that had been described in a police memorandum as a suspected "crack house." The officer had no knowledge of the reliability or age of the memorandum or of the person stopped.

2. *Frisks*

In the above case, the Ontario Court of Appeal indicated that the power of police officers to frisk a detainee depends on the circumstances because "the existence of an articulable cause that justified a brief detention, perhaps to ask the person detained for identification, would not necessarily justify a more intrusive detention complete with physical restraint and a more extensive interrogation."[11] In this case, the officer's inquiry into a bulge in the suspect's pocket and the subsequent seizure of cocaine from the pocket was held to be an unreasonable search that merited the exclusion of the drugs. This case has been criticized for expanding police powers beyond arrest, but it can also be praised as an attempt to regulate low visibility encounters between police and individuals. As a regulatory device, however, it relies on the exclusion of evidence in cases where police hunches were correct and depends on adjudicative determination of the totality of the circumstances in individual cases.

3. *Arrests*

Section 495 of the *Criminal Code* provides that a police officer may arrest without warrant a person who he or she believes on reasonable grounds has committed or is about to commit an indictable offence or a person found committing any criminal offence.[12] This contemplates arrests for attempted indictable offenses. Arrest means the actual seizure of a person's body with a view to detention or words of arrest if the person submits to the arrest.[13] Reasonable grounds require

9. Manitoba Aboriginal Justice Inquiry *The Deaths of Helen Betty Osborne and John Joseph Harper* (1991) (illegal detention of Aboriginal male that led to him being shot by the police); *Report of the Commission on Systemic Racism in the Ontario Criminal Justice System* (1995) c.10 (high levels of investigative stops and dissatisfaction reported by Black respondents).

10. *Simpson* (1993) 79 C.C.C.(3d) 482 at 502 (Ont.C.A.).

11. Ibid at 503 (citing with approval *Terry v. Ohio* 392 U.S. 1 (1968).

12. Section 495 also instructs police officers not to arrest persons for less serious criminal offenses unless necessary to establish their identity or to secure or preserve evidence of the crime or to prevent future crime.

13. *Whitfield* (1970) 9 C.R.N.S. 59 (S.C.C.).

both an honest and a reasonable belief that the suspect has likely committed the crime. Evidence that the police officer was subjectively biased because of the accused's race, nationality, or personal enmity could make even an arrest on objectively reasonable grounds unlawful. Reasonable and probable grounds does not, however, require the establishment of a *prima facie* case and the arrest of a wrong person who matches the description of a suspect and drives the same unusual car is still lawful.[14] Similarly, the fact that a person arrested for causing a disturbance was subsequently acquitted of that offence does not mean that the police could not lawfully arrest him because at the time, he was apparently committing a criminal offence.[15]

An arrest that does not satisfy *Criminal Code* requirements does not necessarily result in a violation of section 9 of the Charter. Even a finding of a Charter violation does not necessarily result in a stay of proceedings or the exclusion of evidence obtained during the arrest.[16] However, such exclusion is not an uncommon result. For example, police officers who arrested three youths identified as hanging around a house that was subsequently broken into were held to have acted without reasonable and probable grounds and without a subjective belief in such grounds, as well as in violation of section 9 of the Charter. A "hunch" of an experienced police officer is not enough. As a result, evidence of stolen goods that the youths led the police to were excluded under section 24(2) of the Charter. Similarly, an arrest of a person satisfying a description as a "male, black 5'8 to 5'11 with a short afro" was invalid because the description did not amount to reasonable and probable grounds.[17] This led to the exclusion of a weapon. A person known to the police who appeared to have swallowed something and walked away quickly when he observed the police was also not validly arrested and narcotics were excluded.[18]

An arrest made with reasonable and probable grounds does not become unreasonable because the police officer continues the investigation, by for example detaining the arrestee for 18 hours in order to conduct an identification parade.[19] But excessive delay could result in exclusion of a confession for example.

a. *Arrest Warrants*. Arrest warrants are used infrequently because of the common use of warrantless arrest powers and because the *Criminal Code* encourages the issuance of a summons which orders the accused to appear in court rather than more intrusive arrests. Warrants require reasonable and probable grounds to believe that the accused committed any criminal offence and that it is necessary in the public interest to arrest the accused.[20] Unfortunately, there is no jurisprudence defining when an arrest is in the public interest.[21] An arrest warrant must name or describe the accused, set out briefly the offence with which the accused is charged and order that the accused be brought before a judge of the territorial jurisdiction.[22] The arrest warrant may be executed anywhere within the territorial juris-

14. *Storrey* (1990) 53 C.C.C.(3d) 316 (S.C.C.).
15. *Biron* (1976) 23 C.C.C.(2d) 513 (S.C.C.).
16. See infra discussion of s.24(2) of the Charter.
17. *Charley* (1993) 22 C.R.(4th) 297 (Ont.C.A.).
18. *Johnson* (1995) 39 C.R.(4th) 78 (Ont.C.A.).
19. *Storrey* (1990) 53 C.C.C.(3d) 316 (S.C.C.).
20. *Criminal Code* s.507.
21. The Supreme Court has found that the denial of bail in the public interest to be excessively vague. *Morales* (1992) 77 C.C.C.(3d) 91 (S.C.C.).
22. *Criminal Code* s.511.

diction of the issuing judge or in the case of fresh pursuit, anywhere in Canada.[23] An arrest warrant issued by a justice in one province, but endorsed by a justice in another province, can be executed in that other province.[24] Where feasible, a police officer is required to produce the warrant and to inform the arrestee promptly of the reasons for the arrest.[25] The latter requirement applies to all arrests and now is specifically guaranteed under section 10(a) of the Charter.

b. *Searches Incident to Arrest.* The police have a common law power to search and seize anything in an arrestee's possession or immediate surroundings to guarantee the safety of the police and the accused, prevent the accused's escape or to gather evidence against the accused that might otherwise be lost. It is not necessary that there be reasonable and probable grounds to believe that the arrestee has evidence or weapons. Such searches may not be conducted in an abusive manner or employ disproportionate constraint. A frisk pat down search when a lawyer was arrested for unpaid parking tickets has been upheld.[26] On the other hand, a rectal search when the accused was arrested for an outstanding traffic violation was an unreasonable search and drugs eventually obtained were excluded.[27] Hair samples, cheek swabs and dental impressions obtained without a warrant from an unwilling accused after his arrest were not legally or constitutionally seized pursuant to common law powers of search incident to arrest.[28] A person under arrest may be photographed[29] and if under arrest for an indictable offence, finger-printed.[30] A person arrested for an indictable offence may also be required to return to the police station for finger printing.[31] The police's discretionary power to take finger prints has been upheld under the Charter as consistent with the principles of fundamental justice and as not constituting an unreasonable search.[32] However, according to *Feeney* in 1997 finger prints obtained after an unlawful arrest will be excluded.[33]

i. *Arrests in Buildings.* In 1986, the Supreme Court held that the police could enter a private dwelling to make a warrantless arrest if there were reasonable and probable grounds for the arrest and was in the building and proper announcement

---

23. Ibid s.514.
24. Ibid s.528.
25. Ibid s.29.
26. *Cloutier v. Langlois* (1990) 53 C.C.C.(3d) 257.
27. *Greffe* (1990) 55 C.C.C.(3d) 161 (S.C.C.).
28. *Stillman* (1997) 113 C.C.C.(3d) 321. The samples were excluded, but a tissue with dna material was admitted into evidence because the police did not force the accused to provide the sample. Parliament has now provided for warrants to seize hair, cheek swabs and blood of dna analysis. For the warrant to be issued, there must be reasonable grounds to believe that a designated serious offence has been committed and that the person was a party to the offence and that dna analysis will provide evidence of whether there is a match with a bodily substance found at the crime. There are statutory requirements to respect the person's privacy when taking the samples and to destroy the sample if the person is acquitted. See *Criminal Code* s.487.05. After *Stillman*, the *Criminal Code* was again amended to allow a warrant to be issued to obtain teeth and other body impressions if there are reasonable grounds to believe an offence has been committed, that the body impression would provide information concerning the crime and it is in the best interests of the administration of justice. See *Criminal Code* s.487.091.
29. *Dilling* (1993) 84 C.C.C.(3d) 325 (B.C.C.A.).
30. *Identification of Criminals Act* RSC 1985 c.I-1.
31. *Criminal Code* s.501(3).
32. *Beare and Higgins* (1988) 45 C.C.C.(3d) 57 (S.C.C.).
33. 115 C.C.C.(3d) 129 (S.C.C.) They have been excluded as evidence unconstitutionally conscripted from the accused.

of the police presence was made.[34] In 1997, this decision was overruled in *Feeney* with the Court stating that the Charter requires, except in cases of hot pursuit,[35] and perhaps exigent circumstances,[36] a search warrant in order to make an arrest in a dwelling house, as well as the announcement of police presence. In general, the individual's privacy interest requires a warrant on the basis that there are reasonable grounds for arrest and reasonable grounds to believe the person is in the dwelling. In *Feeney*, a warrantless entry and search of the accused's trailer after the accused had been observed near where a murder occurred violated section 8 of the Charter. The police were acting on suspicion and did not have reasonable and probable cause for an arrest. Most of the evidence discovered in the search, including the accused's bloody clothing, would likely have been admitted had the police acted in good faith reliance on the previous Court decision, but it was excluded because the police admitted that they did not even subjectively believe they had grounds for an arrest when they entered the trailer. The Court subsequently stayed the application of its new warrant requirement for six months pending a rehearing to consider whether a transition period was warranted. New legislation creating new arrest warrants and defining exigent circumstances exceptions to warrant requirements is being considered. As will be seen, Parliament has frequently responded to decisions striking down warrantless investigative techniques with legislation allowing those techniques but only with a warrant. It has also specifically authorized some warrantless searches presumably on the basis that they can be justified under section 1 of the Charter as reasonable limits on the right against unreasonable search and seizure.

ii. *Arrests in Automobiles.* If a police officer reasonably suspects a driver has been drinking, a breath sample at the roadside may be required forthwith.[37] If there are reasonable and probable grounds to believe that the driver is guilty of a drinking and driving offence, the driver may be required to accompany the police officer and provide a breath sample at the police station.[38] If the person cannot provide a breath sample, he or she may be required to provide a blood sample under medical supervision.[39] A judicial warrant may also be obtained to authorize the taking of a

34. *Landry* (1986) 25 C.C.C.(3d) 1 (S.C.C.).

35. *Macoob* (1993) 82 C.C.C.(3d) 481 (S.C.C.).

36. The Court left open whether there was an exigent circumstances exception to its new warrant requirement, but did indicate that the fact that a "dangerous person is on the loose and there is a risk that he or she will attempt to destroy evidence linking him or her to the crime" *Feeney* (1997) 115 C.C.C.(3d) 129 at 159 did not constitute exigent circumstances. Previously in *Silveria* (1995) 97 C.C.C.(3d) 450 (S.C.C.), the Court suggested that exigent circumstances existed when the police made a warrantless entry into a house after an arrest in order to prevent the destruction of drugs. In that case, the Court based its rulings more on the admissibility of the drugs under section 24(2) of the Charter and warned that in most future cases, evidence would be excluded if the police entered a house without a warrant even with exigent circumstances. There is considerable confusion about the exact nature of exigent circumstances and *Criminal Code* legislation is being considered to provide a non-exhaustive definition of exigent circumstances.

37. *Criminal Code* section 254(2). This section does not authorize the detention of the accused for half an hour to await a road-side breath testing device *Grant* (1991) 67 C.C.C.(3d) 268 (S.C.C), but does justify a 15 minute delay when necessary to ensure the accuracy of the test. *Bernshaw* (1995) 95 C.C.C.(3d) 1 (S.C.C.). Refusal to provide either a road side or police station breathalyser is as serious a crime as drunk driving. *Criminal Code* section 254(5).

38. *Criminal Code* section 254(3).

39. *Criminal Code* section 254(3)(b).

blood sample without the accused's consent if an accident has resulted in death or bodily injury and a breath sample cannot be obtained.[40] The seizure of a blood sample without a warrant or the accused's consent violates section 8 of the Charter and generally results in the exclusion of the blood sample.[41] Blood samples that were obtained for other reasons and could have been legally seized by the use of a warrant may, however, be admitted as evidence.[42]

When a person is arrested for drugs in his car, the police are entitled to search the entire interior of the car and the trunk. In doing so, they are not limited to a search for weapons or evidence which may be easily destroyed.[43] On the other hand, they cannot search the trunk of a car when the accused is arrested for unpaid parking fines or other offenses where there is no evidence of the crime to be found.[44] The Supreme Court has indicated its approval of this latter decision and it apparently applies to other, non-drug, arrests. As long as the accused cannot gain access to the trunk or other interior compartments, a warrantless search of the car's compartment incident to arrest is not necessary to ensure safety or prevent the destruction of evidence. A search warrant should be obtained.

iii. *Dealing With Other People.* A police officer may detain for a reasonable period of time persons within the scope of suspicion. All the occupants of a house could be detained for an hour while a search warrant to search the house was secured.[45] A two hour detention and handcuffing has been held to be unreasonable.[46] There are no clear rulings, but occupants of a car could presumably be detained for a reasonable period. People with a more tenuous connection with the accused, such as fellow patrons of a bar might not be legally detained. Whoever is detained will be entitled to counsel as soon as the police have matters under control.[47]

c. *Arrests Pursuant to an Unconstitutional Statute.* If the police relied in good faith on a statute or a court decision later found to be unconstitutional, evidence obtained from the arrest would likely not be excluded.[48]

4. Searches

Section 8 of the Charter provides: "Everyone has the right to be secure against unreasonable search or seizure." Searches and seizures have been defined by the courts to include state actions that invade a reasonable expectation of privacy without the accused's consent. Use of audio[49] or video[50]-taping by state agents without the consent of all those involved is a search. Thus the Supreme Court invalidated a *Criminal Code* provision which allowed audio-taping of conversations on the basis of the consent of one of the parties, such as a police officer or informer

40. *Criminal Code* section 256.
41. *Poheretsky* (1987) 33 C.C.C.(3d) 398 (S.C.C.); *Dyment* (1988) 45 C.C.C.(3d) 244 (S.C.C.); *Dersch* (1993) 85 C.C.C.(3d) 1 (S.C.C.).
42. *Colarusso* (1993) 87 C.C.C.(3d) 193 (S.C.C.).
43. *Smellie* (1994) 95 C.C.C.(3d) 9 (B.C.C.A.); *Speid* (1991) 8 C.R.R.(2d) 383 (Ont.C.A.).
44. *Belnavais* (1997) 107 C.C.C.(3d) 195 (Ont.C.A.).
45. *Depuis* (1995) 162 A.R. 197 (Alta.C.A.).
46. *Gogol* (1994) 27 C.R.(4th) 357 (Ont.Prov.Div.).
47. *Strachan* (1988) 46 C.C.C.(3d) 479 (S.C.C.).
48. *Hamill* (1987) 33 C.C.C.(3d) 110 (S.C.C.); *Feeney* (1997) 115 C.C.C.(3d) 129 (S.C.C.).
49. *Duarte* (1990) 53 C.C.C.(3d) 1 (S.C.C.).
50. *Wong* (1990) 60 C.C.C.(3d) 460 (S.C.C.).

wearing a "wire," even though the other person may have risked having their conversations overheard or their activities observed.[51] Parliament reacted with legislation allowing judges to authorize consent intercepts with a warrant, as well as new statutory powers authorizing warrantless intercepts in urgent situations and where there is a danger of bodily harm to the person consenting to the interception.[52] Parliament has also authorized judges to issue a warrant authorizing the use of any device or investigative technique that, if not authorized, would constitute an unreasonable search or seizure. The judge must be satisfied of reasonable grounds to believe an offence will be committed, that the search will reveal evidence of the offence, and that the search is in the best interests of the administration of justice.[53] This general warrant provision has been criticized on the basis that it could authorize the use of new technologies for searches without specific legislative approval, but it also provides that it does not authorize searches that invade bodily integrity.

The Supreme Court has ruled that attaching a beeper to a car constitutes a search[54] and Parliament subsequently introduced legislation authorizing the use of a tracking device or a number recorder when a judicial official is satisfied that there are reasonable grounds to suspect an offence has or will be committed, and the device will provide information relevant to the commission of the offence.[55] This requires less than probable cause and its constitutionality has yet to be determined. The taking of bodily samples such as hair samples or bodily impressions without consent constitutes an unreasonable search and seizure,[56] but again Parliament amended the Criminal Code to allow warrants to be authorized on reasonable grounds to obtain such evidence.[57] In all of the above cases, Supreme Court rulings that warrantless investigative techniques were unreasonable searches and seizures provoked Parliament to amend the *Criminal Code* to authorize police search powers usually, but not always, by requiring the police to obtain a warrant.

A person has a reasonable expectation of privacy with respect to blood taken for medical purposes, but not with respect to blood abandoned at the scene of a crime or accident. Courts of Appeal have held that looking into a vehicle stopped at an intersection;[58] observing the accused in a public washroom;[59] photographing people entering public buildings;[60] entering an open residence;[61] entering premises open to the public;[62] or examining a car parked in a driveway[63] all do not amount to searches because they do not invade reasonable expectations of privacy. The Supreme Court has held that those cultivating drugs in a field observable from a

51. At the same time, however, the Court admitted the unconstitutionally seized conversation because there was good faith reliance on a statute. *Duarte* (1990) 53 C.C.C.(3d) 1 (S.C.C.).

52. *Criminal Code* section 184.1-184.4.

53. *Criminal Code* section 487.01.

54. *Wise* (1992) 70 C.C.C.(3d) 193 (S.C.C.).

55. *Criminal Code* section 492.1.

56. *Stillman* (1997) 113 C.C.C.(3d) 321 (S.C.C.).

57. *Criminal Code* section 487.03-487.09, section 487.091.

58. *Hebb* (1985) 17 C.C.C.(3d) 345 (N.S.C.A.).

59. *O'Flaherty* (1987) 35 C.C.C.(3d) 33 (Nfld C.A.); *Le Beau* (1987) 41 C.C.C.(3d) 163 (Ont.C.A.).

60. *Elzein* (1993) 82 C.C.C.(3d) 455 (Que.C.A.).

61. *Martin* (1995) 97 C.C.C.(3d) 241 (B.C.C.A.).

62. *Kouyas* (1995) 136 N.S.R.(2d) 195 (C.A.).

63. *Johnson* (1994) 72 W.A.C.102 (B.C.C.A.).

public highway[64] or those with illegal gambling machines observable from a place of business open to the public[65] have no reasonable expectation of privacy. A demand for a driver's license is not a search because there is no reasonable expectation of privacy given that a license is required to drive.[66] A computer search of a public utility's records of electricity consumption is also not a search because consumers do not have a reasonable expectation of privacy in such information.[67] The Supreme Court has not yet decided whether police examination of bank records invade privacy and lower courts are divided on the issue. The police, like other members of the public, have an implied invitation to knock on someone's front door, but not if they are doing so with the purpose of gathering evidence, in that case by smelling for marijuana.[68]

a. *Search Warrants.* Search warrants are required whenever feasible and must be granted by a neutral and impartial official who can act judicially and generally after reasonable and probable grounds have been established on oath that a crime has been committed and that the search will reveal evidence of the offence.[69] Section 487 of the *Criminal Code* provides for warrants to be issued for the search of buildings, receptacles or places including cars, but not persons. It requires that a judicial official be satisfied by information on oath that there are reasonable grounds to believe that the prescribed items will be found at the place to be searched and will provide evidence of an offence or the whereabouts of a person believed to have committed an offence or anything reasonably believed to have been used for committing any serious offence against a person. A warrant may be granted on the basis of hearsay, but it must, in all the circumstances, establish a credibly based and reasonable probability that an offence has been committed and that the search will reveal evidence of the offence.[70] A tip from an informer will not establish these grounds unless the reliability of the tip is established.[71] There must be a residual judicial discretion as to whether to grant a warrant even if statutory conditions are satisfied.[72]

The warrant must specify both the place to be searched and the offence. It must be carried by the police officer[73] and executed in the day, unless specifically authorized by the justice.[74] If appearance before a justice is impracticable, the information under oath for a warrant may be given by telephone or fax machine.[75] The police officers may seize anything not specified in the warrant if they have reasonable grounds to believe it was used in or obtained by the commission of an offence.[76] The sufficiency of the search warrant will be reviewed by the trial judge with any prior unconstitutionally obtained evidence[77] or inadvertent error[78] not

64. *Boersma* (1994) 31 C.R.(4th) 386 (S.C.C.).
65. *Fitt* (1996) 103 C.C.C.(3d) 224 (S.C.C.).
66. *Hufsky* (1988) 40 C.C.C.(3d) 398 (S.C.C.).
67. *Plant* (1993) 84 C.C.C.(3d) 203 (S.C.C.).
68. *Evans* (1996) 104 C.C.C.(3d) 23 (S.C.C.).
69. *Hunter v. Southam* (1984) 14 C.C.C.(3d) 97 (S.C.C.).
70. *Hunter* (1984) 14 C.C.C.(3d) 97 (S.C.C.).
71. *Debot* (1989) 52 C.C.C.(3d) 207 (S.C.C.); *Garofoli* (1990) 60 C.C.C.(3d) 161 (S.C.C.).
72. *Baron* (1993) 78 C.C.C.(3d) 510 (S.C.C.).
73. *Criminal Code* section 29(1).
74. *Criminal Code* section 488.
75. *Criminal Code* section 487.1.
76. *Criminal Code* section 489.
77. *Grant* (1993) 84 C.C.C.(3d) 173 (S.C.C.); *Feeney* (1997) 115 C.C.C.(3d) 129 (S.C.C.).
78. *Sismey* (1990) 55 C.C.C.(3d) 281 (B.C.C.A.).

used in assessing the warrant's validity. A warrant may be quashed if there was a reckless disregard for truth beyond mere error of judgment or negligence in its preparation. Most warrants are issued by justices of the peace who although independent may not be lawyers. Random audits both before and after the enactment of the Charter have found high levels of legally defective warrants being issued.

There are special and complex provisions to obtain warrants authorizing wiretaps.[79] These can only be issued by judges of the superior courts and require proof that other investigative techniques are not available, as well as reasonable and probable grounds to believe an offence has been committed and the wiretap will provide evidence.[80] Lawyers cannot be wiretapped unless there are reasonable grounds to believe they are parties to a serious offence.[81] In certain cases, targets must be informed after the wiretap warrant has expired.[82] Although editing is allowed to protect informants' identities, the accused has a constitutional right to any information used to obtain a wiretap warrant that is necessary to challenge the sufficiency of the warrant.[83]

b. *Warrantless Searches*. All searches must be authorized by law, the law must be reasonable and the search must be conducted in a reasonable fashion. The prosecutor has the burden to establish the reasonableness of warrantless searches.[84] Section 117.02 of the *Criminal Code* authorizes warrantless searches of places other than dwellings for firearms if there are reasonable grounds to believe that an offence with a firearm has been committed and that a warrant cannot be obtained because of exigent circumstances. Section 11(7) of the *Controlled Drugs and Substances Act*[85] also authorizes warrantless searches of people and places for illegal drugs "if the conditions for obtaining a warrant exist but by reason of exigent circumstances it would be impracticable to obtain one." The latter statute was amended after the Supreme Court limited warrantless searches to cases of exigent circumstances that may result in the destruction of evidence. Exigent circumstances depend on the totality of the circumstances and there is no blanket exception to the warrant requirement for automobiles.[86] The Court has indicated that warrantless searches of dwelling houses violate section 8 even if there are exigent circumstances, but has admitted the evidence under section 24(2) of the Charter because the police acted to prevent a risk that evidence would be destroyed and subsequently secured a warrant to search the house.[87] On the other hand, a warrantless examination of the perimeter of a person's house without reasonable grounds or exigent circumstances and the warrantless search of a home to make an arrest where the police admitted they did not have subjective grounds for an arrest have resulted in the exclusion of evidence.[88] The manner in which warrantless bodily searches are conducted must be reasonable and the use of choke holds without rea-

79. Wiretap warrants are not required for monitoring pagers *Luvovac* (1989) 52 C.C.C.(3d) 551 (Alta.C.A.) and cell phones without a scrambling device. *Criminal Code* section 183.

80. *Duarte* (1990) 53 C.C.C.(3d) 1 (S.C.C.).

81. *Criminal Code* section 186(2).

82. *Criminal Code* Part VI.

83. *Durette* (1994) 88 C.C.C.(3d) 1 (S.C.C.).

84. *Collins* (1987) 33 C.C.C.(3d) 1 (S.C.C.).

85. S.C. 1996 c.19.

86. *Grant* (1993) 84 C.C.C.(3d) 173 (S.C.C.).

87. *Silveria* (1995) 97 C.C.C.(3d) 450 (S.C.C.).

88. *Kokesch* (1990) 61 C.C.C.(3d) 207 (S.C.C.); *Feeney* (1997) 115 C.C.C.(3d) 129 (S.C.C.).

sonable grounds to believe that the person is a drug holder who might swallow drugs has been held to be a serious violation of section 8 of the Charter which merits the exclusion of drugs discovered on the

person.[89] Choke holds which prevent the accused from breathing have, however, been upheld when necessary to stop the swallowing of drugs.[90]

c. *Consent Searches.* Consent searches are governed by the standards for waiver of the accused's constitutional right against unreasonable searches and seizures. In general, the accused must act voluntarily and unequivocally and have enough information to make an informed waiver of his or her right. There was no consent or waiver when a driver opened a gym bag in response to an illegal police inquiry at a traffic spot check. The Court was concerned about allowing police to abuse their limited powers at traffic stops.[91] The Court has also held there was no waiver when a suspect consented to a blood sample being taken with respect to one sexual assault when the police did not inform him that they wanted a blood sample in relation to another sexual assault.[92] The Court reasoned that the accused did not have enough information to make a fully informed waiver. The Supreme Court has also held that a member of the public does not consent to the police knocking on his door when the purpose is to gather evidence against the occupant by smelling for marijuana.[93] A person in a hotel room does not implicitly consent to a police search of that room.[94]

Courts of Appeal have generally been more inclined than the Supreme Court to find consent, for example when an accused offered a police officer his knapsack after the police asked about its contents;[95] when an accused replied "sure do what you want, I have nothing to hide" when the police wished to examine his automobile,[96] when a person agreed to allow the police to "take a quick look" at his car[97] and when, after discussing the matter with his lawyer, the accused agreed to supply a blood sample.[98]

5. *Enforcing the Rules*

Section 24(2) of the Charter provides that where a court concludes that evidence was obtained in a manner that infringed or denied any rights under the Charter, the evidence must be excluded from a criminal trial if its admission would, in all the circumstances, bring the administration of justice into disrepute. Section 24(1) also provides for other appropriate and just remedies for constitutional violations. They include stays of proceedings, sentence reductions and damage awards from civil courts. These remedies are, however, less frequently employed than the exclusion of evidence.

The Supreme Court has developed two tests to determine to whether evidence should be excluded. Under the first test, unconstitutionally obtained evidence that

89. *Collins* (1987) 33 C.C.C.(3d) 1 (S.C.C.).
90. *Garcia-Guittez* (1991) 65 C.C.C.(3d) 15 (B.C.C.A.).
91. *Mellenthin* (1992) 76 C.C.C.(3d) 481 (S.C.C.).
92. *Borden* (1994) 92 C.C.C.(3d) 404 (S.C.C.).
93. *Evans* (1996) 104 C.C.C.(3d) 289 (S.C.C.).
94. *Mercer* (1992) 70 C.C.C.(3d) 180 (Ont.C.A.).
95. *Lawrence* (1990) 59 C.C.C.(3d) 55 (Ont.C.A.).
96. *Zaharov* (1992) 17 W.C.B.(2d) 401 (Ont.C.A.).
97. *Clement* (1995) 100 C.C.C.(3d) 103 (Ont.C.A.) aff'd 107 C.C.C.(3d) 52 (S.C.C.).
98. *Deprez* (1994) 95 C.C.C.(3d) 29 (B.C.C.A.).

will adversely affect the fairness of the subsequent trial will generally be excluded without consideration of the seriousness of the violation or the adverse effects of excluding the evidence on the administration of justice. Any evidence that could not be obtained but for the unconstitutional participation of the accused will be classified as conscriptive evidence which affects the fairness of the trial. This includes statements and other evidence such as hair, blood and breath samples taken from the accused in violation of the right of counsel, but also real evidence that could not have been obtained without the accused's assistance. A knife discovered in the accused's apartment with her assistance will not affect the fairness of the trial because the police would have discovered it in any event.[99] On the other hand, a gun located for the police by an accused at the bottom of a frozen river while the accused was denied his right to counsel was excluded because the police would not have obtained it without unconstitutionally conscripting the accused to help them build their case.[100] Bodily samples taken without a warrant from an unwilling accused have been excluded, but a tissue abandoned by the accused has been admitted because the police did not require the accused to produce this evidence and it was discoverable in any event.[101] Evidence that adversely affects the fairness of the trial will in very rare cases be admitted if, for example, the accused was abusing or incapable of exercising the right to counsel or would inevitably have confessed even if provided with right to counsel warnings.[102]

The second test under section 24(2) is that evidence should be excluded if necessary to avoid judicial condonation of a serious Charter violation. The seriousness of the Charter violation depends on whether the police violated the Charter deliberately or inadvertently. A conclusion that the police could have obtained the evidence without a Charter violation does not mitigate the seriousness of the Charter violation under this test and can aggravate its seriousness by suggesting that the police could have done their job without violating the accused's rights. The Court has not viewed violations committed in good faith as serious and have defined good faith widely to include reliance upon legislation, warrants, policy directives, prior cases, legal advice or accepted practices which were later found to be unconstitutional.[103] Evidence has been excluded to avoid condoning a serious violation when drugs were seized by a choke hold when the police did not have reasonable grounds to believe that the accused was a drug handler;[104] when drugs were seized through a defective warrant and a no knock entry with excessive force;[105] when drugs were seized through an intrusive and unconstitutional rectal search;[106] when drugs were seized after a trespass without reasonable grounds that the police ought to have known was illegal[107] and when bloody clothes and other evidence in a mur-

99. *Black* (1989) 50 C.C.C.(3d) 1 (S.C.C.).
100. *Burlingham* (1995) 97 C.C.C.(3d) 385 (S.C.C.).
101. *Stillman* (1997) 113 C.C.C.(3d) 321 (S.C.C.).
102. *Tremblay* (1987) 60 C.R.(3d) 59 (S.C.C.); *Mohl* (1989) 69 C.R.(3d) 399 (S.C.C.); *Harper* (1994) 92 C.C.C.(3d) 423 (S.C.C.).
103. *Sieben* (1987) 32 C.C.C.(3d) 574 (S.C.C.); *Hamill* (19987) 33 C.C.C.(3d) 110 (S.C.C.); *Duarte* (1990) 53 C.C.C.(3d) 1 (S.C.C.); *Wong* (1990) 60 C.C.C.(3d) 460; *Thompson* (1990) 59 C.C.C.(3d) 225 (S.C.C.); *Generoux* (1992) 70 C.C.C.(3d) 1 (S.C.C.); *Grant* (1993) 84 C.C.C.(3d) 173 (S.C.C.).
104. *Collins* (1987) 33 C.C.C.(3d) 1 (S.C.C.).
105. *Genest* (1988) 45 C.C.C.(3d) 385 (S.C.C.).
106. *Greffe* (1990) 55 C.C.C.(3d) 161 (S.C.C.).
107. *Kokesch* (1990) 61 C.C.C.(3d) 207 (S.C.C.).

der case were seized after the police made a warrantless entry and arrest in the accused's home without even a subjective belief that they had grounds for an arrest and engaged in a pattern of Charter violations.[108] The Supreme Court has, however, admitted drugs seized by a warrantless entry into a house because the police acted in exigent circumstances to prevent the destruction of the evidence and eventually obtained a warrant authorizing the search of the house.[109]

Before evidence is excluded under the second, "serious violation" test (but not the first "fair trial" test), courts will consider the effects of excluding the evidence on the repute of the administration of justice. This requires consideration of the seriousness of the offence charged, the importance of the evidence sought to be excluded and the reactions of reasonable people in all the circumstances. Drug offenses are considered to be very serious and the drugs sought to be excluded very important to the case. An illegally seized blood sample was excluded in one case because other evidence remained to try the accused for causing a fatal traffic accident.[110] In another case, however, such evidence was admitted because it was crucial to the prosecutor's case.[111]

Some have criticized Canadian courts for adopting a quasi-absolute exclusionary rule to protect the fairness of trials and not giving adequate consideration to the harms caused by the exclusion of evidence. At the same time, the Court has taken a contextual approach which mandates exclusion of evidence in order to protect the accused against unfair self-incrimination while allowing a balancing of interests in other contexts. In cases where evidence is not conscripted from the accused, exclusion of unconstitutionally obtained evidence is far from automatic and will generally only occur in response to a very serious violation.

a. *Validity of Search and Use of the Evidence.* Canadian courts distinguish between the validity of a search and the use of evidence obtained from the search. Even if a search is invalid and unconstitutional, the accused has the burden of establishing on a balance of probabilities that the admission of the evidence would bring the administration of justice into disrepute. However, the state has to establish on a balance of probabilities that evidence would inevitably or independently have been obtained[112] and may bear the evidential burden with respect to other matters particularly within its knowledge.

b. *Standing.* An accused must have standing under section 24 of the Charter to request the exclusionary remedy under section 24(2). This means that the accused's own rights must be violated in order to have any unconstitutionally obtained evidence excluded. In the search and seizure context, the accused's reasonable expectation of privacy must have been invaded. An accused does not have a reasonable expectation of privacy or standing to argue that evidence obtained from his girlfriend's apartment should be excluded at his trial, even though he had a key to the apartment and occasionally stayed overnight.[113] This standing requirement restricts the ambit of the Canadian exclusionary rule despite the fact that the exclusion of unconstitutionally obtained evidence is not automatic under section 24(2). Because

108. *Feeney* (1997) 115 C.C.C.(3d) 129 (S.C.C.).
109. *Silveria* (1995) 97 C.C.C.(3d) 450 (S.C.C.).
110. *Dersch* (1993) 85 C.C.C.(3d) 1 (S.C.C.).
111. *Colarusso* (1994) 87 C.C.C.(3d) 193 (S.C.C.).
112. *Bartle* (1994) 92 C.C.C.(3d) 289 (S.C.C.).
113. *Edwards* (1996) 104 C.C.C.(3d) 136 (S.C.C.).

damage suits for violation of Charter rights are rare, it means that even flagrant police violations may not be addressed if the police violate the rights of third parties as opposed to those of the accused.

c. *Fruit of the Poisonous Tree.* In contrast to its standing decisions, the Supreme Court has defined what evidence is obtained in a manner that violates Charter rights in a generous manner. The accused must establish a temporal connection between a Charter violation during the investigation and the evidence sought to be excluded, but not necessarily a causal connection. If drugs were discovered through a legal search, but while the accused was denied his right to counsel, the drugs would still be considered evidence that was obtained in a manner the violated the Charter. They would, however, only be excluded if the Charter violation was serious.[114] Evidence discovered with a valid warrant is still evidence obtained in a manner that violates the Charter if, prior to obtaining the warrant, the police violated the accused's search and seizure rights by a preliminary warrantless search. In some cases, the initial violation and/or a subsequent pattern of violations will be serious enough to require the exclusion of the evidence seized under the warrant.[115] In other cases, however, the evidence will not be excluded because the initial violation is not serious because, for example, the police relied in good faith on a statute that had not yet been found unconstitutional.[116]

There are limits to the reach of the Canadian exclusionary rule. A Charter violation will not be found if both the temporal and causal connection between the Charter violation and the impugned evidence are remote. A witness's testimony at a criminal trial was not obtained in a manner that violated the Charter just because the witness was arrested in an illegal drug raid.[117] On balance, however, the effect of the broad definition of what evidence is obtained in a manner that violates the Charter is to allow for evidence not causally related to a violation to be excluded because the investigation was nevertheless tainted by a serious violation. Flagrant violations that were not the cause of the discovery of evidence will not be ignored by the courts and this could mitigate some of the effects of the standing decisions reviewed above.

d. *Collateral Use.* Only in very limited circumstances will evidence excluded under section 24(2) of the Charter from the prosecution's case in chief be admissible for impeachment purposes. In a case where a statement was excluded because a right to counsel violation affected the fairness of the trial, the Supreme Court decided that admitting the statement for impeachment purposes would also affect the fairness of the trial.[118]

B. Lineups and Other Identification Procedures

1. Lineups

There is no statutory authority or procedure for identification line-ups. Before the Charter, the Supreme Court ruled that the right against self-incrimination did

114. *Strachan* (1988) 46 C.C.C.(3d) 479 (S.C.C.).

115. *Kokesch* (1990) 61 C.C.C.(3d) 207 (S.C.C.); *Feeney* (1997) 115 C.C.C.(3d) 129 (S.C.C.).

116. *Grant* (1993) 84 C.C.C.(3d) 173 (S.C.C.).

117. *Goldhart* (1995) 97 C.C.C.(3d) 385 (S.C.C.).

118. *Calder* (1996) 105 C.C.C.(3d) 1 (S.C.C.).

not protect the accused from being compelled to participate in a line-up.[119] Under the Charter, however, the accused has a right to refuse to participate in a line-up. The results of a line-up have been excluded because the accused did not have a reasonable opportunity to contact counsel before participating.[120] The Court stressed that exclusion was necessary to ensure that the accused was not unconstitutionally forced to assist in building the prosecution's case. A reasonable opportunity to consult counsel, but not counsel's actual attendance is required. Photo line-ups would be permissible because they do not require the accused's participation. Photographing a detained accused[121] and the use of photos when the accused has refused to participate in a line-up[122] have been upheld. Video-taping a person who refused to take part in a line-up has also been upheld.[123] These decisions suggest that the police will often be able to hold identification tests without the accused's unconstitutional participation.

Frailties in identification evidence are generally a matter for the trier of fact. In court identification has been allowed after an out of court identification has been excluded.[124]

2. Other Identification Procedures

The right to silence would seem to protect the accused from being forced to talk for a voice print although there are no reported cases on point. The taking of a person's hair, blood or body impressions in the absence of a warrant or consent would be illegal.[125] The police can, however, obtain warrants to obtain bodily samples for dna testing[126] and to obtain a handprint, fingerprint, footprint, foot impression, teeth impression or impression of any other body part.[127] Both of these new warrant provisions were recently enacted by Parliament in response to Supreme Court decisions holding that taking bodily samples or impressions without a warrant constituted an unreasonable search and seizure.

C. Interrogation

1. Before Formal Charge in Court

Section 10(b) of the Charter provides those subject to arrest or detention with both the right to retain and instruct counsel without delay and a right to be informed of that right. Detention has been interpreted broadly to include not only deprivation of liberty by physical constraint, but also the assumption of control over a person by a demand with significant legal consequences that would otherwise impede access to counsel and psychological compulsion in the form of a reasonable perception of a lack of freedom of choice. Even a brief 5 minute detention

119. *Marcoux* (1975) 24 C.C.C.(2d) 1 (S.C.C.).
120. *Ross* (1989) 46 C.C.C.(3d) 129 (S.C.C.).
121. *Dilling* (1993) 84 C.C.C.(3d) 325 (B.C.C.A.).
122. *D'Amico* (1993) 16 O.R.(3d) 125 (C.A.).
123. *Parsons* (1993) 24 C.R.(4th) 112 (Ont.C.A.).
124. *Thomas* (1993) 24 C.R.(4th) 249 (B.C.C.A.).
125. *Stillman* (1997) 113 C.C.C.(3d) 321 (S.C.C.).
126. *Criminal Code* ss.487.03-09.
127. *Criminal Code* section 487.091.

in the back of a police car requires a right to counsel warning, if the police ask the accused questions.[128] A person who is required to provide a breath sample either at the road side or a police station upon pain of conviction of the offence of refusing to provide a breath sample is detained.[129] A person asked to provide roadside sobriety tests is also detained.[130] However, the denial of the right to counsel with respect to road side breath and sobriety tests has been held to be a reasonable limit justified by traffic safety legislation.[131] Where there is no legislation, the denial of the right to counsel is not justified.[132] Temporary delays in providing the right to counsel are acceptable if the police must search the premises and identify other occupants.[133] Evidence will not be excluded if the Court concludes that the accused was so eager to confess that the right to counsel warning would have made no difference.[134]

A person who is questioned at a police station, but does not know he is a suspect may not be detained.[135] Courts of Appeal have held that an accused questioned in his home;[136] an accused questioned in the back seat of an open police car,[137] an accused asked on the street for identification,[138] an accused whose path was blocked by a police cruiser,[139] a murder suspect who voluntarily came to the police station[140] and even a murder suspect questioned for the second time at the police station but free to leave[141] were all not detained so that the police did not have to provide right to counsel warnings. Nevertheless, a suspect questioned at the police station for four and a half hours but not formally arrested was detained and thus entitled to right to counsel warnings.[142] Despite the Supreme Court's clear and broad definition of detention, the lower courts have introduced some uncertainty as they determine when in particular circumstances a person is or is not subject to detention.

Upon arrest or detention, the police must inform detainees not only that they can consult a lawyer, but about the availability of legal aid for those who cannot afford a lawyer and duty counsel who can provide temporary legal advice regardless of the suspect's financial status.[143] Most provinces have established toll free telephone numbers that allow detainees to contact duty counsel on a twenty four hour basis. The police must inform detainees of available services including the toll

---

128. *Elshaw* (1991) 67 C.C.C.(3d) 97 (S.C.C.).

129. *Therens* (1985) 18 C.C.C.(3d) 481 (S.C.C.) *Thomsen* (1988) 40 C.C.C.(3d) 411 (S.C.C.).

130. *Saunders* (1988) 41 C.C.C.(3d) 532 (Ont.C.A.).

131. *Ratelle* (1996) 105 C.C.C.(3d) 58 (Ont.C.A.).

132. *Gallant* (1989) 95 A.R. 101 (C.A.); *Baroni* (1989) 49 C.C.C.(3d) 553 (N.S.C.A.); *Hill* (1990) 86 Nfld & P.E.I.R. 197 (P.E.I.C.A.).

133. *Strachan* (1988) 46 C.C.C.(3d) 479 (S.C.C.); *Debot* (1989) 52 C.C.C.(3d) 193 (S.C.C.).

134. *Harper* (1994) 92 C.C.C.(3d) 423 (S.C.C.) The accused spontaneously said "I'm the guy you want. Just take me away."

135. *Hawkins* (1993) 79 C.C.C.(3d) 576 rev'd 72 C.C.C.(3d) 524.

136. *Esposito* (1985) 24 C.C.C.(3d) 88 (Ont.C.A.).

137. *Wright* (1990) 56 C.C.C.(3d) 503 (Ont.C.A.).

138. *Grafe* (1987) 36 C.C.C.(3d) 267 (Ont.C.A.).

139. *Lawrence* (1990) 59 C.C.C.(3d) 55 (Ont.C.A.).

140. *Bazinet* (1986) 25 C.C.C.(3d) 273 (Ont.C.A.).

141. *Moran* (1987) 36 C.C.C.(3d) 225 (Ont.C.A.).

142. *Voss* (1989) 50 C.C.C.(3d) 58 (Ont.C.A.).

143. *Brydges* (1990) 53 C.C.C.(3d) 330 (S.C.C.). However, there is no requirement of warning as to right to silence. See TAN 152 and 162-63 infra.

free telephone number,[144] but the Supreme Court has refused to require governments to establish such services despite evidence that they are efficient and practical.

Once a detainee asks to speak to a lawyer, the police must facilitate access to counsel by offering the use of a telephone[145] and not elicit evidence from the detainee until he or she has had a reasonable opportunity to contact a lawyer. The police must hold off eliciting evidence until the suspect has had a reasonable opportunity to contact counsel even if this means that a breath sample is no longer presumed to represent the accused's blood alcohol when driving. Evidence taken in violation of holding off requirements will generally be excluded.[146] This constitutes an indirect but strong penalty on those jurisdictions who do not ensure that all detainees can contact duty counsel shortly after arrest and detention. The police may be required to hold off an identification line-up until an accused has been able to contact counsel of his choice during regular office hours.[147] The detainee should be allowed, within reason, to consult a lawyer of his or her own choice especially if the offence is serious[148] and to consult with that lawyer in confidence and privacy. The detainee must, however, exercise the right to contact counsel with reasonable diligence. A suspect who did not attempt to contact his lawyer when arrested at 7:00pm and two hours later said that he wanted to talk to his lawyer but did not have his home phone number has been held not to have asserted his right to counsel with due diligence.[149] Courts have refused to exclude evidence when the accused was denied his right to counsel because, in a drunk driving case, he was too drunk to exercise the right[150] or rude and obnoxious.[151] Once an accused has been given a reasonable opportunity to consult counsel, questioning may resume without again informing the accused of the right to counsel or providing another reasonable opportunity to consult counsel.[152] This seems to apply even in cases where the accused and/or counsel have indicated a desire not to talk. The right to counsel may, however, be violated by prolonged questioning without counsel being present, police denigration of counsel or the offer of a plea bargain without counsel being present.[153]

The accused's right to counsel can be subject to informed and voluntary waiver. A murder suspect who was too drunk to be aware of the consequences cannot waive her rights to counsel.[154] An accused who answered baiting questions or participated in a line-up before being afforded a reasonable opportunity to consult counsel have not waived their right to counsel.[155] An accused who asked about legal aid, but was not informed about its availability has not waived the right to counsel when he subsequently answered questions.[156] An accused who confessed

144. If the toll free number is not in operation at the time of the detention, it is not necessary to inform the detainee of the number. *Latimer* (1997) 112 C.C.C.(3d) 193 (S.C.C.).

145. *Manninen* (1987) 34 C.C.C.(3d) 385 (S.C.C.).

146. *Prosper* (1994) 92 C.C.C.(3d) 353 (S.C.C.); *Bartle* (1994) 92 C.C.C.(3d) 289 (S.C.C.).

147. *Ross* (1989) 46 C.C.C.(3d) 129 (S.C.C.).

148. *Burlingham* (1995) 97 C.C.C.(3d) 385 (S.C.C.).

149. *Smith* (1989) 50 C.C.C.(3d) 308 (S.C.C.).

150. *Mohl* (1989) 47 C.C.C.(3d) 575 (S.C.C.).

151. *Tremblay* (1987) 60 C.R.(3rd) 59 (S.C.C.).

152. *Hebert* (1990) 57 C.C.C.(3d) 1 (S.C.C.).

153. *Burlingham* (1995) 97 C.C.C.(3d) 385 (S.C.C.).

154. *Clarkson* (1986) 25 C.C.C.(3d) 207.

155. *Manninen* (1987) 34 C.C.C.(3d) 385 (S.C.C.); *Ross* supra.

156. *Brydges* (1990) 53 C.C.C.(3d) 330 (S.C.C.).

after the police had denigrated his counsel of choice also did not waive the right to counsel.[157] On the other hand, an accused who answered questions because he heard voices in his head has waived his right to counsel.[158] With the exception of the last case, the Supreme Court has set high standards for the waiver of the right to counsel.

Section 10(a) of the Charter also requires a person to be informed promptly of the reason for his detention or arrest. This does not require an explicit warning if the matter being investigated was obvious.[159] The right was violated, however, when an accused was not aware that he was also held for a second more serious sexual assault[160] or believed he was being held for drug offenses, not murder.[161] If an attempted murder becomes a murder after the victim dies, the accused should be so informed and have another opportunity to consult counsel.[162] There is no constitutional obligation to inform detainees of their right to silence, but such a warning is customary.

The police may legitimately lie and engage in deception in order to obtain statements.[163]

Nevertheless, the Crown must establish that any statement was voluntary in the sense of not being obtained by fear of prejudice or hope of advantage.[164] If a criminal suspect has asserted the right to silence, the police cannot subvert it by actively eliciting information, but they can use passive means to obtain information, Eg. undercover informants can be used as "listening posts" after the accused asserts the right to silence but they may not actively elicit information.[165]

2. *After Formal Charge*

In general, there is no distinction between the accused's position before or after formal charges in court. The right to counsel under section 10(b) of the Charter is triggered by arrest or detention, not the commencement of formal proceedings. The rules respecting the accused's rights to silence and counsel would be the same both before and after the laying of formal charges.

3. *Enforcing the Rules*

Under the common law, involuntary statements are excluded automatically but can be admitted to the extent that they are confirmed as true by subsequent tangible evidence.[166] Statements taken in violation of the right to counsel in section 10(b) of the Charter[167] or the right to silence protected under section 7 of the Char-

157. *Burlingham* (1995) 97 C.C.C.(3d) 385 (S.C.C.).
158. *Whittle* (1994) 92 C.C.C.(3d) 11 (S.C.C.).
159. *Evans* (1991) 63 C.C.C.(3d) 289 (S.C.C.).
160. *Borden* (1994) 92 C.C.C.(3d) 404 (S.C.C.).
161. *Evans* (1991) 63 C.C.C.(3d) 289 (S.C.C.).
162. *Black* (1989) 50 C.C.C.(3d) 1 (S.C.C.).
163. *Rothman* (1981) 59 C.C.C.(3d) 30 (S.C.C.); *Miller* (1991) 9 C.R.(4th) 347 (Ont.C.A.); *Corak* (1994) 29 C.R.(4th) 388 (B.C.C.A.).
164. *Boudreau* (1949) 94 C.C.C. 1 (S.C.C.).
165. *Hebert* (1990) 57 C.C.C.(3d) 1 (S.C.C.); *Broyles* (1991) 68 C.C.C.(3d) 308 (S.C.C.).
166. *Wray* [1970] 4 C.C.C. 1 (S.C.C.).
167. "Everyone has the right...not to be deprived of (liberty) except in accordance with the principles of fundamental justice."

ter are generally excluded under section 24(2) of the Charter on the basis that the admission of such conscriptive evidence will render a subsequent trial unfair. In a very few cases, the courts have made exceptions to this general presumption. For example, statements obtained in violation of the right to counsel have been admitted when the accused has been rude and obnoxious,[168] has been too intoxicated to exercise his right to counsel[169] or had an irresistible desire to confess.[170]

III. Court Procedures

Most criminal offenses are disposed in the lower trial courts known as the provincial courts. The judges (formerly magistrates) of this court are appointed and paid by each province. In some provinces, they are chosen with the assistance of a nominating panel while in others they are not. They do not have jurisdiction to sit with a jury, but they can hear almost every criminal case short of murder. The most serious criminal cases, including all murder cases, are tried in the superior courts whose judges are appointed by the federal government. These cases may be tried with or without a jury and/or a preliminary hearing conducted by a provincial court judge.

A. Pretrial

1. Initial Court Appearance

After arrest, police officers must release the accused as soon as possible unless detention is required to establish the accused's identity; to secure or preserve evidence relating to the offence, to prevent the continuation of an offence or to ensure the accused's attendance at court.[171] Section 503 of the *Criminal Code* requires the accused to be taken before a judicial official for a first court appearance without unreasonable delay and within 24 hours if practicable. The judicial official then holds a bail hearing in which the prosecutor must generally establish that continued detention is required on the primary ground that detention is necessary to ensure attendance at trial or the secondary ground that detention is necessary for the protection or safety of the public including any substantial likelihood that the accused will, if released, commit a criminal offence or interfere with the administration of justice.[172] A statutory authorization to continue detention when necessary in the "public interest" was struck down by the Supreme Court as an excessively vague infringement of the right not to be deprived of reasonable bail without just cause under section 11(e) of the Charter.[173] At the same time, however, the Court

168. *Tremblay* (1987) 37 C.C.C.(3d) 565 (S.C.C.).

169. *Mohl* (1989) 47 C.C.C.(3d) 575 (S.C.C.)n. 154, *Supra*. This case is in tension with *Clarkson*, but can perhaps be explained by the fact that *Clarkson* concerned an interrogation of a murder suspect while *Mohl* concerned a breathalyser demand to a drunk driver.

170. *Harper* (1994) 92 C.C.C.(3d) 423 (S.C.C.).

171. *Criminal Code* sections 497-499.

172. *Criminal Code* section 515(10).

173. Parliament has recently responded to this decision with an amendment to section 515(10)(c) of the *Criminal Code* which allows the denial of bail on "any other just cause" in-

upheld preventive detention where there is a substantial likelihood that an accused would commit crimes if released[174] and requirements that those charged with drug trafficking show cause why they should be released.[175] Bail decisions can be appealed by the accused and the prosecutor and automatic judicial reviews are required by statute if the accused remains in custody for more than 30 days in less serious matters or 90 days when charged with an indictable offence. *Habeas corpus* can also be used as a remedy for the denial of bail in exceptional cases involving unconstitutionality. [176]

At the first court appearance, the accused may be represented by state-funded duty counsel, but will generally have to apply for publicly funded counsel for subsequent proceedings. In most cases where the accused is charged with an indictable offence, the accused must elect whether he or she desires to be tried in the superior court with a preliminary hearing and/or jury or in the lower provincial court without a preliminary hearing or a jury. Many accused in Canada elect the latter because of a perception that justice in the lower courts is faster, less expensive and the exercise of sentencing discretion more lenient.

2. *Charging Instrument*

Indictments and informations are drafted by police officers and prosecutors. The grand jury has been abolished. There is broad prosecutorial discretion including for many offenses a decision whether to prosecute them by way of indictment or as less serious summary conviction matters. Summary conviction matters are tried in the provincial courts and are generally subject to a maximum of 6 months imprisonment, but in some cases such as sexual assault, 18 months imprisonment. The prosecutor can include in an indictment any offence disclosed by evidence at the preliminary inquiry, even if the accused has not been committed for trial by a judicial official on that offence.[177] The exercise of prosecutorial discretion is subject to Charter review and the common law doctrine of abuse of process. Proceedings can be terminated if there has been irreparable damage to either the accused's rights or to the integrity of the judicial system.[178]

3. *Preliminary Hearings*

Preliminary hearings (inquiries) are only available for indictable offenses where the accused has elected to be tried in the Superior Court with a preliminary inquiry. The prosecutor is required to adduce under oath enough admissible evidence that if believed by the trier of fact would support a conviction. The accused may present evidence and cross-examine witnesses, but is not allowed to seek remedies for vio-

---

cluding "where the detention is necessary in order to maintain the confidence in the administration of justice, having regard to all the circumstances, including the apparent strength of the prosecution's case, the gravity of the nature of the offence, the circumstances surrounding its commission and the potential for a lengthy term of imprisonment." This uses many more words, but in my view, amounts to denial of bail in the public interest.

174. *Morales* (1992) 77 C.C.C.(3d) 91 (S.C.C.).

175. *Pearson* (1992) 77 C.C.C.(3d) 124 (S.C.C.).

176. *Pearson* (1992) 77 C.C.C.(3d) 124 at 133 (S.C.C.).

177. *Criminal Code* section 574.

178. *O'Connor* (1996) 103 C.C.C.(3d) 1 (S.C.C.); *Carosella* (1997) 112 C.C.C.(3d) 289 (S.C.C.).

lations of the Charter. The judge can prohibit the publication of evidence in order to protect the accused's right to a fair trial.[179] The prosecutor may by-pass a preliminary or have a trial after charges have been dismissed at a preliminary by issuing a preferred indictment with the consent of a senior prosecutor.[180] This power has been upheld under the Charter provided the accused has otherwise received sufficient disclosure of the prosecutor's case.[181] With the constitutionalization of disclosure requirements and concern about the length and expense of trials, there is interest in abolishing preliminary inquiry. Many defence lawyers, however, argue that they are necessary as the only means to examine witnesses under oath before trial.

4. *Pretrial Motions*

Pre-trial motions have only recently been used in some Charter matters. Applications for Charter remedies must generally be made to a trial judge and interlocutory appeals are discouraged. In most cases, a Charter ruling would have to be appealed after the verdict. Third parties who allege that their rights are infringed by a publication ban or a subpoena may apply to the trial judge for standing and in some cases can bring interlocutory appeals.[182]

5. *Discovery*

Law reform bodies have long called for the enactment of statutory disclosure obligations, but Parliament did not act. The Supreme Court then interpreted section 7 of the Charter to require the prosecutor to disclose relevant, non-privileged evidence in his or her possession to the accused at an early stage in the proceedings, generally prior to the accused's election as to the mode of trial.[183] Material is relevant if there is a reasonable probability that it will be useful to the accused and no distinction is drawn between inculpatory and exculpatory evidence.

The identity of informers does not have to be revealed unless the informant is an eyewitness to the crimes. The Supreme Court ruled that the prosecutor must disclose all records in its possession concerning the complainant to the accused but Parliament responded with legislation requiring, in sexual cases, that the accused's right to full answer and defence be balanced against the complainant's privacy and equality rights and the social interest in the full reporting of sexual assaults.[184] The accused does not have the right to examine potential witnesses,[185] and this can only be achieved at a preliminary hearing. At present, disclosure obligations are enforced by applications for remedies under section 24(1) of the Charter usually to the trial judge or the superior court if the trial judge has not yet been appointed.

179. *Criminal Code* section 539, 542.

180. *Criminal Code* section 577.

181. *Arviv* (1985) 19 C.C.C.(3d) 395 (Ont.C.A.); *Ertel* (1987) 35 C.C.C.(3d) 398 (Ont.C.A.).

182. *Dagenais* (1994) 94 C.C.C.(3d) 289 (S.C.C.); *O'Connor* (1996) 103 C.C.C.(3d) 1 (S.C.C.).

183. *Stinchcombe* (1991) 68 C.C.C.(3d) 1 (S.C.C.); *Stinchcombe* (1995) 96 C.C.C.(3d) 318 (S.C.C.).

184. *O'Connor* (1995) 103 C.C.C.(3d) 1 (S.C.C.) See now *Criminal Code* sections 278.1-278.91. These new restrictions have been the subject of successful Charter challenges in the lower courts.

185. *Khela* (1995) 43 C.R.(4th) 368 (S.C.C.).

Stays of proceedings will only rarely be justified as a remedy for lack of disclosure[186] and other remedies have included disclosure orders, adjournments, costs and mistrials. Parliament has recently codified procedures and tests for the production and disclosure of the complainant's records in sexual assault cases, but there remains a need for clear and comprehensive codification of all disclosure standards.

B. Trial

1. Nature of Trial

Trials are conducted in an adversary format with lawyers presenting evidence to a judge who usually sits without a jury. The judge decides on the admissibility of evidence and, unlike a jury, is aware of evidence that has been ruled inadmissible. Evidence is ruled inadmissible if it is not relevant; if its prejudicial impact outweighs its probative value; if it is protected by attorney/client privilege and if it is hearsay that is not reliable and necessary in the case.

An accused charged with an indictable offence can generally elect trial by jury. Under section 11(f) of the Charter, the accused also has a right to trial by jury if he or she faces five years imprisonment or more and is not charged with an offence under military law. The jury deliberates in secret and does not give reasons for its verdict. It is composed of twelve people from the place where the trial is held. They must be Canadian citizens and competent in the language of the trial. The jury must be selected in a manner that is fair to both the prosecutor and the accused.[187] Depending on the seriousness of the charge, both the prosecutor and the accused may dismiss four, twelve or twenty prospective jurors without establishing cause.[188] They both have the unlimited ability to have jurors dismissed on grounds of partiality, but the questions that can be asked of prospective jurors are quite limited with only some courts allowing the accused to inquire about racial bias against an accused.[189] Questions arising from the nature of the charge or exploring the general likes and dislikes of prospective jurors are not allowed.

Trial judges generally do not have to give reasons for their verdicts or rulings.[190] A simple statement by a judge that his decision was based on the credibility of the witnesses has been upheld[191], but reasons are required if the evidence is confused and contradictory.[192] A lack of reasons by the trial judge may frustrate the accused's ability to appeal the decision on the basis of legal error. In jury trials, the trial judge must instruct the jury about the relevant law and can also summarize the evidence in the case. The jury never gives a statement of reasons.

---

186. A stay was granted in one controversial case in which a rape crisis centre shredded notes. *Carosella* (1997) 112 C.C.C.(3d) 289 (S.C.C.).

187. *Bain* (1992) 69 C.C.C.(3d) 481 (S.C.C.).

188. *Criminal Code* section 634.

189. *Parks* (1993) 84 C.C.C.(3d) 353 (Ont.C.A.); *Williams* (1996) 106 C.C.C.(3d) 215 (B.C.C.A.).

190. *Burns* [1994] 1 S.C.R. 656.

191. *Barrett* (1995) 96 C.C.C.(3d) 317 (S.C.C.).

192. *R(D).* (1996) 48 C.R.(4th) 368 (S.C.C.).

a. *Guilty Pleas.* Trial judges have a discretion not to accept a guilty plea, but they are *not* required to ensure that guilty pleas are voluntary or have a factual basis and prosecutors need not adduce evidence to justify a guilty plea. However, involuntary pleas have been struck down. Guilty pleas have been approved even when defence is possible.[193] Plea bargaining concerning both charges and sentences occurs openly and is encouraged. An early guilty plea is a significant mitigating factor in sentencing. The accused's right to counsel is violated if the police attempt to plea bargain with the accused when his or her lawyer is not present.[194]

2. *Defendant's Rights*

Section 7 of the Charter has been interpreted to protect the accused's right to present full answer and defence. This includes the right to testify and the right not to be compelled to testify in one's criminal trial. The accused does not have to assert the right not to testify in open court and the trial judge and the prosecutor cannot comment on the accused's decision not to testify.[195] If the accused does testify, then he or she is subject to cross-examination and the use of prior convictions to impeach credibility.[196] The accused also has the right to compel attendance of witnesses and cross-examine them. The accused's right to full answer and defence has been held to be violated when he was not allowed to cross-examine a complainant in a sexual assault trial, on mental health or employment records relevant to issues in the trial,[197] or on the prior sexual conduct of the complainant when relevant to an issue such as mistaken belief in consent.[198] Parliament has responded to these controversial decisions with legislation requiring a balancing of the accused's rights against those of the complainant and the social interest in increased reporting of sexual assault.[199]

The accused has a right to be present at trial so long as he or she does not interfere with the proceedings.[200] The accused is deemed to waive the right to be present if he or she absconds during the course of the trial. The trial can then be conducted in the accused's absence and adverse inferences drawn from the absence.

3. *Lawyers*

Section 10(b), of the Charter providing a right to counsel upon arrest, has not been interpreted as providing a right to legal assistance at trial for accused who cannot afford a lawyer.[201] Nevertheless, the right under section 7 of the Charter not to be deprived of liberty except in accordance with the principles of fundamental justice may be violated if the accused cannot have a fair trial without legal assistance. For example, an accused who could not afford counsel for a long conspiracy trial and did not receive a publicly funded lawyer, was denied her right to a fair

193. *Brosseau* [1969] 3 C.C.C. 129 (S.C.C.); *Adgey* (1973) 13 C.C.C.(2d) 177 (S.C.C.).
194. *Burlingham* (1995) 97 C.C.C.(3d) 385 at 399-400 (S.C.C.).
195. *Canada Evidence Act* R.S.C. 1985 c.C- 5 s.4(6).
196. *Corbett* (1988) 41 C.C.C.(3d) 385 (S.C.C.).
197. *Osolin* (1993) 86 C.C.C.(3d) 481 (S.C.C.); *O'Connor* (1996) 103 C.C.C.(3d) 1 (S.C.C.).
198. *Seaboyer* (1991) 66 C.C.C.(3d) 321 (S.C.C.).
199. *Criminal Code* section 276, 278.1.
200. *Criminal Code* section 650.
201. *Prosper* (1994) 92 C.C.C.(3d) 353 (S.C.C.).

trial and had proceedings stayed until publicly funded counsel was available.[202] The practical availability of counsel depends on legal aid plans administered by the provinces and funded by the provinces, federal government and the legal profession. As a matter of practice, legal aid is available to accused who cannot afford a lawyer where there is a likelihood of imprisonment and sometimes where there is a likelihood of loss of livelihood. Legal aid services in some provinces are supplied by staff lawyers while in other provinces they are supplied by private lawyers who bill the legal aid plan. Lawyers must be competent enough to provide effective assistance of counsel, but there is no right to counsel of choice except in the most serious of cases.

Prosecutors are considered to be Ministers of Justice who are interested in the truth rather than winning.[203] This understanding of the prosecutor's role has led to the imposition of wide discovery obligations on the prosecutor, but not the accused.[204]

4. *Witnesses*

Witnesses can be subpoenaed to testify by both the prosecutor and the accused and they generally do not have the right to refuse to testify on the grounds of self-incrimination.[205] However, compelled testimony and evidence derived from compelled testimony that could not be independently obtained is not admissible in subsequent proceedings against witnesses. Expert witnesses are chosen and paid by the parties to a case and they are examined and cross-examined by the lawyers representing the parties.

5. *Judges*

All judges in Canada are appointed and must have at least 10 years experience at the bar.

6. *Victims*

Crime victims and all other individuals have the right to go before a judicial official to commence a prosecution by establishing reasonable and probable grounds to believe a person has committed a crime. These prosecutions may, however, be stayed or taken over by public prosecutors. Crime victims may provide courts with written victim impact statements to be used at sentencing and courts may require the accused to make restitution to the victim as part of the sentencing process. Crime victims may also apply for compensation from provincial schemes. Witnesses, including victims, may seek relief from subpoenas of confidential information on the basis that such orders may infringe their rights privacy or perhaps equality rights. These claims will be balanced against the accused's right to full answer and defence.[206]

---

202. *Rowbotham* (1988) 41 C.C.C.(3d) 1 (Ont.C.A.); *Rockwood* (1989) 49 C.C.C.(3d) 129 (N.S.C.A.).

203. *Boucher* (1954) 110 C.C.C. 236 (S.C.C.).

204. *Stinchcombe* (1991) 68 C.C.C.(3d) 1 (S.C.C.).

205. The Court has held open the possibility that in rare cases, a witness could obtain an order relieving him or her from the obligation to testify if the dominant goal of the compulsion was to incriminate the witness. *Branch* (1995) 97 C.C.C.(3d) 505 (S.C.C.).

206. *Beharriell* (1996) 103 C.C.C.(3d) 92 (S.C.C.).

C. Appeals

Appeals are taken from provincial courts deciding summary conviction offenses to superior courts and in all other cases to the provincial court of appeal and then to the Supreme Court of Canada. For indictable matters,[207] the accused can appeal matters of law as of right, and matters of fact or the fitness of sentence with leave to a provincial Court of Appeal, usually sitting in panels of three judges. The prosecutor may also appeal questions of law and stays of proceedings as of right and the fitness of sentence with leave to the Court of Appeal. Both the accused and the prosecutor have a right to appeal to the Supreme Court of Canada as of right on a matter of law on which a judge of the Court of Appeal dissents and generally with leave on matters of national importance. Section 11(h) of the Charter contemplates Crown appeals by providing that the accused has double jeopardy protection only after he or she is "finally acquitted of the offence," i.e. after all appeals. Appeal courts have statutory powers to appoint state-funded counsel when "it appears desirable in the interests of justice."[208] This power is not used extensively because of the availability of legal aid for appeals.

1. *Ineffective Assistance of Counsel*

An accused's rights may be violated by ineffective assistance of counsel, but the legal advice must be negligent and result in a reasonable probability of a miscarriage of justice. An accused has been held to be deprived of effective assistance of counsel when one lawyer represents co-accused who might be able to place the blame on each other[209] and when a lawyer did not investigate witnesses who support the accused's alibi.[210] On the other hand, there was no ineffective assistance of counsel when a lawyer did not meet a client charged with sexual assault until the morning of the trial.[211] Litigation over ineffective assistance of counsel is still in an embryonic stage, but is likely to increase.

2. *Other Grounds of Appeal*

An accused's appeal can be allowed on the grounds that the conviction is unreasonable or not supported by the evidence; entails a miscarriage of justice; or is based on an error of law. A legal error made by the trial judge will not, however, require a new trial if the appeal court concludes "no substantial wrong or miscarriage of justice occurred."[212] Courts are reluctant to use this proviso when a Charter violation has been found and will usually order a new trial unless it is clear that there is no basis for the prosecutor's case. Courts have ordered new trials where an accused has been denied full disclosure by the prosecutor;[213] the effective assistance

207. The accused and the prosecutor may appeal errors of law and sentences in summary conviction cases to the superior courts.
208. *Criminal Code* section 684.
209. *Silvini* (1991) 68 C.C.C.(3d) 251 (Ont.C.A.).
210. *McKellar* (1994) 34 C.R.(4th) 28 (Ont.C.A.).
211. *B (L.C.)* (1996) 46 C.R.(4th) 368 (Ont.C.A.).
212. *Criminal Code* section 686(1)(b) (iii).
213. *Stinchcombe* (1991) 68 C.C.C.(3d) 1 (S.C.C.).

of counsel;[214] where the trier of fact could not reasonably have concluded that the accused was guilty beyond a reasonable doubt;[215] and when the accused was denied his right to an interpreter.[216]

3. *Successive Appeals/Collateral Attack*

As Canada has a unitary court system, there are no provisions for successive appeals in different court systems. On an application for the mercy of the Crown, the federal Minister of Justice may order a new trial or appeal and this procedure has been used to reverse several recent miscarriages of justice.[217] This review mechanism has been criticized for its discretionary nature. There have been proposals to establish independent commissions to investigate claims of wrongful convictions, but these have not yet been implemented by Parliament. Civil proceedings may be stayed if they are a collateral attack on a criminal verdict and once appeals have been exhausted, a criminal verdict is *res judicata* even if the law under which the accused has been convicted is subsequently struck down as unconstitutional.[218]

Conclusion

Criminal procedure is partially codified in Canada. It has become considerably more complex with the enactment of a constitutional bill of rights which gives courts the power to interpret rights affecting police powers and the pre-trial, trial, and appeal processes. The constitutional decisions of the Supreme Court now fill many of the gaps in the codified criminal procedure and they have also provoked Parliament to amend the *Criminal Code* to respond to specific rulings. There is still a need for a more comprehensive codification of criminal procedure.

Bibliography

Jamie Cameron (ed.), *The Charter's Impact on the Criminal Justice System* (Toronto: Carswell, 1996)

M.L. Friedland and Kent Roach, *Cases and Materials on Criminal Law and Procedure, 8th ed.* (Toronto: Emond Montgomery, 1997)

Peter Hogg, *Constitutional Law of Canada, 4th ed* (Toronto: Carswell, 1997 as updated)

John Laskin, et al., *The Canadian Charter of Rights and Freedoms Annotated* (Aurora: Canada Law Book, 1997 as updated)

---

214. *Silvini* (1991) 68 C.C.C.(3d) 251 (Ont.C.A.).
215. *W(R)* (1992) 74 C.C.C.(3d) 134 (S.C.C.).
216. *Tran* (1994) 92 C.C.C.(3d) 218 (S.C.C.).
217. *Criminal Code* section 690.
218. *Sarson* (1996) 107 C.C.C.(3d) 21 (S.C.C.).

Alan Mewett, *An Introduction to the Criminal Process in Canada, 3rd ed.* (Toronto: Carswell, 1995)

Kent Roach, *Constitutional Remedies in Canada* (Aurora: Canada Law Book, 1994 as updated)

Kent Roach, *Criminal Law* (Toronto: Irwin Law, 1996)

Roger Salhany, *Criminal Procedure in Canada, 6th ed.* (Aurora: Canada Law Book, 1994 as updated)

Don Stuart, *Charter Justice in Canadian Criminal Law, 2nd ed.* (Toronto: Carswell, 1996)

Don Stuart and Ron Delisle, *Learning Canadian Criminal Procedure, 5th ed.* (Toronto: Carswell, 1997)

Tim Quigley, *Procedure in Canadian Criminal Law* (Toronto: Carswell, 1997)

Supreme Court Law Review (annual reviews of the Supreme Court's jurisprudence)

Criminal Law Quarterly (journal for lawyers, judges and police officers concerning criminal justice)

Canadian Criminal Law Review (journal on the theory and practice of criminal law)

Chapter 3

China

Liling Yue

I. Introduction

China is a centralized state. Its legal system has followed the continental structure; the sources of law are primarily statutes. The legislative power belongs to the National People's Congress (hereinafter NPC). According to the Constitution, provinces[1] only have the power to make local legislation, but not the "basic laws" which include criminal law, criminal procedure law and so on. The main source of criminal procedure law is the Code of Criminal Procedure.[2]

The Chinese Constitution has only provided the basic principles of criminal procedure in the chapters "The Fundamental Rights and Duties of the Citizen" and "The Structure of the State." For example, Article 37 stipulates that "Freedom of the person of citizens of the People's Republic of China is inviolable. No citizen may be arrested except with the approval or by decision of a people's procuratorate (prosecutor) or by decision of a People's Court, and arrests must be made by a Public Security Organ. Unlawful detention or deprivation or restriction of citizen's freedom of the person by other means is prohibited, and unlawful search of the person of citizens is prohibited." Article 125 provides that "Except in special circumstances as specified by law, all cases in the People's Courts are heard in public. The accused has the right to defense."

However, the application of these constitutional principles depends on the Criminal Procedure Code and other laws, such as the Organic Law of the People's Courts[3], the Organic law of the People's Procuratorates,[4] and the Lawyers Law.[5] These statutes provide more details on the role of judges, prosecutors, police and defense counsels, their duties, powers etc. during the criminal proceedings. Besides

1. China has 31 provinces (including Taiwan).

2. The first Code of Criminal Procedure was enacted by the second session of the fifth NPC on July 1,1979, and it was amended by the fourth session of the Eighth NPC on 17th March 1996 in accordance with the " Decision on Amending the Criminal Procedure Law of the People's Republic of China."

3. It was enacted at the Second Session of the Fifth NPC on July 1,1979.

4. It was also enacted at the Second Session of the Fifth NPC on July 1,1979.

5. It was enacted at the 19th session of the Eighth NPC on May 15,1996.

these regulations, the Standing Committee of the National People's Congress (NPC), the Supreme People's Court, the Supreme People's Procuratorate and the Ministry of Public Security (the headquarters of the police) have made binding decisions as to how to implement the Criminal Procedure Law

In addition, the above judicial authorities have also made their own implementation rules, which are enforced within their own jurisdiction. Sometimes these different enactments have created conflicts among these judicial organs. After the new revised Criminal Procedure Law was enacted, the conflicts of application of this law among these judicial institutions has become sharper. In order to solve these problems, these authorities have jointly made "The Stipulation on Certain Issues of Implementation of Criminal Procedure Law"[6] to ensure that the laws are enforced uniformly.

Criminal cases in China haven't played as important a role in law making as in the common law states, but in recent years, the Supreme People's Court has published some typical cases in the "Supreme People's Court's Reports." The Judgments of these cases have the power to influence the decisions of lower courts.

II. Police Procedures

A. Arrest, Search, and Seizure Law

1. Stops and 2. Frisks

There is no law in China covering brief detentions on the street and/or frisks of such detainees by the police. Consequently, it is unknown how frequently such procedures may be used. Chinese law recognizes "detention" (which may extend for up to a month) as one of the five coercive measures[7] that may be used to detain suspects before the formal arrest would be approved by a prosecutor or the chief of police. Criminal detention is for investigative and other purposes discussed below, and is of shorter duration than an arrest. The power to detain a suspect in most cases is exercised by police without the need for approval by a prosecutor or a judge. Prosecutors have the power to order the detention of suspects within the categories of cases they are authorized by law to investigate. The Criminal Procedure Law has specified seven categories of circumstances under which detention may be effected:

- if he is preparing to commit a crime, is in the process of committing a crime, or is discovered immediately after committing a crime;
- if he is identified as having committed a crime by the victim or by an eyewitness on the scene;
- if criminal evidence is found on his person or at his residence;

6. It was enacted in Jan. 19, 1998. It has 14 issues , with 48 articles.

7. There are five different coercive measures *(qiang zhi cuo shi)* to be used to restrict an individual's freedom before trial: Compulsory summons *(juchuan);* Obtaining a surety and awaiting trial *(qubao houshen)*; surveillance of residence *(jianshi juzhu);* detention *(juliu);* arrest *(daibu)*.

- if after committing the crime, he attempts to commit suicide or to escape, or if he is a fugitive;
- if he may possibly destroy or fabricate evidence, or gang up to make false confessions;
- if he does not reveal his true name and address or if his identity is unclear;
- if there is strong suspicion that he is a person who goes from place to place committing crimes; who repeatedly committed crimes; or who has ganged up with others to commit crimes.

The law requires police to interrogate a detainee within 24 hours after a person has been detained. If it is found that the person should not have been detained, he must be immediately released and issued a release certificate.[8] If police deem it necessary to arrest a detainee, they shall, within three days after detention, submit a request to the procuratorate for examination and approval. In practice, there are a large number of suspects detained pending trial. The usual period for which a suspect is detained prior to formal arrest is three to seven days. If the suspect is suspected of belonging to category seven above, however, the period of detention could be extended by up to thirty days.[9] After police submit the request for approval of the arrest, the procuratorate must decide either to approve or disapprove the arrest within seven days.

3. *Arrests*

Arrest in China is the longest and severest measure of restriction of human freedom during criminal proceedings. Arrest may be applied when there is evidence to support the facts of a crime and the criminal suspect or defendant could be sentenced to a punishment not less than imprisonment, and if pretrial release measures, such as residential surveillance, would be insufficient to prevent the occurrence of danger to society.[10] The Criminal Procedure Law also provides special circumstances, under which, even if the above arrest standards have been met, arrest is not appropriate. These circumstances are where the suspect is suffering from grave illness, or is a pregnant woman, or is a woman nursing her baby.

In China most arrests are approved by the prosecutor who issues an arrest warrant. There are only a few arrests ordered by courts. Chinese legislation designed it in this way based on the general theory that the procuratorate, as the supervisory organ of the law, should have the power to issue warrants. When the prosecutor receives the request from the police to order the arrest, the prosecutor should act within seven days. If the prosecutor does not approve the arrest, the police should immediately release the suspect. In practice, most suspects who are arrested await trial in custody. The duration of custodial detention is dependent upon the time taken by the judicial authorities to dispose of the case. This is covered by rules governing the permissible period of investigation, prosecution and adjudication. The period of investigation of a typical case is two months[11]

8. 65 of CPL.
9. 69 of CPL.
10. 60 of CPL. (See the "coercive measures" discussed in fn. 7, *supra*. Ed.)
11. 124 of CPL , "The time limit for holding a criminal suspect in custody during investigation after arrest shall not exceed two months.

and the period for the trial, after the court accepts the case, including investigation and preparing the written judgement, is one month.[12] Unless it has leave of a higher court, the trial court must complete its work within one and a half months.[13]

4. Searches

The right not to be searched illegally is guaranteed by the Constitution. It provides that "unlawful search of the person of citizens is prohibited."[14] It further provides that, "the residences of citizens of the People's Republic of China are inviolable. Unlawful search of, or intrusion into a citizen's residence is prohibited."[15] The Code provides that, for the purpose of gathering criminal evidence and apprehending criminals, investigating personnel may conduct searches of people, articles, residences and other relevant places with connections to criminal suspects, together with those places which might conceal criminals or criminal evidence.[16]

The law does not stipulate if there should be a basis of suspicion to support the search, but when investigating personnel apply for the warrant, they have to show that the search is for the purposes described above. The law also does not describe the limits of the search. The police search wherever they suspect evidence to be hidden and seize whatever they consider to be evidence. The limitation stipulated by law to supervise the search is that, during a search , the person to be searched or his family members, neighbors or other eyewitnesses shall be present at the scene.[17] A record shall be made of the circumstances of a search, and it shall be signed by the investigators and the person searched or his family members, neighbors, or other eyewitnesses.

Conducting a search in China requires a warrant. This warrant is issued by police (Public Security Organs) or prosecutors, but not judges. If an emergency occurs while carrying out an arrest or detention, a search may be conducted without the use of a search warrant.[18] Instead of a search warrant, a detention or arrest warrant may also justify a search. "Emergency" includes suspicious conduct that leads police to believe that the suspect is carrying weapons, including explosives or poison, or trying to destroy or hide the evidence.

Using special investigation measures, such as wiretaps, secret searches and so on is allowed during this phase of investigation. In practice, these measures are usually used to investigate cases of endangering the state security, of civil servants who are suspected of corruption, and other serious commercial crimes. There are strict rules formulated by the investigating authorities to govern applications for such special measures, but we recognize these rules as administrative, not criminal. However, evidence obtained from these measures may not be used at trial directly

12. 138 of CPL.
13. 168 of CPL.
14. 37 of Constitution.
15. 39 of Constitution.
16. 109 of CPL.
17. 112 of CPL.
18. 111 of CPL.

against the suspect or the accused. In practice, such evidence is generally taken as the "clue" to find other evidence.

5. *Enforcing the Rules.*

The amended Chinese Criminal Procedure Law provides that "the use of torture to coerce statements and the gathering of evidence by threats, enticement, deceit or other unlawful methods is strictly prohibited."[19] The law also stipulates that the procuratorate should exercise legal supervision over the criminal procedure.[20] Further provision can be seen in Chapter 3 of Part I, "Initiation of Public Prosecution," which provides that, "In reviewing cases, the procuratorate must ascertain whether the investigation activities were lawful."[21]

In practice, however, although unlawful methods of obtaining evidence are prohibited, there is no rule excluding illegally obtained evidence from being used at trial. There is only "Analysis on Certain Issues of Implementation of Criminal Procedure Law" which was formulated by the Supreme Court after the revised Criminal Procedure Law was enacted. It provides that the testimony of witnesses or victims, or the confession of the accused, which was obtained by torture or threat, enticement, deceit or other illegal means, may not be used as a basis to decide a case.[22] However, this is limited to oral testimony. Physical evidence, including that which was obtained by exploiting illegal interrogation techniques, is not required to be excluded. Since the Criminal Procedure Code was enacted, there has been no case reported which has excluded illegal testimony. If illegally obtained evidence was used for deciding the case, the only issue has been its reliability,[23] not the means by which it was obtained. Thus, to some extent, police misconduct is encouraged by the courts. Physically coerced confessions are generally excluded on reliability grounds, but courts rarely find such torture.

B. Lineups and Other Identification Measures

There are no provisions under Chinese law concerning lineups. In practice, police or prosecutors organize lineups in order to help witnesses or victims recognize the suspect. Frequently this is done without the suspect's knowledge. Taking of fingerprints is routine when suspects are detained in custody. Other measures, such as blood tests, may be taken during the investigation stage. The code provides that if a suspect refuses to be examined, he may be compelled to cooperate.[24]

---

19. 43 of CPL.
20. 8 of CPL.
21. 137 of CPL.
22. 58 of "The Interpretation of Certain Issues on Implementation of Criminal Procedure Law" (stipulated by the Supreme Court).
23. See *Liling Yue* " Status Quo of the Chinese Criminal Evidence Law and the Trends of Reform" in *Proceedings of the First World Conference on New Trends in Criminal Investigation and Evidence,* (J.F.Nijboer, and J.M.Reijntjes, Ed.), p 367.
24. 25. CPL Art. 105.

C. Interrogation

Although Chinese revised Criminal Procedure Law has added a new general principle which is similar to the presumption of innocence,[25] neither the Constitution nor the Criminal Procedure Law has provided the right to be silent. On the contrary, the law has required suspects to answer the questions put by investigative personnel truthfully. Suspects only have the right to refuse to answer questions irrelevant to the case.[26] The law has ignored the issue of who should decide the relevancy to the case. In theory, suspects should have privilege to decide, but in practice, investigative personnel have the power to require the suspect to cooperate. If a suspect insists on silence (it doesn't happen often), and the case is proved later, the defendant may get harsher punishment.

According to the amended criminal procedure law, suspects may only hire a lawyer to give him/her legal advice *after being first interrogated* by the investigating organ or from the day coercive measures (such as detention or arrest) are taken against him.[27] The Criminal Procedure Law doesn't require that counsel be provided to the suspects who can't afford to hire one during the early investigation phase.

III. Court Procedures

In China, most criminal cases are tried in local courts (including district courts in cities, county courts in the countryside). However, the Criminal Procedure Law lists the categories of cases which should be tried in the first instance in the intermediate courts, which are only found in big cities or big districts which include several counties. Those categories are: 1) cases endangering state security; 2) ordinary criminal cases punishable by life imprisonment or the death penalty; 3) criminal cases in which the offenders are foreigners.[28] The higher courts (province level) and the Supreme Court also have jurisdiction to try such cases in the first instance.[29]

A. Pretrial

In China, there are no formal pretrial proceedings, such as a grand jury or a preliminary hearing. Except for a few relatively minor cases, in which the victim

---

25. CPL Art.12 provides that: No one shall be convicted without a verdict pronounced by a People's Court according to the law."

26. 93 of CPL has stated that: "when interrogating a criminal suspect, investigation personnel shall first ask the criminal suspect whether or not he has engaged in a criminal act and let him state the circumstances of guilt or explain his innocence before putting questions to him. The criminal suspect shall answer the questions put by the investigation personnel according to the facts. However, he has the right to refuse to answer questions irrelevant to the case."

27. 96 of CPL.

28. 19 and 20 of CPL.

29. 21 and 22 of CPL.(See the section on "Trial" below).

could take a private charge by himself, most criminal cases are taken charge of by prosecutors. The prosecutorial discretion is restricted by law. Under three kinds of circumstances, prosecutors could use this discretion to decide not to initiate a prosecution: (1) if any of the circumstances provided by Article 15 of the Criminal Procedure Law applies to a suspect; (2) in a minor case, which according to the criminal law, is neither liable for a criminal punishment nor eligible for a criminal exemption.[30]There are nine different circumstances, in which the prosecutor could dismiss under this provision. (3) If the prosecutor still believes the evidence provided by the supplementary investigation is insufficient and that the case does not comply with the terms for prosecution, it may decide not to initiate.[31]

B. Trial

According to the Criminal Procedure law and the Organic Law of the People's Courts of the People's Republic China (hereinafter OLCP),[32] the trier of criminal cases may be composed in two ways, by a single judge or by a panel of judges. Adjudication by a single judge is normally confined to minor cases, such as private prosecutions and other minor criminal cases which can be conducted by summary trial.[33] Most cases are tried by a panel of judges, which comprises either several judges or judges with lay assessors.[34] When local courts or intermediate courts of first instance hear cases, the panel may be composed of either one, two or three professional judges plus however many lay assessors are needed to total three. In the rare cases when high Courts or the Supreme Court try cases at first instance,[35] the panel is composed of seven people, at least three of whom are professional judges. In appellate cases, there are no lay assessors, the panel consisting of three to five judges. During the trial, lay assessors carrying out their duty have equal rights with judges, they together decide the facts and apply the law. Conviction must be done by majority vote, but the opinions of the minority shall be entered in the record.

The typical trial occurs within one month after accepting the case from the prosecutor, and it may not extend beyond one and one half months at the latest. However, with the approval of higher courts and under the circumstances stated in Article126, the period of a trial could be extended another month.[36]

Although Chinese criminal procedure reform has changed the judge's role at trial, making them not so active as before, judges still play a role in organizing and

30. 142 of CPL. These include cases where a legitimate defense would cause undue harm, where a crime has been prepared for but not consummated, etc.

31. 140 of CPL, fourth section.

32. Adopted at the second session of the Fifth National People's Congress on July 1, 1979, and revised according to the Decision Concerning the Revision of the Organic Law of the People's Courts of the People's Republic of China adopted at the Second Meeting of the Sixth National People's Congress on September 2, 1983.

33. 147 of CPL and 10 of OLPC.

34. 38 of Organic Law of People's Courts provides that: "Citizens who have the right to vote and to stand for election and have reached the age of 23 are eligible to be elected people's assessors, but persons who have ever been deprived of political rights are excluded."

35. 37. Since the P.R.C. was founded in 1949, only two cases have been heard in the first instance by the Supreme Court: One involving a Japanese war criminal and the other being the trial of the "Gang of Four." High Courts would only try cases of province-wide importance.

36. 168 of CPL.

controlling the trial. The judgment of the trial has to be in written form and prepared by a judge. Every case has its dossier; the prosecution's part has been prepared by the prosecutor, but the trial part is prepared by the court. (Generally it is made by the Court Clerk who is responsible for making the record of the trial.)

After the indictment is announced, the defendant has the right to make a statement, but needn't swear. There is no system of plea bargaining. No matter whether the defendant pleads guilty or keeps silent, the trial will be conducted anyway. Although Chinese legislation has tried to move the trial model a bit from inquisitorial toward adversarial, it is not a typical adversarial trial. For example, there is also no typical cross-examination. The prosecutor has the power to question witnesses first, no matter which side the witnesses come from. Defendants have the right to apply for the withdrawal of members of the Collegial Panel, the Court Clerk (who makes the record of the trial), the public prosecutor and expert witnesses and interpreters.[37] Defendants have a right to ask questions of the witnesses after they get permission from judges.[38] In practice, the defendant's right to confront the witnesses could not be guaranteed, since there is a large percentage of witnesses who do not appear to give oral testimony at the trial. The written testimony is admissible under the law,[39] and the defendant has the right to state his or her own opinion on this testimony.[40] Defendants and their defender have right to apply for the notification of new witnesses to come to court for the obtaining of new material evidence, and to apply for new expert evaluation or inspection.[41] However, the court is free to accept or ignore such requests. The Criminal Procedure Law hasn't given the power of court to compel the witnesses to attend trial, that means, if witnesses insist on not appearing at the trial and give testimony, the court neither can summon them for attendance nor to give them punishment.

Constitutional and criminal procedure law protects the defendant's right to have counsel. However, due to the Chinese economic situation, it is impossible to appoint a lawyer for every defendant who is indigent. Judges may appoint a lawyer if they consider it is necessary.[42] Disabled defendants, such as the deaf, or mute, or a minor who has not hired a lawyer to present his or her case, are given court-appointed lawyers. Furthermore, every defendant in death penalty cases must have a lawyer.[43]

In theory, the prosecutor's role in criminal proceedings is to supervise the whole proceeding,[44] but in fact, their attitude and actions are aimed more toward to conviction once the defendant has been charged. It is difficult to imagine how prosecutors could manage to maintain the neutral role during the trial, especially where the law has not provided specifically how they should exercise their supervisory role at the trial.

---

37. 154 of CPL.
38. 156 of CPL.
39. 157 of CPL.
40. 157 of CPL.
41. 159 of CPL.
42. 34 of CPL has provided that In case in which a public prosecutor appears in court to bring a public prosecution, the people's court may designate lawyers to undertake the obligation of offering legal assistance to defend a suspect if the latter does not have defenders due to financial difficulties or other reasons.
43. 34 of CPL.
44. 8 of CPL.

Chinese criminal procedure law reform has given victims some rights. The most important is that, if the prosecutor fails to bring the charge, the victim may appeal that decision to a higher procuratorate. If that appeal fails, the victim may present the charge to the court himself.[45] The difficulty for victims is, they have to investigate the case by themselves, to collect and show up evidence. If they fail to do it, they may lose the case.

C. Appeals

Any of the parties, (not including the victim), have the right to appeal the case directly to the next level of the court system within 10 days under any grounds. Defenders or close relatives of defendants may present appeals with the agreement of the defendant. In case the prosecutor considers that a judgment of a first instance court contains an actual error , they shall present a protest to the court at the next level up.[46] The victim only has the right to request the prosecutor to protest the case, they haven't the right to appeal the case directly by themselves. Under the Chinese legal system, the parties can only appeal the case once. The higher court may review both the facts and the application of law and the judgment of first instance. In principle, the law requests that the appeal case should be tried in public, however, the law also allows judges to review the case by reading the file, interrogating the defendant and interviewing their defense counsel if the facts of the case are unclear.[47] If the case is appealed by the defendant, the court of second instance may not increase the punishment on the defendant.[48]

45. 145 of CPL.
46. 181 of CPL.
47. 187 of CPL.
48. 190 of CPL.

Chapter 4

England and Wales

David J. Feldman

I. Introduction

Three matters form a background to understanding English criminal procedure. The first is the UK's constitution. Because the UK has neither an entrenched constitution nor a constitutional Bill of Rights, there has up to now been no constitutional limitation on the power of Parliament to confer on police officers powers which interfere with what in some other jurisdictions would be regarded as fundamental rights. Parliament has progressively expanded police powers and limited the protection of the accused in criminal proceedings for pragmatic reasons, and the courts have contributed to the process by generously interpreting statutory powers and by creating or expanding common-law powers. The European Convention on Human Rights, to which the UK is party, is not yet part of English law and does not give rise to rights enforceable in domestic legal proceedings. However, it will form part of English law when the Human Rights Act 1998 comes into force. That is likely to revolutionize criminal procedure by requiring that public authorities (which include courts) comply with Convention rights, including the right not to be arbitrarily deprived of liberty (Article 5), the right to a fair trial (Article 6), and the right to respect for private and family life, home and correspondence (Article 8).[1] Alongside the ECHR machinery operated by the Council of Europe there is the European Union, much of whose law has direct effect in the UK and is supreme in the event of a conflict with English domestic law. This makes it possible for defendants to rely on directly effective EU law (for example on such matters as free movement of goods and services) as a defence to charges such as illegal importation of goods. Where necessary, English courts can (and the ultimate court of appeal must) refer questions of European Union law to the Court of Justice in Luxembourg under Article 177 of the Treaty of Rome for an authoritative ruling on the interpretation of relevant EU law, staying proceedings pending the outcome.

1. See David Harris, Michael O'Boyle and Colin Warbrick, *The Law of the European Convention on Human Rights* (London: Butterworths, 1995); Jeremy McBride, *The continuing refinement of criminal due process* (1997) 22 E.L.Rev. HRC/1-HRC/16; Sybil Sharpe, *The European Convention: a suspect's charter?* [1997] Crim. L.R. 848-860.

Secondly, there is the constitutional position of the police. There is, formally speaking, no national police force, although regional and national units have been established in the past twenty years to combat serious crime and MI5 has a limited crime-fighting role under the Security and Intelligence Services Act 1994. Police forces are local (currently, with a few exceptions, organized on a county basis), and (except in London) are accountable to police authorities consisting of councillors and magistrates,[2] although police forces are increasingly funded by central government out of general taxation, making local accountability hard to achieve. Constables (a term covering all police officers regardless of rank) hold office under the Crown, rather than being employees of a local chief constable or police authority. In law, every constable is personally responsible for deciding how to use legal powers and perform legal duties. There is thus a tension between the legal responsibility placed on individual constables and police forces and the need for co-ordinated, disciplined police organisation in order to fulfill objectives set for the police by government policy and national legislation.

Thirdly, the investigative function in the process has only recently been separated from the prosecutorial function. Until the Crown Prosecution Service (CPS) was created under the Prosecution of Offenders Act 1985, the police were responsible for most prosecutions, as well as for investigations. The position now is that the CPS is responsible for most prosecution decisions, using material supplied by the police. There are also some specialist agencies which continue to combine investigative and prosecutorial roles, such as the Customs and Excise and the Serious Fraud Office established under the Criminal Justice Act 1987. The process by which prosecution decisions are taken is described later.

II. Police Procedures

Most police powers and the safeguards attaching to them are now contained in statute, particularly the Police and Criminal Evidence Act 1984 (hereafter "PACE"), and the Codes of Practice made by the Home Secretary and approved by Parliament under sections 60 and 66 of PACE—

Code A: the exercise by police officers of statutory powers of stop and search;

Code B: the searching of premises by police officers and the seizure of property found by police officers on persons or premises;

Code C: the detention, treatment and questioning of persons by police officers;

Code D: the identification of persons by police officers;

Code E: the tape recording of interviews by police officers at police stations with suspected persons.[3]

No Code covers arrests. Notes for Guidance contained within the Codes, but not forming part of it, give further guidance to officers and courts interpreting and operating the provisions of the Codes.

2. See Police Act 1996.

3. These Codes are periodically amended, and are published by the Stationery Office.

A. Arrest, Search, and Seizure Law

1. Stops

Stopping and searching people with their consent has always been lawful at common law. Consensual searches are problematic, both because the imbalance of power between constables and ordinary citizens calls in question the genuineness of consent, and because the statutory safeguards do not apply to consensual searches. Notes for Guidance 1D in Code A therefore advise that the police should rely on consent only for routine searches at such places as entrances to sports grounds, or where no power of search exists, and that people who might be incapable of giving an informed consent should not be subjected to a voluntary search. However, the Notes are advisory only. A search conducted in reliance on consent, even if not fully informed or the constable had a power of search, would be lawful.

Additional statutory powers which existed piecemeal in legislation before 1984 were controversial because they tended to be used most often against members of groups which suffer from discrimination, particularly young black males.[4] In an attempt to control abuse of these powers, PACE (as amended) provides for a limited, codified power of stop and search, although some other powers continue to exist alongside it: see Code A, Annex A. PACE and the Code of Practice impose general conditions which must be satisfied before a search may be conducted pursuant to a statutory power, and procedures to be followed when exercising the power. However, more recent evidence suggests that the powers are still used disproportionately against black and Asian people.[5]

The power is usually exercisable only where a constable has reasonable grounds for suspecting that he will find stolen or prohibited articles, or an article which has a blade or is sharply pointed, so as to constitute an offence under section 139 of the Criminal Justice Act 1988, on the person to be detained. "Reasonable grounds" are not defined and are probably indefinable, but Code A, paragraphs 1.6 and 1.7 make it clear that the decision must be based on objective grounds such as the time, place, behaviour of the suspect, and information received from other witnesses. Personal factors alone (such as a person's age, colour, previous convictions, or dress) or stereotypes of the kinds of people likely to be in possession of certain kinds of articles cannot justify a decision to search. If a constable searches a person without his consent and without reasonable grounds for suspicion, the search is unlawful even if it reveals items of the kind for which search the search was made.

There are a number of special search powers which are exercisable on different conditions from those governing searches under section 1 of PACE. These include powers to search for public stores, firearms, crossbows, controlled drugs, dutiable or smuggled goods, intoxicating liquor at designated sporting events, poaching equipment and game, seals and seal-hunting equipment, evidence of lia-

4. Lord Scarman, *The Brixton Disorders*, Cmnd 8427 (London: HMSO, 1981), p 64-5; D. J. Smith and J. Gray, *Police and People in London: the PSI Report* (Aldershot: Gower, 1985), ch. 15; M. McConville, *Search of People and Premises: New Data from London* [1983] Crim. L.R. 604-14.

5. Home Office Research and Statistics Directorate, *Race and the Criminal Justice System* (London: Home Office, 1997).

bility to arrest for a terrorist offence, and evidence of offences against deer, badgers, or other protected wildlife.[6] The locations in which these powers are exercisable varies; some of the powers can be used only against persons, some only against vehicles,[7] and some against either. Broadly speaking, all these powers require reasonable grounds for suspecting that specified articles will be found, and all attract the safeguards of Part I of PACE.

However, some powers do not depend on reasonable grounds for suspicion. Section 60 of the Criminal Justice and Public Order Act 1994 allows a police officer, usually of the rank of superintendent or above, to authorise stops and searches for offensive weapons and dangerous implements in a specified locality for up to 24 hours, extendable for a further 6 hours, without reasonable suspicion if the authorising officer reasonably believes that it is expedient to do so in order to prevent serious violence in the locality which he reasonably believes may take place. Another provision[8] allows a police officer of the rank of Assistant Chief Constable or above (or, in the City of London and Metropolitan Police forces, a Commander), who considers that it is expedient in order to prevent acts of terrorism connected with the affairs of Northern Ireland or another country, to authorise constables to stop pedestrians and vehicles, and to search vehicles and anything carried by a pedestrian, in a specified locality during a period of up to 28 days. This was a response to an I.R.A. bombing operation in the city of London. This power, used to grant successive authorisations, has enabled the police to maintain a security cordon round the city of London for much of the past three years.

Search is permitted under section 1 of PACE[9] for stolen[10] and prohibited articles, and for blades (including folding pocket-knives with a cutting edge more than three inches long) or sharply pointed items. "Prohibited articles" include offensive weapons, and articles made or adapted, or intended by the person having it with him, for use in connection with burglary, theft, taking a motor vehicle without authority, or obtaining property by deception.[11] "Offensive weapons" are defined as articles which are made or adapted for causing injury to any person, regardless of the use to which the person in possession of them intends to put them, and articles which are intended by that person to be used to cause injury, regardless of whether they were originally made or have been adapted for that purpose.[12]

The power conferred by section 1(1) of PACE is a power to detain any pedestrian or vehicle (which includes aircraft, hovercraft, and vessels for floating on water[13]) in a public place (which is widely defined to include places to which the public have access other than a dwelling) for the purpose of the search. The power to stop arises by necessary implication from the power to detain (although a constable in uniform has an independent power under section 163 of the Road Traffic

6. For a list of the main powers, see Code A, Annex A.

7. The term `vehicle' is defined differently for the purposes of different powers.

8. Prevention of Terrorism (Temporary Provisions) Act 1989, section 13A, inserted by Criminal Justice and Public Order Act 1994.

9. As amended by Criminal Justice and Public Order Act 1994, section 140.

10. If, as is likely, `stolen' has the same meaning as under the Theft Act 1968, stolen articles include property obtained by deception: *Director of Public Prosecutions v. Gomez* [1993] A.C. 442, H.L.

11. PACE, section 1(7), (8).

12. PACE, section 1(9).

13. PACE, s section 2(10), 118(1).

Act 1988 to require a driver of a motor vehicle to stop, and a senior police officer may authorise a road check — effectively a road block — for suspects or witnesses under section 4 of PACE). Vehicles may be stopped only by a constable in uniform.[14] Reasonable force may be used if necessary to enable a constable to exercise the power to detain and search.[15]

When a person is searched in public a thorough frisk is permitted, but the person must not be required to remove clothes other than an outer coat, jacket or gloves without his consent. Any coerced search involving removal of more than outer clothing (described in Code A as a "strip search") is permitted only in private, and a person or vehicle may be detained to allow the search to be carried out either at the place where he or it was first detained or "nearby."[16] This may be at a nearby police station or police van if one is available. There must be reasonable grounds for conducting a strip search, and it must be conducted by a constable of the same sex as the person searched.[17] Reasonable force may be used for the purpose if necessary.[18]

The safeguards are mainly procedural. Before conducting a search, a constable must take reasonable steps to bring to the attention of the person to be searched, or the person in charge of the vehicle to be searched, the constable's name and the police station to which he is attached, the object of the proposed search, the constable's grounds for proposing to make it, usually the person's right to a copy of the written record of the search, and (where the constable is not in uniform) documentary evidence that he is a constable.[19] When conducting the search, embarrassment must be kept to a minimum, the co-operation of the person searched must be sought, the search must be no more intrusive than is necessary for the item sought in the light of the grounds for suspicion, and it must be completed within a reasonable time.[20] After the search, the constable must normally make a written record of it,[21] and where an unattended vehicle has been searched a notice giving information about the search must be left on the vehicle.[22] These safeguards apply to all statutory powers to search persons and vehicles unless the legislation conferring the power expressly provides otherwise.

2. *Frisks*

There is no power to "frisk" suspects apart from the powers outlined above, or those which follow an arrest, below.

3. *Arrests*

Arrests fall into two categories: those made under warrant, and arrests without warrant. A court (normally a magistrates' court) can issue an arrest warrant. A

14. PACE, section 2(9)(b).
15. PACE, section 117.
16. PACE, section 2(8). On strip searches see Code C, Annex A, paras. 9-12.
17. Code A, para. 3.5.
18. PACE, section 117.
19. PACE, section 2(2), (3), (4).
20. Code A, paras. 3.1-3.3.
21. PACE, section 3.
22. PACE, section 2(6), (7).

constable may lawfully arrest anyone for whom an arrest warrant has been issued, even if the constable is not personally in possession of the warrant.[23] However, most arrests today are made without warrant. When the Criminal Law Act 1967, section 2 abolished the distinction between felonies and misdemeanors, it created a category of "arrestable offences," now defined in PACE, section 24. Section 25 of PACE introduced a new power to arrest without a warrant in certain circumstances for an offence which does not fall within the category of arrestable offences. A significant number of other statutory powers of arrest without warrant for non-arrestable offences survived PACE,[24] and have since been added to. In addition, there is a power to arrest in order to prevent or end a breach of the peace (in the limited sense of violence or threatened violence to people, or to property in the presence of the owner).[25] However, this chapter concentrates on arrests in relation to criminal investigations.

The original purpose of an arrest for an offence was to secure a suspect in order that he could be charged and brought before a court. This assumed that the police would have enough evidence to justify a charge before making an arrest. In practice, during the twentieth century, the police increasingly relied on interrogation. The Judges' Rules (a set of guidelines for the police developed by the judges then put in the form of a Home Office Circular, having no legal force), which had originally forbidden questioning suspects after arrest, were changed to permit it. In *Holgate-Mohammed v. Duke*[26] the House of Lords held that the police did not exceed their powers of arrest if they arrested a suspect because they reasonably believed that she would be more likely to confess if she was under arrest at a police station than if interviewed at home. This gave the common law's seal of approval to arrest for the purpose of questioning.

However, concern was expressed that controls on detention and interrogation of suspects were inadequate to ensure that purported confessions were genuine and reliable. Following a high-profile miscarriage of justice,[27] the Royal Commission on Criminal Procedure was established in 1979. In the light of its 1981 report,[28] PACE was enacted. It extended powers of arrest, detention and questioning, but imposed a variety of procedural safeguards, which have subsequently been enhanced by tape-recording requirements in PACE and Codes C, D and E. Only PACE deals with arrests.

What Is An Arrest? One must distinguish first between arrests and detentions short of an arrest, including the procedural requirements for a valid arrest; then between "arrestable offences," other offences which carry a power of arrest without warrant, and those which do not. Next, one needs to see the essential precondi-

---

23. Magistrates' Courts Act 1980, section 125(2); *R.* v. *Purdy* [1975] Q.B. 288, C.A.
24. See PACE, section 26 and Sched. 2.
25. See *R.* v. *Howell* [1982] Q.B. 416, C.A.
26. [1984] A.C. 437, H.L.
27. The Confait case: see *Report of the Inquiry by the Hon. Sir Henry Fisher into the Circumstances Leading to the Trial of Three Persons on Charges Arising out of the Death of Maxwell Confait and the Fire at 27 Doggett Road, London SE6*, HC Paper No. 90 of 1977-78.
28. Royal Commission on Criminal Procedure, *Report*, Cmnd. 8092 (London: H.M.S.O., 1981).

tions to a valid arrest. Finally, one must examine the consequences which flow from a lawful arrest.

An arrest is an assertion of lawful authority to detain somebody for the purpose of the criminal process, explicitly telling the arrestee that he is being arrested unless this is impracticable,[29] coupled with either an act of physical restraint over the body of the person arrested[30] or submission by the arrestee to the custody of the arrestor.

Where a person is arrested without being told that he is under arrest, that information must be given as soon as practicable thereafter, unless he has escaped first.[31] The arrestee must also be informed of the ground for the arrest at, or as soon as practicable after, the arrest, unless he has escaped first.[32] By providing expressly that where the arrestor is a constable all this information must be provided even if it is obvious,[33] the Act implies that a lay person who makes an arrest need not give the information if it is obvious. While a period of detention without proper information being given is unlawful, subsequently giving the information will make the detention lawful prospectively, but not retrospectively.[34]

For What Offences Can a Person Be Arrested? Arrestable offences are those which meet the criteria laid down in PACE, section 24. They are offences for which the penalty is fixed by law (the main ones being treason and murder), those for which the maximum penalty which may be imposed on a person aged twenty-one or over on first conviction is or includes imprisonment for a term of at least five years, and a rag-bag of other specified offences relating to customs and excise matters, official secrets, sexual impropriety, misbehaviour at association football matches, unauthorised sale of tickets for sporting events, certain thefts, touting for car hire services, and publishing material intended or likely to stir up racial hatred. It is also an arrestable offence to conspire or attempt to commit any arrestable offence, or to incite, aid, abet, counsel or procure its commission. There is no coherent principle underlying this odd assortment.

In a separate category are offences which are not arrestable offences but which to a power of summary arrest is attached by other statutes. One leading work[35] helpfully classifies these in categories which with slight modification can be summarised as follows: the arrest of persons unlawfully at large; terrorism and related

29. PACE, section 28(1). The use of the words 'I arrest you' or 'you are under arrest' is usual and clear, but anything which in context makes it clear to the arrestee what is being asserted - even mere physical restraint - may suffice: *R. v. Brosch* [1988] Crim. L.R. 743, C.A., particularly if the arrestee is struggling or running off so as to make it unreasonable to expect explanations to be given. On the other hand, if the purpose of the physical restraint is not unambiguous in context (for example, if the detainer may want to administer a breath test to a motorist rather than arrest him) the restraint will not constitute an arrest. See D. N. Clarke and D. Feldman, *Arrest by any other name* [1979] Crim. L.R. 702-707; Glanville Williams, *When is an arrest?* (1991) 54 M.L.R. 408-117; D. Feldman, *Civil Liberties and Human Rights in England and Wales* (Oxford: Clarendon Press, 1993), p 207- 213.

30. *Genner v. Sparks* (1704) 1 Salk. 79; *Hart v. Chief Constable of Kent* [1983] R.T.R. 484, C.A.

31. PACE, section 28(1), (5).

32. PACE, section 28(3), (5).

33. PACE, section 28(2), (5).

34. *Lewis* v. *Chief Constable of the South Wales Constabulary* [1991] 1 All E.R. 206, C.A.

35. Ken Lidstone and Clare Palmer, *Bevan and Lidstone's The Investigation of Crime*, 2nd ed. (London: Butterworths, 1995), p 272-278.

offences; protection of animals; road traffic offences; soliciting for the purposes of prostitution; protective arrest of mentally disordered persons; election offences; unauthorised occupation of premises and aggravated trespass; and public order offences.

Apart from these powers of arrest, section 25(1) of PACE provided for the first time a general power of arrest without warrant where a constable has reasonable grounds for suspecting that any offence, not being an arrestable offence or one carrying a specific power of summary arrest, has been or is being committed or attempted, and that it would be impracticable or inappropriate to serve a summons on the suspected offender for any of a number of "general arrest conditions." These conditions are:

- that the constable does not know and cannot readily ascertain the suspect's name, or has reasonable grounds for doubting the name which the suspect has given;
- that the suspect has failed to give a satisfactory address for service of a summons, or the constable has reasonable grounds for doubting the satisfactoriness of an address;
- that the constable has reasonable grounds for believing that the arrest is necessary to prevent the suspect from causing physical injury to himself or another, suffering physical injury, causing loss of or damage to property, committing an offence against public decency, or causing an unlawful obstruction of the highway, or to protect a child or other vulnerable person from the suspect.

There is also a power to arrest a person convicted of a recordable offence in order to take his fingerprints if he has failed to comply with an instruction to attend a police station for that purpose.[36]

What Are the Essential Preconditions to a Valid Arrest? Although there are slight variations between statutes, there are some general principles. In respect of arrestable offences within the meaning of section 24 of PACE, any person may arrest somebody who is in the act of committing an offence, or whom the arrestor has reasonable grounds for suspecting to be committing an offence. Where an arrestable offence has actually been committed, any person may arrest the person who committed it or whom the arrestor has reasonable grounds for suspecting to have committed it. A constable is protected against legal liability in two further situations: first, where he has reasonable grounds for suspecting that an arrestable offence has been committed by the suspect, even if it turns out that no arrestable offence was committed; and, secondly, where the suspect is, or is reasonably suspected to be, about to commit an arrestable offence. In relation to other statutory powers of summary arrest, including the power to arrest under the "general arrest conditions," the arrestor must be a constable, and sometimes must be in uniform.

What Consequences Flow From a Lawful Arrest? Once a person has been arrested, a number of duties and powers may arise, depending on who has made the arrest and where it took place. A person other than a constable must bring the arrestee before a magistrates' court or deliver him into police custody as soon as is practicable. Normally, however, the arrest is made by a constable. When a consta-

36. PACE, section 27.

ble takes a person into custody for an offence, the arrestee must be taken to a police station as soon as practicable.[37] The protective scheme established for suspects by PACE involves a complex series of procedures overseen initially by the "custody officer" at a police station designated by the chief officer of police for the area as a place for detaining arrested persons, with adequate accommodation for the purpose and at least one trained custody officer on duty.[38] The arrestee is therefore normally to be taken to one of these designated police stations, and must be taken to one if it appears to the constable that it may be necessary to detain the arrestee for more than six hours, unless no police assistance is available or it appears to the constable that the arrestee will cause injury to someone before they can reach a designated station.[39] If first taken to a non-designated station, the arrestee must be moved to a designated station within six hours of arrival, unless he is released earlier.[40]

However, some circumstances justify a delay in taking the arrestee to a police station. First, the constable has power to search a person arrested other than at a police station (normally for weapons) if the constable has reasonable grounds for believing that the person may present a danger to himself or others.[41] Secondly, the constable has power to search the arrestee for anything which might be used to escape from custody, or which might be evidence relating to any offence, if the constable has reasonable grounds for believing that the person may have concealed such an item on him.[42] Thirdly, the constable may search any premises in which the person was when or immediately before he was arrested, for evidence of the offence for which the person has been arrested, if the constable has reasonable grounds for believing that such evidence is on the premises.[43] All these searches must be no more extensive than would be reasonably required to discover items for which search is permitted.[44] Fourthly, the constable may delay taking the arrestee to a police station if the arrestee's presence elsewhere is "necessary in order to carry out such investigations as it is reasonable to carry out immediately."[45] This should not be used merely to evade the requirements of PACE and the Codes, or for purposes unrelated to the investigation.[46] Finally, there are some more extensive powers of detention and search, notably those under the Immigration Act 1971 and the Prevention of Terrorism (Temporary Provisions) Act 1989.

Detention at Police Stations. On arrival at a police station, the custody officer is responsible for decisions relating to his detention and for ensuring that the provisions of PACE and Code C are complied with.[47] First, the custody officer must

37. PACE, section 30(1).
38. PACE, s section 35, 36(1).
39. PACE, section 30(3), (5).
40. PACE, section 30(6).
41. PACE, section 32(1), (8).
42. PACE, section 32(2)(a), (5), (9).
43. PACE, section 32(2)(b), (6). Note also sub- section (7), relating to the permissible extent of a search in premises consisting of two or more separate dwelling units.
44. PACE, section 32(3).
45. PACE, section 30(10).
46. See Lidstone and Palmer, *op. cit.*, p 298-300 and *R.* v. *Kerawalla* [1991] Crim. L.R. 451, C.A.; cp. *R.* v. *Keane* [1992] Crim. L.R. 306, C.A., *R.* v. *Khan* [1993] Crim. L.R. 54, C.A.
47. Where the arrestee is taken to a non-designated station, another officer - if necessary, the arresting officer - must perform the duties of custody officer: PACE, section 36(4), (7). As may be imagined, this is capable of giving rise to some difficult conflicts of interest.

decide whether there is already sufficient evidence to charge the arrested person with an offence, in which case he must either do so or release the person.[48] It is rare for this to happen, as it would limit the power of the police to question the suspect.[49] The custody officer must also release the person, with or without bail, unless there are reasonable grounds to believe that detention without charge is "necessary to secure or preserve evidence relating to an offence or to preserve evidence relating to an offence for which he is under arrest or to obtain such evidence by questioning him."[50] The custody officer normally decides that detention is necessary.[51] A custody record is accordingly opened, in which must be recorded information about the steps taken in relation to the suspect and the grounds for taking them until the arrestee is either released or transferred elsewhere.

Detention without charge after arrest is subject to strict time limits. Except in terrorism investigations under the Prevention of Terrorism (Temporary Provisions) Act 1989, where detention without charge for up to 7 days can be authorised by the Secretary of State, and detention of suspected illegal immigrants under the Immigration Act 1971, the rules are as follows. There is normally a limit of 24 hours from the "relevant time," which is the earlier of the time of arrest or of arrival at the police station.[52] During that time the "review officer," an officer of at least the rank of inspector, checks after no more than six hours and then at intervals of no more than nine hours to see that the conditions for detention continue to be met. The detainee or his legal representative may make representations,[53] although anecdotal evidence leads one to doubt the efficacy of doing so. After 24 hours the detainee must be charged or released, unless the investigating officer can satisfy an officer of the rank of superintendent or above (in the light of any representations from the arrestee or his legal representative) that continued detention is necessary to enable evidence of a "serious arrestable offence" to be secured (usually by questioning) or preserved, and that the investigation is being conducted "diligently and expeditiously,"[54] in which case continued detention may be authorised for up to twelve hours. A "serious arrestable offence" is an arrestable offence within the meaning of PACE, section 24 of PACE which meets statutory criteria of seriousness. Offences such as treason, homicide, rape, kidnaping, hijacking, terrorism, drug trafficking, and grave sexual and firearms offences are always serious arrestable offences. Other arrestable offences are serious if they involve serious harm to the security of the state or public order, serious interference with the administration of justice or the investigation of offences, the death of or serious injury to any person, or substantial financial gain or serious financial loss to any person.[55]

If the investigating officer wants a further period of detention without charge he must bring the detainee (who for this purpose must be given an opportunity to consult and be represented by a solicitor) before a magistrates' court, which may

48. PACE, section 37(7).

49. See Code C, para. 11.4.

50. PACE, section 37(1), (2).

51. Ian McKenzie, Rod Morgan and Robert Reiner, *Helping the Police with Their Inquiries: The Necessity Principle and Voluntary Attendance at the Police Station* [1990] *Crim. L.R.* 22-33.

52. PACE, section 41.

53. PACE, section 40. Ignoring this right makes further detention unlawful: *Re an application for a warrant of further detention* [1988] Crim. L.R. 296.

54. PACE, section 42.

55. PACE, section 116 and Sch. 5, as amended.

grant a warrant of further detention if satisfied of the same matters as the superintendent had to be satisfied of after 24 hours. Warrants of further detention may be extended, so long as the total period of detention without charge does not exceed 96 hours in total from the "relevant time."[56] In 1996, only 271 warrants of further detention were applied for; 263 were granted, and suspects were subsequently charged with serious arrestable offences in 175 (67%) of those cases.[57]

4. Searches

The Position Before the Police and Criminal Evidence Act 1984. At common law, the police were expected to justify entries to premises and searches on them by reference to the occupier's consent, a warrant issued under a statutory power, or a statutory power to enter without warrant, failing which any entry would be unlawful.[58] The existence of a statutory power depended on Parliament having legislated on an activity and having included an entry power in the legislation. While regulatory officials often acquired wide entry powers in this way, the police had no power to obtain a warrant to enter premises to search for evidence of murder. This sometimes led the police to stretch the rules, and the courts increasingly turned a blind eye.[59] Now there is a new power for a magistrate to issue a warrant to enter premises to search for evidence of a serious arrestable offence which is likely to be of substantial value to the investigation, filling lacunae in previous powers to issue warrants. The power does not extend to items subject to legal privilege, excluded material or special procedure material.[60]

Where the police had no warrant and no statutory power to search, and had made no arrest, the courts manufactured for them powers which were in some respects even wider than those following arrest or the grant of a warrant.[61] Such judicial legislation to extend police powers was of questionable legitimacy in a parliamentary democracy. Furthermore, neither legal professional privilege nor equitable and contractual obligations of confidentiality attracted any systematic exemption from the operation of search warrants or of common-law entry and search powers, so the offices of solicitors and accountants could be, and sometimes were, searched for evidence of clients' wrongdoing.[62] The time was ripe for putting the law on a principled footing. The Royal Commission on Criminal Procedure in 1981 made recommendations which were taken into account (although not entirely adopted) when PACE was drafted. The effect of PACE and later legislation is broadly as follows.

Consent. The police continue to be able to justify entries, searches and seizures by showing that the occupier consented. Consensual searches fall outside the pro-

---

56. PACE, s section 43, 44.

57. Wilkins and Addicott, *op. cit.*, p 9-10, Table F and Table 5.

58. *Entick* v. *Carrington* (1765) 2 Wils. 275. See generally David Feldman, *The Law relating to Entry, Search and Seizure* (London: Butterworths, 1986).

59. See e.g. *Pringle v. Bremner and Stirling* (1867) 5 Macph 55 at 60 *per* Lord Chelmsford L.C. (H.L. on appeal from the Court of Session in Scotland); *Elias v. Pasmore* [1934] 2 K.B. 264; *Chic Fashions (West Wales) Ltd. v. Jones* [1968] 2 Q.B. 299, C.A.; *Ghani* v. *Jones* [1970] 1 Q.B. 693, C.A., at 705-6 *per* Lord Denning M.R.

60. PACE, section 8.

61. *Ghani v. Jones* [1970] 1 Q.B. 693 at 708-709 *per* Lord Denning M.R.

62. See, e.g., *Frank Truman Export Ltd. v. Metropolitan Police Commissioner* [1977] Q.B. 952.

visions of the Act, although some guidance is given in the associated Code of Practice (Code B).[63] In practice, the vast majority of entries and searches, and even about one-third of those following arrest (where there is a statutory power to search), are conducted by consent.[64] This poses a number of problems. In particular, there is a risk that occupiers may be improperly pressured to give consent, or may not realise that they have any right to refuse.[65] Issues which then arise are similar to those noted above in relation to searches of the person.

Obtaining Warrants. Most search warrants are issued by magistrates on an application by a constable. Before PACE there was clear evidence that magistrates were not properly performing their constitutional role of scrutinizing the grounds for the application to ensure that the grant of a warrant would be justified.[66] The need for an issuing authority to make an independent assessment of the information supporting the application was explained by the House of Lords in *Inland Revenue Commissioners v. Rossminster Ltd.*[67] However, the good intentions were undermined in each case by a refusal to imply into the legislation a requirement that the warrant must show on its face that such an assessment had been made. This makes it difficult to discover afterwards whether a warrant has been issued on proper grounds. To address these difficulties, PACE provided that applications for warrants are to be supported by a written information and that applicants are to give information and answer questions put by the magistrate. However, recitals still tend to be somewhat formulaic.[68]

PACE also provides a special procedure to give some protection to the press freedom interests involved in searches for journalistic material, and the privacy interests implicated in searches for personal records and the papers of professional or voluntary advisers. Such material is not normally subject to search under warrant. The police have no means of coercing production of items subject to legal privilege.[69] In relation to other material of a confidential or journalistic kind, an application for access or production is made, usually *inter partes*, to a circuit judge. Access to the most sensitive class of confidential material, so-called "excluded material,"[70] may be ordered only if the judge is satisfied that there are reasonable grounds for believing that there is excluded material on premises and that, before the special protections in section 9 of PACE took effect, it would have been possible and appropriate to issue a warrant to search the premises for the material.[71] If

63. *Code of Practice for the Searching of Premises by Police Officers and the Seizure of Property found by Police Officers on Persons or Premises*, especially sections 4 and 5.

64. Lidstone and Bevan, *Search and Seizure*, tables 3.2 and 3.3, p 45-6.

65. See Lidstone and Bevan, *Search and Seizure*; David Dixon, Clive Coleman and Keith Bottomley, *Consent and the Legal Regulation of Policing* (1990) 17 J. Law & Soc. 345-62 at 352-3.

66. K. W. Lidstone, *Magistrates, the Police and Search Warrants* [1984] Crim. L.R. 449- 458.

67. [1980] A.C. 952, H.L., discussed by Feldman, *Law Relating to Entry, Search and Seizure* 72-73, 129-136. See more recently *Attorney-General of Jamaica* v. *Williams* [1997] 3 W.L.R. 389, P.C., on appeal from the C.A. of Jamaica.

68. PACE, section 15; Lidstone and Bevan, *Search and Seizure*, p 19-28.

69. PACE, section 9. "Items subject to legal privilege" are defined in section 10, broadly in line with the common law privilege for lawyer-client communications. See *R.* v. *Central Criminal Court, ex parte Francis & Francis (a firm)* [1989] A.C. 436, H.L.; *R.* v. *Guildhall Magistrates' Court, ex parte Primlaks Holdings Co. (Panama) Ltd.* [1990] 1 Q.B. 262, D.C.

70. PACE, section 11(1).

71. PACE, Sched. 1, paras. 2(3).

an order is made but not complied with, a search warrant may then be issued.[72] The judge may grant access to the less sensitive class of confidential and journalistic material, "special procedure material,"[73] if either the conditions relating to excluded material are satisfied, or there are reasonable grounds for believing that a serious arrestable offence has been committed, that material consisting of special procedure material but not containing excluded material is likely to be of substantial value to the investigation and to be relevant evidence, that other methods of obtaining the material have been tried without success or seemed bound to fail, and that it is in the public interest that the material should be made available.[74] If an order is granted, the person in possession must produce only the material specified. The police are not empowered to search premises. A considerable jurisprudence has developed around the provisions relating to excluded and special procedure material. It seems that judges may currently be too willing to hold, in relation to special procedure material (particularly journalistic material) that it is in the public interest that material should be made available, particularly as the European Court of Human Rights has held that it can breach the right to press freedom under Article 10 ECHR to compel disclosure of a journalist's sources.[75] This is likely to change when the Human Rights Bill takes effect and requires courts to read these provisions in the light of, and so far as possible consistently with, Articles 8 and 10 of the European Convention on Human Rights.

The Form of Warrants. Section 15 of PACE and Code B lay down fairly detailed rules on how applications for warrants are to be made and the supporting paperwork which is needed. Section 15(6) provides that the warrant must specify the name of the applicant, the date of issue, the enactment under which it is made, and the premises to be searched. It must also identify so far as practicable the articles or person to be sought.

Executing Warrants. Warrants stay in force for one month only.[76] When on premises lawfully, the police in searching may use reasonable force if necessary.[77] Due consideration must be shown for the property and privacy of the occupier.[78] A constable must execute the warrant at a reasonable hour unless that would frustrate the purpose of the search.[79] Among other procedural requirements, the constable must produce the warrant to the occupier (although not necessarily before entering), and must provide the occupier with a copy of it.[80] The occupier must also receive a "Notice of Rights and Powers" explaining (*inter alia*) the authority for the search and setting out the scope of the powers under relevant legislation.[81]

72. PACE, Sched. 1, para. 12.
73. PACE, section 14.
74. PACE, Sched. 1, para. 2.
75. *Goodwin* v. *UK* (1996) 22 E.H.R.R. 123, Eur. Ct. H.R. See also A. A. S. Zuckerman, *The weakness of the PACE special procedure for protecting confidential material* [1990] Crim. L.R. 472-8; Feldman, *Civil Liberties and Human Rights* p 452-472, 626-631; Feldman, *Press freedom and police access to journalistic material*, in Eric Barendt (ed.), *Yearbook of Media and Entertainment Law* Vol. 1 (1995), p 43-80.
76. PACE, section 16(3).
77. PACE, section 117.
78. Code B, paras. 5.9-5.10.
79. PACE, section 16(4).
80. PACE, section 16(5); *R.* v. *Longman* [1988] 1 W.L.R. 609, C.A.
81. Code B, para. 5.7.

The search may extend only so far as is required for the purpose for which the search warrant was issued.[82] Failing to abide by these rules makes the entry and search retrospectively unlawful.[83] Nevertheless, if during a search the extent of which is lawful evidence or fruits of any crime are found which fall outside the scope of the warrant, it may usually be seized if the constable has reasonable grounds for believing that seizure is necessary to prevent it being concealed, lost, damaged, altered or destroyed, and that it does not consist of items subject to legal privilege (although officers who are lawfully on premises may seize excluded or special procedure material if they come upon it and have reasonable grounds that it is evidence of any offence and that it is necessary to seize it to protect it from interference). Equivalent provisions apply to material held on computer.[84] Warrants issued under section 8 of PACE are a special case: seizures under them must be for a purpose contemplated by that section.[85]

Other Authorisations Related to Invasions of Privacy. Interceptions of communications on a public telephone system may be authorised by the Home Secretary if he considers it necessary in the interests of national security, to detect or prevent serious crime, or to safeguard the economic well-being of the UK.[86] Information gained cannot be used in court, because in order to protect sources and techniques no evidence can be given about how the information was gained or where it came from.[87] However, where one party to a telephone conversation consents to the interception, or the interception takes place on a private part of the system, no warrant is needed, and the statutory scheme does not apply. This is likely to breach Article 8 ECHR, as interceptions are not in accordance with (i.e. governed by) law,[88] but information gained is nevertheless currently usable in evidence as long as there is no overriding public interest which prevents evidence being given as to its provenance.[89]

Because English law as yet probably contains no right to privacy as such (although there is plenty of privacy-related law),[90] other forms of surveillance require no specific authorisation (although there are Home Office guidelines to the police) unless they involve unlawful behaviour such as trespass to premises. Controversial legislation in 1997 gave the police the opportunity to obtain an authorisation from an "authorising officer" (a chief constable or officer of equivalent rank) for entry to or interference with property or wireless telegraphy.[91] The officer may authorise the taking of such action in respect of such property, or interference with wireless telegraphy in such area, as is specified in the authorisation.[92] This may include

82. PACE, section 16(8).

83. PACE, section 15(1), introduces a statutory doctrine of relation-back to the law of trespass in respect of warrants: *R.* v. *Chief Constable of the Lancashire Constabulary, ex parte Parker* [1993] Q.B. 577, D.C., at 584 *per* Nolan L.J.; *R.* v. *Chief Constable of the Warwickshire Constabular, ex parte Fitzpatrick* [1998] 1 All E.R. 65, C.A.

84. PACE, s section 19, 20.

85. *R.* v. *Chief Constable of the Warwickshire Constabulary, ex parte Fitzpatrick* [1998] 1 All E.R. 65, C.A.

86. Interception of Communications Act 1985, section 2.

87. *Ibid.*, section 9.

88. *Halford* v. *UK*, (1997) 24 E.H.R.R. 523, Eur. Ct. H.R.

89. See *R.* v. *Preston* [1994] 2 A.C. 130, H.L.; *R.* v. *Effik* [1995] 1 A.C. 309, H.L.; *R.* v. *Rasool* [1997] 4 All E.R. 439, C.A.

90. See *R.* v. *Khan (Sultan)* [1997] A.C. 558, H.L.

91. Police Act 1997, section 92.

92. Police Act 1997, section 93(1).

covert entry to, search of and removal of material from private premises, and damage to those premises or that property. Where authorisations relate to dwellings or office premises, or may lead to the acquisition of information regarding confidential personal information or confidential journalistic material, they do not take effect unless approved by a Commissioner[93] (a person who has held high judicial office appointed by the Prime Minister, whose decisions are immune from judicial review[94]). This license to bug and burgle may be issued only where the authorising officer believes (not necessarily on reasonable grounds) that the action is necessary on the ground that it is likely to be of substantial value (a strange and contradictory formulation) in the prevention or detection of serious crime, and that there is no other way in which the objective could reasonably be achieved. A serious crime for this purpose is one which involves the use of violence, or results in substantial financial gain, or is conducted by a large number of persons in pursuit of a common purpose (capable of including much public protest), or is likely to lead to a sentence of at least three years imprisonment.[95] Rather similar powers, though with fewer safeguards, were given to the Security Service (MI5) by the Security and Intelligence Services Act 1994.

5. *Enforcing the Rules*

English law has no general exclusionary rule for improperly obtained evidence. Instead, it distinguished between confessions by the accused and other evidence. The fact that evidence has been obtained by improper or unlawful means does not necessarily (or, except in relation to confessions, even usually) make evidence of the discovery inadmissible or excluded at trial. The judge has a discretion to exclude real evidence obtained in the course of a search if that in all the circumstances admitting it would make the proceedings unfair.[96] Calculations of fairness take account of all the parties, including the prosecution. Real evidence has been excluded where the officer had failed to comply with the requirement to tell the person why he was being stopped and searched,[97] but this is relatively unusual, and the most recent decision of the House of Lords decided that it was not improper for a trial judge to admit evidence obtained by a bugging device attached during a police trespass to the wall of the house of a non-consenting third party, because the public interest in detecting serious crime (in that case drug trafficking) outweighed the interest in privacy.[98] The general approach to exclusion is outlined below, section II.C.3.

B. Identification Parades and Other Identification Procedures

Identification procedures are governed by a Code of Practice (Code D) made under PACE, augmented by statutory provisions empowering the police in speci-

93. Police Act 1997, section 97.
94. Police Act 1997, section 91.
95. Police Act 1997, section 93(2), (4).
96. PACE, section 78.
97. *R.* v. *Fennelley* [1989] Crim. L.R. 142.
98. *R.* v. *Khan (Sultan)* [1997] A.C. 558, H.L.

fied circumstances to take fingerprints and body samples for matching and DNA testing. In a case where there is a disputed identification, an officer not below the rank of inspector and not involved in the investigation, the "identification officer," supervises the identification process. Four methods of visual identification are permitted: a formal identification parade, which is the preferred option; a group identification, where the suspect is viewed by a witness among an informal group of people; a video film of the suspect, if possible made with the suspect's consent; and, if none of the other options is possible, a confrontation with the witness. When seeking the suspect's consent to one of these procedures, the identification officer must tell the suspect of his rights, and also that his refusal to participate may be given in evidence in any subsequent prosecution.[99]

1. Identification Parades

Code D imposes controls to ensure as far as possible that procedures are fairly conducted and that identifications are not contaminated by investigating officers interfering with witnesses. A parade must be held whenever a suspect disputes his identification[100] and consents to a parade, and may be held whenever the officer in charge of the investigation considers it useful and the suspect consents. A video recording or colour photograph of the parade must be taken. Before the parade, the suspect and his legal adviser must be provided with any description of the offender which a witness has already provided. The identification officer must ensure that witnesses can neither communicate with each other, get an advance sight of members of the parade, nor be reminded of any photograph or description of the suspect. Witnesses must not be told whether any earlier witness has made an identification. Appropriate steps must be taken to find out whether witnesses have seen any film or photograph of the suspect in the media. After the parade, the suspect is told whether any witness made an identification.[101]

2. Other Identification Procedures

Group Identifications can, if necessary, take place without the suspect's consent if consent is refused and it is practicable to proceed. They may be covert if necessary. Where the suspect consents, similar safeguards to those relating to parades must be observed.[102] Where there is a *one-to-one confrontation*, safeguards are provided as for parades, *mutatis mutandis*. The witness must be asked, "Is this the person?"[103] *Video identifications* may be conducted either with the suspect's consent or without it, and in the latter case may be conducted covertly. Similar precautions to those relating to a parade must be taken to prevent witnesses colluding or being influenced by police officers.[104]

Fingerprints. Where a detained suspect refuses to consent to being fingerprinted, it may nevertheless be authorised by a police officer of at least the rank of

99. Code D, paras. 2.1-2.15.

100. It need not be held if there is no reason to anticipate a dispute about identity: *R.* v. *Rutherford* (1993) 98 Cr. App. R. 191, C.A.

101. Code D, paras. 2.3-2.6 and Annex A.

102. Code D, paras. 2.7-2. and Annex E.

103. Code D, para. 2.13 and Annex C.

104. Code D, paras. 2.10-2.12 and Annex B.

superintendent if it will tend to prove or disprove the suspect's involvement in the offence.[105] If the suspect resists, reasonable force can be used if necessary.[106]

Body Samples. A person may in some circumstances be required to provide samples of body tissue or body fluids to the police. If the person refuses consent, the consequences depend on the degree of intimacy involved. Where a suspect has been detained, or is not detained but earlier non-intimate samples have proved insufficient to establish the facts, "intimate samples," i.e. samples of blood or urine (except in drink-drive cases), semen or other tissue fluid, or pubic hair, a dental impression, or a swab taken from any body orifice other than the mouth, may be taken. This may be done only if the suspect has consented and the taking has been authorised by an officer of at least the rank of superintendent on the ground that it will tend to prove or disprove the suspect's involvement in a recordable offence.[107] The suspect need not consent, but refusal may lead to adverse inferences being drawn in any subsequent proceedings, and may be treated as corroboration of other evidence.[108]

"Non-intimate samples," which include non-pubic hair, samples from nails, swabs from parts of the body including the mouth but not from other orifices, saliva, and footprints or impressions of any part of the body other than the hand, may be taken without the suspect's consent if he is in custody or has been charged with a recordable offence, and an officer of at least the rank of superintendent authorises it. Such a sample may also be taken if the person has been convicted of a recordable offence. Reasonable force may be used if necessary to take the sample.[109]

The police have established a national DNA register, and samples or fingerprints may be checked against records in the police national computer or DNA register.

3. *Enforcing the Rules*

The identification officer and the officer who authorises the taking of samples or fingerprints have primary responsibility for ensuring that the rules are observed. Where something goes wrong, and a suspect complains that an inappropriate method of identification is used in breach of Code D, it may lead to disciplinary proceedings against the officers concerned, but (following an amendment to PACE by the Criminal Justice and Public Order Act 1994) such breaches are not automatically disciplinary offences. The evidence of any identification may have to be excluded at the suspect's trial. For example, the Court of Appeal quashed convictions in *R.* v. *Graham*[110] where the police had failed to hold an identity parade in a case of disputed identity, and in *R.* v. *Conway*[111] because the trial judge had allowed a witness to identify the accused in the dock, a procedure not authorised by

105. PACE, section 61(3)(b), (4).

106. PACE, section 116.

107. Recordable offences are generally those for which a person may be sentenced to imprisonment.

108. PACE, s section 62 and 65, as amended by Criminal Justice and Public Order Act 1994.

109. PACE, s section 63, 63A, 65, as amended and inserted by the Criminal Justice and Public Order Act 1994.

110. [1994] Crim. L.R. 212, C.A.

111. (1990) 91 Cr. App. R. 143, C.A.

Code D. Similarly where a blood sample has been obtained with the suspect's consent, on the understanding that it would be used only for the purposes of that investigation, it has been held to be wrong to admit evidence derived from the sample in relation to another charge against the same suspect four years later.[112] However, even where there is an impropriety of that kind an appeal may be dismissed if the strength of other evidence is sufficient to uphold the conviction,[113] or the suspect's interests had been adequately protected by other means (e.g. representation by a solicitor),[114] or in the circumstances admitting the evidence would not be unfair notwithstanding the breach.[115] Breaches of the Code do not give rise to a right of action for damages, and would not normally appear to constitute any tort. On the other hand, unlawfully taking a body sample without consent is actionable as a battery.

C. Interrogation

1. *Before Charge*

PACE and Code C provide a complex and comprehensive framework for questioning, which seeks to balance extensive police powers with safeguards against abuse in the manner recommended by the Royal Commission on Criminal Procedure in 1981. Safeguards are of two kinds: procedural and recording requirements to be observed by the police, and rights for suspects which the police have a duty to protect.

At common law there was no legal obligation to answer police questions.[116] However, the previous (Conservative) government launched a major assault on the right to silence, which was seen as an unfair shield for professional criminals. In the light of a careful review of the arguments,[117] the Royal Commission on Criminal Justice recommended by a majority that it would be improper to draw adverse inferences from a refusal to answer questions unless and until the prosecution case had been fully disclosed.[118] However, Parliament had already passed legislation which imposed obligations to disclose information to investigators in connection with terrorism, serious fraud, and money-laundering investigations. These obligations apply to suspects as they do to unimplicated witnesses. The European Court of Human Rights held in *Saunders* v. *United Kingdom*[119] that coerced disclosure of self- incriminating information, which was subsequently used against the person in criminal proceedings, breached the right to a fair trial under Article 6 of the ECHR, but so far the legislation has not been amended. The Criminal Justice and

112. *R.* v. *Nathaniel* [1995] 2 Cr. App. R. 565, C.A. See generally Michael Zander, *The Police and Criminal Evidence Act 1984* 3rd ed. (London: Sweet & Maxwell, 1995), p 239-241.

113. E.g. *R.* v. *Brown* [1991] Crim. L.R. 368, C.A.

114. *R.* v. *Ryan* [1992] Crim. L.R. 187, C.A.

115. *R.* v. *Grannell* (1989) 90 Cr. App. R. 149, C.A.

116. See *Rice* v. *Connolly* [1966] 2 Q.B. 414, D.C.; *Green* v. *D.P.P.* [1991] Crim. L.R. 782, D.C. *Cp. Ricketts* v. *Cox* (1981) 74 Cr. App. R. 298, D.C.

117. Roger Leng, *The Right to Silence in Police Interrogation: A Study of some of the Issues underlying the Debate*, Royal Commission on Criminal Justice Research Study No. 10 (London: H.M.S.O., 1993).

118. Royal Commission on Criminal Justice, *Report*, p. 55, ch. 4, paras. 22 and 24.

119. (1996) 23 E.H.R.R. 313, Eur. Ct. H.R.

Public Order Act 1994 extended this, making it possible to draw adverse inferences in certain circumstances from a suspect's failure to answer questions when interviewed or to give evidence at trial. The current position can be summed up as follows.

The police may ask any questions of anyone. When they have reasonable grounds to suspect that the interviewee has committed an offence they must caution him, informing him of his right to remain silent but also of the facts that "it may harm your defence if you do not mention when questioned something which you later rely on in court" and that "[a]nything you do say may be given in evidence."[120] The caution must be repeated if the person is arrested or charged, and the interviewee must be reminded of it after every break in the interview. Failure to mention matters may tend to undermine assertions or defenses advanced at trial, as adverse inferences may be drawn from the earlier failure to mention them (although there is usually no obligation to disclose them, subject to points considered later).[121]

A special provision applies if the person is arrested, and after caution fails to answer questions relating to incriminating items found in the person's possession or to his reasons for being in the vicinity of the place where an offence has been committed. The court can draw any inferences which seem proper from that failure, although it cannot be the sole evidence on which the defendant is convicted or committed for trial.[122] To allow inferences to be drawn, the officer must first have told the suspect what offence he is investigating, and explained that he considers the factors in question to implicate the suspect in the offence and that a record is being made of the interview which may be given in evidence.[123]

The police must keep a record of all interviews with suspects wherever they take place. This must normally be contemporaneous and written, unless the police can show (and it is very hard to do so) that is impracticable.[124] The interviewee must be shown the record at the end of the interview and given an opportunity to comment on it. Interviews conducted in police stations must also be tape-recorded in accordance with the provisions of Code E. Failure to comply with the recording requirements may lead to the evidence being excluded at trial, particularly if the record-keeping deficiencies make it harder for the police to establish that their evidence is reliable.[125] These provisions cause difficulties in relation to covert surveillance or "sting" operations. Evidence of conversations with undercover officers is likely to be excluded if the court concludes that the main reason for adopting the investigative technique in question was to avoid cautioning the suspect or complying with the provisions about interview records.[126] However, if the court considers that the investigators adopted methods which were legitimate in the circumstances (for example, establishing a jewelry business as a "front" for a police investigation

120. Code C, para. 10.4.

121. Criminal Justice and Public Order Act 1994, section 34; see also section 38(3).

122. Criminal Justice and Public Order Act 1994, section 38(3).

123. Criminal Justice and Public Order Act 1994, s section 36 and 37.

124. See *R. v. Canale* [1990] 2 ALl E.R. 187, C.A.

125. David Feldman, *Regulating Treatment of Suspects in Police Stations: Judicial Interpretation of Detention Provisions in the Police and Criminal Evidence Act 1984* [1990] Crim. L.R. 452- 471.

126. *R. v. Bryce* [1992] 4 All E.R. 567, C.A.

into burglaries and thefts of jewelry) and the records are sufficient to make police evidence reliable, the evidence is likely to be admitted.[127]

PACE gave a right to detained suspects to have someone informed that they are detained, and a right to have access to legal advice.[128] These rights did not exist at common law.[129] The suspect must be informed of his rights, although in respect of serious arrestable offences the police may delay his exercise of either or both of the rights if an officer of the rank of at least superintendent decides that exercise of the right would lead to interference with evidence or people, to physical injury to people, to other suspects (as yet not arrested) being alerted, or to recovery of property, or proceeds of drug trafficking being hindered.[130] In practice only about one-third of detainees seek to exercise the right to legal advice,[131] although it has been suggested that (at least in the past) this was because the police used various ploys to discourage them from doing so.[132] Suspects without advice face particular dangers now that courts can draw adverse inferences from silence: proper advice about the risks and advantages of speaking is vital, and admitting evidence of silence following a refusal to allow access to an adviser may breach the fair trial guarantee in ECHR, Article 6.[133] If the suspect exercises this right, no interview may take place until the advice has been obtained except in cases of urgency.[134] PACE and Code C also give a right to regular meals and at least eight hours of rest in any 24-hour period of detention.[135]

While the arrested suspect is being interviewed, he is outside the protection of the custody officer. The investigating officer is responsible for ensuring that the terms of PACE and the Codes of Practice are complied with during the interview.[136] Making the investigating officer responsible for policing himself is not entirely sat-

---

127. *R.* v. *Christou and Wright* (1992) 95 Cr. App. R. 264, C.A. For full discussion see A. J. Ashworth, *Should the Police be Allowed to Use Deceptive Practices?* (1998) 114 L.Q.R. 108-140.

128. PACE, s section 56, 58.

129. See *R.* v. *Chief Constable of the Royal Ulster Constabulary, ex parte Begley* [1997] 4 All E.R. 833, H.L.

130. PACE, s section 56(2), (5), (5A), and 58(6), (8), (8A). Longer delay is permitted under Prevention of Terrorism (Temporary Provisions) Act 1989.

131. D. Brown, T. Ellis and K. Larcombe, *Changing the Code: Police Detention under the revised PACE Codes of Practice* (London: Home Office Research and Policy Unit/H.M.S.O., 1993), Table 3.4.

132. For the suggestion, see Andrew Sanders and Lee Bridges, *Access to Legal Advice and Police Malpractice* [1990] Crim. L.R. 494-509. For a different view of the evidence, see David Dixon, *Legal Regulation and Police Malpractice* (1992) 1 Social and Legal Studies 515-541.

133. *Murray* v. *UK*, (1996) 22 E.H.R.R. 29, Eur. Ct. H.R.; Michael McConville and Jacqueline Hodgson, *Custodial Legal Advice and the Right to Silence*, Royal Commission on Criminal Justice Research Study No. 16 (London: H.M.S.O., 1993); David Roberts, *Legal Advice, the Unrepresented Suspect and the Courts: Inferences From Silence Under the Criminal Justice and Public Order Act 1994* [1995] Crim. L.R. 483-485.

134. Code C, para. 6.6. For studies of legal advice at police stations, see A. Sanders, L. Bridges, A. Mulvaney and G. Crozier, *Advice and Assistance at Police Stations and the 24 Hour Duty Solicitor Scheme* (London: Lord Chancellor's Department, 1990); John Baldwin, *The Role of Legal Representatives at the Police Station*, Royal Commission on Criminal Justice Research Study No. 3 (London: H.M.S.O., 1993); and M. McConville, J. Hodgson, L. Bridges and A. Pavlovic, *Standing Accused: The Organisation and Practices of Criminal Defence Lawyers in Britain* (Oxford: Clarendon Press, 1994).

135. Code C, paras. 8.6, 12.2. See generally section 8 of Code C; David Feldman, *Regulating Treatment of Suspects in Police Stations: Judicial Interpretation of Detention Provisions in the Police and Criminal Evidence Act 1984* [1990] Crim. L.R. 452-471.

136. PACE, section 39(2).

isfactory, but the risks are to some degree alleviated by the tape-recording requirements noted earlier, and by video-recording which is being introduced where local conditions and technology permit. Special procedures[137] must be followed in relation to juveniles and those who appear to be suffering from a mental handicap or disability, who are entitled to be accompanied at any interview by an "appropriate adult." This may (for example) be a relation or a social-services or health-care professional.[138] An interpreter must be provided for people who have difficulty in understanding English or who appear to be deaf or suffering from a speech handicap.[139]

In relation to techniques of interrogation, Code C, paras. 11.3-11.4 provide that oppression is not to be used, incentives to confess are not to be offered, and questioning the suspect about an offence must stop when the investigating officer decides that there is sufficient evidence for a prosecution to succeed. "Oppression," which makes a confession inadmissible under PACE, section 76(2)(a), may arise from aggressive and/or improper forms of behaviour over a significant period. It has been held to have been present, for example, where the investigating officer misled the custody officer, refused access to a solicitor, breached the recording requirements, and interviewed the suspect several times while in detention;[140] bullied and hectored the suspect and misrepresented to her both the available evidence and the effect of her own previous answers, leading to disorientation and a confession;[141] and shouted at the suspect and repeated allegations several hundred times in a bullying manner, threatening to continue until the police got the answers they wanted, and effectively brain-washing the suspect over 13 hours of interrogation.[142] Incentives or threats designed to induce a confession, or other actions or statements by the police which make the confession unreliable, make the confession inadmissible under section 76(2)(b) of PACE, whether or not the police behaved improperly in the sense of breaching any rules.

Most other rules derive from judicial discussions of the criteria for deciding whether evidence of confessions is admissible or, if admissible, should be excluded in the exercise of the court's discretion. General principles should be treated with caution, since (particularly in relation to the exercise of judicial discretion to exclude evidence) it seems unlikely that judges are in practice following any very clear or consistent theoretical approach to the cases,[143] and there is a tendency to concentrate on the fairness of proceedings rather than the inherent quality of the techniques used.[144] Police action which deprives the court of the best evidence of what

137. See Code C, Annex E.

138. Code C, para. 1.7. For studies of the operation of these provisions see Gisli Gudgonsson, Isabel Clare, Susan Rutter and John Pearse, *Persons at risk during interviews in police custody: the identification of vulnerabilities*, Royal Commission on Criminal Justice Research Study No. 12 (London: H.M.S.O., 1993); Jacqueline Hodgson, *Vulnerable Suspects and the Appropriate Adult* [1997] Crim. L.R. 785-795.

139. Code C, paras. 13.2-13.11.

140. *R.* v. *Ismail* [1990] Crim. L.R. 109, C.A.

141. *R.* v. *Beales* [191] Crim. L.R. 118.

142. *R.* v. *Parris, Abdullah and Miller* (1993) 97 Cr. App. R. 99, C.A.

143. See *R.* v. *Samuel* [1988] Q.B. 615, C.A., at p. 630 *per* Hodgson J.; M. Hunter, *Judicial Discretion: Section 78 in Practice* [1994] Crim. L.R. 558; Zander, *The Police and Criminal Evidence Act 1984* 3rd ed., p 214-246.

144. See Katharine Grevling, *Fairness and the Exclusion of Evidence Under Section 78(1) of the Police and Criminal Evidence Act 1984* (1997) 113 L.Q.R. 667-685.

happened during the interrogation (such as a cynical and calculated refusal to comply with record-keeping requirements) calls in question the reliability of the evidence of confession, and makes it possible, and sometimes necessary, for the court to exclude the otherwise admissible confession under section 78 of PACE.[145] So does conduct which the court regards as amounting to an impropriety undermining the fairness of the proceedings, as where the police misled the suspect's solicitor about the evidence against the accused, and the suspect confessed as a result.[146]

2. *After Charge*

When the suspect has been charged with an offence, questioning must stop, unless he is being investigated in relation to other offences or the police want information about the proceeds of the crime in connection with possible confiscation proceedings.[147] After charge, the suspect is normally entitled to be released on bail, unless there is no satisfactory address for service of a summons, or there are reasonable grounds for believing that he will fail to appear at court, or will interfere with the administration of justice or harm himself, or will (if arrested for an imprisonable offence) commit another offence, or (if a non-imprisonable offence) will cause physical injury to others or damage to property. Bail must not be granted if the accused has previously been convicted in the UK of murder, attempted murder, manslaughter (if sentenced to imprisonment), rape or attempted rape, and has been charged with an offence of the same kind.[148] If bail is granted, conditions (for example as to place of residence or reporting to police stations) can be attached.[149] If bail is refused, the custody officer must ensure that the accused is brought before a magistrates' court as soon as practicable, and in any case not later than the first sitting after charge.[150] The court has power to grant bail with or without conditions, or to remand the accused in custody.[151]

3. *Enforcing the Rules*

Unless the police use physical force or detain a person unlawfully (giving rise to an action for the torts of battery or false imprisonment), the main methods of enforcement are by way of an official complaint or an application to exclude evidence, neither of which give rise to a right to compensation. This position may change in respect to conduct which constitutes a violation of a Convention right if the Human Rights Act 1998 is interpreted by the courts as enabling the creation of new remedies for victims. This section concentrates on issues of admissibility and exclusion of evidence.[152]

---

145. See *R.* v. *Canale* [1990] 2 All E.R. 187, C.A.

146. *R.* v. *Mason* [1987] 3 All E.R. 481, C.A.

147. Code C, para. 11.4.

148. PACE, section 38, as amended and supplemented by Criminal Justice and Public Order Act 1994, s section 25 and 28.

149. Criminal Justice and Public Order Act 1994, section 27. There is a power to arrest a person who fails to comply with a reporting requirement: PACE, section 46A, inserted by Criminal Justice and Public Order Act 1994, section 29(2).

150. PACE, section 46.

151. Bail Act 1976.

152. See John A. Andrews and Michael Hirst, *Andrews and Hirst on Criminal Evidence* 3rd ed. (London: Sweet & Maxwell, 1997), ch. 14.

A Confession by the Accused is admissible only if the accused accepts, or the prosecution proves beyond reasonable doubt, that it was not obtained by oppression or in consequence of anything said or done which was likely to render the confession unreliable.[153] (This statutory rule replaced the common-law test of voluntariness.) If one confession is tainted, but the police re-interviewed the suspect and obtained a new confession, the later statement may be tendered as evidence only in the unlikely event that the factors which vitiated the earlier statement are not still affecting the mind of the suspect.[154] The prosecution may however tender evidence obtained as a result of an excluded confession, as long as no evidence is given of the way in which it was found.[155]

Other Relevant Evidence, including a confession by someone other than the accused, is *prima facie* admissible even if obtained improperly. The English courts have largely maintained their traditional view that it is no part of their role to use the law of evidence to discipline the police for impropriety, although there are cases of very flagrant abuse where they have come close to it.[156] However, the court has a discretion to exclude otherwise admissible evidence in two circumstances. First, there remains a rarely used common-law power, preserved by sections 78(2) and 82(3) of PACE, to exclude evidence from consideration by a jury in order to secure a fair trial where the prejudicial force of the evidence would outweigh its probative value.[157]

Secondly, there is power under PACE, section 78(1) to exclude prosecution evidence (although not that tendered by a co-accused) "if it appears to the court that, having regard to all the circumstances, including the circumstances in which the evidence was obtained, the admission of the evidence would have such an adverse effect on the fairness of the proceedings that the court ought not to admit it." These are broad terms, and are not restrictively interpreted.[158] The question is whether it would make the proceedings unfair to admit the evidence, balancing the public interests in detecting offenders, maintaining civil liberties, and ensuring that we have a law-abiding police force.[159] A breach of the Act or Codes therefore does not automatically lead to exclusion,[160] nor is such a breach or bad faith a necessary precondition for exclusion, although it may be relevant.[161] For a breach of the Codes to lead to exclusion it must be significant and substantial.[162] A breach is likely to be regarded as less significant if the suspect had a solicitor on hand to protect his interests and offer advice,[163] or where it cannot be shown to have affected the sus-

---

153. PACE, section 76(2). See Peter Mirfield, *Silence, Confessions, and Improperly Obtained Evidence* (Oxford: Clarendon Press, 1997); Di Birch, *The Pace Hots Up: Confessions and Confusions under the 1984 Act* [1989] Crim. L.R. 95-116.

154. *R.* v. *McGovern* (1990) 92 Cr. App. R. 229, C.A.; *R.* v. *Glaves* [1993] Crim. L.R. 685, C.A.; Peter Mirfield, *Successive Confessions and the Poisonous Tree* [1996] Crim. L.R. 554-567.

155. PACE, section 76(5), (6).

156. *R.* v. *Canale* [1990] 2 All E.R. 187, C.A. See A. A. S. Zuckerman, *Illegally Obtained Evidence: Discretion as a Guardian of Legitimacy* (1987) 39 Current Legal Problems 55- 70.

157. *R.* v. *Sang* [1980] A.C. 402, H.L.

158. *R.* v. *Brine* [1992] Crim. L.R. 122, C.A.

159. *R.* v. *Hughes* [1988] Crim. L.R. 519, C.A.; *R.* v. *McDonald* [1991] Crim. L.R. 122, C.A.

160. *R.* v. *Pall* [1992] Crim. L.R. 126, C.A.

161. *Matto* v. *Wolverhampton Crown Court* [1987] R.T.R. 337, D.C.; *R.* v. *Brine*, above.

162. *R.* v. *Keenan* (1989) 90 Cr. App. R. 1, C.A.; *R.* v. *Matthews, Dennison and Voss* [1990] Crim. L.R. 190, C.A.

163. *R.* v. *Dunn* [1990] Crim. L.R. 572, C.A.

pect's decision to confess.[164] Failure to caution a suspect and wrongful refusal of access to legal advice are serious and substantial breaches.[165] If a defendant challenges an alleged statement, a failure to comply with the recording provisions will be likely to undermine the court's faith in the police evidence so as to make it unfair to admit the evidence.[166] It will very rarely be proper to admit evidence of an incriminating statement allegedly made after the end of a formal interview which had produced no such statement.[167] It is possible that evidence produced by entrapping the defendant might sometimes be excluded under section 78, thus bypassing the rule that entrapment is no defence in English law.[168]

III. Court Procedures

Criminal offences are divided into three broad categories, and different procedures apply to each. The least serious in terms of their impact on the community and the sentences available on conviction are summary offences, which are always tried by a magistrates' court without a jury. The most serious are indictable offences, always tried at the Crown Court on indictment before judge and jury. Between them fall a growing number of offences which are "triable either way," the mode of trial depending partly on the choice of the defendant and partly, if the defendant opts for summary trial, on the willingness of the magistrates to accept jurisdiction.

Summary Trial. In 1996, 1.92 million defendants were proceeded against in a magistrates' court without a jury, compared with about 86,000 tried before a jury in the Crown Court.[169] Magistrates' courts try all summary offences, and offences triable either summarily or on indictment where the accused has elected for summary trial and the magistrates have accepted jurisdiction. The advantages to the accused of summary trial are that the case may be heard more quickly than a trial on indictment, (Average waiting times in 1996 were 132 days from the date of the offence to completion of the proceedings for indictable offences in magistrates' courts, compared with an average wait of about 100 days after committal before Crown Court trial for those on bail.)[170] and the maximum permitted sentence following conviction is usually lower in a magistrates' court than would be permitted in the Crown Court on indictment. (Although a magistrates' court which feels that its sentencing powers are insufficient in a particu-

---

164. *R.* v. *Walsh* [1989] Crim. L.R. 822, C.A.; *R.* v. *Dunford* (1990) 91 Cr. App. R. 150, C.A.

165. See e.g. *R.* v. *Samuel* [1988] Q.B. 615, C.A.; *R.* v. *Doolan* [1988] Crim. L.R. 747, C.A.; *R.* v. *Manji* [1990] Crim. L.R. 512, C.A.; *R.* v. *Sparks* [1991] Crim. L.R. 128, C.A.

166. *R.* v. *Canale* [1990] 2 All E.R. 187, C.A.

167. *R.* v. *Bryce* [1992] 4 All E.R. 567, C.A.

168. See *R.* v. *Sang* [1980] A.C. 402, H.L.; *R.* v. *Gill and Ranuana* [1989] Crim. L.R. 358, C.A.; *R.* v. *Christou* [1992] Q.B. 979, C.A., and *R.* v. *Bryce* [1992] 4 All E.R. 567, C.A.

169. Home Office, *Criminal Statistics England and Wales 1996*, Cm. 3764 (London: The Stationery Office, 1997), p. 134.

170. *Criminal Statistics England and Wales 1996*, p. 139, Table 6B, and p. 164, Table 6.4.

lar triable-either-way case may remand the accused to the Crown Court for sentence.) On the other hand, conviction rates in contested cases are significantly higher in magistrates' courts (around 70% in 1996) than in the Crown Court (45% in 1996).[171]

Trial on Indictment. This takes place in the Crown Court, with a jury. Some dissatisfaction has been expressed with the jury system, notably in relation to complex fraud cases which the Roskill Committee recommended in 1986 should be tried by judge alone.[172] Although this was not implemented, dissatisfaction with juries as a way of deciding cases is exacerbated by the impossibility of researching how juries actually operate in this country, since the Contempt of Court 1981, section 8 makes it an offence for a juror to disclose such information.[173] On the other hand, people seem emotionally attached to jury trial as a partial protection against arbitrary state action. Trial by jury for the most serious offences is generally regarded as an important quasi- constitutional right in England and Wales. Although fewer than 28,000 contested trials were heard by juries in 1996, compared with about 83,000 heard by magistrates[174] and its value has been doubted,[175] jury trial still has spirited defenders,[176] and its abolition would be politically difficult.

A. Pretrial

The decision to prosecute is usually in the hands of the Crown Prosecution Service, although for some offences the consent of the Attorney-General or the Director of Public Prosecutions is required, and private prosecutions remain possible for most offences.[177] The decision is taken on the basis of guidelines laid down in the non-statutory Code for Crown Prosecutors.[178] First, there must be a "realistic prospect of conviction," in the sense that a properly directed jury or bench of magistrates would be more likely to convict than acquit, taking account of the admissibility or possible exclusion of evidence. Secondly, prosecution must be in the public interest, taking account of a variety of factors including the likelihood that a substantial penalty would be imposed, the characteristics of the offence and the offender, the likely impact on the victim, and the effect on national interests of evidence being made public.

171. *Criminal Statistics England and Wales 1996*, p. 139, Table 6C, and p. 142, Table 6.2.

172. *Report of the Departmental Committee on Fraud Trials*, Chairman: Lord Roskill (London: H.M.S.O., 1986).

173. The Royal Commission on Criminal Justice, *Report*, Cm. 2263 (London: H.M.S.O., 1993), ch. 1, para. 8 recommended that section 8 should be repealed, but that recommendation has not been implemented.

174. *Criminal Statistics England and Wales 1996*, p. 139, Table 6C and p. 142, Table 6.2.

175. See Penny Darbyshire, *The Lamp That Shows That Freedom Lives — Is It Worth the Candle?* [1991] Crim. L.R. 740-752.

176. See e.g. Bruce Houlder, *The Importance of Preserving the Jury System and the Right of Election for Trial* [1997] Crim. L.R. 875-881.

177. See Law Commission Consultation Paper No. 149, *Consents to Prosecution* (London: The Stationery Office, 1997).

178. See Allan Hoyano, Laura Hoyano, Gwynn Davis and Shelagh Goldie, *A Study of the Impact of the Revised Code for Crown Prosecutors* [1997] Crim. L.R. 556-564.

If the accused has admitted the offence, he may be formally cautioned as an alternative to prosecution,[179] particularly if prosecution would not be in the public interest. Cautions are administered for over 100,000 property offences a year, and a growing number of drug offences (about 60,000 in 1996), although the Home Office tried to reduce reliance on them in 1994 because of fears that over-use for inappropriate crimes was bringing them into disrepute.[180] They are an effective and cheap way of dealing with offenders, although their deterrent effect appears to decline with the number of times an offender has been cautioned. Only 11% of those with a first caution in 1994 are known to have re-offended within two years, compared with 30% with a second caution and 42% of those with two or more previous cautions.[181] It has been suggested that the Crown Prosecution Service is too reluctant to prosecute, but evidence of high numbers of judge-directed acquittals in the Crown Court because of weaknesses in the prosecution case cast doubt on that.[182]

If it is decided to prosecute, summary proceedings are initiated by laying a sworn information against the accused before the magistrates' court within six months of the date of the alleged offence.[183] There is usually no time limit in respect of indictable offences. Although it is open to magistrates to refuse to commit a defendant for trial if there has been a delay which in the magistrates' opinion amounts to an abuse of process, making a fair trial impossible, it is a power which is rarely exercised and which must be approached with great care. Proceedings for an indictable offence are normally initiated by bringing the accused before a magistrates' court for committal to the Crown Court for trial.

1. Initial Court Appearance

After being charged by the police, the accused must either be released with or without bail, or be brought before a magistrates' court at its next sitting. If detained, the defendant is likely to be remanded for further hearings, either on bail under the terms of the Bail Act 1976 or in custody. If previously released on police bail, a summons will be issued. The case will be listed for a first hearing. About 19% of those charged with indictable offences and 76% of those charged with summary non-motoring offences were dealt with at that first appearance in 1996, almost all on guilty pleas.[184] For the rest, there will usually be an application for legal aid and for bail. There is a general right to bail,[185] although sureties may be required and conditions imposed where necessary to ensure that the accused will surrender to custody, will commit no offences pending trial, will not obstruct the course of justice, and will make himself available for any pre-trial inquiries.[186]

---

179. However, the caution may be quashed if the suspect confessed only because the opportunity to be cautioned rather than charged had been held out as an inducement: *R.* v. *Metropolitan Police Commissioner, ex parte Thompson* [1997] 1 W.L.R. 1519, D.C.

180. Home Office Circular 18/1994, *The Cautioning of Offenders*; see Roger Evans, *Cautioning: Counting the Cost of Retrenchment* [1994] Crim. L.R. 566-575.

181. *Criminal Statistics England and Wales 1996*, p 104-106.

182. See John Baldwin, *Understanding Judge Ordered and Directed Acquittals in the Crown Court* [1997] Crim. L.R. 536-555.

183. Magistrates' Courts Act 1980, section 127(1).

184. *Criminal Statistics England and Wales 1996*, p. 144, Table 6.4.

185. Bail Act 1976, section 4.

186. *Ibid.*, section 3.

However, bail may be refused in relation to imprisonable offences where necessary for the purposes for which imposition of conditions are permitted if conditions will not achieve the purpose. Where an imprisonable offence is indictable or triable either way, bail may also be refused where the accused was on bail at the date of the alleged offence, or has been arrested for breach of a bail condition, or where detention is necessary for his own protection. Where the offence charged is non-imprisonable, remand in detention is permitted only for the defendant's own protection. If bail is refused, the court must reconsider it of its own motion at every subsequent appearance.[187]

Where the accused is charged with an indictable or either-way offence, the Prosecution of Offences Act 1985, section 22 gives power to impose limits on the maximum permitted period for each stage of proceedings (although no such limits have so far been set) and to impose limits on the time during which a defendant may be remanded in custody pending the next stage of proceedings. The Prosecution of Offences (Custody Time-Limits) Regulations 1987 provide that the maximum periods of custody are to be 70 days between first appearance and committal proceedings or summary trial for an either-way offence; and 112 days between committal and arraignment. After that time has expired, the defendant is entitled to bail as of right, although conditions such as residence, reporting requirements or observance of a curfew may be attached to the grant of bail. The prosecution can apply for an extension of time if they do so before the time limit has expired, and can satisfy the court that there is good and sufficient cause for the extension and that they have acted with all due expedition.[188]

2. *Charging Instrument (Indictment or Information)*

Where the defendant has been charged at a police station, the charge sheet completed at that time will usually form the information which will be the basis for proceedings in the magistrates' court. Where proceedings are begun by summons, the charging instrument is an information sworn by the prosecutor before a magistrate, who signs it. In either case the information recites the brief details of the allegation against the defendant and identifies it as an offence against a named statutory provision or common law. An indictment is similar to an information, but signed by an officer of the Crown Court rather than by a magistrate.

3. *Preliminary Hearing*

For summary offences, which are tried in magistrates' courts, there will be no preliminary hearing. A date will be set by which time prosecution and defence should be ready to proceed, and the trial will then begin (although questions about the admissibility or exclusion of evidence may be tried as preliminary issues, since in a magistrates' court the bench determines all questions of fact and law, and facts emerging during an inquiry as to admissibility may prejudice the bench).[189]

---

187. Bail Act 1976, Sch. 1.

188. Prosecution of Offences Act 1985, section 22(3). For figures on the time actually spent awaiting trial, see *Criminal Statistics England and Wales 1996*, p 139 and 144.

189. See *F.* v. *Chief Constable of Kent* [1982] Crim. L.R. 682, D.C.

In preparation for trial on indictment there will be a committal hearing before magistrates. There are two kinds of committal procedure.[190] Neither now involves the taking of oral evidence. The first procedure involves no consideration of the evidence at all. It may be adopted whenever the defendants are all legally represented, and none has asked the court to consider a submission of no case to answer.[191] In the second type, documentary evidence is submitted by the prosecution (the defence is not permitted to submit evidence at this stage) to the magistrates, who decide whether the papers disclose a sufficient case to justify committal for trial. This procedure must be adopted whenever any of the accused has no legal representation, or the defendant's representative has made a submission of no case to answer.[192] If the magistrates are satisfied that there is a case to answer they commit the defendant for trial. If not, they discharge the defendant. This does not count as an acquittal to ground a subsequent plea of *autrefois acquit*,[193] but a further attempt to commit the defendant will be stopped by a writ of prohibition if the first committal hearing properly considered the case on its merits and there is not strong new evidence, as a further attempt at committal will be regarded as an abuse of process.[194]

4. Pretrial Motions

Pretrial motions in summary proceedings are very limited, and are usually restricted to matters such as bail, legal aid for the trial, and orders restricting pre-trial publicity. Where the defendant first appears charged with a triable-either-way offence, he will be invited to plead either guilty or not guilty before it is decided whether his case should be heard in a magistrates' court or the Crown Court. This procedure, known as "plea before venue," was introduced by section 49 of the Criminal Procedure and Investigations Act 1996.[195] If the defendant pleads guilty, the court proceeds accordingly. A defendant who fails to enter a plea is treated as intending to plead not guilty. The purpose is to reduce the number of "cracked trials," where a case is listed for contested hearing but the defendant actually pleads guilty, leading to a waste of court time.[196] It is expected to relieve delay and congestion in the Crown Court and save costs. However, it may cause difficulty for defendants, who have no guarantee that they will be sentenced by the magistrates' court rather than the Crown Court if they plead guilty. It is also likely to lead to an increase in the number of pre-sentence hearings which are needed to establish contested facts for sentencing purposes.[197]

---

190. Nothing here is said about special arrangements under the Criminal Justice Act 1987 for cases of serious fraud.

191. Magistrates' Courts Act 1980, section 6(2).

192. Magistrates' Courts Act 1980, section 6(1), as amended by the Criminal Procedure and Investigations Act 1996.

193. *R.* v. *Manchester City Stipendiary Magistrate, ex parte Snelson* [1977] 1 W.L.R. 911, D.C.

194. *R.* v. *Horsham Justices, ex parte Reeves* (1981) 75 Cr. App. R. 236n.

195. This inserted s section 17A, 17B and 17C into the Magistrates' Courts Act 1980 with effect from 1 October 1997.

196. In England and Wales there were 16,212 "cracked trials" in the Crown Court in 1996 (some 20% of the total number of cases committed for trial) of which 10,722 resulted from a defendant's unexpected decision to plead guilty: Lord Chancellor's Department, *Judicial Statistics England and Wales for the year 1996*, Cm. 3716, p 63-4 and Table 6.7.

197. See Nicola Padfield, *Plea Before Venue* (1997) 147 N.L.J. 1396-7; Giles Bavidge and Kevin Kerrigan, *Plea Before Venue* (1998) 148 N.L.J. 62-3.

After committal for trial on indictment, there will be a plea and direction hearing (PDH). This innovative procedure is intended to clarify the factual and legal issues in the case and ensure that all parties and the court are properly prepared to deal with them when the trial starts.[198] It is compulsory in all cases. (Other than serious fraud, in which there is a special regime for identifying issues and dealing with pre-trial motions under the Criminal Justice Act 1987.) At the PDH, the defendant is usually arraigned, and enters a plea. If he pleads guilty, sentencing follows. If he pleads not guilty, or an offer to plead guilty to a lesser charge is rejected by the prosecution, both sides must inform the judge of the issues, number of witnesses to be called, exhibits etc., the order in which prosecution witnesses will be called, any points of law which counsel anticipate (including issues concerning admissibility of evidence) and the authorities relied on, any alibi (which ought already to have been disclosed by the defence: see below), any application for a child's evidence to be given by television link or in a pre-recorded interview (see below), the estimated length of the trial, and dates when the witnesses and counsel are available. The judge should then be able to fix a date for the trial and make other necessary rulings. A ruling made before the jury is empaneled, which may include rulings on admissibility of evidence made at plea and direction hearings, is binding unless a judge varies or discharges it, but that may be done only if it appears to be in the interests of justice.[199]

5. *Discovery and Disclosure of Information*

Although the criminal trial is basically adversarial, both defence and prosecution have duties to disclose aspects of their cases before trial. The prosecution's legal duty of disclosure used to be thought to be purely an aspect of the duty to observe the rules of natural justice, at least in relation to summary trials.[200] Later, it was governed by guidelines laid down by the Attorney-General. However, in a series of cases in the early 1990's the Court of Appeal found that failures to disclose information to the defence had contributed to serious miscarriages of justice. The court turned prosecution disclosure requirements into common-law duties, breaches of which (including non-disclosure of information concerning medical or scientific evidence, possible defence witnesses, and the circumstances in which confessions had been obtained[201]) would be likely to lead to a conviction being quashed. As a result, some prosecutions had to be dropped in order to protect sensitive information or vulnerable sources from disclosure. The government, sensitive to complaints from the police, introduced legislation to Parliament to restrict prosecution disclosure and put it on a statutory basis in the Criminal Procedure and Investigations Act 1996. The same legislation imposed a duty on the defence to make advance disclosure of the nature of the defence, as the Royal Commission on Criminal Justice had recommended despite having concluded that "ambush defenses" were rare and made no significant impact on acquittal rates.[202] This built on the

---

198. For the relevant rules see *Practice Direction: Crown Court (Plea and Direction Hearings)* [1995] 1 W.L.R. 1318.

199. Criminal Procedure and Investigations Act 1996, s section 39 and 40.

200. *R.* v. *Leyland Justices, ex parte Hawthorn* [1979] Q.B. 283, D.C.

201. See e.g. *R.* v. *Maguire* 1992] Q.B. 936, C.A.; *R.* v. *Ward* [1993] 1 W.L.R. 619, C.A.; *R.* v. *Keane* [1994] 1 W.L.R. 746, C.A.

202. Royal Commission on Criminal Justice, *Report*, ch. 6, para. 64; note of dissent by Professor Michael Zander at p. 221.

duty to give advance notice of alibi defenses, which had been introduced for trials on indictment by the Criminal Justice Act 1967. The disclosure rules in effect since 1 April 1997 are contained in the 1996 Act and a Code of Practice made by the Home Secretary pursuant to section 23 of the Act. The duties are as follows.[203]

The Investigators have initial responsibility for recording and preserving all information which may be relevant to the investigation, whether gathered in the course of it or generated by the investigators. In particular, they must retain (*inter alia*) draft witness statements where they differ from the final version, and any material casting doubt on the reliability of a confession or of a witness. The material must be retained at least until the latest of three dates: the end of the proceedings if the accused is acquitted; six months after the end of proceedings if convicted; and his release from custody if he is imprisoned. These periods are short in the light of a number of cases in which it has taken years or decades to persuade the Court of Appeal that there has been a miscarriage of justice.

If the defendant is likely to plead not guilty or be tried in the Crown Court, the police must list for the prosecutor any retained material which will not form part of the prosecution case, noting separately any material which the police consider it would not be in the public interest to disclose (such as material prejudicial to national security, information given in confidence, certain information relating to child witnesses, and information relating to police undercover or surveillance operations and other detection techniques). The police should draw special attention to material which might tend to undermine the prosecution case. This part of the process is carried out by a "disclosure officer," who must certify that to the best of his knowledge and belief the Code of Practice has been complied with. Subsequently the disclosure officer must produce amended lists when necessary as the prosecutor gives information about the way in which the case will be presented, if that changes the significance of particular pieces of material.[204] The lists supplied by the disclosure officer must be accurate if the prosecutor is to comply with his disclosure duties.

The Prosecutor's Primary Disclosure duty is to disclose to the defence any material which, in the prosecutor's opinion, might tend to undermine the prosecution case.[205] This requires more than mere relevance, but seems to include material which could raise a new issue which is not apparent from the evidence which the prosecution intended to use, or which gives rise to a real prospect of leading to evidence which might be relevant or raise a new issue.[206] A tendency to undermine does not mean that material must be potentially fatal to the prosecution, but only that it may weaken it. Raising new issues is likely to do so.

The limitations of the duty of disclosure can be illustrated by the pre-Act decision in *R.* v. *Brown*,[207] since the decision would be the same under the 1996 Act. The defence was an alibi. Gordon testified that the defendant had been with him at a party at the time of the attack, and Pinnock testified that he had seen two at-

203. For detailed discussion, see Roger Leng and Richard Taylor, *Blackstone's Guide to the Criminal Procedure and Investigations Act 1996* (London: Blackstone Press, 1997), chs. 1 and 2; John Sprack, *The Criminal Procedure and Investigations Act 1996: (1) The Duty of Disclosure* [1997] Crim. L.R. 308- 320.

204. *Code of Practice on Disclosure*, paras. 5.1-8.1.

205. Criminal Procedure and Investigations Act 1996, section 3.

206. Compare the common law rule set out in *R.* v. *Keane* [1994] 1 W.L.R. 746, C.A.

207. [1997] 3 All E.R. 769, H.L.

tackers and that neither had been the defendant. In cross-examination the prosecution put it to Gordon that he had made a statement to the police (which had not been disclosed to the defence) to the effect that he had been too drunk to remember where the defendant had been. It was put to Pinnock that he had earlier made a statement (disclosed to the defence) implicating the defendant, but had withdrawn it telling the police (and this had not been disclosed) that he had been threatened. The defendant was convicted, and appealed arguing (*inter alia*) that the non-disclosures had undermined the fairness of the trial. The House of Lords held that there was no duty to disclose material which neither undermined the prosecution case nor assisted the defence case, but instead tended to compromise the credibility of potential defence witnesses. It was the responsibility of the defence to make sufficient inquiries to enable it to assess the credibility of its witnesses, and accordingly decide whether to call them.

Defence Disclosure. Within 14 days of the prosecution making its primary disclosure to the defence *in relation to a trial on indictment*, the defence must present a written statement, in general terms, of the nature of the defence (including particulars of any alibi) and the matters on which the defence intends to join issue with the prosecution, with reasons.[208] In deciding how full the statement should be, the defence must balance the natural desire not to give away more information than necessary against the advantages which can be gained from relatively full disclosure. These advantages flow from the prosecutor's duty of secondary disclosure in the light of the defence statement.

This may force the defence to provide information which may enable the prosecution to strengthen its case, breaching the principle that the prosecution must prove its own case. Sprack[209] gives the example of a charge of assault where the accused will claim self-defence, but at the close of the prosecution case the evidence has not established that the defendant struck a blow. The defence submits that there is no case to answer before presenting its evidence. If the prosecution could use the defence statement to establish that the defendant accepted that he had struck a blow, the principle that the burden of proof lies on the prosecution would have been breached. However, Sprack points out that the prosecution could not use the statement in that way unless it could be established that it had been made by the defendant rather than his legal advisers, and should be admitted notwithstanding its hearsay nature. Overcoming the first hurdle may be difficult, and overcoming the second impossible, since the confession exception to the hearsay rule in England and Wales applies only to statements adverse to the person who made it at the time when it was made.[210] A defence statement of this sort would not have been adverse at the time it was made, but would only become adverse at the time when the defence wanted to make a submission of no case. It therefore ought not to be admissible.

In Relation to a Summary Trial, section 6 of the 1996 Act provides that the defence may deliver a defence statement but is not compelled to do so. If they do, the prosecutor comes under a duty to make secondary disclosure.

---

208. Criminal Procedure and Investigations Act 1996, section 5; Criminal Procedure and Investigations Act 1996 (Defence Disclosure Time Limits) Regulations 1997.

209. John Sprack, *Emmins on Criminal Procedure*, 7th ed. (London: Blackstone Press, 1997), p 127-129.

210. Police and Criminal Evidence Act 1984, section 82(1), as interpreted in *R.* v. *Sat- Bhambra* (1988) 88 Cr. App. R. 55, C.A.

The Duty of Secondary Prosecution Disclosure. Whenever the defence makes disclosure, the prosecution must disclose as soon as reasonably practicable any material not already disclosed which, objectively, "might reasonably be expected to assist" the defence disclosed by the defence statement.[211] Paragraph 8.2 of the Code of Practice requires the disclosure officer to re-examine the retained material and draw the prosecutor's attention to anything which might reasonably be expected to assist the defence case as disclosed in the statement. Thereafter, the prosecutor remains under a duty as the case proceeds to review the disclosure requirement in the light of developments.[212]

The duty of disclosure does not apply to anything which has been intercepted under a warrant issued by the Home Secretary under the Interception of Communications Act 1985 (which was intended to avoid such material being used as evidence: see above), or which it would not be in the public interest to disclose. The court, rather than the prosecutor, has final responsibility for deciding whether disclosure of prosecution material is in the public interest. Applications to the court for an order that material be not disclosed are sometimes *inter partes* and sometimes *ex parte*, depending on the degree of sensitivity of the material in question. There are even certain exceptional situations in which the prosecution need not notify the defence that an application not to disclose on the ground of the public interest has been made, for example where even to reveal to the defence the category of material in question would effectively reveal what the prosecution claims it would not be in the public interest to reveal.[213] All this makes the fair treatment of defendants in some cases heavily dependent on the court's sense of fair play, which is in turn dependent on the prosecutor's sense of fairness and the discovery officer's conscientiousness and acuity.

B. Trial

1. Nature of Trial and Tribunal

First instance criminal trials take place in magistrates' courts, the Crown Court, or youth courts, the constitutions of which are outlined in section 5 below, "Judges and magistrates." Criminal trials are essentially adversarial, but the prosecution is required to present the case against the accused in a fair and objective way. The prosecution must normally establish all elements of the offence beyond reasonable doubt, and although the burden of proof is reversed in relation to some issues (the accused may bear the burden of proof on the balance of probabilities in relation to any special defenses which he pleads) he is not generally required to help the prosecution or to prove his own innocence. The procedures vary, however, depending on the court in which the trial is taking place.

211. Criminal Procedure and Investigations Act 1996, s section 7, 13(7).
212. Criminal Procedure and Investigations Act 1996, section 9.
213. *R.* v. *Davis* [1993] 2 All E.R. 643, C.A.

2. *Defendant's Rights*

Under common law and Article 6 of the European Convention on Human Rights the defendant has a general right to a fair trial.[214] This generates a number of more specific rights, of which the main ones are as follows.

The accused has the right not be subjected to proceedings which are an abuse of the process of the court, either because the defendant's fundamental rights have been flouted, or because delay has made it difficult for the defendant to have a fair trial, or because a trial would be contrary to the public interest in the integrity of the justice system.[215] Proceedings were stayed on these grounds when a defendant had allegedly been forcibly brought within the jurisdiction in disregard of relevant extradition rules,[216] and where the prosecution sought to renege on indications that no evidence would be offered against a defendant or that no proceedings would be brought.[217] In *Latif*, a stay was refused where the accused had been entrapped by customs officers, since he was a leading heroin smuggler and the judge had properly weighed "the public interest in ensuring that those that are charged with grave crimes should be tried and the competing public interest in not conveying the impression that the court will adopt the approach that the end justifies any means."[218]

The right to an impartial tribunal leads to strict controls on pre-trial publicity. It is a contempt of court for the press or anyone else to publish anything at any time which is likely to cause substantial prejudice or impede the proceedings. Once proceedings are active, this is an offence of strict liability.[219] Exceptionally prejudicial pre-trial publicity may lead to the quashing of any conviction.[220]

At trial, the right to an impartial tribunal entitled the accused, in a trial on indictment, to a randomly selected jury,[221] although he or the prosecution may challenge for cause (peremptory challenges having been abolished by the Criminal Justice Act 1988, section 118). Grounds for challenge are effectively restricted to (a) ineligibility or disqualification and (b) reasonable suspicion of bias. In addition, the

---

214. See Jeremy McBride, *The Continuing Refinement of Criminal Due Process* (1997) 22 European Law Review HRC/1-HRC/16.

215. See generally *Bennett* v. *Horseferry Road Magistrates' Court* [1994] 1 A.C. 42, H.L.; Andrew L.-T. Choo, *Abuse of Process and Judicial Stays of Criminal Proceedings* (Oxford: Clarendon Press, 1993); Andrew L.-T. Choo, *Halting Criminal Prosecutions: The Abuse of Process Doctrine Revisited* [1995] Crim. L.R. 864-874. The law on this subject is still evolving: *R.* v. *Martin* [1998] 1 All E.R. 193, H.L.

216. *Bennett* v. *Horseferry Road Magistrates' Court* [1994] 1 A.C. 42, H.L.

217. *R.* v. *Bloomfield* [1996] 1 Cr. App. R. 135, C.A.; *R.* v. *Townsend, Dearsley and Bretscher* []1998] Crim. L.R. 126, C.A.

218. *R.* v. *Latif and Shahzad* [1996] 1 W.L.R. 104, H.L., at p. 113 *per* Lord Steyn.

219. Contempt of Court Act 1981, section 2 and Sch. 1. For discussion, see C. J. Miller, *Contempt of Court* 2nd ed. (Oxford: Clarendon Press, 1989); N. V. Lowe and B. E. Sufrin, *Borrie and Lowe's Contempt of Court* 3rd ed. (London: Butterworths, 1995); Feldman, *Civil Liberties and Human Rights in England and Wales*, p 749-765.

220. *R. v. McCann* (1991) 92 Cr. App. R. 239, C.A.; *R. v. Taylor and Taylor* (1994) 98 Cr. App. R. 361, C.A.; D. J. Feldman and C. J. Miller *The Press, Contempt and Judicial Review* (1997) 113 L.Q.R. 36-40.

221. See Juries Act 1974.

prosecution (but not the defendant) may require a juror to "stand by for the Crown." In effect this gives the prosecution a peremptory challenge, although the Attorney-General has directed that the power is to be exercised rarely, and mainly in national security cases or (with the agreement of the defence) if a juror is obviously unsuitable.[222] If grounds subsequently appear for thinking that there is a real likelihood of bias, a conviction will be quashed.[223] In the case of a magistrates' court, one example of this occurs where the clerk retires with the magistrates when they leave court to consider their verdict, except for the limited purpose of advising them on difficult questions of law.[224]

The defendant has a right to counsel, subject to the proviso that the accused must pay for counsel if he does not obtain legal aid, on which see section III,B,3, below. There is a breach of Article 6 ECHR if representation is denied in enforcement proceedings where the ultimate sanction is loss of liberty.[225]

As explained in section IIIA5 above, the defendant has a right to disclosure of material held by the prosecution which might undermine the prosecution's case, balanced by a duty to disclose certain information about his own case. This is an aspect of the fairness principle which the European Court of Human Rights has called "equality of arms."

The defendant is generally entitled to be present at the examination of all witnesses, including hearings to determine whether a witness is competent to testify.[226] Subject to special rules on child witnesses (see section III.B.4 below), the court may hear evidence in the absence of the accused only if his own behaviour makes it impracticable to continue the trial if he is present, or he is too ill to attend but is legally represented and has agreed to evidence being given in his absence, or (in the case of a trial on indictment) he has improperly absented himself from the proceedings.[227]

After a verdict has been given and subject to the outcome of any appeal, nobody may be tried twice for the same offence, and the pleas of *autrefois convict* and *autrefois acquit* are available.

3. *Availability of Legal Assistance and Role of Counsel*

Legal advice and assistance is readily available to defendants who can afford to pay for it themselves. Members of the Bar have an ethical obligation to accept any brief in a case in which they are free to act and where a fee can be agreed. This is facilitated by ensuring that, even where the defendant's assets are frozen by a restraint order in connection with recovery of proceeds of crime, the order is normally relaxed to allow payment of reasonable legal expenses. In some situations legal advice or assistance is available to defendants at the State's expense, mainly

---

222. See *Attorney-General's Guidelines on Exercise by the Crown of its Right of Stand- by*, published at (1989) 88 Cr. App. R. 123.

223. *R.* v. *Gough* [1993] A.C. 646, H.L.

224. *R.* v. *Guildford JJ., ex parte Harding* (1981) 145 J.P. 174.

225. *Benham* v. *UK*, (1996) 22 E.H.R.R. 293, Eur. Ct. H.R.

226. For magistrates' courts see Magistrates' Courts Act 1980, section 4(3). For trials on indictment, see *Lawrence* v. *R.* [1933] A.C. 699, P.C., at 708.

227. Magistrates' Courts Act 1980, section 4(4); *R.* v. *Howson* (1982) 74 Cr. App. R. 172, C.A; *R.* v. *Lee Kun* [1916] 1 K.B. 337; *R.* v. *Jones (No. 2)* [1972] 1 W.L.R. 887, C.A..

through the legal aid scheme. Under the "green form" scheme the Legal Aid Fund pays a solicitor for a small amount of preparatory advice and assistance to the accused, who may have to make a means-tested contribution to the cost. Often the assistance will include preparing an application for legal aid.

Full legal aid by way of representation is granted by the court before which a person is to appear, if it appears to the court to be "desirable to do so in the interests of justice."[228] The court takes account of the seriousness of the consequences which the accused could face if convicted, the significance and complexity of any issues of law, the difficulties which are likely to be faced in investigating the case on his behalf, the ability of the defendant to represent himself, and the risk that a witness might be seriously distressed if forced to be cross-examined by the defendant in person.[229] In some cases legal aid must be granted: where the defendant is committed for trial on a charge of murder, or has already been remanded in custody without representation and is in danger of further remand in custody, or is remanded in custody following conviction for pre-sentence reports to be prepared, or has appealed successfully to the Court of Appeal but that court has granted leave for the prosecution to appeal to the House of Lords.

The effect of a legal aid order is that the State, through the Legal Aid Fund, will bear the reasonable costs of the defence, where the defendant's disposable capital and income are such that he requires assistance in paying them,[230] subject to (a) any limits set down in the order on the type of representation or the type of proceedings which it covers, and (b) any means-tested contribution which the defendant may be required to make. The defendant will normally be allowed to use a solicitor of his choice who will be named in the legal aid order. Sometimes (for example, if there is a highly complex issue of fact or law to be argued) a magistrates' court will grant legal aid for solicitor and counsel, but usually it is allowed for solicitor only. Legal aid in the Crown Court is nearly always for counsel, since solicitors' rights of audience in the Crown Court are very limited.

Where an unrepresented defendant at a magistrates' court has not yet been granted legal aid, a duty solicitor (a private practitioner) can offer advice and claim a fee from the Legal Aid Board.[231] The duty solicitor may also apply for legal aid for the defendant, or make a plea in mitigation or an application for bail, at public expense. In enforcement proceedings where the defendant is at risk of imprisonment, the duty solicitor may represent him, or full representation on legal aid may be obtained.[232] More extensive representation is available by way of an application for legal aid.

4. *Witnesses (Including Expert Witnesses)*

Both prosecution and defence can compel, by summons or subpoena, the attendance of competent and compellable witnesses whose evidence is likely to be

---

228. Legal Aid Act 1988, section 21(2).

229. Legal Aid Act 1988, section 22(2).

230. Sometimes one court can grant legal aid for an appearance before another court. See generally Legal Aid Act 1988, s section 20, 21(5).

231. See Legal Advice and Assistance Regulations 1989 (SI 1989 No 340).

232. Legal Aid and Advice (Amendment) Regulations 1997, introduced in response to the decision of the European Court of Human Rights in *Benham* v. *UK*, above.

relevant. Failure to appear or to answer questions without lawful excuse is punishable as a contempt of court.

The principle of open justice normally entails that witnesses shall give evidence in open court, and that all details of their evidence and identity shall be publishable.[233] However, there are a number of restrictions on this. Some relate to child witnesses, considered below. The other main exceptions to the principle are as follows. First, evidence can be given by written statements if a witness is too frightened of victimization to give evidence in court.[234] Secondly, witnesses are allowed in exceptional circumstances to give evidence anonymously or to provide answers in writing, or to give evidence from behind a screen using voice-distortion equipment, if there would otherwise be a threat to their safety and the arrangements do not unduly prejudice the defendant, balancing the needs of the witnesses against the demands of fairness.[235] Thirdly, there are powers to make orders postponing publication of some evidence presented in open court to prevent a fair trial being prejudiced,[236] and to prohibit publication to protect children from publicity,[237] or to ensure that the objects of allowing witnesses to give evidence anonymously are not thwarted.[238] It is an offence to publish matter likely to lead to the identification of a complainant in a rape case without a court order.[239] Fourthly, courts have power to sit *in camera* where justice could not be done sitting in public.[240] The power is rarely exercised, most commonly in cases involving national security. It must not be exercised merely to save embarrassment to witnesses or parties.[241] When a court sits in private, publication of the details presented may be contempt of court.[242]

Competence and Compellability of Witnesses. The general rule is that anyone is both a competent and a compellable witness, but there are some special qualifications to that principle. The defendant is competent but not compellable.[243] However, if a defendant who is over 14 years old and mentally capable has not given evidence at the conclusion of his defence, the court must draw his attention to the fact that he is permitted to give evidence and that adverse inferences may be drawn if he does not. If the defendant still declines to give evidence, the court or jury "may draw such inferences as appear proper from the failure of the accused to give evidence or his refusal, without good cause, to answer any question."[244] Such infer-

233. *Scott* v. *Scott* [1913] A.C. 417, H.L.; Feldman, *Civil Liberties and Human Rights*, p. 765-781.

234. Criminal Justice Act 1988, section 23.

235. See *Attorney-General* v. *Leveller Magazine* [1979] A.C. 440, H.L.; *R.* v. *Watford Magistrates' Court, ex parte Lenman* [1993] Crim. L.R. 388, D.C.; *R.* v. *Taylor* [1994] T.L.R. 484, C.A,; Gilbert Marcus, *Secret Witnesses* [1990] P.L. 207-223.

236. Contempt of Court Act 1981, section 4.

237. Children and Young Persons Act 1933, section 39 as amended.

238. Contempt of Court Act 1981, section 11. See Clive Walker, Ian Cram and Debra Brogarth, *The Reporting of Crown Court Proceedings and the Contempt of Court Act 1981* (1992) 55 M.L.R. 647-669.

239. Sexual Offences (Amendment) Act 1976, section 4, as amended by Criminal Justice Act 1988, section 158.

240. *Scott* v. *Scott* [1913] A.C. 417, H.L.

241. *R.* v. *Reigate Justices, ex parte Argus Newspapers Ltd.* (1983) 147 J.P. 385, D.C.; *R.* v. *Malvern Justices, ex parte Evans* [1988] Q.B. 540, D.C.

242. Administration of Justice Act 1960, section 12.

243. Criminal Evidence Act 1898, section 1 as amended.

244. Criminal Justice and Public Order Act 1994, section 35.

ences are a matter for the jury, and only exceptionally should a judge remove the matter from their consideration.[245] A defendant giving evidence formerly had to do so before other evidence was called on his behalf, but now the court may allow him to give evidence later.[246]

The Spouse of the Accused is usually both a competent and a compellable witness for the accused, unless they are jointly accused and the spouse whom the co-accused intends to call is still liable to be convicted, in which case she is neither competent nor compellable. A spouse is usually competent to give evidence on behalf of the prosecution or a co-defendant of the accused spouse. However, a spouse is compellable at the instance of the prosecution or a co-accused if and only if the defendant is charged with an offence involving assault on, or injury or threat of injury to, the spouse or someone under the age of 16, or with a sexual offence alleged to have been committed against a person under the age of 16, or with attempting or conspiring to commit, or aiding and abetting etc. the commission of, such an offence. A former spouse who is no longer married to the accused is both competent and compellable as if they had never been married. When giving evidence for or against a spouse, the witness can disclose communications between husband and wife and give evidence as to marital sexual intercourse.[247]

Child Witnesses form a special category, both as to their competence and as to the arrangements for taking their testimony in certain cases. In relation to competence, the Pigot Committee in 1989 recommended that, in place of the previous rules on competence, children under 14 should only give evidence unsworn, but their evidence should be admissible unless the judge considers that they are of unsound mind, incoherent, or incapable of communicating sensibly.[248] The current law gives effect to this recommendation, adding that a deposition of the child's unsworn evidence should be treated as if it had been given on oath.[249] The Pigot Committee stressed the importance of minimizing the stress suffered by young witnesses, particularly in cases of child abuse or domestic violence. To this end, current arrangements represent a compromise between the need to protect children and facilitate the conviction of child abusers and the right of an accused to a fair trial. In cases concerning assault, injury or threat of injury, cruelty to children or sexual abuse involving children, a videotaped interview between the child witness and an adult (who may be a police officer or social worker rather than a lawyer) is to be admissible as the child's evidence-in-chief, as long as the child is available at court for cross-examination, the prosecution has disclosed appropriate details of the circumstances in which the recording was made, and the judge does not feel that admitting it would be contrary to the interests of justice.[250] This puts a heavy responsibility on those conducting interviews without legal training to ensure that

---

245. *R.* v. *Cowan* [1995] 4 All E.R. 939, C.A.; *R.* v. *Condron* [1997] Crim. L.R. 215, C.A.; *R.* v. *Argent* [1997] Crim. L.R. 346, C.A.; Rosemary Pattenden, *Inferences From Silence* [1995] Crim. L.R. 602-611; Peter Mirfield, "Two side effects of sections 34 to 37 of the Criminal Justice and Public Order Act 1994" [1995] *Crim. L.R.* 612-624.

246. PACE, section 79.

247. PACE, section 80.

248. *Report of the Advisory Group on Video Evidence* (1989).

249. Criminal Justice Act 1988, section 33A, inserted by Criminal Justice Act 1991, section 52 and amended by Schedule 9 to the Criminal Justice and Public Order Act 1994.

250. Criminal Justice Act 1988, section 32A, as inserted by Criminal Justice Act 1991, section 54, and amended by Criminal Justice and Public Order Act 1994 and Criminal Procedure and Investigations Act 1996.

they do not "lead" their child witnesses. Several trials have collapsed because the interview techniques have produced evidence held to be unreliable and unfair to defendants.[251]

A child witness who gives evidence in chief or is to be cross-examined following the admission of evidence on video-tape may use a live closed-circuit television link from outside the court, to avoid the stress caused by the formal atmosphere and having to confront the alleged abuser.[252] A defendant representing himself is not permitted to cross-examine such a witness.[253] Only his legal representative may do so. Because a court cannot compel a defendant to accept representation, an unrepresented defendant is thus deprived of the opportunity to cross-examine an important witness. The court also has a general discretion to take steps to make giving evidence less stressful for vulnerable witnesses, particularly children, subject to the overriding requirement for a fair trial for both the accused and the prosecution. For example, where such a witness is giving evidence in court rather than by television link, the judge may allow her to give evidence from behind a screen so that the defendant cannot see or be seen by her,[254] and to be comforted by a social worker if she becomes distressed during her evidence.[255]

Expert Witnesses form a special category, particularly as scientific evidence becomes more important. The freedom of witnesses whom a court accepts as experts to give evidence as to their opinions carries with it responsibilities.[256] There is as yet no systematic accreditation of expert witnesses. The prosecution and defence each pay for their own experts. This gives an advantage to the prosecution so far as greater resources allow them access to particularly experienced experts. A study for the Royal Commission on Criminal Justice[257] illustrated the uses which are made of experts by prosecution and defence, and the reluctance of each side to allow pretrial dialogue between experts on each side. The Commission recommended that there should be far more effort before trial to produce agreed expert opinions, but this has not been implemented. The main requirement is that any party intending to introduce expert evidence of opinion or fact in a trial on indictment (but not summary trial) must disclose a statement of the evidence to be led and the test results, etc., on which it is based. If this is not done, the evidence will not be admissible without the leave of the trial court.[258]

5. *Judges and Magistrates: Role, Selection and Training*

In a summary trial, the bench of magistrates acts as the trier of both fact and law, as well as presiding over the proceedings and, after a conviction, imposing sen-

251. See in a civil context *Re N (a minor) (sexual abuse: video evidence)* [1996] 4 All E.R. 225, C.A.

252. Criminal Justice Act 1988, section 32(1)(b). Under section 32(1)(a), there is also a limited power to take evidence from abroad by live television link in serious cases.

253. Criminal Justice Act 1988, section 34A, inserted by Criminal Justice Act 1991, section 54(7).

254. See, *e.g.*, *R.* v. *X, Y and Z* (1989) 91 Cr. App. R. 36, C.A.

255. *R.* v. *Smith* [1994] Crim. L.R. 458, C.A.

256. See *Andrews and Hirst on Criminal Evidence* 3rd ed., ch. 21.

257. Paul Roberts and Chris Willmore, *The Role of Forensic Science Evidence in Criminal Proceedings*, Research Series No. 11 (London: H.M.S.O., 1993).

258. Crown Court (Advance Notice of Expert Evidence) Rules 1987, made under the provisions of PACE, section 81; *Andrews and Hirst on Criminal Evidence*, p. 158.

tence. Magistrates are appointed by commission for a particular commission area (normally a county), and the jurisdiction of magistrates' courts in relation to summary trials is, in the absence of legislation conferring special powers, limited to offences alleged to have been committed within that area. Justices of the peace must live within 15 miles of the county in which they serve. There are two kinds of magistrates. Most are "lay," i.e. not legally qualified (otherwise known as justices of the peace), who are unpaid and part-time. They sit in panels of at least two and usually three, and are advised on matters of law by their clerk, who is a qualified barrister or solicitor. There are about 30,000 active lay magistrates in England and Wales,[259] appointed on the advice of local advisory committees by the Lord Chancellor, on behalf of (and "in the name of") the Queen.[260] Members of the public and organisations such as political parties, trades unions, or Chambers of Commerce can propose people for appointment. It is increasingly regarded as important to try to ensure that benches are representative of their local communities in terms of gender, age and ethnic balance. However, this is made difficult by the fact that the training provided for magistrates and the commitment to sitting regularly (at least 26 times per year) tend to rule out people who are self-employed or have inflexible jobs. Within a year of appointment the new magistrate must undergo a training course organised by the Magistrates' Courts Committee for their area. This includes an introduction to judicial behaviour, the main rules of law, evidence and sentencing, the problems typically faced in magistrates' courts, and the work of others in the criminal justice system, with visits to courts and penal institutions.

Secondly, there are stipendiary magistrates, who are qualified barristers or solicitors of at least seven years standing. They are appointed by the Queen on the recommendation of the Lord Chancellor.[261] They usually sit full-time (although there are some part-time acting stipendiaries), and hold what is in effect a minor judgeship, mostly in metropolitan areas. They normally sit alone.

The Crown Court, where trials on indictment are heard, is a single national court, but sits in more than 90 centres simultaneously. It has jurisdiction over indictable and triable-either-way offences committed anywhere in England and Wales, and may have its jurisdiction extended by statute to include certain offences alleged to have been committed abroad, such as treason or war crimes. It also sentences defendants whom magistrates' courts have committed for sentence, and hears appeals from decisions of magistrates' courts.

In a trial on indictment, the jury is the trier of fact. The judge determines all questions of law and procedure, including issues relating to the admissibility or exclusion of evidence, and has an overriding duty to secure fairness between prosecutor and accused. He decides on any submission that there is no case to answer or no sufficient case to be left to a jury: over half the acquittals in the Crown Court are judge ordered or directed.[262] He is also responsible for the efficient dispatch of business. However, this does not entitle him to hector witnesses (particularly the defendant when giving evidence) or to interfere too intrusively with the way in

259. Sprack, *Emmins on Criminal Procedure* 7th ed., p. 77.

260. Justices of the Peace Act 1997, section 5; Sprack, *Emmins*, p. 78.

261. Justices of the Peace Act 1997, s section 11, 16.

262. See John Baldwin, *Understanding Judge Ordered and Directed Acquittals in the Crown Court* [1997] Crim. L.R. 536-555, citing *Judicial Statistics England and Wales for the year 1995*, Cm. 3290 (London: The Stationery Office, 1996), Table 6.10.

which counsel conduct the case. Such behaviour is likely to lead to a successful appeal, as undermining the fairness of the proceedings.[263] If the judge is perceived as descending into the arena, it threatens the appearance (if not the reality) of fairness. Any pressure brought to bear on the defendant to drop the defence is likely to vitiate a conviction, so sentence bargaining is deprecated. For example, it is not proper for the judge to tell counsel in chambers that a guilty plea would lead to a lenient sentence.[264] Nor should a judge indicate his view, after the defendant's examination-in-chief, that almost all hope of an acquittal had gone and that it would have gone completely once the defendant was cross-examined,[265] as this is likely to make it difficult for the defendant to do himself justice during cross-examination.

The division of functions between judge and jury leads to a more formal procedure than is found in magistrates' courts. In England and Wales, the judge sums up the facts as well as the law to the jury at the end of presentations by counsel. The jury is told to disregard any indication which the judge might seem to give of his view of the evidence, but the freedom to comment on evidence allows the judge to "steer" the jury in a particular direction (although too obvious a steer may lead to reversal on appeal).

Judges who are entitled to preside over trials on indictment are of three kinds. First, there are recorders and assistant recorders. These are practitioners (either barristers or solicitors) who are appointed as part-time judges to sit in the Crown Court. They are expected to sit for at least forty days per year, and preside over 3% of Crown Court trials.[266] For many of them, appointment as recorder represents a probationary period during which they undergo courses organised by the Judicial Studies Board (including ethnic awareness courses) and their performance on the bench is monitored by the Lord Chancellor's Department. If they are considered to have done well, they will be considered for permanent judicial appointments, typically as circuit judges or High Court judges. Secondly, there are circuit judges. These are full-time appointees who can sit on either civil (county court) or criminal (Crown Court) business. They preside over 77% of Crown Court trials.[267] They will have served time as recorders or assistant recorders, and will continue to attend Judicial Studies Board programmes. Thirdly, there are judges of the High Court ("puisne" judges) who preside over the most serious 3% or so of cases in the Crown Court.[268] These are appointed by the Queen on the advice of the Lord Chancellor from among the ranks of barristers (who will need, in practice, to have sat as part-time judges - assistant recorders, recorders, and deputy high court judges) and circuit judges, some of whom have practiced as solicitors rather than barristers.[269]

---

263. See e.g. *R.* v. *Halusi* (1973) 58 Cr. App. R. 378, C.A.; *R.* v. *Whybrow*, *The Times*, 14 February 1994, C.A. (full text available from Lexis).

264. *R.* v. *Turner* [1970] 2 Q.B. 321, C.A.

265. *R.* v. *Alves* [1996] Crim. L.R. 599, C.A.

266. Lord Chancellor's Department, *Judicial Statistics England and Wales for the year 1996*, Cm. 3716, p. 63.

267. *Judicial Statistics England and Wales for the year 1996*, p. 63. The conditions for eligibility for appointment as assistant recorder, recorder, and circuit judge are set out in the Courts Act 1971, section 16 as amended.

268. *Judicial Statistics England and Wales for the year 1996*, p. 63. There are also deputy circuit judges and deputy High Court judges, who between them preside over 1% of Crown Court trials: *ibid.*

269. Details of the criteria of eligibility for appointment are contained in the Supreme Court Act 1981, section 10, as amended by Courts and Legal Services Act 1990.

The Youth Court is less formal than a magistrates' court. It consists of magistrates who are selected for their special suitability to deal with such cases, who then receive special training. A stipendiary magistrate should not normally sit alone in a youth court. Juveniles (defendants who are less than 18 years old) must be tried summarily in a youth court, unless (a) they are charged with homicide, for which trial on indictment is mandatory, or one of a small number of serious offences and the magistrates consider that he could properly be sentenced to detention for a period similar to that which would be imposed on an adult offender, or (b) they are charged jointly with an adult, or the offence is linked to that of an adult, and the magistrates consider that it to be in the interests of justice that all the defendants should be tried by the same adult court.[270] The public are excluded from youth court sittings, although the press may attend.[271] The press are not permitted to publish anything by which juveniles might be identified.[272]

6. Victims' Rights

With a few special exceptions, outlined below, the general approach to victims has been to set standards of treatment which victims should be able to expect, rather than to create legal rights. Following the adoption by the U.N. General Assembly in 1985 of a *Declaration of General Principles of Justice for the Victims of Crime and Abuse of Power*, the Home Office first published a *Victim's Charter* in 1990. In 1994, it was linked to the *Citizen's Charter* programme, with Charters for a wide variety of public services, which Prime Minister John Major initiated in 1991. The Charters generally establish standards of service and legitimate expectations for users of services. A revised version of the *Victim's Charter* was published in 1996 as part of that programme. *Inter alia*, it sets out the considerations to be borne in mind by police officers and court staff when in contact with victims, and has led to some retraining of officers and staff. It also gives an apparently unqualified undertaking that, if the victim makes a statement to the police about the impact of the offence on him, that will be taken into account by the police, Crown Prosecution Service, magistrates and judge in making decisions. It operates alongside the *Charter for Court Users* (originally the 1993 *Courts Charter*, revised in 1995) which describes the standards of service which victims (among others) can expect at court. However, neither Charter confers legal rights.[273] The reliance on these non-statutory, extra-legal Charters has been criticized by groups like Victim Support, which favour conferring enforceable rights on victims to ensure that the legal system does not add insult to the injury already inflicted on them by the crime.[274] Standards set out in the Charters might give rise to legitimate expectations which could, in appropriate circumstances, be enforced by way of judicial review proceedings. They also now fall within the jurisdiction of the Parliamentary Commissioner for Administration (Ombudsman), who can investigate complaints of injustice caused by mal-administration and recommend compensation.

---

270. See Magistrates' Courts Act 1980, section 24, and Children and Young Persons Act 1933, s section 46 and 53(2); Children and Young Persons Act 1963, section 18.

271. Children and Young Persons Act 1933, section 47.

272. Children and Young Persons Act 1933, section 49.

273. See Helen Fenwick, *Rights of Victims in the Criminal Justice Process: Rhetoric or Reality?* [1995] Crim. L.R. 843-853; Helen Fenwick, *Procedural 'Rights' of Victims of Crime: Public or Private Ordering of the Criminal Justice Process?* (1997) 60 M.L.R. 317-333.

274. *The Rights of Victims of Crime* (London: Victim Support, 1995).

Decision to Prosecute. Under the Code for Crown Prosecutors the impact on victims is one of the public-interest factors to be considered in deciding whether to prosecute a suspect: see section III.A above. The *Victim's Charter* promises that the victim's views will be taken into account. If aggrieved by a decision not to prosecute, he may be able to challenge it by way of an application to the High Court for judicial review. It has been held (on questionable grounds)[275] that where the Attorney-General's consent to prosecution is required his decision is not amenable to judicial review.[276] However, the decisions of other prosecuting agencies, such as the Director of Public Prosecutions, for whom the Attorney-General has political responsibility,[277] the Crown Prosecution Service, and the Inland Revenue Commissioners, are reviewable, although the review power is used sparingly unless the agency has refused to apply their own prosecution guidelines.[278]

Victims as Witnesses. At trial, the victim may have to give evidence. On special arrangements allowing vulnerable witnesses to give evidence in the least stressful way possible see section III.B.4 above.

Sentencing. At the sentencing stage, the Court of Appeal held in *Attorney-General's Reference (No. 2 of 1995)*[279] that the judge could properly receive evidence of the impact which the offence had on the victim. However, the victim has no right to give testimony or present a victim impact statement orally. Some commentators consider that allowing the victim to intervene in that way threatens to introduce subjectivity and arbitrariness into the sentencing process, undermining the due-process rights of the accused and potentially violating his rights under Article 6 of the ECHR.[280] The effects of the offence on the victim may be put before the court by the prosecutor, but are admissible only if contained in a witness statement or deposition which has already been served on the defence and included in the judges' papers. The prosecutor should avoid prejudicially emotive language.[281] If the defence disagrees with factual statements made by the prosecution, the judge must either hear evidence and determine the issue himself or adopt the approach most favourable to the defendant.[282] It is generally considered inappropriate to subject the victim to the cross-examination which this sort of inquiry would entail.

Compensation. Following conviction, courts have power to make compensation orders requiring the defendant (or, in the case of a juvenile defendant, his par-

---

275. See D. J. Feldman and C. J. Miller, *The Law Officers, Contempt and Judicial Review* (1997) 113 L.Q.R. 36-40.

276. In *R.* v. *Attorney-General, ex parte Edey* (unreported, 26 February 1992, C.A., transcript available from Lexis), the Court of Appeal treated as binding the view of the majority in *Gouriet* where the applicant tried to challenge a decision by the Attorney-General not to prosecute for Sunday trading under the Shops Act 1950, section 47.

277. See J. Ll. J. Edwards, *The Attorney General, Politics and the Public Interest* (London: Sweet & Maxwell, 1984), ch. 2.

278. See e.g. *R.* v. *Director of Public Prosecutions, ex parte Chaudhary* [1994] C.O.D. 375, D.C.; cp. *R.* v. *Chief Constable of Kent, ex parte L* [1993] 1 All E.R. 756, D.C.; *R.* v. *I.R.C., ex parte Mead* [1993] 1 All E.R. 772, D.C.; *R.* v. *D.P.P., ex parte C* (1995) 7 A.L.R. 385, D.C.

279. [1996] 1 Cr. App. R. (S.) 274, C.A.

280. See e.g. Andrew Ashworth, *Victim Impact Statements and Sentencing* [1993] Crim. L.R. 498-509; Helen Fenwick, "Procedural 'rights'," above.

281. *R.* v. *Hobstaff* (1993) 14 Cr. App. R. (S.) 632, C.A.

282. *R.* v. *Newton* (1982) 77 Cr. App. R. 13, C.A.

ents[283]) to compensate the victim for personal injury, loss or damage resulting from the offence.[284] The compensation is limited to £5,000 in the magistrates' court but has no statutory limit in the Crown Court.[285] In either court, the order should not be made for a larger amount than the defendant is reasonably able to pay,[286] and usually demands payment by installments rather than a lump sum. These orders are intended to offer a simple and (to the victim) free alternative to civil proceedings in straightforward cases where civil liability is clear. Criminal courts will not embark on an investigation of complex and disputed questions of fact and civil law: in such circumstances, the victim must resort to civil action against the defendant and, where personal injuries have been suffered, apply the state compensation fund under the Criminal Injuries Compensation Scheme.

C. Appeals

The Appeal Structure depends on the court of first instance. Grounds of Appeal are explained here in relation to each type of appeal.

a. *Appeals From Magistrates' Courts to the Crown Court.* This is the normal route of appeal: there were nearly 19,000 such appeals in 1996, with a total or partial success rate of just under 44%.[287] A defendant who has been convicted (but not the prosecution) has a right of appeal to the Crown Court against either conviction or sentence. One who pled guilty may appeal against sentence only[288] unless the Crown Court accepts that the plea was not a genuine admission of guilt. This may occur if the plea was equivocal, or was entered under duress.[289] An appeal against conviction takes the form of a full re-hearing of the case before a circuit judge or recorder and two lay magistrates (without a jury).[290] At an appeal against sentence, the sentencing stage of the first-instance hearing is reprised in full. The court may confirm, reverse or vary the decision of the magistrates, remit the case to the magistrates, or make such other order as it thinks just.[291] This means that the defendant runs the risk that the sentence may be increased:[292] while the House of Lords has taken the view that it is improper for an administrative agency, without an express statutory power, to increase the effective length of a sentence imposed by a judicial

283. Children and Young Persons Act 1969, section 55.

284. Powers of Criminal Courts Act 1973, s section 35, 37, as amended by Criminal Justice Act 1982, section 67 and Criminal Justice Act 1988, s section 104, 105.

285. The Magistrates' Association has issued guidelines on the fairly modest awards which might be considered appropriate compensation for personal injuries.

286. *R.* v. *Huish* (1985) 7 Cr. App. R. (S.) 272, C.A., imposing on the defence team a duty to satisfy themselves that any statement by the defendant about his means or ability to pay is correct before it is put before the court.

287. *Judicial Statistics England and Wales for the year 1996*, p. 67, Tables 6.13 and 6.14.

288. Magistrates' Courts Act 1980, section 108.

289. For example, in *R.* v. *Huntingdon Crown Court, ex parte Jordan* [1981] Q.B. 857, D.C., the accused had been jointly charged with her husband with shoplifting. After pleading guilty, she said that she could have defended herself on the ground that her husband had threatened her with violence to make her commit the offence, but was too frightened of reprisals by her husband to run the defence.

290. Supreme Court Act 1981, section 74.

291. Supreme Court Act 1981, section 48.

292. Supreme Court Act 1981, section 48, as amended by Criminal Justice Act 1988.

authority,[293] that does not apply to a court following a full judicial rehearing of the case. Whatever order the court makes should be supported by reasons showing how it has dealt with each contentious issue.[294]

Either the prosecution or the defendant may appeal to the High Court by way of case stated against the decision of the Crown Court, or apply to the High Court for judicial review of any ruling, on a matter not relating to trial on indictment.[295] There were only 31 such appeals in 1996.[296] The procedures are the same (*mutatis mutandis*) as apply in relation to appeals from and applications in respect of decisions of the magistrates' court to the High Court, described below.

b. *Appeals From Magistrates' Courts to the High Court.* Any party to proceedings who is aggrieved by any decision of a magistrates' court, including either a conviction or an acquittal, has a right of appeal to the High Court on the ground that it was either wrong in law or in excess of jurisdiction.[297] These cases are rare, only 166 such appeals were lodged in 1996.[298] The proceedings are by case stated: the magistrates "state a case" (i.e. set out in writing their findings of fact, their legal rulings, and their decision) for the opinion of the Divisional Court, which makes its decision on the law on the basis of the magistrates' findings of fact unless the appellant is arguing that there was no evidence on the basis of which the magistrates could have reached their conclusion. If the Court decides that the decision was wrong in law, it makes an appropriate order, which may involve remitting the case to the magistrates with a direction to acquit or convict. The appeal is usually heard by a panel of two or three judges sitting as the Divisional Court of Queen's Bench Division, although it can be dealt with by a single judge. The success rate for appellants in 1996 was nearly 45%.[299]

An alternative procedure for challenging a decision of a magistrates' court in the High Court on a question of law is the application for judicial review. This is not, technically, an appeal: it forms part of a civil rather than criminal suit for legal aid purposes, and the High Court cannot substitute its decision for that of the magistrates. Instead, it may, if appropriate, grant orders of certiorari to quash the impugned decision, mandamus to require the magistrates to act in accordance with the law, prohibition to stop them from acting unlawfully, a declaration that the decision is void, or issue an injunction (for example to restrain the enforcement of an unlawful decision). The grounds on which these remedies may be sought are that the decision was made without jurisdiction, vitiated by an error of law or procedural impropriety or unfairness, was so unreasonable in the circumstances that no reasonable court acting properly could have made it, or improperly disappointed the applicant's legitimate expectation.[300] Unlike an appeal by case stated, the ap-

---

293. *R.* v. *Secretary of State for the Home Department, ex parte Venables* [1997] 3 W.L.R. 23, H.L.; *R.* v. *Secretary of State for the Home Department, ex parte Pierson* [1997] 3 All E.R. 577, H.L.

294. *R.* v. *Harrow Crown Court, ex parte Dave* [1994] 1 W.L.R. 98, D.C.

295. Supreme Court Act 1981, section 28.

296. *Judicial Statistics England and Wales for the year 1996*, p. 17, Table 1.14.

297. Magistrates' Courts Act 1980, section 111.

298. Lord Chancellor's Department, *Judicial Statistics England and Wales for the year 1996*, Cm. 3716 (1997), p. 17, Table 1.14.

299. Ibid.

300. For a full treatment of judicial review, see Woolf, Jowell, *De Smith's Judicial Review of Administrative Action* 5th ed. (London: Sweet & Maxwell, 1995).

plicant need not ask the magistrates' court to state a case, but must obtain leave from the High Court to apply. The effects of the remedies which are available are, nevertheless, broadly the same as those following an appeal by case stated.[301]

Either party may appeal from the decision of the Divisional Court in a criminal cause or matter to the House of Lords on a point of law, but only if the Divisional Court certifies that the point of law is of general public importance and either the Divisional Court or the House of Lords grants leave to appeal. This is rare, there was only one such appeal in 1996.[302]

Appeals From the Crown Court in a Matter Relating to Trial on Indictment. The defendant may appeal to the Court of Appeal (Criminal Division) against conviction or sentence, but not as of right: he must either obtain a certificate from the trial or sentencing judge (which is very rarely granted) stating the case is fit for appeal, or be granted leave to appeal by the Court of Appeal.[303] Applications for leave are decided on the papers by a single judge, but an unsuccessful applicant may renew the application to the full court. Legal aid is rarely granted for an application for leave, so the grounds of appeal are often badly drafted. This makes it hard for the Court to identify cases in which there has been a miscarriage of justice.[304] Approximately one-quarter of applications for leave to appeal are successful, and of those appellants granted leave rather under one-third are successful in their appeals against conviction, although the success rate is considerably higher in appeals against sentence.[305]

Appeals against conviction must be heard by three judges, although appeals against sentence may be heard by two. The Court of Appeal must allow such an appeal "if they think that the conviction is unsafe."[306] This is treated as meaning that an appeal should be allowed if the court has a reasonable, or even a lurking, doubt as to the safety of the conviction.[307] It thus requires an overall assessment of the whole case against the appellant on matters of fact and law. Appellants usually seek to identify specific legal errors or procedural irregularities in the course of the trial as a basis for their appeals, such as the trial judge's errors of law or fact in summing up to the jury; misdirections on the onus or standard of proof; mistaken rulings on the admissibility of evidence; and excessive interference in the course of

301. For a comparison of the two procedures, see Sprack, *Emmins on Criminal Procedure*, p 454-455.

302. Administration of Justice Act 1960, section 1; *Judicial Statistics for England and Wales for the year 1996*, p. 10, Table 1.4.

303. Criminal Appeal Act 1968, section 1.

304. See Joyce Plotnikoff and Richard Woolfson, *Information and Advice for Prisoners about Grounds for Appeal and the Appeals Process*, Royal Commission on Criminal Justice Research Study No. 18 (London: H.M.S.O., 1993).

305. In 1996 there were 2,288 applications for leave to appeal against conviction and 6,436 for leave to appeal against sentence. The success rate in respect of applications for leave to appeal was under 25% in respect of both conviction and sentence. The success rate in substantive appeals against conviction was just under 29%, and that in appeals against sentence was nearly 70%: *Judicial Statistics England and Wales for the year 1996*, p. 12, Tables 1.7 and 1.8.

306. Criminal Appeal Act 1968, section 2(1) as amended by Criminal Appeal Act 1995. Before the amendment, the court had to consider whether the conviction was unsafe or unsatisfactory, or the trial judge had erred in law, or there had been a material irregularity in the trial. If any of these circumstances had occurred, the court had a discretion to affirm the conviction if satisfied that no miscarriage of justice had resulted.

307. See *R.* v. *Cooper* [1969] 1 Q.B. 267, C.A.; *Stafford* v. *D.P.P.* [1974] A.C. 878, especially *per* Lord Kilbrandon at 912.

the trial. Nevertheless, this is not essential: an appellant can simply argue that the overall effect of the trial was to produce an unsafe conviction. On the other hand, the court may find that the trial was legally or procedurally flawed yet still dismiss the appeal if satisfied that the error does not make the conviction unsafe. For example, in *R.* v. *Mills, R.* v. *Poole*,[308] the House of Lords held that the prosecution's refusal to disclose witness statements had been a material irregularity, but dismissed the appeal because they did not consider that it had made the convictions unsafe.

Attorney-General's References. As the prosecution cannot appeal from a decision of the Crown Court on a matter relating to trial on indictment, there used to be situations in which the prosecution felt that a ruling against it on a point of law had established a precedent[309] which could prejudice other prosecutions. The Criminal Justice Act 1972, section 36 therefore provided a procedure whereby, following an acquittal of an indictable offence, the Attorney-General can refer to the Court of Appeal any point of law which arose in the case for its opinion. Few cases are referred in this way (usually fewer than ten per year), but the procedure performs a useful function in clarifying the law without putting the particular defendant in renewed jeopardy.

Another form of Attorney-General's reference is, in effect, a prosecution appeal against a sentence which it considers to be unduly lenient. This procedure was introduced by the Criminal Justice Act 1988, sections 35 and 36 to allow the Court of Appeal to lay down guidelines encouraging sentencers to adopt a more severe approach to a class of offence. If the Court of Appeal decides that the sentencer made an error of principle, and that the sentence is so over-lenient that it threatens to damage public confidence in the criminal justice system, the defendant's sentence will be increased.[310] Because this introduces an element of double jeopardy, the uncertainty of having to undergo a second sentencing process will mitigate the sentence. The defendant in the case under review will therefore usually serve a less severe sentence than others committing similar offences in the future may expect.[311] In 1996, 70 sentences were referred under this procedure. As of 17 March 1997, 62 of these references had been heard, and sentence had been increased in 46 of them.[312]

Appeals from the Court of Appeal (Criminal Division). Either the prosecution or the defendant may appeal to the House of Lords on matters relating to trials on indictment, but only if the Court of Appeal certifies that a point of law of general public importance is involved, and either the Court of Appeal or the House of Lords grants leave to appeal. There is no appeal against a refusal by the Court of Appeal to certify that a point of law of general public importance is involved.[313]

1. Ineffective Assistance of Counsel

Generally, this is not in itself a ground of appeal in English law. Incompetent representation in a magistrates' court may be remedied by competent representa-

308. [1997] 3 All E.R. 780, H.L.

309. On the potentially binding effect of Crown Court decisions, see Andrew Ashworth, [1980] *Crim. L.R.* 402.

310. *Attorney-General's Reference (No. 5 of 1989)* (1990) 90 Cr. App. R. 358, C.A.

311. *Attorney-General's Reference (No. 1 of 1991)* [1991] Crim. L.R. 725, C.A.

312. Sprack, *Emmins on Criminal Procedure* p. 427, citing an answer by the Attorney-General to a parliamentary question in the House of Commons on 17 March 1997.

313. *Gelberg* v. *Miller* [1961] 1 W.L.R. 459.

tion in an appeal by way of rehearing to the Crown Court. If counsel's failure results from the court refusing an adjournment so that the defence has inadequate time to prepare its case, it is a breach of the duty of fairness which may lead to the decision being quashed, as in *R.* v. *Thames Magistrates' Court, ex parte Polemis.*[314] However, generally the defendant will not be allowed to argue that the conduct of his own agent made proceedings unfair,[315] although there may be grounds for an appeal if counsel's conduct renders a conviction unsafe.

2. *Other Grounds of Appeal*

See the introduction to section III,C above.

3. *Successive Appeals and Collateral Attack*

The desire for finality dominates this area of law. Save where a case is referred back by the Criminal Cases Review Commission (see section 4 below), only one appeal process is permitted. If the ultimate appeal is unsuccessful, the defendant is not allowed to start again, even if he wants to argue points not taken on the first appeal. The matter is *res judicata.*[316] The search for finality also makes the court unwilling to allow collateral attack on convictions. The courts are likely to strike out, as an abuse of process, applications for habeas corpus or attempts to bring civil actions by defendants where the statement of claim calls in question the result of the criminal proceedings. *Ex hypothesi* the relevant facts will have been proved in the criminal trial beyond reasonable doubt, and there can be no public interest in requiring a private person to prove guilt again in defamation proceedings on the balance of probabilities for the purpose of establishing a defence of justification. In *McIlkenny* v. *Chief Constable of the West Midlands*[317] the *res judicata* doctrine has even been held to prevent a defendant from suing those who arrested, detained and questioned him for battery where the battery had been unsuccessfully alleged as a challenge to the admissibility of a confession during the criminal proceedings. The House of Lords struck out such an action brought by the "Birmingham Six," who had been convicted of the Birmingham pub bombings carried out by the I.R.A. It took a further twelve years, and two further references back to the Court of Appeal, before their convictions were recognized as being unsafe and were quashed.[318]

4. *Criminal Cases Review Commission*

After revelations of miscarriages of justice in a rash of cases the Royal Commission on Criminal Justice in 1993 recommended an overhaul of the process for reviewing convictions when a miscarriage was alleged.[319] Previously the Home Of-

314. [1974] 2 All E.R.1219, D.C.

315. See *Al-Mehdawi* v. *Secretary of State for the Home Department* [1990] 1 A.C. 876, H.L.

316. *R.* v. *Berry (No. 2)* [1991] 1 W.L.R. 125, C.A., approved in *R.* v. *Mandair* [1995] 1 A.C. 208, H.L.

317. [1982] A.C. 529, H.L., affirming [1980] Q.B. 283, C.A.

318. *R.* v. *McIlkenny* [1992] 2 All E.R. 417, C.A. See also the other terrorist-related miscarriage of justice cases, *R.* v. *Maguire* [1992] Q.B. 936, C.A., and *R.* v. *Ward* [1993] 2 All E.R. 577, C.A.

319. *Report*, Cm. 2263, ch. 11. See also Kate Malleson, *Review of the Appeal Process*, Royal Commission on Criminal Justice Research Study No. 17 (London: H.M.S.O., 1993).

fice had been responsible, receiving about 700 cases a year. The Royal Commission took the view that it would be preferable for a specialist body independent of government to review cases and make referral decisions. Accordingly the Criminal Appeals Act 1995 authorised the establishment of a Criminal Cases Review Commission, which took over the review role from the Home Office in April 1997. The new Commission is relatively well resourced and staffed, although it is too early to say how far it will prove adequate to the workload which may be generated.[320] In February 1998 its backlog was about 1,200 cases. As well as receiving applications from alleged victims, the Commission receives references from the Court of Appeal when the Court considers that an appeal before it cannot properly be decided without extensive investigations.

The Commission should make a reference only if it decides that there is a real possibility that the decision in question would not be upheld were a reference made, and that real possibility must usually arise because of evidence or arguments not already considered at trial or on appeal. The Commission can also refer a sentence if there is information or a legal argument which was not considered at trial or on appeal.[321] If the decision or sentence in question originated in the magistrates' court, the case will be referred to the Crown Court, and any issue may then be ventilated. If the case was dealt with in the Crown Court, the appeal will go to the Court of Appeal (Criminal Division), and will be dealt with like any other appeal under the Criminal Appeal Act 1968. This means that the grounds on which the Court of Appeal can allow an appeal must shape the Commission's view as to the existence of a "real possibility" of success.

Bibliography

Andrews, J. A. and Hirst, M., *Andrews and Hirst on Criminal Evidence* 3rd ed. (London: Sweet & Maxwell, 1997).

Archbold's Criminal Pleading and Practice 1997 (London: Sweet & Maxwell, 1997).

Ashworth, A., *The Criminal Process: An Evaluative Study* (Oxford: Clarendon Press, 1994.

Ashworth, A., "Victim impact statements and sentencing" [1993] *Criminal Law Review* 498-509.

Ashworth, A. J., "Should the police be allowed to use deceptive practices?" (1998) 114 *Law Quarterly Review* 108-140.

Baldwin, J., *The Role of Legal Representatives at the Police Station*, Royal Commission on Criminal Justice Research Study No. 3 (London: H.M.S.O., 1993).

Baldwin, J., "Understanding judge ordered and directed acquittals in the Crown Court" [1997] *Criminal Law Review* 536-555.

Bavidge, G., and Kerrigan, K., "Plea before venue" (1998) 148 *New Law Journal* 62-63.

320. See Kate Malleson, *A broad framework* (1997) 147 N.L.J. 1023-1024.
321. Criminal Appeal Act 1995, section 13.

Birch, D. "The Pace Hots Up: Confessions and Confusions under the 1984 Act" [1989] *Criminal Law Review* 95-116;

Blackstone's Criminal Practice 1997 (London: Blackstone Press, 1997).

Brown, D., Ellis, T., and Larcombe, K., *Changing the Code: Police Detention under the revised PACE Codes of Practice* (London: Home Office Research and Policy Unit/H.M.S.O., 1993).

Choo, A. L.-T., *Abuse of Process and Judicial Stays of Criminal Proceedings* (Oxford: Clarendon Press, 1993).

Choo, A. L.-T., "Halting criminal prosecutions: the abuse of process doctrine revisited" [1995] *Criminal Law Review* 864- 874.

Clarke, D. N. and Feldman, D., "Arrest by any other name" [1979] *Criminal Law Review* 702-707.

Darbyshire, P., "The lamp that shows that freedom lives — is it worth the candle?" [1991] *Criminal Law Review* 740-752.

Dennis, I., "The Criminal Justice and Public Order Act 1994: the evidence provisions" [1995] *Criminal Law Review* 4-18.

Dixon, D., "Legal regulation and police malpractice" (1992) 1 *Social and Legal Studies* 515-541.

Dixon, D. *Law in Policing: Legal Regulation and Police Practices* (Oxford: Clarendon Press, 1997).

Dixon, D., Coleman, C., and Bottomley, K., "Consent and the legal regulation of policing" (1990) 17 *Journal of Law & Society* 345-62.

Edwards, J. Ll. J., *The Attorney General, Politics and the Public Interest* (London: Sweet & Maxwell, 1984).

Evans, R., "Cautioning: counting the cost of retrenchment" [1994] *Criminal Law Review* 566-575.

Feldman, D., *Civil Liberties and Human Rights in England and Wales* (Oxford: Clarendon Press, 1993).

Feldman, D., *The Law relating to Entry, Search and Seizure* (London: Butterworths, 1986).

Feldman, D., "Regulating treatment of suspects in police stations: judicial interpretation of detention provisions in the Police and Criminal Evidence Act 1984" [1990] *Criminal Law Review* 452-471.

Feldman, D., "Press freedom and police access to journalistic material," in Barendt, E. (ed.), *Yearbook of Media and Entertainment Law* Vol. 1, 1995 (Oxford: Clarendon Press, 1995), p 43-80.

Feldman, D. J. and Miller, C. J., "The Press, Contempt and Judicial Review" (1997) 113 *Law Quarterly Review* 36-40.

Fenwick, H., "Rights of victims in the criminal justice process: rhetoric or reality?" [1995] *Criminal Law Review* 843-853.

Fenwick, H., "Procedural 'rights' of victims of crime: public or private ordering of the criminal justice process?' (1997) 60 *Modern Law Review* 317-333.

Fisher, Sir H., *Report of the Inquiry by the Hon. Sir Henry Fisher into the Circumstances Leading to the Trial of Three Persons on Charges Arising out of the Death of Maxwell Confait and the Fire at 27 Doggett Road, London SE6*, House of Commons Paper No. 90 of 1977-78.

Grevling, K., "Fairness and the exclusion of evidence under section 78(1) of the Police and Criminal Evidence Act 1984" (1997) 113 *Law Quarterly Review* 667-685.

Gudjonsson, G., Clare, I., Rutter, S. and Pearse, J., *Persons at risk during interviews in police custody: the identification of vulnerabilities*, Royal Commission on Criminal Justice Research Study No. 12 (London: H.M.S.O., 1993).

Harris, D., O'Boyle, M., and Warbrick, C., *The Law of the European Convention on Human Rights* (London: Butterworths, 1995).

Hodgson, J., "Vulnerable suspects and the appropriate adult" [1997] *Criminal Law Review* 785-795.

Home Office, *Criminal Statistics England and Wales 1996*, Cm. 3764 (London: The Stationery Office, 1997).

Home Office Research and Statistics Directorate, *Race and the Criminal Justice System* (London: Home Office, 1997).

Houlder, B., "The importance of preserving the jury system and the right of election for trial" [1997] *Criminal Law Review* 875-881.

Hoyano, A., Hoyano, L., Davis, G. and Goldie, S., "A study of the impact of the revised Code for Crown Prosecutors" [1997] *Criminal Law Review* 556-564.

Hunter, M., "Judicial discretion: section 78 in practice" [1994] *Criminal Law Review* 558-565.

Law Commission, Consultation Paper No. 149, *Consents to Prosecution* (London: The Stationery Office, 1997).

Leng, R., *The Right to Silence in Police Interrogation: A Study of some of the Issues underlying the Debate*, Royal Commission on Criminal Justice Research Study No. 10 (London: H.M.S.O., 1993).

Leng, R. and Taylor, R., *Blackstone's Guide to the Criminal Procedure and Investigations Act 1996* (London: Blackstone Press, 1997).

Lidstone, K., "Magistrates, the Police and Search Warrants" [1984] *Criminal Law Review* 449-458.

Lidstone, K. and Bevan, V., *Search and Seizure under the Police and Criminal Evidence Act 1984* (Sheffield: University of Sheffield Faculty of Law, 1992).

Lidstone, K. and Palmer, C., *Bevan and Lidstone's The Investigation of Crime*, 2nd ed. (London: Butterworths, 1995).

Lord Chancellor's Department, *Judicial Statistics England and Wales for the year 1996*, Cm. 3716 (London: The Stationery Office, 1997).

Lowe, N.V. and Sufrin, B.E., *Borrie and Lowe's Contempt of Court* 3rd ed. (London: Butterworths, 1995).

Marcus, G., "Secret witnesses" [1990] *Public Law* 207-223.

McBride, J., "The continuing refinement of criminal due process" (1997) 22 *European Law Review* HRC/1-HRC/16.

McConville, M., "Search of People and Premises: New Data from London" [1983] *Crim. L.R.* 604-14.

McConville, M. and Hodgson, J., *Custodial Legal Advice and the Right to Silence*, Royal Commission on Criminal Justice Research Study No. 16 (London: H.M.S.O., 1993).

McConville, M., Hodgson, J., Bridges, L. and Pavlovic, A., *Standing Accused: The Organisation and Practices of Criminal Defence Lawyers in Britain* (Oxford: Clarendon Press, 1994).

McKenzie, I., Morgan, R. and Reiner, R., "Helping the police with their inquiries: the necessity principle and voluntary attendance at the police station" [1990] *Criminal Law Review* 22-33.

Malleson, K., *Review of the Appeal Process*, Royal Commission on Criminal Justice Research Study No. 17 (London: H.M.S.O., 1993).

Malleson, K., "A broad framework" (1997) 147 *New Law Journal* 1023-1024.

Miller, C. J., *Contempt of Court* 2nd ed. (Oxford: Clarendon Press, 1989).

Mirfield, P., "Two side effects of sections 34 to 37 of the Criminal Justice and Public Order Act 1994" [1995] *Criminal Law Review* 612-624.

Mirfield, P., "Successive confessions and the poisonous tree" [1996] *Criminal Law Review* 554-567.

Mirfield, P., *Silence, Confessions, and Improperly Obtained Evidence* (Oxford: Clarendon Press, 1997).

Padfield, N., "Plea before venue" (1997) 147 *New Law Journal* 1396-1397.

Pattenden, R., "Inferences from silence" [1995] *Criminal Law Review* 602-611.

Plotnikoff, J. and Woolfson, R., *Information and Advice for Prisoners about Grounds for Appeal and the Appeals Process*, Royal Commission on Criminal Justice Research Study No. 18 (London: H.M.S.O., 1993).

Report of the Departmental Committee on Fraud Trials, Chairman: Lord Roskill (London: H.M.S.O., 1986).

Roberts, D., "Legal advice, the unrepresented suspect and the courts: inferences from silence under the Criminal Justice and Public Order Act 1994" [1995] *Criminal Law Review* 483-485.

Roberts, P. and Willmore, C., *The Role of Forensic Science Evidence in Criminal Proceedings*, Royal Commission on Criminal Justice Research Series No. 11 (London: H.M.S.O., 1993).

Royal Commission on Criminal Justice, *Report*, Cm. 2263 (London: H.M.S.O., 1993).

Royal Commission on Criminal Procedure, *Report*, Cmnd. 8092 (London: H.M.S.O., 1981).

Sanders, A., Bridges, L., Mulvaney, A. and Crozier, G., *Advice and Assistance at Police Stations and the 24 Hour Duty Solicitor Scheme* (London: Lord Chancellor's Department, 1990).

Sanders, A. and Bridges, L., "Access to legal advice and police malpractice" [1990] *Criminal Law Review* 494-509.

Sanders, A. and Young, R., *Criminal Justice* (London: Butterworths, 1994).

Scarman, Lord, *The Brixton Disorders*, Cmnd 8427 (London: HMSO, 1981).

Sharpe, S., "The European Convention: a suspect's charter?" [1997] *Criminal Law Review* 848-860.

Smith, D. J. and Gray, J., *Police and People in London: the PSI Report* (Aldershot: Gower, 1985).

Sprack, J., *Emmins on Criminal Procedure* 7th ed. (London: Blackstone Press, 1997).

Sprack, J., "The Criminal Procedure and Investigations Act 1996: (1) the duty of disclosure" [1997] *Criminal Law Review* 308- 320.

Victim Support, *The Rights of Victims of Crime* (London: Victim Support, 1995).

Walker, C., Cram, I., and Brogarth, D., "The reporting of Crown Court proceedings and the Contempt of Court Act 1981" (1992) 55 *Modern Law Review* 647-669.

Wilkins, G. and Addicott, C., *Operation of Certain Police Powers under PACE, England and Wales, 1996*, Home Office Statistical Bulletin Issue 27/97 (London: Government Statistical Service, 1997).

Williams, G., "When is an arrest?" (1991) 54 *Modern Law Review* 408-117.

Zander, M., *The Police and Criminal Evidence Act 1984* 3rd ed. (London: Sweet & Maxwell, 1995).

Zuckerman, A. A. S., "The weakness of the PACE special procedure for protecting confidential material" [1990] *Criminal Law Review* 472-478.

Zuckerman, A. A. S., "Illegally Obtained Evidence: Discretion as a Guardian of Legitimacy" (1987) 39 *Current Legal Problems* 55-70.

Chapter 5

France

Richard S. Frase

I. Introduction[1]

French pretrial, trial, and appeal procedures are based on a number of underlying principles and concepts, the most important of which relate to the classification of criminal offenses; the organization of the police, prosecutors, and the courts; and the sources of criminal procedural law.

1. In the remainder of this chapter, the following abbreviations will be used.

Material in the French Code of Criminal Procedure (*Code de Procédure Pénale*) will be cited as, e.g., "CPP Art. 16 (para. 1, section 1)." For an English translation of the procedure code as of January, 1987, see Kock & Frase, *The French Code of Criminal Procedure, Revised Edition* (1988). Material in the Criminal Code (*Code Pénal*) will be cited as, e.g., "Crim. Code, Art. 8." (There is no English translation of this new code, which became effective on March 1, 1994.) Unless otherwise noted in this chapter, all quoted material from either the CPP or the Criminal Code represents the author's translation of the current, French-language version (published by Dalloz; also available on Lexis-Nexis).

Major cases are cited by date and court; those reported in the Bulletin des Arrèts de la Cour de Cassation, Chambre Criminelle (Imprimerie des Journaux officiels, various years), are cited by volume (year), case number, and date, e.g.: 1979 Bull.Crim. No. 311 (Nov. 8). (French cases are rarely referred to by the names of the parties.) Other frequently cited sources, and the abbreviations used, in this chapter are as follows Frase, "Introduction," in Frase & Kock, *supra* ("Frase 1988"); Frase, *Comparative Criminal Procedure as a Guide to American Law Reform: How Do the French Do It, How Can We Find Out, and Why Should We Care?* 78 Calif. L.Rev. 539 (1990) ("Frase 1990"); Ministère de la Justice, *Annuaire Statistique de la Justice*, 1991-95 (La Documentation Française, 1997)("Annuaire Statistique"); W. Pakter, *Exclusionary Rules in France, Germany, and Italy*, 9 Hast.Int.& Comp.L.Rev. 1 (1985); Pradel, "France", in: van den Wyngaert et al., eds., *Criminal Procedure Systems in the European Community* (Butterworths, 1993) ("Pradel 1993a"); Pradel, "Les droits de la personne suspecte ou poursuivie depuis la loi no. 93-1013 du 24 août 1993 modifiant celle du 4 janvier précédent. Un législateur se muant en Pénélope ou se faisant perfectionniste?" 41 *Recueil Dalloz Sirey* 299 ("Pradel 1993b"); J. Pradel & A. Varinard, *Les grands arrêts du droit criminel, tome 2: Le procès, La sanction* (Dalloz 1995); Tomlinson, *Nonadversarial Justice: The French Experience*, 42 Md. L.Rev. 131 (1983); A. Sheehan, *Criminal Procedure in Scotland and France* (H.M. Stationery Office, 1975); and G. Stefani, G. Levasseur, & B. Bouloc, Procédure Pénale, 16th Edit (Dalloz, 1996) ("Stefani et al.").

A. Classification of Criminal Offenses

Many procedural rules depend on the nature of the offense charged. In general, more serious offenses are subject to more elaborate procedural safeguards at all stages (pretrial, trial, and post-trial). There are three grades of criminal offense under French law: *Crimes* (the most serious); *délits*, and *contraventions* (the least serious). These three offense types are translated herein as "major felonies," "delicts," and "contraventions." It is important to stress that none of these three categories bears a close resemblance to any category of crime in the United States. Thus, the category of French *crimes* includes the counterparts of only the most serious American felonies (e.g., murder, mutilation, rape, armed robbery, and very high-level drug trafficking). Most American felonies (e.g., aggravated assault, burglary, grand larceny, most drug crimes), as well as many American misdemeanors, are classified as delicts; however, some American misdmeanors are only "contraventions" (a category which also includes most traffic offenses, and many regulatory and public order crimes).

The maximum penalty for major felonies is either life imprisonment or a prison term of ten years or more.[2] Delicts are punishable with a fine and/or a prison term (up to ten years, for the most serious offenses), and/or with public service or with forfeiture of objects or privileges.[3] Contraventions are punishable only with fines (up to 10,000 francs (about $1,700, at 1997 exchange rates) for contraventions of the fifth (most serious) class; up to 20,000 francs, for certain recidivists) or with public service and/or forfeiture of objects or privileges.[4]

B. Organization and Supervision of Police, Prosecution, and the Judiciary

France has a very centralized system of government, without the layers of independent state, county, and city government found in the United States. Thus, French police, prosecutors, judges, and correctional personnel all belong to national civil service hierarchies, and their powers are often strictly regulated by national statutes or regulations. In addition, the French system contains some important structural features designed to improve the performance of the police, prosecutors, and judges.

1. Police

The judicial police,[5] acting on their own initiative or at the direction of judicial authorities or the prosecutor,[6] engage in the investigation and prosecution of

2. Crim. Code Art. 131-1. For an overview of French sentencing laws and practices, *see* Frase, *Sentencing Laws & Practices in France*, 7 Fed. Sent. R. 275(1995).

3. Crim. Code Arts. 131-3 to 131-11.

4. Crim. Code Arts. 131-12 to 131-18. Under the former penal code, in effect prior to March 1994 (see note 1, *supra*), some contraventions were punishable with short jail terms (up to two months, for certain recidivists). The new penal code only allows jailing in cases of willful non-payment of a fine or non-performance of community service.

5. The "administrative" police function includes activities, such as routine patrol and directing traffic, which are designed to prevent crime and maintain or restore public order. Tomlinson, p. 157. Although such activities sometimes lead to evidence used in criminal court, most police

known or suspected offenses. The judicial police function may be exercised by the prosecuting attorney,[7] by members of the two major national police forces (the National Police and the Gendarmerie),[8] and by certain other public officials.[9]

Members of the judicial police are further classified by the Code of Criminal Procedure[10] into three levels, each with different powers: Officers (*officiers de police judiciaire*, hereinafter:"OPJ's); Agents of the judicial police; and Assistant Agents. OPJ's have the broadest powers (for example, only they may direct the investigation of a "flagrant" offense, order investigative detention, or receive delegations of authority from an examining magistrate[11]). Agents have more authority than Assistant Agents (for example, the latter may not exercise the investigatory powers permitted during a "preliminary" investigation).[12] OPJ's are a select group, including the chief prosecutor in each district (*Procureur de la République*), and those members of the National Police or Gendarmerie who have been designated as OPJ's by ministerial decree, from a list of persons declared eligible by statute (e.g., gendarmes with at least three years of service).[13] The Attorney General for each Court of Appeal may also suspend or revoke that status if an OPJ abuses his or her powers.[14]

Most of the work of the judicial police is subject to the direct supervision of the prosecutor's office.[15] The prosecutor must be notified "without delay" of every offense known to the police, and "immediately" if it qualifies as a "flagrant" offense.[16] And although OPJ's have broad powers to take suspects into investigatory

---

powers and admissibility issues are decided according to the Code of Criminal Procedure and other rules governing the "judicial police" function.

6. *See, e.g.*, CPP Arts. 12, 151 to 155.

7. CPP Art. 41 (para. 3).

8. The National Police, under the direction of the Minister of the Interior, is a nation-wide police hierarchy which has gradually absorbed or taken control over most of the municipal police forces (including the Parisian Prefecture of Police, although the latter retains a substantial degree of independence, Stefani et al., para. 278, 282). A second national police hierarchy, the gendarmerie, also provides important administrative and judicial police services. This essentially military corps is under the direction of the Minister of Defense, and covers the entire territory of France; it is therefore particularly important in rural areas, *id.* para. 283-4; Tomlinson, at 157.

9. CPP Art. 16 (para.1, section 1) (mayors and assistant mayors). Certain civil servants (e.g., railway police; public health officials) also enjoy judicial police powers, under special statutes (Pradel 1993a).

10. CPP Arts. 16 to 21-1.

11. See text at notes 35-51, *infra.* It is not clear whether violation of these rules can ever lead to exclusion of evidence, but violation has been held to bar confiscation of certain items as part of the sentence. *See, e.g.*, 1987 Bull. Crim. No. 253 (June 17) (illegal radar detector seized by Agents, not Officers, of the Judicial Police).

12. See text at note 40, *infra.*

13. CPP Arts. 16, 41(para. 3).

14. CPP Arts. 16 to 16-3, 38. See also Arts. 224 to 230 (power of the Indicting Chamber to discipline members of the judicial police).

15. This aspect of the French policing is discussed in Frase 1990 at 557-59.

16. CPP Arts. 19, 40(para. 2), 54. "Flagrant offense" investigations are defined and further discussed at note 36, *infra.* In such cases, arrival of the prosecutor on the scene divests the police of control, CCP Art. 68 (however, it appears that this actually occurs only in very serious cases. Tomlinson at 147). The prosecutor also has certain powers not exercisable by other OPJ's, in these cases: 1) To issue a "warrant for attachment" against anyone who is suspected of having participated in the offense (CPP Art. 70), which directs the police to seize and bring the suspect to the prosecutor, for questioning; 2) to order the police to forcibly bring in non-suspects for questioning, if the latter fail to respond to the requests of the police to appear (CCP Art. 62, para. 2); and 3) during investigatory detention, to deny the suspect of the right to notify his family or

detention (see discussion, *infra*), the prosecutor must be informed promptly of such detention, is given general supervision of all measures taken during detention, and must give written approval for any detention of more than 24 hours.[17] In addition to exercising all of the powers of an OPJ, the prosecutor may direct the police to carry out specified investigative acts.[18] In practice, prosecutors rarely take direct charge of investigations, or order the police to conduct specific investigations, but the possibility of such interventions, and the formal recognition of the prosecutor's power of supervision and independent investigation, may serve a useful function in checking police power.

2. *Prosecutors*

All prosecutors in France serve in a civil service hierarchy (referred to in the aggregate as "official counsel" (*ministère public*), headed by the Minister of Justice (a member of the Prime Minister's "cabinet"). The first level below the Minister of Justice includes the Attorney General (*Procureur Général*) for the Court of Cassation and the Attorneys General for each of the courts of appeal; the latter exercise authority over their own staff, and also over the Prosecuting Attorneys (*Procureurs de la Republique*) for each court of General Jurisdiction within that appellate district.[19] The prosecuting attorneys and their assistants screen criminal complaints to decide whether and what charges to file,[20] prosecute delicts and the most serious contraventions,[21] and direct the work of the judicial police.[22] Prosecution of major felonies is normally the responsibility of the Attorney General for the Court of Appeal.[23]

Although prosecutorial and judicial functions are kept strictly separate, in recognition of the principle of separation of powers, both prosecutors and judges are considered to be "magistrates."[24] The normal path of entry into either branch of the magistrature is by completion of a 31-month training program (following three to five years of university studies in law), and entrance into this program is based primarily on a nation-wide competitive examination. Near the completion of the training program, the candidates choose one or the other branch of the magistrature; those who choose to initially become judges usually stay in the judiciary for life, whereas many of those who choose prosecution later switch to the judiciary. In any case, becoming a prosecutor (or a judge) in France is generally a long-term decision, made at the start of one's legal career.

3. Judges and courts. French criminal court judges are normally appointed after completion of the 31-month training program mentioned above. Like prosecutors, they are part of a nation-wide hierarchy and merit promotion system, but

---

employer, or to order a medical examination of the suspect (CCP Arts. 63-2, para. 2; 63-3, para. 2).

17. CPP Arts. 41 (para. 3) and 63 (para. 1 & 3).

18. CCP Arts. 38, 41 (para. 2), 42.

19. CPP Arts. 34 to 37.

20. See text at note 174, *infra*.

21. CPP Arts. 39 to 48. Normally, the Commissioner of Police is responsible for prosecution of contraventions of the first four classes, but the prosecuting attorney may take charge of any case, if he or she wishes, CPP Art. 45 (para. 1).

22. CPP Arts. 12, 41 (para. 2).

23. CPP Arts. 34 and 39.

24. Tomlinson, at 146; Frase 1990 at 559-64.

in order to maintain their independence, they are considered "unremovable" until the age of mandatory retirement, and are subject to more limited disciplinary procedures.[25]

As described more fully in Part III, a different court has trial jurisdiction over each grade of criminal offense, and pretrial rules sometimes make reference to one or more of these courts. Major felonies are tried in the Assize Court (*Cour d'assises*)[26] which hears only criminal cases; delicts are tried in the Correctional Court (*Tribunal correctionnel*),[27] which is the criminal branch of the court of general jurisdiction *(Tribunal de grande instance*); contraventions are tried in the Police Court (*Tribunal de police*),[28] which is the criminal branch of the court of limited jurisdiction (T*ribunal d'instance*).

Several other important courts or judicial officers should be mentioned at the outset. As discussed in Part II, A, important pretrial investigation and charging functions are exercised by the examining magistrate (*juge d'instruction*), who is chosen from among the judges of the court of general jurisdiction. All decisions by the magistrate to file major felony charges, and many details of the judicial investigation, are reviewed by, or appealable to, the Indicting Chamber (*Chambre d'accusation*), whose three members are chosen from the regional Court of Appeals (*Cour d'appel*). The Court of Appeal itself hears appeals *de novo*, from decisions of the Correctional and Police Courts. The highest judicial court, the Court of Cassation (*Cour de Cassation*), hears appeals on issues of law, from all lower courts. Finally, the constitutionality of newly enacted statutes may be reviewed by the Constitutional Council (*Conseil constitutionnel*), whose nine members are appointed for non-renewable nine-year terms.

None of the other courts mentioned above, even the Court of Cassation, has the power to declare statutes unconstitutional. Moreover, the Constitutional Council may only rule on the constitutionality of a statute prior to the date it is officially promulgated, and (in most cases) only at the request of designated officials.[29] Until recently, only a few criminal procedure laws had been reviewed by the Council. One notable example was the decision of January 12, 1977, invalidating a statute authorizing the police to search any vehicle on the public highway, at any time.[30]

C. Sources of Procedural Law

Unlike the highly constitutionalized American system, most issues of criminal procedure in France are governed by detailed provisions of the Code of Criminal Procedure, which contains over 800 sections (Articles). There are only a few provisions of the French Constitution which relate to criminal procedure (e.g., the presumption of innocence), and there have been (at least by American standards), relatively few decided cases applying constitutional provisions. This is due in part to the strict limits on the timing and jurisdiction of constitutional challenges, noted

25. Tomlinson, at 146; Frase 1990 at 564-67.
26. CPP Arts. 231 to 380.
27. CPP Arts. 381 to 495.
28. CPP Arts. 521 to 545.
29. *See generally*, Tomlinson, at 189-194.
30. Tomlinson, at 189.

above. However, the Court of Cassation has long exercised a broad power of review (somewhat analogous to "due process" review, by American courts), based on the notion of the "rights of the defense" - a vaguely defined group of procedural guarantees (often not based on any specific provision of the constitution or Procedure Code) which are deemed to be implicit in general principles of justice and equity.[31] Another quasi-constitutional source of defense rights is the European Convention for the Protection of Human Rights and Fundamental Freedoms, which is binding on French courts.[32] Provisions of the Convention are having an increasing impact on French procedural law, due to decisions of both the Court of Cassation and the European Court of Human Rights (see generally, chapter —, discussing international procedural norms).

Because French procedural law is so heavily codified, there is relatively little case law. Moreover, even when French courts interpret constitutional or code provisions, their decisions are not viewed as binding precedents, but rather as illustrations of the principles implicit in the constitutional or statutory text. Later decisions cite these principles, and the text itself, rather than the prior decisions. And although legal commentators do cite case law, they rarely discuss the specific facts of the cases (which are only briefly summarized, in reported decisions). In the remainder of this chapter, cases will generally be cited by issue and holding, without extended discussion. However, the facts of five leading (and well-reported) cases are discussed in detail at the end of the chapter (Part C, 2), to illustrate the evolution of French law and law-making over the past forty years.

II. Police Procedures

There are two general principles, applicable to all types of investigations. First, it is generally held that official investigation of the facts should be "fair" (*loyal*), attempting to uncover evidence favorable to the accused as well as unfavorable, avoiding the use of brutal or deceptive methods, and respecting human dignity and "the rights of the defense."[33] Second, all investigatory steps must be thoroughly documented, in writing: Whenever a member of the judicial police or a judge performs any act of investigation, he or she must promptly write an official report (*procès-verbal*), which the suspect, witness, or person searched or questioned is asked to read and sign.[34] The collection of these reports, and other items of evi-

31. *See generally*, Tomlinson, at 166-174. The Constitutional Council has also relied on this concept, which it deems to be included within the "fundamental principles recognized by the laws of the republic" (Constitution of Oct. 27, 1946, Preamble, incorporated in the Preamble of the current Constitution of Oct. 4, 1958), and thus constitutionally protected. Pradel 1993b at 302; Tomlinson at 166, n. 123;190, n. 219.

32. *See, e.g.* 1978 Bull.Crim. No. 346 (Dec. 5) (right to detailed notice of charges; this case (*Baroom*) is discussed further in Part C, 2, *infra*). However, decisions of the Court of Human Rights provide only declaratory and monetary relief, and have no direct effect on criminal charges unless a French court chooses to adopt a similar interpretation of the Convention. 1994 Bull.Crim. No. 166 (May 6).

33. Stefani et al. at para. 36, 531; Sheehan, p. 24; Tomlinson, p.166-167, 176-177.

34. See, e.g., CPP Arts. 19, 20, 62, 92, and 106. *See generally*, Sheehan, p 33-34.

dence, charging documents, etc., is known as the official or procedural file (*dossier*) of the case.[35]

A. Arrest, Search, and Seizure Law

The French do not use the concepts of investigatory "stop," "arrest" and "search and seizure" in the same way as Anglo-American systems. Instead, French law recognizes four types of investigations, and specifies the evidence-gathering and arrest powers available under each: (1) Investigation of "flagrant" offenses; (2) "preliminary" investigations; (3) identity checks; and (4) the formal judicial investigation conducted by an examining magistrate. The latter permits the broadest investigatory powers, but the scope of a flagrant offense investigation is also quite broad. Each of the four types of investigation permits activities which would be considered a stop, a frisk, or an arrest, under U.S. law; flagrant-offense and judicial investigations also permit non-consensual searches and seizures of evidence.

A flagrant offense investigation may be invoked whenever a major felony or a delict (if punishable with imprisonment) 1) "is in the process of being committed," or 2) "has just been committed,"[36]or 3) if, "within the period immediately following the act, the suspect is pursued by clamor, or is found in possession of objects, or presents traces or indications," of having participated in the offense, or 4) if the head of a household requests investigation of an offense committed in the house.[37] The first three of these justifications require the presence of objective, external indications ("*indices apparentes*") that a major felony or jailable delict has been committed (by someone),[38] but actions based on reasonable appearances will be upheld, even if it later appears that the police were mistaken.[39] As discussed below, a flagrant offense investigation conveys a wide variety of temporary detention, interrogation, search, and seizure powers; however, all of these powers must be carried out or approved by an OPJ, a prosecutor, or an examining magistrate.

A preliminary investigation may be invoked in any case, regardless of the nature of the infraction or its recency, and may be conducted by "Agents" of the Judicial Police, as well as OPJ's.[40] Except for summoning of witnesses and temporary "investigatory detention" of suspects (discussed under "Stops," below), no coercive powers are granted; searches of houses and other private places, and seizures of evidence in the course of such an investigation requires the express written consent of the person affected.[41]

---

35. See, e.g., CPP Art. 81 (para. 2 and 3).

36. This language permits some delay in reporting of the offense (e.g., 24 hours, 1991 Bull. Crim., No. 96 (Feb. 26)); but the investigation, if not significantly interrupted, can then continue as long as necessary, Stefani et al., para. 305.

37. CPP Art. 53.

38. 1980 Bull. Crim., No. 165 (May 30). See further discussion in note 48, *infra*, and in Part C, 2 (*Isnard* and *Gomez-Garzon* cases).

39. 1990 Bull. Crim. No. 16 (Jan. 9); 1992 Bull. Crim. No. 110 (Mar.11).

40. CPP Art. 75 et seq.

41. CPP Art. 76. An exception is made for cases involving members of terrorist groups. Art. 706-24.

Identity checks may be conducted by any police officer, but have a very limited purpose and duration (see further discussion under "Stops," below).

A judicial investigation (*information* or *instruction préparatoire*) may be invoked by the prosecutor in any case, and can also be invoked by the victim of a major felony or a delict.[42] Judicial investigation is mandatory when the prosecutor wishes to charge a major felony, and is optional in other cases.[43] The investigation is carried out by a specialized judge of the Court of General Jurisdiction, the Examining Magistrate (*juge d'instruction,* hereinafter: "JDI"). The JDI has discretion to carry out "all acts of investigation that the judge deems useful to the manifestation of the truth,"[44] and thus enjoys very broad powers of arrest and pretrial detention, interrogation of witnesses and suspects, and search and seizure.[45] All of these powers (except the power to interrogate suspects) may also be delegated to another judge or (more often) to an OPJ, by means of a "Rogatory Commission."[46] The JDI also makes charging decisions. (See Section III, A, 2, below.) Most of these investigatory acts, and some of the charging decisions, are subject to review by the Indicting Chamber (*Chambre d'Accusation*), a three-judge panel of the Court of Appeal. In 1993, the Procedure Code was substantially amended, giving the defendant and victim several rights previously exercised only by the prosecutor and/or the JDI, including rights: 1) To request that certain investigative acts be performed; 2) to appeal refusals of such requests to the Indicting Chamber; and 3) to request the Chamber to order exclusion of certain evidence. (See discussion, *infra.*)

1. Stops

French police, without making an "arrest," may detain a person or stop a vehicle under each of the four types of investigation mentioned above. During the course of a "flagrant offense" investigation, OPJ's may: (1) Detain persons on the scene of the offense until completion of the investigation; (2) summon and interrogate any persons capable of furnishing evidence (those who do not appear voluntarily may, with the prosecutor's approval, be forcibly produced); and (3) place suspects in investigatory detention (*garde à vue*) for up to 24 hours (which can be extended to 48 hours, with the approval of the prosecuting attorney).[47] Non-suspects (persons against whom there exists no *indice* suggesting guilt) may only be held long enough to take their statements.[48]

---

42. These and other "victim's" rights may also be exercised by certain associations representing classes of victims or public interests, see discussion in Section III, B, 6, *infra.*

43. CPP Art. 79. Less than ten percent of delict prosecutions involve such an investigation, and the procedure is almost never used for contraventions. Annuaire Statistique at 81.

44. CPP Art. 81 (para. 1).

45. CPP Arts. 92 to 150.

46. CPP Arts. 151 to 55. See text at note 65, *infra.*

47. CPP Arts. 61 to 65. In cases involving terrorist groups, and certain drug violations, investigatory detention may be extended for an additional 48 hours (resulting in a total of 96 hours), with the approval of the JDI (if applicable) or the presiding judge of the court of general jurisdiction. CPP. Arts. 706-23, 706-29.

48. CPP Art. 63 (para. 2). The term *indice* is not defined in the Code, and may mean different things in different contexts. Two leading cases, discussing the kinds of *indices* required to open a "flagrant offense" investigation, are discussed in Part C, 2, *infra.* See also notes 50 and 53, and accompanying text.

Investigatory detention of suspects may also be invoked during a preliminary investigation, but extension for an additional 24 hours ordinarily requires presentation (i.e., appearance) of the suspect before the prosecutor.[49] As in flagrant investigations, OPJ's may also summon (by force, if necessary) and question any persons capable of furnishing evidence; again, non-suspects (those as to whom there is no *indice* of guilt) may only be detained for the time "strictly necessary" to take their statements.[50]

Finally, investigatory detention may be invoked during the course of a judicial investigation, by an OPJ who is carrying out investigations under a Rogatory Commission issued by the JDI.[51] The JDI must be informed promptly of such action, and extensions for an additional 24 hours approval by the JDI (and, ordinarily, appearance of the detainee before the judge). However, there does not appear to be any requirement of individualized suspicion (*indice* of guilt) either at the outset, or at the time of extension.

In practice, investigatory detention is frequently employed. In 1996, the number of persons held in such detention (under any of the three types of investigation described above) represented 43 percent of the total number of persons charged by police with felonies or non-traffic delicts;[52] 18 percent of these detainees were held for more than 24 hours. Although some of these detentions are so brief and localized that they would only be deemed "stops" under U.S. law, most are probably equivalent in duration and other custodial attributes to an American "arrest" (although they do not appear to result in an "arrest record," at least not at the national level).

In addition to the temporary detentions described above, persons may be briefly detained during identity checks. Under this procedure, OPJ's (and under their orders, Agents and Assistant Agents) may demand identification from any person "as to whom there is an indication (*indice*) that he has committed or attempted an offense, is preparing to commit a major felony or delict, is likely to furnish information useful to an inquiry in a case of major felony or delict, or is a person sought by order of a court."[53] Proof of identity may also be demanded in three other cases: 1) On written instructions of the prosecutor, to investigate the offenses he or she specifies, in the places and for the time period specified; 2) "to prevent a breach of the public order, particularly a violation of the security of persons and property," and "regardless of the comportment of the person;"[54] and 3) when any

49. CPP Art. 77.

50. CPP Art. 78. Concerning the meaning of the term "*indice*," see notes 48 & 53.

51. CPP Art. 154. See text at note 65 *infra*.

52. Ministère de l'Interieur, *Aspects de la criminalité et de la délinquance constatées en France en 1996* (La Documentation Française, 1997) at 98, 102.

53. CPP Art. 78-2. Such an *indice* (e.g., trying to conceal a carried item from police view) has been held to validate an identity-check stop, even if police already knew the person's identity, and were watching him because he was suspected of carrying drugs. 1994 Bull. Crim., No. 44 (Feb. 1).

54. This provision is designed to permit identity checks in metro stations and other high crime areas, without regard to individualized suspicion. The Court of Cassation has repeatedly tried to limit these checks, requiring individualized suspicion (1992 Bull. Crim. No. 370 (Nov. 10), or at least some *immediate* threat in the area (Frase 1990 at 580, n. 208). However, the legislature has responded each time by revising the provision to reinstate suspicionless checks (Law No. 93-992 of August 10, 1993; Stefani et al. at para. 303-1, n. 4). *But see* Chambre d'Accusation, Versailles, dec. of June 14, 1994, 1994 Gazette du Palais, no's 336 & 337, p. 15 (robberies committed one week earlier, in same trolley station at same time of day, did not meet threat-to-public-safety standard).

person is found within 20 kilometers of certain borders, or in the public areas of designated ports, airports, train stations, and truck depots open to international traffic. In any of the four cases described above, a person who refuses or is unable to furnish identification may be detained for up to four hours, if this is necessary to permit verification of his identity (which may be proved by an identity card or any other official document which includes a photograph).[55] Certain procedural protections apply to such detentions, and to the creation of police records based on the incident.[56]

The above rules do not distinguish between stops of pedestrians and stops of vehicles. Thus, cars can be stopped to carry out an identity check; to place a suspect in investigatory detention; and to temporarily detain and question potential witnesses.

2. *Frisks*

"Pat-down" weapons frisks (*palpations de sécurité*) are not viewed as full "searches" (*perquisitions*, see *infra*).[57] Although they are not specifically authorized during a preliminary investigation or identity check, they appear to be fairly common, and have been upheld by the Court of Cassation.[58] Once the police obtain evidence that an offense is being or was recently committed (e.g., by finding contraband or evidence), an OPJ may invoke the broad powers of a flagrant offense investigation, which permits a complete search of suspects (*fouille à corps*; *fouille* or *perquisition corporelle*).[59] During a judicial investigation, frisks and other searches of the person (by the JDI or, more often, by OPJ's acting under a rogatory commission) are also broadly permitted. Technically, all such searches must meet the general standard of being "useful to the manifestation of the truth," but the absence of caselaw suggests that this standard is not actually enforced.

3. *Arrests (Seizures of the Person)*

As noted above, persons may be detained and held for up to four hours, under the identity check procedure, and can be held for up to 48 hours in investigatory detention. These seizures require no more than minimal suspicion (some *indice*) that the person has committed an offense; moreover, no individualized suspicion is required for several of these procedures, namely: certain identity checks; initial detentions of witnesses, in a preliminary or flagrant-offense investigation; and all investigatory detentions during a judicial investigation. (See previous discussion.)

In addition to the above powers, suspects may be taken into custody by order of the JDI: 1) For purposes of immediate questioning (the "warrant for attach-

---

55. CPP Art. 78-3; Stefani et al. at para. 304. This period counts against any subsequent period of investigatory detention. Art. 78-4.

56. CPP Art. 78-3 (supervision by prosecutor; advice of rights to notify family or others, and the prosecutor; fingerprinting and photographs only if absolutely necessary; destruction of records of the operation within six months, if no prosecution results).

57. J. Pradel, *Droit Pénal*, vol. II: Procédure Pénale (6th Edit., 1992), para. 264; Stefani et al. at para. 324.

58. Pradel, *supra*, at para. 264 (also noting apparent authorizations for body searches, contained in miscellaneous specialized statutes); Stefani et al. at para. 324; Tomlinson at 183.

59. Pradel, *supra*, at para. 264; Stefani et al. at para. 324; Tomlinson at 182.

ment"); 2) for arrest and subsequent questioning (the "warrant for arrest," which is used when a suspect has fled, or resides outside of France); or 3) for pretrial detention (the "warrant for confinement").[60] Each of these custodial measures requires a written order issued by a JDI or trial judge, specifying the identity of the person sought and the legal and factual nature of the crime of which the person is suspected; warrants for confinement also require an adversary hearing and a finding that pretrial detention is necessary. (See discussion *infra*, Section III, A, 1.) However, none of these three warrants appears to require the judge to have any particular degree of suspicion that the person sought is guilty.

4. *Searches*

During an investigation of a flagrant offense, an OPJ (as well as prosecutors and JDI's) may search the scene of the offense, and seize any evidence, instrumentalities, or fruits of the crime which are found there.[61] If the crime is one which may involve physical evidence, these officials may also enter and search the domicile of all "persons who appear to have participated" in the offense, or (who appear) "to be in possession of papers or objects relating to" the crime, and seize any evidence "useful to the manifestation of the truth." Domicile searches are subject to limitations as to time of day, requirements for the presence of an occupant or other non-police witness, and special provisions designed to protect confidential information; however, no warrant is required, and it is not clear what degree of suspicion is required to justify particular entries, searches, or seizures.[62] It appears that the OPJ's powers are, in most respects, deemed to be as broad as those of a JDI in a judicial investigation.[63]

JDI's have almost complete discretion to search any place and seize any thing that the judge "deems useful to the manifestation of the truth."[64] In addition to personally exercising these broad powers, the judge may also delegate his or her search powers to another judge or to an OPJ, by means of a rogatory commission.[65] The latter are often worded quite broadly, and are far less confining than an Anglo-American search warrant. Although the commission must cite the statutory offense(s) being investigated and at least some of the facts, they need not meet any degree of suspicion, or specify the parties or places to be searched, or things to be seized.[66] Finally, as noted in section II, A, 2, flagrant offense and judicial investigations grant broad power to search the person of suspects.

---

60. CCP Arts. 122 to 136.

61. CCP Art. 54.

62. *Cf.* 1987 Bull. Crim. No. 41 (Jan. 27) (upholding search of premises owned by a suspected fence and known associate of two persons who had just been arrested while committing theft; court appeared to emphasize the "network of proofs" linking owner and the two thieves). *Compare* 1979 Bull. Crim. No. 311 (Nov. 8) (upholding a police order to open a car trunk at a roadblock set up in the wake of an armed kidnapping, with no mention of any individualized suspicion; *see generally* Tomlinson at 184-88).

63. Stefani et al. at para. 507.

64. CCP Art. 81 (para. 1). However, searches of domiciles are subject to most of the same procedural safeguards applicable to searches in a flagrant offense investigation (e.g., time of day; witnessing of the search. Arts. 95 to 97).

65. CCP Arts. 151 to 155.

66. Pakter at 35; Sheehan at 57; 1996 Bull. Crim. No. 60 (Feb. 6).

In contrast to the rules above, police engaged in a preliminary examination may only conduct "searches" (*perquisitions*), enter houses, or seize evidence if they receive the express handwritten consent of the person concerned.[67] However, certain specialized law enforcement agents may receive permission to enter premises and conduct searches in the course of a preliminary investigation, upon application to the presiding judge of the court of general jurisdiction, or his delegate.[68] A similar procedure may be invoked in cases involving terrorism.[69] Although the latter procedures have some similarity to a search warrant application, no actual warrant or other detailed order needs to be issued.

The French procedure code does not expressly regulate searches of places other than houses, nor does French law contain any global definition of a "search" comparable to the Fourth Amendment "reasonable expectation of privacy" concept. However, French courts have applied some of the Procedure Code's restrictions on domicile searches to other searches and seizures. For example, hotel rooms and private offices are treated the same as domiciles;[70] searches of cars and persons, and seizures of mail, require either a flagrant offense investigation against the person or a judicial investigation.[71] In addition, wiretapping and other invasions of informational privacy are regulated by specific provisions of the procedure code which go beyond the normal limitations on evidence gathering.[72] The detailed regulations for wiretapping were enacted in 1991, in response to a European Court of Human Rights case holding that French law did not sufficiently protect the right to privacy recognized under Art. 8 of the European Convention.[73]

As in the U.S., there are many investigatory procedures which are not regulated at all by constitutional or statutory rules. For example, going to someone's house to invite them to come to the police station, or to request them to submit to a test of intoxication, is not a search.[74] Also, the police may, even in a preliminary investigation, obtain bank account information, or observe persons in public by means of binoculars.[75]

---

67. CCP Art. 76.

68. Stefani et al. at 308, n. 2.

69. CCP Art. 706-24 (para. 1).

70. 1914 Bull. Crim. No. 74 (Jan. 31) (hotel); 1987 Bull. Crim. No. 267 (June 24) (private office). Another possible source of guidance are cases under Penal Code Art. 226-1, prohibiting "attacks on privacy" (*la vie privée*) by means of non-consensual voice recording or photography in a "private place" (any area occupied even temporarily, which is not open to others except by permission, e.g., a private boat on the open sea; a hospital room; a store not open for business). *See Code Pénal*, 94th Edit. (Dalloz, 1996), at 270 (annotations).

71. 1953 Bull. Crim. No. 24 (Jan. 22); Conseil Const., Decision of Jan. 12, 1977 (invalidating a statute authorizing police to search any vehicle on the public highway, at any time); Tomlinson at 189; Stefani et al. at para. 324.

72. CCP Art. 100 et seq. (interception of telecommunications); Art. 56 (para. 2) (only the OPJ may read papers and correspondence prior to seizing them, during a flagrant offense investigation); Arts. 56-1 and 56-2 (special requirements for searches of offices of lawyers, doctors, journalists, and audiovisual professionals).

73. *See generally* Tomlinson, *The Saga of Wiretapping in France: What It Tells Us About the French Criminal Justice System*, 73 La. L. Rev. 1091 (1993) ; chap. - *infra* (discussing the European Convention and other international human rights norms).

74. Stefani et al. at para. 539, n. 2.

75. Stefani et al. at para. 324-1.

5. *Enforcing the Rules*

A few of the limitations described above are explicitly covered by an exclusionary rule (so-called "textual nullity") - for example: The safeguards applicable to domicile searches;[76] and some of the limitations applied to identity checks[77] and wiretapping.[78] But most violations give rise to exclusion only if they are deemed to have violated "substantial" provisions of the Code or other laws related to criminal procedure (so-called "substantial" or "virtual" nullity").[79] Textual nullities appear to mandate exclusion, at least of the direct fruits, and may require little or no showing that the violation harmed the defendant's interests;[80] in contrast, courts have - and exercise - considerable discretion when deciding whether to recognize "substantial" procedural rules,[81] and exclusion further requires the court to find that the violation has caused "harm to the interests of the party that it concerns."[82] However, when the violation affects important public interests ("public order" nullities), no showing of prejudice or defendant "standing" is required, nor is there any question of defendant "waiver."[83] Both textual and substantial nullities may also result in exclusion of derivative "fruits" which resulted from the violation, but the exact scope of these rules is unclear.[84] Whatever the nature and scope of the nullity, any excluded evidence is completely removed from the file, and may not be referred to by the attorneys or judges in that case, "on pain of disciplinary pro-

76. CCP Art. 59 (para. 3) (covering violations of Art.s 56, 56-1, 57, and 59; Art. 59 is also incorporated by reference in Arts. 95 and 96 (para. 2), covering searches by JD'Is); CPP Arts. 706-24-1, 706-28, and 706-35 (terrorism, drug, and prostitution cases).

77. CCP Art. 78-3 (para.11).

78. CCP Art. 100-7 (para. 3).

79. CCP Art. 171.; Stefani et al. at para. 609.

80. Chabert & Sur, *Le point en matière de nullités de procédure pénale au fil des cent dernières décisions de la chambre d'accusation de Paris*, 1997 Gazette du Palais, nos. 318 & 319, p. 2, at 3-4 (textual nullities require no showing of prejudice); Roussel, "Le régime des nullités de la procédure pénale après les lois du 4 janvier 1993 et du 24 août 1993," 1996 *Gazette du Palais*, nos. 19 & 20, p. 7, at 8 (same). *But see* 1996 Bull. Crim. No. 316 (Sept. 17) (homeowner must show that violation of Art. 57 rule on search-witnessing prejudiced his interests (other than by providing incriminating evidence).

81. Stefani et al. at para. 609.

82. CCP Arts. 171, 802; Roussel, *supra*. The Court of Cassation has not yet decided whether such prejudice is presumed, or if the moving party must prove it. Stefani et al. at para. 614. *But see* 1996 Bull. Crim. No. 74 (Feb. 13) (presumption of prejudice, when 48-hour limit on investigatory detention is exceeded; see Part C, 2, *infra* ("*X..*" case)).

83. Examples of public order nullities include: Absence of required signatures on investigatory or court documents; violations of territorial or subject matter jurisdiction; violation of statutes of limitation or amnesty; interference with confidentiality of attorney-client communications; failure to administer oath to a witness; absence of the prosecutor or clerk at trial; and denial of public access to trials (Roussel, *supra* at 9-10); Pradel & Varinard at 137-42, 174-76.

84. CPP Arts. 174 (para. 2), 206 (para. 2); Roussel, *supra* at 12; Casorla, *Le droit français*, 63 Revue Int'l Dr. Pén. 183 (1992), at 201, n. 64. Search and seizure violations tend to result only in exclusion of the direct fruits, although later witness statements or confessions are sometimes also excluded. Stefani et al. at para. 615; 1997 Bull. Crim. No. 221 (June 4) (ordering suppression of statements of witness questioned about illegally seized documents): 1953 Bull. Crim. No. 24 (Jan. 22) [Isnard case; see Part C, 2, infra] (illegal body search leading to seizure of physical evidence, investigatory detention, and confession, required suppression of the physical evidence *and* the confession)..

ceedings."[85] This means that trial jurors, and often also the professional judges, never learn of the suppressed evidence. It also means that jointly-tried, co-defendants, whose rights were not violated and who thus might lack standing to raise an objection to the violation, benefit from nullities requested by and granted to other defendants.

The procedures for raising nullities have recently been expanded. The private parties (defendant(s) and civil party(ies)) now have the right to appeal to the Indicting Chamber during the judicial investigation, with a request to exclude evidence; prior to 1993, only the JDI or prosecutor had this power.[86] However, it remains true that trial courts have very limited authority to exclude evidence in cases subject to judicial investigation. All apparent nullities must be brought before the Indicting Chamber prior to transmission of the case by the JDI or the Chamber to the Correctional or Police Court.[87] As for cases which are filed directly in the latter two courts by the prosecutor or the civil party, nullities (of all types, except those related to the court's jurisdiction) must be raised "before any defense on the merits."[88]

Other remedies for violations include disciplinary measures against the offending police officer, prosecutor, or JDI; civil liability of these officials or the government itself; and sometimes criminal liability.[89] Disciplinary action is the most likely of these to be effective. As noted previously (section I, B), OPJ's are subject to several levels of supervision; in addition, all police, as well as prosecutors, are subject to nationwide hierarchical supervision, and prosecutors and judges are career civil servants, whose promotion prospects depend on maintaining a clean record of service. Nevertheless, French academics tend to be skeptical of such administrative remedies, and believe that, in practice, the sole ordinary sanction is exclusion of evidence.[90] It is not known whether the exclusionary and other remedies summarized above have a meaningful effect on police conduct; however, recent efforts to expand exclusionary remedies[91] suggests some dissatisfaction with the effectiveness of the existing remedies.

B. Lineups and Other Identification Procedures

1. Lineups (Identification Parades)

There do not appear to be any formal rules or requirements regulating the use of lineups and other identification procedures. During the course of a judicial in-

85. CPP Art. 174 (para. 3); Stefani et al. at para. 616.

86. Frase 1988 at 16; Stefani et al. at para. 611-1.

87. CPP Arts. 174 (para. 1), 175 (para. 2), 178 (para. 2), 179 (para. 5), 385 (para. 1), and 594. Moreover, if at some point during the judicial investigation any of the parties or the JDI requests the Indicting Chamber to exclude evidence, the private parties (defendant and victim) must raise all exclusion issues then available to them; after that point, any such pre-existing illegalities may only be raised by the prosecutor, the examining magistrate, or the Indicting Chamber itself (Art. 174 (para. 1); 1997 Bull. Crim. No. 66 (Feb. 19); Stefani et al. at para. 611-1), except perhaps for "public order" nullities (Pradel 1993b, at 306).

88. CPP Art. 385 (para. 5); Roussel, *supra* note 80, at 9.

89. Stefani et al. at para. 331, 617.

90. Frase 1990 at n. 256.

91. *See generally* Trouille, "A Look at French Criminal Procedure," 1994 (Brit.) Crim. L. Rev. 735-44.

vestigation, suspects may be viewed by witnesses, for identification purposes; such procedures do not require compliance with the right-to-counsel and other rules applicable to "confrontations" of the suspect and the witnesses (see below), unless the suspect is asked to respond to questions or to a witness's response.[92] During the course of a preliminary investigation, the police may carry out identification procedures, without any particular procedural requirements.[93]

2. *Other Identification Procedures*

The authority to collect voice, handwriting, blood, urine, hair, and other exemplars is poorly defined. JDI's, OPJ's executing a rogatory commission, and OPJ's directing a flagrant-offense investigation, have broad powers to order expert examinations and seize all evidence "which may be useful to the manifestation of the truth."[94] However, there is no general contempt power or other legal basis to formally compel non-testimonial evidence, and legal commentators are of the view that the taking of blood or urine samples requires the express consent of the subject.[95] On the other hand, there is no prohibition on using the subject's refusal as a basis to infer consciousness of guilt, and drunk-driving suspects who refuse to permit the taking of breath, blood, or urine samples are subject to criminal penalties.[96] During preliminary investigations (other than of drunk driving), it is clear that all seizures of evidence require the express written consent of the person concerned.[97] Seizures are also very limited during the course of an identity check; fingerprints and photographs may only be taken under certain circumstances,[98] and the failure of the procedure code to mention any other identification measures implies that they are not allowed.

C. Interrogation

First, a preliminary note about "charging." French procedures for the filing of a "formal charge in court" depend on the level of the offense and the type of investigation. During a judicial investigation, defendants are initially "charged" when they acquire the status and rights of a suspect (*personne mise en examen*).[99] Such defendants may be "charged" a second time when the JDI approves prosecution for a major felony (*crime*) and submits the file to the Indicting Chamber,[100] or approves prosecution on delict or contravention charges by sending the case to be tried in Correctional or Police Court.[101] A third type of "charging" occurs when the Indicting Chamber issues a decree of indictment on major felony charges, or refers the case to Correctional or Police Court on delict or contravention

92. Frase 1990 at n. 172; Stefani et al., para. 534, n. 1, 535, n. 3; Sheehan at 56, n. 75.
93. Stefani et al. at para. 324-1.
94. CCP Arts. 81 (para.s 1 and 8) (JDI powers); Art. 152 (para. 1) (rogatory powers); Arts. 54 (para. 2), 60, and Stefani et al. para. 307 (flagrant offense investigations).
95. Pradel, *supra* note 57, at para. 276; Stefani et al. at para. 36.
96. Art L.1, Traffic Code; Pradel, *supra* note 57, at para. 276.
97. CPP Art. 76 (para. 1).
98. CCP Art. 78-3 (para. 4).
99. CCP Arts. 105, 114.
100. CCP Art. 181.
101. CCP Arts. 178 to 180.

charges.[102] In prosecutions for contravention or delict, when no judicial investigation has been conducted, defendants are charged either by issuance of a citation to appear in court or, for certain delicts, by taking the suspect directly to court.[103]

1. *Before Formal Charge in Court*

Prior to charging by any of the means described above, witnesses and suspects may be held in custody and questioned during an identity check or investigatory detention. They may also be interrogated (usually not in custody) during the early stages of judicial investigation. In addition, persons not in custody may be briefly questioned in various locations by police carrying out a preliminary investigation, but there are no cases or Code provisions governing such questioning.

a. *Identity Checks.* When this procedure is invoked, the police are entitled to insist on proof of identification; persons who refuse or are unable to provide such proof may be detained on the scene, or in a police station, for up to four hours.[104] Although questioning is supposed to relate solely to issues of identification, it seems likely that the police also ask additional investigatory questions. Other than the procedural protections noted previously, there are no formal rules or cases governing questioning at this stage.

b. *Investigatory Detention.* As discussed earlier, OPJ's may place persons in investigatory detention (*garde à vue*) during a flagrant offense investigation; during a preliminary investigation; and when operating under a rogatory commission issued by the JDI in the course of a judicial investigation. However, in the latter case, the rogatory commission does not permit the OPJ to question persons who have acquired the status of a "suspect" (*personne mise en examen*, see below).[105] In other respects, the rules governing interrogation during investigatory detention are similar in all three of the above contexts.[106] At the outset of the detention, the suspect must be informed, in a language he or she understands, of the allowable period of detention (24 hours, with the possibility of extension up to 48 hours, or longer in certain cases), and must also be advised of certain rights.[107] In particular, he has the right: 1) To have his family or employer informed that he is being held in detention; [108]2) to be examined "without delay" by a doctor designated by the prosecutor or OPJ (and, if the detention is extended past 24 hours, to be examined a second time);[109] and (3) after 20 hours of investigatory detention, to speak in private and "without delay" with a retained or appointed attorney, for up to 30 min-

---

102. CPP Arts. 213 to 215.

103. CPP Arts. 389 to 395, 531 to 533. See text at notes 149-154, *infra*.

104. CPP. Arts. 78-2 and 78-3; Stefani et al. at para. 304, 304-1. See text at note 53, *supra*.

105. CPP Arts. 105 (para. 1), 152 (para. 2).

106. *See* CPP Arts 77 (para. 5) and 154 (para. 4), incorporating the provisions of Arts. 63-1, 63-2, 63-3, 63-4, 64, and 65.

107. CPP Arts. 63-1 to 63-4; *see generally* Pradel 1993b. *But see* 1997 Bull. Crim. No. 66 (Feb. 19) (one-hour delay in formal notification of detention and advice of rights was valid; OPJ didn't have sufficient *indices* of suspect's guilt when questioning began (apparently, in a hospital); defendant was initially being questioned only as a witness, under Art. 62).

108. With the approval of the prosecutor or JDI, exercise of this right may be denied "for reasons of the necessities of the investigation" (e.g., to prevent destruction of evidence or escape of other suspects). CPP Art. 63-2 (para. 2).

109. A medical exam may also be requested by the suspect's family, and may be ordered by the prosecutor, OPJ, or JDI at their own initiative. CPP Art. 63-3.

utes.[110] Counsel is not allowed to be present during questioning,[111] and does not have access to the police files or the detention record, although counsel must be advised of "the nature of the infraction," and may insert written "observations" (e.g., comments on the suspect's mental or physical state; requests that other suspects be questioned or searched) in the detention record. For certain offenses, the right to counsel only attaches after 36 hours of detention (for conspiracy, aggravated pimping, or extortion) or 72 hours (for drug and terrorism cases). Although the police have no contempt or other legal power to compel statements, suspects do not receive any "right-to-silence" warning at any stage of police detention or questioning. However, investigatory detention records must include the dates and times of interrogation, rest, and release; the results of any medical exam (including the doctor's views as to the appropriateness of continued detention); counsel's written observations; and a record (including the suspect's signature) documenting compliance with the advice-of-rights summarized above.[112]

c. *Interviews of Witnesses (non-parties) During a Judicial Investigation.* The JDI may forcibly summon and hear as a witness any person (other than charged suspects or the civil party) "whose deposition appears to be useful."[113] Except for convicts and persons under the age of 16, witnesses are heard under oath; they can be fined (up to the maximum allowed for a contravention) for refusing to appear and answer questions.[114] However, any person named in the civil party's complaint may refuse to be heard as a witness, and may demand some of the rights applicable to interrogations of charged suspects (see below).[115] After a suspect has been charged (*mise en examen*), he is given rights to counsel and other rights (described in section 2 below), and may not be heard as a mere witness.

2. Interrogation After Defendant Is Formally Charged

After the defendant has been charged with a contravention or delict (by receipt of a citation, or order of "immediate appearance" in court), the investigation is considered to be complete, and there is normally no further pretrial interrogation. However, there is no formal prohibition on continued investigation. Occasionally, the trial court (or, before opening of the trial, the prosecutor) will decide that further inquiries are needed and request the opening of a judicial investigation.[116] It may also be possible to conduct a (further) preliminary investigation, and invoke (further) investigatory detention (unless the total allowable period of such detention has already been used).

After a suspect has been initially charged (*mise en examen*) by the JDI, he or she will almost always be subject to (further) questioning, but is entitled to certain rights. Such initial charging occurs automatically for persons named in the prose-

110. CPP Art. 63-4. If the suspect is a minor, the right to counsel attaches at the outset of detention. Pradel 1993b, *supra*, at 301.

111. *But see* CPP Art. 70 (para. 2) (during investigation of a "flagrant" major felony, when a judicial investigation has not yet been opened, if a person who was summoned for questioning by the prosecutor appears with counsel, the person may only be questioned in counsel's presence).

112. CPP Arts. 63-1 (para. 2), 63-3 (para. 4), 63-4 (para. 4), 64 and 65.

113. CPP Arts. 101 and 109.

114. CPP Arts. 103, 108, and 109; Sheehan, p. 55, n. 73.

115. CPP Art. 104.

116. Stefani et al. at para. 317.

cutor's request to open a judicial investigation; it can also occur during the investigation, as soon as there exists against any person "grave and concordant indications that he has participated in the acts being investigated.[117] In addition, the JDI *may* (but need not) charge anyone as to whom there is any evidence of guilt in connection with the offenses under investigation, and charging results automatically from the issuance of a warrant for appearance, arrest, or detention.[118] Finally, the civil party (see *infra*, Section B, 6), enjoys some of the same rights as a charged suspect, during the investigation.

At the first appearance of a charged suspect before the JDI, the suspect must be informed of the legal and factual nature of the offenses being investigated and with which he is charged.[119] He must also be advised of his rights to request that certain acts of investigation be carried out, and/or that certain evidence be excluded from the investigatory (and trial) record. If the suspect has not already chosen counsel, he is advised of his right to select counsel or have counsel appointed (which is guaranteed to all indigents).[120] The suspect is further advised that he may not be questioned at this hearing unless he consents and counsel is present. However, if the suspect wishes to make a statement (without prompting or comment by the judge), the statement will be received;[121] suspects at this stage may also be interrogated or confronted without their consent in exigent circumstances (when a witness is about to die, or important evidence about to disappear).[122]

Following the suspect's first appearance, the "parties" (charged suspect(s) and civil party(ies)) may only be interrogated or "confronted" (with each other or with one or more witnesses) in the presence of their lawyers, unless they waive this right or the lawyer fails to appear, after being "duly called" at least five working days in advance.[123] As discussed more fully in section III, A, 5, *infra*, counsel has liberal access to the dossier of the investigation before and after the hearing. Charged suspects and civil parties are not placed under oath, and there is no formal sanction if they refuse to speak. With the judge's permission, the prosecutor and the attorneys for the parties may pose questions of the accused, the victim, or the witnesses; if the request is refused, the text of the proposed question must be inserted in the dossier of the investigation.[124] Sessions are not electronically recorded, and the written record (which the parties are asked to read and sign) generally includes only the substance of the interrogation, not the verbatim text.[125]

After the initial appearance of the charged suspect, he or she need not be further advised of any right to remain silent. Although suspects cannot legally be

117. CPP Art. 105. However, many observers have complained about belated charging (*inculpations tardives*), designed to avoid the right to counsel. Stefani et al. at para. 528, n. 4. This may have become less of a problem since the elimination, in 1993, of the former requirement in Art. 105 of proof that delayed charging was "designed to defeat the rights of the defense."

118. CPP Art. 80-1 (para.s 1 and 2).

119. CPP Art. 116 (para. 1). All of these required rights advisories may also be given by registered letter, if the JDI chooses to charge by that means, or by a notice communicated by an OPJ acting on the judge's orders and signed by the suspect. Art. 80-1 (para. 3).

120. Defendants also have the right to request appointment of an interpreter, to permit effective consultation with counsel. 1994 Bull. Crim. No. 394 (Dec. 6).

121. CPP Art. 116 (para. 3); Stefani et al. at para. 532.

122. CPP Art. 117.

123. CPP Art. 114 (para. 1 and 2).

124. CPP Art. 120.

125. Stefani et al. at para.534.

compelled to speak, or formally punished for refusing, the expectation seems to be that they will ordinarily respond to most questions, and react to confrontation sessions.

Once the judicial investigation is closed, and the matter referred either to the Indicting Chamber or the Correctional or Police Court, there is normally no further pretrial interrogation unless the Chamber or trial court orders further investigations.

3. *Enforcing the Rules*

The following discussion builds on the previous description of exclusionary rules ("nullities") and other remedies. (See section II, A, 5.)

French law appears to recognize a concept similar to, but narrower than, the U.S. "involuntary confession" doctrine. As noted in Part I, French authorities are expected to avoid the use of unfair, brutal or deceptive methods of evidence-gathering, and to respect human dignity and the rights of the defense. In particular, torture is forbidden by Art. 3 of the European Convention on Human Rights, and by the European Convention for the Prevention of Torture; the former convention also forbids the use of "inhuman or degrading punishments or treatments." These principles have not yet generated much case law,[126] but it does appear that French courts will exclude confessions obtained by means of a drugs ("truth serum"), and possibly also the polygraph (lie detector).[127] On the other hand, French courts have traditionally been lax in controlling the use of psychological pressure, and some authors have suggested that the police are given more latitude than judges, in the use of deception.[128] Also, French courts generally admit evidence obtained in a questionable manner by private parties (e.g., by the victim).[129]

Violations of procedural rules related to confessions also may result in exclusion of evidence. Prior to the reforms of 1993, violations of the procedures required at the suspect's first appearance before the JDI, and at subsequent interrogations, were subject to a "textual" nullity provision, explicitly requiring exclusion not only of the illegal acts themselves but also all subsequent proceedings.[130] The current law gives courts more discretion, generally requiring violation of "substantial formalities" which have "caused injury to the complaining party,"[131] but it seems likely that exclusion will continue to be ordered in many of these cases.[132]

As for violations of the rules governing interrogations during investigatory detention (e.g., allowable duration; required records), French courts were formerly very reluctant to apply exclusionary remedies. These detention provisions have

126. *But see Tomasi v. France*, Eur. Ct. Hum. Rts. dec. of Aug. 27, 1992 (number and intensity of blows received by suspect established a violation of Art. 3).

127. Stefani et al. at para. 56.

128. Tomlinson at 179-80; Pakter at 10, 13.

129. Stefani et al. at para. 56.

130. *See* Frase 1988 at 16 (discussing former Art. 170 (para. 1)).

131. CPP Art. 171. However, some violations (e.g., questioning under oath of a charged suspect (*personne mise en examen*)) are deemed "public order nullities," and thus require no showing of prejudice to the interests of the accused. Chabert & Sur, *supra* note 80, at 4-5; Roussel, *supra* note 80, at 9; Pradel & Varinard at 176.

132. Stefani et al. at para. 609.

never been subject to explicit (textual) nullity, and although the Court of Cassation once stated that such violations might lead to exclusion if it were shown that "the search for and establishment of the truth was fundamentally tainted,"[133] this rule was very rarely invoked.[134] More recently, however, the Court has held that a violation of the maximum limit of 48 hours resulted in a *presumption* of prejudice to the accused's interests, and thus invalidated the procedure and the resulting confession (even though the confession was obtained *before* the end of the 48th hour of detention).[135] In another case,[136] the Court held that failure to give the required warnings until 16 hours after detention began (due to unavailability of the only interpreter contacted by police) invalidated a confession, even though it was made after the warnings, and there was no violation of the suspect's rights to counsel, medical exam, and family-notification. Finally, lower courts have excluded confessions obtained after failure to grant appropriate access to counsel after 20 hours of detention.[137] This dramatic shift in French law appears to reflect two watershed developments in 1993: The clear legislative intent to increase the rights of suspects during police questioning, and a decision of the Constitutional Council which declared that the right to consult an attorney after 20 hours forms part of the constitutionally protected "rights of the defense."[138]

III. Court Procedures

As previously noted in Part I, French criminal charges are tried in one of three courts; major felonies are tried in the Assize Court; delicts are tried in Correctional Court; and contraventions are tried in Police Court. The Assize Court consists of three professional judges (the "court proper") and nine lay jurors who, together with the judges, decide on both guilt and sentence.[139] The Correctional Court consists of either three professional judges or a single judge, depending on the of-

133. 1960 Bull. Crim. No. 156 (Mar. 17).

134. Pakter at 13; Pradel & Varinard at 182-83 (criticizing the narrow scope of this rule, and citing only one, very usual case in which exclusion was ordered).

135. 1996 Bull. Crim. No.74 (Feb. 13) (total detention of 52 _ hours, including a 9-hour detention for the same offense, six years earlier). This case ("X.. ") is further discussed in Part C, 2, *infra*. *See also* two unreported decisions of the Paris Indicting Chamber, cited in Chabert & Sur, *supra* note 80, at 5, n. 12.

136. 1996 Bull. Crim. No. 443 (Dec. 3).

137. *See, e.g.*, Trib. Gr. Inst. D'Aix-en-Provence, dec. of Dec. 22, 1993, reported in 1994 Recueil Dalloz Sirey no. 40, *Jurisprudence*, p. 566 (failure to provide interpreter was equivalent to denial of counsel, and required the annulling of the entire record of investigatory detention).

138. Trouille, *A Look at French Criminal Procedure*, 1994 (Brit.) Crim. L. Rev. 735-44 (discussing 1993 procedure code reforms); Pradel 1993b at 300-302 (discussing Conseil Constit., dec. no. 93-326 of Aug. 11, 1993).

139. CPP Arts. 240, 243 to 253, 296 (para. 1). Felonies committed by military personnel, or involving terrorist groups, state security, or certain serious drug or conspiracy violations, are tried to a court consisting only of seven judges. Arts. 698-6, 702, 706-25, and 706-27. As of 1997, an Assize Court reform proposal was pending, which would create a smaller, first-instance trial court of two lay and three professional judges, with *de novo* appeals heard by the larger Assize Court described in text.

fense;[140] the Police Court always consists of a single judge.[141] About half of all trials occur in Police Courts, about half in Correctional Courts, and less than one-half of one percent in Assize Courts; if adjudications without trial ("penal orders") are included, Police Courts handle about three-quarters of all criminal matters (excluding parking and other minor violations subject to pre-set (i.e., scheduled) fines).[142]

A. Pretrial

1. *Initial Court Appearance and Pretrial Detention*

Except in limited circumstances (defendants subject to the "immediate appearance" procedure described below; persons seized under warrants of attachment or arrest, issued by a JDI), French domestic law does not regulate how soon after arrest suspects must be brought to court.[143] For most offenses, investigatory detention may only last for 48 hours, but the expiration of this period does not necessarily require immediate charging or arraignment (although this can occur, especially under the "immediate appearance" procedure). Many defendants are released at this point, with or without a specified later court date.

The procedures at the suspect's first appearance before the JDI were previously described in Part II, C, 2. The procedures governing the accused's first appearance in the trial court depend on the level of the offense. In major felony cases, once the decree of indictment issued by the Indicting Chamber has become final, the accused is transferred to the jail in the place where the Assize Court sits.[144] If he has not

140. CPP Arts. 398 (para.s 1 & 3) and 398-1. Delicts triable by a single judge include all traffic offenses, various assaults and threats, non-support, most thefts, receiving stolen property, criminal damage to property, and certain minor drug crimes. However, such offenders must be tried by a three-judge court if they are held in pretrial detention.

141. CPP Art. 523.

142. Annuaire Statistique, p. 92-99. Penal orders and scheduled fines are discussed in text at notes 273-74, *infra.*

143. CPP Art.s 126 to 133 provide that defendants arrested on a warrant must be released after 24 hours, if they have not been questioned by the JDI (or, in some cases, the prosecutor). The immediate appearance procedure is discussed in text, *infra.*

The European Convention on Human Rights contains a "prompt arraignment" rule in Art. 5.3: All arrested persons "shall be brought promptly before a judge or other officer authorized by law to exercise judicial power." However, French courts have held that investigatory detention of up to 48 hours does not violate this provision, because any detention beyond the first 24 hours must be approved by the prosecutor, "a magistrate of the judicial order whose mission is to supervise the application of the law." 1992 Bull. Crim., No. 105 (Mar. 10). Moreover, even substantial delays at later stages, in violation of the general "speedy trial" requirements of Art. 6.1, do not require reversal of the conviction. *See* Cour de Cass., Ch. Crim., dec. of April 29, 1996, reported in: 1997 Recueil Dalloz-Sirey, no. 148, *Sommaires Commentés*, at p. 148 (delay of over 13 months between trial and issuance of the judgment of conviction).

French statutes of limitation require that some act of investigation or prosecution occur within a certain period after the offense: 10 years, for major felonies (or, for certain terrorist offenses, 30 years); 3 years, for delicts; and 1 year, for contraventions. CPP Arts. 6 to 9, 706-25-1. The limitations on the duration of pretrial detention, discussed in text, *infra*, also serve to indirectly limit excessive delays in arraignment.

144. CPP Art. 269. Assizes are held in Paris, and in each department. Art. 232. Sessions are held every three months (or more often, if necessary). Art. 236.

been detained, he is notified that he is to appear before the presiding judge of the Assize Court on a certain date.[145] As soon as possible thereafter, that judge (or another judge delegated by him) interrogates the accused about his identity, and makes sure that proper notice of the decree of indictment was given.[146] The accused is then asked to designate counsel to assist in his defense; if he does not have or does not choose counsel, one is appointed for him, without regard to any claim of indigency.[147] At the trial itself, counsel is obligatory.[148]

In delict cases, where the suspect has been held in investigatory detention, he may be initially "arraigned" by being brought before the prosecutor.[149] At this time, the prosecutor will: 1) Inform the defendant of the charges; 2), receive any declarations which the accused wishes to make; 3) inform the accused of his right to retained or appointed counsel; and 4) notify the chosen attorney (or, if appointed counsel is needed, the President of the local Order of Advocates). The prosecutor will then decide whether to: a) Request a judicial investigation; or b) release the suspect on his promise to appear for trial ("convocation by official reports"), giving the suspect a trial date at least 10 days and no more than two months later; or c) release the suspect outright, if prosecution seems unlikely or uncertain;[150] or d) if the case appears ready for trial, order the defendant's continued detention and prompt arraignment in Correctional Court.[151]

The latter procedure ("immediate appearance") is authorized for delicts punishable with two to seven years imprisonment (or in the case of "flagrant" delicts, one to seven years). If arraignment on the same day is not possible, continued detention must be approved by a judge of the Correctional Court (following the general pretrial detention procedures and prerequisites described below). Arraignment must occur on or before the second working day thereafter, or defendant will be released from custody. At the arraignment (at which counsel must be present, or have been duly summoned or waived), the judge advises the defendant that he cannot be tried that same day unless he consents, in the presence of his counsel. If no consent is given, or the matter does not appear to the judge to be ready for trial, the trial date can be postponed for a minimum of two weeks, and a maximum (unless defendant expressly consents) of six weeks. Pretrial detention may be continued by a further order of the court, according to the general rules described below. In all "immediate appearance" cases, pretrial detention may not last more than two months after defendant's first appearance in Correctional Court.[152]

Defendants who remain at liberty are cited (by the prosecutor or the civil party) to appear for trial in Correctional Court. Trials in Police Court, on contravention charges, are almost always initiated by citation, and pretrial detention is not allowed. The citation will indicate the factual and legal nature of the offense, and the place and time of the required court appearance (which must be at least ten

145. CPP Arts. 215-1, 239, and 272.
146. CPP Arts. 272 and 273.
147. CPP Arts. 274 and 275.
148. CPP Art. 317.
149. CPP Art. 393; Sheehan at 38-39.
150. In such cases, subsequent prosecution by citation, or opening of a judicial investigation, are still permissible.
151. CPP Arts. 393, 394 (arraignment before the prosecutor); Arts. 395 to 397-6 (immediate appearance procedures).
152. CPP Art. 397-3.

days after service of the citation).[153] If it was issued by the civil party, the citation must indicate that party's name and address, and may also indicate the factual and legal basis for an award of damages. Jurisdiction can also be obtained by voluntary appearance of the accused, or by remand from the JDI or Indicting Chamber.[154]

At the accused's appearance for trial in Correctional or Police Court, the court will confirm his identity, state how the court obtained jurisdiction, and decide if an interpreter is needed.[155] In Correctional Court, counsel may be appointed upon defendant's request, and is obligatory "when the accused is subject to an infirmity which would compromise his defense."[156] In Police Court trials, retained counsel is permitted, but there is no provision for appointed counsel.[157]

Pretrial Detention orders. Except for the limited custody permitted under the investigatory detention and identity check procedures, pretrial detention must be judicially approved, either by the JDI, or by the Assize or Correctional Court. These judges may also order conditional release ("pretrial supervision").[158]

Persons charged with any major felony may be detained if the magistrate finds, after holding an adversary hearing, by an order stating specific reasons, (1) that pretrial supervision is insufficient, and (2) that pretrial detention a) "is the only way" to prevent interference with the evidence or witnesses, "fraudulent conspiracy among defendants and accomplices," harm to the accused, or continued or renewed crime by or flight of the accused; or b) is "the only way" to end the exceptional and persistent disturbance of the public order, caused by the seriousness or circumstances of the offense;[159] or c) is appropriate because defendant has violated the terms of his pretrial supervision. Such defendants may only be held for one year, but detention may be extended for additional six-month periods if the above requirements are met.[160]

Pretrial detention can be ordered in delict cases, upon compliance with the hearing, order, and justification requirements above, but only if the delict is punishable with at least two years imprisonment (one year, for "flagrant" delicts).[161]

---

153. CPP Arts. 550 to 555; Stefani et al. at para. 504.

154. CPP Arts. 388, 531.

155. CPP Arts. 406 to 408, and 535.

156. CPP Art. 417.

157. Stefani et al. para. 684; CCP Arts. 531 to 543.

158. CPP Arts. 138 to 143. Conditions of release may include any of the following: restrictions on travel, domicile, or frequentation of specific places; supervision by designated authorities; limits on professional activities; required educational programing; surrender of identity documents or driver's license; avoiding association with designated persons; required treatment or medical examination; limits on checking account privileges; surrender of weapons; deposit of security to guarantee the rights of the victim; and proof of contribution to family expenses or required alimony. Money bail may also be required, but use of this option is rare. Stefani et al. at 553; Ministère de la Justice, *Compte Général de l'administration de la justice pénale*, 1978, p. 23, 25 (955 bailed defendants, out of a total of about 80,000 subject to pretrial detention or release orders).

159. CPP Arts. 141-2, 144, and 145. The vague "public order" concept was disapproved by the European Court of Human Rights in Letellier v. France, Jt. of June 26, 1991. The Court stated that such a justification could only be allowed in exceptional cases, upon proof of an actual threat to public order (by others) if defendant were to be released. *See also* 1990 Bull. Crim., No. 296 (Aug. 7) (judge failed to specify why continued detention was needed due to the continued intensity of public emotion).

160. CPP Art. 145-2; Stefani et al. at para. 569.

161. CPP Art. 144. These offense-severity limits do not apply if defendant has violated the terms of his pretrial supervision. Art. 141-2.

Such an order is limited to four months, but it may be extended. If the accused's current offense and prior convictions are not very serious, such detention may only be extended once, for a two-month period.[162] In other cases, detention may be extended for a four-month period (totally eight months) and, in "exceptional cases," may be extended even further; in such cases, detention may not exceed one year, if the maximum sentence for the current offense is five years or less, or two years, if the maximum is less than ten years.[163] In addition to each of these limits, a further two months of detention is allowed between the end of the judicial investigation and defendant's trial in Correctional court.[164]

At the termination of the judicial investigation, suspects referred for trial in Police Court must be released from pretrial detention or supervision, and the Police Court itself has no power to initiate such measures; defendants are simply issued citations to appear.[165] In contrast, suspects charged with felonies may be (and usually are) further held in custody pending review by the Indicting Chamber, while awaiting trial, and during the trial.[166] In cases of delict, the JDI may continue pretrial detention for up to two more months, pending the accused's appearance in Correctional Court.[167] The Correctional Court itself may continue pretrial detention[168] (and may continue or initiate pretrial supervision[169]), but may only initiate pretrial detention if the accused (1) has violated the conditions of pretrial supervision,[170] or (2) has been brought to court under the "immediate appearance" procedure previously noted.[171]

Any person held in pretrial detention who subsequently obtains a dismissal or acquittal may apply to a special commission for an indemnity.[172]

In practice, pretrial detention seems to be used sparingly, at least by American standards: only about 10 percent of all prosecuted defendants (excluding minor traffic cases) have ever been held in pretrial detention, and only about five percent were still detained at the time of final disposition of their charges.[173]

2. *Charging Instruments and Procedures*

Major felony cases require issuance of a decree of indictment by the Indicting Chamber (see section 3, below). All other cases are charged by the prosecutor or the civil party; the only "charging instrument" in such cases is the citation described above, in the absence of which defendants receive oral advice as to the nature of the charges prior to or upon initial appearance in court. Defendants also

162. CPP Art. 145-1 (para. 2).
163. CPP Art. 145-1 (para. 1 & 3).
164. CPP Art 179 (para. 4). Defendants who violate pretrial supervision conditions may be re-incarcerated, and the detention time limit starts over. Stefani et al. at para. 569.
165. CPP Arts. 178, 179, 213 (para. 3), and 531.
166. CPP Arts. 181 (para. 2) and 215 (para. 2); Sheehan, p. 51.
167. CPP Art. 179 (para.s 3 & 4).
168. CPP Art. 464-1.
169. CPP Art. 141-1.
170. CPP Art. 141-2 (para. 2).
171. See text at note 151, *supra*.
172. CPP Arts. 149 to 150.
173. Frase 1990 at 601. The figures in text include pretrial detention ordered by JDI's or trial judges, or incurred during the "immediate appearance" procedure. They do not include defendants held by the police in investigatory detention.

have broad access to the investigatory file (*dossier*) of the case (see section 5 below).

The French prosecutor has broad discretion to refuse to invoke the criminal law, even in cases of provable guilt, or to charge less serious crimes than the evidence would permit.[174] For example, the prosecutor may choose to treat an offense as a delict even though it could have been prosecuted as a felony; the case is then sent directly to Correctional Court, without requesting opening of a judicial investigation - a process known as "correctionalization." "Contraventionalization" is an analogous procedure which allows provable delicts to be sent to Police Court and tried as contraventions. However, the victim has an independent power to insist on prosecution (see section III, B, 6, below), and certain cases may be instituted directly by administrative officials (e.g., customs violations).[175] Moreover, once the prosecutor has requested a judicial investigation, or sent the case directly to Correctional or Police Court, the prosecution lacks any formal power (akin to the common law *nolle prosequi*) to dismiss or reduce charges; at least in theory, such charges may only be dismissed or reduced by the court (although in practice, courts often defer to the wishes of the prosecutor).[176] Finally, cases cannot be sent to the Assize Court without the approval of major felony charges by both the JDI and the Indicting Chamber (see below); certain other cases cannot be filed in any court without the approval of the victim or an administrative agency.[177]

3. *Preliminary Hearing*

The only French equivalent of the U.S. preliminary hearing are the reviews conducted by the JDI and by the Indicting Chamber.[178] Such reviews are mandatory for major felonies. Investigation by a JDI is optional for delicts and contraventions, and is only used when the lesser investigatory and detention powers of the police are deemed insufficient; only about eight percent of delict trials are preceded by a judicial investigation, and the procedure is almost never used in contravention cases.[179] In optional judicial investigation cases, the Indicting Chamber will only review nullity issues, not the charges themselves. There is no provision for the Correctional or Police Court to review the sufficiency of the charges, prior to the start of the trial itself.

If the JDI determines that the facts constitute a major felony, the entire case (including nullity issues) must be reviewed by the Indicting Chamber.[180] For this purpose, the Chamber holds a non-public hearing at which the attorneys, but usually not the parties or witnesses, attend and present their oral or written arguments.[181]

174. CPP Art. 40 (para. 1); Sheehan, p. 18, 41-43. See also Art. 41 (para. 7) (authorizing "mediation," and eventual non-prosecution, with the consent of the defendant and the victim); Code of Public Health, Art. 628-1 (pretrial diversion and treatment of drug addicts). In 1995, prosecution was declined in 80 percent of matters screened by French prosecutors (excluding contraventions of the first four classes). Annuaire Statistique, p. 81. This figure has remained about the same since the late 1970's. *See* Frase 1990 at 614.

175. Sheehan, p. 31.

176. Id., p. 18.

177. Id., p. 41-42.

178. CPP Arts. 79, 181, 191 to 218.

179. This proportion declined steadily, from 1974 through 1984, but has since remained fairly constant. Frase 1990 at 667, n. 640; Annuaire Statistique at 81.

180. CPP Arts. 181, 191 to 218.

181. CPP Arts. 197 to 201; Sheehan, p. 66.

The pretrial screening rules above do not distinguish between defendants held in custody and those who remain at liberty.

4. *Pretrial Motions*

Motions may be made during a judicial investigation (usually to the JDI; occasionally to the Indicting Chamber), and may also be made at the outset of trial. At any time during the judicial investigation, the prosecutor may request the JDI to carry out "any investigative steps which appear (to the prosecutor) to be useful to the manifestation of the truth, and any security measures" (e.g., arrest and detention of suspects).[182] If the magistrate refuses any aspect of the request, an order stating reasons must be issued within five days. The prosecutor may appeal any order of the JDI (as well as failures to respond to requests) to the Indicting Chamber.[183] The charged suspect (*personne mise en examen*) and the civil party may request the JDI to take their own statement; question a particular witness; conduct a confrontation with another suspect, civil party, or witness; visit and examine the crime scene; or order another suspect or civil party to produce a particular piece of evidence.[184] The Magistrate must comply, or issue an order stating reasons, within one month, and failure to do either is immediately appealable by the requesting party to the Indicting Chamber. The suspect may also appeal orders related to pretrial detention or supervision, and those assuming jurisdiction, permitting civil claims to be filed, and denying a request for expert evidence; the civil party may appeal orders affecting his civil claim, or related to expert evidence (but may not appeal solely on issues related to pretrial detention of the accused).[185] Finally, the prosecutor and all charged suspects and civil parties may request the Indicting Chamber to declare a nullity and exclude evidence from the official file (*dossier*).[186] All nullity issues must be raised before the close of the judicial investigation.

When there has been no prior judicial investigation, nullity issues related to prior proceedings may be raised in Correctional or Police Court, but only before any defense on the merits[187]

5. *Discovery*

Counsel for the defendant (or defendant personally if acting *pro se*, even if he or she is a lawyer)[188] may inspect the full dossier of the case at certain stages of pretrial procedure, and immediately prior to trial. In addition, when the right to counsel attaches after 20 hours of investigatory detention, counsel must be informed about "the nature of the infraction being investigated," but may not inspect the dossier until the end of investigatory detention.[189]

182. CPP Art. 82.
183. CPP Arts. 82 (para. 4) and 185.
184. CPP Arts. 81 (para.s 8 to 11) and 82-1.
185. CPP Arts. 186 and 186-1.
186. CPP Art. 173 (para.s 2 & 3).
187. CPP Art.385 (para. 5).
188. "X..." v. France, Eur. Ct. Hum. Rts. dec. of March 18, 1997 (former French rule, denying *pro se* defendants access to dossier, violated "equality of arms" principle). 1978 Bull. Crim., No. 52 (Feb. 9); Stefani et al. at para. 534.
189. CPPArts. 63-4 (para. 3), 393 (para. 3), and 394 (para. 2).

During a judicial investigation, after a suspect has been charged (*mise en examen*), defense counsel must be allowed to consult the dossier at the suspect's first appearance before the magistrate, and at least four working days before the first interrogation of the suspect or audition of the civil party.[190] Thereafter, defense attorneys may consult the dossier at any time during working hours, "subject to the needs of the investigation," and may obtain (at their own expense) copies of some or all of the dossier.[191] Whenever the Indicting Chamber holds a hearing, either on an interlocutory appeal from decisions of the JDI, or when reviewing felony charges proposed by that magistrate, the dossier is available, in the office of the clerk of the Chamber, at least 48 hours before the hearing, if the accused is detained, or five days ahead, in other cases.[192]

When the case is sent for trial in the Assize Court, the accused and the civil party have access to the dossier at all times after the accused's first appearance before the presiding judge of the Court.[193] In Correctional and Police Court trials, the parties may consult the dossier at any time after notice of the trial date has been given.[194]

B. Trial

1. *Nature of Trial*

As noted previously, lay jurors are only found in the Assize court, which tries major felony cases; delicts are tried in Correctional court, before one or three professional judges; contraventions are tried in Police Court before a single professional judge. Professional judges are assigned to court sessions in advance. Their professional careers and advancement were described in Part I. The specific trial procedures applicable in the Assize, Correctional, and Police Courts differ substantially, with more serious offenses being subject to more elaborate procedural safeguards. Before considering these courts separately, however, it is useful to examine the common features of trials in all three courts.

To begin with, there are no defendant pleas in French criminal courts. Thus, there is no direct French counterpart to the Anglo-American guilty plea, and no bargaining of charge or sentence leniency in return for such a plea; in principle, all cases are tried, and the accused's confession or admission of the charges has no formal effect on the method of adjudication. Nevertheless, there are a number of procedures and practices, especially in Police and Correctional Courts which, like plea bargaining, are designed to save time and discourage unnecessary litigation. Various trial substitutes avoid trial completely, in most Police Court matters, and trials in Correctional Court can be substantially shortened if the defendant, before or during the trial, admits most of the alleged facts.[195] Moreover, defendants understand that such cooperation is likely to reduce their sentence.

---

190. CPP Arts. 114 (para. 3) and 116 (para. 3).

191. CPP Art. 114 (para.s 3 & 5). Unless the JDI objects, counsel may give copies of dossier material to their clients (defendant or civil party), but further dissemination by the latter is punishable with fine of 25,000 francs. *Id.,* Arts. 114 (para. 6 & 7), 114-1.

192. CPP Art. 197 (para. 3).

193. CPP Arts. 278 (para. 2), 279, and 280. These first appearance procedures are discussed in text at note 144, *supra.*

194. CPP Art. 394 (para. 2). See text at notes 149-154, *supra.*

195. Frase 1990 at 627-8, 637-39.

When a trial is held it must, absent exceptional circumstances, be open to the public.[196] It must also, in principle, be "oral, and adversary" - "the court may base its decision only on the evidence that is brought out in the course of the trial and subject to debate by the parties."[197] Until recently, this principle was only loosely applied in Correctional and Police Courts, where written proofs were often simply read aloud in court, and police reports were often presumed to be correct.[198] However, recent decisions applying the European Convention on Human Rights have imposed stricter standards. Art. 6.3.d of the Convention grants the accused the right "to examine or have examined witnesses against him and to obtain the attendance of witnesses on his behalf under the same conditions as witnesses against him;" Art. 6.1 further grants a general right to a "fair trial" (*procès équitable*). The European Court of Human Rights, and the French Court of Cassation, have held that these provisions require the trial court to grant defendant's request to summon and question a witness unless the witness is clearly unavailable, or his testimony would be irrelevant, or the accused had an adequate opportunity to confront and question the witness in prior proceedings, or there is a serious risk of witness intimidation or retaliation; detailed reasons must be given for any refusal to call the witness.[199]

In all three trial courts the accused's prior record of convictions is always admissible. Except for exclusions based on lawyer-client and other professional privileges, or on "nullities" (illegally-obtained evidence, see discussion *supra*), French trial courts are bound by very few legal restrictions on the nature of evidence they may receive; "offenses may be established by any manner of proof, and the judge shall decide according to his thorough conviction."[200] Several factors seem to explain the absence of the kinds of detailed evidence rules found in many English-speaking systems: (1) Fact-finding in France is dominated by professional judges, not lay jurors; (2) trial procedure is not divided into separate "guilt" and "sentencing" phases, so all evidence bearing on sentence must be admitted at the same time as evidence bearing on guilt; and (3) as to both guilt and sentence, the French believe it is better to judge the whole person (including his past behavior and character), not just his current charges - "One judges the man, not the acts."[201]

---

196. CPP Arts. 306, 400, and 535.

197. CPP Art. 427 (para. 2).

198. Frase 1988 at 28-29, 31.

199. Pradel 1993a at 120; *Kostovski v. the Netherlands*, Eur. Ct. Hum. Rts, dec. of Nov. 20, 1989 (Convention violated where sole, unidentified prosecution witness was questioned only by a pretrial judge, and without the presence of prosecutor, defendant, or counsel); *Delta v. France*, Eur. Ct. Hum. Rts. dec. of Dec. 19, 1990 (defendant and his counsel never had an opportunity to question key prosecution witnesses); 1991 Bull. Crim. No. 115 (Mar. 6) (trial in Assize court violated Convention); 1989 Bull. Crim. No. 13 (Jan. 12) (trial *de novo* in Court of Appeals violated Convention; this case (*Randhawa*) is also discussed in Part C, 2, *infra*). *But see Doorson v. the Netherlands*, Eur. Ct. Hum. Rts. dec. of Mar. 26, 1996 (trial as a whole was not unfair, where defendant was identified by numerous anonymous witnesses who feared for their safety; identity of witnesses was known to pretrial judge, who heard witnesses in presence of defendant's counsel, and the witnesses corroborated each other's testimony).

200. CPP Art. 427 (para. 1).

201. ("*On juge l'homme, pas les faits.*") See Pugh, *The Administration of Criminal Justice in France: An Introductory Analysis*, 23 Louisiana Law Review 1, 10 (1962). See also CPP Arts. 331 (para. 5) and 444 (para. 1) (witnesses may testify not only as to the charges, but also as to the accused's "character and morals").

The conduct of the trial itself is controlled and directed almost entirely by the presiding judge. The trial usually begins with the sequestration of the witnesses,[202] after which the court interrogates the accused and receives his statements, if any;[203] the parties and attorneys then have limited rights to question the accused, usually through the intermediary of the presiding judge.[204] The accused is not put under oath, and cannot be legally compelled to answer any of the questions, but he cannot prevent the questions from being asked, nor can he prevent the court from drawing adverse inferences from his silence.[205] Next, the witnesses cited by the parties are individually questioned by the court (in the order determined by the court), after which the attorneys have limited rights to pose their own questions.[206] Witnesses are asked to state their name, age, profession, domicile, and whether they are related to, or employed by, any of the parties.[207] Witnesses testify under oath unless they are under sixteen years of age, have a criminal record, are related to one of the accused, are a defendant in the same trial, or have entered the case as a civil party.[208] Testimony is generally given in narrative form, although the presiding judge may interrupt to clarify ambiguities, preserve order, or prevent digressions.[209] Inconsistent witnesses may also be questioned jointly, and the accused may be asked, during or after a witness's testimony, to respond to that testimony.[210]

After the last witness is heard, the parties make their closing arguments - first the civil party, then the prosecution, then the defense; the first two may respond to the defense arguments, but the accused or his counsel shall always have the last word.[211] The court then deliberates on issues of both guilt and sentence (there is no separate sentencing hearing) and, if applicable, also on issues of civil liability. If the defendant is convicted, he or she may be ordered to pay costs to the civil party, and will also be assessed a fixed tax payable to the court (the former system of variable costs was abolished in 1993).[212] In Correctional and Police Courts, the court must render a written judgment order, citing the reasons for the decision (including the principal facts supporting guilt, as well as the law violated); in the Assize Court, however, the judgment order is simply the mixed court's verdict (guilty or not guilty as to each offense; findings of aggravating or mitigating circumstances; and the sentence imposed).[213]

---

202. CPP Arts. 325, 436, and 536.

203. CPP Arts. 328. 442, and 536. This interrogation normally begins with an examination of the background of the accused, including his prior convictions, followed by a reading of the details of the charge and important items of evidence contained in the dossier. Sheehan, p. 72-73.

204. CPP Arts. 312, 442, and 536.

205. Sheehan, p. 73; Pakter, p. 26, n. 183.

206. CPP Arts. 329 to 332, 454, and 536. Defense and prosecution attorneys rarely engage in rigorous cross-examination, but presiding judges or counsel for the civil party sometimes do.

207. CPP Arts. 331 (para. 2), 445 (para. 1), and 536.

208. CPP Arts. 331 (para. 3), 335, 446 to 448, and 536; Stefani et al. at para. 679; Sheehan, p. 74.

209. CPP Arts. 309, 331 (para. 4); Sheehan, p. 74. In principle, non-expert witnesses may only consult documents with the court's permission, in "special" cases, but this rule is not strictly adhered to. CPP Arts. 168 (para. 1), 452; Sheehan, p.74, 83.

210. Sheehan, p. 74.

211. CPP Arts. 346 and 460.

212. Law of Jan. 4, 1993, arts. 120 to 143. For example, the tax for decisions of the Assize court is 2,500 francs (about $420, at 1997 exchange rates); decisions of the Police Court, whether by trial or penal order, cost 150 francs. General Tax Code, § 1018A.

213. CPP Arts. 348 to 366, 485, 543; Stefani et al. at para. 708.

The description above assumes that the accused has been present throughout the trial; however, defendants may also be tried *in absentia*, and the results are sometimes binding on the accused as if he had been present.

a. *Trials in the Assize Court.* The Assize court has full jurisdiction to try any case transferred to it by the indicting chamber, and it may try only such cases (including related delict and contravention charges).[214] At least 24 hours before the start of trial in the Assize court, the accused must serve on the prosecution and civil parties the names of all cited defense witnesses and experts, and the prosecution and civil parties must serve the names of their cited witnesses on the accused.[215] Opposing parties may object to the hearing of a witness who was not properly noticed.[216]

The trial itself begins with the selection of nine trial jurors from the session list called for that term of court.[217] The names of prospective jurors are selected by a rather complex procedure, based on electoral lists.[218] Legal qualifications to be a juror include age (at least 23), retention of full political, civil, and family rights, and ability to read and write in French; police officers and certain high government officials are disqualified.[219] The trial jurors are chosen by lot, but the prosecution is allowed four peremptory challenges, and the defense is allowed five (no matter how many defendants there are).[220] The court must also order the selection of one or more alternate jurors.[221] There is no questioning of prospective jurors by the parties or by the court.

The trial, once begun, must continue without interruption to judgment, and may only be recessed to allow the court to eat and sleep.[222] (Assize court trials generally last from one to three days). In addition to maintaining courtroom order, the presiding judge has power to do whatever he or she may deem necessary to discover the truth, including citation of additional witnesses.[223] The trial proper begins with a reading of the decree of indictment, by the clerk.[224] Next the president interrogates the accused and directs the testimony of the witnesses. (See summary of trial procedures, above.) The other two judges and the jurors may, with the president's approval, ask questions of the accused or of any witness,[225] and the parties may submit questions to be asked by the president.[226] Each witness must remain in

---

214. CPP Arts. 214 and 231.

215. CPP Art. 281.

216. CPP Arts. 329 and 330.

217. CPP Arts. 282, 288 to 305. Session lists (35 jurors and 10 alternates) are drawn by lot from an annual list of prospective jurors for each Assize court. Arts. 266 to 267.

218. CPP Arts. 259 to 265.

219. CPP Arts. 255 to 258-1.

220. CPP Arts. 298 to 301. The reasons for challenges may not be revealed. Art. 297 (para. 2). Prosecution challenges are rare. Sheehan, p. 82, note 31.

221. CPP Art. 296 (para. 2).

222. CPP Art. 307. The case may also be remanded to (and recommenced at) the next term of court. Art. 343.

223. CPP Art. 310. The presiding judge may order, under his control, sound reproduction; all other recording or photography is prohibited, subject to substantial fines, Art. 308, and there is generally no written transcript of testimony. Arts. 333 and 379.

224. CPP Art. 327.

225. CPP Art. 311. The presiding judge, the other judges, and the jurors have the duty not to indicate their opinion as to guilt. Arts. 311 and 328. See Part C.2, *infra*, discussing several cases where convictions were reversed for violation of Art. 328.

226. CPP Arts. 312 and 332 (para. 2).

the courtroom until the court retires to deliberate, unless he or she is excused by the president.[227] After the last witness is heard, the parties make their closing arguments on the criminal charges.

The arguments finished, the president reads the specific questions to which the court and jury must respond.[228] The jurors are also instructed that, to convict the accused, they must be "thoroughly convinced" of his guilt.[229] The judges and jurors then retire to deliberate. In principle, nothing may be considered by them that has not been presented orally at the trial, either by means of testimony, reading of documents, or inspection of physical evidence.[230] After deliberating, the judges and jurors vote by secret ballot.[231] Conviction requires the votes of at least eight of the twelve members (and thus, at least five of the nine jurors).[232] If the vote is for conviction, the court proceeds to vote (again, by secret ballot) on the penalty.[233] Each member proposes a penalty, which must receive a majority of the ballots to prevail (however, imposition of the maximum allowed penalty requires at least eight votes). The members continue to ballot until they arrive at a penalty. On the third and subsequent ballots, the most severe penalty proposed on the preceding ballot is stricken from the list of available penalties.

At the end of deliberations, the court returns to the courtroom. After the accused is brought in, the president announces the court's verdict and reads its responses to the specific questions posed. The decision on the civil claim is made by the three professional judges alone, and damages may be awarded even if the accused has been acquitted.[234] The civil party may also be ordered to pay damages to the accused, if acquitted.[235]

The accused may sometimes be tried *in absentia*. The trial is "deemed to be adversary" (*réputé contradictoire*), and thus binding as though the accused were present, when the accused who is already in custody refuses to voluntarily enter the courtroom (he can also be forcibly led into court),[236] or is expelled from the courtroom for disruptive behavior.[237] In cases of default judgment of an accused not in custody, a different procedure (*jugement par contumace*) is used.[238] An abbreviated, non-adversary trial is held, but the convicted accused who later surrenders or is arrested must be retried according to the normal procedures described above.

---

227. CPP Art. 334. However, witnesses or accuseds may be ordered to retire temporarily, during testimony of other witnesses or accuseds. Arts. 338 and 339.

228. CPP Arts. 348 to 351.

229. CPP Art. 353 (jurors are asked: "Avez-vous une intime conviction?").

230. *See* CPP Art. 347 (para. 3), specifying that the dossier of the case must be deposited with the clerk, and may not be taken into the conference room. It may, however, be consulted during deliberations, in the presence of official counsel and the attorneys. Art. 347 (para. 4). Also, judges and jurors may take and retain notes, during the trial, Art. 340, and the decree of indictment is retained throughout the deliberations, Art. 347 (para. 3). The decree includes not only a summary of the alleged facts, but also information on the accused's background and prior record. Sheehan, p. 67.

231. CPP Arts. 356 to 358, 362.

232. CPP Art. 359. This rule also applies to any vote refusing extenuating circumstances.

233. CPP Art. 362.

234. CPP Arts. 371 and 372.

235. CPP Art. 371 (para. 1).

236. CPP Arts. 319 and 320.

237. CPP Art. 322.

238. CPP Arts. 627 to 641.

b. *Trials in Correctional Court.* The Correctional Court has jurisdiction to hear charges of delict (and related contravention charges).[239] It may receive jurisdiction by any of the following means: (1) Voluntary appearance of the parties;[240] (2) citation, issued at the request of the prosecutor, or the civil party;[241] (3) "convocation by official reports," issued by the prosecutor at the end of investigatory detention;[242] (4) the "immediate appearance" procedure;[243] or (5) remand ordered by the JDI or the Indicting Chamber.[244]

The accused has the right to be assisted by retained or appointed counsel, but counsel is not obligatory unless the accused "is subject to such an infirmity as to compromise his defense."[245] Prior to or at the trial, counsel (but not the accused, him or herself) has the right to inspect the official file (*dossier*) of the case.[246] Trial witnesses may be summoned and compelled to testify by means of citation, issued at the request of the civil party, the prosecutor, or the defense.[247] Any witnesses who appear in court without having been regularly cited may also be heard, with the court's permission, provided they were present at the opening of the trial.[248] In practice, the parties often do not bother to cite or produce many witnesses, preferring instead to rely on their pretrial statements, contained in the dossier; this is especially likely in cases which had a judicial investigation.[249]

The trial itself normally begins with the presiding judge verifying the identity of the accused, and noting how the court obtained jurisdiction.[250] The president then proceeds to the examination of the accused and the witnesses.[251] (See previous summary of trial procedures.) Unlike the procedure in Assize court, the clerk keeps detailed notes of all testimony (but not a verbatim transcript);[252] also, the trial may be continued to a later date, if necessary.[253] However, almost all trials are completed within one day; most take less than half a day, and many last less than an hour.

The Code specifically provides that "offenses may be established by any manner of proof, and the judge shall decide according to his thorough conviction" (*in-*

239. CPP Arts. 381 and 382 (para. 4).
240. CPP Arts. 388 and 389.
241. CPP Arts. 388, 390, 390-1, and 550 to 566.
242. CPP Arts. 388, 393, 394, and 397-6. See text at note 149, *supra*.
243. CPP Arts. 388, 393, and 395 to 397-7. See text at note 151, *supra*.
244. CPP Arts. 179, 213, and 388.
245. CPP Art. 417 (para. 4).
246. CPP Art. 393 (para. 3). See text at note 35, *supra* .
247. CPP Arts. 397-5, 435 to 441; 551 (para. 1). The latter article, dealing with citations generally, only provides for issuance of citations at the request of the prosecution or the civil party, but in practice defendants can request bailiffs to cite witnesses; moreover, this procedure appears to be mandated by Art. 6.3.d of the European convention on human rights, granting defendants "compulsory process" rights equal to those enjoyed by the prosecution. Stefani et al. at para. 678, 678-1. See Part C.2, *infra* (*Randhawa* case).

Although this rarely occurs in practice, the court may, on its own motion, call for expert evidence, or order a supplementary judicial investigation. CPP Arts. 434 and 463.

248. CPP Art. 444 (para. 3).
249. Sheehan, at p. 29 & 74.
250. CPP Art. 406.
251. CPP Arts. 436 to 457.
252. CPP Art. 453.
253. CPP Art. 461.

time conviction).[254] However, in the case of police or other written reports, these general principles are subject to three important qualifications. First, such a report has probative value only if it is regular in form, and only as to matters personally observed by its author in the course of his prescribed duties.[255] Second, certain reports (e.g., of labor violations) are presumed true (as to the basic facts reported, not necessarily the broader inferences) unless contrary proof is offered in writing, or by witnesses (*not* including the accused, who is not considered a "witness").[256] Third, a few reports (e.g., by customs officials) are presumed true, as to basic facts, until they are proved (by a separate, rather complex, procedure) to have been forged.[257]

After all evidence is received, and final arguments completed, the court may immediately announce its verdict and sentence; alternatively, the court may announce the judgment later the same day, after retiring to deliberate (often on several cases at once), or it may postpone announcement of the judgment to a specified later date.[258] The judgment must contain both reasons and a disposition.[259] The Code further specifies that the court may found its decision only on the evidence "brought to [it] in the course of the trial, and discussed before [it] by the parties."[260] However, unlike the procedure in Assize court, the Correctional Court retains access to the dossier both at trial and during deliberations,[261] and judgements sometimes rely on material in the file which was not specifically mentioned in court.

If the accused is found guilty of a delict or a contravention (or both), the court pronounces the sentence and decides on the civil party's claim, if any.[262] Except in very limited cases,[263] the court may not decide the civil claim if the accused has been acquitted of all criminal charges, but it may grant damages to the acquitted defendant, against the civil party.[264]

When an accused who received notice of the trial date fails to appear, without a valid excuse or permission of the court, he may be tried *in absentia* and the result will be binding as though he were present (*réputé contradictoire*).[265] A similar rule

254. CPP Art. 427 (para. 1). See also Art. 428 ("confessions, like all types of evidence, are left to the free appreciation of the judges").

255. CPP Art. 429.

256. CPP Arts. 431 and 432.

257. CPP Arts. 433 and 642 to 647-4. The Court of Cassation has held that these rules do not violate the presumption of innocence and fair trial provisions of the European convention on human rights. Stefani et al. at para.s 38, 700. *See also* 1989 Bull. Crim., No.33 (Jan. 30) (presumption of illegal importation or attempted exportation, in Art. 418 of the Customs Code, did not violate the European Convention).

258. CPP Art. 462.

259. CPP Art. 485.

260. CPP Art. 427 (para. 2).

261. CPP Art. 347.

262. CPP Arts. 464, 466, and 467. The Correctional Court must return the case to the prosecutor, without judgment, if it finds the offense constitutes a major felony. Art. 469.

263. CPP Art. 470-1 (non-intentional injury). See also Art. 468 (absolved accused).

264. CPP Art. 472.

265. CPP Arts. 410 (para. 2) & 417. Alternatively, the court may continue the case and issue an arrest warrant, if the offense is punishable with at least two years imprisonment. Art. 410-1. In less serious cases, the accused may request to be judged *in absentia*, and if the request is granted his counsel may still be heard. Art. 411. See also Art. 416 (accused who is ill may be heard, with counsel, out of court).

applies when the accused is expelled from court for disruptive behavior, or absents himself after the trial has begun.[266] When it appears that the non-appearing accused had no notice of the trial date, a default judgment may be entered, which permits the accused to petition for rehearing.[267]

c. *Trials (and trial substitutes) in Police Court.* When a trial is held in Police Court (which is rare), the procedure is generally the same as in Correctional Court, with the following major exceptions: (1) The court always consists of a single judge;[268] (2) the court's jurisdiction may only be based on voluntary appearance of the parties, citation, or remand from the JDI or Indicting Chamber;[269] (3) there is no provision for appointed counsel, but retained counsel may appear (and in minor cases, may be heard even if the accused is absent);[270] (4) the court has no power to try or impose sentence for a delict, even one involving disruption of the trial;[271] and (5) the category of written reports which are presumed true (as to basic facts) in the absence of contrary proof is much broader, including almost all reports by members of the judicial police.[272]

Thus, trials in Police Court are almost always brief and simple. Nevertheless, the vast majority of contravention charges are adjudicated without trial; indeed, most are handled without any involvement of the Police Court whatsoever. Most contraventions may be (and generally are) handled by payment of pre-set (scheduled) fines.[273] A second, so-called "simplified" or "penal order" procedure applies to almost any contravention, and permits the imposition of a fine with no hearing or trial.[274] The prosecutor initiates the procedure, and the Police Court determines the amount of fine to be paid. However, if the Police Court believes that a trial or sanctions other than a fine would be preferable, or either the prosecutor or the accused objects to the court's proposed fine, the case is automatically set for trial in the Police Court.

2. *Defendant's testimony*

As noted above, defendants have the right to testify, but do not take an oath. With the permission of the presiding judge, they may be cross-examined by the prosecutor, although this is infrequent in practice. However, the judge's questioning often takes a very "adverse" form if the defendant denies guilt (many trial judges are former JDIs or prosecutors). Defendants may refuse to answer particular questions, but are not expressly advised of this right, nor may they prevent questions from being posed. Comment on the failure to answer some or all questions, and adverse inferences based on silence, are not prohibited.

French law has traditionally held that defendants who fail to appear without a valid excuse may not be represented by counsel. Art. 417 (para. 1); Stefani et al. at para. 675. However, the European Court of Human Rights has held that this violates Arts. 6.1 ("fair trial") and 6.3.c (right to counsel) of the Convention. *Poitrimol v. France*, dec. of Nov. 23, 1993.

266. CPP Arts. 405 and 413.

267. CPP Arts. 412, 487 to 494-1.

268. CPP Art. 523.

269. CPP Art. 531. The accused tried in Police Court may not be subjected to pretrial detention, or even pretrial supervision. See text at note 165, *supra*.

270. CPP Art. 544 (para. 2) [offenses punishable by fine only].

271. CPP Arts. 535 (para. 2) and 540.

272. CPP Art. 537 (para.s 2 & 3). See text at note 256, *supra*..

273. CPP Arts. 529 to 530-3.

274. CPP Arts. 524 to 528-2.

3. *Lawyers*

Defendants may be represented by retained counsel in any case, and must be represented in Assize court; they have a right to appointed counsel in both Assize and Correctional Court. The trial is primarily conducted by the presiding judge, and lawyers play relatively passive roles. Attorneys may exercise a limited number or peremptory challenges to jurors, in Assize court trials (see above).

In theory, the prosecutor (as well as the police and judges) is supposed to be "fair" and even-handed in the pursuit of the truth, searching for and presenting all evidence of innocence as well as of guilt.[275] Indeed, prosecutors are considered to be "magistrates," and share a common training and similar career ladder.[276] In practice, however, prosecutors normally act as advocates in favor of guilt and more severe punishment, although they are probably not as adversarial as U.S. prosecutors.

4. *Witnesses*

Witnesses are obtained for trial by being issued citations, which are served by a bailiff (*huissier de justice*). Under Art. 6.3.d of the European Convention on Human Rights, defendant must be allowed to compel the attendance of witnesses in his favor on the same grounds as the state obtains prosecution witnesses.[277] Cross-examination of adverse witnesses is only permitted with the permission of the presiding judge, and is rare in practice. The summoning and questioning of such witnesses by the court was formerly discretionary, but now appears to be required (unless the witness is clearly unavailable or of no value). In general, a witness has no right to refuse to testify on ground that doing so would incriminate him.[278]

5. *Judges*

Judges are always appointed, and are usually graduates of the national magistracy school (See discussion in Part I, B, 3.)

6. *Victims*

Any person injured by a criminal offense (and certain other persons or associations representing injured persons)[279] may initiate prosecution, or may join a prosecution already commenced; in either case, they receive most of the rights of a party to the prosecution (e.g., notice of hearings, right to be heard, appeal rights), and may demand an award of damages (determined under the applicable rules of

---

275. See text at note 33, *supra*.

276. See Part I, B, 2, *supra*.

277. See discussion of witness-citing rules, text at notes 199, 215, & 247, *supra*.

278. Stefani et al. at para.530.

279. CPP Arts. 2 to 2-16. Insurance companies often enter criminal cases, either as civil party, Sheehan, p. 20-21, or as intervenors representing the victim, the accused, or the "person civilly responsible" (e.g., parents; employers). Art. 388-1 et seq.

civil liability) from the criminal court. Except for felonies and certain delicts involving non-intentional injuries, acquittal bars an award of damages.[280]

The civil party may join a case initiated by the prosecutor at any time during the judicial investigation,[281] or before the prosecutor's final arguments in Correctional or Police Court.[282] To initiate prosecution for a felony, the civil party must file his claim with the JDI; victims of a delict may either use this method, or (if the offender's identity is known) may initiate prosecution directly in Correctional Court.[283] Victims of a contravention must file directly in Police Court.[284] The prosecuting attorney is permitted to state his views on the case to the JDI, but may only submit a petition not to investigate if "the facts cannot legally support a prosecution," or "would not permit a penal sanction."[285] Unless excused by reason of indigency, the civil party must deposit a sum to cover his possible liability for abuse of process.[286] If the case later ends in dismissal or acquittal, a civil party who initiated prosecution may be assessed a civil fine, and/or may be ordered to pay damages to the defendant.[287]

Under some circumstances, the victim may also petition a government commission for an award of damages from the state.[288]

C. Appeals

Decisions of the Correctional or Police Court may be appealed *de novo* to the Court of Appeals,[289] with further appeals on issues of law to the Court of Cassation. Certain issues may be appealed by the prosecution and the civil party, as well as by the defense. Decisions by the Assize courts are only reviewable on issues of law, in the Court of Cassation.[290]

Review by the Courts of Appeal. Final decisions of the Correctional Court as to guilt, innocence, dismissal, or sentence may be appealed by the accused, the prosecuting attorney, the attorney general for that appellate district, and certain administrative authorities; final decisions regarding civil liability may be appealed by the accused, the civil party, the person civilly responsible for the accused, or an insurer of one of these parties.[291] More limited appeal rights apply to final decisions

---

280. CPP Arts. 371 (para. 1), 372, 464 (para. 2), 466, 470-1, 539 (para. 2), and 541 (para. 2).

281. CPP Art. 87 (para. 1).

282. CPP Arts. 421 and 536.

283. CPP Arts. 85, 388, 392, and 551.

284. CPP Arts. 531, 533, and 551.

285. CPP Art. 86 (para. 7).

286. CPP Art. 88.

287. CPP Arts. 91, 371 (para. 1), and 472.

288. CPP Arts. 706-3 to 706-14.

289. Interlocutory appeals of certain decisions of the JDI may also be brought to a special panel of the Court of Appeals (the Indicting Chamber). See text at notes 28, 86-88, & 178-186, *supra*.

290. *But see* note 139, *supra*, discussing a pending Assize court reform proposal.

291. CPP Arts. 497 and 509 (para. 2).

of the Police Court.[292] With some exceptions, execution of the trial court judgment is suspended during the appeal.[293]

Appeals are heard by the criminal chamber of the regional Court of Appeals (*cour d'appel*), which consists of three judges.[294] The appeal hearing is, in principle, a trial *de novo* on all issues of fact, law, or sentencing raised by the appeal. The rules of trial procedure (including right to counsel) are the same as those used in the Correctional Court, with the following exceptions:[295] (1) The hearing begins with an oral report of the case by one of the two associate judges ("counselors"); (2) witnesses other than the accused are only heard if the court so orders;[296] and (3) final arguments begin with the appellant (although the accused still has the last word). On appeal only by the accused, the person civilly responsible, the civil party, or an insurer of one of these parties, the Court of Appeals may not impose a judgment less favorable to the appellant than the judgment appealed from.[297]

In recent years, about four percent of trial convictions (excluding penal orders) in Correctional and Police Courts combined have been appealed; on the average, about 12 percent of these appeals resulted in acquittal of the defendant.[298]

Review by the Court of Cassation. There are two kinds of review by this Court. Petitions for Review are limited to issues of law; Petitions for Revision are a form of collateral attack, limited to cases of newly-discovered evidence. (See section 3, below.)

Petitions for Review are used to resolve legal issues raised by final decisions of Indicting Chambers, Courts of Appeal, and Assize courts, as well as final decisions of the Correctional and Police Courts which were not subject to review by the Court of Appeals.[299] Any party may petition for review of a decision adversely af-

---

292. The accused, the person civilly responsible, and the prosecutor may only appeal on criminal aspects if the Police Court imposed a drivers license suspension or a fine exceeding the maximum for a second class contravention, or if the conviction offense was a fifth class contravention. CPP Art. 546. The Attorney General's former right to appeal any police court judgement was struck down as incompatible with the "equality of arms" required under the European Convention. 1997 Bull. Crim. No. 170 (May 6, 1997).

293. CPP Arts. 506, 515-1, and 549.

294. CPP Arts. 496 to 520 and 546 to 549.

295. CPP Arts. 512, 513, and 549.

296. However, decisions of the European Court of Human Rights and the Court of Cassation suggest that the appeals court must hear a witness requested by the defendant, or explain why such hearing is impossible or inappropriate, at least if the witness was also refused in the trial court. *Delta v. France*, dec. of Dec. 19, 1990; 1989 Bull. Crim. No. 13 (Jan. 12). See also text at note 198, *supra*. *But see* 1988 Bull. Crim. No. 161 (Apr. 18) (no violation, where defendant had failed to request hearing of the witness in the trial court).

297. CPP Art. 515 (para. 2). However, upon appeal by one party, all other parties (including the prosecutor) have five additional days to file their own appeals. Art. 500.

298. Annuaire Statistique, p. 95, 99, 103. This source no longer reports separate figures for Correctional and Police Court cases. In 1984, about five percent of final delict convictions, and about one-half of one percent of contravention convictions (by trial; excluding penal orders) were pronounced by courts of appeal. Frase 1990 at 682, n. 742. There are also no separate figures on prosecution, defense, and civil party appeals, or on appeal outcomes (other than the number of acquittals).

299. CPP Arts. 567 to 621. The petition for review may not be used to raise issues not presented below, or to attack trial court decisions which a party could have appealed, but did not. Arts. 567 & 599. Also, such petitions may not be used to contest the sufficiency of the evidence to convict. 1988 Bull. Crim. No. 161 (Apr. 18); Sheehan, p. 92. However, the recognized grounds

fecting his interests, but decrees of acquittal in the Assize Court may only be reviewed for the purpose of clarifying the law, without prejudice to the accused.[300]

The petition is filed with the criminal chamber of the Court of Cassation. An accused sentenced to an executed prison term exceeding six months must surrender into custody, or be dispensed from doing so by the trial court; otherwise, his petition is forfeited.[301] The hearing resembles that in the court of appeal; one judge reports on the case, and the parties make their arguments.[302] Counsel is not required, but legal aid (*aide juridictionelle*) is available for the accused who requests it.[303] If the Court annuls the decision below, in whole or in part, it usually remands the case to a different court of the same rank as the court which rendered the annulled decision (occasionally, no further proceedings are needed, or permitted).[304]

In recent years, Petitions for Review leading to a decision on the merits have represented less than one percent of all trial court convictions (excluding penal orders); among such decisions on the merits, the average reversal rate has been about 11 percent (including decisions favorable to the prosecution and civil party, as well as those favorable to the defendant).[305]

1. *Ineffective Assistance of Counsel*

It does not appear that this is a ground of appeal or other post-trial review in France. Even in the Assize Court, where counsel is obligatory, the absence of counsel during the trial, through no fault of the court or prosecution, is not a grounds for reversal.[306] Similarly, the failure of counsel to appear after being "duly summoned" does not prevent the JDI from proceeding with the interrogation of the suspect.[307]

2. *Other Grounds for Appeal*

In light of the 11-12% reversal rates in the appeals and cassation courts (resulting in the acquittal of over 3,000 defendants per year, and an unknown number of reversals favorable to the prosecution or civil party), it is clear that there are many effective legal and factual grounds for appeal in France. Reversals based on such factors as improper prosecutorial argument or improper conduct by a trial judge are rare.[308] However, use of illegally obtained evidence has often been a basis for reversal. (See cases discussed in part II, especially sections A, 5 and C, 3, *supra*.)

---

for reversal include the insufficient reasoning (*défaut de motifs*) or lack of legal basis (*manque de base légale*) of the lower court's judgment. The Court of Cassation sometimes cites one or both of these two grounds when reversing convictions based on very meager evidence. *See, e.g.*, 1989 Bull. Crim., No. 13 (Jan. 12). This case (*Randhawa*) is discussed further in Part C, 2, *infra*.

300. CPP Art. 572.

301. CPP Art. 583.

302. CPP Arts. 587 (para. 2) and 601 to 603.

303. Law of July 10, 1991, Art. 7; Stefani et al. at para. 777.

304. CPP Arts. 609 to 613; Stefani et al. para. 783.

305. Annuaire Statistique, p. 92-105.

306. 1976 Bull. Crim. No. 291 (Oct. 14); 1957 Bull. Crim. No. 614 (Oct. 9).

307. CPP Art. 114 (para. 1); Stefani et al. at para. 534.

308. However, a number of cases have reversed convictions because the presiding judge in the Assize court revealed his opinion as to the accused's guilt, in violation of CPP Art. 328 (para. 2). *See, e.g.*, 1989 Bull.Crim., No. 259 (June 14) (judge asked defendant, "Don't you think that you're denying the evidence, and that you have an untenable position?"); 1991 Bull. Crim., No.

The remainder of this section discusses some of the more important cases in which convictions have been reversed on appeal. Because these are "leading" cases (and some could even be described as "revolutionary"), most are not "representative" of other cases from the same period, or even later periods. They are discussed here in order to illustrate the considerable evolution of French law over the past forty years, and the willingness of the Court of Cassation to both infer and expand new procedural rights for defendants.

Isnard *(1953)*. One of the earliest and most important cases reversing a conviction on appeal was a 1953 decision[309] involving an illegal body search which lead to seizure of physical evidence (betting slips), questioning of the suspect, and a confession. The Court of Cassation held that both the physical evidence and the confession must be suppressed. The case is significant for several reasons. First, the Court held the search illegal, even though no Procedure Code provision specifically regulates body searches, nor are such searches expressly prohibited in the course of a preliminary investigation. The Code does specify that searches of houses (*perquisitions*) during a preliminary inquiry require express written consent. The Court apparently felt that body searches are so intrusive that they should be covered by ("assimilated" to) the rules on house searches. Absent consent, the latter are only permitted under a flagrant offense investigation (or a judicial investigation, but none was open at the time).

Second, the Court in *Isnard* narrowly construed the definition of a flagrant offense (and thus, the scope of such investigations). Although the Code literally says a crime is "flagrant" when it is in the process of being committed (which it was, here - the suspect was in possession of illegal gambling materials), the Court held that the opening of a flagrant offense investigation requires the police to observe objective evidence (*indices apparents*) of this offense - a requirement of "individualized suspicion" which has since been extended by legislation to other decisions (placement in investigatory detention; some identity checks). Mr. Isnard had previously been charged with illegal gambling, but there was no external sign or other evidence that he was committing this crime, or had recently done so, when he was stopped on the street. Subsequent cases have given more specific content to the nature and sources of the individualized suspicion required. (See *Gomez-Garzon*, discussed *infra.*)

Third, the Court held that these violations required suppression of the resulting evidence, even though the exclusionary rule ("nullity") provisions of the Code at that time only expressly applied to judicial investigations. Moreover, the Court excluded both the immediate fruits of the illegal search (the betting slips) and the "derivative fruits" (defendant's confession), thus applying a version of the "fruit of the poisonous tree" doctrine. The Court stated that all of these operations were covered by a single police report, constituting "a single unit," and that the confession was not "freely given." It does not appear that the Court viewed the confes-

16 (Jan. 9) (at the start of trial, presiding judge gave all parties and members of the court a draft of the questions which the court would have to decide; the last page of the draft included a finding of guilt). *See generally* Pradel & Varinard at 263-67 (discussing these two cases and others, applying Art. 328).

309. 1953 Bull. Crim. No. 24 (Jan. 22); also reported in 1953 Recueil Dalloz, Jurisprudence at 533, commentary by C. Lapp, and in 1953 Juris-Classeur périodique, la semaine juridique, No. 7456, and discussed in Tomlinson at 181-83.

sion as coerced, but rather saw it as the product of the earlier illegalities - not an independent act. The scope of French "fruits" rules continues to be uncertain, and relatively few later cases expressly discuss this issue, but the implicit rule of Isnard's case has often been cited: Derivative fruits which are the necessary product of a substantial illegality must be suppressed. (See Part II.A, 5, *supra.*)

Gomez-Garzon (1980). The *Isnard* case held that police need objective signs (*indices apparents*) that a crime has been committed, before they may open a flagrant offense investigation.[310] In an important 1980 case,[311] the Court of Cassation held that the required degree of suspicion had *not* been met when police searched the defendant's hotel room based on a "confidential report" that the defendant was selling drugs. In addition to this report, the police knew that the defendant had previously been implicated in drug sales; had recently moved from a house to the more anonymous setting of the hotel; and had admitted using cocaine in the past (although denying that he presently possessed it). Subsequent cases have held that anonymous tips are insufficient unless confirmed by further independent investigation.[312]

Baroom (1978). One of the most important developments in the criminal appeals caselaw of the past twenty years has been the growing willingness of French courts to apply the provisions of the European Convention on Human Rights (which became applicable in France on May 3, 1974). A 1978 decision of the Court of Cassation[313] was one of the first reported cases to cite the Convention as a basis for reversing a conviction. Defendant had been charged with a weapons violation ordinarily punishable with up to three years of imprisonment, but with up to five years for certain recidivists. The charging documents did not mention any possible recidivist enhancement, and the Correctional Court imposed a sentence of six months. Defendant appealed, after which the prosecution also appealed (thus allowing the sentence to be increased on appeal). The Court of Appeals invoked the recidivist enhancement on its own motion, and sentenced Mr. Baroom to the maximum (five-year) penalty.

The Court of Cassation, reversed, saying that it was not clear defendant had been properly informed of the possible enhancement, or given a chance to defend himself on this point (in particular, to argue that the prior conviction was only a default, not a final judgment). The Court cited both Art. 427 of the Procedure Code (limiting judgments to evidence that was produced and discussed at trial) and Arts. 6 and 13 of the Convention (fair trial rules; requirement that national courts provide "an effective remedy"). Although the decision built upon prior cases applying Art. 427, the Court gave special emphasis to the Convention (which had *not* been cited in Baroom's petition for review). Art. 6.3.a of the Convention was quoted almost verbatim, both in the opinion and in the headnote summary published in the official case report: "Every accused has the right to be informed in detail of the nature and cause of the accusation against him." Subsequent cases in the

---

310. However, once the investigation is properly commenced, a lesser degree of individualized suspicion is required to search particular places. See note 62, *supra*.

311. 1980 Bull. Crim. No. 165 (May 30); also reported at: 1981 Recueil Dalloz-Sirey, Jurisprudence at 533, commentary by W. Jeandidier.

312. Stefani et al. at para. 305.

313. 1978 Bull. Crim. No. 346 (Dec. 5); also reported in: 1979 Recueil Dalloz-Sirey, Jurisprudence at 50, commentary by S. Kehrig.

Cassation and lower courts have increasingly involved discussion of the requirements of the Convention; most often, French law is found to be in compliance, but many convictions have been reversed on this ground.

Randhawa (1989). In the late 1980's, French courts began to make much more frequent use of the provisions of the European Convention, particularly the provision of Art. 6.3.d, granting the accused "the right to examine or have examined witnesses against him." One of the first cases to reverse a conviction on this ground was a 1989 decision of the Court of Cassation.[314] The defendant Randhawa cited two adverse witnesses to attend his trial *de novo* in the Court of Appeals, and formally requested the Court to hear them. However, Art. 513 of the Procedure Code provides that witnesses are only heard if the Court of Appeals so orders. The appeals Court refused the request, stating that "it would not be useful to the manifestation of the truth" to hear these witnesses because they had already been heard during pretrial police and judicial proceedings (albeit not in the presence of defendant or his counsel), and their statements had been provided to the defense. The Court then found defendant guilty, basing its judgment entirely on the statements of these two witnesses (one had identified defendant from a photograph; the other had made conflicting statements during the course of various proceedings).

The Court of Cassation reversed, basing its decision entirely on Art. 6.3.d of the Convention (and on the general "fair trial" concept of Art. 6.1). The Court stated that a trial court may only deny hearing of a requested witness if it gives specific reasons showing that hearing the witness would be impossible or very difficult, or that there is a risk of intimidation or reprisals against the witness; the Court also implied that the trial court can refuse to hear a witness if defendant had an adequate opportunity to question the witness in previous proceedings, or if the testimony of the witness would be unimportant. Despite these limitations, cases such as *Randhawa* give French defendants far greater rights of "confrontation" than were traditionally recognized in France and other systems based on the Civil Law model. *Randhawa* is all the more remarkable because it was decided one year *before* the first case in the European Court of Human Rights, holding that French trial procedures violated Art. 6.3.d of the Convention.[315]

"X.." (1996).[316] The Convention was also cited in a recent case[317] excluding evidence because of a violation of the 48-hour limit on investigatory detention. In a remarkable, and perhaps revolutionary decision, the Court of Cassation held that violation of the 48-hour (extended) limit results in a *presumption* of prejudice to the interests of the accused, thus requiring the annulment of all official reports of the detention (including defendant's confession). As noted earlier, there are no textual nullity provisions associated with the Procedure Code's limits on the duration of investigatory detention, and the Court had previously been extremely reluctant to infer "substantial" nullity and exclude evidence; defendants had to show that "the search for and establishment of the truth was fundamentally tainted," which in practice could rarely be shown. The presumption of prejudice may suggest that

314. 1989 Bull. Crim. No. 13 (Jan. 12); also reported in: 1989 Recueil Dalloz-Sirey, Sommaires Commentés at 174.

315. *Delta v. France*, Eur. Ct. Hum. Rts., dec. of Dec. 19, 1990.

316. "X.." is the French equivalent of "Doe."

317. 1996 Bull. Crim. No. 74 (Feb. 13); also reported briefly in: 1996 Recueil Dalloz-Sirey no. 29, *Sommaires Commentés*, at 258.

the Court views these durational limits as raising issues of "public order," thus dispensing both with the former focus on "the truth" and with the requirements of Art. 802 (under which defendants invoking non-public-order nullities must show prejudice to their interests).[318] Alternatively, the Court may simply view extended detention as inherently "prejudicial."

The "X.." case is even more remarkable, given its unusual facts. Although the defendant was held a total of 52 _ hours, this included a 9-hour detention during a preliminary investigation of the same offense (statutory rape of defendant's stepdaughter), over six years earlier. At that time, prosecution was declined, but the victim later filed another complaint, and a judicial investigation was opened. Defendant was then detained for another 43 _ hours. The Court held that these two periods of detention must be added together. Finally, the Court annulled the official report of the detention, and defendant's confession, even though the confession occurred *before* the 48-hour limit had been reached (during most of the 4 _ hours which exceeded that limit, defendant was resting, and was then promptly released by the JDI). Although defendant later recanted his confession, the Court did not discuss how the subsequent durational violation may have (or should be presumed to have) contributed to the confession. Rather, the Court seemed to be concerned with the violation of *liberty* caused by the 52_-hour detention, and viewed annulment of the entire detention record as the appropriate remedy. The Court cited Arts. 5.1 and 5.3 of the European Convention, which guarantee "liberty and security of the person," and require that all arrested or detained persons be brought "promptly before a judge or other officer authorized by law to exercise judicial power."

It is still too early to tell what long-term effects the "X.." decision will have, but it certainly suggests that the Court of Cassation is now much more willing to strictly enforce the procedural protections applicable to investigatory detention. The case also illustrates the Court's growing willingness to base its decisions on provisions of the European Convention, and to give those provisions a broad interpretation.

3. *Successive Appeals/Collateral Attack*

As noted above, decisions of the Correctional and Police courts are subject both to appeal de novo, in the Court of Appeals, and to subsequent review on the record (petition for review) in the Court of Cassation. In addition convictions entered by Correctional courts, courts of appeal, and Assize courts are subject to collateral attack by means of a Petition for Revision, requesting annulment of the conviction based on certain post-trial events or newly discovered evidence.[319] The petition is filed in the Court of Cassation by the Minister of Justice, or by the accused or his representative. The petition procedure applies only to convictions for felony or delict, where (1) subsequent evidence suggests that the supposed homicide victim is still alive; or (2) another person has been found guilty of the same offense, and that person and the accused cannot both be guilty; or (3) a witness against the accused was later convicted of perjury; or (4) new evidence suggests

318. 1996 *Recueil Dalloz-Sirey, Sommaires Commentés* at 258. *See generally* Part II.A.5, *supra*.

319. CPP Arts. 622 to 626.

doubt as to the accused's guilt.[320] A decision of annulment results in remand for retrial unless retrial is impossible, or the accused is clearly innocent.[321]

320. CPP Art. 622.
321. CPP Art. 625; Stefani et al. at para. 795.

Chapter 6

Germany

Thomas Weigend

I. Introduction

The main source of German criminal procedure law is the *Code of Criminal Procedure* (CCP). The *Code of Criminal Procedure* originates from 1877. It has since been amended several times, but its general structure remained the same. The German Constitution (Basic Law of 1949) contains few provisions relating directly to criminal procedure,[1] but some of the individual rights guaranteed by the Constitution do have special relevance in the context of the criminal process. This is true, e.g., for the guarantees of the freedom of movement (art. 2 section 2, 2nd sentence Basic Law), the inviolability of the home (art. 13 Basic Law), and the secrecy of the mail and of telecommunications (art. 10 Basic Law). The jurisprudence of the Federal Constitutional Court[2] therefore has great relevance for the interpretation of criminal procedure law although the interpretation of the *Code of Criminal Procedure* is the task of "ordinary" courts.

Although criminal procedure law is exclusively Federal law, most criminal courts are State courts. Only at the highest level in the hierarchy of "ordinary" (i.e., other than constitutional) courts is there a Federal court, i.e., the Federal Court of Appeals. The Federal Court of Appeals, which has five panels dealing with criminal matters, is the most influential authority on the interpretation of criminal law and criminal procedure law. Although lower courts are not formally bound by decisions of the Federal Court of Appeals, they usually adhere to its rulings because

1. See, e.g., art. 101 section 1 Basic Law (prohibiting the creation of *ad hoc* courts for individual matters), art. 103 section 1 Basic Law (guaranteeing the right to be heard in court), art. 103 section 3 Basic Law (prohibiting more than one criminal prosecution for the same offense), art. 104 section 2 Basic Law (limiting detention without judicial authorization to the day following arrest).

2. The Federal Constitutional Court, situated in Karlsruhe, hears, *inter alia*, citizens' complaints of violations of their basic rights (*Verfassungsbeschwerde*). The Court can only decide upon constitutional issues, not interpret other state or federal law, yet the Court sometimes interprets statutes in a novel way in order to bring them into conformity with the requirements of the Constitution. See, e.g., BVerfGE 19, 342 (1965) (interpreting para. 122 section 3 CCP, which permits pretrial detention in homicide cases without any further condition, as containing a - rebuttable - presumption that the suspect may abscond unless detained).

whenever a conflict of opinion appears on points of law the case can and often will eventually be decided by the Federal Court of Appeals.

II. Police Procedures

A. Arrest, Search, and Seizure Law

Art. 13 Basic Law contains a specific protection of the home (*Wohnung*). It reads, in relevant part:

1) The home is inviolable.
2) Searches may be ordered only by a judge, and if there is danger in delay also by other organs as provided by statute, and may be conducted only in such form as provided by statute.
3) ...

The Federal Constitutional Court has interpreted the term "home" very broadly; it has extended the protection of art. 13 Basic Law, e.g., to restaurants and to places of business.[3]

The freedom of movement, which is relevant to the law of arrest and detention, is protected by art. 2 Basic Law, which reads:

1) ...
2) Everyone has a right to life and to bodily integrity. The freedom of the person is inviolable. These rights can be abridged only on the basis of a statute.

Art. 104 Basic Law contains a more specific guarantee of the individual's freedom against detention:

1) The freedom of the person can be interfered with only on the basis of a formal statute and only in conformity with the procedures prescribed therein. Detained persons must not be mentally or physically maltreated.
2) Only a judge can determine the permissibility and duration of a detention. If someone has been detained without a judicial order, the judge's determination must be brought about without delay. The police must not, on their own authority, keep someone in detention longer than until the end of the day following seizure (*Ergreifen*). Specifics must be regulated by statute.
3) Every person provisionally detained on the suspicion of having committed a criminal act must be brought before a judge not later than on the day following arrest (*Festnahme*), and the judge has to inform him of the reasons for the arrest, to interrogate him and to give him an opportunity to raise objections. The judge must without delay either issue a reasoned detention order (*Haftbefehl*) or order release.
4) A relative of the detainee or a person whom he trusts must without delay be informed of any judicial decision ordering or extending detention.

---

3. See BVerfGE 32, 54 (1971). A prison cell has, however, been held not to be a "home," BVerfG NJW 1996, 2643.

The powers to take someone into provisional or regular detention before trial, to search persons and places, and to seize evidence have all been regulated in the *Code of Criminal Procedure*.[4] These provisions thus limit the constitutional freedoms described above. According to the jurisprudence of the Federal Constitutional Court, statutory powers to interfere with basic rights of the individual, even if explicitly granted by the constitution, have to be interpreted in the light of the constitutional value system. This means that limitations of basic rights, e.g., searches and seizures, can be imposed in individual cases only when they are the least intrusive means to achieve the purpose of the statute and when the intrusion into the individual's rights is not out of proportion with the legitimate end sought.[5]

1. Stops

There is no German counterpart to the American "stop" as a brief detention on the street. German law does, however, authorize police to take the measures necessary for establishing the identity of persons suspected of having committed a criminal offense (or even a mere administrative infraction) (*Identitätsfeststellung*; para. 163b section 1 CCP). If the suspect's identity cannot immediately be determined, the suspect can be held as long as is required for the necessary inquiries (para. 163c section 1 CCP). For the purpose of determining the suspect's identity, his person and effects can be searched and his fingerprints taken. If a suspect has been searched for indications of his identity (e.g., a passport or a characteristic tattoo) and contraband has been found in the course of that search, the relevant objects can be seized and used as evidence.[6]"Suspicion" (*Verdacht*) has been defined very loosely in this context: A suspect is everyone who might become subject to a criminal prosecution; even insignificant and uncertain indications of his of her involvement in criminal activity can establish "suspicion."[7] The definition of suspicion is not of great relevance here because even non-suspects can be held for up to twelve hours if it is necessary, for the purposes of a criminal investigation, to establish their identity; however, non-suspects cannot be searched or fingerprinted without their consent (para. 163b section 2 CCP). Identity checks can be undertaken (without prior judicial authorization) by any police officer. If it is necessary to detain a person, para. 163c section 1 CCP requires that the individual be brought before a judge without delay; but judicial approval need not be sought if obtaining a judicial hearing would take up more time than establishing the individual's identity (which is often the case). Even with judicial consent, detention for the purpose of establishing a person's identity cannot last longer than twelve hours (para. 163c section 3 CCP).

Police cannot stop or detain a person merely for the purpose of interrogating or questioning him. There is, in fact, no obligation on the part of a citizen to obey

4. See paras. 94 (seizure), 102, 103 (search), 127 (provisional detention) CCP. For details, see below.

5. See, e.g., BVerfGE 7, 198 at 208-209 (1958); BVerfGE 30, 292 at 316-317 (1971); BVerfGE 69, 1 at 35 (1985).

6. *Kleinknecht/Meyer-Goßner*, Strafprozeßordnung, 43rd ed. 1997 (hereinafter: *Kl/M- G*), para. 163b n. 22; *Wache*, in: *Pfeiffer* (ed.), Karlsruher Kommentar zur Strafprozeßordnung und zum Gerichsverfassungsgesetz mit Einführungsgesetz, 3rd ed. 1993 (hereinafter: Karlsruher Kommentar), para. 163b n. 21.

7. *Wache*, in: Karlsruher Kommentar, para. 163 n. 9 with further references.

a "summons" to appear at the police station or even to talk with police who visit him at his home or work-place.

2. *Frisks*

German criminal procedure law does not provide for protective searches for weapons. It should be noted, however, that State police law typically authorizes police to search an individual (not for the purpose of detecting evidence of a crime but) for the purpose of preventing commission of an offense or of another disturbance of the public peace and order.[8] Police thus routinely frisk anyone whom they believe to be armed in order to "prevent commission of an offense."

3. *Arrests*

The law of arrest is closely connected with the general concept of detention before trial: The *Code of Criminal Procedure* uses the term "provisional arrest" (*vorläufige Festnahme*), which signifies that arresting a suspect is regarded as a preliminary measure preceding detention. Moreover, the requirements for provisional arrest are largely identical with those of pretrial detention.

Pretrial detention generally presupposes the existence of two elements: There must be "urgent suspicion" that the *Beschuldigte* (i.e., a suspect against whom a criminal investigation is being conducted) has committed a criminal offense, and detaining him must be necessary for the protection of the integrity of the criminal process because the suspect, if left at large, would flee from justice or tamper with evidence (para. 112 CCP[9]). If these requirements are fulfilled, a judge[10] can, upon

---

8. See, e.g., para. 39 section 1 *Polizeigesetz des Landes Nordrhein-Westfalen* (Police Code of the State of North Rhine-Westfalia) of February 24, 1990.

9. Para. 112 CCP reads (in relevant part):

"(1) Pretrial detention can be ordered against a suspect when he is urgently suspected of having committed an offense and when grounds for detention exist. Pretrial detention must not be ordered when it is out of proportion with the significance of the matter and with the expected penalty or measure of rehabilitation and security.

(2) A ground for detention exists if it has been determined, on a factual basis,

1. that the suspect has absconded or is in hiding,
2. that, based on the circumstances of the individual case, there exists a risk that the suspect will flee from justice (danger of flight),
3. that the suspect's conduct gives rise to the urgent suspicion that he will
   a) destroy, alter, hide, conceal or falsify evidence,
   b) impermissibly influence co-defendants, witnesses or expert witnesses,
   c) cause others to perform such acts

and that therefore there exists a risk that the finding of the truth will be rendered more difficult (danger of obstruction).

(3) ..."

10. The "judge" to which the Code refers is a designated magistrate of the nearest *Amtsgericht* (county court, i.e., the lowest level of State courts). County courts usually have judges on weekend duty so that arrest determinations can be made in due course.

application of the public prosecutor, issue an arrest warrant to be executed by a police officer (para. 114 CCP).

If a judge cannot be reached as quickly as is necessary for the timely detention of the suspect, a prosecutor or police officer (para. 127 section 2 CCP) or, if the suspect has been caught in the act, any citizen (para. 127 section 1 CCP) can provisionally arrest anyone who is under "urgent suspicion" of having committed a criminal offense. The suspect must then, without undue delay, and not later than by the end of the day following arrest, be brought before a judge, who determines whether the requirements of pretrial detention are fulfilled.[11] If that is not the case, the suspect must be released immediately; in the alternative, the judge must issue an order of pretrial detention (para. 128 CCP). The difference between a stop for the purpose of *Identitätsfeststellung* (para. 163b CCP) and a *vorläufige Festnahme* (para. 127 CCP) does not turn on the intensity or length of the intrusion but on its purpose: any deprivation of liberty for the purpose of preventing flight or destruction of evidence is a provisional arrest, whereas detention for the purpose of determining an individual's identity is *Identitätsfeststellung*.

It cannot generally be said that an illegal arrest leads to the exclusion of evidence obtained from the suspect during detention. Evidence has been held inadmissible when the suspect's pretrial detention was abused for the purpose of obtaining a confession to an undercover police informer placed in the suspect's jail cell.[12] In another decision of the same year, the Federal Court of Appeals stated generally that an illegal detention "can" make inadmissible statements elicited from the suspect during detention.[13] On the particular facts of the case, however, the Court found that no interrogation had taken place: the suspect had been allowed to talk with his girlfriend in the presence of a police officer, and during that conversation had made incriminating statements. Postponing the suspect's presentation to a judge until the very end of the day following arrest has been held not to violate the requirements of para. 128 section 2 CCP, hence a confession made on the second day of detention was regarded as admissible.[14] Although the question of the legality of an arrest may thus be relevant to the admissibility of evidence obtained during detention, there is not much case law on this issue. This may have to do with the fact that the statute defines very broadly the prerequisites for a legal arrest and pretrial detention. The legal concepts have, moreover, been interpreted in a "user-friendly" fashion so that it is difficult for a suspect to show that his arrest was not in conformity with the law.

Paras. 112 and 127 section 2 CCP require "urgent suspicion" of criminal wrongdoing by the suspect *and* either danger of flight or danger of evidence-tampering as prerequisites of detention. "Urgent suspicion" exists when there is a great

---

11. The majority of suspects who end up in pretrial detention are not arrested on a judicial warrant but are first provisionally arrested by a police officer on the basis of para. 127 section 2 CCP. According to the empirical study of *Gebauer*, Die Rechtswirklichkeit der Untersuchungshaft in der Bundesrepublik Deutschland, 1987, p. 215, 76% of all pretrial detention orders were preceded by a police provisional arrest.

12. BGHSt. 34, 362 (1987). The Federal Court of Appeals held that the authorities in that case had employed illicit "coercion" (*Zwang*) prohibited by para. 136a CCP.

13. BGH NStZ 1988, 233.

14. BGH NStZ 1990, 195.

likelihood that the suspect has unlawfully and culpably committed a criminal act.[15] This is a fairly loose standard which does not accord much protection to the suspect. It must further be taken into account that, at the stage of the judge's determination on pretrial detention, any evidence presented tends to be prosecution evidence, because the defense has usually not yet had an opportunity to collect counter-evidence.

"Danger of flight" exists when specific facts indicate that the suspect will try to abscond and thus make trial impossible.[16] In practice, danger of flight will often be assumed if a suspect has strong ties to a foreign country, is unemployed and/or without a home and a family in the community or has a strong incentive to flee because he must expect long-term imprisonment if convicted.[17] The alternative reason for ordering pretrial detention, i.e., a danger that the suspect, if left at large, might try to unduly influence witnesses or to destroy incriminating evidence, has been cited in only a small percentage of detention cases;[18] the possibility of authorizing detention on these grounds does, however, play an important role in interrogations: police tend to tell suspects that silence can be regarded as an indication of a suspect's general willingness to obstruct the course of justice, including the destruction of evidence. A separate ground for pretrial detention exists when the suspect, if left at large, must be expected to commit serious offenses similar to those of which he is suspected (*Vorbeugehaft*); this provision applies only to a limited number of offenses, e.g., arson, rape, robbery, larceny, aggravated assault, and drug offenses (para. 112a CCP).

4. Searches

Searches (*Durchsuchungen*) can be defined as activities by law enforcement officers by which they openly[19] seek to obtain objects which a person carries[20] or

15. *Kl/M-G*, para. 112 n. 5; *Lemke*, in: Heidelberger Kommentar zur Strafprozeßordnung, 1997 (hereinafter: Heidelberger Kommentar), para. 112 n. 4. In a 1979 decision, the Federal Court of Appeals declared that "urgent suspicion" requires a high probability, based on the result of the investigation, that the suspect is guilty, but that the judge need not regard the suspect's *conviction* as likely (BGH, cited in: *Pfeiffer*, Aus der Rechtsprechung des Bundesgerichtshofs in Strafsachen zum Verfahrensrecht, NStZ 1981, 93 at 94). By this rather cryptic statement, the Court probably meant to say that probability must be assessed on the basis of information presently available to the decision-maker and that he should not speculate about possible new evidence which might prevent conviction of the suspect. In a later decision, the Federal Court of Appeals emphasized that "urgent suspicion" requires more than merely "some probability" (*gewisse Wahrscheinlichkeit*) and that there must exist admissible evidence by which the suspect's guilt can be proved with "great likelihood," BGH NStZ 1992, 449. For an even more stringent probability requirement, see *Paeffgen*, in: *Rudolphi* et al., Systematischer Kommentar zur Strafprozeßordnung und zum Gerichtsverfassungsgesetz (looseleaf), para. 112 n. 9 (suspect's guilt must "suggest itself").

16. According to paras. 230, 231 CCP, the defendant cannot be tried *in absentia*. Only few exceptions of this rule exist, e.g., when the maximum sentence is only a minor fine (para. 232 CCP) or when the defendant has purposely rendered himself unfit for trial (para. 231a CCP).

17. See *Gebauer* (n. 11), p. 236.

18. According to the study of *Gebauer* (n. 11), p. 232, danger of evidence-tampering was cited as the *only* reason for pretrial detention in only 1.3% of the cases. This danger may play a greater role in decisions to provisionally arrest a suspect (these decisions are usually made by police officers on the spot, and their reasons are not recorded).

19. Surreptitious gathering of evidence, e.g. by means of "bugs" or hidden cameras, is not regarded as a "search," *Herdegen*, in: Bonner Kommentar zum Grundgesetz, 1993, Art. 13 n. 52

which are situated on private premises.[21] Searches thus interfere with the right of privacy (as protected by art. 2 section 1 in connection with art. 1 section 1 Basic Law) and/or the inviolability of the home (as protected by art. 13 section 1 Basic Law). The constitutionally protected "home" also covers places of business[22] as well as front or back gardens separated from public streets by a fence or a hedge.[23] The exact limits of what consitutes a search have not been much litigated because the legal requirements of a search are very easy to meet. One commentator is of the view that "searches" of buildings are limited to situations in which a person physically enters the building; peeping into an apartment from the street, even by means of binoculars, would thus not be a search and would be permissible without a warrant; yet the same author thinks that viewing or listening by means of "technical devices," e.g. infrared cameras or beepers fixed to cars, would require special statutory authorization.[24]

German law generally accords very little protection to persons and buildings against searches for the purpose of criminal prosecution. Art. 13 Basic Law, which generally declares the sanctity of the home "inviolable," explicitly allows searches if authorized by a judge or, if delay would jeopardize the effectiveness of the search, by other officers designated by law (art. 13 section 2 Basic Law). Consequently, paras. 102, 103 CCP grant broad authority to search suspects and non-suspects alike for possible evidence. A search is permissible when-ever there is suspicion (*Verdacht*)[25] that a criminal offense has been committed. In that case, a suspect can be searched whenever it is expected that the search will lead to the detection of evidence; the suspect's home as well as his belongings can also be searched in order to arrest the suspect (para. 102 CCP). It should be noted that the Code uses the term *Verdächtiger*, not the expression *Beschuldigter* which denotes someone who is the object of an investigation; this means that a rather vague suspicion is a suffi-

---

with further references. There are special rules on wiretaps (paras. 100a, 100b CCP) and on video and accustic surveillance of premises (paras. 100c, 100d CCP). These measures are permissible only when certain serious offenses are being investigated and must be authorized by a judge (although the prosecutor can order surveillance in cases of "danger in delay," his authorization is valid for only three days); a further requirement (largely neglected in practice) is that other, less intrusive means of investigation have previously been exhausted or are evidently inexpedient.

20. This includes the search for objects an individual has hidden in a body orifice; see *Amelung*, in: Kommentar zur Strafprozeßordnung (Reihe Alternativkommentare; *Wassermann*, gen. ed.) (hereinafter: Alternativkommentar), vol. 2/1, 1992, para. 102 n. 23.

21. In BVerfGE 51, 97 at 106-107 (1979), the Federal Constitutional Court has defined the search of a home as a state agent's purposeful seeking for persons or objects in order to find something which the home owner does not wish to lay open or to deliver. This definition has aptly been criticized as too narrow because art. 13 section 1 Basic Law protects the sphere of the home even with respect to matters the individual does not generally wish to keep secret; *Kunig*, in: *von Münch/Kunig* (eds.), Grundgesetz, vol. 1, 4th ed. 1992, art. 13 n. 26; but see *Herdegen* (n. 19), art. 13 n. 51 (denying existence of a "search" when officers enter a building to view "evident matters").

22. See text at n. 3, *supra*.

23. BGH StV 1997, 400.

24. *Amelung*, in: Alternativkommentar, para. 102 n. 22. These instrumentalities would not fall under the definition of a "search" because they are not being used openly (see text at n. 19, *supra*).

25. Searches require a lesser degree of suspicion than pretrial detention; any indication, based on criminalistic experience, that an individual may have committed an offense, is sufficient; see BVerfG StV 1994, 353; *Kl/M-G*, para. 102 n. 2.

cient basis for a search.[26] Yet even an individual as to whom there exists no suspicion whatsoever can be searched if there are facts indicating that the suspect or traces of an offense (e.g., scars stemming from an assault) or objects which can be seized might be found on the individual or in his home (para. 103 CCP). Homes and places of business are generally protected from night time searches, but this protection does not apply when there is danger in delay (para. 104 section 1 CCP) - which will often be the case.

Given the low substantive barriers against searches, one would expect certain formal safeguards to exist. The law does provide some, but with little practical effect. Searches are to be authorized by judicial order (para. 105 section 1 CCP),[27] usually upon motion of the prosecutor and without a hearing.[28] Judicial search orders must be in writing and must specify the places to be searched as well as the items expected to be found.[29] The Federal Constitutional Court has declared that the requirement of specificity follows from the constitutional principle that the state must not interfere more than necessary with the citizen's private sphere; the judge must therefore circumscribe as precisely as possible the limits of the search. In practice, however, the requirement of specificity seems to be frequently ignored.[30] Because of the need to tailor judicial search warrants to the actual requirements of the investigation, such warrants lose force if circumstances change significantly and can in any event be used for only six months.[31]

These requirements for judicial search warrants are, however, of little practical relevance because the great majority of searches are conducted without any prior judicial authorization: police usually assume that there is "danger in delay," i.e., that the time loss involved in presenting the matter to a judge would lead to the disappearance of the evidence sought. They therefore order the search on the spot and carry it out immediately.[32] If the police, in the course of executing a judicial war-

---

26. See *Kl/M-G*, para. 102 n. 3; *Rudolphi*, in: Systematischer Kommentar, para. 102 n. 5.

27. There has been some debate as to whether a search can be conducted on the basis of an arrest warrant. The majority of State courts have held that a judicial arrest warrant implicitly confers authority to enter and search the suspect's home (but not the home of a non-suspect); OLG Düsseldorf NJW 1981, 2133; OLG Celle StV 1982, 561; *Kl/M-G*, para. 105 n. 6; *Nack*, in: Karlsruher Kommentar, para. 105 n. 4; but see, *contra*, *Amelung*, in: Alternativkommentar, para. 105 n. 14; *Rudolphi*, in: Systematischer Kommentar, para. 105 n. 4. In practice, this is a moot issue: if a police officer appears at the suspect's house with an arrest warrant and does not see the suspect at the door, he will assume that there is "danger in delay" and order (and immediately carry out) a search of the house without bothering about a judicial order; see *Kaiser*, Notwendigkeit eines Durchsuchungsbefehls bei strafprozessualen Zwangsmaßnahmen?, NJW 1980, 875 at 876.

28. Only in cases of emergency and if no representative of the prosecutor's office can be reached can the judge act *sua sponte*, i.e., upon informal motion of the police (para. 165 CCP). In either case, the judge bases his decision exclusively on the information he has received from the police dossier; hearing the opponent would usually be equivalent to frustrating the purpose of the search, hence a prior hearing is not required in this situation (para. 33 section 4 CCP).

29. See BVerfGE 44, 353 at 372 (1977); BVerfG NStZ 1992, 91; BVerfG NJW 1994, 3281.

30. See, e.g., *Bandisch*, Mandant und Patient, schutzlos bei Durchsuchung von Kanzlei und Praxis?, NJW 1987, 2200 at 2203; *Baur*, Mangelnde Bestimmtheit von Durchsuchungsbeschlüssen, wistra 1983, 99.

31. BVerfG StV 1997, 394. The Federal Constitutional Court has developed this time limitation on judicial warrants for searches of the home directly from art. 13 Basic Law in connection with the constitutional principle of proportionality.

32. *Amelung*, in: Alternativkommentar, para. 105 n. 8; *Nelles*, Kompetenzen und Ausnahmekompetenzen der Strafprozeßordnung, 1980, pp. 215, 220 (Only about 10% of searches were

rant, happen to find other items indicating criminal conduct (e.g., during a search for specified stolen goods, the police happen to find illegal drugs), they can, if they are "auxiliary officers" of the prosecutor,[33] immediately start a new investigation (e.g., for a drug offense) and seize the item as evidence on the basis of "danger in delay" (para. 98 section 1 CCP). Even if the police officers who conduct a search do not have authority to order seizure (because they are not "auxiliary officers") they can provisionally seize a "chance find" and take it to the prosecutor's office (para. 108 section 1 CCP).

Because of the broad permissibility of searches under German law, there is no need for special rules on searches incident to arrest. To the extent such searches are conducted not for the purpose of detecting evidence or the proceeds of an offense but for the protection of arresting officers, they can be based on State police law (see *supra* II.A.2.). Police can (and often do) avoid the "strictures" of search law by obtaining the consent of the person to be searched or of the owner or tenant of the relevant premises.[34] In order for his consent to be valid, the individual must first be informed of the purpose of the search and the right to withhold consent,[35] consent given on the basis of a misapprehension caused by the police officer (e.g., when the officer poses as a repairman) is invalid.[36]

The legality of a search can be submitted to judicial review, yet traditionally courts have often rejected such cases, arguing that the issue was moot when the search had ended. In a recent decision, however, the Federal Constitutional Court has declared this jurisprudence to be in violation of art. 19 section 4 Basic Law, which guarantees judicial review of any state action possibly violating individual rights.[37] The Court held that anyone whose home or person was subjected to a search can demand a declaratory judgment on the legality of the search.

5. *Enforcing the Rules*

There is no general exclusionary rule which would make illegally obtained evidence inadmissible. Para. 136a section 3 CCP does provide for inadmissibility of statements elicited by certain forbidden means, e.g., violence, hypnosis or illegal threats. In other instances of violations of procedural rules by law enforcement personnel, German courts weigh the seriousness of the violation against the public interest in determining the truth. In a recent case,[38] which concerned the admissibility of unwarned self-incriminating statements, the Federal Court of Appeals reaffirmed the principle that the truth should be sought, but not at any cost. The court emphazised, on the other hand, that a functioning system of criminal justice

---

conducted upon judicial order.); *Sommermeyer*, Schutz der Wohnung gegenüber strafprozessualen Zwangsmaßnahmen, ein Phantom?, JR 1990, 493 at 496.

33. Most police officers (except the lowest ranks of the police force) are at the same time auxiliary officers of the prosecutor's office (*Hilfsbeamte der Staatsanwaltschaft*) and as such have special emergency powers in the criminal process.

34. If there are several co-owners or co-tenants of a building or flat, each of them must consent to the search; *Schäfer*, in: *Löwe/Rosenberg*, Die Strafprozeßordnung und das Gerichtsverfassungsgesetz. Großkommentar (hereinafter: *Löwe/Rosenberg*), 24th ed. 1986, para. 102 n. 8.

35. Id.

36. *Herdegen*, in: Bonner Kommentar (n. 19), art. 13 n. 45.

37. BVerfG StV 1997, 393.

38. BGHSt. 38, 214 (1992).

must exist in a state based on the rule of law (*Rechtsstaat*). Although the court refused to give hard and fast rules on the exclusion of illegally obtained evidence, it noted that violation of a rule which has the purpose of safeguarding the defendant's basic procedural rights normally leads to exclusion. Generally, the outcome of the courts' weighing of interests is difficult to predict in any individual case because it depends, *inter alia*, on the grievousness of the violation (which is greater when law enforcement officers act in conscious disregard of the law), the importance of the individual interest infringed upon, the relevance of the piece of evidence for the resolution of the case, and the seriousness of the offense.

Special rules apply to evidence belonging to an individual's most private sphere, e.g., a diary containing notes on intimate thoughts and feelings. To the extent that using this information would violate the dignity of the person (as protected by art. 1 section 1 Basic Law), this evidence must not be seized and, even if it was properly seized (because the contents were not known to the officer or the evidence was offered voluntarily by a private individual) may be inadmissible in court.[39]

The fruits of illegal searches are usually held admissible in criminal proceedings. In a 1989 decision, the Federal Court of Appeals assumed *arguendo* that a (second) search of the defendant's apartment lacked the requisite judicial authorization. Leaving open the general question of admissibility in this situation, the Court declared that the evidence found in the apartment should not be excluded if the judge would, on a proper motion, have authorized the search and if the objects found were otherwise admissible.[40]

Only in exceptional cases have courts held otherwise. In 1977, the Federal Constitutional Court held unconstitutional the search for and seizure of client files of a drug counselling agency because the intrusiveness of the search was, under the circumstances of the case, out of proportion with the legitimate interests of law enforcement.[41] Although the issue of the files' admissibility in criminal proceedings was technically moot, the Court declared that their inadmissibility was an immediate consequence of the unconstitutionality of their seizure.[42] In a 1985 decision, the Berlin High Court (*Kammergericht*)[43] held inadmissible documents which the police had found when they searched defendant's apartment on a judicial warrant which specifically authorized a search for a firearm allegedly in the defendant's possession. The circumstances clearly indicated that the police had set out for a "fishing expedition" in the defendant's home in abuse of the limited judicial warrant. The Berlin court regarded this (intentional) violation of the defendant's rights (and the flouting of the judge's authority) as so serious that the need to provide a remedy outweighed the public interest in clearing up the alleged offence. Some legal

---

39. See BVerfGE 34, 238 (1973); 80, 367 at 373-383 (1989). In the 1989 diary case, the "majority" (in fact, four out of eight justices) found that a murder defendant's diary was not absolutely protected from inspection and use in court because it contained descriptions of the writer's feelings toward others and therefore went beyond pure introspection.

40. BGH NJW 1989, 1741 at 1744. *Accord*, *Amelung*, in: Alternativkommentar, para. 105 n. 50; *Kl/M-G*, para. 94 n. 21; *Nack*, in: Karlsruher Kommentar, para. 94 n. 18; *Rudol- phi*, in: Systematischer Kommentar, para. 105 n. 30.

41. BVerfGE 44, 353 (1977).

42. Id. at 383-384.

43. Kammergericht StV 1985, 494. For similar decisions of lower courts, see Landgericht Bonn NJW 1981, 292; Landgericht Bremen StV 1984, 505.

writers would go even further and argue in favor of exclusion whenever a search is illegal, basing their view on the need to ensure respect for the requirements of art. 13 Basic Law and of the criminal procedure rules flowing from the inviolability of the home.[44]

A general standing requirement for challenging the admissibility of evidence has been introduced by the Federal Court of Appeals in a different context, i.e., when a witness' privilege against self-incrimination was disregarded. In that case,[45] the witness' statement was held to be admissible against the defendant because the violation had not infringed upon the defendant's "legal sphere" (*Rechtskreis*). Although there seems to exist no Court of Appeals decision on this point in the context of searches, it can be assumed that fruits of an unlawful search would be excluded (if at all) only if the defendant or his home had illegally been searched.

According to the majority view, inadmissibility of illegally obtained evidence does not extend to derivative evidence. The Federal Court of Appeals has, e.g., held admissible the statements of witnesses located by means of an illegal wiretap[46] or of a coerced confession.[47] These decisions can be explained by the fact that German courts do not exclude evidence in order to deter police misconduct but on a "clean hands" rationale. Because derivative evidence is not itself tainted by a violation of procedural rules, the interest of justice outweighs any remaining defect in the process of finding the item in question. German courts also sometimes rely on the "hypothetical clean path" doctrine, arguing that relevant evidence should not be excluded when there was a "technical fault" in securing it but the item could have been obtained by legal means. In a case decided by the High Court of Celle,[48] a police officer acquired a blood sample of a suspect from a nurse after the suspect had undergone emergency surgery. Although the police officer had acted illegally,[49] the court admitted the blood sample, arguing that it would be formalistic to exclude it since the officer could have obtained *another* blood sample by immediately ordering a physical examination of the suspect in accordance with para. 81a CCP.[50] It should be noted that courts apply the "hypothetical clean path" analysis to justify even the admission of evidence *directly* obtained by illegal means.[51]

To the extent evidence is deemed inadmissible (e.g., because it had been obtained by the coercive methods specifically outlawed in para. 136a CCP) it is totally banned and cannot be introduced for limited purposes. However, the meaning of "exclusion" of evidence in the German system differs from the respective Anglo-American concept. In Germany, professional judges sitting on a criminal court are usually aware even of "excluded" facts (e.g., a defendant's coerced con-

---

44. For a recent overview, see *Krekeler*, Beweisverwertungsverbote bei fehlerhaften Durchsuchungen, NStZ 1993, 263.

45. BGHSt. 11, 213 (1958); see also BGHSt. 38, 214 at 220 (1992).

46. BGHSt. 32, 68 (1983); see also BGHSt. 35, 32 (1987) (holding admissible defendant's confession to an expert witness made eight days after the defendant had been confronted with an illegally recorded tape of his self-incriminating remarks).

47. BGHSt. 34, 362 at 364 (1987).

48. OLG Celle JZ 1989, 906.

49. He failed to inform the nurse of the fact that she was not obliged to hand the blood sample over to the police (cf. paras. 53, 53a, 97 CCP).

50. For similar cases, see BGHSt. 24, 125 at 130 (1971); OLG Zweibrücken NJW 1984, 810.

51. For a critique of this jurisprudence see *Rogall*, Hypothetische Ermittlungsverläufe im Strafprozeß, NStZ 1988, 385; *Svenja Schröder*, Beweisverwertungsverbote und die Hypothese rechtmäßiger Beweiserlangung im Strafprozeß, 1992.

fession) because they will have examined the prosecutor's file before trial. Exclusion thus requires the judges to delete the relevant information from their minds and to base their judgment on a fiction rather than on the facts known to them. Even if a judge is willing to obey the command of the law and to disregard excluded information, it is psychologically difficult for him to make a decision he knows to be unrelated to the "real" facts of the case. Judges may thus try to reach a verdict which can be reconciled with the "real" facts, knowing that they must not mention some of these facts in the oral or written explanation given for the judgment. Exclusion of evidence thus just makes it more difficult for the court to *justify* a decision which may well have been influenced by the "excluded" evidence.

The situation is somewhat different with respect to lay judges,[52] because they do not have access to the file,[53] they know only what has been mentioned at the trial. If a piece of evidence has been recognized as inadmissible before trial and has therefore not been introduced or mentioned at the trial, lay judges can participate in finding the judgment without ever knowing of that evidence.[54] Yet given lay judges' limited input into the court's actual decision-making, the fact that they are (sometimes) unaware of the existence of excluded evidence does not make exclusion of evidence less fictitious in practice.

B. Lineups and Other Identification Procedures

1. Lineups

There is no explicit statutory basis for compelling suspects to participate in a lineup before trial. Courts and legal authors nevertheless largely agree that lineups are permissible and that suspects as well as witnesses can be compelled to take part in them. The Berlin High Court (*Kammergericht*) has based the permissibility of lineups on para. 58 section 2 CCP,[55] while legal writers cite para. 81a CCP[56] or para. 81b CCP,[57] the Federal Constitutional Court has relied on an analogy to both provisions to justify compelling a suspect to participate in a lineup.[58]

---

52. Lay judges sit together with professional judges on all but the most petty and most serious criminal cases; see text at notes 108-111, *infra*.

53. See BGHSt. 13, 73 (1958); a recent decision (BGH NJW 1997, 1792) indicated that this rule may soon change.

54. If "inadmissible" evidence has been introduced or mentioned at the trial, the presiding judge will inform the lay judges that they have to disregard that piece of evidence. In that case, the same problem as with professional judges arises.

55. Kammergericht NJW 1979, 1668 at 1669; *accord*, BGHSt. 34, 39 at 49 (1986) (*dictum*); *Kl/M-G*, para. 58 n. 9. Para. 58 section 2 CCP reads: "Before trial, a confrontation with other witnesses or with the defendant is permissible only if it appears necessary for the further proceedings." This provision refers only to the rights and duties of witnesses and therefore seems inapposite as a basis for compelling the *suspect's* participation in a lineup; see *Odenthal*, Die Gegenüberstellung im Strafverfahren, 2nd ed. 1992, pp. 65-67.

56. See, e.g., *Dahs*, in: *Löwe/Rosenberg*, 24th ed. 1987, para. 81a n. 38; *Odenthal* (n. 55), pp. 70-72. Para. 81a CCP authorizes "bodily examinations" of a suspect, though only by judges, prosecutors and expert witnesses.

57. See, e.g., *Roxin*, Strafverfahrensrecht, 24th ed. 1995, p. 249. Para. 81b CCP authorizes the police to take photographs, fingerprints, measurements and "similar measures" of the suspect.

58. BVerfGE 47, 239 at 251-252 (1978).

There are no strict legal rules on how a lineup should be conducted. Courts and commentators agree that "live" lineups are more reliable that photo lineups, yet it is permissible to show a witness several photographs when a lineup of persons is not practicable.[59] The outcome of a lineup should be recorded, but this need not be done by videotaping the procedure.[60] Even if a lineup was methodically flawed, its result is admissible, though the court, in its written judgment, must show that it was aware of the defect and of the ensuing limited value of any identification[61]. If the suspect does not have counsel, the fact that a lineup is to be conducted does not make it necessary to appoint an attorney for him. Since the Code is silent on the issue, there may not even exist a right for the suspect to have retained (or previously appointed) counsel present during the lineup.[62]

2. Other Identification Procedures

The availability of other identification procedures hinges on the interpretation of the privilege against self-incrimination. German courts have interpreted the maxim "*nemo tenetur seipsum accusare*" (no one can be compelled to accuse himself) - not explicitly formulated in German law, but deemed to have constitutional rank[63] - to prohibit any compulsion to self- incriminatory *activities* on the part of a suspect or witness. A suspect can therefore not be compelled to speak up for the production of a voice sample,[64] to produce a hand-writing sample (but hand-written notes can be seized from the suspect's possession), to perform a test nor even to urinate or to exhale into a breathalyzer.[65] Passivity, on the other hand, can be demanded and even compelled: it is thus permissible to take a blood sample, even if the suspect has to be subdued for that purpose. Other body fluids as well as hair samples can be taken, by force if necessary, on

---

59. See *Odenthal* (n. 55), p. 54 (citing study showing that properly conducted photo lineups need not be less reliable that "live" lineups).

60. Cf. *Kl/M-G*, para. 58 n. 12.

61. BGH NStZ 1982, 342; Kammergericht NStZ 1982, 215; cf. BGHSt. 40, 66 at 69-70 (1994) (concerning recognition of suspect's voice); *Dahs*, in: *Löwe/Rosenberg*, 24th ed. 1985, para. 58 n. 14; *Eisenberg*, Beweisrecht der StPO, 2nd ed. 1996, pp. 516-517; but see *Kühne*, Strafprozeßlehre, 4th ed. 1993, pp. 168-169 (arguing for inadmissibility of results of "botched" lineup).

62. For a decision explicitly denying a right to counsel, see Kammergericht NJW 1979, 1669; for the contrary position, see *Dahs*, in: *Löwe/Rosenberg*, 24th ed. 1987, para. 81a n. 38; *Odenthal* (n. 55), pp. 76-78.

63. The Federal Constitutional Court has derived the privilege against self-incrimination from the guarantee of the dignity of the person (art. 1 Basic Law) and the fair trial principle; BVerfGE 38, 105 at 113 (1974); BVerfGE 56, 37 at 43 (1981); BVerfG NStZ 1995, 555; for critical analyses, see *Lorenz*, "Operative Informationserhebung" im Strafverfahren, JZ 1992, 1000 at 1005-1006; *Verrel*, Nemo tenetur - Rekonstruktion eines Verfahrensgrundsatzes, NStZ 1997, 361.

64. BGHSt. 34, 39 at 45-46 (1986); BGHSt. 40, 66 at 71-72 (1994). In the latter decision, the Federal Court of Appeals indicated the admissibility of the statement of a witness who, upon invitation of the police, "overheard" an interrogation of the suspect by a police officer and on this basis identified the suspect's voice as the voice of someone who had raped her.

65. See *Dahs*, in: *Löwe/Rosenberg*, 24th ed. 1987, para. 81a notes 17-20; *Pelchen*, in: Karlsruher Kommentar, para. 81a n. 4; *Rogall*, in: Systematischer Kommentar, vor para. 133 n. 141.

66. The taking of a urine sample with a catheter is regarded as impermissible because of the significant health risk involved; see *Dahs*, in: *Löwe/Rosenberg*, para. 81a n. 51; *Kl/M-G*, para. 81a n. 21; *Lemke*, in: Heidelberger Kommentar, para. 81a n. 17. (There are no court decisions on this issue.)

the basis of para. 81a CCP,[66] which authorizes examinations of the body as well as bodily "intrusions" to the extent necessary for the investigation.[67] Blood samples can even be taken from non-suspects if that is "indispensible" for determining the truth (para. 81c section 2 CCP). Examinations of the body have to be authorized by a judge, yet if there is "danger in delay" (e.g., when the blood alcohol contents of a suspect have to be determined) a prosecutor or a member of the "auxiliary" police can order the examination (para. 81a section 2 CCP).

C. Interrogation

1. Rules on Interrogations

An interrogation (*Vernehmung*) can be defined as a confrontation of a suspect or a witness with a state agent who demands information.[68] Suspects against whom an investigation is being conducted must, at the beginning of any interrogation, be informed (a) of the offense of which they are suspected, (b) that they are free, according to the law, to make or not to make a statement with respect to the alleged offense,[69] (c) that they can consult a defense attorney at any time, even prior to being interrogated, (d) that they can demand police or prosecutors to take exonerating evidence (para. 136 section 1 CCP). This information must be given at the beginning of each interrogation by a judge, a prosecutor (para. 163a section 3 CCP) or a police officer (para. 163a section 4 CCP), regardless of whether the suspect is in custody or whether formal charges have been filed against him. The required information need not be given in any particular form. In order to avoid problems of proof, however, police tend to have suspects sign a preformulated statement confirming that they have been advised of their rights.[70]

It should be noted that the relevant information has to be given only to suspects, i.e., to persons whom the interrogator actually *treats* or *should treat* as suspects,[71] and the suspect has to be advised of his rights only in connection with *interrogations*, so that spontaneous declarations of a suspect can be recorded (and

67. Intrusive measures (i.e., those piercing the skin) must be performed by a physician (para. 81a section 1 CCP).

68. BGHSt. 40, 211 at 213 (1994); BGHSt. 42, 139 at 145 (1996). In both cases, the Federal Court of Appeals required that the official capacity of the interrogator is evident. The Court thus excluded from the definition of an "interrogation" inquiries of an undercover agent or a police informer. When the Court's definition of an interrogation is not met, no warnings need be given. See also *Rogall*, Systematischer Kommentar, para. 136 n. 6.

69. The suspect need not be informed of the fact that any statement he makes can be used against him.

70. Interrogations by a judge must be formally recorded (para. 168a section 1 CCP).

71. In the initial stages of an investigation, the courts leave it to the discretion of the police and prosecutors whether they treat a person possibly involved in the offense as a suspect (*Beschuldigter*) or as a mere witness; only if individualized suspicion has become "strong" is it absolutely necessary to give the warnings in accordance with paras. 136, 163a CCP; see BGHSt. 38, 214 at 227-228 (1992). The privilege against compelled self-incrimination applies, of course, to everyone, not only to suspects. A witness can therefore refuse to answer any question if the reply would tend to incriminate him or a close relative (para. 55 CCP). Witnesses must also be informed of that right, but the information needs to be given only when an actual danger of self-incrimination arises, not at the beginning of every interrogation.

later used as evidence) even if no warning was given.[72] Police sometimes engage in so-called informal questioning (*informatorische Befragung*) of witnesses and suspects before they begin a formal interrogation. If a situation needs to be clarified, it is perfectly legal for the police to ask questions of by-standers without giving them information on the applicable law.[73] But the courts go further; they permit police officers to conduct lengthy "informal" interviews with suspects before informing them of their rights and admit information obtained in the course of such talks as evidence.[74]

There are no formal time limits for interrogations. Statements obtained when the suspect or witness was exhausted or had been tormented are, however, not admissible as evidence (para. 136a section 1, 3 CCP). A statement must be excluded if the person who made it was at the time so exhausted that his freedom of will was substantially impaired; the state of exhaustion need not have been brought about by the interrogation itself, nor need the interrogator have been aware of it.[75]

A suspect's relatives must be informed of his detention (para. 114b CCP), but access need not be granted during an interrogation. When a suspect is interrogated by a prosecutor or a judge he has a right to have (retained) counsel present, and counsel must, if practicable, be informed of the time and location of the interrogation (paras. 168c section 1, 5; 163a section 3 CCP). It should be noted that suspects do not have a right to have counsel *appointed* during the investigation stage of the criminal process; this is true even for indigent defendants. In felony cases as well as in other instances of possible severe sanctions and/or special impairment of the defendant's ability to defend himself, para. 140 CCP does provide for the (mandatory) appointment of counsel. As a rule, however, the presiding judge appoints counsel for the defendant only after formal charges have been filed, i.e., when the investigation has been completed (para. 141 section 1 CCP). Only upon special motion of the prosecutor's office can the presiding judge appoint counsel at an earlier date (para. 141 section 3 CCP). In larger cities, bar associations provide attorney hotlines through which suspects can reach a private attorney even outside normal office hours.

There is no right to have (even retained) counsel present during *police* interrogations,[76] the suspect can, however, claim his right to remain silent and simultaneously offer to make a statement in the presence of counsel. The suspect has, moreover, the right to consult with counsel *before* any police interrogation (and must be informed of that right; see above). If the suspect wishes to talk with his attorney and the police prevent him from doing so before he makes a statement, that state-

72. BGH NJW 1990, 461; *Achenbach*, in: Alternativkommentar, para. 163a n. 22; *Rogall*, in: Systematischer Kommentar, vor para. 133 n. 44.

73. *Achenbach*, in: Alternativkommentar, para. 163a n. 23; *Roxin*, Strafverfahrensrecht, p. 179.

74. BGH NStZ 1983, 86; *accord*, *Kl/M-G*, Einleitung n. 79; *Geppert*, Notwendigkeit und rechtliche Grenzen der "informatorischen Befragung" im Strafverfahren, Festschrift für Oehler, 1985, p. 323. Some writers recognize a need for informal questioning only as long as there exists no individualized suspicion; *Hanack*, in: *Löwe/Rosenberg*, 24th ed. 1984, para. 136 n. 7; *Rogall*, in: Systematischer Kommentar, vor para. 133 notes 42-45.

75. BGHSt. 1, 376 at 379 (1951); BGHSt. 13, 60 (1959) (confession made after suspect had been without sleep for 30 hours was excluded); but see BGHSt. 38, 291 (1992) (statement admitted although suspect later claimed that he had found no sleep in his cell during the night before interrogation).

76. *Roxin*, Strafverfahrensrecht, p. 131; *Wache*, in: Karlsruher Kommentar, para. 163a n. 28.

ment must be excluded.[77] If a suspect says that he wishes to speak with counsel but has not yet retained an attorney, police must make reasonable efforts to assist the suspect in finding an attorney willing to represent him.[78] The police need not, however, indefinitely refrain from questioning a suspect after he has expressed a desire to find and consult with an attorney. If the suspect has tried to reach an attorney but has failed to do so (because the interrogation took place after midnight) the police can continue to "encourage" the defendant to talk, and an ensuing statement has been held admissible.[79] German law does not contain a strict rule that questioning must stop once the suspect has demanded to talk with counsel or has declared that he wishes to remain silent. Although the police must not exert pressure or threaten the suspect in order to make him talk, commentators emphasize that an interrogator need not just accept the suspect's wish to say nothing but can inform him of possible disadvantages of remaining silent.[80] Waiver of the right to remain silent or to consult with counsel does not require any form - if the suspect talks, his privilege to remain silent is deemed waived.

Tricks and fraudulent tactics of the police to make a suspect talk are generally discouraged by the courts. Para. 136a section 1 CCP specifically prohibits attempts to influence a suspect's or witness' determination whether to make a statement by "deception" (*Täuschung*), and any ensuing statement is declared inadmissible (para. 136a section 3 CCP). The Federal Court of Appeals applies the law strictly whenever interrogators positively make false statements but tolerates the withholding of available information even if the effect is deceptive. In one case, the suspect had allegedly hidden stolen goods in a coin-operated locker in a train station. When the suspect was interrogated by a police officer, he said, "Why do you ask me what I did? You have cameras at the train station which record everything, don't you?". The police officer confirmed the suspect's assumption although he knew that there had in fact not been any surveillance in place, and the suspect made a confession, which was held admissible.[81] In another case, the police had found the dismembered body of a murder victim. They interrogated the victim's room-mate, whom they suspected of having killed the victim, telling him that they investigated the case of a "missing person." The statements the suspect made in response were held inadmissible, because the police officer had purposely mislead him about the dimension of the case.[82] In a third case, the police told a suspect that they had "overwhelming evidence" of his guilt when in fact they had only an unfounded suspicion; the ensuing confession was held inadmissible.[83] With respect to questions of law, the distinction between active and passive misinformation does not apply: the interrogator must, e.g., correct a suspect's mistaken notion that he is

77. BGHSt. 38, 372 (1992).

78. BGHSt. 42, 15 (1996).

79. BGHSt. 42, 170 (1996). This decision can hardly be reconciled with the decision of another panel of the Federal Court of Appeals cited in note 78; for an analysis, see *Herrmann*, Das Recht des Beschuldigten, vor der polizeilichen Vernehmung einen Verteidiger zu befragen, NStZ 1997, 209.

80. *Hanack*, in: *Löwe/Rosenberg*, 24th ed. 1984, para. 136 n. 24; *Kl/M-G*, para. 136 n. 8; *Rogall*, in: Systematischer Kommentar, para. 136 n. 34.

81. BGH NJW 1986, 2770.

82. BGHSt. 37, 48 at 52-53 (1990).

83. BGHSt. 35, 328 (1988).

under a legal duty to confess.[84] It should be noted that the courts generally limit the concept of "deception" to *intentional* misrepresentations,[85] whereas the impact of the false information on the suspect's mind is the same when the officer is only negligent or acts in good faith, the German term *Täuschung* has indeed the meaning of a willful deception.

The law is murky and contested with respect to police informers. The Federal Court of Appeals does not regard an informer's "talk" with a suspect as an interrogation, even when the informer had been instructed by the police.[86] The Court nevertheless applies, by analogy, the prohibition of certain methods of interrogation listed in para. 136a CCP to police informers' attempts to obtain information from the suspect. The suspect's statements would thus be inadmissible if the informer had brought them about by coercion or threats.[87] The fact that the informer does not disclose the fact that he works for the police or that the police are listening in on the conversation is not regarded as a "deception" in the sense of para. 136a CCP and therefore does not lead to exclusion of the suspect's statement.[88] The Court has, however, held that placing a detained suspect in a cell together with a police informer instructed to elicit incriminating information is unlawful "coercion" because pretrial detention has the exclusive purpose of holding someone for trial and loses its legitimacy when it is abused for other purposes (i.e., for surreptitiously collecting evidence against the suspect).[89]

2. No Impact of Formal Charging

The fact that formal charges against the suspect have been filed is irrelevant to the permissibility of interrogations. Likewise, the fact that the defendant has (retained or appointed) counsel does not preclude law enforcement personnel from interrogating him in the absence of counsel.

3. Enforcing the Rules

Statements made after violations of the above-mentioned rules have occurred are generally inadmissible. Para. 136a section 3 CCP explicitly prohibits the use of any statement by a suspect or witness[90] made when his freedom of the will was impaired by maltreatment, exhaustion, interference with his body, administration of drugs, torture, deception, hypnosis, illegal compulsion or threats, illegal promises or measures interfering with his memory or with his

84. *Boujong*, in: Karlsruher Kommentar, para. 136a n. 22; *Hanack*, in: *Löwe/Rosenberg*, 24th ed. 1984, para. 136a n. 36; *Kl/M-G*, para. 136a n. 17.

85. BGHSt. 31, 395 at 399 (1983); BGHSt. 35, 328 at 329 (1988); BGH StV 1989, 515. It is permissible to ask the suspect suggestive or confusing questions; *Boujong*, in: Karlsruher Kommentar, para. 136a n. 20; *Rogall*, in: Systematischer Kommentar, para. 136a n. 54; but see *Hanack*, in: *Löwe/Rosenberg*, 24th ed. 1984, para. 136a n. 43 (emphasizing proximity to deception).

86. BGHSt. 42, 139 at 145-147 (1996).

87. BGHSt. 39, 335 at 348-349 (1993); BGHSt. 40, 66 at 71-72 (1994).

88. BGHSt. 39, 335 at 348 (1993); BGHSt. 42, 139 at 149 (1996).

89. BGHSt. 34, 362 (1987).

90. Para. 69 section 3 CCP makes the prohibition of certain measures of interrogation applicable to witnesses.

ability of introspection. If any of these prohibited measures was applied at the time the statement was made, exclusion does not require a showing that the statement was in fact involuntary. It will normally be assumed (and does not require proof) that the statement was actually caused by the illicit method brought to bear upon the declarant.[91] The statement is inadmissible even if the suspect or witness now consents to its use (para. 136a section 3 CCP). This rule does, of course, not preclude the declarant from stating the same facts again in open court.

A mere omission of informing a suspect of his rights (see 1., *supra*) has not been regarded as a "deception," but the Federal Court of Appeals has nevertheless held statements inadmissible when the interrogator had not informed the suspect of his right to remain silent[92] and to consult with counsel.[93] With respect to the privilege against self-incrimination, the Court found that omission of the required warning uncontrollably jeopardized the suspect's ability to avail himself of the privilege so that the suspect's (conclusive) waiver had to be presumed involuntary.[94] Given this rationale, it was logical for the Court to recognize an exception if it could be proved that the suspect was in fact aware of his right to remain silent.[95]

Other effective methods to enforce police obedience to the rules are not available. There exists the theoretical possibility of initiating criminal[96] or disciplinary proceedings against an offending police officer, but these means are in practice applied only in cases of massive brutality.

Inadmissible confessions must not be introduced in court even by indirect means; e.g., an expert witness cannot build his expert opinion on a confession coerced by the police.[97] Evidence *derived* from unwarned or coerced statements[98] has, however, been held admissible because German courts do not recognize a "fruit of the poisonous tree" doctrine.[99] Courts also admit "untainted" later confessions even if the declarant had not been informed of the fact that his earlier statement could not be used in court.[100]

91. BGHSt. 13, 60 at 61 (1959); *Boujong*, in: Karlsruher Kommentar, para. 136a n. 38.

92. BGHSt. 25, 325 (1974) (warning not given in judicial interrogation); BGHSt. 38, 214 (1992) (warning not given in police interrogation).

93. BGHSt. 42, 15 at 21-22 (1996); see also BGHSt. 38, 372 (1992) (inadmissibility of statement when suspect was prevented from consulting with counsel).

94. BGHSt. 38, 214 at 220-222 (1992).

95. Id. at 224-225. The Court explains that knowlegde of the right to remain silent can be assumed when the suspect makes a statement in the presence of counsel but that knowledge cannot be inferred from the fact that the suspect had previously been prosecuted or convicted.

96. Para. 343 Penal Code provides: "Whoever, as an officer called upon to participate in a criminal proceeding ... bodily mistreats another person, otherwise applies force, threatens the application of force or mentally torments another person in order to cause that other person to say or declare something with respect to the proceedings or to refrain from doing so shall be punished by imprisonment between one and ten years." In 1995, two persons were convicted of that offense; *Statistisches Bundesamt*, Fachserie 10 (Rechtspflege), Reihe 3: Strafverfolgung 1995, 1997, p. 32.

97. *Kl/M-G*, para. 136a n. 29.

98. Given the general manner in which the Federal Court of Appeals has rejected the "fruit of the poisonous tree" doctrine, there can be no doubt that the court would also admit into evidence derivative fruits of illegal searches.

99. BGHSt. 34, 362 at 364 (1987).

100. BGHSt. 37, 48 at 53 (1990); BGH NStZ 1988, 419.

III. Court Procedures

A. Pretrial

1. *Initial Court Appearance*

A suspect does not appear in court before trial unless he has been arrested and the prosecutor wishes him to be held in pretrial detention. In that case, a hearing before a judge takes place not later than by the end of the day following arrest (paras. 115, 128 CCP). At that hearing, the judge has the dossier of the police investigations; the prosecution is often represented by the police officer in charge of the case. The suspect is present and must be given an opportunity to rebut the allegations made against him (para. 115 section 3 CCP). If the suspect has (retained) counsel, the latter has a right to be present and must be informed of the time of the hearing (para. 168c secs. 1, 5 CCP). The judge should try to set the hearing at a time convient for the defense attorney, but the time limit of paras. 115, 128 CCP (end of the day following arrest) cannot be waived.[101] The purpose of the hearing is to determine whether the statutory requirements for an order of pretrial detention (urgent suspicion and danger of flight or obstruction of evidence; para. 112 CCP[102]) are fulfilled. Even if they are, the suspect can demand suspension of the detention order if less intrusive measures, e.g., an order to report to the police at fixed intervals, not to leave the community without judicial permission and/or to post a financial security, are sufficient to guarantee the defendant's presence at the trial (para. 116 section 1 CCP). If the suspect is kept in pretrial detention, he can at any time demand a judicial review of the continued necessity to detain him (para. 117 CCP); upon defendant's motion, a hearing must be held every two months if detention continues (para. 118 section 3 CCP).

2. *Charging Instrument*

The decision to charge is the exclusive domain of the public prosecutor's office; there is no direct participation of any other agency. The prosecutor is obliged by law to file charges whenever there is "sufficient" suspicion that the suspect has committed a crime (para. 170 section 1 CCP).[103] The standard of sufficiency to be applied in this context is likelihood that the suspect will be convicted after trial. The required prognosis leaves some leeway to individual prosecutors' appraisal of the strength of the evidence. German prosecutors tend to err in favor of bringing charges because a non-conviction is not regarded as a personal (or institutional) defeat to the extent it would be in a partisan system of justice.[104]

---

101. *Boujong*, in: Karlsruher Kommentar, para. 115 n. 11.

102. For details, see II.3., *supra*.

103. Para. 170 section 1 CCP reads: "If the investigation has provided sufficient grounds for public accusation, the prosecutor's office brings an accusation by filing formal charges with the appropriate court."

104. The rate of acquittals in German courts nevertheless is below 3% (*Statistisches Bundesamt* [n. 96], pp. 42-43: 2.8%). An additional 13% of cases have been dismissed by the courts (id.); such dismissals, which usually occur at the trial, are sometimes employed as alternatives to acquittals.

The victim of an offense can challenge a prosecutor's refusal to bring charges for lack of sufficient evidence. If an intra-office review of the matter does not lead to a reversal of the decision not to bring charges, the victim can present the issue to the State Court of Appeals, which can direct the prosecutor's office to file an accusation (paras. 172-175 CCP). Although victims' efforts to force an accusation are seldom successful in practice, the mere existence of the possibility of judicial review provides a check on arbitrary dismissals by prosecutors.

With respect to less serious offenses,[105] which make up the great majority of offenses reported to the police, prosecution is in fact discretionary: Para. 153 CCP permits the prosecutor to refrain from prosecution when the suspect's guilt appears insignificant and when there is no public interest in prosecution, and para. 153a CCP provides for dismissal of "convictable" cases in exchange for a payment by the suspect to the state or to a charitable organisation.[106] Both provisions are used quite frequently by prosecutor's offices as tools for weeding out cases of lesser significance.

3. *Preliminary Hearings*

Preliminary hearings, i.e., hearings to review the strength of the prosecution case before trial, are not a feature of the German criminal process. The professional judge members of the trial court do review the prosecution case before setting it for trial; yet they do so without a hearing on the basis of the formal accusation and the dossier of the investigation submitted by the prosecutor's office. The defense can - but rarely does - submit a brief in response. Because admitting the case for trial requires only "sufficient suspicion" (*hinreichender Tatverdacht*), only about 1% of accusations are rejected at this stage,[107] usually because of the court's differing view on the applicable law.

4. *Pretrial Motions*

The defendant can ask the court to take certain evidence before trial (paras. 201, 202 CCP). Because the court has discretion to reject such motions at this stage, most defendants prefer to wait until the trial with making demands for the taking of evidence. The issue of inadmissibility of evidence can be raised before trial, but the court will not usually rule on it until it has discussed the matter with the parties at the trial.

B. Trial

1. *Nature of Trial*

Criminal courts in Germany find the facts, establish the applicable law and impose sentence. Depending on the seriousness of the case, courts consist of between

105. These are defined as offenses with a statutory minimum punishment of less than one year imprisonment (*Vergehen*).

106. With respect to more serious offenses eligible for dismissal, the court must agree with non-prosecution; yet courts almost never object.

107. *Statistisches Bundesamt*, Rechtspflege, Reihe 2: Gerichte und Staatsanwaltschaften 1995, 1997, p. 84.

one and five judges. Although there is no jury, lay persons participate, as co-equal judges, in the adjudication of the broad middle range of criminal matters.

If only a fine or imprisonment of up to two years is the expected sanction, the case is tried without lay participation by a single professional judge (*Strafrichter*) (para. 25 Code of Court Organisation; hereinafter: CCO). Other cases of lesser seriousness are decided by panels consisting of one professional judge and two lay judges (*Schöffengerichte*; paras. 24, 28, 29 section 1 CCO).[108] Panels of three professional and two lay judges (*Große Strafkammer*)[109] sit on trials of the most serious offenses. There is no lay participation in trials of serious offenses against the security of the state, which take place before panels of five professional judges of the State Court of Appeals (*Oberlandesgericht*; paras. 120, 122 section 2 CCO).

Lay judges also participate in second instance adjudication: when a case is tried *de novo* upon a general appeal (*Berufung*), it is heard by the *Kleine Strafkammer* consisting of one professional judge and two lay judges (para. 76 section 1 CCO). Lay judges are, however, not involved in the decision of appeals on legal grounds (*Revision*).

To the extent that lay judges are members of criminal court panels, their participation is limited to the trial and the ensuing decision-making phase. They are not involved in the admission or preparation of cases for trial (paras. 30 section 2, 76 section 1 CCO). With respect to the judgment, lay judges have a strong position. In the smaller panels (*Schöffengericht* and *Kleine Strafkammer*), they have a majority (2:1); in the larger panels (*Große Strafkammer*), decisions adverse to the defendant cannot be made against the votes of the lay judges because such decisions require a two thirds majority (para. 263 section 1 CCP).

The process of selecting lay judges is fairly complicated. Lay judges must be German citizens; people younger than 25 years or older than 70 years of age, persons who have lived in the community for less than one year, cabinet members, judges, prosecutors, attorneys, police officers and clergymen shall not be called to serve (paras. 33, 34 CCO).[110] Every four years, each city or district council establishes, by a two thirds majority, a list of persons eligible for service as lay judges. The final selection is made by a commission consisting of a county court judge, a civil servant, and ten members elected by the district council (para. 40 CCO). This commission selects[111] the requisite number of lay judges for each county court and district court. Assignment of these lay judges to particular cases is then made by lot (para. 45 section 2 CCO).

As a result of the selection process, lay judges do not exactly represent a cross section of the German population: In 1985, only 37% of all lay judges were

---

108. In complex cases, the court, upon motion of the prosecutor, can request an additional professional judge to serve on the *Schöffengericht*, which then consists of two professional and two lay judges (para. 29 section 2 CCO).

109. In cases not involving the death of the victim, the *Große Strafkammer* can also sit with only two professional and two lay judges (para. 74 section 2 CCO).

110. Certain groups of persons, for whom serving as a lay judge would create particular hardship, can decline to serve (para. 35 CCO); this includes, e.g., physicians, pharmacists, and persons who have to care for a family.

111. The law requires that each lay judge be selected individually by a majority of two thirds of the commission. The commission must not draw lots (BGHSt. 33, 41 [1984]) nor can it simply adopt the proposals of political factions of the city council (BGHSt. 35, 190 [1988]).

women, and 29% were public servants.[112] Lay judges as well as professional judges can be challenged for bias,[113] but there are no peremptory challenges.

Trials can last from a few minutes to several years. A typical *Schöffengericht* (county court) case may take half a day, cases tried before the *Große Strafkammer* usually take a few days. Para. 229 CCP states that a trial cannot be adjourned for more than ten days,[114] if there was a longer interruption, the trial must start again from the beginning. This rule is meant to guarantee speed and continuity of the fact-finding process. It sometimes leads to counterproductive results, however, when courts "bide time" by holding very brief sessions every ten days just to keep the trial alive.

Inadmissible evidence is excluded from the trial, but professional judges usually are aware of it from the dossier of the case (see II.A.5., *supra*).

The professional judge(s) who sit on the court must prepare a written opinion explaining which facts were found to be true, how the law was applied and on what grounds the sentence was based (para. 267 CCP). The written judgment is often quite detailed and lengthy, including a thorough evaluation of the evidence adduced at the trial. The written judgment can be greatly abbreviated if all parties have waived appeal (para. 267 section 4 CCP). When an appeal has been filed, the judgment is transferred to the appeals court.

German law does not provide for formal pleas. Even if the defendant admits his guilt, the court remains obliged to find the facts necessary for conviction (para. 244 section 2 CCP).[115] However, if the defendant gives the court a credible and detailed description of how he committed the offense and if neither the prosecution nor the defense offer further evidence, the court will usually be satisfied that the defendant's statement provides a sufficient basis for the judgment and will refrain from calling additional witnesses.[116] From this possibility of reasonably limiting the effort of "finding the truth," the German equivalent of plea bargaining has developed. In complex cases, the defense sometimes intimates to the court that the defendant would be ready to make a statement and to refrain from demanding the taking of further evidence in exoneration if he could be certain that his sentence would not exceed a certain maximum. The court, after hearing the opinion of the prosecutor, then indicates what the approximate sentence might be in case of the defendant's cooperation. If all sides agree, the defendant makes a (limited) confession in open court, is convicted on this basis, receives the previously agreed sentence, and the proceeding is thus significantly shortened. The legality of this "shortcut to justice" is still in doubt. The Federal Court of Appeals has made it clear that

---

112. See the figures from official (otherwise unpublished) statistics cited in *Rennig*, Die Entscheidungsfindung durch Schöffen und Berufsrichter in rechtlicher und psychologischer Sicht, 1993, pp. 478, 480. Members of ethnic minorities are largely excluded because only German citizens can serve as lay judges.

113. A judge will be recused from a case if there is "concern of bias," i.e., if there exist circumstances which are apt to cause an objective observer to doubt the judge's impartiality (para. 24 CCP).

114. An interruption of 30 days is possible when the trial has already lasted for ten days or more (para. 229 section 2 CCP).

115. Para. 244 section 2 CCP reads: "In order to find the truth, the court must, *ex officio*, extend the taking of evidence to all facts and pieces of evidence relevant for its decision."

116. *Gollwitzer*, in: *Löwe/Rosenberg*, 24th ed. 1985, para. 244 n. 33; *Schlüchter*, in: Systematischer Kommentar, para. 244 n. 28.

informal "discussions" among the court and the parties before and during the trial are not *per se* illegal but that the court must not unilaterally deal with the defense and that the judges cannot make a firm offer of a fixed sentence before having heard all relevant evidence.[117] Practitioners seem to have found ways to respect these limitations and yet to arrive at satisfactory "deals." Because of the uncertain legal status of this practice, agreements are usually not made in public but in judges' chambers or on the telephone, and the defense has to rely on an informal, non-binding "hypothetical" sentence offer by the court.[118]

2. Role of Lawyers

The trial is primarily conducted by the presiding judge, who determines the sequence in which proof is taken, is responsible for the completeness of the evidence (para. 244 section 2 CCP[119]), and interrogates the defendant, witnesses and expert witnesses (para. 238 section 1 CCP[120]). All other judges (including lay judges) as well as the prosecutor, the defense attorney, the victim or his representative - if present -[121] and the defendant himself have the right to ask additional questions of witnesses and expert witnesses (para. 240 CCP). The parties can also demand that the court take additional evidence, and the court can deny such a motion only if the evidence offered is obviously redundant or irrelevant.[122]

The prosecutor is deemed a neutral officer of the law. The prosecutor's office is bound by the law to investigate evidence tending to exonerate the suspect as well as incriminating evidence (para. 160 section 2 CCP). This neutral role extends to the trial and post-trial phase: the prosecutor can - and sometimes does - ask the court, at the end of the trial, to acquit the defendant for lack of sufficient evidence, and the prosecutor's office can bring an appeal against a conviction in favor of the defendant (para. 296 section 2 CCP). In fact, however, after the prosecutor has made up his mind to file formal charges he will usually attempt to obtain a conviction. Especially when the defendant is represented by counsel, the prosecutor usually defines his role as an advocate, not as a neutral arbiter. Yet this rule is not without exceptions. In routine cases, the accusation is prepared and filed by one member of the prosecutor's office and the case is represented in court by another, who may well have different views on the strength of the prosecution case in light

---

117. See, e.g., BGHSt. 37, 298 (1991); BGHSt. 38, 102 (1991); BGHSt. 42, 46 (1996).

118. For an overview of the problems of "plea bargaining" in Germany, see *Herrmann*, Bargaining Justice - a Bargain for German Criminal Justice?, 53 University of Pittsburgh Law Review 755 (1992).

119. See n. 115, *supra*.

120. Para. 238 section 1 CCP reads: "The presiding judge conducts the trial, interrogates the defendant and takes the evidence."

121. Victims of certain offenses against the person have the right to join the prosecution as "subsidiary prosecutors" (*Nebenkläger*). When they do, they - or their attorneys - have extensive participation rights at the trial as well as the right to appeal against an acquittal; see paras. 395, 397, 400 CCP.

122. Para. 244 secs. 3-5 CCP does not grant the court discretion to deny motions to take additional evidence but permits it to reject such "offers of proof" (*Beweisantrag*) only if a specific reason for rejection (listed in the Code) applies. A mistaken rejection of an offer of proof often leads to reversal of the judgment. For that reason, offers of proof are welcome bargaining chips for the defense in attempting to make the court promise a lenient sentence in exchange for cooperation (see text at notes 117-118, *supra*).

of the evidence presented at the trial and may therefore ask the court to acquit the defendant.[123]

3. *Witnesses*

It is the responsibility of the presiding judge to subpoena the necessary witnesses for trial (para. 214 section 1 CCP). The presiding judge gathers from the dossier (and sometimes from a defense brief filed before trial) which witnesses need to be heard at the trial. The parties (including the defendant) have two options for introducing additional witnesses: they can make a formal "offer of proof" to the court, demanding that a certain witness be heard for the truth of a fact asserted by the party (*Beweisantrag*),[124] or they can have the witness subpoenaed directly by the bailiff (para. 220 CCP). In the latter case, the witness is bound to appear at the courthouse for the trial, but a valid "offer of proof" is still necessary to oblige the court to hear him (para. 245 CCP).

The defendant himself is not regarded as a witness. He can make statements in court, but he is not sworn to tell the truth and cannot be punished if he does not. His statements are nevertheless part of the trial evidence and can form the basis of the judgment.

The defendant has an absolute right to remain silent, flowing from the privilege against self-incrimination (see II.C.1., *supra*). After the formal charges have been read by the prosecutor, the presiding judge asks the defendant whether he wishes to make a statement, and the defendant can refuse to do so without having to give reasons. The defendant can later change his mind, and the fact that he did not make a statement at the earliest opportunity or that he remained silent throughout cannot be used as evidence of his guilt,[125] nor can the sentence be enhanced because the defendant remained silent.[126] Witnesses can refuse to answer questions if the reply would create a danger for the witness or one of his relatives of being prosecuted for a criminal offense or an administrative infraction (para. 55 section 1 CCP). German law recognizes a large number of testimonial privileges. Relatives of the defendant can generally refuse to testify (para. 52 CCP).[127] Members of certain professions, e.g., physicians, clergymen, attorneys, tax accountants, and drug counsellors, can withhold information obtained in the course of their professional activities unless the person who gave the information formally authorizes the professional to testify (para. 53 CCP).

Expert witnesses are regarded as neutral helpers of the court, not as supporters of one party. The law therefore provides for appointment of experts by the judge (para. 73 section 1 CCP). In practice, however, prosecutors often appoint ex-

---

123. The prosecutor is precluded from withdrawing criminal charges once the case has been set for trial (para. 156 CCP). If the prosecutor determines, in the course of the trial, that evidence of the defendant's guilt is too weak to support a conviction, his only choice is to ask the court for acquittal. The court is, however, not bound by the prosecutor's wishes.

124. See n. 122, *supra*, and accompanying text.

125. BGHSt. 20, 281 (1965); for further references, see *Rogall*, in: Systematischer Kommentar, vor para. 133 n. 199.

126. BGH StV 1981, 276; *Hanack*, in: *Löwe/Rosenberg*, 24th ed. 1984, para. 136 n. 28; *Rogall*, in: Systematischer Kommentar, vor para. 133 n. 207.

127. The privilege belongs to the witness, not to the defendant. The defendant can thus not (legally) influence a relative's decision whether to testify.

perts during the investigation stage of the process,[128] and the court retains the same expert for reasons of expediency. The defense can try to introduce additional experts in the same way as they can nominate witnesses (see *supra*), but its chance of success is often limited because of financial considerations. Because the fees of expert witnesses called by the court are part of court costs (to be borne by the defendant if he is convicted, and otherwise by the state), the law gives the court broad discretion in ruling on "offers of proof" for hearing additional expert witnesses; only if the expert nominated by a party has research facilities clearly superior to those of the expert appointed by the court or if the court expert's opinion is self-contradictory or otherwise defective (para. 244 section 4 CCP) must the court appoint an additional expert. If the court refuses to do so, the defense still has the option of directly serving a subpoena on the desired expert witness,[129] but a party subpoena must be accompanied by the expected expert fee plus expenses in cash (para. 220 section 2 CCP). At the trial, all expert witnesses give their opinions orally[130] and then are interrogated by the presiding judge. The parties can ask additional questions, as with other witnesses.

Theoretically, the German system of court-appointed expert witnesses should make for a neutral, detached role of experts, in contrast to the "hired gun" syndrome in adversarial systems. In practice, however, the influence of the police and the prosecutor's office on the selection of experts is strong. Defense counsel complain that experts tend to favor the side responsible for their selection, i.e., the prosecution — a situation exacerbated by the seemingly neutral position of experts, which makes it difficult (by law as well as in fact) to counter the testimony of a court-appointed expert by testimony of a "private" expert invited by the defense.[131]

C. Appeals

Appeals are possible against all judgments except those rendered by courts of appeal. The defendant as well as the prosecution have the right to appeal; whereas the defendant can only appeal against judgments of conviction (but he can limit the appeal to the sentence), the prosecutor's office can appeal both acquittals and convictions. With respect to the latter, the appeal can be in favor of the defendant if the prosecutor finds that the defendant should have been acquitted or that the sentence was too severe (para. 296 section 2 CCP). The victim can appeal against an acquittal if he has joined the prosecution as a "subsidiary prosecutor."[132]

Two kinds of appeals are available: general appeals (*Berufung*) and appeals on legal grounds (*Revision*). Figures about the "success" of appeals are not available.

---

128. Authority to do so is derived from para. 161a section 1 CCP, which provides that witnesses and expert witnesses are obliged to appear and to testify at the prosecutor's office.

129. If an expert subpoenaed by a party is present in the courthouse, the court must hear him unless his opinion is evidently irrelevant (para. 245 section 2 CCP).

130. Expert witnesses customarily file a written version of their opinion with the court before trial. Yet the judgment can be based only upon their oral testimony.

131. See *Widmaier*, Zur Rechtsstellung des nach Paragraphen 220, 38 StPO vom Verteidiger geladenen Sachverständigen, StV 1985, 526; *Tondorf/Waider*, Der Sachverständige, ein "Gehilfe" auch des Strafverteidigers?, StV 1997, 493.

132. See n. 121, *supra*.

The great majority of appeals are filed by defendants.[133] With respect to general appeals, about one third of appeals were withdrawn,[134] which indicates an expectation on the part of the appellant that the appeal will be dismissed. In cases of appeals on legal grounds, only a small minority are decided by judgment after an oral hearing, whereas the great majority are rejected without a hearing as "obviously unfounded" or granted as "obviously founded."[135] Although the statistics do not distinguish between these two kinds of dispositions, it is safe to assume that the great majority of them were rejected as "obviously unfounded."

General Appeal. A party which feels aggrieved by a judgment of a single professional judge or a *Schöffengericht* only has to file a one-sentence letter ("I hereby appeal against the judgment.") within a week after the judgment has been announced.[136] This is sufficient to oblige the three-judge panel of the district court (*Kleine Strafkammer*; cf. paras. 74 section 3, 76 section 1 CCO) to hold a new trial on the issues of guilt as well as sentence (paras. 314, 322 section 1 CCP).[137] An exception exists, however, with respect to petty offenses sanctioned by not more than 15 day fines; in these cases, the appeals court can deny review if it finds, in its unreviewable discretion, that the appeal is evidently without merit (paras. 313, 322a CCP).

At the level of the appeals court, the trial process begins again at the starting point. The appeals court is obliged to collect and present all the evidence necessary to arrive at the judgment, and it cannot limit itself to a review of the first instance judgment but must take new evidence if necessary (para. 323 section 3 CCP). If the appeals court comes to the same conclusion (with respect to both the verdict and the sentence) as the first instance court it rejects the appeal and upholds the original judgment. If not, the appeals court renders its own judgment based on the evidence presented at the second trial. Only if the county court had erroneously assumed jurisdiction is the case remanded to the appropriate court (para. 328 CCP).

Appeal on Legal Grounds. Appeal on legal grounds *(Revision)* is available against almost every judgment based on a trial. State courts of appeal hear appeals in cases originating in county court (para. 121 section 1 CCO).[138] Appeals in cases originally tried in district court or in a State Court of Appeals (which has first instance jurisdiction in serious cases involving the security of the state, including terrorism; para. 120 CCO) go directly to the Federal Court of Appeals (para. 135 section 1 CCO).

---

133. In 1995, 85% of general appeals and 95% of appeals on legal grounds were filed by the defendant; *Statistisches Bundesamt*, Fachserie 10 (Rechtspflege), Reihe 2: Gerichte und Staatsanwaltschaften 1995, 1997, pp. 98, 108.

134. *Statistisches Bundesamt* (n. 133), p. 98.

135. Dispositions without a hearing occured in 86% of cases disposed of by State Courts of Appeals and in 88% of cases in the Federal Court of Appeals; id. at pp. 108, 112.

136. The appellant is of course free to submit a brief in support of the appeal (cf. para. 317 CCP), and the prosecutor's office usually does so. Yet written argument in support of the appeal has no influence on the court's duty to re-investigate the whole matter at the new trial.

137. *Berufung* can be (and in practice often is) limited to the sentence (para. 318 CCP); in that case, the conviction becomes final, and the trial at the district court deals only with the issue of sentence.

138. Parties can challenge county court judgments by means of *Berufung* and then file *Revision* against the district court judgment rendered upon the new trial. They can also file *Revision* directly against the judgment of the county court (para. 335 CCP); this is advisable only if the appellant agrees with the county court's findings of fact but wishes to challenge the application of the law.

An appeal on legal grounds must allege a violation of the law (para. 337 section 1 CCP); erroneous or incomplete fact-finding by the trial court can thus, in principle, not be grounds for *Revision*. Appeals on legal grounds must be submitted in writing, and they must be accompanied or followed by an explanation of the grounds for appeal (*Revisionsbegründung*) authored by an attorney (paras. 341 section 1, 345 section 2 CCP).

Grounds for Appeal. An appeal on legal grounds leads to reversal of the judgment if the appeals court determines that a) the trial court failed to apply or misapplied a relevant rule of substantive or procedural law and b) that the trial court's judgment is based (*beruht*) on that error (para. 337 CCP). German courts have construed requirement (b) in a very liberal fashion, reversing judgments whenever it is *possible* that the court's error had an influence on the verdict or the sentence. In other words, an error is regarded as harmless only if it is logically impossible that the judgment would have been different if the trial court had not committed the error. It follows that various *procedural* errors lead to reversal if the defendant, but for the error, might have persuaded the court to find in his favor. The Federal Court of Appeals has, e.g., reversed a judgment because the defendant was not given an opportunity to have the "last word" after closing statements of the prosecutor and the defense attorney, as required by para. 258 section 3 CCP.[139] In another case, the judgment was reversed because a court erroneously failed to swear a witness; the Federal Court of Appeals reasoned that the trial court may have given insufficient weight to that witness' testimony and that, in any event, the defendant was misled by the reason the court gave for not swearing the witness.[140]

With respect to some (procedural) errors, para. 338 CCP establishes an irrebuttable presumption that they influence the judgment. These errors (if alleged and found to be true on appeal) thus lead to "automatic" reversal of the judgment (*absolute Revisionsgründe*). This list of "deadly sins" includes the following: the court did not have jurisdiction; a judge who was excluded by law (para. 22 CCP) or who should have been recused for cause (para. 24 CCP) participated at the trial; a person whose attendance at the trial the law requires (i.e., the defendant, a representative of the prosecutor's office, or, in a case of "necessary defense," defense counsel) was not present for (part of) the trial; the public was excluded from the trial without sufficient cause; the written judgment was not filed within five weeks after the end of the trial;[141] a ruling of the court unlawfully and significantly restricted the rights of the defense. The last ground for reversal, which appears to give special protection to the rights of the defense, is in fact largely superfluous because any *significant* interference with defense rights will almost always have the potential of affecting the judgment and thus lead to reversal according to the general clause of para. 337 CCP. Because the role of defense counsel is not as crucial to the fairness of the trial as it is in adversary systems, ineffectiveness of the assistance of counsel is not a ground for automatic reversal. It has, however, been regarded as reversible error for the presiding judge to appoint an attorney who had an obvious conflict of

139. BGHSt. 3, 368 (1953).

140. BGHSt. 8, 155 (1955). The trial court had made the mistake of regarding the witness as a possible accessory in the offense and had therefore failed to make him testify under oath (cf. para. 60 CCP).

141. This ground for automatic reversal has mainly disciplinary purposes (i.e., to give judges a strong incentive to write and file judgments in time); the assumption that the judgment is based on the delay in filing it is fictitious.

interest because he had previously represented the victim of the offense in his claims for damages.[142]

If it appears from the written judgment that the court had based its verdict on evidence which should not have been admitted, the judgment is clearly "based on" an erroneous application of the law, which leads to reversal according to para. 337 CCP.

It should be noted that appeals on legal grounds cannot be based on the claim that the fact-finding was erroneous. An appeals court would therefore reject out of hand a *Revision* which maintains that the defendant should not have been convicted because he did not in fact commit the offense or because a key prosecution witness did not tell the truth. But even a claim that the trial court misinterpreted or failed to take into account a witness' testimony would not help the appellant because the appeals court has no means of checking the trial court's fact-finding:[143] the appeals court neither takes evidence nor considers the prosecutor's dossier, and the formal minutes (*Protokoll*) of the trial usually say nothing about the contents of testimony.[144]

Yet the Federal Court of Appeals has in recent years consistently expanded the scope of its review, upon *Revision*, of the trial courts' findings of facts.[145] One method of achieving such review is the so-called *Aufklärungsrüge*, a claim that the trial court violated its obligation, under para. 244 section 2 CCP, to collect all the relevant evidence. In making this claim of a procedural violation, the appellant alleges that the judgment rests on an insufficient factual basis because the trial court failed to follow certain leads (which the appellant must describe in some detail) which should have given it reason to introduce additional evidence. Another method of expanding review on *Revision* to the trial court's fact- finding is to examine the internal consistency of the judgment, especially its compatibility with the laws of logic, and the completeness of the evaluation of the evidence.[146] Appeals courts (sometimes) perform this kind of review in response to challenges of the substantive correctness of the judgment. If they find the interpretation the trial court gave to a certain piece of evidence unpersuasive, they do not (and cannot) call into question the trial court's factual findings as such but reverse the judgment on the ground that it did not take account of "obvious" (*naheliegende*) alternative interpretations and thus fails to give a coherent and complete explanation of the judgment. If, e.g., the trial court declares that it believed the testimony of prosecution

142. BGH StV 1992, 406 at 407.

143. BGHSt. 2, 248 (1952); BGHSt. 15, 347 (1961). For a defense attorney's view on this problem, see *Schlothauer*, Unvollständige und unzutreffende tatrichterliche Urteilsfeststellungen, StV 1992, 134.

144. If the *Protokoll* does contain substantive information, the Federal Court of Appeals permits the appellant to challenge the trial court's fact-finding as being contrary to the contents of the *Protokoll*; see, e.g., BGHSt. 38, 14 (1991) (a witness' statement was noted *verbatim* in the *Protokoll* in accordance with para. 273 section 3 CCP, and the trial court's judgment contained a different version of that statement); yet the appeals court will not disturb the *interpretation* the trial court has given to a document or statement; *Kl/M-G*, para. 337 n. 15; *Pikart*, in: Karlsruher Kommentar, para. 337 n. 3.

145. For analyses of this development, see *Hanack*, in: *Löwe/Rosenberg*, 24th ed. 1985, para. 337 notes 120-179; *Pelz*, Die revisionsgerichtliche Überprüfung der tatrichterlichen Beweiswürdigung, NStZ 1993, 361.

146. See BGHSt. 10, 208 (1957); BGH NStZ 1986, 325; *Pikart*, in: Karlsruher Kommentar, para. 337 notes 28-29.

witness A and not the conflicting testimony of defense witness B, the appeals court can reverse the judgment if it finds that the trial court did not sufficiently explore potential self-serving motives of witness A for incriminating the defendant and thus failed to give a persuasive explanation for its evaluation of the evidence. In a controversial case,[147] the Federal Court of Appeals reversed a conviction for aiding manslaughter based on the following facts: the defendant's wife had given birth to a girl of whom the defendant was not the father. A few days after the birth, the defendant picked up his wife and the baby at the hospital with a taxi. When the taxi stopped en route to defendant's home, he took the baby, who lay in a bag, and left the taxi. The baby was never seen or heard about thereafter. The Federal Court of Appeals found that the judgment below, which had assumed from these circumstances that the defendant was involved in the violent death of the baby, lacked a sufficiently reliable factual basis and was therefore legally defective. This judgment is a good example of the recent trend of appeals courts to second-guess trial courts' fact-finding.

List of Abbreviations

AlternativkommentarKommentar zur Strafprozeßordnung (Reihe Alternativkommentare; *Wassermann*, gen. ed.), 3 vols., 1988-1996

BGH*Bundesgerichtshof* (Federal Court of Appeals)

BGHSt.*Entscheidungen des Bundesgerichtshofs in Strafsachen*

(Decisions of the Federal Court of Appeals)

BVerfG*Bundesverfassungsgericht* (Federal Constitutional Court)

BVerfGE*Entscheidungen des Bundesverfassungsgerichts*

(Decisions of the Federal Constitutional Court)

CCOCode of Court Organisation

CCP*Code of Criminal Procedure*

Heidelberger Kommentar*Lemke* et al., Heidelberger Kommentar zur Strafprozeßordnung, 1997

JR*Juristische Rundschau* (a law journal)

JZ*Juristenzeitung* (a law journal)

Karlsruher KommentarKarlsruher Kommentar zur Strafprozeßordnung und zum Gerichtsverfassungsgesetz mit Einführungsgesetz (*Pfeiffer*, ed.), 3rd ed. 1993

Kl/M-GKleinknecht/Meyer-Goßner, Strafprozeßordnung, 43rd ed. 1997

Löwe/Rosenberg Löwe/Rosenberg, Die Strafprozeßordnung und das Gerichtsverfassungsgesetz. Großkommentar

NJW*Neue Juristische Wochenschrift* (a law journal)

NStZ*Neue Zeitschrift für Strafrecht* (a law journal)

147. BGH StV 1981, 33.

OLG*Oberlandesgericht* (Federal Court of Appeals)

StPO*Strafprozeßordnung* (*Code of Criminal Procedure*)

Systematischer Kommentar*Rudolphi* et al., Systematischer Kommentar zur Strafprozeßordnung und zum Gerichtsverfassungsgesetz (looseleaf)

wistra*Zeitschrift für Wirtschaft, Steuer, Strafrecht* (a legal journal)

Chapter 7

Israel

Eliahu Harnon
Alex Stein

I. Introduction

Israeli rules of criminal procedure and evidence are grounded in parliamentary legislation and in the common law principles, as developed and interpreted by courts (primarily, by the Supreme Court). Although the Israeli Parliament (the Knesset) authorizes administrative agencies to issue regulations concerning various issues in the area of criminal procedure, it is a well established principle of the Israeli law that any procedure that has a negative impact on fundamental human rights must be grounded in primary legislation. Recently, this principle has been reinforced by the constitutional Basic Law: Human Dignity and Liberty (1992) that confers upon people charged with crimes a number of important constitutional rights. These rights include:

- The right to dignity and physical integrity;
- freedom of movement, which includes the right against detention and extradition;
- the right to privacy that includes protection from searches and intrusions into private communications;
- the right to property that includes protection from seizures and fines.

  None of these rights, however, is guaranteed unreservedly. Each of these rights can be limited and even annulled by ordinary legislation, providing that the legislation satisfies the following three conditions:

- It fits the "values of the State of Israel as a Jewish and democratic state;"
- it does not qualify the right in question by an "unnecessary" or "unbalanced" limitation;
- it has been legislated for "a proper purpose."

The last two conditions thus seem to correspond with the American "compelling governmental interest" doctrine that licenses imposition of restrictions upon constitutional rights in the United States.

The Basic Law also contains a "preservation of laws" clause, according to which prior legislation remains unaffected by the Basic Law even when it does not satisfy the above conditions. However, the courts nowadays interpret pre-existing legislation in congruence with the Basic Law.[1] This interpretive constitutional alignment of the legislation minimizes the legislation's detrimental effects upon human rights.

Apart from this and other Basic Laws,[2] Israel does not have a written constitution or bill of rights. Subject to the provisions made by the Basic Laws, statutes enacted by the Knesset enjoy absolute authority and may infringe on the constitutionally unprotected rights.

The Supreme Court has, however, gradually created what might be termed a "Judicial Bill of Rights." This Bill of Rights is part and parcel of the Israeli common law. It contains a judge-made presumption that accords legislation an intention to protect rather than to infringe upon human rights and freedoms. In this way, courts have developed a variety of fundamental rights that affect criminal procedure and evidence. The right to confront adverse witnesses is one of such rights. Other relevant rights, such as the right of silence and the privilege against self-incrimination, derive primarily from statutory sources.

The principal statutes regulating the Israeli criminal procedure and evidence contain the following:

- Criminal Procedure Law [Consolidated Version] 1982 (hereafter: CPCV).
- Evidence Ordinance [New Version] 1971 (hereafter: Evidence Ordinance).
- Criminal Procedure Law (Powers of Enforcement—Arrest) 1996 (hereafter: CPEA). Driven by the principles of the developing Israeli Constitution, this important piece of legislation severely restricts the arrest powers by laying down strict conditions and time-limits for arrest. Complaints have already been heard from police officers that the new law of arrests is an impediment to the law-enforcement.
- Criminal Procedure Law (Powers of Enforcement—Body Searches) 1996 (hereafter: CPES).
- Criminal Procedure Ordinance (Arrest and Search, New Version) 1969 (hereafter: CPO; A&S).

More specific aspects of criminal procedure are regulated by other statutes and administrative regulations. As for the law of criminal evidence, this is largely built upon rules and principles, as developed at common law in England. These rules and principles - such as the rule against hearsay, the rule against opinion, the rule against disposition and character and the principles governing the admission and gathering of identification evidence—have been incorporated by the Israeli case law. The same is largely true about the principles regulating trial testimony and impeachment. Unlike the laws of criminal procedure, which are almost entirely codified, our Evidence Ordinance covers only a small amount of laws of evidence.

Subject to a few derogations, Israel has joined the following international conventions concerning fundamental human rights:

1. Ganimat v. State of Israel, 49(4) PISKEY DIN (hereafter: P.D.) 584 (1995).
2. Such as The Basic Law: Freedom of Occupation.

- Convention on the Prevention and Punishment of the Crime of Genocide (1948).
- International Convention on Civil and Political Rights (1966).
- International Convention on the Elimination of all Forms of Racial Discrimination (1966).
- Convention on the Elimination of all Forms of Discrimination Against Women (1979).
- Convention Against Torture and Other Cruel, Inhuman, or Degrading Treatment or Punishment (1984).
- Convention on the Rights of the Child (1989).

In Israel, international conventions (except those that are merely declaratory of the customary international law) do not automatically become part and parcel of the domestic law. The principle of direct applicability, applied in a few other countries with regard to international conventions, is not part of the Israeli law. It is only the customary international law that is automatically domiciled in our legal system. In order to become part of the Israeli domestic law, international conventions (as well as other covenants and agreements) need to be formally incorporated by an Act of the Knesset. Apart from the Convention on the Prevention and Punishment of the Crime of Genocide (1948), none of the above-mentioned conventions have become part of Israeli domestic law. Even so, in interpreting parliamentary legislation, Israeli courts tend to invoke the presumption that the Knesset did not intend to violate the international obligations of the State of Israel. Consequently, legislation is interpreted in correspondence with the conventions signed by the Israeli government. In this way, international conventions effectively become part of the Israeli domestic law.

II. Police Procedures

A. The Law of Arrest, Search, and Seizure

1. Stops

a. *Questioning a Witness* A police officer in the rank of Inspector and above, and any other officer acting under special authorization, are permitted to question any individual thought to possess information pertaining to the investigation of a crime.[3] Any person questioned in these circumstances must answer correctly all questions that are put to him, with the exception of those whose answers would be self-incriminating.[4] Failure to do so constitutes a crime, which (*inter alia*) justifies the application of the "suspect" rules (described below in paragraph 2). Formal criminal proceedings against the refusing witness also may be initiated.

b. *Questioning and Detaining a Suspect.* In the presence of a "reasonable suspicion" that a person has committed a crime, a police officer is permitted to request the suspected person to give his name and address. If practicable, the officer may

3. Criminal Procedure Ordinance (Testimony), section 2(1).
4. Ibid, section 2(2).

conduct questioning on the spot, of both suspects and witnesses. If questioning outside of the police station is not feasible, the officer may request the suspect to accompany him to a police station.[5] The legal requirement that the suspicion be "reasonable" entails that it ought to be based on objective evidence, rather than on mere guesswork or subjective "gut-feelings." If the suspect refuses to give his name and address, or if he refuses to accompany the officer to a police station, the suspect may be arrested[6] so long as the crime of which he is suspected constitutes an "arrestable offense."[7] Arrestable offences include felonies and misdemeanors punishable by incarceration for a period longer than three months or by fine (if the fine exceeds the statutory minimum that goes through inflationary adjustments).[8] As for witnesses, as already mentioned, these must answer any questions (subject to the privilege against self-incrimination). A witness also must appear for questioning at the police station, if so requested by a police officer. Non-compliance with this request constitutes a criminal offence.[9]

c. *Searches and Stops of Vehicles.* Automobiles can be searched, similarly to other premises, in accordance with the rules outlined above. In addition, an automobile can be searched without warrant if there is a suspicion that it carries an illegal weapon or explosive. This power can be exercised without "probable cause," i.e., on broad discretionary grounds, by any authorized police officer or guard,[10] and it exists in relation to vessels as well.[11] A vessel also can be searched whenever it is deemed necessary for public safety and the vessel to be searched requests entry to or is situated in an Israeli seaport.[12]

A specific search power with regard to automobiles was conferred on the police by the Dangerous Drugs Ordinance.[13] This power allows search of any automobile whenever the search is deemed necessary for preventing and detecting prohibited drug-trafficking,[14] and the same applies to any aircraft or vessel entering an Israeli airport or seaport.[15]

Any automobile also can be stopped and searched without a warrant, whenever a police officer has a reasonable ground to believe that the search is required in connection with an arrestable offence.[16]

2. *Frisks*

Police may search anyone whenever it is deemed necessary for public safety and, in particular, when there is a suspicion that the person subjected to a search or a frisk is carrying a knife, a firearm or any explosive substance.[17] This power can

5. CPEA, sections 67, 68.
6. Ibid, section 23(b).
7. Ibid, section 23(a)(7).
8. Penal Law 1977, sections 24 & 61. The sum, recently adjusted, stands of approximately 2,400$US.
9. Ibid, sections 286, 287.
10. Ibid, section 2(a)(5).
11. Ibid.
12. Ibid, section 2(a)(3).
13. The Dangerous Drugs Ordinance [New Version] 1969, section 28(b)(1).
14. Ibid.
15. Ibid, section 28(b)(4).
16. CPEA, section 71. For "arrestable offences," see our discussion of arrest powers.
17. Ibid, sections 2(a)(1), 2(a)(4)

be exercised without "probable cause," i.e., on broad discretionary grounds, by any authorized police officer or guard. A similar power was given to the police in relation to persons suspected of carrying prohibited drugs. This power, however, cannot be exercised without a probable cause: there must be an objective reason to believe that the person to be searched or frisked is carrying drugs.[18]

3. *Arrests of Suspects*

Arrests in Israel are divided into two categories:

- Arrests carried out in accordance with a judge's warrant;
- arrests carried out instantaneously without a warrant by an authorized officer.

a. *Arrests by Warrant.* Arrest warrants can be issued against a suspect at any stage of police investigation. Having received and reviewed an application for arrest made by a police officer, a judge can issue an arrest warrant if:

- The judge has a "reasonable suspicion" that the suspect has committed an arrestable offense;[19] and:
- the judge is convinced that the police investigation would be jeopardized if the suspect is not arrested, or that the personal security of an individual, the community's safety or the security of the State of Israel would be facing danger on the part of the suspect, if he is not arrested.[20]

Exceptionally, an arrest warrant may be issued solely for the purposes of the suspect's interrogation by the police (i.e., even in the absence of dangerousness). In such a case, the arrest period must not exceed 15 days.[21]

The required "reasonable suspicion" may be based upon any relevant evidence, even when the latter is not admissible in a criminal trial. There is also a "necessity requirement" that accords an unbending preference to the minimal curtailment of the suspect's freedoms.[22] This requirement is an offshoot of the broader "minimization of the individual's harm" principle, which is firmly embedded in the law of arrests[23] and in the Israeli constitutional law in general.[24] An arrest warrant therefore can be issued only if the objective of the arrest cannot be attained in a way that would be less damaging to the suspect's freedom, *e.g.*, by releasing the suspect on bail and by stipulating in the bail conditions that the suspect will not leave his home and will avoid any contact with prospectant witnesses.[25] As long as an investigation continues, the suspect has no right to inspect the investigative materials. This right and the parallel prosecution's duty to disclose the investigative materials come into existence only upon bringing an indictment against the suspect, i.e., when a criminal trial is opened and the suspect is formally turned into

---

18. The Dangerous Drugs Ordinance [New Version] 1969, section 28(b)(2). Police may also frisk and/or search, without cause, people entering airports, courthouses, and other public buildings.
19. See supra nn.7-8 and accompanying text.
20. CPEA, section 13(a)(1)(2).
21. Ibid, section 13(a)(3).
22. Ibid, section 13(b).
23. Ibid, section 1(b).
24. See Basic Law: Human Dignity and Liberty (1992), and particularly sections 1, 1A, 5, 8.
25. CPEA, section 13(b).

"accused." At the same time, the suspect has the right to participate in the arrest proceeding by questioning the police officer (which guarantees partial disclosure of the investigative materials) and by presenting his own testimony and argument. In the case of a warrant issued in the suspect's absence, the suspect must be brought before a judge within 24 hours of the warrant's execution.[26]

The initial detention period following arrest is limited to 15 days and it can be judicially extended.[27] Detention exceeding 30 consecutive days can be authorized by a judge only upon application confirmed by the Attorney General.[28] The total period of detention prior to bringing an indictment against the suspect is 75 days. This period can be extended on special grounds only by a Supreme Court Justice.[29]

A person suspected of a crime against state security may be arrested under a different set of provisions. Any such suspect may be arrested for 15 days by a senior police officer,[30] an arrest that subsequently can be extended up to four months by consecutive 30-day arrests ordered by a Supreme Court Justice. Applications for such extensions need to be brought by the Attorney General.[31]

Once an indictment was brought against a suspect, the suspect is turned into "accused," and the trial court may order that the accused be detained until the end of the trial. Such an order can be issued only upon finding that the accused's release on bail, regardless of the bail conditions, would present:

- *A danger to the proceedings*, which would be the case when the accused is likely to tamper with evidence, to intimidate the prospectant witnesses or to abscond;
- *A danger to the community*, which would be the case when the accused is likely to commit further crimes.

In the absence of dangerousness, as described above, the accused cannot be detained during his trial.[32] Dangerous or not, the accused also cannot be detained in the absence of *prima facie* evidence that substantiates the accusations specified in the indictment.[33] In a number of cases, the prosecution's burden is alleviated by a presumption of dangerousness, activated by an indictment charging the accused with one of the offences listed in the statute. The list includes drug offences, offences involving severe violence or cruelty, offences punishable by life imprisonment, such as murder, offences against state security and offences involving domestic violence (that need not be severe).[34] The accusation pointing to an offence that activates the presumption also must be substantiated by *prima facie* evidence. Finally, the accused would be arrested during his trial if found to have jumped bail or have otherwise violated the bail conditions.[35]

---

26. Ibid, section 17(c).
27. Ibid, section 17(a).
28. Ibid, section 17(b).
29. Ibid, sections 59, 62.
30. The Penal Law, 1977, section 125.
31. Ibid, section 124.
32. CPEA, section 21(a)(1).
33. Ibid, section 21(b). The Supreme Court has held in this connection that the prosecution's evidence must be subjected to a serious scrutiny that goes far beyond the examination of the evidence in rulings concerning direct dismissal of charges ("no-case-to-answer"). Zada v. State of Israel, 50(2) P.D. 133 (1995).
34. Ibid, section 21(a)(1)(c).
35. Ibid, section 21(a)(2).

The accused is entitled to the assistance of counsel during these proceedings, and unless he has voluntarily waived this right, an attorney must be provided to him by the Public Defender's Office.[36] In this context too, the court is obligated to achieve the goal of arrest in the way that is least damaging to the accused's freedom.[37] Personal factors, such as age, occupation, community ties and criminal record of the accused, have to be taken into account in the court's decision. There is also a provision enabling these factors to be presented and analyzed in a special report that has to be prepared by a probation officer or a social worker.[38] The severity of a crime with which the accused is indicted also must be accounted for, along with the circumstances in which it was allegedly committed. This factor alone does not, however, establish the dangerousness of the accused for the purposes of his detention pending trial. If the issue of dangerousness cannot be resolved unambiguously, the court should hold that the prosecution did not discharge its burden of proof and the accused must be released on bail. As already mentioned, this burden is reversed and the risk of erroneous arrest is shifted to the accused whenever the presumption of dangerousness comes into play.

There is, therefore, a strong presumption in favor of releasing the accused on bail, subject to conditions that would ensure the proper enforcement of the criminal law.[39] Bail conditions also cannot be excessive with regard to the amount of money that needs to be deposited as a bond.[40] Imposition of excessive bail conditions would not only violate the statute. It would also be unconstitutional.[41]

If an accused is detained prior to trial, the trial normally must begin within 30 days after the post-indictment arrest. In exceptional circumstances, the beginning of the trial may be postponed by the trial court for additional 30 days or for a shorter period (as determined by the President or the Vice-President of the trial court).[42] If the trial has not begun within the required period, the accused would normally be released from custody, with or without bail. On highly exceptional grounds, however, a Justice of the Supreme Court may order that the accused will remain in custody for a period not exceeding 90 days, and such orders may be renewed consecutively.[43] Once the trial of an arrested accused has begun, it must end within 9 months in order to retain the accused under arrest.[44] If the trial did not end within 9 months, a Justice of the Supreme Court may extend the post-indictment arrest for additional periods, not exceeding 90 days each, on highly exceptional grounds.[45] Normally, the accused would have to be released from custody, with or without bail.

Decisions made by trial judges with regard to arrest and bail are subject to appeal and renewed hearings.

b. *Arrests Without a Warrant.* Warrantless arrests constitute an exception to the principle that judicial warrant is required for an arrest. A police officer may ar-

36. Ibid, sections 21(b)(2), 21(c).
37. Ibid, section 21(b)(1).
38. Ibid, section 21A.
39. Ibid, section 21(b)(1).
40. Ibid, section 46.
41. Binkin v. State of Israel, 48(1) P.D. 290 (1993).
42. CPEA, section 60.
43. Ibid, section 62.
44. Ibid, section 61.
45. Ibid, section 62.

rest a person reasonably suspected by him of having committed an arrestable offense,[46] if one of the following conditions are satisfied:

- The suspect committed the offence in front of the arresting officer, and because of this the officer believes that security of an individual or of the community at large would be further endangered by the suspect, if he remains free;
- the officer has a reasonable suspicion that the suspect will not appear for questioning at the police station, or will further endanger society or security of the State, or will disrupt the future proceedings (*e.g.*, by tampering with evidence or by harassing witnesses), if he remains free;
- the offence of which the suspect is suspected appears on the list of offences that activate the presumption of dangerousness in relation to the suspect (as specified above with regard to detention during trial);
- the suspect was released on bail, and there is a reasonable suspicion that he breached one of the bail conditions or is about to abscond;
- there is a reasonable suspicion that the suspect is escaping from a lawful custody;
- the suspect refuses to comply with the officer's requirements that are based on the officer's authority to stop and question suspects, or otherwise disturbs the officer to exercise this authority (*e.g.*, the suspect refuses to provide his name and address or to accompany the officer to the police station when properly requested to do so).[47]

The "minimization of the harm" principle applies here as well. An officer authorized to arrest a suspect under one of the above conditions is allowed to execute the arrest only when the arrest's objective cannot be attained by a less severe curtailment of the suspect's freedom, i.e., by stopping and questioning the suspect and by requiring him to come to a police station without being arrested.[48]

Private people are not authorized to carry out an arrest, but are allowed to stop a suspect and detain him until a policeman arrives, in the following circumstances:

- The suspect is suspected to have committed—in the presence of the detaining person—a violent offence, a felony, theft or an offence that caused tangible damage to property;
- another person, who calls for help, points to the suspect and identifies him as a perpetrator of one of the above-mentioned offences;
- in each of the above cases, there must be a suspicion that the suspect will escape or that his identity is not known; the suspect must be handed over to a police officer without delay, and the total period of the suspect's detention by a private person must not exceed three hours.[49]
- The detaining person also may use reasonable force, if the suspect resists detention, provided that the use of force will not cause injury to the suspect.[50]

---

46. Ibid, section 23.
47. CPEA, section 23(b).
48. Ibid, section 23(c).
49. Ibid, section 75(a)(b).
50. Ibid, section 75(c).

A "reasonable suspicion" for purposes of arrest is a two-fold requirement:

The arresting officer must consider, subjectively, all the facts and circumstances that are known to him—both those that cast suspicion on the suspect, and those that exonerate the suspect—and if the consequence is, objectively, a picture according to which an ordinary person would bring the suspect under suspicion, a reasonable suspicion has been established.

There is, therefore, an objective as well as a subjective standard in this two-fold requirement. The objective standard requires that the arresting officer's suspicion be based upon objective evidence that would lead a rational officer to suspect the suspect of committing the alleged crime. Under the subjective standard, the officer's decision to arrest the suspect must be formed *bona fidei* on the basis of this evidence alone.

When is a person considered to have been arrested? There is no formal definition of "arrest" in the Israeli law. There are, however, certain basic features that characterize arrests, as opposed to stops and non-custodial questioning of people. By focusing upon these features we can arrive at a functional definition of arrest. The primary purpose of arrest is preservation of public order, which was brought under imminent danger, whereas stops and questioning have been devised to serve the preliminary investigation of a crime. Accordingly, arrest powers include the officers' power to use a reasonably necessary force in executing arrests. The authority to stop people and subject them to non-custodial interrogation does not include this power. The same holds true with regard to the power of arresting officers to put handcuffs on the suspect's hands.[51] There is no such power outside of the arrest authority.

The arresting officer must identify himself and explain to the suspect the reason for his arrest at the earliest opportunity, unless it is apparent, under the circumstances, that the suspect is well-aware of this information or is likely to escape, to conceal or destroy evidence or to assail the arresting officer.[52] The arrested suspect must immediately be brought to a police station, unless circumstances of an urgent nature (specified in the statute) make this impossible, or if the suspect voluntarily agrees to accompany police officers to another place in order to gather additional evidence or to prevent its destruction.[53] At the police station, the arrest is reviewed by the officer in charge. After giving the suspect an opportunity to present his claims,[54] the officer in charge has to examine whether the suspect is legally arrested.[55] If this is not the case, the officer must release the suspect immediately.[56] The officer, however, may still arrest the suspect if there are other grounds for arresting him.[57] People appearing for non-custodial questioning also may be arrested by the officer in charge, if there are legal grounds for arresting them.[58] The officer in charge is authorized to release suspects on bail in accordance with his discretion. There is, however, no such discretion with regard to a person suspected of escaping from a lawful custody. Such a person would remain under arrest.[59]

51. CPO(A&S), section 19; CPCV, section 26(2).
52. CPEA, section 24. See also Attorney General v. Kedoshim, 10 P.D. 972 (1956).
53. CPEA, section 25.
54. CPEA, section 28.
55. CPEA, section 27(a).
56. CPEA, section 27(b).
57. CPEA, section 27(c).
58. CPEA, section 27(d).
59. CPEA, section 27(e).

Once the arrest is confirmed, the officer in charge must inform the suspect of the reasons for his arrest, of the suspect's right to inform a person close to him about his arrest, of the suspect's right to appoint and meet with an attorney (either privately appointed or designated by the Public Defender's Office) and of the time limits within which the suspect may be held under arrest prior to appearing before a judge.[60] The officer must also inform the suspect about his right to remain silent, about the fact that any statement of the suspect might be used as evidence against him and also about the adverse inferences that might be drawn against the suspect at his trial, if he decides to remain silent.[61] (See also section II, C, 1.)

The suspect must be brought before a judge within 24 hours[62] or, in exceptional cases, within 48 hours of his arrest. If 48 hours have elapsed and the suspect did not appear before a judge, the suspect must immediately be released.[63] In this case, his arrest would become illegal, which would have a number of legal consequences that are specified below. A judge before whom the suspect was brought may extend the suspect's arrest for a period not exceeding 15 days.[64] Such an extension can be granted only on the grounds justifying an arrest warrant, which have already been discussed. The judge's decisions concerning arrest and bail are subject to appeal and review, as indicated earlier.

c. *Arrest Warrants and Private Property.* An arrest warrant is not limited to a specific location and thus allows the arresting officer to enter any property (private and public alike) where, according to the officer's reasonable suspicion, the arrestee might be found.[65] In such circumstances, the occupier of the property must allow the arresting officer to enter the property. If the occupier refuses to do so, the officer may enter the property by using reasonable force.[66]

The Israeli law contains no explicit provision as to whether police are authorized to forcibly enter private property in order to arrest a suspect lawfully, but without a judicially issued warrant. In the leading case, *Birman v. State of Israel*,[67] the Supreme Court held that the authority does exist as attendant upon the police authority to search private premises during the course of pursuit of a person who escaped from legal custody or was requested to stop by a police officer and refused to do so.[68] "Pursuit" in this context need not to be "hot," nor even continuous. As held by the Supreme Court, "pursuit" of a suspect need not be continuous and may extend over long periods of time, weeks or months, depending on the particularities of the case. The officer entering private premises must, of course, have a reasonable belief that the suspect is there.

d. *Searches Attendant Upon Arrest.* (i). *Bodily Searches.* The arresting officer (at the scene of the crime or elsewhere) or an officer receiving the arrestee into his custody is authorized to search the arrestee's clothes and pockets, as well as any container carried by the arrestee. Objects found may be taken from the arrestee, in

60. CPEA, section 32.
61. CPEA, section 28(a).
62. CPEA, section 29(a).
63. CPEA, section 31(b).
64. CPEA, section 17(a).
65. CPCV, section 26(1).
66. CPO(A&S), section 45.
67. 33(3) P.D. 326 (1978).
68. Ibid.

which case they have to be listed. Their list must be signed both by the officer and by the arrestee (unless the latter refuses to cooperate). A copy of the list must be given to the arrestee. The arrestee's legal belongings are returned to the arrestee under a court's order at the end of the proceedings (or earlier, if they are not used as evidence).

A more thorough physical search, called an "outer search," may be carried out if the police have a reasonable suspicion that evidence is to be found thereby. The extent of the permitted search depends upon whether the suspect has agreed to it. If the suspect agrees to the search, it may include: 1) Undressing and being photographed nude, 2) providing imprints of body parts, 3) removal of substance from under fingernails, 4) cutting of fingernails, 5) taking material from nostrils, 6) giving hair samples, 7) removing material from the surface of the body, 8) examination of skin, 9) giving urine samples, saliva samples, breath samples, and/or cell samples from the cheek's interior.[69] If the suspect does not consent to the search, he may be forced to comply with a search falling under categories 1-3 and 6-8 (excluding the taking of dental impressions and the removal of hair from covered parts of the body). In order to carry out an outer search without the suspect's consent, the suspect must first be given an opportunity to explain the reasons behind his refusal. The suspect also must be told that his refusal might give rise to adverse inferences at his trial. After this has been done, a permit for the search may be issued by an officer of the police.[70]

An "inner search," which may include taking blood, ultrasound imaging, x-rays, and a gynecological scan, is allowed to be carried out if the suspect is being held for a felony offense. No "inner search" may be carried out unless a physician, after having examined the suspect's medical history and conditions, has issued a permit according to which there are no health reasons to prevent it.[71] The suspect is warned that refusal to be searched or to confer with the physician regarding his medical history and health conditions may be used as evidence against him.[72] If the suspect does not agree to the inner search, the police may perform it only on the basis of a judicial order. This order will be granted if the court is satisfied that the value of the evidence to be attained by the search outweighs the possible damage to the suspect.[73] A gynecological scan, even consensual, can be carried out only under judicial order.[74]

Both "outer" and "inner" searches must be carried out in a way that least damages the dignity, privacy and health of the suspect.[75] They must be carried out by members of the suspect's sex, unless urgency requires otherwise, or if the suspect agrees to be examined by medical personnel of the opposite sex.[76]

(ii). *Dealing with People other than Suspects*. Presence of people other than the suspect at the scene of an arrest does not by itself authorize a frisk or a search of

69. CPES, sections 1, 3(a).

70. Ibid, sections 3(b)-(g), 11. Blood samples may be taken also in non-felony cases: see id., section 4(b).

71. CPES, sections 1, 4.

72. Ibid, sections 4(c)(d)(h) and 11.

73. Ibid, sections 4(h), 7, 8.

74. Ibid, section 4(f).

75. Ibid, section 2(d).

76. Ibid, section 2(h).

these people's belongings. If, on the other hand, an individual is found within or near a place which is being searched, and the police have a reasonable suspicion that the individual is hiding an object which is being sought, the individual may also be searched.[77] The police have no general authority to frisk such people solely on the suspicion that they may be armed.

4. *Searches*

Police have the general authority to examine and seize any item found in plain view when it is believed to be connected with the commission of a crime. They have no general authority to frisk or search people solely on the suspicion that they may be armed (subject to narrowly defined exceptions, such as those related to airport searches). There is also no authority for police to enter a private property for the purpose of examining what may not be clearly seen from outside of it. A suspicion that stolen property is located on the premises may justify the issuance of a search warrant, but it does not authorize a warrantless search (even if the latter consists of no more than a stroll up the driveway to see if the car parked in an open garage is the one reported to have been stolen). All forms of police trespass are illegal in the absence of a specific grant of authority.

Investigation which does not require physical trespass, but does involve an invasion of privacy, such as peeking through windows, opening mail or attaching a "bug" to a vehicle, are forbidden by the Protection of Privacy Law 1981. Broadly speaking, the list of activities prohibited by this Act is based on a "reasonable expectation" of privacy. Wiretaps, discussed in greater detail below, are regulated by the Secret Monitoring Law 1979.

a. *Search Warrants.* The general rule is that searches of private property, whether an open field or a house, require the issuance of a judicial search warrant based upon probable cause. The law provides for exceptions to this principle by authorizing warrantless searches in the following situations[78]:

- The police officer has a reasonable suspicion that a felony is being perpetrated or has just been committed on the premises;
- the owner or occupier of the premises turns to the police for assistance;
- a person found on the premises turns to the police for assistance and there is a reasonable belief that a crime (not necessarily a felony) is being committed on the premises;
- an escaped prisoner is believed to be on the premises.

A search warrant may be issued by a judge when:[79]

- It is required for obtaining evidence in the course of a criminal investigation (or for a criminal trial), or;
- when the judge is satisfied that either a stolen property or an object connected to a criminal activity (past or future) is located on the premises, or;
- when the premises are being used in facilitating an offence, or;

77. CPO(A&S), section 29.
78. Ibid, section 25.
79. Ibid, section 23.

- when the judge is satisfied that the investigated offence is (or was) directed against a person located on the premises.

Evidence examined by the judge for the above purpose may include hearsay or any other evidence that may not be admissible for conviction purposes, as long as the evidence rationally tends to establish one the grounds for issuing a search warrant. For obvious reasons, hearings concerning search warrants are usually conducted *ex parte*. Search warrants must specify the investigated offence (in general terms), the place to be searched and the items sought by the police (when these are known). There are no formal limitations with regard to the hours during which a warrant may be executed. Under the present law, midnight is as acceptable a time for carrying out a search as morning or noon. However, any search ought to be conducted in a way that does not unduly infringe the dignity and the privacy of the individual involved. Set by the Basic Law concerning human dignity and freedom, this new constitutional limitation is yet to be clarified by the courts. Search warrants are not required to have an expiration date and are usually issued without time limits. This practice, however, is likely to be changed in view of the constitutional provisions set by the Basic Law.

Searching officers are authorized to enter the premises by using reasonable force only when refused admission to the premises.[80] Evidence found during the course of a search may be seized by the police even if it was not specified in the warrant. All searches—those conducted pursuant to a warrant and those that are not—must be carried out in front of two witnesses who are not police officers. This requirement does not apply only when exigent circumstances make its implementation impossible, or when a judge authorizes a search without witnesses, or when the occupier of the searched premises requests that witnesses not be present.[81] The police are required to inform the person affected by the search of his or her right to witnesses.

b. *Wiretaps*. The Secret Monitoring Law criminally prohibits the recording of conversation by anyone who is not a party to it, unless *one* of the parties to the conversation has consented to the recording. The police may obtain a judicial permit to allow such recording in connection with a felony. Prior to issuing the permit, the judge is required to balance the ensuing invasion of privacy against the needs of the criminal investigation.[82] Conversations taking place in areas where there is no reasonable expectation of privacy (defined in the statute as a "public domain") can be intercepted by the police on the basis of a special authorization issued by a senior officer.[83] The statute also regulates wiretapping and surveillance in cases of emergency, as well as in cases involving state security, to which different rules apply.[84] The statute severely restricts the possibility to intercept conversations protected by evidentiary privileges (such as the attorney-client or the doctor-patient privileges). Wiretapping of such conversations for purposes of a criminal investigation may be authorized only by judges and only in exceptional casesection[85] Violation of the statute constitutes a criminal offence, punishable by imprisonment

80. Ibid, section 45.
81. Ibid, section 26.
82. Secret Monitoring Law 1979, section 6.
83. Ibid, section 8.
84. Ibid, sections 4, 5, 7.
85. Ibid, sections 9, 9A.

not exceeding five years, and is also actionable in torts. Evidence obtained through illegal wiretapping is inadmissible in courts, subject to a carefully drafted "good faith" exception that applies only in "serious felony" cases (which refers to cases involving crimes punishable by at least seven years of incarceration).[86]

c. *Warrantless Searches.* Searches that can be conducted without a warrant include:

- Searches ancillary to the searched person's arrest;
- searches made in connection with illegal narcotics;
- searches allowed by special statutory provisions, such as those dealing with tax and currency offences and with activities defined as criminal under the consumer protection laws.

d. *Consent Searches.* Restrictions imposed by the law on police searches aim at protecting the individual. If an individual willingly consents to a search, the search may be carried out even when no warrant has been issued. The general rules regulating searches (described above) will, however, continue to apply, subject to explicit waiver, which should be both voluntary and informed. Police officers are required to inform the searched person of his right to have witnesses, who are not police officers, present during the execution of the search. They also are obligated to inform the searched person of his right not to submit himself or his property to a warrantless search. Moreover, the Supreme Court held, in connection with consensual bodily searches, that they should be conducted in a way that gives maximal protection to the suspect's dignity, an inalienable constitutional right that cannot be waived.[87]

5. *Enforcing the Rules*

If police have acted illegally in arresting, searching and interrogating a person, or have otherwise violated a person's right, the afflicted person can file a complaint which will be investigated by a special department in the Attorney General's Office. The result of any such investigation may be a disciplinary action and, in appropriate cases, a criminal prosecution. In most cases, police misconduct will also be actionable in torts and the aggrieved person will be able to seek compensation. However these procedures are rarely used and are unlikely to deter police misconduct.

Heretofore, Israeli courts have continually ruled that illegally obtained evidence is admissible, subject to three statutory exceptions:

- Involuntary confessions, i.e., confessions elicited from suspects by eliminating or severely curtailing their free will through illegal means, such as violence, physical or psychological torture, threats, intimidation and unlawful promises.[88]

86. Ibid, section 13.
87. State of Israel v. Guetta, 46(5) P.D. 705 (1992).
88. Evidence Ordinance, section 12(a).

- Information obtained through unlawful eavesdropping (subject to a limited discretion of the court to admit the evidence on special grounds, despite its illegal origin).[89]
- Information obtained by an unlawful infringement of privacy (subject to a broad discretion of the court to admit the evidence).[90] This rule could have a significant impact on the development of a broad exclusionary rule, if the conception of privacy were interpreted broadly. This conception however, has not been interpreted in this way. Instead, it has been limited to the informational type of privacy, which made it inapplicable in cases involving police brutality, as well as in most cases that involve illegal searches.[91]

The Supreme Court explicitly held that these are exceptions to the general rule that favors the admissibility of illegally obtained evidence. If the way in which a piece of evidence was obtained reduces its weight, then the weight of the evidence should be reduced as dictated by the canons of rationality. Illegal conduct of the police must be tackled in another proceeding, and the accused will not go free just because of the constable's misconduct. Consonantly with this view, the "fruits of the poisonous tree" doctrine also has been rejected.[92]

This approach to illegally obtained evidence may be undergoing revision. There is growing academic literature urging courts to interpret the Israeli Constitution as embodying an exclusionary rule.[93] Following this literature, the District Court of Nazareth has recently ruled inadmissible a voluntary confession not preceded by an adequate police warning that ought to have informed the suspect about his basic rights.[94] Furthermore, as has recently been ruled by the Supreme Court, the trial court has the power to dismiss an entire indictment "in the interests of justice," if it finds the indictment to be based upon evidence that was obtained by violation of the accused's constitutional rights.[95] How these new principles will develop is difficult to predict. It seems likely, however, that the emerging exclusionary doctrine will be applied only in response to a violation of one of the constitutional rights, which is both grave and malicious, and that Israeli courts will follow the Canadian "discretionary exclusion model," taking all relevant factors into account, as opposed to the American law that adopted a rigid exclusionary rule qualified by a limited number of exceptions. The list of constitutional rights that protect people suspected and accused of crimes is broad enough to turn the emerging doctrine into a powerful vehicle for tackling police misconduct. The Basic Law: Human Dignity and Liberty extends constitutional protection to per-

---

89. Secret Monitoring Law 1979, section 13.

90. Protection of Privacy Law 1981, section 32.

91. Military Court of Appeal v. Va'aknin, 42(3) P.D. 837 (1988).

92. See, e.g., State of Israel v. Eluz, 45(4) P.D. 289, 304 (1991).

93. See A. Barak, The Constitutionalization of the Israeli Legal System as a Result of the Basic Laws and Its Effect on Procedural and Substantive Criminal Law, 31 Israel L. Rev. 3, 19 (1997); E. Harnon, Illegally Obtained Evidence - Has the Law Been Affected by the Basic Law on Human Dignity and Freedom?, 13 Bar-Ilan Law Studies 139 (1996).

94. State of Israel v. Ouda (delivered by the Nazareth District Court on 31.12.1997 and not yet published). This issue is currently awaiting the Supreme Court's decision in another case. (Chief Military Prosecutor v. Issacharov).

95. Katz v. Attorney General (delivered on 21.5.97 and not yet published).

sonal liberty, as well as to dignity, privacy and property of the individual. This Law also has been interpreted as conferring upon individuals the general right to due process.[96]

B. Lineups and Other Identification Procedures

1. Lineups

Under the Israeli law, a compulsory lineup does not violate the suspect's privilege against self-incrimination. Similarly to its American counterpart, the Israeli privilege against self-incrimination extends only to communicative (testimonial), as opposed to physical, evidence.[97] Because standing in a lineup involves no communication on the part of the suspect, it was held not to be covered by the privilege.[98] A suspect's refusal to stand in a lineup also allows adverse inferences to be drawn against him, unless he provides a reasonable explanation.[99] This rule is easily understood as a supplement to the statutory provisions that prescribe adverse inferences against the accused who decided to exercise the right of silence by not testifying in his defense,[100] as well as against a suspect invoking the right of silence when questioned by the police after being given a proper warning.[101] A suspect, however, cannot be physically forced to stand in a lineup, but if he refuses to do so, the police may conduct a photo-lineup or a lineup where the witness is called to identify the suspect out of a random crowd of people (e.g., at a refectory, the courtyard, etc.).

According to the case law, a lineup must comply with the following principles (which, subject to necessary modifications, apply to any alternative lineup):

- The lineup must consist of at least eight people, resembling the suspect in age, height, weight, dress and appearance. The suspect may choose his exact location among the lineup participants; however, he may not object to any person's participation in the lineup;
- the suspect must be informed of his right to the presence of counsel. The lineup may be carried through without presence of counsel, provided that the police has taken appropriate measures to inform counsel of the lineup (or, in extreme cases, if the witness objects to counsel's presence out of fear of reprisals[102]);
- in order to enable the court to form a first-hand impression of the lineup, the lineup should be photographed, preferably in color, or videotaped (in addition to a full written memorandum of the course of the lineup that the police is required to provide);
- the lineup must be arranged so as not to let the witness see the suspect beforehand, or receive any information concerning the suspect's identity.

---

96. See Zada, supra n.33; Barak, supra n.93.
97. Evidence Ordinance, section 47; Khoury v. State of Israel, 36(2) P.D. 85 (1982).
98. Kariv v. State of Israel, 32(2) P.D. 729 (1978).
99. See, e.g., Charbon v. State of Israel, 36(1) P.D. 90 (1981).
100. CPCV, section 162.
101. CPEA, section 28(a).
102. See Meiri v. State of Israel, 32(2) P.D. 180 (1978), subsequently qualified by Gali v. State of Israel, 40(4) P.D. 169, 176 (1986).

Where several witnesses are required to identify the same suspect, a separate lineup should be conducted for each of them, and they are to have no contact with one another;

- police officers must refrain from suggesting the "right" answer to the witness, whether through words or discreet gestures;
- any response or unusual behavior by the witness, the suspect or the suspect's attorney must be recorded in the lineup memorandum.

Failure to inform counsel of a lineup has, in one case, resulted in the nullification of the lineup's probative value. However, this view no longer prevails; instead, counsel's absence does not in itself invalidate the lineup. The same holds true in respect of other flaws in the lineup procedure, although such flaws do, indeed, impair the lineup's probative value, and may, on occasion, reduce it to zero.[103]

2. *Other Identification Procedures*

A suspect cannot be compelled to give a voiceprint, since voiceprints have yet to be recognized as reliable and, indeed, admissible means of identification (although the police do use voice-specialists for investigation purposes). Identification of suspects by a witness participating in a "voice lineup" has, however, been accepted by case law as admissible evidence.[104]

C. Interrogation

1. *Before Formal Charge*

A police officer interrogating a suspect must not take his statement prior to warning him that he is entitled to remain silent, that anything he chooses to say may be used against him as evidence in court, and that exercising the right to silence may strengthen the prosecution's evidence in the ensuing criminal trial.[105] Until recently, this rule served only as a guideline, and non-compliance with it did not lead to an exclusion of the defendant's admission of guilt. A confession could be excluded only when it was not "free and voluntary," e.g., when it was obtained through the exercise of unlawful means such as violence, threats, inducement, severe psychological pressure, and the like. As mentioned above with regard to illegal arrests (section II, A, 5), the voluntariness requirement for admissibility of confessions has been supplemented in a recent trial court decision by a broad constitutional principle (akin to the American *Miranda* doctrine) that renders inadmissible a confession made at custodial interrogation, if the confession was not preceded by a proper warning of the suspect. Whether this ruling will be entrenched in the Israeli law and used as a basis for evidentiary exclusion remains to be seen.

A new statute concerning arrests has recently been enacted.[106] This statute specifies the suspect's rights attendant upon arrest, including the rights with regard

103. See Meiri and Gali, ibid; Malka v. State of Israel, 36(4) P.D. 309 (1982).
104. Charbon v. State of Israel, 36(1) P.D. 90 (1981).
105. CPEA, section 28(a).
106. This is the CPEA of 1996, as amended in 1997.

to detention conditions and counseling privileges. The new statute provides that an arrestee should be held in adequate conditions, which will not impair his health or personal dignity. The statute also provides that an arrestee is entitled to satisfactory sanitation conditions, to a bed, a mattress and blankets, to reasonable lighting and ventilation conditions and to sufficient food. An arrestee is also entitled to a daily walk in open air and to visiting, mail and phone privileges, although these rights can be restricted for investigation purposes.[107]

According to the same statute, an arrestee has a right to consult and be represented by an attorney. If an arrestee requests to see an attorney, or if an attorney appointed to him by a friend or a relative asks to see him, the request must be carried out immediately, subject to the power of the officer in charge of the investigation to postpone such a meeting.[108] If the officer in charge believes that putting off the interrogation might harm the investigation considerably, or obstruct the arrest of other suspects or the obtainment of further evidence, he can authorize in writing a delay of up to 24 hours in the meeting between the suspect and the attorney.[109] A delay of up to 48 hours also can be authorized, if it is necessary for the protection of human life or for the prevention of a crime.[110] In extreme cases, people suspected of espionage, high treason, terrorism and the like can be prevented from meeting with a lawyer for a period of up to 21 days, subject to the fulfilment of certain specified conditions, including judicial review.[111] The court can and normally should appoint a public defense attorney for an arrestee who asks for an attorney, but cannot afford one.[112]

A suspect may assert his right to silence, and may also refuse to answer specific questions in fear of self-incrimination (or for any other reason). However, asserting these rights does not preclude further interrogation, since these rights only relieve the suspect of criminal liability (ordinarily faced by a witness refusing to answer police questions on grounds other than self-incrimination). For this reason, the suspect's assertion of the right to silence, not only in court, but also at police interrogation, can serve to strengthen the prosecution's evidence.[113] The suspect may waive his rights to counsel and to silence, whether explicitly or implicitly. Any such waiver will be effective subject to a few restrictions imposed on police deception.[114]

The right of silence and the privilege against self-incrimination apply separately to each and every question of the interrogation. Therefore, volunteered statements may be used as evidence, but do not prevent the suspect from reasserting his rights (as opposed to a defendant who chooses to testify at trial on his own behalf: In these circumstances, the testifying defendant cannot reassert the right to silence).[115]

Police deception is not regarded as a violation of the suspect's rights, as long as it does not constitute a criminal offence or undermines the search for truth.[116]

---

107. See, e.g., CPEA, section 9.
108. Ibid, section 34(b)(d).
109. Ibid, section 34(e).
110. Ibid, section 34(f).
111. Ibid, section 35.
112. CPCV, section 15(c)(d)(f)(g); The Public Defenders Law, 1995, section 18(a).
113. CPEA, section 28(a); CPCV, section 162. See also Mandelfrost v. State of Israel, 43(1) P.D. 818 (1989).
114. See, e.g., Bitter v. State of Israel, 41(1) P.D. 52 (1987); Katz v. Attorney General (delivered on 21.5.97 and not yet published).
115. Evidence Ordinance, section 47(c).
116. See supra n.114.

Threats and promises cannot be used in obtaining confessions. Any such action amounts to a criminal offence[117] and is likely to render the ensuing confession "involuntary" and thus inadmissible.[118] Jailhouse informants can be used in order to elicit incriminating evidence from the arrestee. The Secret Monitoring Law, 1979, does not preclude the undercover recording of such an encounter, since the law does not prohibit monitoring of a conversation when one of its participants (the informant, in our case) has given his consent to the monitoring.[119] In addition, a prison cell is considered public domain, and therefore does not require a court warrant for wiretapping; an authorization from a senior police office is sufficient for monitoring prison-cell conversations.[120]

2. *After Defendant is Formally Charged*

Although post-indictment interrogation of a defendant is rare, rules that apply to such an interrogation do not differ from those that apply to interrogation that precedes the indictment. Jailhouse informants can be used both as listening posts, and for inducing defendants to confide in them regarding offences they have been charged with. Electronic bugs also can be used in order to obtain the defendant's confession. Confessions obtained through the use of both techniques can be used as direct evidence in a trial, and also can be employed in order to find further evidence.

3. *Enforcing the Rules*

Failure of the police to give the requisite warnings has never, until recently, been grounds for excluding a confession in court unless other actions of the police render the confession "involuntary." As noted, the *Ouda* case, discussed above, has changed this and the issue is pending before the Supreme Court.

III. Court Procedures

Magistrate Courts try offences punishable by fines or by prison sentences of up to 7 years. However, drug offences punishable by prison sentences of more than 7 years also can be tried in a Magistrate Court at the discretion of the District Attorney, provided that the defendant is not sentenced to a prison term of more than 7 years.[121]

The District Courts' jurisdiction is residuary, and therefore these courts try all offences which are not tried by the Magistrate Courts.[122] Nevertheless, when a defendant is accused of one of the specified corruption offences punishable by a prison sentence ranging between 5 and 7 years (bribery, corporate fraud and the like), the District Attorney may decide to prosecute him in a District Court.[123] The

117. The Penal Law 1977, section 277.
118. Muadi v. State of Israel, 38(1) P.D. 197 (1982).
119. The Secret Monitoring Law 1979, section 1.
120. Ibid, section 8(1)(c).
121. The Courts Law [Consolidated Version] 1984, section 51.
122. Ibid, section 40.
123. Ibid, section 51(a)(1)(b) and Part II of the Second Supplement to the Courts Law.

District Court of Jerusalem also has an exclusive jurisdiction over all antitrust offences (regardless of the imposed punishment).[124]

Appeals against judgments (both convictions and acquittals) delivered by Magistrate Courts are heard by the District Courts. The courts' jurisdiction is determined separately for every offence; therefore, a defendant will stand trial at the Magistrate Court even if prosecuted for 2 offences, each punishable by a prison sentence of 4 years. Appeals against judgments (both convictions and acquittals) rendered by a District Court in its capacity as a trial court are heard by the Supreme Court.[125] There is no right to appeal against a judgment rendered by a District Court in its capacity as a Court of Appeals: Second appeals, heard by the Supreme Court, are possible only after obtaining a special leave to appeal from the Supreme Court. No such leave can be obtained on the grounds of an error of fact or an error in law allegedly committed by the District Court. The Supreme Court will accept the case for a second-appeal review only if the case raises an unsettled legal issue of general significance.[126] The same principle applies to additional hearings conducted by the Supreme Court with regard to its own rulings made in its ordinary appellate capacity. Such hearings are conducted before extended panels of at least 5 justices.[127]

In extraordinary circumstances, a convicted defendant can successfully petition for a new trial, thus re-opening the final judgment. Broadly speaking, this possibility becomes viable when a newly discovered evidence makes the defendant's conviction *prima facie* overturnable (that is unsafe and unsatisfactory) Furthermore, under a recent statutory amendment, a new trial can be ordered even without new evidence, if there are grounds to believe that miscarriage of justice has occurred in the former trial.[128] Heard by a Supreme Court Justice, such a petition also can be brought by the Attorney General. The latter, however, cannot bring a petition for re-opening a case of an acquitted defendant: Unlike an ordinary prosecutorial appeal, this would violate the defendant's right against double jeopardy. If the Justice hearing the petition orders a new trial, the defendant's conviction is quashed and the new trial is held afresh by an authorized trial court (if the prosecution insists on indicting the defendant).[129]

A. Proceedings Prior to Trial

1. *Initial Court Appearance*

See discussion in the Introduction, section I.

2. *Charging Instrument*

Prosecution is by indictment issued by the prosecutor. Prosecutorial discretion is essentially in the hands of the Attorney General and his representatives: The

124. See ibid, sections 40(1); 51(a)(1). The District Court of Jerusalem obtained the exclusive jurisdiction over antitrust offences from the designating order issued by the Minister of Justice pursuant to CPCV, section 6(c1).

125. The Courts Law, ibid, section 41(a).

126. Cheniyon Haifa Ltd. v. Matzat Or (Hadar Haifa) Ltd., 36(3) P.D. 123 (1982).

127. The Courts Law [Consolidated Version] 1984, section 30.

128. Ibid, section 31; Kozali v. State of Israel (delivered by the Supreme Court on 16.2.1999 and not yet published).

129. Azaria v. State of Israel (delivered in June 1997 and not yet published), para. 35.

State Attorney, the District Attorneys and other public prosecutors (predominantly affiliated to police forces).[130] In practice, it is the District Attorneys who decides whom to prosecute, subject to combined statutory and case law guidelines. The District Attorney must prosecute when there exists sufficient evidence—both credible and admissible—pointing to the defendant's guilt, unless he or she believes that there is no public interest in prosecuting.[131] Public interest should be considered in light of the gravity of the offence, its consequences to both society and the victim, its frequency, the time elapsed between the act and the prosecution, the personal circumstances of the suspect, the victim's position as to prosecution and prosecutorial priorities. Above all, public interest should be considered in view of the basic interests of equality before the law, and the need to punish for offences.[132] The indictment itself is not judicially reviewed prior to the proceedings, but judicial review of decisions as to whether or not to prosecute may always be sought at the Supreme Court in its capacity as the High Court of Justice.[133] Furthermore, as recently held by the Supreme Court, a trial court is authorized to quash an indictment "in the interests of justice" for reasons such as gross abuse of prosecutorial discretion and severe police misconduct that violated one of the defendant's constitutional rights.[134]

Under a special statute, an investigation into the cause of a suspicious death may be conducted judicially. The judge conducting such an investigation may issue an indictment order, under which the District Attorney is obliged to bring the specified indictment against the named person.[135] If an investigation ended without issuing an indictment order, findings and conclusions made by the judge need only be considered by the District Attorney in deciding whether to indict the suspect. Apart from this, the District Attorney's discretion remains unfettered.[136] The Attorney General is authorized to stay and subsequently reopen (subject to a time limitation) any criminal proceeding.[137] The prosecution also may decide to drop charges at any stage of the trial, which would result in the defendant's acquittal if the charges were dropped after the defendant pleaded not guilty.[138] If the charges were dropped prior to pleading, the indictment will be quashed and can later be resubmitted (subject to the limitation-of-action rules).[139]

3. *Preliminary Hearings*

These are discussed above in regard to post-indictment detention. In addition, a preliminary hearing may be conducted with a view to narrow the scope of the disputed facts by determining which facts are genuinely in dispute and which can be stipulated; furthermore, the accused and the prosecution may agree upon admission of evidence that is otherwise inadmissible, waive the foundational and other formal requirements, such as authentication, with regard to both documents

130. CPCV, section 12.
131. Ibid, section 62.
132. Ganor v. Attorney General, 44(2) P.D. 485 (1990).
133. Ibid.
134. Yafet v. State of Israel, 50 (2) P.D. 221 (1996).
135. The Investigation of Felonies and Causes of Death Law 1958, section 32.
136. Refael v. Attorney General, 22(2) P.D. 776 (1968).
137. CPCV, sections 231–232.
138. Ibid, sections 93, 94(a).
139. Ibid, section 94(a).

and physical evidence, and so forth. All this becomes possible only when the accused is represented by counsel.[140]

4. *Pretrial Motions*

Suppression of evidence by exclusionary rules can take place only when the prosecution submits the evidence in question. Failure to raise an objection at the earliest opportunity to the submission of such evidence will ordinarily result in its admission (provided that the accused is represented by counsel[141]). This forfeiture principle will not be activated and the "first opportunity" will not be considered missed, if the evidence is admitted at a time when the accused was reasonably unaware of the grounds of its inadmissibility.[142]

Pretrial motions concerning jurisdiction, ill-drafted indictment, double jeopardy, immunity, limitation of action, etc., are generally brought at the opening of the trial, before the defendant answers the charge. However, motions other than concerning venue or a technical defect in the indictment are generally allowed to be brought at any stage of the trial and even on appeal.[143] A motion for disqualifying the judge (for reasons such as clear and imminent bias[144]) must be brought at the earliest opportunity, whenever it arises.[145] As for discovery related motions, these can be brought by the accused at any reasonable time. As with any other intermediary decision, rulings on pre-trial motions and on admissibility of evidence can generally be appealed against only at the end of the trial. This principle is qualified by two exceptions: 1) Rulings on judge-disqualification motions can be appealed against immediately;[146] 2) a ruling concerning the accused's right to evidential discovery is also subject to an intermediary appeal.[147]

5. *Discovery or Inspection of Investigatory Material*

The defendant is entitled to inspect and copy the investigatory material concerning the charge.[148] This entitlement applies to any evidence or information that might help the defense.[149] The prosecution is not allowed to submit any evidence that was not subject to discovery.[150] The right to discovery is limited by recognized privileges,[151] such as the public interest immunity.[152] Most privileges recognized in Israel (by statute or by case-law) are not absolute. Virtually any of them can be removed judicially "in the interests of justice," when the privileged evidence is nec-

---

140. Ibid, section 144.

141. See, e.g., Evidence Ordinance, sections 10B, 12(b); CPCV, section 144; Bashiri v. State of Israel, 34(3) P.D. 393, 467–468 (1978) (requiring the court to help unrepresented defendants with raising objections against inadmissible evidence).

142. Marziano v. State of Israel, 46(4) P.D. 539, 550–551 (1992).

143. CPCV, sections 149–151.

144. The Courts Law [Consolidated Version] 1984, section 77A.

145. CPCV, section 146.

146. Ibid, section 147.

147. Ibid, section 74(e).

148. Ibid, section 74(a).

149. Lavie v. State of Israel, 28(2) P.D. 505 (1974).

150. CPCV, section 77(a).

151. Ibid, section 78.

152. Evidence Ordinance, sections 44-46.

essary for protecting a substantive right which is of greater social value than the secrecy sought to be protected by the privilege. In most cases involving privileges, the accused therefore may petition for disclosure, and the court will have to decide whether the necessity to disclose the privileged information in the interests of justice outweighs the interest in its non-disclosure.[153] If the court decides in favor of the accused, the prosecution will have the choice of either disclosing the information or dropping the indictment.[154] The Supreme Court recently has clarified in this connection that the court must remove the privilege and order disclosure in any case where the privileged evidence is potentially capable of casting a reasonable doubt upon the prosecution's case, let alone when it tends to positively establish the accused's innocence.[155] As was held in this and several other cases, protection of an innocent person from wrongful conviction is the primary objective of the law of criminal procedure and evidence. This objective overrides the objectives and values associated with evidentiary privileges, including the privilege protecting the security of the State. The supremacy of this objective is now mandated by the emerging Israeli Constitution.[156]

The accused, for his part, is not obligated to discover any evidence, save for expert opinions sought to be adduced by him as part of the defense evidence.[157]

B. Trial Proceedings

1. *Nature of Trial*

Only bench trials exist in Israel. The Israeli defendant therefore does not have a right to a jury trial and is tried by a single professional judge or (depending on the severity of the crime in question) by a panel of three professional judges (in a District Court and, most exceptionally, in a Magistrate Court).[158]

In most trials, the accused enters into a guilty plea, with or without plea-bargaining. In trials where the accused plead not guilty, time consumed by the proceedings depends on the particularities of each case. In the absence of empirical studies, it is difficult to estimate the approximate length of a typical contested trial. A criminal trial normally must be conducted successively, day by day, subject to special circumstances.[159] However, due to a severe overload on the court system, those special circumstances have become the rule, and in practice almost no trial continues daily. If the accused is detained pending trial, the trial must end within nine months, subject to a special discretion to extend this period that was bestowed by statute on a Supreme Court Justice.[160]

Under the Israeli law of evidence, any relevant evidence is admissible, subject to several exclusionary rules, and any potentially relevant evidence is due to be dis-

---

153. Ibid., sections 44(a), 45, 49(a), 50(a), 50A(a).

154. Greenberg v. State of Israel, 47(4) P.D. 766, 770 (1993).

155. Mazrib v. State of Israel (delivered on 8.5.1997 and not yet published); Greenberg, ibid, Livni v. State of Israel, 38(3) P.D. 729 (1984).

156. Mazrib, ibid.

157. CPCV, sections 82–84.

158. The Courts Law [Consolidated Version] 1984, sections 37, 47.

159. CPCV, section 125.

160. CPEA, sections 61-62.

closed, subject to a number of evidentiary privileges.[161] Every person is both competent[162] and compellable as a witness, with a few exceptions, including young children, insane and mentally retarded people[163] and, in limited circumstances, the accused's spouse, children and parents.[164]

The rules governing evidentiary exclusion are broadly divided into four categories: 1) The rule against hearsay;[165] 2) the rule rendering inadmissible evidence concerning general disposition and character of the accused[166] (the "judge the act, not the actor" principle); 3) the opinion rule under which only expert, as opposed to lay, opinions are allowed as evidence in criminal trials;[167] 4) the four separate rules rendering inadmissible illegally obtained evidence, as follows: a) evidence obtained unconstitutionally (as mentioned above, this rule is yet to become clear);[168] b) evidence obtained by illegal wiretapping;[169] c) evidence obtained in violation of the defendant's (informational) privacy;[170] d) involuntary confessions.[171] Application of rules (a) and (c) involves some discretionary elements, which are rather limited in the application of rules (b) and (d). Rule (b) is qualified by a good-faith exception applicable in trials for offences punishable by imprisonment for 7 years or more.

Rulings on evidential admissibility are made by the trial judge. The judge, of course, is required to disregard evidence that has been ruled inadmissible. Since the judge is also required to deliver a reasoned judgment in writing justifying his or her decision, the judge cannot consciously rely upon inadmissible evidence. Any such reliance would result in overturning the verdict on appeal, unless the error committed by the judge was found to be harmless. If there are reasons to believe that inadmissible evidence might have been relied upon by the judge unconsciously and thus affected the verdict, the verdict also may be overturned on appeal.[172]

Criminal proceedings in Israel are based on the adversarial system: It is the task of the prosecutor and the defense to conduct evidentiary inquiries and to present their respective evidence and contentions. The court plays a more passive role and is not expected to initiate production of evidence or examination of witnesses. The court, however, is not completely free of responsibility in these matters, and may, and in some cases is obligated to, assist an unrepresented defendant.[173] When the

---

161. Evidence Ordinance, sections 44–52, lays down the principal statutory privileges. To these the Supreme Court added two additional privileges: A privilege protecting confidentiality between journalists and their sources and a bank-client privilege. There are also numerous statutory privileges that apply to many other kinds of information and relationships: See, e.g., the Rights of Patients Law 1996, sections 21(c)(d); 22(b)(e). For full discussion of the Israeli evidentiary privileges, see A. Stein, The Bank-Client Evidentiary Privilege, 25 Mishpatim 45 (1995).

162. Evidence Ordinance, section 2.

163. See generally, Jabari v. State of Israel, 49(2) P.D. 332 (1995).

164. Evidence Ordinance, sections 3-6; 8.

165. The Attorney General v. The Judge Conducting a Preliminary Inquiry, 13 P.D. 5 (1959).

166. Shayovitz v. Attorney General, 19(3) P.D. 421 (1965).

167. Tenenholtz v. Popelovitz, 8 P.D. 1570, 1574 (1953); Evidence Ordinance, section 20.

168. State of Israel v. Ouda (delivered by the Nazareth District Court on 31.12.1997 and not yet published).

169. The Secret Monitoring Law 1979, section 13.

170. The Protection of Privacy Law 1981, section 32.

171. Evidence Ordinance, section 12(a).

172. Evidence Ordinance, section 56; CPCV, section 215; Ploni v. State of Israel, 50(3) P.D. 225 (1993).

173. See, e.g., Zeiger v. State of Israel, 27(1) P.D. 505, 511 (1973); Bashiri v. State of Israel, 34(3) P.D. 393, 467-468 (1978).

parties have concluded presenting their cases, the court may summon a witness to testify, even if that witness has already testified in the trial, and may order that further evidence be brought before him.[174] The court also may examine a witness following the examinations of the parties, and may ask any clarifying questions throughout the examinations. Additionally, the court may summon an expert witness to testify concerning matters requiring expertise.[175] As held by the Supreme Court, all the above powers should be exercised with great caution, and only on rare occasions.[176]

Keeping accurate records of court proceedings is an inherent part of the trial itself, and must be done by the judge herself, by mechanical means, such as tape-recording, or by a stenographer. The trial file also must include the indictment and any other documentation relevant to the trial or admitted as evidence.[177] The transcript serves as evidence to its content's accuracy, and cannot be disputed on appeal, unless permitted, on special grounds, by the Appellate Court.[178] In practice, transcripts are made either through tape-recording or by hired stenographers working on wordprocessors, and judges can keep track of them through on-line monitors.

The defendant cannot confess to having committed a crime, but only to the facts with which he has been charged. It remains for the court to determine whether those facts constitute a crime. The court must accept a guilty plea and act upon it, unless it suspects that the admission was not "true and sincere."[179] The court also may reject a guilty plea where the public interest requires that the facts be established judicially, and not solely on the basis of the defendant's admission.[180]

At any stage of the proceedings, including appeal, the defendant may apply for the court's permission to withdraw his admission.[181] The Supreme Court ruled in this connection that contrary to the strict wording of the statute, such a permission should be given whenever the defendant makes a good faith application for his admission's withdrawal.[182] As a rule, the defendant may be convicted solely on the basis of his admission in court, without the prosecution having to offer testimony or recite evidence.

Plea bargaining between the prosecution and the defendant is allowed, in respect to both the sentence and the indictment. A plea bargain must be made in a written agreement or documented in the court's transcript. The prosecution must always inform the court of the existence and conditions of a plea bargain. When a plea bargain is concluded prior to the commencement of the trial, and the prosecution agrees, as part of the bargain, to remove some of the charges from the in-

---

174. CPCV, sections 167, 175.

175. Ibid, sections 111, 167.

176. See, e.g., Kanir v. State of Israel, 35(3) P.D. 505 (1981); Gindil v. State of Israel, 41(4) P.D. 543, 547-548 (1987).

177. CPCV, sections 134-136.

178. CPCV, sections 137-139.

179. Ibid, section 154.

180. Such was the case in the trial for the attempted arson of the El-Akza Mosque, where it was important to ascertain that Israeli authorities had nothing to do with the arson. There also was some doubt as to whether the accused was mentally stable. See State of Israel v. Rohan, 68 Psakim Mehozi'im (District Court of Jerusalem) 344 (1969).

181. CPCV, section 153.

182. Samahat v. State of Israel, 45(5) P.D. 798 (1991).

dictment or to substitute a less serious offence for a more serious one, changes effected by the bargain will bind the court because at this stage the prosecution exercises an exclusive discretion over the indictment instrument and is authorized to amend it unilaterally, without the court's permission. Even at a later stage, the prosecution can achieve the same result by informing the court that it will not bring evidence relating to one of the charges originally brought against the accused.[183] As for promises of the prosecution with respect to the sentence, the rule is that the court is in no way obligated by the plea bargain.[184] The court must clarify this to the defendant, who may consequently retract his plea. The prevalent opinion in the Supreme Court holds, that a plea bargain will not be endorsed by the court if a significant discordance exists between the appropriate sentence and the one agreed upon by the parties.[185] Under a new Bill concerning plea bargaining, this principle is proposed to be replaced by a rule requiring stricter adherence to the bargain: A court-imposed sentence will be allowed to deviate from the sentence agreed upon by the parties only in extreme cases, where the bargain contradicts public policy in sentencing.[186] This position currently reflects only a minority opinion at the Supreme Court,[187] but is widely believed to represent the lower courts' actual practice. At the same time, the Bill provides greater standing to alleged victims of crimes: prior to entering into a plea bargain, the prosecutor will be required to ascertain the victim's condition and will be statutorily advised to consult the victim.[188]

2. *Defendants*

Every defendant has the right to testify in his own defense, in which case he will be subjected to full cross-examination, but may also refrain from testifying altogether.[189] If the defendant refrains from testifying (thus exercising the right of silence), his refusal can serve to strengthen the prosecution's evidence, and, in appropriate cases, even satisfy a formal corroboration requirement.[190] It may be cited in the written judgment as among the bases of conviction.

Both the defendant and the prosecution are entitled to cross-examine adverse witnesses.[191] However, the defendant's confrontation right has been severely curtailed since 1979, when a statute amending the Evidence Ordinance (by adding section 10A), interpretively expanded by the case-law, had recognized the admissibility of recorded out-of-court statements given by alleged "turncoat witnesses" or by

183. Assis v. Judge Ostrovsky, 45(1) P.D. 661 (1990).

184. Bahmoutzki v. State of Israel, 26(1) P.D. 543 (1972); Arbiv v. Attorney General, 40(2) P.D. 393 (1986); Keshet v. State of Israel, 40(3) P.D. 472 (1986).

185. See, e.g., Markowitz v. State of Israel, 47(2) P.D. 45 (1993) (the majority opinion).

186. The Criminal Procedure Bill (Amendment No. 19) (Plea Arrangements) 1995.

187. See, e.g., Markowitz v. State of Israel, 47(2) P.D. 45, 55-58 (1993).

188. The Criminal Procedure Bill (Amendment No. 19) (Plea Arrangements) 1995, the proposed CPCV, section 155c(d). For a detailed discussion of this and related issues, see E. Harnon, Plea Bargaining in Israel - The Proper Functions of the Prosecution and the Court and the Role of the Victim, 31 Israel L. Rev. 245 (1997).

189. CPCV, section 161.

190. Ibid, section 162.

191. Ibid, section 174. See also the Law Amending the Law of Procedure (Examination of Witnesses) 1957, sections 1–2.

witnesses allegedly kept out of the way.[192] The resulting broad exception to the hearsay rule was motivated not only by the war against crime, which requires tackling the problem of witness-intimidation, but also—and, perhaps, primarily—by the growing faith in the trial judges' capacity to establish the truth and to adequately protect the accused from the risk of wrongful conviction.[193] This latter factor is responsible for the general shift in the law of evidence from evidential admissibility to evidential weight.

3. *Assistance of Counsel*

Every defendant has a right to counsel. Every defendant may appoint to himself an attorney of his own choice. In cases involving offences against state security, the attorney must undergo authorization by the Ministry of Defense and undertake the appropriate obligations with regard to any secret information. According to the newly enacted Public Defenders Law, 1995 (including the relevant amendments in the Criminal Procedure Law [Consolidated Version], 1982), the accused is entitled to a free public defender under each of the following circumstances:

- He is charged with murder, with a capital offence, or with an offence punishable by a prison sentence of no less than 10 years;
- he is under 16 years of age and is brought to trial before a court which is not a Juvenile Court (*i.e.*, when a juvenile accused is tried as an adult);
- he is dumb, blind, or mute, or is suspected to be mentally ill or feebleminded;
- the prosecution applied for an order to detain the accused during the trial;
- the accused is indigent, according to the criteria set by the Minister of Justice, and is not tried for one of the petty offences, also specified by the Minister;
- the court is in the opinion that a fair trial cannot be conducted when the accused is unrepresented.[194]

Ineffective assistance of counsel may constitute a ground for appeal only in extreme cases, where the possibility of miscarriage of justice—i.e., the risk of wrongful conviction—is evident.[195]

4. *Judges*

Israeli judges are sworn-in and thus formally appointed by the President of the State after the decision concerning their appointment was made by a special committee, comprised of the Chief Justice (President of the Supreme Court), two other Supreme Court Justices, the Minister of Justice and another cabinet minister, two members of Parliament (the Knesset), and two representatives of the Bar. This Appointments Committee is chaired by the Minister of Justice.[196] A person is qualified

---

192. State of Israel v. Tubul, 42(4) P.D. 309 (1985); State of Israel v. Chage Yichye, 47(3) P.D. 661 (1991); Machadjna v. State of Israel, 38(4) P.D. 767 (1981); Abuhatzera v. State of Israel, 36(4) P.D. 141 (1981); Chazan v. State of Israel, 41(1) P.D. 512 (1985).

193. See, in particular, State of Israel v. Tubul, 42(4) P.D. 309, 353-358 (1985).

194. CPCV, section 15; The Public Defenders Law 1995, section 18.

195. Sokolovskaya v. State of Israel, 48(1) P.D. 1, 5–8 (1991). See also *Kozali*, supra n.128.

196. Basic Law: The Judiciary, section 4.

to be appointed to judicial office (as a Magistrate, District or Supreme Court judge) if she is a qualified legal practitioner (an attorney, a judge, or a civil servant) or if she is a university teacher of law. For each judicial position, the statute also specifies a minimal length of the candidate's professional experience: 5 years for a Magistrate Court judge, 7 years for a District Court judge and 10 years for a Supreme Court justice. Holding a judicial office at a Magistrate Court for 4 years also qualifies the judge for appointment to a District Court, and 5 years at a District Court qualify the judge for the Supreme Court. A person also can be appointed to the Supreme Court if she is considered by the Judicial Appointments Committee a "distinguished jurist."[197]

5. *Victims*

Every person may complain to the police that an offence was committed.[198] The complainant thus does not have to be the victim, though in practice most complaints are brought by the victims of crimes. The complainant is entitled to be informed in writing of any official decision not to investigate an offence or not to prosecute.[199] Upon such a decision, the complainant may lodge an objection with the Attorney General[200] (unless the offence complained about is listed amongst not very severe offences that can be prosecuted privately by the victim himself).[201] Against the Attorney General's decision the complainant may initiate a judicial review by petitioning to the High Court of Justice.[202]

If the court finds the defendant guilty, it may order him to compensate the victim. A compensation order does not prevent the victim from bringing a civil lawsuit against the defendant. In any such lawsuit, the final criminal verdict would usually serve as conclusive evidence against the convicted defendant.[203] The victim's condition as a result of the offence may serve as evidence in sentencing proceedings, especially in cases involving sexual offences.[204]

C. Appeals

These are discussed at the beginning of section III.

---

197. The Courts Law [Consolidated Version] 1984, sections 2–4.

198. CPCV, section 58.

199. Ibid, section 63.

200. Ibid, section 64.

201. Ibid, sections 68-72. A reform committee recently has recommended to significantly reduce the list of offences that can be prosecuted privately.

202. Shor v. Attorney-General, 11 P.D. 285 (1957); Ganor v. Attorney-General, 44(2) P.D. 485 (1990).

203. Evidence Ordinance, sections 42A-42E; The Courts Law [Consolidated Version] 1984, section 77(a).

204. CPCV, section 187.

Chapter 8

Italy

Rachel VanCleave

I. Introduction

Italy, traditionally a civil law country, adopted a Code of Criminal Procedure in 1989 dramatically moving away from its historically inquisitorial system of criminal justice to a system infused with adversarial elements, resulting in a mixed system. These changes may be organized broadly into three categories. First, are changes which restructured the nature of criminal investigations. The 1989 Code implemented checks on the previously discretionary power of the police conducting investigations, abolished the inquisitorial "investigative judge" and allocated primary investigatory responsibility to the public prosecutor, with the newly created judge for preliminary investigations (*giudice delle indagini preliminari* or *g.i.p.*) responsible for overseeing the course of the investigations.

Second are reforms designed to make criminal trials more consistent with the democratic principles of orality, immediacy and publicity. Thus, trials in Italy are open to the public, persons testifying do so live, in open court and in a direct and cross-examination format conducted by the prosecutor, defense attorney and attorney for the private party. Somewhat ironically, the democratic reforms to the trial have made the trial more complicated and time-consuming requiring the less democratic reform which implemented a form of plea-bargaining, historically unheard of in inquisitorial systems. Thus, the third category of reforms include devices created to dispose of cases with greater efficiency by either moving a case to trial quickly, bypassing the preliminary hearing phase, or allowing cases to be resolved at the preliminary hearing phase, eliminating the need for a trial.

Due to the rather dramatic and revolutionary changes made by the 1989 Code, there have been many amendments to resolve some of the tensions created by the Code and to repair the Code after the Italian Constitutional Court has found some provisions in violation of the Italian Constitution. Nonetheless, the process of fine-tuning the Code is not complete and amendments continue to be enacted and provisions continue to raise constitutional questions.

II. Police Procedures

The 1989 Code as initially enacted limited the scope of police discretion. Subsequent amendments have retreated somewhat from several of the strict limitations. For example, the original 1989 Code required the police to report crimes and turn over evidence to the prosecutors within forty-eight hours of receiving "news of the crime" (*notizia del reato*).[1] This provision was subsequently changed to require the police to notify the prosecutor "without delay."[2]

In addition, the Code limits the types of investigatory acts which the police may perform on their own initiative, especially once they have notified the prosecutor of the crime. After this point, the prosecutor controls the investigation enlisting the help of the police by delegating to them the authority to conduct certain investigatory procedures which the police could not otherwise perform on their own. Although the prosecutor has primary control over the investigations, and the Code has made the prosecutor a "party" at trial, the Italian prosecutor has a duty to investigate facts and circumstances which exculpate or otherwise favor the defendant.[3] This is due to the fact that while prosecutors are not judges, they do come under the umbrella term "magistrates" (*magistrati*) under article 107 of the Italian Constitution.[4]

A. Arrest, Search, and Seizure Law

The Italian Constitution article 13 provides that "[p]ersonal liberty shall be inviolable."[5] And further that "[t]here shall be no form of detention, inspection, or search of the person, nor any other restriction whatsoever of personal liberty, except by decision, wherein the reasons are stated, of the judicial authorities, and only in cases and in the manner prescribed by law."[6] The Constitution also states that in "exceptional cases on necessity and urgency, expressly provided for by law, the police may take provisional measures, of which the judicial authorities must be notified within forty-eight hours."[7] Article 14 sets out a similar protection of the home.[8] The constitution thus states in broad terms the sanctity of personal liberty and of the home, yet expressly permits legislation to abrogate these broad rights in cases of necessity and urgency. Indeed, there are numerous provisions in the *Code*

---

1. C.P.P. art. 347(1) (1989).
2. C.P.P. art. 347(1) as amended by decreto-legge June 8, 1992, n. 306, art. 4(a).
3. C.P.P. art. 358.
4. Chapter IV of the Italian Constitution is entitled "The Judiciary" and within this chapter are provisions relating specifically to prosecutors. Cost. arts. 107(5) and 112.
5. Cost. Art. 13(1) (Italy, 1948). Translation is from Mauro Cappelletti et al., The Italian Legal System 283, app. A (1967).
6. Id., art. 13(2). See also art. 2 which provides inter alia "[t]he Republic recognizes and guarantees the inviolable rights of man, both as individual and in the social organizations wherein his personality is developed."
7. Id., art. 13(3).
8. "The home is inviolable. No inspection, search, or [seizure] shall be carried out therein except in the cases and in the manner established by law in accordance with the guarantees prescribed for the protection of personal liberty." Const. Art. 14 (1)(2) (Italy, 1948).

of Criminal Procedure as well as in other laws which authorize the police to act upon their own initiative in the absence of a judicial decree.

1. Stops

No specific term which translates to a "stop" is used under the Italian system. However, article 351 of the penal Code makes it a misdemeanor to refuse to provide public officials personal identifying information, or to provide false information.[9] There is no apparent limit on the requirement to provide such information to public officials, which of course includes the police. Article 349 of the *Code of Criminal Procedure* gives the police the authority to acquire such identification information from one suspected of a crime as well as from others who may have information about a crime.

2. Frisks

There is no lesser form of a search in Italy. Where the police have stopped a suspect pursuant to article 384 described below, they may search the individual or the place of arrest only if the situation is one of urgency and there is not time to obtain a search warrant.[10] Thus, there is no distinction as to the degree of intrusiveness of a search. If they suspect that a person is armed, they may search him pursuant to the "Public Safety" law discussed supra p. 19-20. No particular level of suspicion is required.

3. Arrests

The Italian Code distinguishes between an arrest (*arresto*), under articles 381 and 382, and detention of one suspected of a crime (*fermo di indiziato di delitto*), under article 384. While the requirements for each are different, the purpose and result are essentially the same. Neither an arrest nor a stop is necessary to formally initiate the criminal process under the Italian system. Rather an arrest and a stop are provisional measures used either to protect the public safety or for investigative purposes. Consequently, an arrest or a stop may be the first step in an effort to impose some form of preventive detention[11] or as a means of acquiring information from the person arrested or stopped.

First, as to arrests, the police are required to arrest anyone caught in *flagranza* committing, attempting, or having completed a non-negligent (*non colposo*), crime for which the penal law prescribes a sentence of life imprisonment or where the sentence set out in the criminal code imposes a minimum of at least five years and a maximum of at least twenty years.[12] This provision then lists specific crimes for which arrest is obligatory but would not otherwise come under this provision based on the punishment prescribed, such as certain crimes against the state, and

9. This is punishable by one month in jail or four hundred thousand lire (about $266.00). C.P. 351.

10. C.P.P. art. 352(2).

11. See infra.

12. C.P.P. art. 380(1).

the crime of engaging in the trade of slaves.[13] Article 381 lists the types of crimes for which the police have the power to execute an arrest, but are not required to do so. Once again, however, such arrests are permissible only where the individual arrested was caught *in flagranza.*[14] In addition, an arrest under article 381 is not purely discretionary, but must be based on the seriousness of the offense as well as the dangerousness of the suspect.[15] Article 381 defines the crimes for which an arrest is possible, but not required, as non-negligent offenses for which there is a maximum sentence of at least three years, or as to negligence offenses for which there is a maximum sentence of at least five years.[16] As with the provision for mandatory arrests, article 381 lists specific crimes for which an arrest is permissible, but the prescribed sentence is different than that set out in paragraph one of article 381.[17]

Article 384 sets out the requirements for a detention of one suspected of a crime (*fermo di indiziato di delitto*) who is not caught *in flagranza.*[18] There must be specific elements which indicate a danger of flight, and there must be serious circumstantial evidence (*gravi indizi*) of guilt, not mere suspicions.[19] In elaborating on this standard, the Supreme Court has stated that where the circumstantial evidence would lead one to "reasonably conclude that the crime charged occurred and that the suspect committed it," the statute is satisfied.[20] Furthermore, the evidence need not amount to that necessary to bind the defendant over for trial.[21] Therefore, where the police come upon the suspect unexpectedly and discover drugs where the

---

13. The offenses for which an arrest is mandatory are as follows: crimes against the state set out in articles 241–313 of the penal code for which there is a sentence of at least a five year minimum or a maximum of at least ten years; looting (C.P. art. 419); crimes against the public safety set out in articles 422–452 of the penal code for which there is a sentence of at least a three year minimum or a maximum of at least ten years; aggravated theft (C.P. art. 625); robbery or extortion by use of violence (C.P. arts. 628 & 629); illegal manufacturing of weapons (legge April 18, 1975, n. 110, art. 2(3); crimes involving illicit drugs (Decreto del Presidente della Repubblica, Oct. 9, 1990, n. 309); terrorist crimes; establishment of secret or military societies (legge Jan. 25, 1982, n. 17, art. 1; legge April 17, 1956, n. 561, art. 1); organized-crime conspiracies (C.P. art. 416bis); association for purposes of delinquency (C.P. art. 416) where one of the crimes set out in subparts a-d, f, g, or i of C.P.P. art. 380(2) is the subject of the association. C.P.P. art. 380(2a-m); The American Series of Foreign Penal Codes: The Italian Penal Code (Edward M. Wise, trans. 1978).

14. The state of flagranza is defined to include one who is in the process of committing a crime as well as one who is pursued by the police immediately after the commission of a crime and one who is caught in possession of objects or traces indicating that he has just committed a crime. C.P.P. art 382.

15. C.P.P. art. 381(4).

16. C.P.P. art. 381(1).

17. The offenses listed here are as follows: a form of misappropriation of public funds based on another's error (C.P. 316); corruption based on an omission or delay of one's official duties which benefits oneself or another (C.P. 319(4) and 321); use of violence or threats against a public official (C.P. 336(2)); putting into commerce or administering harmful medicines or food (C.P. 443 and 444); child abuse (C.P. 530); causing bodily injury (C.P. 582); larceny (C.P. 624); destruction of property with aggravating circumstances (C.P. 635(2)); certain types of fraud (C.P. 640); embezzlement (C.P. 646); alteration of weapons or manufacture of explosives (Legge April 18, 1975 n. 110, arts. 3 and 24(1)). C.P.P. art. 281(2a-m).

18. See C.P.P. art. 382 for a definition of stato di flagranza.

19. C.P.P. art. 384(1).

20. Cass. I, sent. 1090, (March 9, 1992).

21. Cass. Sez. VI, sent. 1552 (Jan. 25, 1993) (discussing the standard for preventive detention which is the same as that for a fermo, as discussed under the heading "preventive detention").

suspect had been standing, and the police know that the suspect has been involved in drug deals, the circumstantial evidence is sufficient for a *fermo*.[22] In addition to the requirement of serious circumstantial evidence, the crime involved must also be serious, that is, punishable by life imprisonment, or by a statutory minimum of at least two years and a maximum of more than six years imprisonment,[23] or be a crime involving weapons or explosives. Before the public prosecutor has taken over the investigations[24] the police may carry out a detention on their own initiative.[25] After the police have notified the public prosecutor of the crime,[26] the police act upon directions from the prosecutor unless there is a danger that the suspect may flee and there is not sufficient time to wait for action by the prosecutor.[27] As mentioned above, the police may conduct a bodily or premise search upon performing a *fermo*. After detaining the person and taking them into custody, the police proceed as they would if they had arrested the individual.[28] Thus, the difference between a detention and an arrest is based in part on the seriousness of the offense and in part on whether the defendant is caught *in flagranza*. In addition, it seems that the Code contemplates that arrests will occur before the filing of the *notizia del reato* and thus before the prosecutor has taken over the investigations. Therefore the rules regarding arrests limit the types of provisional measures the police may perform on their own initiative. A detention, on the other hand, generally is a measure taken after the filing of the *notizia del reato* and therefore usually occurs upon delegation by the prosecutor. In any event, a prosecutor will typically request the judge of the preliminary investigations, who must validate the detention, to order that the person detained or arrested be held under preventive detention, pending the investigation.[29]

As to both arrests and detentions, upon taking the individual into custody, the police immediately notify the prosecutor, and advise the suspect of the right to an attorney.[30] Within 24 hours of the arrest or detention the police must make the person available to the prosecutor, and transmit the transcript of the detention or arrest which includes the nomination of an attorney by the person, the date, time and place of the stop or arrest, and an explanation of the reasons for the detention or arrest.[31] Before requesting a judicial hearing to validate the arrest, the prosecutor may interrogate the individual upon giving timely notice to the defense attorney.[32] The Code gives this power to the prosecutor where it is necessary to evaluate the legitimacy of the detention or arrest or to further the investigations.[33] During the

---

22. See Cass., Dresia (Jan. 15, 1991).
23. C.P.P. art. 384(1).
24. See C.P.P. art. 348(1 and 3).
25. C.P.P. art. 384(2).
26. See C.P.P. art. 330 et seq., describing the different avenues by which the public prosecutor and the police might receive notice of a crime, notizia di reato. See also article 347 requiring the police to refer to the prosecutor any notice of a crime.
27. C.P.P. art. 384(3).
28. See C.P.P. art. 386, and infra.
29. Preventive detention is discussed briefly, infra.
30. C.P.P. art. 386 (1).
31. C.P.P. art. 386 (3).
32. C.P.P. art. 388(1).
33. Article 389(1) provides that where it is evident that the arrest or stop was erroneous or not within the bounds provided for by law, the prosecutor, per an order explaining the error, is to order that the person be immediately released.

interrogation the prosecutor is to tell the individual the offense for which he or she was detained or arrested.[34] The prosecutor may decide, before a hearing validating the arrest or detention has taken place, whether the person detained or arrested should be placed under house arrest, per article 284, or remain in jail, if the prosecutor believes this is necessary to avoid prejudice to the investigations.[35] Immediately following the arrest or detention, the suspect has the right to confer with the defense attorney unless the prosecutor issues a decree postponing this right for no more than five days following the arrest or detention.[36] However, since the suspect must be brought before a preliminary hearing judge, *giudice per le indagini preliminari (g.i.p.)*, within 48 hours of the arrest or detention, the prosecutor in actuality may only suspend the suspect's right to confer with her attorney for up to two days.[37]

Article 389 provides for immediate release of one detained or arrested by either the police or the prosecutor as soon as it becomes apparent that the arrest or detention was made of the wrong person, or was not done in accordance with the law or the requirements discussed above were not complied with. Where the police decide to release the individual pursuant to article 389 they are to inform the prosecutor of this right away.

In addition, the Code provides for the forced appearance (*accompagnamento coattivo)* of a suspect where his presence is needed for an act to be done during an evidentiary hearing[38] such as an interrogation[39] or confrontation.[40] Such forced appearance is by order of the judge.

Preventive Detention. There is another way in which one may be deprived of one's constitutional right of liberty even if not yet facing formal charges. These types of arrests come under the category of preventive detention measures (*misure cautelari*).[41] Article 273 provides that "no one may be held under preventive detention unless there are grave [or serious] circumstantial evidence of guilt." The Code, under article 274, permits use of this device in the following situations:

a) fear that the investigations could be jeopardized by the tampering or destruction of evidence;

b) a fear that the defendant or suspect will flee;

---

34. C.P.P. art. 388(2).

35. C.P.P. art. 386 (5).

36. C.P.P. art. 104 (4). Paragraph three of the same article gives the judge this power during the course of the preliminary investigations upon the request of the prosecutor. However, immediately following an arrest or stop, the prosecutor has this power until the suspect is brought before a judge.

37. C.P.P. art. 390 (1).

38. C.P.P. art. 399.

39. See, infra sect. II C.

40. A "confrontation" or confronto, described in articles 211–212, is a procedure in which more than one individual is questioned contemporaneously because there are contradictions or inconsistencies as to material facts between or among their declarations, or separate testimonies. This may occur during the preliminary investigations and be conducted by the prosecutor according to article 364, or the prosecutor may delegate this authority to the police per article 370. In addition, the judge may conduct the procedure during an "evidentiary hearing" (incidente probatorio), per article 392(e), or at trial under article 212. See also Fortuna at 795.

41. C.P.P. arts. 272–315, as amended by legge August 8, 1995, n.332 (this law specifically addressed changes to the Code in the area of preventive detention).

c) a fear that the defendant or suspect will commit a violent crime or one similar to that under investigation.

The Supreme Court has stated that the standard for "serious circumstantial evidence of guilt" is the same as that for a *fermo*.[42] A prosecutor can request a court to impose preventive detention following the individual's arrest or *fermo*, pending resolution of the charges filed. However, the imposition of preventive detention does not require that such charges be filed. In other words, one who is arrested or subject to a *fermo* faces criminal charges and may also be subject to one of the *misure cautelari*, but precautionary measures may be imposed on suspects who are not yet facing formal criminal charges, and may not ever face formal charges. In fact, after criticisms that this device was being used as an investigatory technique aimed at provoking confessions or statements against others, especially in political corruption cases, the legislature amended this book of the Code to provide for greater personal guarantees.[43] For example, the Code now states that a danger that evidence may be destroyed or tampered with may not be based upon the suspect's refusal to make a statement.[44]

The Code provides that only a judge has the authority to impose a form of preventive detention, but only upon the request of the prosecutor and only if one of the above exigencies is present. Aside from detention in prison,[45] the most serious restriction of liberty, the Code provides for other forms including house arrest,[46] prohibition on travel outside the country,[47] and a requirement that the individual report to a specific police office on specific days at certain times.[48] Where a judge has imposed one of these measures during the preliminary investigations, a suspect may be held from three months to one year depending on the punishment prescribed for the suspected offense.[49] Again, while a request for some form of preventive detention is usually in conjunction with a request to validate an arrest or a stop, a prosecutor may also request an order of preventive detention even where there has been neither an arrest or stop of the individual.

4. *Inspections, Searches, and Seizures*

a.*Inspections.* The Italian Code of Criminal Procedure distinguishes between inspections (*ispezioni*)[50] and searches (*perquisizioni*).[51] Inspections are mainly observations of places like the scene of a crime, things such as objects found at the scene of a crime, and persons such as the victim to determine their injury, or the suspect to note, for example, signs of a fight.[52] The purpose of an inspection is solely descriptive; that is, to determine the traces or effects of the crime.[53] This is in

42. Cass. I, sent 1090 (March 9, 1992).
43. See Ennio Amodio, Nuove Norme sulle Misure Cautelari e sul Diritto di Difesa 2-3 (1996). The law amending this section of the Code is legge Aug. 8, 1995, n. 332.
44. C.P.P. art. 274(1).
45. C.P.P. art. 285.
46. C.P.P. art. 284.
47. C.P.P. art. 281.
48. C.P.P. art. 282.
49. C.P.P. art. 303(a).
50. C.P.P. arts. 244–246.
51. C.P.P. arts. 247–251.
52. D'Ambrosio, at 251.
53. Fortuna at 390-391; Loris D'Ambrosio and Piero Luigi Vigna, La Pratica di Polizia Giudiziaria 346 (5th ed. 1995).

contrast to a search, the object of which is to locate things subject to seizure or persons to arrest. In addition, when conducting an inspection the police or the judicial authority may only use their eyes and not their hands.[54] Article 244 provides that an inspection may proceed upon a decree by a judicial authority which includes both judges and prosecutors, containing the reasons for the inspection. The Code does not state that a specific level of suspicion is required for an inspection, however, it seems that this investigatory act is limited to observations at the scene of the crime. An inspection is permissible when it is necessary to assess the traces or other material effects of a crime.[55] The police may conduct an inspection only upon delegation by the prosecutor[56] or in situations where waiting for the prosecutor would result in alteration or destruction of the traces or effects of the crime, unless a bodily inspection is involved.[57] Generally, only a judicial authority may conduct an inspection of a person,[58] unless there are urgent circumstances in which case the police may make only certain types of observations relating to the suspect's exterior. Examples include, tatoos, scars, birthmarks, bruises, the age of the person, odor of alcohol, and the attitude of the person.[59] Where the police conduct the inspection under such urgent circumstances the Code requires that the inspection itself as well as the observations made be documented by means of a written record created during the course of the inspection, or, where circumstances do not permit this, immediately after.[60]

Where the inspection is of a place, the judicial authority may include in the decree an order that no one on the premises may leave during the inspection.[61] In addition, the defendant, or whoever has actual access to or control over the premises, if present at the time of the inspection, must receive a copy of the decree or warrant authorizing the inspection.[62] However, if the defendant does not receive a copy of the decree the legality of the inspection is not affected.[63] Rather, the public official may be guilty of criminal trespass where the place is a home, punishable by up to one year.[64]

If an inspection of an individual is involved, the Code provides in article 245 that the individual must be told of his or her right to have a trusted individual present. This does not necessarily mean a defense attorney, but someone whom the individual trusts, as long as acquiring that person's presence would not unduly delay the inspection. Generally an inspection of an individual is limited to observations to determine traces or effects of a crime, such as an injury sustained during the crime.

On situations where the police perform an emergency or urgent inspection because waiting for the prosecutor could result in alteration or destruction of the

---

54. Cordero, at 716.
55. C.P.P. art. 244(1).
56. C.P.P. art. 348.
57. C.P.P. art. 354 (2 & 3); D'Ambrosio, at 251.
58. C.P.P. art. 354(3).
59. D'Ambrosio, at 251; Codice Spiegato, at 282, 284.
60. C.P.P. art. 357; D'Ambrosio at 247.
61. C.P.P. art. 246(2).
62. C.P.P. art. 246(1).
63. Fortuna, at 391.
64. C.P. 615(2) makes it a crime for a public official to enter a person's home without observing the formal requirements like those set out in the provisions on inspections in article 246 of the Code of Criminal Procedure.

thing, place or person to be inspected, the police are not required to notify the attorney of the suspect or defendant, even though the attorney may be present during the inspection, and even though the police must advise the suspect or defendant of the right to have an attorney present.[65] Otherwise, the defense attorney must be notified at least twenty-four hours before an inspection takes place.[66]

b. *Searches. (i) With Warrants.* Searches (*perquisizioni*), in contrast to inspections, are carried out for the purpose of securing evidence, fruits of the crime, and the accused for the criminal proceeding.[67] In addition, the police and the judicial authorities are not limited to mere visual observations, but may use their hands as well as technological mechanisms such as x-rays.[68] Nonetheless, the two are regulated in a similar manner. The general rule is that a judicial authority, a judge or a prosecutor, must issue a search warrant. More than mere suspicion is required for a search since the Code uses the term "*fondato motivo*"[69] which translates best to "well-founded grounds" for believing that such relevant evidence may be discovered or the defendant may be found in a particular place.[70] The warrant must also be supported by a hypothesis, or indication of the nature of the crime to which the objects or persons sought relate,[71] even if this only generally indicates the relationship between the suspected crime and the things sought. In this regard, the Supreme Court (*Corte di Cassazione*) quashed a search warrant on the grounds that the judge and prosecutor had only listed the penal code provisions they believed the defendant had violated, without indicating what types of things they expected to find in relation to those crimes.[72] The purpose of such a requirement is to ensure that searches are limited to the discovery of evidence to support criminal prosecution of a certain crime and not be permitted to become a tool for filing charges, or fishing expeditions.[73]

The judicial authority may carry out the search, or delegate this to the police with the same decree.[74] Where the prosecutor conducts the search he is to ask the suspect, if present, whether that person has a defense attorney and if not assigns a defense attorney who has the right to be present during the search.[75] Similar to when one must submit to a bodily inspection, where one is to be corporally searched, the Code allows the individual to have present someone he trusts, and requires that the search be conducted in a manner which is respectful of dignity and

65. C.P.P. arts. 365 & 364(3) provide that the defense attorney is to be told of an inspection conducted by the police or the prosecutor, respectively, however article 354(3) makes an exception for urgent or emergency inspections. See also D'Ambrosio at 247 and Cordero at 714.

66. C.P.P. art. 364(3).

67. C.P.P. art. 247(1); Fortuna at 393.

68. D'Ambrosio, at 229.

69. C.P.P. art. 247(1); Aniello Nappi, Guida al Codice di Procedura Penale 245 (6th ed. 1997).

70. This is similar to the standard for a fermo and for preventive detention discussed above in section A3. The Supreme Court has stated that a search warrant may not be based upon mere suspicions; rather, there must be "important circumstantial evidence pointing to a probability that the subject of the search will be found on the person or in the place to be searched." Cass. V, ord. 899 (May 23, 1992).

71. Nappi, at 245.

72. Cass. I, sent. 2379 (May 19, 1994).

73. See Giustino Gatti, Codice di Procedura Penale Annotato con la Giurisprudenza 247 (1997).

74. C.P.P. art. 247(3).

75. C.P.P. art. 365.

modesty.[76] Such bodily searches also include searches of those things which a person has in their possession, such as purses, luggage and the clothing worn by the individual,[77] as well as the trunk of a car.[78] In addition, before such a search, the individual must receive a copy of the search warrant.

As to searches of places, the Code also requires that the defendant, if present, as well as the person having access to the place, be given a copy of the warrant and told of their right to have an attorney present, or any trusted person.[79] Where none of these persons are present the copy of the warrant is delivered to a cohabitant, neighbor, or the superintendent of the building.[80] If no one is present, the police may file the copy of the warrant in their offices and post a notice on the door advising that a search has taken place. In any event, the absence of anyone at the place to be searched will not preclude a search.[81] Searches of places include not only places of residence, but also those places in which one conducts personal activity, including work or employment. This is clear from the Code because article 250 refers to searches of places generally, while article 251 refers specifically to places of residence when limiting the time of day such searches may be performed.[82] Article 251 provides that searches of residences and those "closed places adjacent" to residences may not begin before seven o'clock in the morning nor after eight o'clock in the evening, except in urgent situations. Courts have concluded that such "closed places adjacent" to a residence include trailers and the passenger compartments of cars parked nearby.[83] In contrast, searches of non-residential premises, such as barns and warehouses, may be conducted at any time. Furthermore, open places such as fields, streets or abandoned premises are not covered by the protections established for searches.[84]

(ii) *Warrantless Searches*. While the Code requires that warrants be issued before a search may occur, in certain circumstances the police may proceed on their own initiative. Article 352 provides an "exigent circumstances" exception: that where an individual is caught in the act of committing a crime (*in flagranza*)[85] or is someone who has escaped custody, the police may conduct a search of the person or of a place without having first obtained a warrant. The police must have grounds for believing that fruits of the crime, or other relevant traces are hidden on the person or in the place, or that a suspect or fugitive is hidden in the place searched.[86] This article also provides that police may conduct a warrantless search when executing an order of preventive detention, an order of imprisonment of a defendant, one who has been convicted of a crime for which arrest is mandatory or otherwise enumerated in article 380, or even one who has been stopped for crimes set out in that article. However, the article requires the same basis (*fondo*) for conducting such a search as for a search warrant as well as the existence of particularly

76. C.P.P. art. 249; See article 245(2) with regards to bodily inspections.
77. Fortuna, at 394; D'Ambrosio, at 228.
78. Fortuna, at 394.
79. C.P.P. art. 250(1).
80. C.P.P. art. 250(2).
81. Codice di Procedura Penale: Spiegato Articolo per Articolo 289.
82. Fortuna, at 395.
83. Cass. VI, sent. 2922, Nov. 5, 1990.
84. D'Ambrosio, at 231.
85. C.P.P. art. 382 includes also one caught immediately after the commission of a crime within the definition of in flagranza.
86. C.P.P. art. 352(1).

urgent circumstances which do not permit the delay of waiting for a warrant.[87] Where the police conduct a warrantless search they must transmit, without delay or at least within 48 hours, to the prosecutor information regarding where the search was conducted, as well as a written record of the search per article 357. The prosecutor then has 48 hours to validate the search if the requirements are satisfied.[88] In the context of a warrantless search the Code provides that although the defense attorney has the right to be present, the police are not required to notify the attorney of the search.[89]

(iii) *Searches of Defense Attorneys.* The Code of Criminal Procedure has one article devoted to the special protections applied to searches and inspections of defense attorneys. Article 103 provides that there are only two situations in which a search of a criminal defense attorney's office may occur. One is where the attorney, or one employed by the attorney, is a criminal defendant or where the purpose of the search or inspection is to discover traces or other materials effects of a crime or to find specific persons or things.[90] The protection is not limited to investigative activity relating to specific cases in which the defense attorney is employed, but includes all criminal cases of the defense attorney.[91] Furthermore, the protection is not limited to the offices of the defense attorney, but extends to other places where the attorney has direct access, such as the attorney's home.[92] Article 103 further provides that papers and documents relating to defensive work are not subject to seizure, unless they constitute fruits of the crime.[93] Similarly, this protection applies to documents relating to any defensive work, not simply that which involves the particular crime under investigation.[94] When a search, inspection or seizure is permitted, it must be performed by a judicial authority, a prosecutor or a judge, and the local forensics office must be notified and allowed to have a representative present during the activity.[95] Therefore, this is not an investigative practice which the prosecutor may delegate to the police. The purpose of such protections is to ensure that criminal defendants obtain effective representation.[96] In addition, the Code provides that in no event may conversations between a defense attorney and the client or expert witnesses be intercepted by wiretap or electronic eavesdropping.[97]

(iv) *Special Laws.* The above represents the rules under the Code of criminal procedure relating to searches. However, in Italy there are several "special laws" (*leggi speciali*) which expand the ability of the police to conduct searches and inspections, justified by the need to ensure public safety. The following are some examples. A law entitled *Public Safety* (*pubblica sicurezza*) gives police the authority to search any place, without a warrant, in which they suspect to find weapons, ammunition or explosive materials, even if their suspicions are based on mere circumstantial evidence.[98] Within at least forty eight hours of such a search the police

87. C.P.P. art. 352(2).
88. C.P.P. art. 352(4).
89. C.P.P. art. 356.
90. C.P.P. art. 103(1).
91. Cass. Sez. Un. November 12, 1993, Grollino.
92. Cass. Sez. Un. November 12, 1993, DeGasperin.
93. C.P.P. art. 103(2).
94. Cass. Sez. Un. November 12, 1993, Grollino.
95. C.P.P. art. 103(3).
96. Cass. Sez. VI, Oct. 27, 1992, sent. 3804.
97. C.P.P. art. 103(5).
98. R.D. June 18, 1931, n. 773, art. 41.

must notify the prosecutor, and even though the police need not notify the defense attorney, such attorney may be present at the search.[99] It appears that the standard for a search for weapons is not as strict as the "serious circumstantial evidence" required for detention, discussed above.[100]

Another law entitled *Prevention of Racketeering Conspiracy and Other Serious Crimes Dangerous to Society*,[101] allows the police to search vehicles and other means of transport, luggage and other personal effects[102] for the ransom proceeds of a kidnaping or weapons, ammunition, explosive materials, currency or other things of value which are the objects or fruits of enumerated crimes.[103] The enumerated crimes are racketeering conspiracy, and related crimes,[104] money laundering,[105] aggravated robbery,[106] aggravated extortion,[107] kidnaping,[108] and a crime which best translates as making economic or investment use of illegally obtained money or other things of value (*impiego di denaro, beni o utilità di provenienza illecita*).[109] Police may conduct such searches pursuant to this law where they have grounds for believing that they will find any of the things listed above, there are urgent circumstances which do not allow time to obtain a warrant, and the search is within certain activity planned to prevent or suppress the enumerated crimes.[110] The quantum of evidence required for a search under this law is stated as "well founded grounds" which appears to be less that the stricter standard for detention but more than required for a search for weapons. This means that an individual officer may not conduct a spontaneous search under this law.[111]

The law regarding *Narcotics and Psychotropic Substances—Prevention, Cure and Rehabilitation of Addicts*[112] similar to the law relating to serious crimes, gives law enforcement the authority to search vehicles and other modes of transportation, luggage and personal effects when such officials have "well founded grounds" to believe that they will find illegal narcotics.[113] In addition, the same requirements for the law described above also apply to these types of searches for drugs. Given these numerous exceptions to the warrant requirement, which largely swallow the rule, it appears that Italy's history of terrorism and organized crime, which considerably lengthened the road to reform, continues to limit personal guarantees, at least in regard to searches.[114]

---

99. C.P.P. arts. 352(4) and 356; D'Ambrosio at 235.

100. See sect. II A3, Supra.

101. Legge March 19, 1990, n. 55.

102. Another urgent anti-mafia law permits searches of buildings to turn up individuals who have evaded arrest, as well as weapons. D.L. June 8, 1992, n. 306, art. 25-bis.

103. Legge March 19, 1990, n. 55, art. 27.

104. C.P. art. 416-bis.

105. C.P. art. 648-bis.

106. C.P. art. 628(3).

107. C.P. art. 629(2).

108. C.P. arts. 289-bis, 620.

109. C.P. art. 648-ter.

110. Legge March 19, 1990, n. 55, art. 27(1).

111. D'Ambrosio, at 240.

112. D.P.R. October 9, 1990, n. 309.

113. D.P.R. October 9, 1990, n. 309, art. 103(2).

114. See Mario Chiavario, Procedura Penale: Un Codice tra "Storia" e Cronaca 64-65, 85-86 (1996) (discussing the history of the new Code of criminal procedure and the concerns that the new Code would be ineffective in fighting terrorism and organized crime).

(v) *Wiretaps.* The Italian Constitution provides that "Freedom and secrecy of correspondence shall be inviolable. They may be limited only by a judicial decision wherein the reasons are stated, under the guarantees established by law."[115] Articles 266-271 of the criminal procedure code set out the parameters for electronic monitoring for investigative purposes. The Code provides that such monitoring and recording of communications is allowed as to certain types of crimes, such as those punishable by more than 5 years imprisonment, including life imprisonment, crimes involving illegal drugs, weapons or explosive materials, and smuggling.[116] Second, the Code requires that the prosecutor obtain a judicial decree authorizing any such recordings and that the decree be based on serious suspicions (*gravi indizi*) of criminal activity and that it be absolutely necessary in order to proceed with the investigations.[117] However, the Code also provides that when the delay of waiting for a judicial order would seriously impair the investigations, the prosecutor may order the wiretap.[118] In such urgent situations the prosecutor must seek judicial validation (*convalida*) within 24 hours, and if the judge does not validate the prosecutor's order within 48 hours, the wiretap is essentially considered void *ab initio*, and the results may not be used.[119]

The police may record conversations by wiring an individual or by placing bugs in a particular place.[120] However, in order to monitor recordings in a place of residence there must be a "well-based belief that criminal activity is occurring therein."[121] The Constitutional Court held that a pen register comes within the provisions regarding wiretaps, thus imposing the same requirements.[122] Initially, a wiretap may remain in effect for only fifteen days after which it may be extended for intervals of fifteen days by judicial decree as long as the requirements stated above are still satisfied.[123] However, a special law concerning organized crime allows a wiretap to remain in place for forty days, and be extended for up to twenty days at a time upon the prosecutor's order which a judge must then validate.[124]

c.) *Seizures.* Article 252 provides that the objects found pursuant to a search are to be seized. The next thirteen articles set out the details regarding seizure of objects.[125] Seizures, along with inspections, searches and wiretaps are considered means of searching for evidence (*mezzi di ricerca della prova*). The criminal procedure code also allows for seizure or confiscation of objects for purposes other than evidentiary, however, the present discussion is limited to seizure for evidentiary purposes. Article 253 states that a judicial decree stating the supporting reasons may order the seizure of fruits of the crime (*corpo del reato*) and objects which are otherwise relevant to the crime. Examples of fruits of the crime include a weapon used in a homicide,[126] and a marked bill used in an illicit drug transaction, as well

---

115. Const. Art. 15. The translation is taken largely from Mauro Cappelletti et al., The Italian Legal System 284 (1967).
116. C.P.P. art. 266(1).
117. C.P.P. art. 267(1).
118. C.P.P. art. 267(2).
119. C.P.P. art. 267(2). The notion of "use" of evidence is discussed in section A5 below.
120. C.P.P. art. 266(2).
121. C.P.P. art. 266(2).
122. Cort. Cost. n.81/1993.
123. C.P.P. art. 267(3).
124. Legge, May 31, 1991, n. 152, art. 13(2).
125. C.P.P. arts. 253-265.
126. D'Ambrosio, at 318.

as the vehicle used by the defendant in the commission of drug trafficking.[127] As to objects which are relevant to the crime, the Supreme Court has held that this concept is broader than the definition of "fruits of the crime" but that there must nonetheless be a connection between the objects seized and the crime charged.[128] The court stated that this connection is to be determined on a case by case basis.[129]

As with inspections and searches, the police may conduct a seizure on their own initiative pursuant to article 354(2) where there are urgent circumstances. In such situations the police must then deliver to the prosecutor the written record of the procedure within forty-eight hours, for the prosecutor to validate the seizure. In addition, while the defense attorney has the right to be present, there is no requirement that the police notify the defense attorney of the seizure.[130] On the other hand, where the police act pursuant to a judicial decree and upon delegation of authority by the prosecutor the police must notify the suspect, if present, of the right to have an attorney present unless waiting for the attorney would result in undue delay of the seizure.[131]

The Code sets out specific rules regarding certain types of seizures. For example, as to seizures of objects in a bank, documents, account information or the contents of a safe deposit box, the Code provides that either a judicial authority or the police upon delegation may examine (or search) such things where the bank agrees to provide the authorities with this opportunity.[132] However, when a bank refuses this request, only the prosecutor may proceed with a forced seizure of the objects.[133] As to seizures of a suspect's correspondence and sealed envelopes, generally only a judicial authority may conduct such a seizure, thus providing additional protections for an individual's correspondence.[134] However, despite this additional protection, as well as the protections discussed above with respect to the limitations placed on searches of an attorney's office, the Supreme Court held that where attorney-client correspondence is discovered during a search of the suspect, neither the search or seizure is invalid.[135] In addition, a police officer may conduct such a seizure after receiving oral authorization, in cases of emergency, from a judicial authority.[136]

5. *Enforcing the Rules*

Article 191 of the Code includes a sweeping provision which states that "evidence acquired in violation of prohibitions established by law may not be used."[137] Further, that the parties may raise this issue at any stage in the proceedings and that the judge, *sua sponte* may declare evidence unusable.[138] Despite this broad language, in practice this provision has limited effect. First, as already discussed there

127. Cass. VI, May 21, 1992, n. 1794.
128. Cass. VI, Jan. 11, 1991, n. 32.
129. Id.
130. C.P.P. art. 365.
131. D'Ambrosio, at 319.
132. C.P.P. art. 248.
133. C.P.P. art. 248(2) and 255.
134. C.P.P. art. 254.
135. Cass. VI, June 27, 1995, n. 2588.
136. C.P.P. art. 353.
137. C.P.P. art. 191(1).
138. C.P.P. art. 191(2).

are a number of special laws which allow the police to conduct searches and seizures on their own initiative in several circumstances. Second, interpretations by the Supreme Court have narrowed the application of this provision in the context of searches and seizures by finding that the sanction only applies where there has been a violation of an express and specific prohibition.[139] While it is well-established that evidence obtained by torture or other violation of personal dignity is excluded from consideration for purposes of judgment, it is unclear the extent to which an illegally performed search affects evidence subsequently seized.[140] Some panels of the Supreme Court[141] have held that where the object seized is fruit or proof of the crime (*corpo del reato*),[142] or otherwise relevant to the crime, the police are required to seize such evidence under article 253 and therefore the illegitimacy of the search does not render the seizure illegitimate.[143] Such cases rely on the argument that searches and seizures have different requirements and are actions which are independent of each other.[144] Further, such cases rely on the fact that the police who conduct an illegal search are subject to prosecution under penal code article 609 which punishes public officials who conduct a search or inspection in abuse of their power with up to one year imprisonment.[145]

However, one panel of the Supreme Court has held that under the 1989 Code it is no longer possible to deny the connection between a search and a seizure.[146] In this case the court held that where the decree for the search was wholly lacking any reasons supporting the search, the subsequent seizure of documents discovered during a residential search was also illegitimate. The court reached this result, despite the fact that the documents seized were useful for subsequent investigations. This case represents not merely a departure from decisions of other panels, but also from the analysis used before the 1989 Code which required a court to find a close link between the illegal search and subsequent seizure on a case-by-case basis before holding the seizure illegitimate.[147]

The Supreme Court has recently had opportunities to clarify the issue en banc, but it has not succeeded.[148] In one case the court held that where a residential search was performed without a warrant and not pursuant to any code provision or special law permitting the police to act without a warrant the *search* was null.[149]

---

139. Cass. I, sent. 6922, June 11, 1992; Cass. I., sent. 1357, Feb. 4, 1994. Article 191 is not only an "exclusionary rule" but it also applies to how evidence is produced at trial. For example, where at trial a witness responds to a leading question by the party who called the witness, prohibited under article 499(3), the response may not be used for purposes of the judgment under article 191. Cass. I, sent. 3187, March 18, 1992.

140. Article 188 prohibits the use of methods or techniques designed to influence one's ability to remember or evaluate facts. See also Nappi, at p. 146; Cordero, at 584.

141. The Corte di Cassazione is divided into several criminal and civil panels. Royal Decree No. 12, Jan. 30, 1941, art. 67.

142. The definition of corpo del reato includes both fruit of the crime and corpus delicti. Francesco de Franchis, Dizionario Giuridico 590 (1996).

143. Cass. II, sent. 4827, May 2, 1995. See also Nappi, at 253.

144. Cass. VI, sent. 1557, May 22, 1991.

145. Id. See also Cordero, at 581–2.

146. Cass. V, ord. 899, May 23, 1992.

147. Francesca Maria Molinari, Invalidità del decreto di perquisizione, illegitimità del sequestro in Riv. Ital. Dir. Proc. Penale 1127, 1130 (1994).

148. See Nappi, at 253–4.

149. Cass. Sez. Un., sent. 5021, May 16, 1996.

The subsequent *seizure* of thirty-one grams of cocaine was not usable,[150] under article 191, unless it came within article 253 which permits the seizure of fruit of the crime or other evidence relevant to the crime, which it clearly did. The court reasoned that since the Code requires seizure of such evidence, the way in which it was obtained is irrelevant. In the opinion, the court makes a distinction between proof or evidence (*prova*) and means of finding evidence (*mezzi di ricerca della prova*). The Code itself categorizes inspections, searches and seizures as means of finding evidence.[151] The court then stated that article 191 refers to evidence, and a search is not evidence but merely a means or method of finding or acquiring evidence. The reasoning which holds that evidence constituting the *corpus delicti* must be seized and therefore the way in which it was discovered is irrelevant, dramatically narrows the language of article 191 and its usefulness as a curb on illegal searches, and yet is the prevailing interpretation.[152]

Even where there is a violation of a specific prohibition, evidence so seized may be used if it constitutes *corpo del reato*. For example, article 103 which sets out strict requirements for the inspection or search of a defense attorney's office, also states that "the results of inspections, searches, seizures or wiretaps obtained in violation of the preceding rules may not be used."[153] However, an exception is made for objects which constitute *corpo del reato*.[154]

Article 267, which sets out the requirements for wiretaps,[155] also has a specific provision which renders results of the wiretap unusable where the prosecutor fails to obtain timely judicial validation of a wiretap initiated by the prosecutor under urgent circumstances. Article 271 further provides that wiretaps performed in cases where they are not permitted or in violation of certain rules, may not be used.[156] In addition, the results of such wiretaps are to be destroyed unless the judge determines that these constitute *corpo del reato*.[157] Thus, while such evidence may not be relied upon for the verdict, it will not be destroyed. Moreover, the results may be used to support a request for preventive detention where the wiretap merely failed to conform to "formal" rather than "substantive" requirements.[158] In addition, the Supreme Court has held that where the results of a wiretap, otherwise unusable, provide the basis for a new *notitia criminis*, a subsequent wiretap, properly performed to investigate the new crime, is not affected by the illegitimacy of the prior wiretap.[159]

Thus it seems that with a very few exceptions, the broad language of article 191 has not been realized in application.

---

150. The Italian Code of Criminal Procedure uses the word "unusable" (inutilizzabilità) rather than "exclusion" (esclusione) indicating that the purpose behind these rules is to set out which evidence a judge may or may not rely on in reaching a judgment.

151. Book III, title III is entitled "Mezzi di ricerca della prova."

152. See Cordero, at 581–2; Nappi, at 256.

153. C.P.P. art. 103(7).

154. C.P.P. art. 103(2).

155. See supra.

156. C.P.P. art. 271(1).

157. C.P.P. art. 271(3).

158. Cass. I, sent. 4745, Jan. 27, 1992.

159. Cass. I, sent. 7759, July 11, 1994.

B. Lineups and Other Identification Procedures

The Code divides identification procedures into three categories: "summary information" (*sommarie informazioni*) as to the identity of an individual, pretrial identification of an individual which the prosecutor conducts (*individuazione*), and identification of an individual which a judge conducts at an evidentiary hearing or at trial (*ricognizione*).

Italian law requires that persons must respond to police requests for "summary information" regarding that person's identity.[160] All persons must provide basic information upon request. This information includes one's name, any alias or pseudonym, parents' names, date and place of birth, citizenship, residency, and profession.[161] The police may verify a suspect's identification by means of fingerprints, photographs, and other methods.[162] However, a potential witness may not be subjected to such procedures. While the police may collect and verify information regarding the identification of individuals, the prosecutor has the authority to conduct an *individuazione* of an individual.[163]

The prosecutor may proceed with such a pretrial identification parade if it is necessary for the immediate continuation of the investigations.[164] However, the Code does not specify the manner in which the prosecutor is to conduct the procedure, except to provide that where a witness may be intimidated or otherwise influenced by the subject to be identified, the prosecutor is to follow the precautions outlined in another section dealing with *ricognizioni* at a preliminary hearing or at trial.[165] Where the prosecutor conducts an *individuazione*, there is no requirement that defense counsel be present,[166] nor that there be a transcript of the procedure.[167] This identification procedure may be used to identify both persons and things, yet there is no requirement that the person or thing be physically present for purposes of identification; the prosecutor may use photographs or other such reproductions.[168]

Alternatively, the prosecutor may request that the judge for the preliminary investigations hold an evidentiary hearing (*incidente probatorio*) for the purpose of

160. Codice Penale (C.P.) art. 651 (imposes punishment of up to one month imprisonment or fine up to the equivalent of about $200.00 for refusal to furnish such information).

161. Ennio Fortuna, Manuale Pratico del Nuovo Processo Penale 513 (4th ed. 1995). See also Regio decreto, May 6, 1940, n. 635, art. 294 (requiring individuals to show their identification papers upon any request by the police).

162. C.P.P. 349(2).

163. C.P.P. art. 361. Under article 370, the prosecutor may delegate this procedure to the judicial police, however, the police may not act on their own initiative in this regard.

164. C.P.P. art. 361(1).

165. C.P.P. art. 214(2). Identification of a voice may also be done as part of this procedure.

166. In Sentenza n.265 (1991) the Constitutional Court declined to find article 361 unconstitutional for failing to require the presence of defense counsel. The Court affirmed that defense counsel must be present during preliminary investigative acts only as required by article 364; where the prosecutor engages in interrogations, inspections or confrontations. The reasoning of the Court was that the sole purpose of the procedure was investigatory and not for evidentiary purposes. See also, Franco Cordero, Procedura Penale 707 (3rd ed. 1995).

167. Fortuna, at 555.

168. Cordero, at 707.

conducting a *ricognizione*,[169] or wait until trial. In either case the judge conducts the procedure. If the judge performs the identification procedure the Code requires the judge to follow a specific method which may temper some of the negative aspects of the prosecutorial pretrial identification.[170] Specifically, the judge is to ask the person called to describe all the details the witness[171] remembers.[172] The judge next asks the witness whether he has already been asked to identify the person or object in question, if before or after the alleged crime he has seen a picture or other reproduction, if the person or thing was described to him before, and other questions which might impact the credibility of the identification.[173] The judge must then obtain at least two other persons who look as much like the suspect or defendant as possible, including how they are dressed, and allow the suspect or defendant to select his place among them before recalling the witness.[174] The Code provides that identifications of objects are to be conducted in the same way,[175] as are identifications based on senses other than sight.[176] Where more than one person is called to identify the same object or person, the judge is to conduct each procedure separately.[177] In addition, defense counsel must be present at both evidentiary hearings[178] and trial.[179] Furthermore, the Code requires that each step in the procedure be recorded in the transcript or the entire procedure and its results are void.[180]

C. Interrogation

The Code makes a clear distinction between suspects and defendants. An individual becomes a defendant (*imputato*) only after the prosecutor has initiated formal criminal proceedings.[181] Until there are formal charges, a person who is being investigated by the police or the prosecutor is referred to as a suspect (*indiziato* or *persona sottoposta alle indagini preliminari*).[182] The purpose of this distinction appears to be to maintain consistency with provisions of the Code which distinguish the different phases of the process, as well as to avoid the stigma attached to the word defendant where one has not been formally charged.[183] Despite this distinc-

169. C.P.P. art. 392(1)(g). A suspect may also request an evidentiary hearing. C.P.P. art. 392(1).

170. C.P.P. arts. 213-217.

171. I have used the term witness here, but a co-defendant might also be called upon to make an identification, and such a person is not considered to be a "witness" because one accused of a crime is not allowed to give sworn testimony. Nuovo Dizionario Giuridico 1716 (4th ed. 1996) (defining testimone as third persons called to provide factual information).

172. C.P.P. art. 213(1).

173. Id.

174. C.P.P. art. 214(1).

175. C.P.P. art. 215.

176. C.P.P. art. 216.

177. C.P.P. art. 217.

178. C.P.P. art. 401.

179. C.P.P. art. 484(2).

180. C.P.P. art. 214(3).

181. C.P.P. art. 60.

182. .C.P.P. art. 61.

183. Fortuna, at 204.

tion, the Code provides that unless otherwise indicated, a suspect is to have the same rights and guarantees as a defendant.[184] The Code also sets out the rules governing the use of statements made by a suspect or a defendant.

1. *Before Formal Charges are Fileda*

a. *Declarant Not Yet a Suspect.* As to someone who is not yet a suspect but makes statements to the police,[185] once such a person reveals incriminating evidence, the police are required to interrupt the individual and warn him that investigations may begin against him, and that he has a right to name a defense attorney.[186] Such pre-warning statements may not be used against the person who made them for purposes of the judgment, but may be used against others incriminated by the declarant. If the declarant from the beginning of the questioning should have been considered either a defendant or a suspect, the statements may not be used against either the suspect or an incriminated by the suspect.[187] Nonetheless, the declarant or those incriminated by him may still be the object of investigations based on the same statements.[188] Thus, incriminating statements made when the declarant should have been treated as a suspect from the beginning of the questioning may be used for investigative but not evidentiary purposes.

b. *Statements by a Suspect.* Where a suspect refuses to provide identification information to the police, the police may bring the individual to the police office and detain him for a period of time absolutely necessary to identify the person, but in any event for no more than 12 hours.[189] If they believe he has given false information he can also be held up to twelve hours.[190] In addition, the Code requires that the police immediately notify the prosecutor that, and the time at which, an individual was brought to the police offices for identification purposes. If the prosecutor believes that it is unnecessary to detain the person for this purpose, the prosecutor is to order the police to release the individual.[191]

Before the police may request other information useful for the investigation of a crime (*sommarie informazioni*) from a suspect, who has not been stopped or arrested, the police must invite the individual to name a defense attorney or to have counsel appointed.[192] The police must then notify counsel of the questioning before it occurs and the defense attorney must be present during the questioning.[193] If the suspect does not name an attorney, article 350 refers the police to another article in the Code which sets out the procedure for assigning a defense attorney to sus-

184. C.P.P. art. 61.

185. C.P.P. art. 351. This article gives police the authority to obtain information relating to the crime from any person who may provide information useful to the investigation.

186. C.P.P. art. 63.

187. C.P.P. art. 63(2). The Supreme Court has stated that this prohibition on the use of such statements extends only to those who were involved with the declarant in related or connected crimes, not to those involved in different crimes with the defendant. Cass. Sez. Un., sent. 1282 (Dec. 13, 1996).

188. Ennio Fortuna et al., Manuale Practico del Nuovo Processo Penale 207 (4th ed. 1995).

189. C.P.P. art. 349(4).

190. Id.

191. C.P.P. art. 349(5).

192. C.P.P. art. 350(2).

193. C.P.P. art. 350(3).

pects and defendants.[194] There is nothing to indicate that a suspect may waive the right to have counsel present. Where a suspect makes statements in the absence of counsel, such statements may not be used at trial except for purposes of impeachment.[195] In addition, the individual must be warned of his right to remain silent.[196] The Code also requires the police to prepare a transcript of the questioning.[197]

The Code distinguishes between two types of statements made in the absence of counsel. First, are those statements made at the scene of the crime or immediately thereafter in response to police questions which are necessary for the immediate continuation of the investigations.[198] The Code states that responses to such questions may not be documented nor used (even to impeach), unless defense counsel happened to be present.[199] Though the Code does not state that such non-use is limited to trial, the Supreme Court has so limited this provision. For example, such responses may be used for purposes of imposing precautionary measures (*misure cautelari*),[200] or determining whether the alternate procedure, summary trial (*giudizio abbreviato*),[201] may be used.[202]

Second are spontaneous statements made by the suspect after the police had advised him that he has a right to an attorney.[203] As mentioned earlier, these may not be used in the prosecutor's case-in-chief,[204] should the case go to trial, except for purposes of impeachment.[205] The Supreme Court has held that such statements may be used for other, non-investigatory purposes. For example, statements made by the defendant to the police in the absence of counsel may be considered by a judge who is evaluating whether to impose precautionary measures (*misure cautelari*),[206] or whether to issue a search warrant.[207] Furthermore, such statements may be used against a co-conspirator.[208] Thus, it appears that the limitation on the use of statements made to the police without counsel present applies only to the prosecutor's case-in-chief and only where the case is disposed of by a trial rather than by one of the alternative procedures.

194. Article 97 provides that court-appointed counsel (difensore di ufficio) is to come from a list which the court has. Subpart 4 of this article provides for substitute court-appointed counsel where the attorney previously appointed does not appear and counsel is required for the particular procedure or act. Such substituted counsel may be any defense attorney who is immediately available. In fact, this author observed numerous occasions where the bailiff went out into the court halls to find an attorney to represent a defendant whose court-appointed attorney had failed to appear.

195. C.P.P. art. 350(7). See also C.P.P. art. 503(3) (provides for impeachment of the person under examination at trial).

196. C.P.P. art. 64(3).

197. C.P.P. art. 357(2)(b). Articles 134–142 set out the requirements for documenting interrogations and other acts.

198. C.P.P. art. 350(5).

199. C.P.P. art. 350(6).

200. Cass. I, sent. 4725 (Oct. 13, 1995).

201. Discussed infra section IIIA(4b).

202. Cass. I, sent. 697 (Jan. 30, 1997).

203. C.P.P. art. 350(7).

204. C.P.P. art. 350(7).

205. C.P.P. art. 503(3).

206. Cass. III, sent. 2230 (July 2, 1996); Cass. IV, sent. 1249 (June 25, 1992).

207. Cass. III, sent. 166 (Feb. 25, 1995).

208. Cass. IV, sent. 5144 (May 21, 1996).

The police may conduct this type of questioning when the case has not yet been turned over to the prosecutor. Once the prosecutor takes charge of the case, police questioning may occur only upon delegation of this power to the police by the prosecutor.[209] At the interrogation the suspect is told that an attorney will be appointed to assist the suspect (*difensore di ufficio*), or that he may nominate his own attorney (*difensore di fiducia*).[210] Whether defense counsel is appointed or is private, the prosecutor must provide notice to such counsel at least 24 hours before an interrogation is to take place,[211] unless in situations of absolute urgency where there is reason to believe that any delay could prejudice the search for or security of sources of evidence in which case the prosecutor must notify defense counsel without delay, or at least in a timely manner.[212] If the interrogation proceeds without counsel (even in "absolute urgency"), it is considered null and statements obtained from the suspect may not be used against the suspect, but may be used against other suspects.[213] However, if the case proceeds to trial, and the defendant does not appear (*contumace*), is absent, or refuses to be questioned, upon request, the transcripts of such statements made by the defendant to the prosecutor, the judge for the preliminary investigations, or the police who are acting upon the prosecutor's delegation, are read at trial and thus become part of the trial dossier.[214] The Code does not state that the prosecution may use such statements for impeachment purposes.[215] The suspect has the right to refuse to answer questions regarding the crime under investigation,[216] but this will be noted in the transcript of the interrogation.[217]

As to general rules governing interrogations, the Code provides that methods or techniques likely to violate a suspect or defendant's "freedom of self-determination" (*libertà di autodeterminazione*) or to alter one's ability to remember and evaluate facts, are prohibited even where the defendant consents to such.[218] This prohibits techniques such as hypnosis or use of drugs,[219] as well as methods of using promises or threats; each answer must be made intentionally and consciously.[220] (It is unclear whether deceit is permitted.)

Following an arrest or stop (*fermo*) of an individual, the prosecutor must notify the judge for the preliminary investigations (*giudice per le indagini preliminari* or *g.i.p.*)[221] who will schedule a hearing to decide whether to validate[222] the arrest

---

209. C.P.P. art. 65 states that judicial authorities (the prosecutor and the judge) may interrogate a suspect or defendant. Article 370 provides that the prosecutor may delegate to the police the authority to perform certain "acts" including interrogation.

210. C.P.P. art. 364(2).

211. C.P.P. art. 364(3).

212. Even if defense counsel has not yet received notice, counsel may be present at the interrogation. C.P.P. art. 364(5).

213. Cass. VI, sent. 3735 (Nov. 19, 1994).

214. C.P.P. art. 513(1).

215. C.P.P. art. 514 (Aside from the express exceptions stated in the Code, no statements may be read into the record at trial.)

216. C.P.P. art. 64(3) (requiring the prosecutor to advise the suspect of this right).

217. C.P.P. art. 65(3).

218. C.P.P. art. 64(2) and art. 188.

219. Codice di Procedura Penale: Spiegato Articolo per Articolo 111 (1996).

220. Franco Codero, Procedura Penale 239 (3rd ed. 1995).

221. C.P.P. art. 390(1).

222. C.P.P. art. 390(4).

and whether to order that the individual be held pursuant to the provisions governing preventive detention.[223] During this hearing, defense counsel must be present.[224]

2. *After Defendant is Formally Charged (Declarant is a Defendant)*

As mentioned above, the label "defendant" (*imputato*) is not acquired until the prosecutor has decided to exercise his or her power to initiate criminal proceedings. At this point, the prosecutor presents to the judge for the preliminary investigations a request to either hold a preliminary hearing in order to decide the sufficiency of the evidence to proceed to trial, drop the charges (*archiviazione*)[225] or to proceed to one of the special proceedings discussed below. At the preliminary hearing the defendant may request to be interrogated.[226] This interrogation is governed by the rules set out earlier[227] regarding the prohibited methods and techniques and the requirement that the defendant be told of his right to remain silent and of his right to have an attorney appointed if he does not have a private attorney. The sections of the Code involving questioning by the police or interrogation by the prosecutor refer to the person under investigation, or the suspect (*persona sottoposta alle indagini* or *indiziato*), indicating that once one becomes a defendant (*imputato*) neither the police or the prosecutor may further question or interrogate the defendant except during court proceedings such as the preliminary hearing or at trial, at the option of the defendant.

3. *Enforcing the Rules*

Article 191, discussed above regarding invalid searches and seizures, is also pertinent to the issue of statements obtained from the defendant. The Code contains specific provisions regulating the circumstances under which statements may not be used. For example, article 63 provides that where an individual not yet considered a suspect makes incriminating statements before the police have interrupted him and warned him that such statements may result in an investigation against him and that he may have an attorney, such statements may not be used against the individual, but may be used for investigatory purposes.[228] The Supreme Court has also held that such statements may be used against another.[229] However, where the individual should have been treated like a suspect from the beginning,[230] the statements may be used against neither the declarant nor others.[231] The court has narrowed this second rule such that it does not prohibit the use of statements against others who are not involved in the same crime or in a related crime with the declarant. Therefore, such statements may be used against a third person for purposes of a different crime.[232]

223. C.P.P. art. 390(5), see also articles 272 et seq.
224. C.P.P. art. 391(1).
225. C.P.P. art. 408.
226. C.P.P. art. 421 (2).
227. C.P.P. arts. 64 and 65.
228. C.P.P. art. 63(1).
229. Cass. VI, sent. 6007, May 30, 1991; Cass. VI, sent. 5226, May 20, 1993.
230. C.P.P. art. 63(1).
231. Cass. VI, sent. 6425, June 1, 1994.
232. Cass. Sez. Un., sent. 1282, Dec. 13, 1996.

While the Code limits the use at trial of spontaneous statements or other statements made without counsel present to the police, such statements may be used in a hearing on the issue of preventive detention.[233] In addition, such statements may be used in the alternative procedure, abbreviated trial (*giudizio abbreviato*).[234]

III. Court Procedures

Article 111 of the Italian Constitution expressly establishes the *Corte di Cassazione* (Supreme Court), and article 134 the *Corte Costituzionale* (Constitutional Court). The Constitution provides that, except as to decisions of the military courts in time of war, "recourse shall always be allowed to the Supreme Court, on the ground of violation of law, against judgments as well as orders affecting personal liberty."[235] This court is divided into panels of judges and is to ensure the uniform interpretation of the law.[236] The Constitutional Court has jurisdiction over "disputes regarding the constitutionality of laws of the State and the Regions."[237] The other courts are established by legislative acts.

There are three courts of first instance and their jurisdiction is based upon the type of crime involved.[238] The *Corte di assise* has jurisdiction over the most serious crimes; those punishable with life imprisonment, the most severe punishment under Italian law, or those crimes for which the maximum sentence is not less than 24 years, except for attempted homicide.[239] This court is composed of six lay judges and two professional judges.[240] The *Pretura* is another court of first instance having jurisdiction over the least serious offences, those punishable by a maximum of no more than four years, or a monetary fine, or a combination of prison and fine.[241] The *Pretura* is composed of a single professional judge. Finally, the *Tribunale*, the third court of first instance has jurisdiction over all crimes not coming within the jurisdiction of either the *Corte di Assise* or the *Pretura*.[242] Three professional judges make up the *Tribunale*.

There are two intermediate courts of appeal, the *Corte di assise di appello* and the *Corte di appello*. The *Corte di assise di appello* is made up of two professional judges and six lay judges and hears appeals from the *Corte di assise*.[243] The *Corte di appello* consists of three professional judges and hears appeals from the *Tribunale* and the *Pretura*.[244]

---

233. Cass. I, sent. 4725, Oct. 13, 1995.

234. Cass. I, sent. 697, Jan. 30, 1997. Giudizio abbreviato is discussed infra.

235. Cost. Art. 111(2).

236. Royal Decree No. 12, Jan. 30, 1941, art. 65.

237. Cost. Art. 134.

238. Article 4 provides that to determine the jurisdiction of the different courts it is necessary to consider the punishment set out for the crime, excluding enhancements for recidivism and the circumstances of the crime, unless the law establishes a different type of punishment for certain aggravating circumstances.

239. C.P.P. art. 5(1).

240. Legge n. 287, April 10, 1951, art. 3.

241. C.P.P. art. 7.

242. C.P.P. art. 6(1).

243. C.P.P. art. 596(2); Legge n. 287, April 10, 1951, art. 4.

244. C.P.P. art. 596(1); Royal Decree n.12, Jan. 30, 1941, arts. 2–3.

In addition to these jurisdictional aspects of the judiciary in criminal cases, there is a burgeoning body of law regarding issues akin to recusal of judges. Provisions in the criminal procedure code relate to recusal of judges based on personal interests or where the judge or an immediate family member was harmed by the crime, for example.[245] Article 34 also sets out situations of "incompatibility" (*incompatibilità*). This provision provides that where a judge has taken part in a judgment at one instance or phase of the proceedings, the same judge may not participate as a judge in the same case at another phase of the proceedings.[246] Specifically, this article prohibits a judge from participating in a trial when that judge has issued a conclusive order or ruling in the preliminary hearing, provided for an immediate trial,[247] issued a conviction by penal decree,[248] or ruled on an appeal against a sentence of dismissal.[249] The purpose of this provision is to ensure that the defendant will be tried before an impartial judge who has not had an opportunity to prejudge the defendant based upon the judge's prior involvement in the case. While article 34 sets out the specific instances in which a judge may not participate in the defendant's trial, the Constitutional Court has expanded this list by finding the provision unconstitutional to the extent that it does not include these other instances. For example, the Constitutional Court has held that the where judge for the preliminary investigations (*g.i.p.*) has rejected a motion to dismiss charges, that same judge may not then preside over a request for an abbreviated trial (*giudizio abbreviato*).[250] In addition, the court has held that the *g.i.p* who imposes preventive detention may not be a judge at trial.[251] In all, the Constitutional Court has issued about fifteen opinions which expand the application of article 34 in order to ensure thatjudges who decide the merits of a case, whether at trial or by means of an abbreviated procedure, are impartial.[252]

A. Pretrial

Criminal proceedings under the Italian code begin with the notice of a crime (*notizia di reato*) which may be received by either the police[253] or the prosecutor.[254] The police or the prosecutor may receive the notice of a crime from the reporting of a crime (*denuncia*) by an individual who has knowledge of a crime,[255] or by a public official who discovers that a crime occurred while such official was carrying out his or her duties.[256] Notice might also come from the victim of the offense in the form of a *querela*.[257]

---

245. C.P.P. arts. 36–37.
246. C.P.P. art. 34(1).
247. This refers to giudizio immediato which is discussed infra, sect. A 4d.
248. Decreto penale is discussed infra, sect. A 4e.
249. C.P.P. art. 34(2).
250. Corte cost., Nov. 12, 1991, n. 401.
251. Corte Cost., Sept. 16, 1995, n. 432.
252. See Nappi, at 69-72.
253. C.P.P. art. 55.
254. C.P.P. art. 330.
255. C.P.P. art. 333.
256. C.P.P. art. 331.
257. Article 425 of the Code of criminal procedure provides that where a querela is required, but lacking, the prosecution may no longer be pursued.

Receipt of the notice of the crime marks the beginning of the investigative phase, the aspects of which are discussed in section II above. Upon registration of the name of the person suspected of the crime, the prosecutor has six months to complete the investigations.[258] As to certain serious crimes, such as murder, terrorist acts, or illegal manufacture, importation or sale of weapons,[259] the investigative period is one year.[260] Article 406 allows for extensions of the investigative period, but also provides that notice of such a request must be served on the suspect, thus the investigation loses its secrecy unless the crime involved is mafia conspiracy, kidnaping for ransom, or conspiracy to traffic in illegal narcotics.[261] As to these crimes the secrecy of the investigation may be maintained. Nonetheless, as to most crimes the maximum period for the preliminary investigations is eighteen months or two years for the more serious crimes.[262]

1. *Initial Court Appearance (Evidentiary Hearing)*

As indicated earlier, a judge called the *giudice per le indagini preliminari* (*g.i.p.*) is a creation of the 1989 Code and is the judicial authority who oversees the preliminary investigation. One proceeding which the *g.i.p.* conducts during the investigative phase is the evidentiary hearing (*incidente probatorio*).[263] The main purpose of such a hearing is to preserve as early as possible testimony by one who may not be available at trial or one whose testimony might be compromised by threats of violence or by offers or promises of money for false testimony. As discussed earlier, a judge might also conduct an identification (*ricognizione*) of an individual at an evidentiary hearing where there is urgent need.[264] The Code requires the presence of both the prosecutor and the defense attorney.[265] The suspect need not be present unless his presence is required in order to perform a procedure such as a *ricognizione*, in which case, the judge may order the compulsory presence of the suspect.[266]

2. *Charging Instrument (or Dismissal)*

Upon conclusion of the preliminary investigative stage, the prosecutor must determine whether there is sufficient evidence to request that the defendant be bound over for trial (*rinvio a giudizio*), or that the charges be dismissed (*archivazione*).[267] In order to fulfill one important goal of unclogging the criminal justice system,[268] the 1989 Code broadened the requirements for dismissals. Dismissals were previously limited to cases where the notice of the crime was manifestly groundless.[269]

---

258. C.P.P. art. 405(2).

259. The crimes to which the longer investigative period applies are listed in subpart 2(a) of article 407.

260. C.P.P. art. 405(2).

261. C.P.P. art. 406(3bis).

262. C.P.P. art. 407(1-2).

263. C.P.P. arts. 392-404.

264. C.P.P. art. 392(1)(g).

265. C.P.P. art. 401(1).

266. C.P.P. art. 399.

267. C.P.P. art. 405(1).

268. See Gazzetta Ufficiale della Repubblica Italiana, Oct. 24, 1988, n. 250, supp. Ord. 106-108 (Report of the Preliminary Project).

269. See Nappi, at 312.

The current Code permits dismissal where the "elements acquired during the preliminary investigation are insufficient to support a conviction."[270] In addition to expanding the definition of the groundlessness of the charges generally, the Code also specifies other reasons for dismissing a case under article 411. These are where there has been a general amnesty or pardon as to the particular crime,[271] prosecution is barred by the statute of limitations,[272] the *querela* has been withdrawn,[273] or upon the defendant's payment of a monetary fine where the offense is an infraction (*contravvenzione*).[274] In addition, article 411 provides for a dismissal where the law does not criminalize the conduct, and where a condition for proceeding (*condizione di procedibilità*) is lacking.[275] Where the judge denies the request for a dismissal, the judge sets the date for the preliminary hearing.[276] In addition, the judge may order the prosecutor to conduct further investigations, indicating the date by which these must be completed.[277]

Where the prosecutor does not request dismissal, he requests instead that the defendant be bound over for trial (*rinvio a giudizio*).[278] Included in this request are the following: general identification information about the defendant, statement of the facts of the crime, including aggravating and mitigating circumstances, an indication of the sources of evidence, and a request that the judge enter judgment on the motion to bind the defendant over for trial.[279] The judge then sets a date for the preliminary hearing (*udienza preliminare*), which must take place within 30 days of the request.[280]

3. *Preliminary Hearing*[281]

The purpose of this pretrial phase is to filter out cases which are not likely to result in a conviction and to serve as a bridge between the investigative phase and the trial for those cases where the case proceeds to trial.[282] The Code provides that the preliminary hearing is to occur in the *camera di consiglio* which translates to the judge's chambers. This means that the hearing is not conducted in open court.[283] At the hearing the judge will have the written documentation provided by the prosecutor, and upon determining that all parties are present and were properly notified, will allow the prosecutor to present a summary of the results of the preliminary investigation and an argument as to why these support binding the defen-

---

270. D.lgs., July 28, 1989, n. 271, art. 125 (Le norme di attuazione, di coordinamento e transitorie del codice di procedura penale) (this law translates approximately to "temporary rules pertaining to giving effect to the new Code and coordinating it with other laws").
271. C.P. art. 151.
272. C.P. art. 157.
273. C.P. art. 152.
274. C.P. art. 162.
275. Such situations include where a querela has not been filed and it is required. Other such conditions are set out in Book V, Title III of the Code of Criminal Procedure, articles 336-346.)
276. C.P.P. art. 409(5).
277. C.P.P. art. 409(4).
278. C.P.P. art. 405(1).
279. C.P.P. art. 417.
280. C.P.P. art. 418(1).
281. The Code does not provide for a preliminary hearing in the pretura. Stefani, at 3.
282. Nappi, at 336.
283. C.P.P. art. 420; de Franchis, at 470.

dant over for trial.[284] The defendant may request to make an unsworn statement, then the attorneys of any civil party[285] may make an argument and lastly the defense attorney presents an argument. The Code provides that the prosecutor and defense attorney are each permitted one rebuttal argument.[286] If, at this point, the judge believes that it is possible to make a decision on the request to bind the defendant over for trial, the preliminary hearing is declared closed. Alternatively, the judge may indicate to the parties additional or incomplete areas for investigation, and accept such evidence from the parties where it supports committing the defendant to trial or indicates that a judgement of inability to proceed (*non luogo a procedere*) is required.[287] In addition, if during the course of the preliminary hearing it appears that the charges filed are inconsistent with the facts presented, the prosecutor may modify the charges.[288]

Upon conclusion of the preliminary hearing the judge is to deliberate immediately and subsequently announce a judgment of inability to proceed, or commitment of the defendant to trial.[289] Where the judge decides that the case may not go further, the judgment is essentially one of acquittal (*non luogo a procedere*). Article 425 provides that a sentence of *non luogo a procedere* is required when any of the conditions for proceeding to trial are lacking, that the crime did not occur or that the defendant did not commit it, that the act did not constitute a crime, or that the defendant is not criminally responsible (*non imputabile*),[290] or otherwise not punishable (*non punibile*).

4. Special Proceedings

Book VI of the Code sets out five special proceedings designed to provide alternatives to trial in an effort to streamline the criminal process and unclog the courts. Two of these proceedings permit a judgment without trial, application of punishment upon the request of the parties, or agreed punishment (*applicazione della pena su richiesta delle parti*),[291] and abbreviated trial (*giudizio abbreviato*).[292] Two other special proceedings bypass the preliminary hearing phase bringing the defendant to trial directly. These are called the "direct trial" (*giudizio direttis-*

284. C.P.P. arts. 420 and 421(2).

285. The victim of the crime (persona offesa dal reato), as well as the person who suffered monetary damages (soggetto al quale il reato ha recato danno), may choose to become a civil party (parte civile) to the criminal proceedings, pursuant to articles 90 and 74 respectively of the Code of criminal procedure, rather than filing a separate civil suit. Often the victim and the person suffering damages are one and the same, but in the event they are not, for example where the decedent in a homicide is the victim while those suffering damages are the surviving relatives, the Code allows both to become civil parties. Others who may be joined in the criminal action are the person or entity responsible for the defendant (responsabile civile), and the person responsible for paying any criminal fines imposed on an insolvent defendant (persona civilmente obbligata per la pena pecunaria). See C.P.P. arts. 83 and 89, respectively.

286. C.P.P. art. 421(2).

287. C.P.P. art. 422(2).

288. C.P.P. art. 423.

289. C.P.P. art. 424. Where it would not be possible to announce the judgment right away, the Code gives the judge 30 days from the preliminary hearing to issue the judgement.

290. The Penal Code provides that one who is not capable of forming the requisite intent is not chargeable. C.P. art. 85.

291. C.P.P. arts. 444–448.

292. C.P.P. arts. 438–443.

simo),[293] and the "immediate trial" (*giudizio immediato*).[294] The fifth proceeding, penal decree (*procedimento per decreto*), which existed under the old Code only as to cases in the *pretura* but has been expanded under the 1989 Code to case in the *tribunale* as well, permits a sentence of payment of a monetary fine, one-half the statutory minimum, without either a preliminary hearing or trial.[295]

a. *Applicazione della pena su richiesta delle parti.* This mechanism has been called "bargaining as to the punishment" (*patteggiamento sulla pena*) indicating that it had its roots in American plea bargaining, but is really only similar in concept "imposition of a sentence agreed upon by the parties, without trial."[296] It differs in the following respects. First, this mechanism is only applicable to less serious crimes. Article 444 provides that the defendant and the prosecutor may request a substituted sanction, such as probation or a monetary fine, a sentence of imprisonment reduced by one-third, or a combination of a substituted sanction and imprisonment, as long as the sentence of imprisonment, after considering all the circumstances and the one-third reduction, does not exceed two years. Second, the defendant, without the prosecutor's agreement, may request the judge to impose a particular sentence under this procedure. The prosecutor's refusal to consent to the requested judgment will preclude use of this procedure. However, upon conclusion of the trial, if the judge finds that the prosecutor's refusal was unjustified, and the defendant's request appropriate, the court is to impose the sentence originally proposed by the defendant.[297] Third, use of this procedure does not require the defendant to admit guilt. While the Code provides that application of the requested penalty is equivalent to a conviction, it also states that the conviction is extinguished in five years for more serious crimes (*delitti*) or two years for infractions, if the defendant does not commit another serious crime or a similar infraction.[298] Finally, the incentive for opting for this procedure is limited to the one-third reduction in sentence specifically provided by the Code.[299]

Due to the principle of mandatory prosecution under article 112 of the Italian Constitution, the prosecutor has very little room to negotiate with respect to the charge under this procedure of party-agreed punishments. Nonetheless, where a particular article of the penal code sets out alternative sentencing possibilities depending upon the seriousness of the offense, the prosecutor and the defendant might agree that the defendant's conduct was less serious, thus permitting a final sentence under two years. For example, the crime of receipt of stolen goods under article 648 of the penal code sets out a term of imprisonment of two to eight years. The next paragraph provides that in less serious cases, usually where the value of the goods is lower, the term of imprisonment is a maximum of six years, but no minimum sentence is required.[300] In this type of situation, the prosecutor and the defendant might agree that the case is less serious, and present their agreed upon sentence using the paragraph which does not require a minimum.

---

293. C.P.P. arts. 449–452.
294. C.P.P. arts. 453–458.
295. C.P.P. art. 459(2).
296. Relazione del Progetto Preliminare, Gazz. Uff., Oct. 24, 1988, n.250, supp. ord. N.2, 104.
297. C.P.P. art. 448(1).
298. C.P.P. art. 445(2).
299. C.P.P. art. 444(1).
300. C.P. art. 648(1 and 2).

The defendant and the prosecutor individually, or jointly, may request the judge to approve an agreed-upon sentence in lieu of trial right up until the opening of the trial.[301] Furthermore, where the judge denies a request, the parties may continue to make a request up until this point in the procedure. The Code provisions governing party-agreed punishments do not set out the standard by which the judge is to determine whether the request is appropriate. However, the Constitutional Court has held that article 444 is unconstitutional to the extent that it "does not expressly permit the judge to consider whether the agreed sentence promotes the constitutional goal of rehabilitation."[302] Furthermore, the court stated that the judge is required to state written[303] reasons for accepting the agreed sentence and those reasons must be more than simply that the parties have agreed.[304] The judge evaluates the party-agreed sentence on the basis of the evidence accumulated this far in the prosecutor's dossier.[305] However, the court may not modify the request in any way, but must accept all aspects of the request or reject it.[306] Nonetheless, the court retains the duty to dismiss the case under article 129 of the criminal procedure code if it determines that the events charged did not occur, that the defendant did not commit them, that they do not constitute a crime, that prosecution is barred, or that a condition for proceeding is lacking.[307]

b. *Giudizio Abbreviato.* This mechanism has been dubbed bargaining as to the procedure, even though no bargaining occurs. In contrast to the party-agreed mechanism, only the defendant can request an abbreviated or summary trial, though the prosecutor's consent is required.[308] Typically, the defendant makes this request either before or at the beginning of the preliminary hearing.[309] Upon such a request the court is to determine whether it is possible to decide the matter "on the state of the evidence" (*allo stato degli atti*), that is based upon the evidence acquired by the prosecutor during the preliminary investigations.[310] The judge will receive the written record, hear oral arguments from the prosecutor and the defense attorney, and perhaps a statement from the defendant, before adjourning to decide whether it is possible to adjudicate the case, and if so, the verdict and sentence. Where the judge accepts the request and finds the defendant guilty the sentence which would otherwise be imposed is reduced by one-third.[311] In contrast to the party-agreed sentence mechanism, the summary trial procedure is available as to all crimes except those punishable by life imprisonment.[312]

---

301. C.P.P. art. 446(1).
302. Corte cost., July 2, 1990, n. 313.
303. Const. Ant. III.
304. Id.
305. Nappi at p. 489.
306. Nappi, at 495–96.
307. C.P.P. art. 129(1).
308. C.P.P. 438(1).
309. As discussed infra the defendant may also request this procedure in response to direct trial or immediate trial requested by the prosecutor. See Carmine Covino, "Patteggiamento" e Giudizio Abbreviato 125–126 (1995) (referring to the use of summary trial described in the text as "typical" and the use as described in this footnote as "atypical").
310. C.P.P. art. 440(1).
311. C.P.P. 442(2).
312. As originally enacted, the Code provided for a reduction to thirty years where the penal code required life imprisonment. The Constitutional Court subsequently found this unconstitutional because the drafters of the criminal procedure code went beyond their delegated authority. Corte, cost. April 23, 1991, n. 176.

As originally drafted, the provisions regarding summary trial did not indicate the effect of the prosecutor's refusal to consent to the procedure. However, the Constitutional Court held that if, following trial and a conviction, the court determines that the refusal to consent was unjustified, the court can grant the defendant a one-third reduction in the sentence imposed.[313] In addition, the Constitutional Court held that where the *g.i.p.* denied the request for summary trial, and after a trial and conviction the trial court determines that the case could have been adjudicated *allo stato degli atti*, the trial court may grant the defendant the one-third sentence reduction. Thus, the Constitutional Court has added judicial review of both the prosecutor's refusal to consent to and the *g.i.p.*'s refusal to accept a defendant's request for summary trial.

The mechanism of party-agreed punishment is less burdensome than the summary trial, but applies to a very narrow category of crimes. Abbreviated trial applies to all crimes but seeks to ensure a greater degree of inquiry as to the defendant's guilt. Thus it appears that the drafters of the new Code sought to balance efficiency concerns as well as concerns regarding the accuracy of criminal convictions in coming up with two alternatives to trial. However, the abbreviated trial has also been called the "inquisitorial alternative" because it involves the use of investigative acts as proof or evidence and eliminates the protections of a trial in open court.[314] In contrast to the ordinary trial there is no oral or live presentation of evidence, except perhaps a statement by the defendant. Rather, the judge decides guilt or innocence and the sentence based on the evidence contained in the prosecutor's dossier.

c. *Giudizio Direttissimo*. The mechanism of direct trial allows a case to proceed to trial, bypassing the preliminary hearing phase. This procedure also omits the pretrial phase involving the submission of lists of evidence and witnesses to be presented at trial. Only the prosecutor may request this procedure and only in one of the following situations: 1) where the defendant was arrested *in flagranza*, in which case the prosecutor may bring the defendant before a trial judge to request a validation of the arrest and a request for direct trial;[315] 2) where the defendant was arrested *in flagranza* and the arrest was validated by a *g.i.p.*, in which case the prosecutor has fifteen days to request direct trial;[316] or 3) where during the course of interrogation the defendant confesses, in which case the prosecutor issues a summons requiring the defendant to appear in court within 15 days.[317] In addition, where the arrest has not been validated, if the defendant consents, the case may be immediately set for trial.[318] In these situations, evidence of guilt is overwhelming, making conviction likely, thus justifying skipping the preliminary hearing.

The Code provides that cases resolved by direct trial must proceed according to the Code provisions for trial.[319] In addition, the judge is to warn the defendant of the right to request either a summary trial or party-agreed sentence,[320] thus giv-

313. Corte cost., Feb. 8, 1990, n. 66. Subsequently the court extended this to situations where summary trial was requested in response to the procedures allowing the case to proceed directly to trial. Corte cost., April 18, 1990, n. 183.

314. Nappi, at 465.

315. C.P.P. art. 449(1).

316. C.P.P. art. 449(4).

317. C.P.P. art. 449(5).

318. C.P.P. art. 449(2).

319. C.P.P. art. 451(1).

320. C.P.P. art. 451(5).

ing the defendant an opportunity to receive a reduction in punishment where evidence of guilt is strong.

d. *Giudizio Immediato.* Immediate trial also bypasses the preliminary hearing phase, but not the pretrial phase. The prosecutor may request this procedure where evidence of guilt is obvious, the individual has been interrogated,[321] and less than ninety days have passed since the registration of the notice of the crime.[322] Use of immediate trial is not limited to the situations listed for direct trial.[323] Rather, the important requirement is that either guilt or innocence be unequivocal.[324] The judge, without a hearing, decides whether to set the case for trial. Similar to the trial pursuant to the direct trial procedure, under immediate trial, the judge must inform the defendant of the right to request either the party-agreed punishment mechanism or summary trial in response to the prosecutor's request.[325] The Code also allows the defendant to request the procedure of immediate trial.[326]

e. *Procedimento per Decreto.* The resolution of cases by penal decree had been limited to cases in the *pretura* under the prior Code, but has now been extended to cases in the *tribunale* under the 1989 Code. The penal decree procedure resolves the case without either a preliminary hearing or a trial, but only where a monetary fine is sought, even where the relevant penal code procedure would allow for imprisonment.[327] The procedure involves the prosecutor's request for the imposition of a penal decree which the judge accepts or rejects.[328] Upon the judge's acceptance, a conviction is entered against the defendant.[329] The defendant then has fifteen days to demand a trail.[330] The fine sought may amount to a reduction of up to one-half of the minimum fine permissible under the statute, thus encouraging defendants not to demand a trial.[331]

5. *Discovery*

Where the matter is not resolved by one of the special procedures or by dismissal, the case is set for trial. At this point, the prosecutor transmits to the court the dossier for trial which includes documentation showing that the requirements for proceeding exist, the written record of "non repeatable acts" performed by both the police and the prosecutor, transcripts of any evidence acquired by an evidentiary hearing and by letters rogatory outside of Italy, *corpus delicti*, and other objects relevant to the crime.[332] This is different from the prosecutor's dossier which includes all other documentation, acts and evidence.[333] The defense attorney

321. C.P.P. art. 453(1).
322. C.P.P. art. 454.
323. See sect. III A4c, Supra.
324. Nappi at p. 458.
325. C.P.P. art. 456(2).
326. C.P.P. art. 453(3). A defendant is likely to request this where he or she is confident of an acquittal. Nappi, at 455.
327. C.P.P. art. 459(1).
328. C.P.P. art. 459(1).
329. C.P.P. art. 460.
330. C.P.P. art. 461(1).
331. C.P.P. art. 459(2).
332. C.P.P. arts. 416, 431; Eraldo Stefani, L'Accertamento della Verità in Dibattimento: La Difesa e L'Accusa nella Formazione della Prova 3–4 (1995).
333. See C.P.P. art. 433.

has the right to view the contents and make copies of the prosecutor's dossier as well as the trial dossier.[334] While there is no defense dossier, the Code does provide a mechanism by which the defense attorney can insert the results of any defense investigation into the prosecutor's dossier.[335]

6. *Pretrial Acts*

After the order committing the defendant to trial, the Code sets out procedures to be followed before trial. These are controlled primarily by the president of either the *tribunale* panel or the panel of the *Corte di assise.*[336] One of these is the examination of evidence and the prosecutor's dossier by the parties, discussed above.[337] Another provision allows for the taking of evidence before trial in situations of urgency, a procedure somewhat similar to the evidentiary hearing which might occur during the preliminary investigatory stage.[338] Article 468 requires parties to submit lists of those witnesses, experts and technical consultants they intend to call to testify at trial, and an indication of the circumstances to which they will testify.[339] Upon request, the president authorizes by decree the summons (*citazione*) of such witnesses, excluding any testimony prohibited by law, and that which is redundant.[340] In addition, this article provides that a party may request the admission of transcripts of evidence from another criminal proceeding along with the list of persons that party intends to call at trial.[341] Finally, the court may order a dismissal pursuant to article 469, providing yet another filter in an effort to streamline and unclog the system.

B. Trial[342]

1. *Nature of Trial*

One of the three significant changes under the 1989 Code discussed earlier is the nature of the trial.[343] Under the new Code, the parties are given a greater role while the role of the court is dramatically reduced.[344] The trial is open to the public and the Code requires that evidence be presented orally rather than through written summaries as under the prior Code.[345]

---

334. C.P.P. arts. 433(2) and 431(1), respectively.

335. C.P.P. art. 367. This article allows the defendant to submit what amounts to a brief (memoria). See de Franchis, Dizionario Giuridico 971. Such a brief may include evidence discovered by the defense during its investigations. Stefani, at 6.

336. See supra discussion regarding the different courts. The Code sets out in articles 549-567 procedures which are peculiar to cases in the pretura, most significantly is the elimination of the preliminary hearing.

337. C.P.P. art. 466.

338. C.P.P. art. 467.

339. C.P.P. art. 468(1).

340. C.P.P. art. 468(2).

341. C.P.P. art. 468(4bis).

342. Cost. Art. 25(1) (Italy, 1948) ("No one shall be denied the right to be tried by his natural and lawfully appointed judge") Cappelletti, at 286.

343. See supra Introduction.

344. Stefani, at xii.

345. C.P.P. art. 471(1) (trial is open to the public); Law No. 81 of Feb. 16, 1987, Raccolta Ufficiale delle Leggi e dei Decreti della Repubblica Italiana I 220, art. 2, directive 2 (adoption of the oral method).

After certain introductory procedures, the prosecutor begins by concisely stating the facts supporting the charge and indicates the evidence which he seeks to have admitted. Next, the attorneys for any civil parties and the defense attorney indicate the facts they intend to prove and request the court to admit such evidence.[346] Requests for the admission of evidence is for evidence not set out in the list required under article 468 prior to trial. Such evidence may nonetheless be admitted where there the requesting party could not have made the request earlier.[347]

The president of the relevant panel informs the defendant of the right to make declarations at any point during the proceedings as long as such comments are relevant to the charge and do not unduly hinder the trial.[348] The prosecutor then calls the state's witnesses in the order in which these where initially listed.

The testimony is presented in a direct and cross-examination format conducted by the parties, though the judges may ask questions of the witnesses as well. The Code prohibits the use of leading questions by the party who called the witness.[349] While the presentation of the evidence is mainly in the hands of the parties, the presiding judge may interrupt to ensure that the questions are relevant, the responses are genuine and that the examination is conducted in a manner which is respectful of the individual. In addition, the Code permits the president to order, sua sponte, the consideration of new sources of evidence.[350] The Constitutional Court overruled an objection to this provision in which the argument was that the new Code puts the responsibility for evidence in the hands of the party.[351] The court refused to find that the accusatory procedures had changed the goal of the trial to the ascertainment of a formal or procedural truth. Rather, the court declared that the goal remains that of determining the actual or material truth, and that it is the responsibility of the impartial judge to ensure that such truth comes out.[352]

While the Code provisions seem to envision a trial that proceeds from beginning to end over the course of as many consecutive days as needed, trials are regularly begun, cut short and then continued two to three months later. Therefore, many trials end up being broken up into three or more "hearings" over the course of six months to one year. Judges seem concerned that their dockets will become overcrowded if they heard only one trial over the course of two or more consecutive days.[353] However, it is ironic that one important goal of the new trial procedures is to further the principle of orality, yet where the trial is broken up in this way, judges will have to resort to the written record since they are unlikely to remember the testimony from two to three months earlier.

The standard used for deciding the case is the "free conviction of the judge" (*libero convincimento del guidice*),[354] which is common in countries with a civil law tradition. The Code requires that the verdict and sentence be based on a ma-

---

346. C.P.P. art. 493.
347. C.P.P. art. 493(3).
348. C.P.P. art. 494(1).
349. C.P.P. art. 499(3).
350. C.P.P. art. 507.
351. Corte Cost., March 26, 1993, n. 111.
352. Id.
353. This is based on the author's observations and conversations with judges, prosecutors and defense attorneys at the Tribunale in Rome during the fall of 1996.
354. C.P.P. art. 192(2).

jority vote, when the case is heard by a panel of judges.[355] In the event of an evenly split vote, which is possible in the *Corte di assise*,[356] the decision more favorable to the defendant prevails.[357] The Constitution requires that the court then prepare a written judgment stating the reasons supporting the verdict and sentence.[358]

a. *Guilty Pleas. See* sect. III 4, *supra.*

2. Defendant

The Italian Constitution declares that "everyone shall have the inviolable right of defense in every phase and stage of any legal proceedings."[359] At trial, the Code states that the defendant is to appear as a free person, except to the extent that certain precautions against flight or violence are necessary.[360] As indicated above, the defendant has the right to make statements relevant to the charges at any time during the proceedings. However, the defendant may not give sworn testimony.[361] The prosecutor may call the defendant to be examined, but the defendant may refuse to be examined upon taking the stand. Where the defendant does not appear for the trial, or refuses to submit to questions, the judge, upon request of a party, is to order the reading of statements made by the defendant to the prosecutor, to the police upon delegation by the prosecutor, or to the judge during the preliminary investigation or the preliminary hearing.[362]

3. Lawyers

A defendant may name no more than two attorneys of his choice (*difensore di fiducia*),[363] or may have one appointed (*difensore di ufficio*) from a list compiled by the *Consiglio dell'ordine forense*, a type of bar or legal association.[364] A 1990 law provides that the State will pay for the legal expenses of indigents whether the counsel is selected by the defendant[365] or appointed by the court.[366] However, if the offense is a misdemeanor (*contravvensione*), the State will not pay the legal fees, unless the misdemeanor is joined with or connected to a crime (*delitto* or *reato*).[367] As discussed earlier, the new Code creates a more active role for the defense attorney with the use of examination and cross-examination of those giving statements to the court. In addition, the defense attorney has the power to engage in investi-

355. C.P.P. art. 527(3).
356. See supra sect. III.
357. C.P.P. art. 527(3).
358. Const. Art. 111.
359. Cost. Art. 24(2), Cappelletti, at 286.
360. C.P.P. art. 474.
361. C.P.P. art. 197.
362. C.P.P. art. 513(1). This provision was recently amended to prohibit the use of these statements against others unless such persons have consented. Legge, 1997, n. 267, in Guida al Diritto, N. 30, p.13 (Aug. 9, 1997).
363. C.P.P. art. 96(1).
364. C.P.P. art. 97(2). See also de Franchis at 560 (translating the term).
365. Legge, July 30, 1990, n. 217, art. 9.
366. Id., art. 8.
367. Id., art. 1(8).

gatory acts to discover evidence favorable to the defendant.[368] However, since the Code does not provide for a defense dossier, the results of such investigations must be included in the prosecutor's dossier, pursuant to article 367 discussed above,[369] or, where the attorney's client is still only a suspect (not yet bound over for trial) such information may be presented directly to the judge.[370]

In addition to increasing the role of the defense attorney at trial, the new Code similarly increases the role of the prosecutor. However, the prosecutor remains part of the judicial branch.[371] Despite an unsuccessful attempt to separate the careers of judges and prosecutors,[372] the debate still continues and the tensions inherent in having an adversarial trial system where one "party" is also considered a member of the "neutral" judiciary have yet to be resolved. Notably, in political corruption cases the power of the prosecutors is most criticized.[373]

4. *Judges*

Both prosecutors and judges are considered members of the judiciary (*magistratura*).[374] Thus, both take the same entrance examinations, have the same salary, and may move from one branch to the other.[375] To be eligible to take the examination, one must be between the ages of 21 and 30 and satisfy certain "physical and moral requirements."[376] The rather rigorous entrance examination is part oral and part written and covers "subjects such as civil, Roman, criminal and administrative law...[and] constitutional, ecclesiastical, international, labor, and social welfare law,...civil and criminal procedure."[377] The examination scores are then ranked and vacant posts are assigned based on the scores. However, before taking a post one must first serve a one-year apprenticeship rotating among prosecutors and judges. Advancement depends upon the availability of positions and is based on se-

---

368. The norms for putting into effect, coordinating and making the transition to the new Code of Criminal Procedure, attached to Decreto Legislative July 28, 1989, n. 271, art. 38(1) (Hereinafter, disp. att.).

369. See supra sect. III A 5.

370. Decreto legislativo, July 28, 1989, n. 271, art. 38(2bis), as amended by legge Aug. 8, 1995, n. 332, art. 22. Article 18 of this law amended article 335 of the criminal procedure Code to provide notice to a suspect of the fact that he is being investigated, except as to certain types of crimes. C.P.P. art. 335(3 & 3bis).

371. See supra n.4 and accompanying text.

372. Disegno di legge, Sept. 30, 1996, n. 1383.

373. See e.g., Vittorio Bufacchi, The Success of 'Mani Pulite': Luck or Skill? in Italy: Politics and Policy 189, 194 (Robert Leonard & Rafaella Nanetti, eds. 1996) (discussing the "unorthodox methods used by Milan magistrates"). On the other hand, this author observed a case involving possession of illegal drugs for distribution where the defendant had had several court-appointed attorneys by the time of the closing arguments phase of the trial. The prosecutor urged the Tribunale to consider the fact that this was a case which really should have been resolved by summary trial, entitling the defendant to a one-third sentence reduction. This mechanism is only available upon request of the defendant, who in this case was apparently not advised of this.

374. Cost. arts. 107(5), 112.

375. Ottavio Campanella, The Italian Legal Profession, 19 J. Legal Prof. 59, 83–84 (1994-95).

376. Id., at 84–85 (quoting G. Leroy Certoma, The Italian Legal System 72, W.E. Butler ed., 1985).

377. Id.

niority and merit, which can include the timely disposition of cases as well as scholarship, especially to the higher courts. Judges may be dismissed for cause but otherwise tenure continues until the age of 70. Since prosecutors and judges are both members of the *magistratura* it is possible for them to go from one branch to the other.

5. Victims

The victim of a crime has the right to name an attorney for representation.[378] One who is unable to afford an attorney is entitled to one paid by the state.[379] A victim also has a right to receive notification as to certain facts involving the case,[380] has the right to ask the prosecutor to conduct an evidentiary hearing,[381] receive notice of such,[382] and to attend such a hearing where the victim must examine a witness.[383] Furthermore, the victim has the right to submit briefs and suggest elements of proof.[384] When a victim decides to become a civil party to the criminal action the victim will be represented by counsel and have an opportunity to present evidence and to cross-examine witnesses.[385]

C. Appeals

Article 111 of the Italian Constitution states "recourse shall always be allowed to the Court of Cassation on the ground of violation of any law, against judgments as well as sentences affecting personal liberty, whether pronounced by courts of ordinary or of special jurisdiction."[386]

The Code uses the umbrella term of *impugnazioni* for different types of appellate review of criminal judgments. Under this heading are procedures for an appeal (*appello*),[387] recourse to the Court of Cassation (*ricorso per Cassazione*),[388] and the extraordinary remedy of revision (*revisione*).[389] As discussed in section III above, appeals are heard by the *Corte di assise di appello* and the *Corte di appello*. This intermediate appellate review is considered a trial proceeding of second instance (*secondo grado di giudizio*)[390] because such appeals include not only issues of law but also those of fact.[391] On appeal the court may review the evidence presented at the trial or may hear the introduction of new evidence upon request of a party, or

378. C.P.P. art. 101.
379. Legge, July 30, 1990, n. 217, art. 1(1).
380. See e.g., C.P.P. art. 341 (victim has the right to be notified of the time and place of non-repeatable technical assessments).
381. C.P.P. art. 394.
382. C.P.P. art. 398(3).
383. C.P.P. art. 401(3).
384. C.P.P. art. 90(1).
385. C.P.P. art. 505.
386. Cost. Art. 111(1), Cappelletti, at 305.
387. C.P.P. arts. 593-605.
388. C.P.P. arts. 606-628.
389. C.P.P. arts. 629-647.
390. See Nappi, at 665.
391. C.P.P. art. 581(1c); Codice di Procedura Penale: Speigato Articolo per Articolo 670 (1996).

on its own motion.[392] Thus, the judgment at trial is not afforded a status of finality.

Consistent with this lack of finality, the Code permits appeals by the defendant or the prosecutor of convictions as well as dismissals.[393] The Italian Code provides for different types of dismissals such as a declaration of innocence (*assoluzione*),[394] and where a condition for proceeding is lacking.[395] Thus a defendant might appeal one form of an acquittal for a more favorable form. After a decision by the *Corte di Appello*, one may appeal to the Supreme Court as to errors of law, as discussed below.

1. *Ineffective Assistance of Counsel*

There is nothing in the Code to allow this type of claim on appeal. However, the Supreme Court has stated that the prosecutor has an interest in appealing a conviction or acquittal in order to obtain the exact application of the law, even if this favors the defendant, thus ensuring that the defendant does not suffer the adverse effects of a judge's error.[396] This is another example of the tensions created by the shift to an adversarial trial system while the prosecutor's continue to be part of the judiciary.

2. *Other Grounds of Appeal*

Recourse may be made to the Supreme Court (*Corte di Cassazione*) for issues of law, such as incorrect application of the law, failure to take certain evidence, and failure of the court to set out reasons justifying the result, or the complete illogic of such reasons.[397] The Supreme Court has the power to reverse a judgment without remand in the following situations, *inter alia*, where the act committed does not constitute a crime, for jurisdictional defects, where a judicial order is not authorized by law, or the conviction was based on mistaken identity.[398] The Court may also amend the decision or the punishment.[399] The Supreme Court also reviews denials of requests for revision (*revisione*) from the *Corte di appello*.[400]

3. *Collateral Attacks*

The intermediate appellate court also has jurisdiction over requests for revision (*revisione*).[401] This extraordinary remedy is a collateral attack of an otherwise final conviction only where there is new evidence which alone, or in connection with evidence introduced at trial, demonstrates that the convicted person must be ab-

392. C.P.P. art. 603(1).
393. C.P.P. art. 593(1).
394. C.P.P. art. 530(1).
395. See supra sect. III A 3.
396. Cass. Sez. Un., sent. 6203, June 23, 1993.
397. C.P.P. art. 606.
398. C.P.P. art. 620.
399. C.P.P. art. 619.
400. C.P.P. art. 634(2).
401. C.P.P. art. 633(1).

solved,[402] or the conviction was based on false or fabricated evidence.[403] This remedy is not available for a condemned individual who seeks a more favorable dismissal or a lesser punishment.[404]

---

402. C.P.P. art. 630(1c). By absolved, the Code intends that where the prosecution should not have proceeded per article 529, the defendant was innocent per article 530, or prosecution is barred by the statute of limitations under article 531. C.P.P. art. 631.

403. C.P.P. art. 630 (1d).

404. C.P.P. art. 629.

Chapter 9

Russian Federation

Catherine Newcombe[1]

I. Introduction

This chapter offers a broad overview of a criminal justice system in transition. At present, the legal system of the Russian Federation is a hybrid of sorts: old rules and practices reminiscent of the Soviet era co-exist with new, democratic procedures based on the rule of law. This overview attempts to provide a practical and necessarily general understanding of Russia's fledgling criminal justice system, with an emphasis on areas of significant progress as well as those presenting serious challenges.

As heir to the Continental European Inquisitorial model,[2] the primary source of criminal law and procedure in Russia is found in its codified system of laws, consisting principally of the Criminal Code (*Ugolovnii Kodeks RSFSR*) and the Code of Criminal Procedure (*Ugolovno Protsessualnii Kodeks RSFSR*). Although a new Criminal Code (CC) came into force on January 1, 1997, a new Code of Criminal Procedure (CCP) remains in draft form, awaiting debate and passage by the Russian Parliament.[3] The draft CCP is expected to become law sometime in 1999, or

1. Ms. Newcombe received her LL.B from McGill University (1993) and her B.A. from Amherst College (1988). She is an attorney with the American Bar Association's Central and East European Law Initiative (ABA/CEELI) where she works on the DOJ/CEELI Criminal Law Reform Project, a partnership between the U.S. Department of Justice and ABA/CEELI focused on criminal law reform in Central/Eastern Europe and the former Soviet Union. The author would like to thank Mr. Vasiliy Vlasihin, Counsel to ABA/CEELI's Moscow Office, Dr. Vladimir Brovkin of the Center for Study of Transnational Crime at American University, Mr. Nikita Filatov, Esq. of St. Petersburg, and Mr. Peter Roudik of the Library of Congress for their assistance in preparing this chapter.

2. Criminal law and procedure in contemporary common law (accusatorial) and continental/civil law (inquisitorial) jurisdictions represent a combination of both legal traditions. However, historically, "[t]he principle features [of the inquisitorial system] include first, attenuation or elimination of the figure of the private accuser and appropriation of that role by public officials; and second, the conversion of the judge from an impartial referee into an active inquisitor who is free to seek evidence and to control the nature and objectives of the inquiry. In addition, the relative equality of the parties ...[is] drastically altered...the contest is between the individual (the accused) and the state." John Henry Merryman, The Civil Law 127 (2nd ed., 1985).

3. Russia has a federal criminal justice system, and thus, both the CC and the CCP are federal laws. As of the writing of this chapter, the draft CCP has passed the first of three readings by the

perhaps later. The CCP currently in force dates back to the Soviet Era[4] but has been heavily amended so as to give effect to changes accompanying the fall of the USSR.

The Constitution of the Russian Federation[5] (RF Constitution) also contains several articles connected to criminal procedure, as well as various provisions securing civil liberties. Specifically, it guarantees the right to freedom and personal inviolability (Art. 22); the privacy of telephonic and mail communications (Art. 23); and the inviolability of the home (Art. 25). It also establishes a presumption of innocence (Art. 49); the right to qualified legal counsel (Art. 48); the right to a jury trial in certain cases (Art. 47); as well as prohibitions against double jeopardy (Art. 50) and self-incrimination (Art. 51). Further, the RF Constitution requires a judicial decision in order to conduct a search or seizure, as well as to arrest, take into custody, or detain an individual (Art. 22). A transitional provision of the Constitution, however, provides that the current procedures for the latter events (arrest, custody, and detention) will continue in effect until the adoption of a new Criminal Procedure Code implementing the constitutionally-mandated changes.[6] Hence, members of the Russian judiciary have yet to acquire the decision-making powers in these important matters.

As is the case in other civil law systems, judicial decisions have no precedential value in Russia and thus are not technically a source of law. Nonetheless, the Supreme Court of Russia has the authority to issue "Guiding Explanations" for lower courts on specific areas of the law, including criminal law and procedure. These opinions do not provide interpretations of the law but rather focus on its application with the goal of establishing some sort of consistency in judicial decision-making. In practice, these explanations are followed by all Regional and District Courts as well as affected state agencies and officials.[7] As such, they are arguably a source of law in Russia.[8]

The primary participants in the Russian criminal justice process are the procurator,[9] investigator, representative of an Agency of Preliminary Investigation or In-

---

State Duma (the Lower House of the Russian Parliament). A second reading is currently scheduled for sometime during the Fall of 1998. All references to the CCP or Criminal Procedure Code refer to the CCP currently in force. The Fall 1997 version of the Draft CCP Code is the version of the Draft CCP used in this chapter. It is referred to as the Draft Criminal Procedure Code or draft CCP. A copy of this draft is on file with the author.

4. The CCP was passed on October 27, 1960.

5. The Constitution of the Russian Federation was ratified on December 12, 1993.

6. *See* Article 6, The Constitution of the Russian Federation (1993), Second Part, Concluding and Transitional Provisions.

7. For a more detailed discussion of "Guiding Explanations," *See* T. Foglesong, "Habeas Corpus or Who Has the Body? Judicial Review of Arrest and Pretrial Detention in Russia," 14 Wis. Int'l L.J. 541, 568–9 (1996). With the exception of the appellate courts, lower courts are not legally bound by the "Guiding Explanations." However, the guidelines explicitly urge compliance by all lower courts, and in practice, such compliance exists.

8. In addition to the criminal and criminal procedure codes, rules promulgated by the Ministry of Justice, the Procuracy, and other law enforcement agencies are also considered sources of criminal law in Russia.

9. The 1995 Law on the Procuracy of the Russian Federation defines the powers of the Procuracy in Russia today. The elimination of the Procuracy's supervision over the Judiciary by amendments to the law in 1992, significantly reduced the power of the Russian Procuracy from that which existed during the Soviet era. For more specific information on the Russian Procuracy, *See* Law on the Procuracy of the Russian Federation (November 24, 1995), Sobranie Zakonadatel'stvo RF, No. 47 (1995). *See also*, Russia: Law Amending Law on RF Prosecutor, FBIS-SOV-96-017-S (January 25, 1996).

quiry,[10] judge, defense counsel (*advokat*)/defender (*zashchitnik*), accused/defendant (*obvinaemyi/podsudimyi*), and victim (*poterpevshiye*) or victim's representative.[11] Procurators are essentially prosecutors. They represent the government in court and also supervise and prepare the records of the preliminary investigation[12] — the dossier (*delo*) or case file[13] — which forms the basis of the government's case against the defendant. Additionaly, in more serious cases, such as murder, the Procuracy is required to conduct the investigation.[14] Investigators are lawyers[15] who conduct and supervise the investigation of a criminal matter. Although procurators exercise supervisory authority over them, criminal investigators are authorized to undertake a number of investigative activities, including making an arrest, ordering a search and seizure, compelling document production, and calling witnesses and experts. They also document such activities in the dossier.[16] Representatives of Preliminary Investigation and Inquiry Agencies are responsible for the actual investigative legwork, such as interviewing witnesses and inspecting crime scenes.[17] Finally, in Russia, victims are considered parties to criminal proceedings. A lasting legacy of both Tsarist and Soviet Russia, however, is that the procurator continues to stand at the top of the criminal justice system in terms of influence and legal authority — followed by the investigator, the judge, and defense counsel. Improvements in the status of judges and defense attorneys are being made, albeit slowly.

A criminal case may be initiated based on sufficient indicia of crime, whether acquired, for example, by means of a crime scene investigation, confession, or a citizen complaint. Subject to the overall supervision of the Office of the Procurator General, a procurator or investigator may formally issue a case initiation decree.[18] In some instances, a court may also issue a case initiation decree. Next, depending

---

10. The Agencies of Preliminary Investigation and Inquiry are listed in Articles 125 and 117, respectively, of the current CCP.

11. In Russia, suits arising out of claims for material damages caused by criminal activity are merged with the actual criminal proceeding. Hence, civil plaintiffs and defendants are also parties to Russian criminal cases. Thus, when a verdict and sentence are issued, civil damages may also be awarded. *See* Article 29 of the current CCP.

12. *See* Articles 211–213 of the CCP.

13. "The dossier is actually a complete record of the pretrial proceedings, and it informs the judges, the defense attorney, and others about the testimony of key witnesses and the evidence that is to be presented. The judge who reads the dossier ahead of time knows fairly well what is going to happen during the trial." Erika Fairchild, Comparative Criminal Justice Systems 127 (1993).

14. According to the current CCP, the Procuracy conducts the preliminary investigation of offenses, such as murder, kidnapping, rape, banditry, computer crimes, as well as crimes committed by judges, prosecutors, and law enforcement officers.

15. *See* Foglesong, *supra* note 7 at pp. 551–553.

16. Criminal investigators may be from the Ministry of Interior (MVD), the Federal Security Service (FSB), the Federal Service of Tax Police, or the Procuracy depending on which of these agencies has the statutory authority to investigate the particular crime in question. *See* Article 127 of the CCP. *See also* Arrest and Detention section.

17. These agencies consist of several law enforcement agencies, including the MVD and FSB. In essence, they are the Russian equivalents of police officers and detectives.

18. See Article 116 of the CCP. They may also refuse to initiate a case. *See* Article 113 of the CCP. In May of 1995, Russia's Constitutional Court held that an individual has the right to contest the decision of a procurator to close a case. Unfortunately, the Court's opinion does not address whether a person has the right to contest a decision not to open a criminal case. *See* Torture

on the type of crime, an inquiry (*doznaniye*) or a preliminary investigation (*predvaritelnoye sledsviye*) is conducted by representatives of Agencies of Inquiry (*e.g.* police) or Investigation (*e.g.* criminal investigators), respectively. [19] The vast majority of cases involve a preliminary investigation.[20]

The 60-day preliminary investigation period, which is frequently extended by procurators,[21] is the time frame in which investigators and representatives of the Agencies of Preliminary Investigation conduct searches and seizures, interrogate suspects (*podozrevaemyiye*) and/or accused persons (*obviniaemyiye*),[22] interview witnesses, and compile other evidence on which to base an indictment. Also during this time, the CCP permits law enforcement officials, under certain circumstances, to detain suspects as well as to apply other "measures of restraint" (*meri presecheniye*) against accused persons.[23] Preliminary investigations are essentially secret proceedings that are closed to the public. The preliminary investigation procedures discussed below govern the investigation of all cases, whether ultimately tried before a judge or a jury.[24]

Defense counsel and the accused may also collect evidence during the preliminary investigation but are not legally required to do so. In reality, few defense attorneys actually conduct their own independent investigations during this stage of a criminal proceeding largely because the law gives them very limited rights of investigation.[25] Under the current CCP, suspects and accused persons and/or their counsel must petition the agencies conducting the preliminary investigation in order to obtain evidence. Of course, defense attorneys may file objections to im-

---

in Russia: This man-made Hell (Amnesty International, April 1997) (EUR 46/04/97) 6 (hereinafter cited as "Amnesty").

19. The CCP specifically excludes the requirement of a preliminary investigation for some types of criminal acts, such as simple battery and defamation. *See* Article 126 of the current CCP. In those cases, a more brief Inquiry is conducted by representatives of Inquiry Agencies. *See* Articles 117–120, 363, and 414–416 of the CCP.

20. An abbreviated form of prosecution called "Protocol Form" (*Protokolnaya Forma*) is available for a number of minor crimes (such as assault and battery) where the identity of the perpetrator is known. In short, the police or another Agency of Inquiry investigate the crime (i.e. take statements from victims and witnesses, examine crime scheme, etc.). Based on the information gathered during the Inquiry, the head of the Inquiry Agency formulates the charge(s) which is then forwarded to the appropriate procurator for review. The procurator then has the discretion to either dismiss the case, forward it for preliminary investigation, or send it directly to court. *See* Articles 414–419 of the CCP.

21. *See* Article 133 of the CCP. According to Article 133, district procurators (among others) have the authority to extend a preliminary investigation for up to three (3) months; regional procurators and others of equal status may extend the preliminary investigation for up to six (6) months in cases of "special complexity"; and the Procurator General of the Russian Federation or his deputy may authorize extensions beyond six (6) months but only in "exceptional" cases. Unfortunately, little practical guidance exists as to what types of cases fall into the categories of "special complexity" and "exceptional." In practice, it appears to be purely a matter of procuratorial discretion. Further, in practice, such investigatory time frames are often violated by procurators claiming burdensome caseloads.

22. *See* discussion in *Interrogation* section *infra*.

23. *See* Articles 90 and 122 of the CCP as well as Articles 93–108 of the draft CCP. *See also* discussions in *Arrest and Detention* and *Court Procedures* sections *infra*.

24. *See* Article 139 of the CCP.

25. The draft CCP includes provisions which give defense counsel the authority to conduct an independent investigation.

proper investigatory activity.[26] However, even if a suspect or accused person has a lawyer, it is frequently difficult to procure evidence from the state, in part, because defense counsel may only attend those investigative proceedings that the suspect or accused has a legal right to attend.[27] Once the preliminary investigation has been completed, the investigator in charge forwards a recommendation on the disposition of the case to the procurator. At his discretion, the procurator may then send an indictment to the court, close the case, or send the matter back for additional investigation.[28] If the procurator forwards an indictment, it is then reviewed by a judge with the legal authority to commit the case to trial.

In Russia, courts of general jurisdiction are organized in a three-tiered hierarchy. At the lowest level are the District Courts;[29] which serve a city or rural district. They hear criminal cases in which the maximum punishment is less than five (5) years imprisonment. As the courts of first instance, they hear the vast majority of criminal cases.[30] Above them are the Regional Courts (Oblast or Krai Courts and also the Supreme Courts of Autonomous Republics),[31] which are the courts of first instance for more serious crimes, such as murder. They have jurisdiction over crimes for which the maximum punishment is more than five (5) years imprisonment and are the appellate courts for the District Courts. In nine of Russia's 89 regions, these courts may also conduct jury trials. At the highest level is the Supreme Court (*Verhovnii Sud*).[32] A draft law presently under consideration provides for the creation of a level of courts beneath the District Courts — the Justice of the Peace Courts (*Miroviye Sudi*). The law envisions that the judges[33] at this lowest level will have jurisdiction over relatively minor criminal matters, including arrest and detention hearings.[34] Finally, Russia's Constitutional Court has exclusive jurisdiction over those cases that involve challenges to the constitutionality of legislation or government action.[35]

---

26. For example, defense counsel must file a motion requesting that a particular witness be questioned; he cannot officially question the witness on his own. The investigator is required to grant the request if the testimony is relevant to the case; if not, the decision to grant the petition is at his discretion. *See* Article 131 of the CCP. Victims (victims' representatives) as well as civil plaintiffs and defendants are also afforded similar rights under Article 131.

27. Unless, of course, the suspect/accused and/or defense attorney is asked to participate by the investigator. *See* Articles 51 and 48, respectively, of the current CCP and draft CCP. *See* also discussion in *Lawyer* section *infra.*

28. *See* Articles 211–217 and 221–223 of the CCP. *See also* discussion in *Court Procedure* section *infra.*

29. *See* Article 35 of the CCP.

30. They hear approximately 90 percent of all criminal cases.

31. See Article 36 of the CCP. The Moscow and St. Petersburg City Courts are also regional courts.

32. The Russian Judicial System has three branches: the Constitutional Court, a single body with no courts underneath it; the arbitration (commercial) court system with district and circuit courts of arbitration topped by the High Court of Arbitration; and the system of courts of general jurisdiction with the Supreme Court at the highest level.

33. Under the proposed law, the judges will be called Justices of the Peace.

34. The draft law on the Justices of the Peace was rejected by the Federation Council (the Upper House of the Russian Parliament) late in 1997. A reconciliation committee made up of members of both Houses is presently revamping the draft law.

35. Late last year, however, arbitration and general jurisdiction court judges received the right to apply the RF Constitution and international conventions to which the Russian Federation is a party, directly to matters before them. As such, these judges may rule on the constitutionality of a particular activity. *See* "On the Judicial System of the Russian Federation," signed by President Yeltsin on December 31, 1996 and in force as of January 1, 1997. Further, in February of 1998,

II. Police Procedures

A. Arrest, Search and Seizure Law

1. Stops and 2. Frisks

Russia does not have a procedure identical to the U.S. conception of "stop and frisk." However, under Russia's Administrative Offenses Code, a person may be detained by law enforcement authorities for up to three hours for, among other things, the purpose of establishing identity or preventing administrative offenses.[36] In practice, it appears that sufficient grounds (*dostatochniye ocnovaniye*) must exist to stop a person despite the fact that the Administrative Offenses Code contains no such standard. Once an individual is stopped, the detaining official may conduct a protective frisk for weapons, a check on outstanding warrants, and/or a personal search (*dosmotr*).[37]

The Administrative Offenses Code requires that an official written report (*protokol*)[38] of the stop be recorded. The detaining official's full name and position; where and when the *protokol* was made; information about the detainee; and the reasons for the detention must all be entered in the *protokol*. If a frisk, background check, or personal search is conducted, it must also be recorded in the *protokol*. Both the detainee and the official detaining him must sign the *protokol*. In the event that the former refuses to sign, an entry to that effect must be made in the *protokol*.

3. Arrest (arrest; privod) *and Detention* (zaderzhaniye)[39]

Since the constitutional provisions requiring judicially-sanctioned arrests and detentions have not been implemented by a revised criminal procedure code, such decisions remain, as during the Soviet era, the exclusive domain of the Russian Procuracy.[40] Although police and investigators generally execute them, current law

---

the Russian Parliament ratified the European Convention on Human Rights. Thus, Russian judges now also have the authority to apply its provisions to the cases that come before them. There are indications that Russian judges increasingly view their right to apply the RF Constitution and international conventions directly as an effective tool for promoting international standards of due process in Russia. In fact, using such authority, a Moscow Oblast Court judge recently held that sending a case back for additional investigation constitutes a violation of international standards prohibiting double jeopardy. *See* discussion at pp. 306–307 *infra*.

36. *See* Articles 239–246 of the Kodeks RSFSR Ob Administrativnix Pravonarousheniyakh (Administrative Offenses Code). Article 239 lists the circumstances under which such stops may be conducted and Article 241 lists those who may carry them out.

37. *See* Article 243 of the Administrative Offenses Code. Such a search requires the presence of two lay witnesses. *See* discussion of lay witnesses in *Search and Seizure* section *infra*.

38. A *protokol* is an official written record that memorializes certain proceedings, such as interrogations, confrontations, detentions, and searches. *See* Article 240 of the Administrative Offenses Code.

39. The Russian term *zaderzhaniye* means both to apprehend and arrest an alleged criminal on the spot and to detain him for a period of time before a formal charge is filed.

40. The current draft CCP provides for the transfer of such authority to judges. *See* Article 89 of the CCP and Article 90 of Draft CCP.

vests members of the Russian Procuracy with the sole authority to issue arrest and detention orders.

Under Article 122 of the CCP (and Article 87 of the Draft CCP), warrantless arrest and detention is sanctioned in cases where a person is suspected of committing a crime punishable by some period of imprisonment and either (1) he is caught in the act of committing the crime *(flagrante delicto)* or immediately afterwards, (2) he is identified as having committed the crime by an eyewitness,[41] or (3) traces of the crime are found on his person, in his possession, or in/around his dwelling.[42] Article 122 also authorizes officials to execute such arrests and detentions if there is "other information" giving authorities reason to suspect criminal activity and the suspect attempts to flee or fails to prove permanent place of residence or identity.[43] Official commentary on the CCP and the CCP itself fail to define "other information." Whether such information exists or not seems to be a matter of procuratorial discretion.

In Russia, a criminal suspect (*podozrevaemyi*)[44] may be held, interrogated, and personally searched for up to three days (72 hours),[45] or up to ten days in "exceptional circumstances,"[46] before he must be charged as an "accused" or released.[47] In addition, a procurator must be notified in writing about the detention within 24 hours of its occurrence, and within 48 hours of such notification, he must decide whether to continue to hold or release the suspect from custodial detention.[48] However, human rights groups report that, in practice, suspects are often held beyond these statutory time limits without any formal decree.[49]

---

41. Victims are included in the eyewitness category.

42. *See* Articles 122 and 127 of the CCP and Article 87 of the Draft CCP.

43. Identification and arrest may occur simultaneously.

44. A suspect is an individual who is detained on suspicion of having committed a crime pending a decision as to whether enough evidence exists to charge him as the "accused."

45. *See* Article 122 of the CCP.

46. *See* Article 90 of the CCP. Once again, neither legislation nor cases indicate what circumstances are considered "exceptional." Thus, whether a case is considered "exceptional" appears to be purely a matter of procuratorial discretion. *See also* Foglesong, *supra* note 7 at p. 553.

47. An individual is considered an "accused" when an investigator officially declares that there is sufficient evidence to formally charge him with the commission of a crime. The legal instrument used to identify a person as an accused is called the "accusatory indictment." If the suspect is not formally charged as the accused within this 3 or 10 day period, he must be released. *See* Articles 143–149 of the CCP. *See also* discussion in *Interrogations* section *infra*.

48. It is important to note that Article 6 (Second Part, Concluding and Transitional Provisions) of the RF Constitution preserves the procedures for arrest, pretrial detention, and custody of criminal suspects and accused persons under the current criminal procedure code until the passage of a new RF criminal procedure code incorporating the Constitution's mandates. Consequently, Article 22 of the RF Constitution, which limits detentions to 48 hours, does not yet apply to detentions of a criminal nature. Article 90 of the draft criminal procedure code does implement the constitutionally-mandated 48-hour time limit on such detentions, and if this draft code comes into effect, the current 72-hour maximum will be reduced to the 48-hour limit required under the RF Constitution.

49. *See* Amnesty, *supra* note 18 and The Moscow Center for Prison Reform's publication, "In Search of A Solution: Crime, Criminal Policy and Prison Facilities in the Former Soviet Union" (Human Rights Publishers, Moscow 1996) (hereinafter the "MCPR publication"). *See also* International Commission of Jurists trial observers mission to Moscow: Report on the trial of Aju Mariam in the Gagarinski Inter-Municipal Court in Moscow (December 1997) (hereinafter the "ICJ Report") on file with the author. *See also*, U.S. Department of State: Russia Country Report on Human Rights Practices for 1997 at p. 9, available at the following website: www.state.gov/www/global/human_rights/1997_hrp_report/russia (hereinafter "Russia Human Rights Report").

In addition, Article 147 of the CCP authorizes the arrest (*privod*)[50] of any accused person who is officially summoned to appear before investigators but fails to do so. Such arrests may occur without a preliminary summons if the accused has no permanent address or is attempting to elude investigators. Finally, Article 89 of the CCP permits arrest and custodial detention (*zakliucheniye pod strazhu*), among other measures of restraint, where there are reasonable grounds to believe that an accused person will flee, obstruct the preliminary investigation, or continue to engage in criminal activity. The same article also authorizes arrest and custodial detention as a means of ensuring the execution of any judgment against the accused.[51] Although these same articles provide for bail and personal sureties, most accused persons in Russia are arrested and placed in custodial detention pending trial.[52]

The right to a lawyer (defender) attaches at the moment an individual is arrested and detained[53] or formally charged with a crime, whichever occurs first.[54] The current CCP also requires that both suspects and accused persons be informed of their right to a defense.[55] Unfortunately, most suspects and accused persons do not, in fact, have lawyers at the early stages of a criminal prosecution, most often because they cannot afford an attorney and the government is unable to secure one in a timely matter.[56] Finally, it is important to note that Russian law permits both licensed attorneys and non-lawyers (e.g. members of a union or other social organization and close relatives) to act as defense counsel in criminal proceedings.[57] However, whether both classes of defense counsel may represent suspects and accused persons at the pretrial investigation stage remains unaddressed by Russian courts.[58]

In theory, both arrest and detention decisions must be justified by a showing of cause. In reality, before 1992, they were unreviewable and often arbitrary decisions made by the procurator. By virtue of amendments to the CCP in 1992,[59] the Russ-

---

50. *Privod* describes the procedure used by duly authorized law enforcement officials to bring a subject to proceedings, if necessary, with the use of force. *See* Article 111 of the draft CCP.

51. *See* Article 89 of CCP and Articles 94 and 104 of the Draft CCP.

52. For a more detailed discussion of custodial detention, see section entitled *Measures of Restraint and Pretrial Detention, infra.*

53. In fact, the right to counsel attaches at the moment a person is informed of the decision to use such measures of restraint.

54. *See* Article 48 (2) of the RF Constitution (1993). *See also* Articles 46 (3) and 47(1) of the CCP and Articles 41 - 44 of the draft CCP.

55. *See* Articles 123 and 149 of the CCP.

56. Local government efforts to secure attorneys are frequently delayed due to insufficient financial and/or manpower resources.

57. Article 48(2) of the RF Constitution reads: Every person who has been detained, taken into custody or charged with a crime shall have the right to a lawyer (*advokat*)/defender (*zashchitnik*) from the moment of, respectively, detention or indictment. The term *advokat* refers to a professional lawyer while the word *zashchitnik* contemplates anyone who carries out the function of defense counsel in court. *See Review of the Constitutionality of Article 47(4) of the Criminal Procedure Code of the RSFSR in connection with complaints by citizens B.V. Antipov, P.L. Gitis, and S.V. Abramov* (VKS, January 28, 1997, No. 1).

58. In the case cited in note 57, the Russian Constitutional Court ruled that it lacked the institutional competence to decide this question.

59. "O Vnesenii izmenenii I dopolnenii v Ugolovno-protsessual'nyi kodeks RSFSR, VEDOMOSTI S"EZDA NARODNYKH DEPUTATOV I VERKHOVNOVO SOVETA ROSSIISKOI FEDERATSII, NO. 25, May 23 1992, Art. 1389. The law allows for judicial review of the legality of an arrest, the use of detention as a measure of restraint, and the extension of the time-period of pretrial detention beyond the two-month limit. In its April 27, 1993 Guiding Instructions,

ian judiciary has been given the authority to review the legality of procuratorial arrest and detention decisions.[60] Current law directs that within 24 hours of receipt of a petition contesting an arrest and detention decision,[61] it must be transferred to the district procurator who must, within 24 hours, forward a copy of the complaint with supporting documentation justifying the arrest and detention to the court. Within three days of receiving these materials from the procurator, the court is required to conduct a closed hearing with the procurator,[62] the detainee, and his defender (*zashchitnik*) present, to examine the matter. The law also states that a procurator's failure to supply documentation is a ground for nullifying the arrest and detention order and releasing the detainee. The CCP further provides that the judge's decision in these cases is not subject to appeal by the petitioner[63] or protest[64] brought by the procurator.[65] Finally, the judge who hears this matter is prohibited from presiding over the related criminal case if it subsequently goes to trial.

Once again, the reality is that few Russians "... are ... running to the law."[66] Many are unaware that they have the right to contest their arrest and detention, and those who do want to appeal often lack qualified legal assistance to draft the complaint.[67] In addition, general delays in the court's receipt of materials, if any, from the Procuracy, as well as a widespread lack of participation by procurators have prevented the effective implementation of judicial review of arrest and detention decisions.[68] As a result, it generally takes courts ten days to a month to process such appeals.[69] Moreover, Russian courts, on the whole, remain slow to question or even overturn procurators' decisions in these matters for a number of reasons, including "misgivings about their role as custodians of pretrial justice [and] fears

---

the Supreme Court of Russia affirmed the availability of judicial review of arrest and pretrial detention decisions for all suspects and defendants, including those detained under Article 90 of the CCP. *See* MCPR publication, *supra* note 49 at pp. 80-82 for a detailed analysis of the law and its application in practice. *See* Articles 220-1 and 220-2 of the CCP.

60. *See also Pretrial Detention* section *infra.*

61. A May 1995 Constitutional Court decision broadened the category of individuals who could contest the validity of an arrest and detention decision to include not only the detainee but also defense counsel or other legal representative of the detainee. *See* Amnesty, *supra* note 18 at p. 5.

62. The presence of the procurator is mandatory in these proceedings.

63. According to Article 220–2, if the complainant's appeal is not granted, reconsideration of the custodial detention may only occur if it is once again selected as a means of restraint after having been either canceled or modified by those conducting the investigation.

64. *See* explanation of protest in *Appeals* section *infra.*

65. The Russian Supreme Court's detailed instructions as to how the judiciary should properly decide these cases is contained in the following documents: Ruling No. 3 of the Plenum of the Supreme Court of the Russian Federation on the Practice of Judicial Examination of the Legality and Validity of Arrests or Extension of the Period of Retention in Custody (April 27, 1993) and Judicial Review of Lawfulness and Grounds for Arrest (Judicial Practice) (A.P. Kunitsyn, ed., Soloex Publishers, Moscow 1994). Both documents are on file in English with the author.

66. This was the conclusion a Supreme Court study in March 1993. *See* Foglesong, *supra* note 7 at p. 566.

67. Others fear that appealing would aggravate their situation or doubt that the court will be able to change the charges. *See* MCPR's informal poll of approximately 50 prisoners in Moscow's Butyrskaya Prison. MCPR, *supra* note 49 at p. 81. *See also* Russia Human Rights Report, *supra* note 49.

68. *See* generally Foglesong, *supra* note 7; MCPR publication *supra* note 49; and ICJ Report, *supra* note 49.

69. *See* ICJ Report, *supra* note 49.

of freeing potential criminals."[70] Further, there is a large backlog of cases for a comparatively smaller number of judges who sit in dilapidated courtrooms with antiquated case processing systems. Thus, Russian law enforcement continues to enjoy broad discretion and authority to arrest and detain individuals with limited supervision by the courts. Indeed, as one expert has commented: "The law of criminal procedure in Russia ... confers on police unusually broad powers to arrest [and detain] suspects and ... considerable time before charges must be laid to build a case."[71]

4. Search (**Obisk**) *and Seizure* (**Viyemka**)[72]

Under the Russian Constitution, a court order must be obtained in order to intercept private communications (phone, mail, etc.) or to conduct searches and seizures in private homes.[73] However, implementing legislation in the form of a revised criminal procedure code giving the courts exclusive authority over the aforementioned activities has yet to be passed by the Russian Parliament. Thus, the current Russian Criminal Procedure Code continues to vest the Procuracy with overall authority to approve search and seizure activity.[74]

Under the current CCP, prior to conducting a search, an investigator is required to demonstrate in a "reasoned decree" (*motivirovannoe postanovlenie*) that there are sufficient grounds (*dostatochniye ocnovaniye*) to believe that instruments and/or fruits of crime, as well as other objects of relevance to the case, are located on a given premises or in someone's possession.[75] Only with prior procuratorial approval of said reasoned decree, though, may the search actually be conducted. Where there can be no delay, the CCP allows an investigator to commence a warrantless search with an unsanctioned decree. The investigator, however, is required to inform a procurator within 24 hours.[76] Seizures must also be based upon an investigator's reasoned decree, with the proviso that the items to be removed are significant to the case and their exact location is known.[77] With the exception of seizures of government secrets and postal-telegraphic communications,[78] the Criminal Procedure Code requires no prior procuratorial or court approval for seizures.[79] The CCP outlines the required elements of a legally executed search and seizure. They include the following: the execution of the search and seizure during

70. *See* Foglesong, *supra* note 7 at p. 578. In his article, Foglesong analyzes judicial review of arrest and detention decisions in Russia.

71. *See* Foglesong, *supra* note 7 at p. 554.

72. See generally, Articles 167–177 of the CCP and Articles 194–200 of the draft CCP.

73. *See* Articles 23 and 25 of the RF Constitution (1993). *See also* Article 12 of the CCP.

74. *See* Article 211 of the CCP. A procurator's supervisory powers include the authority to rescind illegal and groundless decrees issued by investigators or representatives of the Agencies of Inquiry.

75. *See* Article 168(1) of the CCP. It reads in part: "The investigator, having sufficient grounds to believe, that the instruments of crime, articles and valuables gained through criminal activity as well as other articles or documents that may have significance in the case are located on some premises or any other place or in someone's possession." Searches may also be conducted to find persons and corpses.

76. *See* Article 168(3) of the CCP.

77. *See* Article 167 of the CCP.

78. *See* Articles 167 and 174 of the CCP.

79. *But see* Article 211 of the CCP which gives the procurator the authority to rescind illegal and groundless decrees issued by representatives of the Agencies of Inquiry or investigators.

the daytime[80] except in instances that "cannot suffer delay"; the presence of civilian witnesses (*ponyatiya*)[81]and those subjected to the search;[82] an initial request to voluntarily hand over the items that are being sought; the use of measures to prevent the public disclosure of facts concerning private life unless significant to the case; the removal of only those items having a connection to the case under investigation; and the preparation of a search and seizure *protokol*.[83]

While conducting a search or seizure, the investigator has the right to open locked or secured premises, to control the movement and interaction of persons on the premises,[84] and to conduct personal searches of persons at the place of the search or seizure activity provided there are sufficient grounds to believe that they are concealing items relevant to the case.[85] Specifically, Article 172 of the Russian CCP authorizes law enforcement authorities to conduct a personal search[86] of any individual who is either (1) being arrested and taken into custody or (2) on the premises of a place where a search or seizure is being conducted and there are sufficient grounds to believe that said individual is concealing evidence of potential significance to the case. By law, personal searches need no judicial order or procuratorial approval beforehand, but they must occur in the presence of civilian witnesses.

In sum, the search and seizure provisions of the Russian CCP provide few constraints on the scope of investigative activity. The evidentiary justification for both search and seizure — "sufficient grounds" (*dostatochniye ocnovaniye*) — remains undefined in the CCP and, as such, provides much latitude for procuratorial discretion. The language of the code is similarly vague with regard to the types of searches and seizures that cannot "suffer delay" and hence may be carried out by an investigatory decree only reviewed by a procurator after the fact. Indeed, the decision to search and seize remains a unilateral calculation on the part of procurators and investigators without the benefit of the judgment of an independent judicial referee. Finally, it is important to note that Russia has enacted a Law on Operational-Search Activity.[87] This law regulates both the open and undercover collection of information by means of wiretaps, informants, controlled buys/sells, and other investigative methods[88] for the stated purposes of exposing and preventing crimes; identifying persons who have committed, are committing, or planning to commit illegal acts; and searching for persons who are hiding to escape investigation, court proceedings, or punishment. However, the materials collected pur-

80. The CCP defines "night" as 10pm–6am.

81. *See Enforcing the Rules* section at pp. 17–18.

82. If the subject(s) of the search/seizure are not present, family members who have reached the age of majority or other qualified representatives may fulfill this requirement. *See* Article 169 of the current CCP.

83. *See* Articles 170 and 176 of the CCP.

84. *Id.*

85. *See* Article 172 of the CCP and discussion in text below.

86. *See* Article 172 of the CCP.

87. The Law on Operational-Search Activity, SOBRANIE ZAKONODATELSTVO (Official Gazette, SZ RF) 1995, No. 33, Item 3349) (hereinafter "LOSA"). The Law on Operational-Search Activity (144-FZ) came into force on August 12, 1995. The law was amended on July 18, 1997. It applies to several agencies, including the operational sub-units of the Federal Security Service (FSB), the Tax Police, and the Ministry of Interior (MVD). *See also Wiretaps* and *Informants* sections *infra*.

88. For a list of operational-search activities permitted under the law, *see* Article 6 of LOSA, *supra* note 87.

suant to this law do not constitute legally cognizable evidence and thus cannot be used to prosecute criminal misconduct unless made to conform to the current rules of criminal procedure regulating the collection, verification, and evaluation of evidence.[89] According to Russian experts, the practical effect of the Law on Operational-Search Activity is minimal because flaws in the legislation itself cause courts to reject information collected pursuant to this law. In fact, many organized crime and corruption cases have been discontinued due to the impossibility of using methods sanctioned by the CCP to confirm the information collected under this law. The results of operational-search activity, however, are often used to secure evidence that is admissible in court.

Wiretaps

As discussed above, the Law on Operational-Search Activity[90] permits certain law enforcement authorities to monitor phones and other types of communication.[91] According to the law, agencies authorized to conduct operational-search activity[92] may only install wiretaps and other devices to monitor communication pursuant to a court order[93] provided there is information about an illegal act (for which preliminary investigation is mandatory) that is being prepared for, is being committed, or has been committed; the persons involved in such activity; and/or any events or acts creating a threat to Russia's state, military, economic, or environmental security. After receiving a request from an authorized agency seeking to use a wiretap, a judge's decision must be based on the materials submitted with the request, and any additional information demanded from the agency.[94] The court's decision may be appealed by either the agency seeking to conduct the operational-search activity or by the person potentially subjected to such activity.[95]

The law allows judicial approval after the fact in cases of emergency "which may lead to the commission of a grave crime, and also if there is information on [...] events or actions, creating a threat to the political, military, economic, or environmental security of the Russian Federation."[96] In these instances, operational-search activity, such as wiretapping, may be commenced by the head of an investigative body without prior court approval, but a judge must be notified within 24

---

89. *See* Article 11 of LOSA, *supra* note 87. The draft CCP contains a similar provision. Article 85 of the draft code reads as follows: "The results of operational-search activity, obtained in compliance with the Federal Law on "Operational-Search Activity," may be used as proof in criminal cases pursuant to provisions of this Code regulating the gathering, verification, and evaluation of evidence."

90. *See* LOSA, *supra* note 87.

91. In a recent article, though, Peter Solomon states that in some regions, such as Sverdlovsk, the courts began hearing wiretap applications in 1994. Peter H. Solomon, Jr., "The Persistence of Judicial Reform in Contemporary Russia," 6(4) East European Constitutional Review 50 (Fall 1997).

92. *See* Article 13 of LOSA, *supra* note 87.

93. *See* Article 8 of LOSA, *supra* note 87.

94. However, the judge cannot order or be supplied with materials on "the persons implanted into organized criminal groups, on the staff of secret workers of the bodies engaged in the operational-search activity, and on the persons rendering assistance on the confidential principle and on the tactics of carrying out operational-search measures." *See* Article 9 of LOSA, *supra* note 87.

95. Article 5 of LOSA provides a right of appeal to those who allege that their constitutional rights have been violated. *See* LOSA, *supra* note 87.

96. *See* Article 8 of LOSA, *supra* note 87.

hours. The judge, in turn, must issue an order either allowing or terminating the activity within 48 hours of its commencement.[97] What precisely falls within the confines of "emergency" and "security," though, remains undefined by law or legal commentary. Finally, in some instances, the law also permits operational-search activity to proceed without a court order provided there is valid written consent.[98] Again, however, the results of wiretaps conducted pursuant to the Law on Operational-Search Activity are not considered legal evidence unless they conform to current rules of criminal procedure.

5. *Enforcing the Rules*

Article 50 of the Russian Constitution specifically states that illegally obtained evidence is inadmissible in court. Article 69 of the CCP reiterates this abolition by stating that illegally obtained evidence cannot be used at trial. In practice, these are rather toothless provisions, particularly in the non-jury trial regions of Russia, for several reasons.

First, the current CCP contains no detailed exclusionary rules and there is no "fruit of the poisonous tree" doctrine. Consequently, law enforcement agencies routinely use wiretaps to obtain additional evidence admissible in a criminal case. Furthermore, members of the Russian Procuracy exercise a fairly low level of supervision over the activities of criminal investigators. Moreover, under pressure to reduce Russia's ever-increasing crime rate, it is reported that many procurators regularly turn a blind eye to illegal investigatory activities.[99] However, even if challenged, a questionable investigative action is not automatically held in abeyance pending the resolution of the complaint.[100]

Second, the lack of meaningful participation by the defense attorney at the preliminary stages of a criminal matter—especially in non-jury trial regions—further hinders the possibility, not only of contesting potentially illegally obtained evidence, but also of introducing exculpatory evidence early on in a criminal prosecution.[101] In jury trial regions, the situation is much better: "The critical responses of the first juries to the often sloppy and illegal methods of investigators ... forced procurators to take a more critical look at the file in cases set for jury trial, which has led to procurators themselves moving to exclude illegally seized evidence or amending the indictment to charge lesser offenses."[102] Even if evidence is not excluded at a preliminary hearing, Russian defense attorneys have become increasingly adept at reducing its credibility in the eyes of the jury.

---

97. *Id.*

98. *Id.*

99. *See* Amnesty, *supra* note 18 and MCPR, *supra* note 49.

100. *See* Article 218 of the CCP.

101. Article 51 of the CCP outlines the rights and obligations of defense counsel. The current draft CCP allows the defense to conduct its own independent investigation. If passed, the new CCP would arguably promote a more adversarial criminal justice system in Russia.

102. Stephen C. Thaman, "Reform of the Procuracy and Bar in Russia" 3(1)Parker Sch. J. E. Eur. L. 1, 18 (1995). *See also* Case of the MARTYNOV BROTHERS (Saratov Regional Court) in an unpublished memorandum, dated January 24, 1994, from Stephen C. Thaman to CEELI on file with the author (hereinafter "CEELI Memorandum").

Third, judicial review of investigative activity is quite limited under the current CCP. Nonetheless, judges are currently excluding evidence obtained through investigative misconduct.[103] In one of Russia's first jury trials, the presiding judge excluded a large amount of the government's evidence on the grounds that it was obtained illegally. As a result, the prosecution's charges were significantly reduced and the defendants received substantially lower sentences.[104] It is anticipated that with time and experience, Russian judges will become more secure in their new role as independent reviewers of executive action and increasingly adept at the task of judicial review.[105]

Finally, it is interesting to note that a unique procedural requirement has been retained from the Soviet era, in part, as a means of deterring official misconduct. According to Articles 135 and 169 of the CCP, those who conduct a search[106] are required to secure two civilian witnesses (*ponyatiya*) to observe and attest to its proper execution. The failure to secure these witnesses renders the search invalid and any evidence gathered inadmissible in court. In practice, the attesting witness requirement has become increasingly difficult to fulfill. Many Russian legal professionals and law enforcement officials see this rule as an unnecessary throwback to the Soviet era, which more often than not impedes the effectiveness of searches and other investigative activity.[107] Also, Russians citizens, generally speaking, do not want to be involved in such activity. Others, however, view the attesting witness requirement as a necessary and meaningful check on law enforcement activities.

B. Lineups and Other Identification Procedures

1. Lineups

Under Russian law, persons and objects may be presented to a witness, victim, suspect, or accused person for identification. A written record of the identification presentation is required, and the entire proceeding must be conducted in the presence of civilian witnesses (*ponyatiya*). Before any actual identification is made, the person being asked to make the identification is questioned about the circumstances under which he has previously observed the person or object, asked to describe any distinguishing characteristics, and warned about the consequences of re-

---

103. *See* note 35 *supra*. Again, as of January 1, 1997, Russian judges have the authority to apply the RF Constitution and more recently the European Convention on Human Rights directly to the matters brought before them. *See* the federal law "On The Judicial System of the Russian Federation" (December 31, 1996), Article 5, Clause 3. *See also*, Sergei Pashin, "New Opportunities for Development of Russia's Judicial System," 2(19) Constitutional Law: Eastern-European Review (1997)(hereinafter "Pashin").

104. *Id.*

105. An additional practical issue is whether there will be a sufficient number of adequately trained judges who possess the political will to deal effectively with their new responsibilities under the RF Constitution.

106. By law, the attendance of at least two civilian witnesses is also required during a crime scene examination, line-up, and confrontation.

107. Most officials complain that it takes too much time to secure these witnesses and that the surprise element of searches is jeopardized by the civilian witness requirement. Nonetheless, the civilian witness requirement has been retained in Articles 59 and 185 of the draft CCP.

fusing to provide an identification or knowingly giving a false identification.[108] The person or object being identified must be presented with no less than three other similar looking individuals or objects. Additionally, the person being identified has the right to choose where he stands among them.[109] Photo arrays are permissible if it is impossible to secure the presence of the person or object to be identified. All photo arrays must contain a photograph of the person (object) for which identification is sought and at least three additional photos of other persons (objects) bearing a close resemblance to the former.

2. Other Identification Procedures

Article 186 of the current CCP permits investigators to obtain handwriting and other specimens from suspects and accused persons. Such specimens may also be obtained from victims and witnesses but only when necessary to determine whether such persons either left traces at the scene of the crime or had contact with material evidence. Additionally, fingerprints and blood samples may only be taken from a suspect after he has been formally committed to custody. If, however, the suspect is also a defendant in an active criminal case, he may be legally compelled to provide such evidence at any time. Furthermore if he has ever been a criminal defendant, his fingerprints may also be obtained from a record bank. Additionally, the criminal procedure code gives investigators the right to conduct examinations of accused persons, suspects, witnesses, and victims in order to locate signs of criminal activity on their body or the presence of specific features.[110] Finally, the CCP also allows investigatory agencies to call on "specialists" and "experts" to assist in criminal investigations.[111]

C. Interrogation

1. Before Formally Charged as the Accused

As discussed earlier, an individual suspected of committing a crime may be held, interrogated, and otherwise investigated for up to 72 hours before being formally placed in custody.[112] In fact, the CCP requires immediate interrogation of suspects.[113] In addition, because the code defines witnesses broadly to include any person having "knowledge of significance" regarding a crime, suspects are often erroneously ques-

---

108. Article 164 -166 of the CCP and Article 209–210 of the draft CCP. Article 210(9) of the draft CCP adds a provision allowing for the identification to occur in such a way that the person being identified cannot see the person making the identification.

109. In one of Russia's first jury trials, the victim's identification of a stolen television set was excluded because the television in question was not presented with other televisions of a similar make. See Case of SLONCHAKOV/CHERNIKOV (Moscow Regional Court), CEELI Memorandum, *supra* note 102.

110. *See* Article 181 of the CCP.

111. *See* Articles 133^1, 183, and 186 of the CCP. For example, those investigating a case often use these provisions to secure ballistics experts. Experts also participate at the trial stage. *See* discussion in *Experts* section *infra*.

112. *See* Article 122 of the CCP and discussion in *Arrest and Detention* section *supra*.

113. *See* Article 123 of the current CCP. In exceptional cases, this period may be extended for up to ten days. The "exceptional" nature of a case is not determined by a court. Instead, it is, essentially, an exercise of unreviewable discretion by the procurator. *See* Article 90 of the CCP and discussion in *Arrest and Detention* section *supra*.

tioned as witnesses and thus not advised of their constitutional rights and incorrectly informed that they are liable under the criminal code for refusing to testify or falsifying testimony.[114] Further, at this point, despite a legal right to counsel, few suspects in custody actually have an attorney present. In the absence of counsel, the use of threats/promises, intimidation, and even physical force is not uncommon. Consequently, many suspects tend to provide incriminating evidence during this period.[115]

2. *After Formally Charged as the Accused*

Once officially identified as the accused, rules of criminal procedure once again mandate an immediate interrogation. The accused's right to counsel also attaches at this time if he has not previously been subject to some measure of restraint (e.g. detention).[116] Some Russian legal experts contend that the "immediacy of the interrogation required by the Criminal Procedure Code, however, may interfere with the individual's right to counsel because the examination may take place before the individual has sought legal representation."[117] By law, the interrogation begins with the investigator asking the accused whether he declares himself guilty. The accused is then asked whether he has any exculpatory evidence that he wishes to offer regarding the charge. Interrogations may not take place at night,[118] except where delay cannot be tolerated. Moreover, those who stand accused in the same matter must be interrogated individually, and measures must be taken to ensure that they do not communicate with one another.

An important guarantee for both suspects and accused persons is Article 51 of the RF Constitution, which states that no one may be compelled to give evidence against himself and other close relatives (e.g. spouse, parents, children).[119] Articles 52 and 46 of the CCP give suspects and accused persons, respectively, the right to know what kind of criminal activity they are accused or suspected of as well as the right to provide explanations. However, the criminal procedure code fails to specifically indicate when they must be advised of their Article 51 right against self-incrimination, and whether this mandatory warning is impliedly guaranteed in these provisions of the criminal procedure code is the subject of much disagreement among Russia's legal academics. Nonetheless, based on Article 69 of the CCP and Article 51 of the RF Constitution, Russian judges (particularly those in jury trial regions) have zealously excluded any statements made by suspects and accused persons who have not been advised of their rights against self-incrimination. For ex-

---

114. *See* Articles 181 and 182 of the Russian Criminal Code. *See* Case of Aju Mariam in ICJ Report, *supra* note 49.

115. *See* ICJ Report, *supra* note 49. *See also* Case of SLONCHAKOV/CHERNIKOV (Moscow Regional Court in CEELI Memorandum, *supra* note 102. In that case, the judge excluded the statements of the two defendants because they were erroneously questioned as witnesses rather than as suspects and, thus, were not properly informed of their rights.

116. Article 47 of the CCP and Article 48 of the RF Constitution. *See* discussion, *supra* at pp. 290–291.

117. K. Ratnikov and C. Strick, "A Survey of the Rules of Evidence in Russian Criminal Procedure," 2 Parker Sch. J. E. Eur. L. 321, 353(1995) (hereinafter "Ratnikov"). *See also* Article 123 of the CCP.

118. *See* note 80 *supra.*

119. Article 34(9) of the CCP defines "close relatives" as parents, children, adoptive parents, adoptive children, brothers and sisters, grandparents, grandchildren, husbands, and wives. *See also* Article 308 of the Criminal Code.

ample, in the Martynov Brothers case,[120] the judge suppressed the statements of the defendant brothers at a preliminary hearing because they were not advised of their rights prior to being interrogated.[121]

Further, it is a criminal offense in Russia to use threats or other illegal actions in order to compel a suspect, accused person, victim, or witness to provide testimony.[122] Moreover, such evidence is at once a violation of the RF Constitution and without legal force.[123] In reality, however, the law seems largely ignored. Human Rights groups regularly receive reports of threats, ill-treatment and even torture by law enforcement officials attempting to obtain "confessions," which remain a mainstay of most criminal prosecutions in Russia.[124] Even Russia's Presidential Human Rights Commission admits there are problems.[125] According to some Russian legal scholars, this unfortunate situation arises because the criminal procedure code does not outline any explicit procedures for reviewing the petitions of defendants alleging such abuses. Hence, judges tend to disregard such allegations and admit questionable evidence.[126] In 1995, though, the Supreme Court of Russia overturned and sent back for supplementary investigation, a case involving the confessions, allegedly obtained by torture, of three individuals who had been convicted and sentenced to death.[127] Also, lower courts are increasingly excluding such suspect evidence, particularly in jury trial regions.[128]

Confrontation

Confrontation is an investigative technique used by investigators and procurators when there is conflicting testimony among witnesses, victims, and suspects/accused persons.[129] During a confrontation, the participants are each asked to relate

120. *See* Case of the MARTYNOV BROTHERS (Saratov Regional Court) in CEELI Memorandum, *supra* note 102.

121. *See also* Case of SLONCHAKOV/CHERNIKOV (Moscow Regional Court) in CEELI Memorandum, *supra* note 102.

122. *See* Article 302 of CC (1997) and Article 20 of the CCP. It is also a crime to fabricate evidence under Article 303 of the CC.

123. *See* Article 50 RF Constitution (1993).

124. More often than not, these reports are from detainees held in pretrial detention facilities. *See* Amnesty, *supra* note 18 at p. 37. In a recent New York Times article, Judge Sergei Pashin of the Moscow Appeals Court stated, "[O]ften, in the cases that come before [me], confessions are beaten out of suspects—and even out of people rounded up as witnesses." "Russians Lament Crime of Punishment" by Alessandra Stanley, New York Times, January 8, 1998 at p. A1 (hereinafter "Russians Lament"). *See also* Russia Human Rights Report, *supra* note 48 at pp. 5–8. It is important to note that, by law, a criminal conviction cannot be based on a confession alone. Article 77 of the CCP requires corroborating evidence to convict.

125. In 1995, the Commission reported that "the number of officials charged with unlawful detention, the use of force against suspects and witnesses, and the falsification of evidence had almost doubled since previous years." *See* Amnesty, *supra* note 18 at p. 18

126. *See* Ratnikov, *supra* note 117 at p. 349.

127. *See* the case of Mikhail Yurochko, Yevgeny Mednikov, and Dmitry Elsakov in Amnesty, *supra* note 18 at pp. 37-38. Unfortunately, the latest reports indicate that these defendants remain in a detention facility awaiting trial.

128. Perhaps, the new authority that Russian judges have to apply the RF Constitution and the European Convention on Human Rights directly to their cases will encourage the judiciary to more aggressively exclude evidence obtained in violation of constitutional guarantees and/or international human rights standards.

129. See Articles 162 and 163 of the CCP.

their version of the events in question, and, with permission, the participants may also question each other. A confrontation *protokol* is drawn up following the proceeding and included in the case file. The general purpose of a confrontation proceeding is to provide the investigator or procurator with an opportunity to acquire a more complete understanding of the differences in testimonies, to assess their relative credibility, and/or to resolve inconsistencies.

Informants; Controlled Buys; and Threats/Promises

The Law on Operational-Search Activity[130] permits the use of informants in criminal investigations.[131] Exemption from criminal liability, monetary remuneration, as well as state protection for themselves and their families are among the rights that may be granted to those who contract with investigative bodies as informants.[132] Russian criminal procedure law, though, does not allow testimony from those who cannot be identified nor does it consider as evidence, information obtained from a source that cannot be named. In addition, because the confidentiality of cooperation agreements between informants and law enforcement authorities is protected under Russia's State Secrecy law, informants may only be declassified pursuant to a decision by the head of the agency conducting the operational-search activity. Further, informants must give their written consent to have their information disclosed.[133] Hence, only when declassified informants consent to testify as official witnesses may their information be introduced as evidence in a criminal prosecution.

The Operational-Search law also sanctions the use of controlled-buys/deliveries and undercover operations.[134] The law requires that such activities be approved by the head of the agency intending to conduct such activity, and in certain circumstances, the law specifically exempts from criminal liability those who commit unlawful acts in the course of exposing other criminal activity.[135] Once again, however, the results of this type of investigative activity are not automatically considered usable evidence in a criminal prosecution. Further, the relationship between this provi-

---

130. *See* LOSA, *supra* note 87.

131. *See* Articles 15, 17, and 18 of LOSA, *supra* note 87.

132. *Id.*

133. *See* Article 12 of LOSA, *supra* note 87.

134. Article 8 of LOSA states, in part: "The test purchase or the controlled delivery of things, substances and products, whose free realization is forbidden or whose circulation is restricted, as well as the operational experiment or the operational implanting of the official persons of the bodies, engaged in the operational-search activity, as well as of persons, who render them assistance, shall be effected on the grounds of the decisions approved by the head of the body, engaged in the operational-search activity. The carrying out of the operational-search experiment shall be admitted only for the purposes of exposing, preventing, suppressing, revealing a grave crime, as well as for the purpose of exposing and identifying the persons, who are preparing, committing, or have perpetrated crimes." *See* LOSA, *supra* note 87.

135. "The person from among the members of the criminal group, who has committed an unlawful action, which has not entailed grave consequences, and who has been drawn into cooperation with the body, engaged in the operational-search activity, and has actively assisted in exposing the crimes, has recompensed the damage he has done or has made good the inflicted harm in another way, shall be exempt from the criminal responsibility in conformity with the legislation of the Russian Federation." Article 18(4) of LOSA, *supra* note 87.

sion in the Law on Operational-Search Activity and Russia's entrapment laws is unclear. Finally, while Russian procurators and investigators commonly use "threats/promises,"[136] and probably use jailhouse informants[137] regularly, it is difficult to obtain any rules governing the use of these investigative tools.

3. *Enforcing the Rules*

Unfortunately, Russia's authoritarian legacy[138] has been slow to disappear. Indeed, progress has been made since the fall of communism, but corruption and due process abuses remain widespread. They are particularly serious problems within the law enforcement community, and thus, coerced confessions, fabricated evidence, and bribed testimony remain commonplace. Furthermore, highly publicized anti-crime campaigns have placed a priority on results rather than on the means used to achieve them. "[U]nder the guise of fighting crime, there [has been] a tendency to expand the powers of security and law enforcement agencies to the detriment of Constitutional rights and guarantees" concluded the Russian Presidential Commission on Human Rights.[139] The same Commission also reported that in 1995, more than 20,000 MVD employees were disciplined for engaging in illegal activities in the course of conducting investigations.[140]

III. Court Procedures

A. Pretrial

In essence, the pretrial stage of a criminal prosecution remains, both in law and practice, the exclusive domain of Russian procurators and investigators. Nonetheless, as discussed previously, court hearings on procuratorial arrest and detention decisions may take place before cases reach trial. Plea bargaining has not been adopted in Russia. Accordingly, all cases must eventually go to trial if they are docketed and not

---

136. In practice, law enforcement officials frequently threaten detainees with a night in pretrial detention as a means of making detainees talk or sign *protokols*. As a result, many detainees are so frightened that they need no prompting to sign documents or to talk to law enforcement officials.

137. Amnesty International and The Moscow Center for Prison Reform report that corrections officials sometimes use "press-cameras" (*pressovshchiki*) in SIZOs and prisons. In return for privileges, *pressovshchiki* extract confessions and "deal with" troublesome prisoners. *See* Amnesty *supra* note 18 at pp. 39–40.

138. In 1987, a series of exposés on the Soviet criminal justice system appeared in several of the USSR's leading news publications. They detail numerous cases where evidence was fabricated, innocent citizens were wrongfully accused, and other similar abuses. *See Literaturnaya Gazeta* 52 (1986), 13; *Sovetskaya Rossiya*, June 14, 1986; *Moskovskiye Novosti*, nos. 16, 25, 41 and 50 (1987); *Nedelya*, nos. 42 and 51 (1987); and *Ogonek*, nos. 33 and 49 (1987). More recently, allegations of planted evidence have been lodged against Russian law enforcement. *See* Case of Aju Mariam in ICJ Report, *supra* note 49 and "Judge Is Accuser, Arbiter" by Mumin Shakirov in Moscow Times, April 3, 1998.

139. Amnesty, *supra* note 18 at p. 18.

140. Amnesty, *supra* note 18 at p. 18. *See also* Russia Human Rights Report, *supra* note 49 at pp. 7-8.

closed.[141] Thus, any confession by the accused simply becomes part of the totality of evidence considered by a judge or jury in determining guilt or innocence.[142]

Once the preliminary investigation has concluded and a complete dossier (*delo*) has been compiled, the lead investigator must come to one of the following conclusions supported by appropriate explanation and documentation: indict; forward the case to court for a decision on the necessity of taking measures of a medical nature; dismiss the case; or transfer the case to a court for administrative sanctions. If the investigator concludes that sufficient evidence exists to indict, he must inform the victim and/or his representative(s) and the civil plaintiff(s)/defendant(s) that they have a right to review the dossier and file appropriate motions.[143] Upon their petition, the investigator must forward the dossier to them for review. After the aforementioned parties have familiarized themselves with the dossier, the investigator must provide the same opportunities to the accused and counsel. [144] The investigator then draws up the formal indictment, which he submits, along with the entire dossier, to the appropriate procurator.[145] Having received the formal charge and dossier from the investigator, it is then incumbent upon the procurator to review the case to ensure that (1) there is indeed a crime attributable to the accused, (2) there are no circumstances warranting the discontinuation of the matter, (3) there has been a thorough and objective investigation, (4) the demands of the CCP have been met by the investigating agencies, and (5) the initial accusation and the formal indictment are well-founded and in accord with the law. The procurator has five days from the date he receives the case to decide whether to indict and forward the case to court, close the case, or return it for additional investigation.[146] He also has the right to exclude, reduce, or increase the criminal charges contained in the formal charge drafted by the investigator as well as to create a new indictment altogether. If he decides that more serious charges are in order, they must be clearly supported by the facts in the dossier. If not, then the procurator must return the case for supplemental investigation.[147]

1. Initial Court Appearance and 2. Charging Instrument

If, at his discretion, the procurator files an indictment in a criminal case,[148] he sends the indictment and entire case file to the appropriate court with notification as to whether he considers it necessary to appear before the court to support the indictment.[149] The CCP only requires the participation of a procurator at jury trials and if

141. The Moscow City Courts are interested in establishing a pilot program on plea bargaining based, in part, on the fact that plea bargaining would help reduce heavy caseloads and that it is a useful tool for penetrating organized crime groups.

142. Articles 69 and 111 of the CCP. *See also* Article 77 of the CCP.

143. *See* Articles 200 and 201 of the CCP.

144. *See* Articles 201–204 of the CCP. Defense council may file motions for additional preliminary investigation with the investigator, who, in most instances, has the discretion to grant or refuse such requests.

145. *See* Articles 205–207 of the CCP. The procurator may or may not have previously participated in the investigation.

146. *See* Article 214 of the CCP. *See* discussion in the text below regarding the referral of jury trial cases for supplemental investigation.

147. *See* Article 215 of the CCP.

148. *See* Articles 211-217 of the CCP.

149. At this point, the case file becomes the official court record.

the trial judge so orders.[150] At this time, notice of the specific court to which the case has been forwarded is also served on the defendant. In non-jury trial regions, the defendant makes his initial appearance at a preliminary hearing held by a professional judge.[151] Having received the indictment and case file from the procurator, the judge will review them to decide whether the case should be placed on the trial docket.[152]

In jury trial regions, the procurator enjoys greater responsibility for the indictment and trial. Inquisitorial rules allowing the court, on its own initiative, to close or conduct a case in spite of a procurator's decision to the contrary in his absence, have been abolished. The jury trial judge must adhere to the procurator's decision, for example, not to proceed because of insufficient evidence. Similarly, the court cannot unilaterally send a case back for further investigation; there must be a motion to do so by one of the parties based on new evidence. Finally, once the indictment has been handed down, a defendant must promptly petition for a jury trial. Failure to do so constitutes a complete waiver of one's right to a jury trial.

3. *Preliminary Hearing and Pretrial Motions*

Non-Jury Trials

Within 14 days of the date on which the procurator forwards the formal indictment, a professional judge must decide whether the case should be committed for trial. At this preliminary administrative proceeding, the judge[153] who, alone, reviews the matter has a number of options. Specifically, he has the authority to place the case on the trial docket, remand it for supplementary investigation, or transfer it to another court because of improper jurisdiction or venue. He may also suspend or dismiss it. The judge must also decide whether the procurator's formal indictment is legally sound, whether any means of restraint imposed on the defendant should be changed or revoked, and whether any petitions of the various parties should be granted.[154] If the judge resolves to docket the case for trial, he must set the date, time and place of trial and decide who will be summoned to participate in the case (*i.e.* interpreters, witnesses, experts, etc.).[155] Additionally, he must provide all of the parties with an opportunity to review the dossier, and furnish the defendant and his counsel with a copy of the indictment.[156] By law, trial is required to

---

150. *See* Articles 228 and 428 of the CCP. *See also* Decree No. 44 (August 18, 1994) issued by the General Procurator of the Russian Federation in which the Procurator General obliges all those subordinate to him to participate in trials involving organized crime, banditry, pre-meditated murder, and smuggling, as well as cases involving other dangerous crimes, crimes committed by juveniles, and cases where the importance and complexity of the procedural issues make the participation of the procurator necessary. A recent article in the Moscow Times indicates the frustration that many defense attorneys experience when procurators do not show up to present their cases. *See* Judge is Accuser, Arbiter, *supra* note 138.

151. As in many other civil law jurisdictions, Russia has both professional and lay judges. See section entitled *Judges infra*.

152. *See* Articles 221-223[1] of the CCP.

153. Should the case eventually go to trial, the judge who docketed the matter is not barred from presiding over it at trial.

154. *See* Articles 221–223[1] of the CCP.

155. *Id.* He must also determine whether the case will be heard by a single judge or a panel and whether the case will be heard in an open or closed proceeding.

156. See Articles 236-237 of the CCP.

begin within two weeks of a case's docketing, but these time limits are frequently violated. In fact, it is not uncommon for defendants to wait several months, usually all the while sitting in pretrial detention, for their cases to come to trial.[157]

Jury Trials

Once a defendant (*podsudimyi*) has petitioned for a jury trial, a preliminary hearing is held on the decision to indict and evidentiary matters. Motions submitted by the parties and other procedural matters, such as verifying the defendant's election of a jury trial, are also considered at this time. All parties must be present at this proceeding.[158] Pretrial motions to suppress evidence, although a relatively new procedure for which there is little case precedent or guidance, are now more or less routine in Russia's jury trial regions.[159] Increasingly, jury trial judges are preliminarily excluding information on defendants' prior convictions as inadmissible under the new jury trial law. They are also striking evidence that has a prejudicial effect outweighing any probative value.[160] A significant drawback, however, is that suppressed evidence often comes back in through in-court testimony. For example, a defendant's prior bad acts, once preliminarily excluded, are often revealed by a victim or witness who is asked to relate "what happened" in an uninterrupted narrative in court.[161]

Measures of Restraint and Pretrial Detention

At any time during the pretrial stage of a criminal prosecution, the accused may be subjected to one of several "measures of restraint" (*meri presecheniya*), including bail, a signed guarantee not to leave the jurisdiction, and custodial detention—provided there are sufficient grounds to believe that he may flee, obstruct the preliminary investigation, or continue to engage in criminal activity.[162] In order to execute any one of these measures against the accused, a "reasoned decree" detailing the foundations for the selection of a particular measure of restraint must be submitted by the person conducting the investigation, prosecutor, or court.[163] In the case of bail or custodial detention, prior procuratorial authorization of an investigator's decree is required. Further, the CCP gives procurators rather broad authority to apply, alter (*i.e.* change the particular measure of restraint or lengthen/shorten the term of its application), or remove measures of restraint.[164]

157. See case of Aju Mariam, *supra* note 49.

158. See Article 432 of the CCP.

159. In Russian jury trials, all parties may move to suppress evidence. Jury trial proceedings are covered in Articles 420-466 of the CCP.

160. For example, based on this standard, a judge denied the introduction into evidence of photographs of a victim's decomposed body. See Case of SLONCHAKOV/CHERNIKOV (Moscow Regional Court) in CEELI Memorandum *supra* note 102.

161. Witness preparation is relatively rare in Russia, particularly in non-jury trial regions. In the eight regions that have jury trials, witness preparation is more and more common.

162. *See* Article 89 of CCP and Article 90 of the Draft CCP. In "exceptional" cases, Article 90 of the CCP allows such measures to be applied against a suspect. *See* discussion in *Arrest and Detention* section *supra*.

163. Articles 91 and 95 of the CCP and draft CCP, respectively, also mandate that consideration be given not only to the type of crime but also to the gender, occupation, age, health, and family situation of the accused.

164. *See* Articles 211 and 213 of the CCP.

The judge who commits the case to trial and the trial judge also retain this authority.[165]

Although the criminal procedure code provides a variety of restraint measures, the reality in Russia is that custodial detention (*zakliucheniye pod strazhu*) is the rule as opposed to the exception. Bail is rarely used, even if the accused is neither a flight risk nor has committed a dangerous crime. Most experts agree that "[t]wo factors strongly encourage a high rate of detention in Russia: the institutional politics of fighting crime and the legal regime of arrest and detention...[T]he law of criminal procedure...erects few obstacles to the arrest and detention of citizens and the state places a high priority on expunging crime, especially through preventative measures."[166] In fact, for crimes such as kidnapping, robbery, arson, bribery, and drug trafficking, the CCP allows law enforcement officials to hold an accused in custody pending trial based purely on the objective "dangerousness" of the crime.[167] By law, upon presentation of the decree applying a particular measure of restraint, the accused must be informed of his appeal rights. However, the procurator's discretion to order custodial detention is left unchecked unless the detainee files a *habeas corpus*-type of appeal to the courts.[168] Even if such an appeal is filed, the chances of release are slim given the political pressure to control crime by incarceration and the courts' lack of confidence and experience in exercising judicial review.[169] The result is that Russia's pretrial detention facilities are filled with many individuals without criminal records and persons, more often than not, accused of relatively minor offenses.[170] Human rights reports reveal that once in pretrial detention, detainees are often subject to abuse, and even torture. In addition, conditions in Russia's SIZOs (pretrial detention facilities) are abysmal. Intense overcrowding compounded by unsanitary conditions has led to the rampant spread of tuberculosis and other communicable diseases.[171]

Under current law, the maximum term of detention pending trial is two months, but this term may be extended in certain circumstances for up to 18 months.[172] An additional six months of detention is also possible if granted by a

---

165. *See* Articles 222-223 of the CCP.

166. *See* Foglesong, *supra* note 7 at pp. 549-55.

167. Article 96 CCP. *See* case of Aju Mariam in ICJ Report, *supra* note 49. Ms. Mariam was charged with unlawful purchase and possession of drugs with intent to supply and unlawful sale of drugs to another under Article 224(3) of the Criminal Code. Ms. Mariam had no prior criminal record but her alleged crime is considered "objectively dangerous" under Article 96 of the CCP. Her lawyer's petition to release her from a detention facility was denied, in part, because of her alleged crime's classification as "dangerous" under Article 96.

168. A detainee may also file a complaint against the extension of the term of detention. *See* Articles 220-1 and 220-2 as well as the discussion of judicial review of arrest and detention decisions in *Arrest and Detention* section *supra*.

169. *See* Solomon, *supra* note 91. In his article, Mr. Solomon notes the following: "[T]he courts have reviewed nearly 20% of these decisions and overturned some 20% of those reviewed. As a result, some 4% of suspects and accused placed in detention before trial have gained release."

170. The Moscow Center for Prison Reform has collected hundreds of reports of detainees like Elena Voronina — a mother of two small children without a criminal record who was detained on a charge of stealing 5 kilos of biscuits. *See* Amnesty, *supra* note 18 at pp. 29–34. *See also* Russians Lament, *supra* note 124.

171. Detainees must sometimes sleep in shifts because there are not enough beds. *See* Russians Lament, *supra* note 124. *See also* Russia Human Rights Report, *supra* note 49 at p. 7.

172. *See* Article 97 of the CCP. It provides district and county prosecutors (and prosecutors of equal status) with the authority to extend the period of detention for up to three (3) additional months if it is not possible to complete the preliminary investigation and there are no grounds for

court upon procuratorial petition that the accused have this time to review the materials in the completed dossier.[173] In reality, the vast majority of defendants in pretrial detention remain incarcerated for periods far exceeding the appropriate legal maximum. This situation exists for several reasons. First, Russia has no legislation akin to the American "Speedy Trial Act." Trials are regularly delayed because of the overwhelming caseloads of individual judges.[174] Second, once commenced, trial proceedings are frequently adjourned because participants, especially witnesses, fail to appear. Hence, defendants generally wait more than a year for their cases, once docketed, to actually reach trial. Further, as discussed above, the overwhelming majority of these defendants linger in jail during this considerable period of time. Some estimates indicate that by the time most of those in pretrial detention finally go to trial, they will have already served the amount of prison time that they could potentially receive as punishment, if convicted.[175]

B. Trial

1. Nature of Trial

The vast majority of Russia's criminal trials are based on the inquisitorial procedure of the civil law system. Although a positive development for rule of law reform, only a small number of criminal cases in Russia are actually tried by a jury. At present, jury trials are only available in nine (9)[176] out of the eighty-nine (89) administrative regions in Russia. Further, jury trials are only available for certain serious crimes, such as murder, rape, and kidnapping. [177] Additionally, a defendant must elect to have his case decided by a jury. Thus, at first instance, most criminal

changing the measure of restraint. Regional prosecutors have the power to extend the term of detention for up to six (6) months in cases of "extreme complexity." In "exceptional" cases in which persons are accused of "grave and especially grave crimes," the Deputy Prosecutor General and the Procurator General of the Russian Federation may extend the term of detention for up to a year and up to a year and a half, respectively. Once again, whether a particular case fits into one of these special circumstances is within the sole discretion of members of the Procuracy.

173. The 18-month clock begins to tick at the moment of the detention. The provision permitting a six month extension of detention to allow the defense to review the completed dossier was contained in an amendment to the CCP passed on December 31, 1996. Most regarded it as a significant step backwards on the road to criminal justice reform in Russia, but others saw it as an effective means of stemming the rising tide of criminality in Russia. It is controversial for another reason. Many claim that the amendment is in direct contravention of a Russian Constitutional Court decision of June 13, 1996 which held that provisions disallowing the conditional release of an accused from pretrial detention after the conclusion of the preliminary investigation were unconstitutional. *See* Amnesty, *supra* note 18 at p. 6.

174. *See* the chronological timetable of the case of Aju Mariam. Her case was delayed for more than two and one half years. ICJ Report, *supra* note 49.

175. *See* Amnesty, *supra* note 18. Time served in pretrial detention facilities is subtracted from any sentence that a convicted defendant may receive.

176. In 1993, Russia re-invigorated its jury trial system which began as one of the populist reforms under Tsar Alexander II in the late 17th century. Moscow, Saratov, Krasnodar, Rostov, Stavropol, Ivanovo, Ryazan, Altai, and Simbirsk (Ulyanovsk) are the nine regions that presently have jury trials. Despite requests from approximately 12 regions, there are currently no plans to implement the jury trial system in any other areas.

177. *See* Articles 36 and 421 of the CCP.

cases come before a single judge or a panel of judges,[178] but rarely before a professional judge and jury.

A troubling aspect of Russian criminal trials is the fact that in Russia's 89 non-jury trial regions, the judge may remand the case for additional investigation at any time during the proceeding. This inheritance from the Soviet era raises concerns about whether the Russian Constitution's prohibition on double jeopardy has any meaningful content at all. Practically speaking, this situation also encourages cases to languish unresolved for years. Such delays in the disposition of criminal cases not only hinder efforts aimed at reducing the huge numbers of cases pending in Russian courts, but also further extends the time that detained defendants spend in jail.

Judicial proceedings in Russia, at both bench and jury trials, are rather informal events and often exhibit a lack of any formalized procedure. The judges, procurators, and defense attorneys constantly interrupt witnesses and each other. Further, spectators seated in the public viewing areas regularly shout out their reactions to the testimony of witnesses and the defendant. In fact, it is not uncommon to hear extremely prejudicial outbursts such as: "*You are a scoundrel! You are a devil! You murdered my daughter!!*" Such interjections usually go unchecked by the judge and rarely receive any objection from either prosecution or defense.[179]

The most distinguishing visual characteristic of Russian courtrooms is the jail cell located in full view of all present, even the jury.[180] Instead of sitting at a table with counsel, a defendant must sit or stand in this cell or as it is commonly called "the cage," throughout all courtroom proceedings.[181] The defendant asks questions and gives testimony from the cage. If there are multiple defendants, they are often placed altogether in the cage. With permission from the presiding judge, defense counsel may confer with his client by walking over to the cage and whispering through the bars. Initially, the decision to place defendants in a cell—a contraption that arguably erodes the presumption of innocence—was a financial one. Unfortunately, it appears that the cost of hiring a guard for every defendant at

---

178. By law, single judges may only hear cases for which the maximum punishment is no more than five years imprisonment. With the consent of the accused, though, single judges may also hear other types of cases. *See* Article 35(2) of the CCP. All other cases are heard by a three judge panel, comprised of either a professional judge and two lay assessors or three professional judges. Additionally, a three-professional judge panel, with the consent of the defendant(s), may hear any type of criminal case, except for those cases within the jurisdiction of the District Courts (*See* discussion in text at p. 287). Further, a 15 December 1996 amendment to the CCP provides that a panel of three professional judges must hear any case involving a crime(s) punishable by a maximum penalty of greater than 15 years, life imprisonment, or capital punishment. As a result, regional court judges have been significantly impaired in their ability to hear other cases since the aforementioned cases comprise approximately 80 percent of all cases heard by regional judges. *See* Pashin, *supra* note 103. It is important to note that despite the wording of the legislation, Russia, as a member of the Council of Europe, has agreed to abolish capital punishment. *See also*, discussion in text on p. 287.

179. *See* generally, Richard Andrias, "Jury-Trials, Russian-style," 11(2) Criminal Justice 14 (Summer 1996) (hereinafter "Andrias").

180. In jury trials, the cage is often located directly across from the jury box.

181. In addition, the Ministry of the Interior (MVD) has issued orders instructing MVD guards that they cannot allow anyone, even defense counsel, to approach the defendant in the courtroom. A new law on the Marshal's Service (FZ-118, July 21,1997) now gives the Marshals responsibility for judge and courtroom security.

every criminal proceeding throughout Russia continues to be too costly, even in the post-Soviet era, to abolish the use of the cage.[182]

Features of Non-Jury Trials

In non-jury trials, Russia employs the inquisitorial process which is distinguished by a trial proceeding in which all participants[183] inquire into the factual circumstances surrounding the criminal act. As the principal truth seeker, the judge is charged with the primary role in making evidentiary findings and determining the veracity of testimony. Hence, a procurator's election not to appear to present a particular case does not prevent the trial from moving forward.[184]

Bench trials generally proceed as follows. The judge[185] announces the beginning of the trial and takes participant attendance. Witnesses are then excused until the time that they are slated to testify. Next, challenges to the inclusion of participants as well as motions regarding new witnesses and evidence are heard. The judge concludes this stage of the trial by summarizing each party's rights and obligations at trial.[186]

The judge commences the judicial inquiry (*sudebnoye sledstviye*) by reading the indictment or directing the procurator to read it, which essentially consists of a long and detailed recitation of the findings of the preliminary investigation. The judge then asks the defendant whether he understands the charges against him and whether or not he pleads guilty. The defendant must answer himself. Upon his request, the defendant must be given an opportunity explain his answer, but few defendants actually avail themselves of this right.[187] The judge then asks the defendant to testify if he so desires, but advises the defendant of his right not to incriminate himself.[188] Next, the court examines the evidence in the case. Having read the dossier, and thus knowing all the facts and findings in the matter, the judge calls for and examines evidence and asks questions of the attorneys, witnesses, and defendant. Under Russian rules of evidence, experts' conclusions and *protokols* (*i.e.* witness, search and seizure, line-up, crime scene examination *protokols*) are automatically admissible.[189] Although Russia's criminal procedure code mandates that court decisions be based on primary and direct evidence produced in live court, the reality is that judges commonly fill in the evidentiary gaps from trial with

---

182. In his article "Trial By Jury in the New Russia: A Travelogue," 15 Dick. J. Int'l L. 151, 158 (1996), Professor Gary Gilden describes an instance where the judge ordered that the defendant sit with his attorney at the counsel table, only to be refused by the guard on duty who stated: "You have your instructions, I have mine." Russian judges have no recourse in these situations. The Regional Court in Ryazin, however, is an exception to the rule. Instead of a "cage," this regional court uses a dock similar to that used in Great Britain.

183. The participants consist of the judge, procurator, defense attorney, victim or victim's representative, and defendant.

184. *See* discussion in text in section entitled: *Initial Court Appearance and Charging Instrument.* If the procurator fails to show up, by law, the trial may continue according to Article 251 of the CCP. See also Article 228 of the CCP.

185. If the case is heard by a panel, the chairman of the panel (a professional judge) generally takes the lead with respect to the judicial duties described in the text.

186. *See* Articles 267–277 of the CCP.

187. *See* Article 278 of the CCP.

188. At the trial of Aju Mariam, the trial judge advised Ms. Mariam of her right not to incriminate herself. *See* ICJ Report *supra* note 49 at p. 13, para. 3.12.

189. If justified by the evidence, the court may also introduce new charges. *See* Article 255 of the CCP.

the contents of the case file. For example, if witnesses fail to appear at trial without legal excuse,[190] their statements are often improperly taken from the case file and read into the court record. Thus, the procurator, given his active participation in the preparation of the case file, practically speaking, has the upper hand at trial.

The defendant and the witnesses[191] testify in no particular order. Their statements are not elicited through direct and cross examination. Instead, witnesses and defendants deliver free-form narratives, often containing hearsay. Their testimonies are subject to few, if any, restrictions on content, in part, because the culpability and penalty phases of a criminal matter occur in a single proceeding in Russia. However, if there are substantial inconsistencies between in-court testimony and pretrial statements, the latter are admissible. If witnesses are absent with a legal excuse, their pretrial statements are also admissible. Following their testimony, witnesses may remain in the courtroom while others testify (including other witnesses) and may be asked to respond to additional questions. Although the judge takes the lead, all parties may ask questions of those testifying.[192] In practice, the procurator and the defense attorney ask few questions of either the witnesses or the defendant, and they rarely object to statements made in testimony. If improper evidence or questioning is given, it is usually the judge, not the attorneys, who announces its inadmissibility.

Pleadings follow the examination of evidence. Again, all parties have the right to make oral arguments and rebuttals with the proviso that they concern only the evidence presented in court. By law, the last rebuttal always goes to the defendant.[193] The court may neither place time restrictions on nor permit any questions during the defendant's last word. However, the judge may stop the defendant for irrelevancies and reinitiate questioning if the defendant informs the court of new and relevant facts.

Following the defendant's last word, the single judge or panel retires to decide the case in private. If the case is heard by a panel, the verdict is determined by a vote. A simple majority is needed to convict. Since the guilt and sentencing phases are combined, the court returns with both a verdict and punishment.

Features of Jury Trials

Russian jury trials are adversarial proceedings with the attorneys generally taking a larger and the judge a more diminished role in the courtroom.[194] Only professional judges may preside over jury trials, and they are conducted in the following manner.

---

190. What precisely qualifies as a legal excuse for failure to appear is undefined in the CCP. *See* Article 286 of the CCP.

191. Experts are included in this category.

192. After the judge has completed his questioning, questions may be asked by the parties in the following order: procurator, victim or victim's representative, and defense counsel and/or defendant.

193. *See* Articles 46 and 297 of the CCP.

194. In fact, the language of the CCP requires such: "The preliminary hearing and the jury trial are based on the principle of adversariness. Equal rights are guaranteed to the parties, for whom the judge, while maintaining objectivity and impartiality, creates the necessary conditions for a thorough and complete investigation of the facts." (Art. 429 of the CCP).

Once a jury panel has been selected, the judge instructs the jurors that he has the authority to rule on questions of law and punishment,[195] whereas they have the responsibility for deciding the defendant's guilt or innocence. The judge further instructs the jury that the parties are equal, that the defendant is presumed innocent until proven guilty, that the jury must hear all of the evidence before pronouncing guilt or not, and that jurors must be objective, fair, and just. With the jury present, the judge then asks the defendant whether or not he admits guilt but warns the defendant about self-incrimination before giving him the opportunity to testify.[196] Next, the victim or victim's representative is advised as to his rights and duties. The procurator then presents the charges against the defendant. In Russian jury trials, neither the prosecution nor the defense has the right to make an opening statement to the jury.[197] On the whole, witness testimony resembles more of a narrative than an examination by attorneys which, as noted earlier, is a situation that facilitates the disclosure of inadmissible evidence. As in non-jury trials, victims and defendants are allowed to question witnesses.[198] Jurors are also entitled to question witnesses and defendants, but only via written questions forwarded to the judge. Finally, the use of exhibits and diagrams and other explanatory aids for the jury is rare.

Following a summation by the judge of the evidence presented by the prosecution and defense, the jury retires to deliberate. Jurors arrive at a verdict by completing a juror questionnaire.[199] It usually consists of three questions: "Did the prosecution prove that the alleged incident took place? If so, did the prosecution prove that this defendant was involved? If so, did the prosecution prove that he is legally responsible?" A defendant is found guilty only if all three questions are answered in the affirmative by all jurors. However, after three hours of deliberation, the standard falls to a majority of jurors answering all three questions with a "yes." An acquittal occurs if at least half of the jurors answer any one question in the negative. Finally, based on mitigating circumstances, the jury also has the authority to recommend leniency in the defendant's sentence.[200]

Gradually, Russian jury trial judges and attorneys are casting off their inquisitorial tendencies as they struggle to accept the increased responsibilities associated with trying a case in front of a jury. They are also developing effective trial advocacy skills and jury selection techniques.[201] Still, the civil law system and mind-set greatly influence this common law process. Russian judges are hesitant to give up their traditional role as the primary inquisitors, and procurators still generally receive deferential treatment by all parties. In sum, Russian jury trials are a unique mix of adversarial and inquisitorial rules strung together in a rather informal proceeding.[202]

---

195. *See* further discussion in *Jurors* section *infra*.

196. *See* section entitled *Defendant infra*.

197. The draft CCP, however, gives both sides the right to make an opening statement.

198. The order of questioning is also the same. *See* text at p. 308 and note 183, *supra*.

199. *See* Andrias, *supra* note 179 at pp. 17–18.

200. *See* Articles 445 and 449 of the CCP.

201. Many Russian lawyers have participated in trial advocacy training programs conducted by US and European instructors.

202. The future of jury trials in Russia is unclear. Many Russian attorneys readily support jury trials as an effective check on both procuratorial discretion and adherence by all parties to the rules of criminal procedure. Others oppose jury trials, arguing that a lay jury cannot meaningfully appreciate the complexities of a criminal case. Moreover, the financial and manpower resources needed to support jury trials are strong disincentives for their expansion.

1. Defendants

In Russia, every defendant has the right to a defense.[203] Criminal defendants also have the right not to testify,[204] and the fact that they do not testify cannot be held against them. The defendant and the jury, if there is one, are specifically instructed to this effect.[205] If the defendant chooses not to testify, however, any statements made by him during the preliminary investigation may be disclosed. As noted earlier, these same statements may also be introduced if there are significant contradictions between a defendant's in-court testimony and pretrial statements.[206] Finally, the defendant may offer arguments and explanations in addition to relating the facts,[207] and unlike witnesses, the defendant does not have to sign a statement promising to tell the truth.

2. Lawyers

The right to qualified legal counsel is guaranteed by Article 48 of the RF Constitution and Article 47 of the CCP.[208] As discussed previously, both lawyers and non-lawyers are permitted to act as defense counsel in a criminal matter.[209] Defendants must be represented by counsel at jury trials. According to the CCP, the participation of defense counsel in non-jury trials[210] is only mandatory in cases in which (1) public procurators participate; (2) juveniles are involved; (3) persons, who because of a mental and/or physical handicap (i.e. deaf, mute, or blind), cannot adequately defend themselves; (4) persons cannot speak the language (Russian) in which the judicial proceedings are conducted; and (5) persons are accused of crimes for which the death penalty may be imposed.[211] The rights and obligations of defense counsel are outlined in Article 51 of the CCP and include the right to participate in interrogations, file petitions, and meet alone with clients without limitation as to quantity and length of such meetings.[212] In practice, defense attorneys frequently incur difficulty not only in securing meetings with their clients in custody, but also in preserving attorney-client privilege and privacy at client meetings in correctional institutions.

If an individual cannot afford a private defense lawyer, the procurator (or the person conducting the preliminary investigation, usually the investigator) or court will appoint a public defender.[213] But, as noted earlier, securing a lawyer—partic-

---

203. *See* Article 48 of the RF Constitution and Article 19 of the CCP. Subject to a few minor exceptions, defendants are obliged to appear at trial. See Article 246 and 247 of the CCP.

204. Article 51 of the Russian Constitution (1993).

205. Article 451 of the CCP.

206. *See* Articles 281 and 246 of the CCP.

207. *See* Article 298 of the CCP.

208. *See also* Articles 48 and 50 of the CCP.

209. Article 47 of the CCP permits not only advocates (members of the official College of Advocates), but also private attorneys (not members of a Collegia), representatives of professional unions and other social organizations (where the matter involves a member), as well as close relatives and other persons (with permission of a judge) to act as defense attorneys. *See* discussion in *Arrest and Detention* section. See also Article 249 and 250 of the CCP.

210. Article 49 of the CCP.

211. The participation of a defender is mandatory at the pretrial stage of criminal prosecutions in cases involving juveniles; persons with a mental and/or physical defect; and persons accused of crimes for which the death penalty may be imposed. With respect to the last category, Russia, as a member of the Council of Europe, has agreed to abolish capital punishment.

212. *See also* Articles 48 and 50 of the CCP.

213. *See* Article 47 of the CCP and Article 48 of the RF Constitution.

ularly at the pretrial stage—is often problematic. Further, the quality of public defenders is generally quite low in Russia [214] since they are paid roughly $8USD per day of court-approved work. According to Sergei Pashin, a judge of the Moscow City Court, the present fee-for-service system of providing legal assistance to indigent citizens suffers greatly from the fact that attorneys assigned to these cases frequently delay hearings in these matters in order to attend the proceedings of their well-paying clients.[215]

3. *Witnesses and Experts*

While witnesses are considered court witnesses, as opposed to witnesses for a particular side, they may be called by both prosecution and defense. By law, witnesses are required to appear when officially summoned (subpoenaed), to relate all they know about the particular case and to answer all questions during both the preliminary investigation and at trial. At the pretrial stage, a witness' statement is officially recorded in a *protokol* which is signed by the witness at the conclusion of his testimony. [216]

In Russia, it is a criminal offense for a witness to refuse to testify or to give false testimony.[217] In accordance with constitutional privileges, exceptions are made for those who refuse to give testimony against themselves or against a spouse or a close relative.[218] Witnesses may not be asked leading questions. At trial, answers to leading questions will be struck by the judge, even if no objection is made by counsel. More importantly, the factual information that witnesses relate in their testimony is only admissible if the source of the information is indicated.[219] In practice, it appears that witness summonses are rather sporadically enforced, and the absence of witnesses often delays trial proceedings.[220] Furthermore, interference with witness testimony and witness intimidation are common, particularly in high profile and organized crime cases.[221]

In Russia, experts or committees of experts may be summoned to assist with pretrial investigations and trials[222] if special knowledge of "science, technology, art,

---

214. For example, in the case of Aju Mariam, the first court- appointed attorney did not explain to Ms. Mariam the case against her and then failed to show up for her initial appearance before a judge. *See* ICJ Report, *supra* note 49 at p. 8.

215. Pashin, *supra* note 103 at p. 12.

216. *See* Article 73 and 74 of the CCP. According to Article 32 of the CCP, a witness' statement made during the preliminary investigation and recorded in a witness protokol is admissible in exceptional circumstances where the witness is prevented from appearing in court (*i.e.* illness, death, or absence from forum). In practice, this standard is often applied very loosely, if at all, which some assert is a legitimate ground for appeal. *See* Ratnikov, *supra* note 117 at p. 348.

217. *See* Article 307 of the Criminal Code. Witnesses are informed of these rules and sign the *protokol* indicating that they understand them prior to giving testimony.

218. *See* Articles 308 of the Criminal Code and Article 51 of the RF Constitution. Witness testimony, however, is often excluded because investigators fail to advise witnesses of this privilege.

219. Article 74 of the CCP.

220. *See* ICJ Report, *supra* note 49 at p. 11.

221. Articles 176(8) and 324(5) of the draft CCP include provisions for the protection of the identities of witnesses and victims during the investigation and trial stages of a criminal matter.

222. *See* Article 78 of the CCP. Article 184 of the CCP outlines the procedures that those conducting the pretrial investigation must follow when conducting expert consultations. At the pretrial stage, in addition to other rights, the suspect or accused has the right to challenge the expert selected, present additional questions to the expert, and request that an expert be chosen from a list that he proposes. *See* Article 185 of the CCP.

or craft" is required.[223] Experts may also analyze handwriting and other specimens submitted to them for comparative examination. Like witnesses, experts are neutral participants. Persons possessing the appropriate expertise needed are summoned and paid by those conducting the investigation or by the court. By law, experts must furnish an objective conclusion in the form of a written report.[224] They are criminally liable for refusing to provide a conclusion or knowingly providing a false conclusion.[225] Further, experts are obliged to appear at trial when called, but in practice, most do not testify in court and instead submit a written report that is automatically admissible at trial.

Experts have the right to familiarize themselves with relevant materials; to petition for additional pertinent materials; and with permission, to be present during certain proceedings and pose questions to those being interrogated. By law, suspects/accused persons/defendants and counsel must be presented with a copy of any expert's report. They also have the right to provide explanations, file objections, request additional questions be asked of the expert, and petition for an another expert consultation. The procurator or persons conducting the investigation must answer such requests from the defense, but in most instances they are not required to fulfill them. In fact, more often than not, the procurator or investigator declines to carry out these requests.

At trial, experts are permitted to ask questions of the defendant, victim, and witnesses related to the opinion they have been asked to render. Likewise, each one of the parties may submit written questions to the expert. All parties may also ask the expert to clarify or supplement his conclusion. Neither the court nor those conducting the pretrial investigation are bound to accept the conclusion of an expert; however, if they do not accept it, they must provide the reasons for doing so.[226] Finally, experts tend to be expensive and are, therefore, used sparingly in Russia.

4. *Judges*

A fair number of Russian judges have significant experience as practicing attorneys, mostly as procurators, but many have also been judges since graduation from law school.[227] As is the case in other civil law jurisdictions, Russia has a separate cadre of non-professional judges called lay assessors[228] who hear both civil and criminal cases alongside professional judges. They are ordinary citizens, age 25 or older, elected to serve as lay judges by the community. Lay assessors

223. *See* Article 78 of the CCP. According to Article 79 of the CCP, expert consultation is required to establish the cause of death; the nature of bodily injury, the mental or physical state of a suspect, accused person, witness, or victim when questions arise as to his capacity and responsibility; as well as the age of the accused, suspect, or victim in cases where it is a material issue.

224. *See* Article 191 of the CCP.

225. *See* Article 182 of the CCP.

226. Article 80 of the CCP.

227. Further, according to Judge Sergei Pashin, approximately 29 percent of Russia's sitting judges have worked as a judge for three (3) years or less. *See* Pashin, *supra* note 103.

228. Lay Assessors are commonly referred to as "Nodders," as they seldom disagree with the professional judge. A new law dealing with the selection, tenure, and qualifications of lay assessors is expected to be passed in 1999.

are generally senior citizens who are assigned to a particular judge for a year-long term, but the position is really more or less permanent.[229] Lay judges have the same authority as professional judges to read the dossier, examine evidence, call and question witnesses, as well as to decide guilt and sentencing. Only professional judges, however, are allowed to preside over jury trials.

Finally, a recent concern of many members of the Russian judiciary is courtroom security. A new law on the Marshal's Service was passed in the summer of 1997 in an attempt to remedy this situation.[230]

5. *Victims* (poterpevshiya)

The Russian Constitution provides that "[t]he rights of victims of crimes or of abuses of power are protected by law [and the] state guarantees the victim's access to justice and to compensation for damages caused."[231] Accordingly, in Russia as in most European nations, a victim's civil claims may be joined to the criminal proceeding.[232] Further, as a result of reforms during the Khrushev era, victims are parties to criminal proceedings, which affords them significant rights of participation in both bench and jury trials. Specifically, victims and their official representatives have the right to testify,[233] to present evidence, to review materials from the completed preliminary investigation, to question witnesses and the defendant at trial, and to appeal court decisions.[234] In jury trials, the victim or his representative may object to a procurator's decision to dismiss the case. Victim testimony may include facts as well as opinions, but like witnesses, victims must identify the source of their knowledge. Otherwise, the information they impart cannot be used as evidence. Finally, it is an offense under the Criminal Code for a victim to refuse to provide testimony or to give false testimony.[235]

Although arguably a positive development for victims' rights, the expansive role of the victim in Russia may in fact be undermining new constitutional guarantees of due process. For example, victim testimony, questioning and verbal interjections during trial often contain prejudicial information, such as prior bad acts, that were preliminarily excluded based on the presumption of innocence. This is particularly problematic in jury trials as jurors may be influenced by such remarks.[236]

---

229. *See* Pashin, *supra* note 103 at p. 4. A presidential decree (*Ukaz Presidenta* RF, No. 41, January 23, 1997) continued the terms of then-sitting lay accessors.

230. *See* note 181 *supra*.

231. *See* Section I, Chapter 2, Article 54 of the Constitution of the Russian Federation (1993).

232. Thus, civil damages, if any, are awarded along with the verdict and sentence.

233. *See* Article 75 of the CCP. *See also* Articles 303 and 308 of the CC.

234. *See* Article 53 of the CCP.

235. *See* Article 308 of the Criminal Code. Again, exceptions are made for those who refuse to give testimony against themselves, their spouses, or close relatives. The CCP also provides victims with other means of taking legal action against an accused. *See* Articles 27 and 53 of the CCP.

236. *See* Scott P. Boylan, "Coffee from a Samovar: The Role of the Victim in the Criminal Procedure of Russia and the Proposed Victims Rights Amendment to the United States Constitution Compared," 4(1) U.C. Davis J. Int'l Law & Policy 103 (Winter 1998). In his article, Mr. Boylan contends that Russia's creation of an official, constitutional role for the victim before guilt is established, in and of itself, defeats the realization of a true presumption of innocence.

6. *Jurors*

Jury pools are derived from local housing lists. Jury duty is mandatory and when they are paid, jurors are fairly well compensated for their time.[237] Prospective jurors must be citizens of the Russian Federation between 25 and 70 years old and have no criminal convictions or mental incapacities. Twelve jurors, foreperson included, and two alternates hear each case. The prosecution and defense have two peremptory challenges each, plus theoretically unlimited challenges for cause. Those lawyers practicing in Russia's jury trial regions seem to have only two major complaints about the jury selection process: the lawyers' inability to question the jurors directly and the minimal amount of information provided by the court on prospective jurors. These failings have the effect of reducing challenges for cause.

C. Appeals

In Russia, appeals may take one of the following forms: pretrial appeals of alleged law enforcement misconduct; appeals of unenforced verdicts[238] and sentences (cassation); and supervisory review. Each proceeding differs in terms of its availability and scope. Under the CCP, oral or written complaints against the actions of an Agency of Inquiry or Investigation may be lodged with a procurator directly or through those whose conduct is questioned. If the latter receive the complaint, they must forward it along with any explanations to the Procuracy within 24 hours. Upon receipt of a complaint, a procurator has three days to review it and inform the complainant of his decision in the matter. If the procurator rejects the complaint, he must set out his reasons for doing so.[239] Complaints against a decision or the conduct of a procurator are directed to the appropriate higher level procurator.[240] Because the appeals discussed previously are all directed to and decided by the Procuracy, subjects them to a potentially one-sided and biased analysis.

In Russia, the standard appellate procedure is cassation (*kassatsiya*).[241] If the court of first instance is a district court, then the regional court will hear the appeal; appeals from the regional courts are heard by the Supreme Court. Jury trial cases may only be reviewed by a cassational panel of the Russian Supreme Court.[242] In jury trial cases, as a general rule, only legal errors and omissions (*e.g.* violations of criminal procedure rules) may be subject of cassational review.[243] In

---

237. Judge Sergei Pashin notes that in 1996, 35 percent of jurors summoned, actually reported to court. He explains that the low juror appearance rate is due to poorly maintained jury lists and sporadic juror remuneration. *See* Pashin, *supra* note 103 at p. 4.

238. Cassational appeals are appeals of judgments that have not yet entered into force.

239. *See* Articles 218 and 219 of the CCP.

240. *See* Article 220 of the CCP.

241. *See* generally, Articles 325–355 of the CCP. When the prosecutor petitions for cassational review, it is called a cassational protest but when launched by the defendant, it is called a cassational appeal. When a victim or civil plaintiff/defendant appeals, it is referred to as a private cassational appeal.

242. *See* Article 464 of the CCP.

243. *See* Article 465 of the CCP.

all other cases, appeals may be based on factual and/or legal grounds.[244] All parties (procurator, victim, and defendant) may petition for the cassational review of an unenforced verdict or sentence in a criminal case within one week (7 days) of the court's decision.[245] In fact, the procurator has a legal duty to lodge an appeal on behalf of the state or the defendant based on any illegalities that may have occurred at trial. Both guilty verdicts and acquittals may be appealed by all parties.[246] Some claim, however, that right to appeal acquittals offends the RF Constitution's prohibition against double jeopardy.[247]

The panel of three professional judges reviewing a case on cassational appeal is not restricted to the grounds of the appeal filed by the parties.[248] Having heard the case, the appellate panel may order one of the following judicial remedies: uphold the original decision; cancel the original decision and send the matter back for further investigation or re-trial;[249] cancel the original decision and dismiss the case; or modify the original decision.[250] Grounds for setting aside or modifying a verdict include: incomplete or biased preliminary or court investigation; inconsistency between the factual circumstances of the case and the verdict; significant violation(s) of the rules of criminal procedure; and erroneous application of criminal law.[251] The only limitation on the panel's discretion is that it may neither charge the defendant with a more serious crime nor apply a harsher sentence if the defendant has appealed the case.[252] The same is true if the case is reversed and remanded to the court of first instance, unless the severity of the charge is the reason for the reversal. But, if the reviewing panel sends the case back for supplemental investigation and new facts support a more serious crime, a higher charge and sentence are permitted.

Further appellate review takes the form of supervisory review (*nadzornaya instansiya*), which consists of higher-court review of only those issues of fact and law presented in the case record. By law, only members of the Procuracy or the courts may bring such appeals. The defendant and his counsel are excluded from these proceedings unless the reviewing court, at its discretion, requests their participation. Following its examination of the case, the reviewing court has several options, including returning the case for new investigation or trial at either the cassational or trial level; dismissing the case altogether; or reducing the sentence.[253] Supervisory review is also the procedure used to re-open a criminal case post conviction based on the discovery of new evidence.[254]

---

244. *See* Article 337 of the CCP.

245. Article 328 of the CCP requires that these appeals be filed within seven days of the date on which the judgment is rendered. If the defendant is in custodial detention, the appeal must be filed within seven days of his being served with the judgment. Article 329 of the CCP allows this period to be extended upon petition showing good cause.

246. *See* Articles 328-341 of the CCP.

247. *See* Article 50 of the RF Constitution. *See also* note 35.

248. If matters of fact are reviewed on appeal — only those facts contained in the written record—may be considered by the panel. *See* Article 338 of the CCP.

249. *See* Article 348 of the CCP.

250. *See* Article 339 of the CCP.

251. *See* Articles 345-347 of the CCP.

252. *See* Article 340 of the CCP. This is not the case when the procurator or victim files the appeal or in the case of supervisory review.

253. Articles 371-383 of the CCP describe the supervisory review process.

254. *See* Articles 384-390 of the CCP.

The exclusion of the defendant and counsel from this type of appellate review results in a rather unbalanced proceeding. Further, because neither the defendant nor defense counsel may independently avail themselves of this appellate proceeding, their legal recourses are greatly limited. Of course, they have the right to petition the Procuracy to file a protest on their behalf or to re-open a case on the basis of new evidence but, arguably, this is qualitatively inferior to having the independent right to take such action. Finally, in practice, appellate review at both the cassational and supervisory review levels is often plagued by the fact that court proceedings are poorly recorded, if at all.[255]

1. *Ineffective Assistance of Counsel*

As noted earlier, Article 48(1) provides every person with a right to qualified legal counsel in Russia. However, ineffective assistance of counsel appears to be a growing problem, particularly with respect to indigent defendants. Indeed, this situation is, in part, a direct consequence of allowing those who have no formal legal education to act as defense counsel. To date, however, there appear to be no recorded instances in which a Russian defendant has lodged, or won, an appeal claiming that the incompetence of his defense counsel led to material violations of criminal law or to his conviction.[256] However, discontented clients may, and increasingly do, file complaints with the Chairman of the local Court, the Russian Supreme Court, and/or one of the local Collegia of Advocates regarding the professional conduct of defense counsel.[257] In turn, the Collegia have the authority to investigate such complaints and, if appropriate, to penalize and/or disbar a member attorney.[258]

---

255. This situation has also facilitated the ease with which court records may be falsified. *See* Pashin, *supra* note 102 at p. 12.

256. However, a justice of the RF Constitutional Court raised, but unfortunately did not address, this issue in *dicta* in a case concerning the constitutionality of Article 47 of the CCP. *See* note 56 *supra*.

257. In St. Petersburg, there are about two to three complaints filed with the Collegia each month.

258. In St. Petersburg, approximately five to seven attorneys are disbarred each year based on such complaints.

Chapter 10

South Africa

P.J. Schwikkard
S.E. van der Merwe

I. Introduction

A. Sources

The sources of South African criminal procedure are constitutional provisions, national statutes, common law rules and case law.

1. Constitutional Provisions

The Constitution of the Republic of South Africa Act 108 of 1996 is the supreme law of South Africa. Chapter two of the Constitution contains a justiciable Bill of Rights. Neither statutory rules nor common law rules nor executive acts nor judicial decisions may limit any right entrenched in the Bill of Rights, unless a court with the necessary jurisdiction finds that such a limitation is a constitutionally permissible limitation in terms of section 36(1) of the Constitution.[1] The present Constitution came into operation in February 1997 and was preceded by a so-called interim Constitution[2] which came into operation in April 1994. Prior to the latter date, South Africa never had a Bill of Rights. The new constitutional dispensation not only represents a complete break with the *apartheid* era, but also re-

1. Section 36 of the present Constitution provides as follows:
(1) The right in the Bill of Rights may be limited only in terms of law of general application to the extent that the limitation is reasonable and justifiable in an open and democratic society based on human dignity, equality and freedom, taking into account all relevant factors, including—
(a) the nature of the right;
the importance of the purpose of the limitation;
the nature and extent of the limitation;
the relation between the limitation and its purpose; and
less restrictive means to achieve the purpose.
(2) Except as provided in subsection (1) or in any other provision of the Constitution, no law may limit any right entrenched in the Bill of rights.
2. The Constitution of the Republic of South Africa Act 200 of 1993.

places parliamentary sovereignty with a Constitution which is the supreme law and which can therefore prevent a repetition of the legislative and executive excesses of the past.[3]

Section 35 of the Constitution deals with the rights of arrested, detained, accused and sentenced persons. The drafters of section 35 drew, richly and correctly, not only from local statutory and common law procedural rights, but also from international instruments such as the International Covenants on Civil and Political Rights (1966), regional documents such as the European Convention on the Protection of Human Rights and Fundamental Freedom (1950) and national charters like the Canadian Charter of Rights and Freedoms (1982), They also drew from decisions of the Supreme Court of the United States, most notably *Miranda v Arizona*.[4] The result is that South Africa now sports—from a world-wide comparative perspective and as far as we could establish—one of the most elaborate and detailed provisions dealing with the individual who gets drawn into or who is trapped in the criminal justice system. Section 35 of the Constitution forms the corner-stone of the South African criminal justice system and warrants full quotation:

> (1) Everyone who is arrested for allegedly committing an offence has the right—
>
> (a) to remain silent;
>
> (b) to be informed promptly—
>
> (i) of the right to remain silent; and
>
> (ii) of the consequences of not remaining silent;
>
> (c) not to be compelled to make any confession or admission that could be used in evidence against that person;
>
> (d) to be brought before a court as soon as reasonably possible, but not later than—
>
> (i) 48 hours after the arrest; or
>
> (ii) the end of the first day after the expiry of the 48 hours, if the 48 hours expire outside ordinary court hours or on a day which is not an ordinary court day;
>
> (e) at the first court appearance after being arrested, to be charged or to be informed of the reason for the detention to continue, or to be released; and
>
> (f) to be released from detention if the interests of justice permit, subject to reasonable conditions.
>
> (2) Everyone who is detained, including every sentenced prisoner, has the right—
>
> (a) to be informed promptly of the reason for being detained;
>
> (b) to choose, and to consult with, a legal practitioner, and to be informed of this right promptly;

3. See generally *Dugard Human Rights and the South African Legal Order* (1978) 250-275 and Mathews *Freedom, State Security and the Rule of Law : Dilemmas of the Apartheid Society* (1986) 32–215 for examples and critical analyses of these past excesses.

4. 384 US 436 (1966).

(c) to have a legal practitioner assigned to the detained person by the state and at state expense, if substantial injustice would otherwise result, and to be informed of this right promptly;

(d) to challenge the lawfulness of the detention in person before a court and, if the detention is unlawful, to be released;

(e) to conditions of detention that are consistent with human dignity, including at least exercise and the provision, at state expense, of adequate accommodation, nutrition, reading material and medical treatment; and

(f) to communicate with, and be visited by, that person's—

(i) spouse or partner;

(ii) next of kin;

(iii) chosen religious counsellor; and

(iv) chosen medical practitioner.

(3) Every accused person has a right to a fair trial, which includes the right—

(a) to be informed of the charge with sufficient detail to answer it;

(b) to have adequate time and facilities to prepare a defence;

(c) to a public trial before an ordinary court;

(d) to have their trial begin and conclude without unreasonable delay;

(e) to be present when being tried;

(f) to choose, and be represented by, a legal practitioner, and to be informed of this right promptly;

(g) to have a legal practitioner assigned to the accused person by the state and at state expense, if substantial injustice would otherwise result, and to be informed of this right promptly;

(h) to be presumed innocent, to remain silent, and not to testify during the proceedings;

(i) to adduce and challenge evidence;

(j) not to be compelled to give self-incriminating evidence;

(k) to be tried in a language that the accused person understands or, if that is not practicable to have the proceedings interpreted in that language;

(l) not to be convicted for an act or omission that was not an offence under either national or international law at the time it was committed or omitted;

(m) not to be tried for an offence in respect of an act or omission for which that person has previously been either acquitted or convicted;

(n) to the benefit of the least severe of the prescribed punishments if the prescribed punishment for the offence has been changed between the time that the offence was committed and the time of sentencing; and

(o) of appeal to, or review by, a higher court.

(4) Whenever this section requires information to be given to a person, that information must be given in a language that the person understands.

(5) Evidence obtained in a manner that violates any right in the Bill of Rights must be excluded if the admission of that evidence would render the trial unfair or otherwise be detrimental to the administration of justice.

It is important to bear in mind that section 35 of the Constitution is not a codification of South African criminal procedure. In *S v Zuma*[5] it was held that the right to a fair trial in section 25(3) of the interim Constitution (which is substantially similar to section 35(3) of the present Constitution) encompasses more than the rights enumerated by the drafters.

The interim Constitution and the present Constitution have had a profound effect on the South African criminal justice system, and more particularly criminal procedure. Statements obtained by the police from an arrested person without the police having informed the arrested person of his or her constitutional right to silence or constitutional right to counsel, have been excluded.[6] Prior to constitutionalization, these failures would merely have been considered as "factors" or "circumstances" which could have assisted the court in determining whether the statement had been made freely and voluntarily and without undue influence. Since constitutionalization, several legislative provisions placing an onus (burden of proof) or evidential burden upon an accused to disprove certain facts which were statutorily presumed, have been declared unconstitutional—largely on the basis that these statutory presumptions were in conflict with the constitutional presumption of innocence.[7]

The legislature has, on the basis of constitutional provisions, also responded pro-actively in repealing statutory provisions which were clearly irreconcilable with constitutional provisions. One example is the former statutory rule in terms of which an Attorney-General in certain circumstances had the right to withhold bail for 90 days, and to have been able to do so without judicial intervention.[8] This statutory power was repealed shortly after constitutionalization.[9] It was clearly in conflict with the individual's constitutional right to have access to a court of law, as well the individual's constitutional right to be presumed innocent.

2. *National Statutes*

The most important statutory—as opposed to constitutional—source of South African criminal procedure, is the Criminal Procedure Act 51 of 1977 which came into operation in July 1977 and which has been amended thirty four times since then. This Act supplements the constitutional provisions referred to above, determines the powers of the police and prosecutorial authorities in the criminal process and regulates the process from the accused's first appearance in court to final appeal. But the Criminal Procedure Act is not an all-embracing code. It is supplemented by various other national statutory provisions like the Magistrates' Court Act 32 of 1944, the High Court Act 59 of 1959, the Extradition Act 67 of 1962, the Drugs and Drug Trafficking Act 140 of 1992, the South African Police

5. 1995 (1) SACR 568 (CC).

6. *S v Agnew & another* 1996 (2) SACR 535 (C); *s v Marx & another* 1996 (2) SACR 140 (W).

7. *S v Zuma* supra, *S v Bhulwana* 1995 (12) BCLR 1579 (CC).

8. The now repealed s 61 of the Criminal Procedure At 51 of 1977.

9. By section 4 of the Criminal Procedure Amendment Act 75 of 1995.

Services Act 68 of 1995, the Interception and Monitoring Prohibition Act 127 of 1992; the Attorney-General Act 92 of 1992, and the Investigation of Serious Economic Offences Act 117 of 1991.

3. *Common Law Rules*

In those very rare instances where there are no constitutional and statutory rules in respect of a certain issue, the court must rely on available common law rules. Principles which govern certain procedural remedies such as an application for recusal of a presiding officer on account of real or perceived bias and the remedy known as *habeas corpus*, stem from the common law. As far as criminal procedure is concerned, the English law serves as the common law of South Africa—even though the Roman-Dutch law of the seventeenth century is in theory the common law.[10]

4. *Case Law*

The doctrine of precedent (*stare decisis*) applies in South Africa. Judicial decisions concerning the interpretation and application of constitutional, statutory and common law rules create precedents which bind lower courts. Thus, a decision of the High Court is binding on all regional and district magistrates' courts, the High Court, in turn, is bound by decisions of the Supreme Court of Appeal which, in turn, is—as far as constitutional issues are concerned—bound by decisions of the Constitutional Court. Section 167(3)(a) of the Constitution provides that the Constitutional Court "is the highest court in all constitutional matters."

II. Police Procedures

A. Arrest, Search, and Seizure

1. *Stops*

The nomenclature of South African criminal procedure, unlike its American counterpart, does not include such labels as "stops" and "frisks," such concepts being subsumed under the more general terms of arrest, detention, search and seizure. Whilst arrested persons will be detained whether they are physically incarcerated or in lawful police custody, the term detention also has a broader meaning. Persons who have not been arrested may be said to be detained when a police official deprives them of their liberty by physical constraint or by demand or direction. See also II,C,1 below.

2. *Frisks*

In paragraph 11,A,3,e below, it is pointed out that a police officer may search an arrested person. It is generally accepted that a warrantless and superficial bod-

10. Geldenhuys and Joubert *Criminal Procedure Handbook* 2ed (1996) 16.

ily search (like patting down the outer clothing of a person) may precede a formal arrest if consent is given or where a police officer believes on reasonable grounds that he or she is dealing with a situation where personal or public safety requires such a limited intrusion.

3. *Arrests*

Section 12(1) of the Constitution[11] provides:

Everyone has the right to freedom and security of person, which include the right—

(a) not to be deprived of freedom arbitrarily or without just cause;

(b) not to be detained without trial;

(c) to be free from all forms of violence from either public or private sources;

(d) not to be tortured in any way; and

(e) not to be treated or punished in a cruel, inhuman or degrading way.

The general rule is that the purpose of an arrest must be to bring a person before a court to be charged and tried. (Except, where a person is reasonably suspected of committing a serious offence[12] they may be detained for purposes of investigation.[13] See also II,A,3,h below.) As arrest clearly constitutes an infringement of a persons freedom of movement, privacy and dignity, it has been argued but not yet decided that the presumption of innocence demands that arrest only be used where a summons or written notice to appear before court would be ineffective.[14]

An arrest may be made with or without a warrant. In both instances statutory authorization is required. For an arrest to be effected, unless the person to be arrested submits to custody, there must be an actual touching of the person's body, or forced confinement.[15] In terms of s 39(3) of the Criminal Procedure Act[16] "[t]he effect of an arrest shall be that the person arrested shall be in lawful custody and that he shall be detained in custody until he is lawfully discharged or released from custody." An arrestee must be taken to a police station as soon as possible or to any other place expressly stipulated in the warrant of arrest.[17] Failure to do so will make the detention unlawful, as will failure to bring the detainee before a court within forty-eight hours of the arrest.[18]

A "reasonable suspicion" on the part of the arrestor that a person has committed an offence is a prerequisite for a lawful arrest made with or without a warrant.[19] The test applied is an objective one; consequently, the circumstances giving rise to the suspicion must be such as would ordinarily cause a reasonable person to

11. The Constitution of the Republic of South Africa Act 108 of 1996.

12. Set out in the First Schedule to the Criminal Procedure Act.

13. Sections 40(1)(*b*) & s 50 of the Criminal Procedure Act.

14. Du Toit et al. *Commentary* 5-1. *S v More* 1993 (2) SACR 606 (W). Cf *Tsose v Minister of Justice* 1951 (3) SA 10 (A).

15. Section 39(1) of the Criminal Procedure Act 51 of 1977.

16. *Id* Section 51.

17. *Id* Section 50(1).

18. *Id* Section 50; section 35(1)(d) of the Constitution of the Republic of South Africa Act 108 of 1996.

19. Sections 40 & 43 of the Criminal Procedure Act of 1977.

form the suspicion that the arrestee had committed an offence.[20] If a person is arrested unlawfully, his detention subsequent to the arrest will also be unlawful until such time as his continued detention is ordered by a magistrate in terms of section 50(1) of the Criminal Procedure Act.[21] When the lawfulness of an arrest or detention is challenged the arrestor bears the burden of proving lawfulness.[22]

Whilst there is no case authority directly in point there can be little doubt that if an arrest is made in terms of a statute that is later declared unconstitutional the lawfulness of the arrest will not be impugned.[23]

a. *Use of Force in Effecting an Arrest.* Section 49 of the Criminal Procedure Act provides:

> If any person authorised under this Act to arrest or to assist in arresting another, attempts to arrest such person and such person
>
> (a) resists the attempt and cannot be arrested without the use of force; or
>
> (b) flees when it is clear that an attempt to arrest him is being made, or resists such attempt and flees,
>
> the person so authorized may, in order to effect the arrest, use such force as may in the circumstances be reasonably necessary to overcome the resistance or to prevent the person concerned from fleeing.
>
> (2) Where the person concerned is to be arrested for an offence referred to in Schedule 1 or is to be arrested on the ground that he is reasonably suspected of having committed such an offence, and the person authorized under this Act to arrest or to assist in arresting him cannot arrest him or prevent him from fleeing by other means than by killing him, the killing shall be deemed to be justifiable homicide.

As private citizens may, in the circumstances specified in section 42 of the Criminal Procedure Act, arrest a person without a warrant. The protection afforded by section 49 applies to both police officers and private persons. The burden of proof rests on the person relying on section 49 to establish on a balance of probabilities that all the requirements of the section have been met.[24] In each instance the use of force must be reasonably necessary in the circumstances to overcome resistance or to prevent the person from fleeing. Whilst an objective test is applied in determining the reasonableness of the force, reasonableness will be assessed in the context of the particular circumstances of the case before the court. The key question to be answered in each case is whether the person resisting or fleeing arrest could have been brought under control by less severe means.[25] Section 49(2) has been criticized for providing too much protection to an arrestor charged with murder or culpable homicide. Whilst many of the offences listed in Schedule 1 of the Criminal Procedure Act are serious, it also includes relatively minor of-

20. Du Toit et al. *Commentary* 5–9. *R v Van Heerden* 1958 (3) SA 150 (T) 152.

21. *Minister of Law and Order, Kwandebele v Mathebe* 1990 (1) SA 114 (A) 122D; *Isaacs v Minister of Law and Order* 1996(1) SACR 314 (A).

22. *Minister of Law and Order v Parker* 1989 (2) SA 636 (A).

23. *Key v Attorney-General, Cape Provincial Division* 1996 (2) SACR 113 (CC); Part 17 of Schedule 6 of the Constitution of the Republic of South Africa 1996.

24. *R v Britz* 1949 (3) SA 293 (A); *R v Labuschange* 1960 (1) SA 632 (A); *S v Swanepoel* 1985 (1) SA 576 (A); *Macu v Du Toit* 1983 (4) SA 629 (A).

25. *Macu v Du Toit* 1983 (4) SA 629 (A).

fences. Consequently, in theory, a person who shoots a street urchin fleeing arrest whom he suspects of petty theft will be protected by section 49(2). It is not surprising that the Supreme Court of Appeal has tried to curb the ambit of this section by requiring that an oral warning and warning shot be given (if this is reasonable in the circumstances). It has also been suggested that the arrestor should try and shoot the suspect in the legs.[26] In *Government of the Republic of South Africa v Basdeo*[27] the court, in denying a soldier the protection of section 49(2), held that "such an awesome power plainly needs to be exercised with great circumspection and strictly within prescribed limits."[28] The soldier's conduct fell outside the scope of section 49(2). His conduct was negligent.

b. *Duties of Advisement on Effecting an Arrest.* If an arrest is made without a warrant the arrested person must be immediately informed of the reason for her arrest. In the case of an arrest with a warrant the arrestor must on demand provide a copy of the warrant.[29] Failure to fulfill these requirements will result in the arrest and subsequent detention being unlawful,[30] unless the arrestee was clearly aware of the reason for her arrest or made it impossible for herself to be so informed.[31] In *Minister van Veiligheid en Sekuriteit v Rautenbach*[32] the court held that as the arrest of a person deprived him of his liberty it was necessary that he be informed as soon as practicably possible of the reason for the drastic curtailment of one of his fundamental rights and that this objective could only be obtained through a strict application of the statutory requirement. See also II,C,1 below.

c. *Arrest Without a Warrant.* Generally arrest should be effected in terms of a warrant, the circumstances in which arrest may be made without a warrant being enumerated in the applicable legislation.

Section 40 of the Criminal Procedure Act lists the following circumstances in which a peace officer may arrest a person without a warrant. These include a person:

(a) who commits or attempts to commit any offence in his presence;

(b) whom he reasonably suspects of having committed an offence referred to in Schedule 1 other than the offence of escaping from lawful custody;

(c) who has in his possession any implement of housebreaking or car breaking... and who is unable to account for such possession to the satisfaction of the peace officer;

(d) who is found in possession of anything which the peace officer reasonably suspects to be stolen property or property dishonestly obtained;

(e) who is found at any place by night in circumstances which afford reasonable grounds for believing that such person had committed or is about to commit an offence;

---

26. *Matlou v Makhubedu* 1978 (1) SA 946 (A). See also *Minister van Veiligheid en Sekuriteit v Rautenbach* 1996 (1) SACR 720 (A).

27. 1996 (1) SA 355 (A).

28. At 369D-E.

29. Section 39(2) Criminal Procedure Act 51 of 1977.

30. *S v Dladlha* 1975 (1) SA 762 (T); *Brand v Minister of Justice* 1959 (4) SA 712 (A).

31. *S v Mxinwa* 1992 (2) SACR 477 (N); *S v Ngidi* 1972 (1) SA 733 (N); *R v September* 1959 (4) SA 256 (C); cf *Botha v Lues* 1983 (4) SA 496 (A).

32. 1996 (1) SACR 720 (A).

(f) who willfully obstructs him in the execution of his duty;

A peace officer may require persons whom she has the power to arrest to furnish their full names and addresses and may arrest, without a warrant, a person who fails to do so.[33] Persons who, in the opinion of the peace officer, may be able to give evidence in regard to the commission or suspected commission of any offence, may similarly be compelled to supply their names and addresses.[34]

d. *Arrest With a Warrant.* A warrant of arrest may be issued by a magistrate or justice of the peace upon the written application of an attorney-general, public prosecutor or commissioned police officer.[35] As commissioned police officers are justices of the peace (along with other categories of persons who are not judicial officers) there need not necessarily be any judicial consideration of the application for a warrant. The application must: set out the offence alleged to have been committed; claim jurisdiction; state that from information taken on oath there is a reasonable suspicion that the person in respect of whom the warrant is applied for has committed the alleged offence.[36] However, in practice in forming a reasonable suspicion an applicant may go beyond the sworn information available.[37]

e. *Searches Incident to Arrest.* A police officer may search a person on arrest and seize any article in that person's possession or custody or under her control, that may be connected with or afford evidence of the commission or suspected commission of an offence.[38] It is accepted practice for the police to search the immediate area (like the area where the arrestee was immediately prior to his arrest) in which they make the arrest. The courts have not been called upon to establish the permissible parameters of such a search. The person making the arrest may place in safe custody any object found on the person arrested and which might be used to cause bodily harm to himself or others.[39]

Section 48 of the Criminal Procedure Act, permits a person who is authorised to make an arrest and who knows or reasonably suspects that the person to be arrested is on any premises including dwellings to break open, enter and search such premises for the purposes of effecting the arrest. Arrestors may only resort to such drastic measures if they have failed to gain entry after first audibly demanding entry and saying why they wish to enter the premises.

f. *Ascertainment of Bodily Features or Conditions Following Arrest.* In terms of section 37 of the Criminal Procedure Act police officials have extensive powers with regard to the ascertainment of bodily features once a person has been arrested or formally charged in a court. Any police official may require an arrested or charged person to make themselves available for identification in such condition, position or apparel as the police official may determine.[40] Line-ups are discussed in paragraph II,B,1 below. A police official may also take such steps as he may deem necessary in order to ascertain whether such a person has any mark, characteristic

33. Section 41 of the Criminal Procedure Act of 1977.
34. *Id.*
35. *Id* Section 43.
36. *Id* Section 43.
37. Du Toit et al. *Commentary* 5-18.
38. Section 23(1)(*a*) of the Criminal Procedure Act of 1977.
39. Section 23(2) of the Criminal Procedure Act of 1977.
40. *Id* Section 37(1)(*b*).

or distinguishing feature or shows any condition or appearance.[41] Police officials are also authorised to take photographs.[42] A police official herself may not take a blood sample[43] but may request any registered medical practitioner or nurse to do so.[44] Furthermore, if any registered medical practitioner attached to any hospital is on reasonable grounds of the opinion that the contents of the blood of any person admitted to such hospital for medical attention or treatment may be relevant at any later criminal proceedings such medical practitioner may take a blood sample of such person or cause such sample to be taken.[45]

At common law the debate as to whether the ascertainment of bodily features without the consent of an accused infringed the common-law privilege against self-incrimination was settled by the Supreme Court of Appeal in *Ex parte Minister of Justice: In re Matemba*[46] who found that the privilege against self-incrimination applied only to testimonial utterances. Under South Africa's new constitutional dispensation it has been argued that the compulsory ascertainment of bodily features constitutes an impairment of the right to dignity and the privilege against self-incrimination. Whilst the matter has yet to come before the Constitutional Court, it has been held in two High Court decisions that the compulsory taking of fingerprints does not infringe the constitutional right to dignity, and as it does not constitute testimonial evidence it cannot be said to infringe the privilege against self-incrimination.[47]

Section 225(2) of the Criminal Procedure Act provides that evidence obtained not in accordance with section 37, or against the wish or will of the accused, will still be admissible. For example, in *S v Britz*[48] the court held that the fact that the nurse taking the blood sample had not taken the appropriate sanitary precautions in drawing the blood specimen was irrelevant to admissibility. There can be little doubt that the application of section 225(2) will be subjected to constitutional scrutiny in the future,[49] especially in view of section 35(5) of the Constitution which is discussed in paragraph II,A,5 below.

g. *Powers Conferred Under the Police Act 68 of 1995*. The objects of the police service are to prevent, combat and investigate crime, to maintain public order, to protect and secure the inhabitants of the Republic and their property and to uphold and enforce the law.[50] Whilst members of the police service have wide powers to stop and search persons and property, these must be done in the performance of their legislatively designated functions.[51]

A member of the South African Police Services may without warrant, where it is reasonably necessary for the purposes of control over the illegal movement of people or goods across the borders of the Republic, search any person, premises, other place, vehicle, vessel or aircraft, or any receptacle at any place in the Repub-

41. *Id* Section 37(1)(*c*).
42. *Id* Section 37(1)(*d*).
43. *Id* Section 37(1)(c).
44. *Id* Section 37(2)(a).
45. *Id* Section 37(2)(b).
46. 1941 AD 75.
47. *S v Huma(2)* 1995 (2) SACR 411 (W), *S v Maphumulo* 1996 (2) SACR 84 (N).
48. 1994 (2) SACR 687 (W) .
49. Cf *Msomi v Attorney-General of Natal* 1996 (8) BCLR 1109 (N).
50. Section 205 of the Constitution of the Republic of South Africa Act 108 of 1996.
51. Section 13(1) of the South African Police Services Act 68 of 1995.

lic and any foreign state, or in the territorial waters of the Republic, or inside the Republic within 10 kilometres or any reasonable distance from such territorial waters and seize anything found in the possession of such person or upon at or in such premises, other place, vehicle, vessel, aircraft or receptacle and which may lawfully be seized.[52]

In circumstances where it is necessary, in order to restore public order or to ensure the safety of the public in a particular area, the National or Provincial Police Commissioner may give written authorization for a particular area to be cordoned off.[53] Such an area may not be cordoned off for more than 24 hours.[54] A police official who has received such authorization may, within the cordoned off area, search any person, premises or vehicle, or any receptacle and seize any article referred to in section 20 of the Criminal Procedure Act. Anyone whose rights are effected by such action may demand a copy of the written authorization.[55]

The National or Provincial Commissioner may similarly authorize the setting up of a roadblock where it is necessary for the police in the performance of their constitutionally designated functions.[56] If the purpose of the roadblock would be defeated by the delay in obtaining such authorization, in certain specified instances, a roadblock may be set up without prior authorization.[57] When such a roadblock is set up the police may exercise the same powers of search and seizure as in the case of a cordoned off area referred to above.[58]

For the purposes of investigation, a police official may without authorization, cordon off the scene of an offence or alleged offence and any adjacent area. Where it is reasonable in the circumstances, in order to conduct an investigation, a police official may prevent any person from entering or leaving an area so cordoned off.[59]

h. *Arrest and Detention of Witnesses for Purposes for Interrogation.* Section 185 of the Criminal Procedure Act provides for the detention of potential state witnesses in relation to certain particularly serious offences.[60] This is permissible where the Attorney General is of the opinion that the personal safety of such person is in danger or that he may abscond, be tampered with or intimidated.[61] It will also be allowed where the Attorney-General deems it to be in the interests of such person or the administration of justice that he be detained in custody.[62] Application for such a detention must be made to a judge by way of affidavit excepting where the Attorney-General is of the opinion that the object of obtaining such an order

52. *Id* Section 13(6).
53. *Id* Section 13(7)(a).
54. *Id* Section 13(7)(b).
55. *Id* Section 13(7)(c).
56. See *Id* section 13(8).
57. *Id* Section 13(8)(d).
58. Section 13(7)(g) of the South African Police Services Act 108 of 1995. See also section 11 of the Road Traffic Act 29 of 1989; section 41 54 of the Arms and Ammunition Act 75 of 1969; section 11 of the Drugs and Drug Trafficking Act 140 of 1992; s 4 of the Game Theft Act 105 of 1991, s 4 of the Customs and Excise Act 91 of 1964; s 143 of the Liquor Act 27 of 1989; s 81 of the Diamonds Act 56 of 1986.
59. Section 13(11)(a) & (b) of the South African Police Services Act 68 of 1995.
60. Listed in Part III of Schedule 2 of the Criminal Procedure Act of 1977.
61. .*Id* Section 185(1)(a).
62. *Id* Section 185(1)(a).

would be defeated if the person was not detained without delay. In such a case application must be made to a judge in chambers within 72 hours.[63]

4. Search

Section 14 of the Constitution[64] reads as follows:

Everyone has the right to privacy, which includes the right not to have

(a) their person searched;

(b) their property searched;

(c) their possessions seized; or

(d) the privacy of their communications infringed.

The general provisions conferring powers of search and seizure on the police are to be found in the Criminal Procedure Act. Whilst many of these constitute a prima facie infringement of section 14 of the Constitution they fall within the ambit of the limitations clause which permits the reasonable and justifiable limitation of entrenched rights.[65] The constitutionality of many of the relevant provisions are yet to face judicial scrutiny and consequently the precise parameters of police powers in this area remain uncertain. It should be noted that there are numerous other Acts conferring powers of search and seizure on designated persons.[66]

To date the South African courts have not been called upon to investigate the scope of the concepts search and seizure. In terms of the Criminal Procedure Act the power to search will only arise where the object of that search is to find a particular person or seize a specified category of article. Section 20 of the Act permits the state to seize anything -

(a) which is concerned with or is on reasonable grounds believed to be concerned in the commission or suspected commission of an offence, whether within the Republic or elsewhere;

(b) which may afford evidence of the commission or suspected commission of an offence whether within the Republic or elsewhere; or

(c) articles which are intended to be used or are on reasonable grounds believed to be intended to be used in the commission of an offence.

The reasonableness of the required suspicion or belief is tested objectively on all the facts before the court.[67] The courts will consider whether the seizure is necessary for the investigation and proof of some offence.[68] A document which is subject to legal professional privilege may not be seized.[69]

---

63. See also section 12 of the Drugs and Drug Trafficking Act 140 of 1992.

64. The Constitution of the Republic of South Africa Act 108 of 1996.

65. *Id* Section 36.

66. For example, the Investigation of Serious Economic Offences Act 117 of 1991; the Drugs and Drug Trafficking act 140 of 1992; the Arms and Ammunition Act 75 of 1969.

67. *Ndabeni v Minister of Law and Order* 1984 (3) SA 500 (D).

68. *Highstead Entertainment (Pty] Ltd t/a `The Club' v Minister of Law and Order* 1994 (1) SA 387 (C); *Choonara v Minister of Law and Order* 1992 (1) SACR 239 (W).

69. *Sasol (Eiendoms) Bprk v Minister van Wet en Orde* 1991 (3) SA 766 (T); *Bogoshi v Van Vuuren NO v Director Serious Economic Offences* 1996 (1) SACR 785 (A).

a. *Search Warrants.* Search and seizure without a warrant is only exceptionally permitted. A search warrant may be issued by a magistrate or justice of the peace who, after considering information on oath, has reasonable grounds for believing that an article, which can be of use in proving a criminal case,[70] is in the possession or under the control or upon any person or upon or at any premises within his area of jurisdiction[71]. "Premises" includes any vehicle, boat or aircraft. It has been held that the decision to issue a search warrant may only be set aside on administrative grounds.[72] A search warrant may also be issued by a judicial officer presiding at criminal proceedings where it appears to the judicial officer that such article is required in evidence at such proceedings.[73] Police officials who are justices of the peace (i.e., of the rank of captain or above) may issue search warrants as well as warrants for arrest.

The warrant must be clearly worded[74] and authorize both search and seizure.[75] The warrant will authorize a police official to seize the article in question and to that end authorize such police official to search any person identified in the warrant, or to enter and search any premises identified in the warrant and to search any person found on or at such premises.[76] The articles to be seized need not be described in detail and can be described in terms of type or class,[77] however, this does not allow articles to be described in terms that are too broad or general.[78] A search warrant can be issued on any day and will remain in force until it is executed or canceled by the person who issued it, or if such person is not available by a person with like authority.[79]

Where the police are authorised to search persons or premises they are required to do so with strict regard to decency. A woman may only be searched by a woman (and presumably a man by a man).[80] In executing warrants officials are required to act reasonably and only as authorized by the warrant.[81] The Act stipulates that a warrant must be executed by day, unless the person issuing the warrant authorizes the execution by night.[82] There is no distinction made with regard to the manner of search in relation to arrested or detained persons. After a warrant has been executed any person whose rights in respect of any search or article seized can demand a copy of the warrant.[83] A person may ask to see the warrant before the search and seizure commences.[84]

b. *Search Without a Warrant.* If the relevant person concerned consents to the search and seizure, a police official need not have a warrant to search that person

70. *Cine Films (Pty) Ltd v Commissioner of Police* 1971 (4) SA 574 (W).
71. Section 21(1)(1) of the Criminal Procedure Act of 1977.
72. *Divisional Commissioner of SA Police, Witwaterrand Area v SAAN* 1966 (2) SA 503 (A).
73. Section 21 of the Criminal Procedure Act of 1977.
74. *World Wide Film Distributors v Divisional Commander, South African Police* 1971 (4) SA 312 (C).
75. *Nusas v Divisional Commander, South African Police* 1971 (2) SA 553 (C).
76. Section 21(2) of the Criminal Procedure Act.
77. *Cine Films (Pty) Ltd v Commissioner of Police* 1972 (2) SA 254 (A).
78. *Smith, Tabata & Van Heerden v Minister of Law and Order* 1989 (3) SA 627 (E).
79. Section 21(3)(b) of the Criminal Procedure Act of 1977.
80. *Id* Section 29.
81. *Divisional Commissioner, South African Police v SAAN* 1966 (2) SA 503 (A).
82. Section 21(3)(a) of the Criminal Procedure Act of 1977.
83. *Id* Section 21(4).
84. Du Toit et al. *Commentary* 2-3.

or container or premises for the purpose of seizing any article referred to in section 20 of the Criminal Procedure Act. Whether or not the requisite consent was given will be tested objectively on the facts before the court.[85] The person who gives the consent must have the authority to do so. In *S v Motloutsi*[86] the court held that the consent of a lessee of premises to the search of a room sub-let to another was invalid as the goods in the room were not under the lessee's custody or control and the lessee had no right to pry into the accused's private possessions. Search and seizure without a warrant is also permitted where a police officer believes on reasonable grounds that a search warrant would be issued on application and if he reasonably believes that the delay in obtaining such a warrant would defeat the object of the search.[87] The existence of reasonable grounds will be tested objectively,[88] the onus being on the state to prove that reasonable grounds existed at the time when the police conducted their search.[89] The actions of a person conducting a search without a warrant may be reviewed by a court on the merits. If, for example, it is found that there was no urgency or immediate risk of destruction of vital evidence, the conduct of the police officer would generally be considered unreasonable.

c. *Permissible Force in Conducting a Search.* A police official who may lawfully search any person or premises, with or without a warrant, may use such force as may be reasonably necessary to overcome any resistance against such search or against entry of the premises, including the breaking of any door or window of such premises. However, before taking such action the police official must first audibly demand admission to the premises and state the purpose for which he seeks to enter such premises.[90] This is not required where the police official concerned is on reasonable grounds of the opinion that any article which is the subject of the search may be destroyed or disposed of if admission is first demanded.[91] Examples are where the officer concerned reasonably believes that drugs may be flushed down the toilet or tossed out of a high-rise building.

d. *Interception and Monitoring Prohibition Act 127 of 1992.* A police officer may make written application to a judge of the High Court for a directive permitting the interception of a postal article or telecommunication or the monitoring of telecommunications. Such application will be granted if the judge is convinced that a serious offence that has been, or is being, or will probably be committed, cannot be investigated properly in any other manner or that the security of the Republic is threatened or that the gathering of information concerning a threat to the security of the Republic is necessary.[92] The constitutionality of this provision has not yet been tested. However, it is most likely that these provisions will be found to fall within the parameters of the limitations clause.

---

85. *Hako v Minister of Safety & Security* 1996 (2) SA 891 (Tk).
86. 1996 (1) SACR 78 (C).
87. Section 22(b) of the Criminal Procedure Act of 1977.
88. *Ndabeni v Minister of Law & Order* 1984 (3) SA 500 (D).
89. *Alex Cartage (Pty) Ltd v Minister of Transport* 1986 (2) SA 838 (E); *S v Mayekiso* 1996 (2) SACR 298 (C).
90. Section 27(1) of the Criminal Procedure Act of 1977.
91. *Id* Section 27(2).
92. Section 2 & 3 of the Interception and Monitoring Prohibition Act 127 of 1992.

5. *Enforcing the Rules*

The rules governing arrests, searches and seizures can be indirectly enforced in several different ways. The South African Police Services may hold an *internal disciplinary enquiry*. The aggrieved citizen may also lay a *criminal charge* of assault or trespassing (or any other applicable crime) against the police official concerned. He or she may, furthermore, take *civil action* against the police official or South African Police Services on the basis that a delict (known as "tort" in some countries) was committed, i e, an actionable invasion of personal rights such as the right to privacy or bodily integrity. Fear of publicity, ignorance and the risk of costs (in civil actions) have led to a situation where criminal and civil actions are seldom taken by aggrieved citizens.

It took South African courts many years to come to the conclusion that evidence obtained in breach of the rules which govern arrest, search and seizure, should as a rule be excluded. For several decades they had admitted such evidence on the basis of the general English common law rule that relevance is the test for admissibility and that a court should therefore not be concerned with the manner in which the evidence had been procured.[93] The essence of their argument was that the relevance—and therefore the probative value—of evidence cannot be impaired by the unlawful method employed in acquiring such evidence. In 1927 it was decided in *R v Mabuya*[94] that relevant evidence obtained by police officials in the course of an unlawful search of a private dwelling, should be admitted. Exactly sixty years later, it was also held in *S v Nel*[95] that evidence of private but "tapped" telephone conversations should be received, despite the fact that the prosecution had failed to prove that proper authorization for the recording of these conversations had been authorized in terms of (the then-existing) section 118A of the Post Office Act 44 of 1958. Both *Mabuya* and *Nel* can hardly be described as decisions which served as an incentive to the police to act in accordance with the rules governing arrest, search and seizure.

However, immediately prior to constitutionalization there was a sudden judicial awareness of the danger of indirectly permitting the state and its officials to obtain evidence in an illegal manner. *S v Hammer*[96] provides a good example. In this case an eighteen year old accused who was in police custody had received permission to write a letter to his mother. He asked a police official to deliver his letter to his mother. The police official agreed to do so but never did so. The police official read the letter and handed it to the prosecution. The court accepted that whilst the police official might have been entitled to read the letter in his capacity as a censor in terms of prison regulations, he had no right to hand the letter to the prosecution. The court held that evidence of the contents of the letter had to be excluded not only because this evidence had been obtained in breach of the accused's right to privacy, but also because it had been unfairly obtained.

The interim Constitution—unlike the present Constitution—made no provision for the exclusion of unconstitutionally obtained evidence. However, the High

---

93. See generally Van der Merwe "Unconstitutionally Obtained Evidence: Towards a Compromise between the Common Law and the Exclusionary Rule" 1992 *Stellenbosch Law Review* 173 178.

94. 1927 CPD 181.

95. 1987 (4) SA 950 (W).

96. 1994 (2) SACR 496 (C).

Court was quick to acknowledge that there had to be a discretionary exclusionary rule which could protect constitutional rights and force the police to operate within the law. In *S v Motloutsi*[97]—which was decided under the interim Constitution—the accused was charged with robbery. The defence objected to the admission of evidence relating to the finding and seizure by the police of bloodstained banknotes to the value of almost R10 000-00 which were hidden in a music system. The music system belonged to the accused and was in a room which had been sublet to the accused by one M who in turn rented the house from a local authority. The room of the accused was searched by the police. They did so without a search warrant and in the absence of the accused who was in custody at that stage and who had not consented to this warrantless search. M, the lessee, had however consented to the search of the accused's room. As was pointed in paragraph A,2,B above, the court held that M's consent to the search of the room which had been sublet to the accused, was invalid: The articles seized were not in the lessee's custody or under his control, and the lessee had no right to pry into the accused's private possessions. The court concluded that the police had acted outside the scope of section 22(a) of the Criminal Procedure Act,[98] that they were aware of their unlawful conduct and that there had therefore been a conscious and deliberate breach of the accused's constitutional right to privacy. The court, however, expressly refused to apply a rigid mandatory exclusionary rule like the one in *Mapp v Ohio*.[99] Instead, it preferred to exercise a discretion to exclude. In so doing, the Court relied heavily on the Irish case *The People v O'Brien*[100] and came to the conclusion that the evidence of the banknotes (the real evidence, as it were) and the discovery thereof, had to be excluded because there had been a conscious and deliberate violation of the accused's right to privacy in the absence of any extraordinary circumstances (such as the imminent destruction of vital evidence).

The present Constitution—which was not in force at the time of the decision in *Motloutsi* and which only came into force in February 1997—seeks to clarify the uncertainty which had prevailed shortly before constitutionalization and during the period when the interim Constitution was in force. Section 35(5) of the present Constitution provides that evidence "obtained in a manner that violates any right in the Bill of Rights must be excluded if the admission of that evidence would render the trial unfair or otherwise be detrimental to the administration of justice." Unfortunately, written judgments reflecting the judicial application and interpretation of section 35(5) were not yet available at the time of writing this chapter. However, the following observations can be made:

(a) Section 35(5) does not require "standing" as is the case in, for example, the United States. Thus, if A's house is illegally searched by the police, any evidence they acquire against B will be inadmissible against B at B's trial (provided, of course, that the court is satisfied that the other requirements of section 35(5) are present). B can rely on section 35 despite the fact that A's house, and not his, was illegally searched. It is submitted that this approach is consistent with the deterrence rationale of the exclusionary rule.

97. 1996 (1) SACR 78 (C).

98. This section provides for a warrantless search and seizure if valid consent is given by a "person who may consent" to the search and seizure.

99. 367 US 643 (1961).

100. 1965 IR 142.

(b) It is submitted that the words "obtained in a manner that violates," require a causal connection between the evidence and the violation.

(c) Exclusion is mandatory once the court is also satisfied that admission of the evidence would "render the trial unfair" *or* "otherwise be detrimental to the administration of justice." The latter criterion was obviously borrowed from section 24(2) of the Canadian Charter of Rights and Freedoms, which requires exclusion if, having regard to all the circumstances, the admission of the evidence would "bring the administration of justice into disrepute." It is to be expected that the Canadian decisions on this point will be useful to South African courts in their interpretation of section 35(5), especially since section 39(1)(c) of the Constitution expressly states that in interpreting the Bill of Rights, a South African court may consider foreign law.

It has been suggested that the admission of unconstitutionally obtained evidence will be detrimental to the administration of justice if such admission would undermine public support of the legal system.[101] However, it cannot be argued that the public's dismay at the exclusion of unconstitutionally obtained evidence can in principle assist the court in determining whether admission would be "detrimental to the administration of justice." In *S v Makwanyane*[102] the Constitutional Court, in holding the death penalty unconstitutional, noted that whilst public opinion did have some relevance, "it is not a substitute for the duty vested in the Courts to interpret the Constitution and to uphold its provisions without fear or favour." A similar approach, it seems, should be adopted in the interpretation of section 35(5). It can safely be assumed that a public opinion poll would probably indicate that the majority of South Africans would, because our high incidence of crime, be perfectly happy if courts were to admit unconstitutionally obtained evidence. This opinion, however, should not be relied upon in determining whether admission would be "detrimental to the administration of justice."

The exclusion of statements obtained by the police during interrogation in breach of constitutional provisions relating to the rights of detained and arrested persons, is discussed in paragraph II,C,3 below.

B. Lineups and Other Identification Procedures

1. Lineups (Identification Parades)

Line ups—referred to as identification parades in South Africa—are authorised by section 37 of the Criminal Procedure Act. However, there are no detailed statutory rules setting out the procedure to be followed at this kind of parade. Courts have often expressed their concern at this state of affairs. The eighteen rules as set out below are based on internal police directives and cases where courts have found it necessary to set certain guidelines for the police. Given this situation, some academics have suggested that the following eighteen "rules" are fair to the accused and can at the same time enhance the quality of any identification that may result:[103]

101. Schwikkard, Skeen and Van der Merwe *Principles of Evidence* (1997) 150.
102. 1995 (3) SA 391 (CC).
103. Du Toit et al. *Commentary* 3-7 to 3-12.

(1) The proceedings at the parade should—at the time of parade—be recorded by the police official in charge of the parade.

(2) The police official in charge of the parade (as referred to in Rule 1 above) should not be the investigating official, i.e. should not be the official who is charged with the investigation of the crime in respect of which the parade is held.

(3) Suspects should be informed of the purpose of the parade and the allegations against them and should, further, be given an opportunity to obtain a legal representative to be present at the parade.

(4) A suspect should be informed that his refusal to take part in a parade can at a possible later criminal trial be adduced as evidence against him and, further, that the court might draw adverse inference from such refusal or non-compliance.

(5) The parade should in principle consist of at least eight to ten persons, but a greater number is desirable.

(6) It is generally undesirable that there should be more than one suspect on the parade; and if a second is placed on the parade, the two suspects should be more or less similar in general appearance and the persons on the parade should be increased to at least twelve to sixteen.

(7) If the same identifying witnesses are involved in two parades, then the suspect should not be the only person appearing in both, nor should a suspect be added to a parade, already inspected by the identifying witnesses, for purposes of a second parade.

(8) The suspect and persons in the parade should be more or less of the same build, height, age and appearance and should have more or less the same occupation and be more or less similarly dressed.

(9) It is extremely desirable that at least one photograph should be taken of all the persons (including the suspect) at the parade, depicting them as they appeared in the line-up and standing next to each other.

(10) The police official in charge of the parade should inform the suspect that he may initially take up any position and change his position before any other identifying witness is called.

(11) A suspect should be asked whether he is satisfied with the parade and, further, whether he has any requests.

(12) It is, generally speaking, wise for the police official in charge of the parade to comply with any reasonable request made in terms of Rule 11 above, especially as regards to change of clothing.

(13) Identifying witnesses should be kept separately, should not be allowed to discuss the case while waiting to be called upon to attend the parade, should not be allowed to see the parade being formed or re-formed and should be kept under the supervision of a police official who is neither the one in charge of the parade nor the investigating official.[104]

(14) Identifying witnesses should be prevented from seeing any member of the parade before they are brought in for purposes of making an identifica-

104. *R v Nara Sammy* 1956 (4) SA 629 (T).

tion, and in particular should not be allowed any opportunity of seeing the suspect in circumstances indicating that he is the suspect, before or after the parade.

(15) A police official—who is neither the investigating official nor the official in charge of the parade nor the official charged with supervising the identifying witnesses—should escort one identifying witness at a time from the place of office where the latter is kept to the parade; and after such identifying witness's inspection of the parade, such official should escort the witness to an office or place where the witness can have no contact with witnesses who are still waiting to inspect the parade. The police official who escorts the identifying witness may not discuss the case with him.

(16) The supervising official referred to in Rule 13 above and the escorting official referred to in Rule 15 above, should not know who the suspect is; and the line-up should be formed and re-formed in their absence.

(17) The official in charge of the parade should inform each identifying witness that the person whom the witness saw may or may not be on the parade and, further, that if he cannot make a positive identification, he should say so.

(18) The official in charge of the parade should request the identifying witness to make his identification by touching the shoulder of the suspect. And, in the event of any identification being made in this manner, it is desirable that a photo be taken of the actual act of identification. Touching of the shoulder should not be required where the witness is reluctant to do so.

Failure to observe one or more of the above rules merely affects the weight of the evidence of identification and therefore does not lead to the exclusion of such evidence except in respect of rule 3 above. In *S v Mhlakaza and others*[105] evidence of an identification parade was excluded by the court because the accused had not been given a reasonable opportunity to obtain legal representation. The court held that the accused were on constitutional grounds entitled to have their legal representatives present at the parade, despite the fact that at that stage there had been no formal arraignment.

In *S v Hlalikaya and others*[106] the court held that an accused is not entitled to be legally represented at a so-called "photo identification parade," i.e., a procedure at which witnesses are presented with a series of photographs of persons (sometimes referred to as a "rogue gallery") which include the suspect and other people, and are requested to identify the person involved in the alleged crime. The constitutional right to legal representation, held the court, was not applicable to pre-trial investigative procedures which require no co-operation from the accused. *Hlalikaya* is therefore clearly distinguishable from the decision in *Mhlakaza*.

There is an ethical rule of practice that the prosecution must disclose, to the court and the defence, the fact that a witness had at an earlier parade made an incorrect identification.

105. 1996 (2) SACR 187 (C).
106. 1997 (1) SACR 613 (SECLD).

2. *Other Identification Procedures*

The ascertainment of bodily features and conditions following an arrest, was discussed in paragraph II,A,1,f above.

The taking of blood samples, photographs, finger-prints, palm-prints, foot-prints, hair samples etc, is permitted by section 37 of the Criminal Procedure Act, provided the person has been lawfully arrested or released on bail. Reasonable force may be used in obtaining such samples or prints.[107] A trial court has the statutory power to order the taking of bodily samples or prints.[108]

C. Interrogation

1. *Before Being Formally Charged in Court*

The police may question any person regarding an offence. However, if such a person is detained or arrested the police are required to advise that person of their relevant rights before questioning them, and, if charged, bring them to court within (normally) 48 hours. On the basis that the South African courts have held that the right to a fair trial ensues from the inception of the criminal process,[109] the combined effect of provisions contained in the Constitution,[110] the Criminal Procedure Act[111] and the Judges' Rules[112] can be summarised as follows: whenever a person is arrested or detained she must be promptly advised of her right: to remain silent; the consequences of not remaining silent; the right to consult with a legal practitioner, and that if she cannot afford the services of a legal practitioner that she may apply for legal aid and that a legal practitioner will be assigned to her if substantial injustice would otherwise result.[113] Where such person is under the age of 18 then she must also be advised of her right to parental assistance.[114] The appropriate warning must be repeated at each stage of the pre-trial procedure where the co-operation of the accused is sought and which would necessitate an abandonment of her constitutional rights.[115] Evidence elicited during an interrogation that has not been preceded by the requisite warning will run the risk of exclusion in terms of section 35(5) of the Constitution as discussed in II,A,5 above. At the time of writing there has been no reported case on exclusion, in terms of section 35(5), of statements to the police in the absence of warnings.

To date the courts have not clarified the meaning of the word "detention." However, it can be argued that in the South African context, the term includes in

107. *S v Binta* 1993 (2) SACR 553 (C).

108. Section 37(3) of the Criminal Procedure Act 51 of 1977.

109. *R v Kuzwayo* 1949 (3) SA 761 (A); *S v Lwane* 1966 (2) SA 433 (A); *S v Dlamini* 1973 (1)
SA 144 (A).

110. Section 35(1)(b) & (c),(2)(a),(b) & (c), (3)(f),(g),(h) & (j) of the Constitution of the Republic
of South Africa Act 108 of 1996.

111. Section 73 of the Criminal Procedure Act 51 of 1977.

112. Judges Rules 2 & 3.

113. *S v Brown* 1996 (2) SACR 49 (NC).

114. *S v M* 1993 (2) SACR 487 (A); *S v Kondile* 1995 (1) SACR 394 (SE).

115. *S v Mathebula* 1997 (1) BCLR 123 (W).

addition to physical constraint, compulsion to obey a demand or direction of an agent of the state. Such compulsion will arise when criminal liability will be a consequence of non-compliance, or if the person reasonably believes that they do not have a choice as to whether or not to comply. Consequently, suspects who are questioned by the police in their homes will not be detained as the police have no power to compel a suspect to answer questions. However, if a suspect reasonably believes that she must answer the questions put to her then she will be detained and must be advised of her rights. For all practical purposes, she would then be an arrested person. It can also be said that a person is detained when a reasonable person would feel that she is not free to go—in which event the required warnings must be given.

There is a paucity of judicial or legislative direction as to the conditions under which interrogation should take place and the appropriate manner of interrogation. Some guidance is to be found in section 35(2) of the Constitution which provides that detained persons have the right to conditions of detention that are consistent with human dignity, including at least exercise and the provision, at state expense, of adequate accommodation, nutrition, reading material and medical treatment.[116] Detainees also have the right to communicate with, and be visited by, their spouse or partner; next of kin; chosen religious counsellor and chosen medical practitioner.[117] They have such access prior to questioning.

a. *Undue Influence.* The police may not act in manner that would unduly influence a person in making an incriminating statement. Undue influence will be said to exist where a person's freedom of will is impaired in any way. The test for undue influence is subjective.[118] The issue is what the accused honestly believed. In most instances a threat or promise will be found to constitute undue influence. Rule 10 of the Judges Rules provides that when two or more persons are charged with the same offence, and a voluntary statement is made by any one of them, the police, if they consider it desirable, may furnish each of the other persons with a copy of such statement, but nothing should be said or done by the police to invite a reply. The police should not read to a person a statement so furnished, unless such person is unable to read it and desires that it be read over to him. If a person desires to make a voluntary statement in reply, the usual caution should be administered. Non-compliance with rule 10 has been held to constitute undue influence,[119] and has accordingly led to exclusion of the statement.

b. *Entry to Premises for the Purposes of Interrogation.* A police official in the course of her investigation may, if she reasonably suspects that a person who may furnish information pertaining to the offence is on any premises, without warrant enter such premises for the purpose of interrogating such person and obtaining a statement. However, a police official must have the consent of the occupier before entering any private dwelling.[120] The person who is the subject of the interrogation retains the right to be duly warned of his rights. Having entered for purposes of in-

116. Section 35(2)(e) of the Constitution.

117. *Id* Section 35(2)(f).

118. *S v Mkwanazi* 1966 (1) SA 736 (A).

119. *S v Colt* 1992 (2) SACR 120 (E). In this case the accused was an unsophisticated and unintelligent person with limited education. The court found that the "trickery or stratagem" of the policeman who confronted the accused on more than one occasion with a statement made by a co-accused, amounted to undue influence.

120. Section 26 of the Criminal Procedure Act.

terrogation, the police may only conduct a search in circumstances set out in II,A,4,b above. Reported cases on this specific point do not exist.

c. *Powers Relating to Witnesses.* A witness who declines to make a statement to the police can, in terms of section 205 of the Criminal Procedure Act, be compelled to appear before a magistrate and answer questions put by a prosecutor. A witness who in such circumstances refuses to answer a question will be committing an offence unless he can claim a lawful excuse for not answering. The constitutionality of section 205 was considered in *Nel v Le Roux*[121] on the basis that it infringed the right to remain silent and a number of other constitutionally protected rights. The Constitutional Court held that the section was not unconstitutional but there may well be circumstances in which the manner of its application was unconstitutional. The witness may claim the privilege against self-incrimination and this privilege will only fall away if indemnity (immunity) in terms of section 204 of the Criminal Procedure Act is invoked. In terms of this section a witness can be made an offer of indemnity and then be required to answer questions. Such a witness is entitled to legal representation.

d. *Continued Interrogation* After Assertion of Rights. Generally, continued interrogation after an accused has asserted his right to remain silent will be viewed as undue influence.122 Similarly, if a person requests counsel, interrogation will not be permissible in the absence of such counsel.123 It is submitted that if due to indigence a person cannot afford counsel and the state finds itself unable to provide counsel, interrogation must cease. However, the courts have not yet accepted this view.

e. *Waiver.* If an arrested or detained person has been duly warned and does not claim either the right to remain silent or the right to counsel, the police may question them. Waiver of these rights can be oral and also need not be express. The onus of establishing waiver rests on the government. Waiver must be clearly and unequivocally proved. In determining whether any particular conduct constitutes waiver, the whole of the conduct of the person in question will be examined. At all time the court will take cognisance of the fact that people do not lightly abandon rights.[124] If information is given after an accused has asserted his rights the courts will examine the circumstances carefully to establish whether the accused did so voluntarily or because he was ignorant as to the ambit of the rights claimed.[125] In terms of the Judges' Rules a person in police custody who makes a voluntary statement must not be cross-examined. However, questions may be put to him solely for the purpose of removing elementary or obvious ambiguities.[126]

f. *Tricks.* In *R v Masinyana.*[127] the accused was falsely told by a policeman that the evidence against the former was very strong. The accused then confessed. His confession was excluded because he was found to have been unduly influenced by the policeman's statement.

g. *Traps and Undercover Operations.* The use of traps and undercover operations is often a means of obtaining statements from suspects. The use of traps and

121. 1996 (1) SACR 572 (CC).
122. *S v Mpetha(2)* 1983 (1) SA 576 (C).
123. *S v Agnew* 1996 (2) SACR 535 (C); *S Mhlakaza* 1996 (2) SACR 187 (C).
124. *S v Mathebula* 1997 (1) BCLR 123 (W).
125. *S v Marx* 1996 (2) SACR 140 (W).
126. Rule 7.
127. 1958 (1) SA 616 (A).

undercover operations is regulated by section 252A of the Criminal Procedure Act. A duly authorised person may make use of a trap or engage in an undercover operation in order to detect, investigate or uncover the commission of an offence, or to prevent the commission of any offence. Evidence obtained in this manner will be admissible if that conduct does not go beyond providing an opportunity to commit an offence: Provided that where the conduct goes beyond providing an opportunity to commit an offence a court may admit evidence so obtained subject to subsection (3). Section 252A(2) contains an extensive list of factors that the court must consider in determining whether the conduct goes beyond providing an opportunity to commit an offence. Subsection (3) confers a discretion upon the court to exclude evidence where the conduct in question goes beyond providing an opportunity to commit an offence where the evidence was obtained in an improper or unfair manner and the admission of such evidence will render the trial unfair[128] or would otherwise be detrimental to the administration of justice. In considering the admissibility of evidence the court is required to weigh up the public interest against the personal interest of the accused.[129]

2. *After Defendant Is Formally Charged*

Once an accused has been formally charged the police may still question her. However, if the accused has exercised her right to legal representation such questioning may not occur in the absence of such legal representative. This is also the case where the accused has indicated that she wishes to have legal representation but has not had a reasonable opportunity to obtain such representation.[130] The police may no longer question the accused once the accused has pleaded. Questioning may only take place or proceed if the accused waives her right to counsel. They accused may, presumably, be requested by the police to waive this right. There are no decided cases on this issue.

3. *Enforcing the Rules*

In terms of both the common law and the Criminal Procedure Act a distinction has been drawn between informal admissions and confessions. A statement made out of court by an accused which is adverse to her case, but which does not admit to all the elements of the crime charged, is categorized as an informal admission. Before a statement will constitute a confession it must be "an unequivocal acknowledgment of guilt, the equivalent of a plea of guilty before a court of law."[131] This distinction between informal admissions and confessions is significant because the requirements of admissibility are far more onerous in respect of confessions than is the case with admissions. The only requirement that must be met before an admission will be accepted into evidence is voluntariness.[132] Before a confession will be admitted into evidence it must not only have been made voluntarily but also in sound and sober senses and without undue influence.[133] Where a confession is

---

128. See *S v Nortje* 1996 (2) SACR 308 (C).
129. Section 252A(3)(b). This section echoes section 35(5) of the Constitution.
130. *S v Mhlakaza* 1996 (2) SACR 187 (C).
131. *R v Becker* 1929 AD 167.
132. Section 219A of the Criminal Procedure Act of 1977.
133. *Id* Section 217(1).

made to a police official who is not a magistrate or a justice of the peace who is not a member of the South African Police Service, the confession must be confirmed or reduced to writing in the presence of a magistrate or justice of the peace.[134]

The courts have given a very expansive interpretation to the meaning of the word "voluntary." Any informal admission will only be found to be involuntary if it has been induced by a promise or threat proceeding from a person in authority.[135] A person in authority is "anyone whom the [accused] might reasonably suppose to be capable of influencing the prosecution."[136] In the case of confessions the requirements that the statement be made "freely and voluntarily" and "without undue influence" are treated as separate requirements, each having a distinct meaning.[137] The voluntary requirement is assigned the same meaning as it has in the case of informal admissions. Undue influence will be present where some external factor operates so as to extinguish the accused's freedom of will[138] and need not emanate from a person in authority.[139] Even if a statement is found to have been made voluntarily it will be excluded if it was induced as a consequence of undue influence.[140]

As a result of the distinction made between admissions and confessions, absence of advice as to the right to remain silent and the right to legal representation was only of significance in relation to confessions and were only factors to be considered in determining whether undue influence was present. A significant change has been brought about by the Bill of Rights. The Bill of Rights makes no distinction as regards the treatment of admissions and confessions and introduces a new ground for the exclusion of evidence obtained in the absence of an appropriate warning. Section 35(5) of the Constitution provides that evidence obtained in a manner that violates any right in the Bill of Rights must be excluded if the admission of that evidence would render the trial unfair or otherwise be detrimental to the administration of justice. Thus a statement which is made voluntarily and without undue influence may still be excluded if it was obtained in circumstances that infringe constitutionally guaranteed rights,[141] for example, where the right to a fair trial would be infringed.[142] Whilst failure to properly advise an accused will constitute an infringement of the right to fair trial, it will not automatically result in exclusion of the relevant statement, as the limitations clause (cited in footnote 1 supra) must be applied before the constitutional exclusionary clause comes into play.[143]

a. *Facts Discovered as a Consequence of an Inadmissible Admission or Confession.* A "pointing out" in terms of section 218 of the Criminal Procedure Act has been defined as "an overt act whereby the accused indicates physically to the

134. *Id* Section 217(1).

135. *R v Barlin* 1926 AD 459; *S v Yolelo* 1981 (3) SA 1002 (A).

136. Hoffmann & Zeffertt *South African Law of Evidence* 4ed (1988) 203.

137. *S v Radebe* 1968 (4) SA 410 (A).

138. *R v Kuzwayo* 1949 (3) SA 761 (A).

139. *R v Masinyama* 1958 (1) SA 616 (A).

140. *S v Pietersen* 1987 (4) SA 98 (C).

141. *S v Melani* 1996 (1) SACR 335 (E); *S v Marx* 1996 (2) SACR 140 (W); *S v Zuma* 1995 (1) SACR 569 (CC); *S v Ntuli* 1996 (1) SACR 94 (CC).

142. *S v Mathebula* 1997 (1) BCLR 123 (W).

143. Section 36 of the Constitution. See *Mathebula* supra. In this case (decided under the interim Constitution) it was held that a judge is duty bound to uphold all the provisions of the Constitution, including the limitations clause. The court held that waiver could validly constitute a limitation, but that the prosecution had failed to prove a valid waiver.

inquisitor the presence or location of something or some place actually visible to the inquisitor."[144] Evidence of a pointing out will be admissible even if no concrete facts are discovered as a result of the pointing out. It is only necessary to show that the accused knew of a fact relevant to his guilt.[145] However, statements accompanying the pointing out may not be admitted into evidence[146] and the courts have held that an otherwise inadmissible confession in the guise of a pointing out remains inadmissible.[147] Until the 1990's section 218 was interpreted so as to permit evidence from a pointing out to be admitted into evidence no matter what the degree of impropriety in obtaining it. The courts did so on the basis of the reliability theory.[148] In *S v Sheehama*[149] the court noted that the reliability argument was dependent on an element of discovery and was therefore not applicable where the pointing out simply confirmed already known facts. This approach led the courts to express disapproval of police practices that might compromise the discovery element in a pointing out. The courts have found the following practices to be undesirable: a member of the investigating unit being involved in the pointing out;[150] the involvement of any person in conducting the pointing out who has prior knowledge of the relevant places or objects;[151] and using an interpreter, during the course of the pointing out, who is attached to the investigation unit.[152] In the *Sheehama* case it was held that the pointing outs were inadmissible as they had not been freely and voluntarily made. The accused had received a routine warning from a police officer, which was, however, so inaccurately relayed by the interpreter that the accused was under the impression that he was compelled to make such pointing outs as should be required of him.

The reliability theory was expressly rejected by the Supreme Court of Appeal in *S v January; Prokureur-Generaal, Natal v Khumalo*.[153] The court in equating a pointing out with a statement by the accused held that section 218 did not permit evidence obtained as a result of an involuntary pointing out to be admitted. Where a pointing out cannot be separated from the confession, or where it constitutes a confession itself, all the requirements necessary for a confession must be met.[154] Clearly, evidence obtained as a consequence of a pointing out may also be excluded if obtained unconstitutionally and a pointing out obtained in absence of an appropriate warning will be excluded.[155] Even where an accused has been properly warned on arrest he should again be warned when asked to make a pointing out or confession.[156] The same considerations apply to facts discovered as a consequence

144. *S v Nkwanyama* 1978 (3) SA 404 (N).
145. *R v Tebetha* 1959 (2) SA 337 (A).
146. *R v Nhleko* 1960 (4) SA 712 (A).
147. *S v Mbele* 1981 (2) SA 738.
148. *R v Samhando* 1943 AD 608.
149. 1991 (2) SA 860 (A).
150. *S v Mbele* 1981 (2) SA 738 (A). The court held that there were irregularities in the pointing out and accompanying statements, which raised a reasonable doubt whether the accused had acted voluntarily.
151. *S v Nyembe* 1982 (1) SA 835 (A). The evidence was not excluded.
152. *S v Mahlabane* 1990 (2) SACR 558 (A). In this case the evidence was excluded because there was a reasonable doubt that the accused had acted freely and voluntarily.
153. 1994 (2) SACR 801 (A). See also *S v Sheehama* supra.
154. *S v Mjikwa* 1993 (1) SACR 411 (N); *S v Yawa* 1994 (2) SACR 709 (SE).
155. *S v Melani* 1996 (1) SACR 335 (E).
156. *S v Marx* supra.

of information given by the accused where the information forms part of an inadmissible statement.[157]

b. *Inadmissible Confessions Which Subsequently Become Admissible.* A confession excluded by section 217(1) is "unconditionally... inadmissible"[158] and as a general rule cannot become admissible by virtue of waiver or consent on the part of the accused. Consequently the prosecution is prohibited from introducing evidence of an inadmissible confession either in evidence in chief or in the course of cross-examination of the accused or other defence witnesses. However, in terms of section 217(3) of the Criminal Procedure Act an inadmissible confession will become admissible against the maker—(a) if he adduces any evidence, either directly or in cross-examining any witness, of any oral or written statement made by him either as part of or in connection with such confession; and (b) if such evidence, is in the opinion of the judge or judicial officer presiding at such proceedings, favourable to such person. The effect of (a) is, inter alia, to ensure that an accused does not elicit or adduce selective portions of a document, which, when read as a whole, could be out of context.

4. Derogation of Rights During State of Emergency

Section 37 of the Constitution provides for the suspension of certain rights on the declaration of a state of emergency declared by Parliament. However, rights specified in the Table of Non-Derogable Rights are not capable of suspension. During a state of emergency the appropriate warnings need not be given to persons who are merely detained. However, arrested persons must still be advised of their right to remain silent but they need not be advised of their right to legal representation. Accused persons will still retain their right to legal representation and to be informed promptly of this right.

III. Court Procedures

1. Criminal Courts

The most important criminal *trial* courts are:

a. *The District Magistrates' Courts:* These courts are known as "lower courts." Their penal jurisdiction is limited to twelve months imprisonment and fines not exceeding R20 000-00. These courts also have no jurisdiction in respect of murder, rape and high treason.

b. *The Regional Magistrates' Courts*: The penal jurisdiction of these courts—which are also known as "lower courts"—is limited to ten years imprisonment and fines not in excess of R200 000-00. Regional magistrates' courts may try all cases, except high treason.

c. *The High Court*: Imprisonment and fines imposed by the High Court have no limits, subject to maxima that may be specified by statute in respect of certain

157. See *S v Ismail* 1965 (1) SA 446 (N); *S v Mokahtsa* 1993 (1) SACR 408 (C).
158. *R v Perkins* 1920 AD 307; *S v Nkata* 1990 (4) SA 250 (A).

offences. The High Court may try all cases, but does in practice only deal with the most serious offences. There are nine divisions of the High Court. These divisions have appellate jurisdiction in respect of all cases decided in the lower courts. Appeals against any of the decisions of any of the divisions of the High Court, are to the Supreme Court of Appeal. The Supreme Court of Appeal is not a trial court and has appellate jurisdiction only, except in cases of contempt of court committed in court. The Constitutional Court as referred to in paragraph I,A,4, is also not a trial court.

Trial procedures in the lower courts and High Court are—except for a few minor differences—exactly the same.

2. *Methods to Secure Attendance*

The accused's attendance at his trial in a lower court can be secured by a summons (issued by a prosecutor) or by a written notice (issued by a peace officer and stipulating that an admission of guilt fine can be paid prior to the trial date) or by an arrest. Attendance in the High Court is secured by serving an indictment (issued by the Attorney-General) on the accused. This is reserved for serious criminal offences.

An arrested person's first appearance is in the district magistrates' court from where the case may be remanded to the regional magistrates' court if the seriousness of the offence so requires. An indictment to stand trial in the High Court may also be served on an accused at his appearance in one of the lower courts, and the case may be remanded to the High Court once a trial date is available.

The court in which an accused appears for remand or trial, must inform the accused of his right to legal representation. This right is discussed more fully in III,C,3 below.

A. Pretrial

1. *Initial Court Appearance*

Section 35(1)(d) of the Constitution and section 50 of the Criminal Procedure Act 51 of 1977 require that an arrested person must be brought before a court as soon as reasonably possible, but not later than 48 hours after the arrest, or the end of the first court day after the expiry of the 48 hours if the 48 hours expire outside ordinary court hours or on a day which is not an ordinary court day. But even before the expiration of the 48 hour period (or the period as deemed), an arrested person is entitled to arrange a "first appearance" in order to bring a bail application. In *S v Du Preez*[159] it was held that the police, as part of the state machinery, are obliged to assist in making it possible for the accused to entertain such an early application. An accused must, at any rate, upon arrest or at his first appearance be informed of his right to apply for bail.[160] In all instances, however, the court may

159. 1991 (2) SACR 372 (Ck) See also *Novick v Minister of Law and Order* 1993 (1) SACR 194 (W).

160. Section 50(6) of the Criminal Procedure Act 51 of 1977. In terms of section 59 of this Act the police may grant bail in respect of certain minor offences.

remand a bail application for a period not exceeding seven days if the court is satisfied, inter alia, that it has insufficient information available to determine the bail application.[161]

In *Minister of Law and Order v Kader*[162] it was held that the magistrate presiding at the first appearance of the accused, must "guard against the accused being detained on unsubstantial or improper grounds and [must] ensure that his detention is not unduly extended." The trial of the accused hardly ever proceeds on the first appearance of the accused, except in respect of those cases where the prosecutor decides to proceed on a trivial offence (for example, public drunkenness instead of assault) and the accused has also waived his right to legal representation. Section 35(1)(e) of the Constitution requires that an arrested person must, at his or her first court appearance, either be charged or released or informed of the reason for continued detention. Most cases are remanded to a trail date or for further investigation. In these instances the court is obliged to consider the status of the accused pending trial. Here, too, a constitutional criterion has been set: The accused has the right to be released from detention if the interests of justice permit, subject to reasonable conditions.[163]

An accused may be released on warning, i.e., without paying bail but on condition that he re-appears at the appointed date. Failure to re-appear is an offence.

An accused under eighteen years may be released without bail into the care of his parents or guardian, or a probation officer. These people then have—within limits—the duty to secure the further court attendance of the juvenile concerned.

In deciding whether release on warning or bail would be in the interests of justice, the courts are essentially required to consider the following risks: The risk of the accused absconding; the risk of interference by the accused with the police investigation or state witnesses; the risk of the accused committing further crimes if released on bail. The latter consideration creates the possibility of bail being refused on the basis that some form of "preventive detention" is justified. The High Court has stressed that a court should be most cautious in refusing bail on the basis that there is a risk that an accused might commit further crimes. However, in *S v Patel*[164] it was held that bail can properly be refused if the court is satisfied that an accused has a propensity to commit the crime charged and that he might continue to commit such crimes if released on bail.

In *S v Visser*[165] it was held that bail is non-penal in character; and therefore neither the amount set for bail nor the refusal of bail may be influenced by punitive considerations, for example, to punish the alleged offender or to deter other possible future offenders from committing a similar crime (which, in this instance, was drunken driving).

The onus is upon the prosecution to show that the release would not be in the interests of justice. But there is a statutory provision[166] which creates a reverse onus, requiring the accused to show that the interests of justice do not require his

161. Sections 50(6)(a) and 60(6)(b) of the Criminal Procedure Act of 1977.
162. 1991 (1) SA 41 (A).
163. Section 35(1)(f) of the Constitution.
164. 1970 (3) SA 565 (W).
165. 1975 (2) SA 342 (C).
166. Section 60(11) of the Criminal Procedure Act of 1977.

or her detention in respect of certain serious offences, for example, murder, rape, robbery with aggravating circumstances, dealing in drugs, fire-arms or explosives, and fraud and theft involving amounts in excess of R500 000-00. The constitutionality of this provision is suspect but has as yet not been tested in a court of law.

Failure to appear on the required date, or breach of any other bail condition which the court may have imposed (such as a duty to report to the police every 24 hours), is a criminal offence and will also, as a rule, lead to the re-in statement of detention.

2. *Charging Instrument*

A prosecutorial investigation—such as the one found in the United States where, usually in complex cases, a grand jury is used to subpoena witnesses—does not exist in South Africa. The investigation of crime is conducted by the police who will submit their docket (file, dossier) to the prosecutor who decides on the basis of statements in the docket, whether there are reasonable prospects of a successful prosecution. The prosecutor may direct and control the investigation but does not participate actively in any investigative work.

Potential witnesses who refuse to give statements to the police, may in terms of section 205 of the Criminal Procedure Act at the instance of the prosecutor be subpoenaed to appear before a magistrate or judge for questioning. At these proceedings witnesses are entitled to legal representation and to exercise their privilege against self-incrimination. If a witness invokes self-incrimination, the prosecution can offer an indemnity to the witness.[167] In this event the witness is obliged to answer; and if the magistrate or judge concludes that the witness answered the questions frankly and honestly, the witness is indemnified from prosecution and can be used as a prosecution witness at a subsequent trial. The constitutionality of section 205 of the Criminal Procedure Act was considered by the Constitutional Court in *Nel v Le Roux NO and others*[168] and found constitutional, largely on the basis that the provisions of section 205 were, in the court's view, as narrowly tailored as possible to meet the legitimate State interest of investigating and prosecuting crime.

3. *Preliminary Hearing*

The preliminary hearing ("preparatory examination") provided for in sections 123 to 143 of the Criminal Procedure Act 51 of 1977 has become obsolete.[169] The reason for this is that the prosecution has the right, and prefers, to proceed by way of summary trial,[170] i.e., a trial which is not preceded by an adversarial hearing where a judicial finding is made whether there is sufficient evidence to proceed. It is generally claimed and accepted that a summary trial expedites matters.

There is, however, a so-called "abbreviated preparatory examination." This term is really a misnomer as the examination focuses on the accused. Actual or potential prosecution witnesses are not examined. The object of the judicial exami-

167. *Id* Section 204.

168. 1996 (1) SACR 572 (CC).

169. Over the past five years, less than a dozen preparatory examinations have been held country-wide.

170. Sections 112 to 122D of the Criminal Procedure Act of 1977.

nation of the accused is to identify the nature of the defence, find some common ground and establish the issues for purposes of a possible[171] subsequent trial. The accused is entitled to legal representation at the abbreviated preparatory examination. He must also be informed of his right to silence. Failure to do so is a grave irregularity which results in the inadmissibility, at a subsequent trial, of answers given by the accused. Judicial examination of the accused also follows immediately after plea at the trial. The nature, purpose, and ambit of such questioning are dealt with in more detail in paragraphs III,B,e and III,B,f below.

4. *Pretrial Motions*

Pretrial motions to suppress evidence on account of exclusionary rules, do not form part of South African criminal procedure. Objections to the admissibility of, for example, confessions or admissions, are dealt with at the trial stage in terms of a procedure known as the "trial-within-a-trial" (referred to as a *voir(e) dire* in some other countries). The main trial is temporarily suspended while the prosecution and defence have an opportunity to lead evidence about the circumstances in which the evidence in dispute was procured. Admissibility must then be determined by the presiding officer (judge or magistrate) and the assessors,[172] unless the presiding officer is of the opinion that it is in the interests of justice to decide the matter alone.[173] In those instances where the assessors are not lawyers, they are normally excluded from participating in the trial-within-a-trial. Once a decision has been made to exclude or admit the evidence, the main trial proceeds again and the assessors, if they were excluded, rejoin the main trial.

One of the main purposes of a trial-within-a-trial is to protect the constitutional right of the accused to refuse to testify on the merits. At the trial-within-a-trial the accused can testify and be cross-examined concerning the evidence in dispute, but may not be cross-examined on the merits of the case. The accused thus retains the right to choose whether to testify at the main trial, a right which he need only exercise if he is not discharged[174] by the court at the end of the state's case. This right is discussed more fully in paragraph III,B,2 below.

5. *Discovery*

In *S v Shabalala v Attorney-General of Transvaal and Another.*[175] The Constitutional Court held that an accused's constitutional right to a fair trial ordinarily entitles him or her to pre-trial discovery of all statements and reports in the police docket. The Constitutional Court, however, also ruled that the prosecution could resist such discovery on one or more of the following grounds: Protecting the identity of an informer or the methods of police investigation, or that disclosure would create a reasonable risk of intimidation of prosecution witnesses.

---

171. An accused who gives a plausible explanation in the course of judicial examination at the abbreviated preparatory examination, often finds that the charge against him is reduced from a serious offence (like murder) to a less serious one (like culpable homicide which merely amounts to the negligent killing of a human being).

172. Assessors are discussed in IIIBd below.

173. Section 145 of the Criminal Procedure Act of 1977.

174. *Id* Section 174.

175. 1995 (2) SACR 761 (CC).

Statements which are exculpatory (or *prima facie* likely to be helpful to the defence) must be disclosed, as well as all statements obtained by the police from the accused. The prosecution has no right to have access to the statements held by the defence.

B. Trial

1. Nature of Trial

The public trial of an accused before an ordinary court must begin and conclude without unreasonable delay.[176] The trial is an adversarial proceeding, except in so far as the accused may be questioned by the court immediately after having tendered his plea. This procedure—which must respect the right to silence—is discussed more fully in paragraph III,B,f below. The prosecution is required—because of the presumption of innocence—to prove its case beyond a reasonable doubt on the basis of admissible evidence which the accused can challenge. The trial rights of the accused are discussed in paragraph III,B,2 below.

a. *Speedy Trial.* A court must investigate any delay, in the completion of proceedings pending before it, which appears to the court to be unreasonable and which could cause prejudice to the accused or his or her legal adviser, or to the prosecution or any witness.[177] The court is required to consider the following factors,[178]*inter alia*: the duration of the delay; the reasons advanced for the delay; whether any person can be blamed for the delay; actual or potential prejudice caused to the accused or the prosecution by the delay, for example, a weakening of the quality of the evidence, the possible death or disappearance or non-availability of a witness, the loss of evidence and costs. If the court finds that the completion of the proceedings is being delayed unreasonably, it may make any order deemed fit to eliminate the delay or prevent further prejudice.[179] Where the accused has not yet pleaded to the charge, the court may order that the case against the accused be struck off the roll and not be resumed without the written instruction of the Attorney-General. Where the accused has pleaded to the charge and the prosecution or defence, as the case may be, is unable to proceed with the case or refuses to do so, the court may order that the proceedings be continued and disposed of as if the case for the prosecution or the defence, as the case may be, has been closed.[180]

In *Wild and Another v Hoffert No and Others*[181] the court held that neither of the applicants had advanced or claimed substantial grounds for claiming that the delay of almost two years in the commencement of their trial had resulted, or would probably or inevitably result, in them not having a fair trial as guaranteed by the Constitution. The court accordingly refused to order a stay of prosecution. In coming to this conclusion, the court also relied heavily on principles enunciated

176. Sections 35(3)(c) and 35(3)(d) of the Constitution as read with section 152 to 154 of the Criminal Procedure Act of 1977.

177. Section 342A(1) of the Criminal Procedure Act of 1977.

178. *Id* Section 342A(2).

179. *Id* Section 342A(3)(c).

180. *Id* Section 342A(3)(d).

181. 1997 (2) SACR 233 (N).

by the Supreme Court of Canada in *R v Askov*[182] and the Supreme Court of the United States in *Barker v Wingo.*[183]

In *Du Preez v Attorney-General, Eastern Cape*[184] it was held that the constitutional right to trial within a reasonable time, only arises once the accused has been advised by a competent authority that he is to be prosecuted. However, in *Coetzee and others v Attorney-General, KwaZulu-Natal, and Others*[185] it was held that the right to have a trial commence without unreasonable delay, does not arise only when the accused is arrested or served with a summons or indictment. Such a delay, held the Court, would cut down the accused's right unnecessarily. The Court nevertheless held that having regard to all the circumstances and especially the reasons for the delay, there were no grounds for an order to stay prosecution.

South African courts have not decided that lapse of a certain period would be presumptively prejudicial. They have repeatedly emphasized that each case must be determined according to its peculiar circumstances.

b. *Public Trial.* All pretrial, trial and post trial court proceedings are in principle open to the public and the media. There are exceptions to this rule, for example, where the accused is not yet 18 years-old or where the court is satisfied that publicity might result in harm to a witness. The court may also prohibit publication of a complainant in a sexual offence. These exceptions are probably constitutionally permissible limitations of the accused's constitutional right to a fair trial.

c. *Ordinary Court.* The constitutional right of the accused to be tried by an "ordinary court" means that the accused must be tried by a permanent court which has the necessary substantive, territorial and penal jurisdiction. A "special court" may not be set up. It is for this reason that section 148 of the Criminal Procedure Act is probably unconstitutional. This section gives the State President the power to appoint a so-called "special superior court" of three judges in certain circumstances, for example, where the charge relates to the security of the State.

Double jeopardy is strictly applied in South Africa.[186] An acquittal or conviction on the merits by a competent court in respect of a charge which also has an impact in another national jurisdiction, is a bar to a second prosecution in the other jurisdiction.

In terms of section 35(3)(m) of the Constitution an accused has the right not to be tried for an offence in respect of an act or omission for which he has previously been either acquitted or convicted.

d. *Trial by Judge or Magistrate Sitting Without Assessors.* Trial by jury in the High Court declined from about 1920 until 1969 when it was finally abolished. Over these years it was gradually replaced by the appointment of assessors who assist the presiding judge in fact-finding in the High Court. Less than three years ago legislation also provided for the use of assessors in the lower courts where magistrates preside. The judge or magistrate appoints two assessors per case. Assessors

182. [1990] 59 CCC (3d) 449.

183. 407 US 514 (1972).

184. 1997 (2) SACR 375 (E).

185. 1997 (1) SACR 546 (D). It should be noted that one division of the High Court is not bound by the decision of another.

186. *S v McIntyre* 1997 (2) SACR 333 (T). Even convictions or acquittals outside the borders of South Africa, are taken into account for purposes of the double jeopardy rule.

in the lower courts[187] and the High Court[188] can to some extent be compared with jurors as they are, like jurors, finders of fact. But assessors, unlike jurors, must give reasons for their finding and also have joint deliberations in chambers with the judge or magistrate, as the case may be. Judges and magistrates give reasons for their decision. These reasons form part of the record and is available to any appeal court.

A judge or magistrate is at all times either a sole finder of fact or, where assessors have been appointed, a co-finder of fact. In the latter instance the decision of the majority is the verdict of the court.

Persons appointed as assessors in the High Court must be experienced in the administration of justice (such as legal practitioners or law lecturers) or must have skill in any matter which may be considered at the trial (such as accountants or pathologists). These requirements do not apply, but may be considered, when assessors are appointed for purposes of a criminal trial in the lower courts. The appointment of assessors by magistrates in the lower courts is—unlike the appointment of assessors by judges in the High Court—essentially aimed at promoting the notion of lay participation in the adjudication of facts in a criminal trial. Presiding officers in lower courts (i.e., magistrates and regional magistrates) are in terms of legislation required to take the following factors into account in determining the appointment of assessors:[189] the cultural and social environment from which the accused originates; the educational background of the accused; the nature and seriousness of the offence and the probable punishment in the event of a conviction. However, at the moment less than 20% of cases in the lower courts involve assessors.

The accused may request, but has no absolute right to insist, that assessors be appointed or not be appointed. The judge or magistrate has a discretion. However, in the regional court two assessors must be appointed if an accused is charged with murder, unless the accused requests that the trial should proceed without assessors. In the event of such a request, the regional magistrate is nevertheless left with a discretion to appoint assessors.

There is no system of peremptory challenges if assessors are appointed. Removal of an assessor must be applied for on common law grounds such as real or perceived bias.

It is generally accepted that the use of assessors in the High Court and lower courts is successful. In *S v Gambushe*[190] the High Court held on appeal that the presiding officers in lower courts must instruct their lay assessors on relevant principles of law governing the evaluation of evidence.

e. *Guilty Pleas.* If the accused pleads guilty to a trivial offence the court may convict forthwith. However, if the accused pleads guilty to an offence which merits a fine of more than R1 500-00 or imprisonment without the option of a fine, the court must question the accused to establish the validity of the plea of guilty.[191] In

187. Section 93*ter* of the Magistrates' Courts Act 32 of 1944.
188. Section 145 of the Criminal Procedure Act of 1977.
189. Section 93*ter*(2)(a) of the Magistrates' Courts Act 32 of 1944.197 (1) SAR 638 (N).
190. 1997 (1) SACR 638 (N).
191. Section 112(1)(b) of the Criminal Procedure Act of 1977.

S v Mkize[192] it was held that the questions and answers must at least cover all the essential elements and facts of the crime which the prosecution in the absence of the plea of guilty would have been required to prove. The purpose of the questioning, held the High Court in *S v Baron*,[193] is to protect an accused form the adverse consequences of an ill-considered plea of guilty. Where the court is in doubt that the accused is in law guilty, the court is required to record a plea of not guilty.[194] The prosecution must then prove its case by adducing evidence in respect of those facts which are in issue. A full trial is then conducted and the accused has the rights which he would have had, had he pleaded not guilty.

A plea of *nolo contendere* is not permitted. If an accused refuses to plead to the charge, a plea of not guilty is recorded and the prosecution must then prove its case.[195]

Plea bargaining, as a process which involves an undertaking by the judge or magistrate that in the event of a plea of guilty a certain sentence will be imposed, is not permitted. In practice, the prosecution and defence do occasionally—and without involving the court—come to an agreement that the prosecution will drop certain charges in exchange for a plea of guilty to others. The South African Law Commission is presently investigating the possibility of introducing some form of formal plea bargaining, largely because of congested court roles.[196]

f. *Pleas of Not Guilty.* Where an accused pleads not guilty, the court may ask him whether he wishes to make a statement indicating the basis of his defence.[197] The Supreme Court of Appeal has held that the accused must be informed that he is under no obligation to make a statement indicating the basis of his defence.[198]

If a statement is made, the court may put further questions to establish the issues. The court may also ask the accused whether facts which are not in issue, may be recorded as formal admissions. However, the accused must also be informed that he can refuse to consent to such formal admissions,[199] in which even the prosecution must prove those facts. Once this procedure is completed, the prosecution is required to lead evidence in support of its allegations.

The South African plea and trial procedure where a plea of not guilty is tendered, can be described as a *sui generis*-procedure.[200] Judicial examination is employed as an attempt to establish the facts in issue, and thereafter the trial proceeds along adversarial principles. The accused has the right to testify, or refuse to testify, after the closure of the prosecution's case.

g. *The Accused's Rights at Trial.* One of the most fundamental trial rights of the accused is his right to be present when being tried[201]—a trial right which is

192. 1978 (1) SA 264 (N).

193. 1978 (2) SA 510 (C).

194. Section 113 of the Criminal Procedure Act of 1977.

195. *Id* Section 109. A refusal to plead does not amount to contempt of court. See *S v Monnanyane* 1977 (3) SA 976 (O).

196. *Interim Report on the Simplification of Criminal Procedure: Project 73* (1995).

197. Section 115(1) of the Criminal Procedure Act 51 of 1977.

198. *S v Daniels* 1983 3 SA 275 (A).

199. *S v Daniels* (supra).

200. See generally Van der Merwe, Barton and Kemp *Plea Procedures in Summary Criminal* Trials (1983) 15.

201. Section 159 of the Criminal Procedure Act of 1977.

guaranteed by section 35(3)(e) of the Constitution. But serious and continued disruptive behaviour is sufficient ground for the trial court to order the removal of the accused. Such an order must be preceded by a warning[202] which must be recorded.[203] Evidence led in the absence of the accused, must be recorded. An accused who has been removed may at a later stage, depending upon his conduct, once again attend the trial.

The accused has a so-called passive defence right which incorporates his constitutional right to be presumed innocent, to remain silent, not to testify during the proceedings and to be a non-compellable witness.[204] In *S v Brown*[205] the High Court held that no adverse inference may be drawn against an accused merely by virtue of the fact that he has exercised his constitutional right to silence.

The accused also has a so-called active defence right which incorporates his constitutional right to adduce and challenge evidence.[206] The accused may testify in his own defence. He may also call defence witnesses in terms of a compulsory process and, where necessary, at state expense.

The right to challenge evidence, includes the right to cross-examine prosecution witnesses.[207] Much emphasis is therefore placed upon the oral presentation of evidence (the principle of orality). Although hearsay evidence cannot be tested by conventional safeguards such as confrontation and cross-examination, it may in the court's discretion be admitted in certain circumstances. One of the factors to be considered by the court in its discretionary admission of hearsay, is that such admission would deprive the accused of his constitutional right to cross-examine the original observer or declarant.[208]

2. *Lawyers' Role*

In terms of section 35(3)(g) of the Constitution the accused's right to a fair trial includes the right "to have a legal practitioner assigned ... by the state and at state expense, if substantial injustice would otherwise result, and to be informed of this right promptly." The High Court has held that in determining whether the accused is entitled to legal representation at state expense as provided in the Constitution, the following two questions must be addressed:[209] First, can the accused pay for his own legal representation? If not, will substantial injustice otherwise result if legal representation is not furnished by the state? Relevant to the latter question are factors such as the complexity of the proceedings and the potential consequences for the accused if convicted (for example, imprisonment).

The accused is not entitled to state-appointed counsel of *his* choice,[210] nor is he entitled to specify that state-appointed counsel be chosen from a particular category of lawyers based on race, gender, or religious belief.[211]

---

202. *R v Pauline* 1928 TPD 643.
203. *S v* Mokao 1985 (1) SA 350 (O).
204. Section 35(3)(h) of the Constitution.
205. 1996 (2) SACR 49 (NC).
206. Section 35(3)(i) of the Constitution.
207. *K v Regional Court Magistrate NO, and others* 1996 (1) SACR 434 (E).
208. *S v Ramavhlale* 1996 (1) SACR 839 (A).
209. *Legal Aid Board v Msila & others* 1997 (2) BCLR 229 (E).
210. *S v Vermaas; S v Du Plessis* 1995 (2) SACR 125 (CC).
211. *S v Ngwepe* 1995 (1) SACR 486 (T).

South African courts have as yet not decided whether the right to counsel includes the right to effective assistance of counsel. It is submitted that this would indeed be the case. But in *S v Bennett*[212] it was held that where an accused at the trial fails to take any steps to terminate his counsel's mandate and also expressed no dissatisfaction with the latter's conduct of the case, he is not entitled to challenge the correctness of the verdict on appeal on the ground that his counsel had been negligent in the conduct of his defence. The Supreme Court of Appeal has held that counsel is—for the duration of his mandate—in complete control of the mode of presentation of the defence case.[213] The decision whether to testify or not, is something which the accused himself must decide after having been properly advised by counsel.[214]

Breach of legal professional privilege, is a grave irregularity which automatically vitiates the proceedings.[215] The same approach applies to a case where counsel had a conflict of interest, such as representing two accused whose defences were mutually exclusive.[216]

3. *Witnesses*

The prosecution as well as the defence have a right to compel witnesses to appear at trial. A witness is entitled to refuse to answer questions on the basis that his answer would incriminate him. However, if he is offered indemnity by the prosecution he is obliged to answer.[217] Failure to do so is an offence.

a. *Expert Witnesses.* In terms of adversarial principles, the parties choose and call their own expert witnesses. The result is that an expert witness at times tends to be partisan, asserting the cause of the party who called him. However, courts are aware of this danger.[218] The court may of its own accord call an expert witness.

An expert witness' opinion is ignored where it is based on some hypothetical facts which have no relation to the facts in issue or which are entirely inconsistent with other facts found proved.[219] This problem often occurs where a psychiatrist relies solely on the accused's version of events in assessing his mental condition for purposes of determining criminal responsibility.[220]

The court has the power to order that expert witnesses—such as a ballistics expert[221] or psychiatrist[222]—can be called by an indigent accused at state expense. This is necessary in order to ensure that there is "equality of arms."

---

212. 1994 (1) SACR 391 (C).

213. *R v Matonsi* 1958 (2) SA 450 (a). In *R v Baartman* 1960 (3) SA 535 (A) it was held, for example, that cross-examination which is shared between counsel and his client, is irregular.

214. *S v Majola* 1982 (1) SA 125 (A).

215. *S v Mushimba* 1977 (2) SA 829 (A).

216. *S v Naidoo* 1974 (3) SA 706 (A).

217. Section 204 of the Criminal Procedure Act 51 of 1977.

218. Schwikkard, Skeen and Van der Merwe *Principles of Evidence* (1997) 91.

219. *S v Mkohle* 1990 (1) SACR 95 (W); *S v Venter* 1996 (1) SACR 664 (A).

220. *S v Loubscher* 1979 (3) SA 47 (A).

221. *S v Huma* 1995 (1) SACR 407 (W).

222. *R v Linda* 1959 (1) SA 103 (N); section 78 of the Criminal Procedure Act 51 of 1977.

4. *Judges and Magistrates*

Judges preside in the High Court, the Supreme Court of Appeal, and the Constitutional Court. Judges are appointed by the President on the advice of the Judicial Service Commission[223] which is an independent body consisting of, inter alios, the President of the Constitutional Court, the Chief Justice, one Judge President, four practising lawyers, and some members of the National Assembly.[224] Judges normally have extensive practical experience. They retire, as a rule, at age seventy. They have security of tenure and can only be removed if the Judicial Service Commission finds incapacity or gross incompetence or gross misconduct *and* if the National Assembly calls by at least two-thirds for removal of the judge concerned.[225]

Magistrates were largely drawn from the ranks of prosecutors, but any lawyer can now apply to be appointed. Magistrates are civil servants. They do not enjoy the same security of tenure as judges. There is also an independent body which makes recommendations on the appointment of magistrates.

Judges and magistrates must ensure that the procedural and evidential rules are observed in the course of the trial. The parties conduct their respective cases and the judge or magistrate may not descend into the arena by, for example, cross-examining a prosecution or defence witness.[226] But questions put to clarify ambiguities or areas not covered by the parties, are permissible. A judge or magistrate also has the power to call a witness, except an accused, where the evidence of such witness appears essential for the just decision of the case.[227] Witnesses, including accused persons, who have testified, may also be re-called by the court if the court considers it essential for the just decision of the case.[228]

5. *Victims*

South Africa does not have a general statute dealing with the rights of victims of crime. In practice the prosecution will normally consult a victim before withdrawing a serious charge or accepting a plea of guilty to a lesser charge. Victims are on occasion also called to testify in aggravation of sentence.

Victims cannot compel the prosecutor to withdraw or proceed with the case. But if a prosecutor declines to prosecute, the victim may in certain instances institute a private prosecution[229] after having obtained a *nolle prosequi* certificate from the Attorney-General. The private prosecution can only proceed if the individual complainant can prove some substantial and peculiar interest in the issue of the trial, arising out of some injury which the victim (or the victim's spouse or child) individually suffered as a consequence of the alleged offence. A private prosecution is therefore not possible in respect of so-called victimless crime, for example, a fail-

---

223. Section 174(6) of the Constitution.
224. Section 178(1) of the Constitution.
225. Section 177(1) of the Constitution.
226. 1982 (1) SA 828 (A).
227. Section 196 of the Criminal Procedure Act of 1977; *R v Beck* 1949 (2) SA 626 (N).
228. *Id* Section 167; *R v Gani* 1958 (1) SA 102 (A).
229. *Id* Sections 7 to 17.

ure to pay tax. Private prosecutions are seldom instituted but are still considered necessary as a safety value to avoid unlawful personal retaliation.[230]

A criminal court may, upon conviction, order an accused to pay compensation to a victim for damages to or loss of property.[231] Such an order has the effect of a civil judgment and precludes a civil action for proprietary damages by the accused concerned. In all other matters, an acquittal or conviction by a criminal court, is no bar to a civil action for damages at the instance of any person who has suffered as a result of an (alleged) offence.[232]

C. Appeals

In terms of section 35(3)(h) of the Constitution an accused's constitutional right to a fair trial includes the right of appeal to, or review by, a higher court. Appeal and review are different methods aimed at setting aside a conviction or sentence, and are therefore discussed separately.

1. Appeals[233]

An accused has an absolute right to appeal to the High Court against a lower court's decision on fact or law. If the High Court confirms the lower court's finding or if the High Court was indeed the trial court, i.e., the court of first instance, an appeal to the Supreme Court of Appeal is only possible with leave of the High Court. If leave to appeal is refused by the High Court, the accused may petition the Chief Justice for leave to appeal to the Supreme Court of Appeal. The most common grounds of appeal are that the court *a quo* had concluded against the weight of evidence that there was proof beyond reasonable doubt, had misinterpreted a rule of substantive law, or had imposed a shockingly inappropriate sentence.

The state pays for the copies of the trial record as well as counsel if the accused is indigent and the conviction and sentence have serious consequences. The state pays for purposes of the first level of appeal.

If an appeal is successful, the accused may only be charged again if the court of appeal had set aside the conviction on one or more of the following grounds: That the trial court was not competent (for example, had no substantive jurisdiction to try the case); that the indictment was invalid or that there was some other "technical irregularity or defect in the procedure" (for example, where a witness was inadvertently not required to take the oath or make an affirmation). In all other instances the double jeopardy rule prevails. The same approach applies in respect of successful reviews as set out in the next numbered paragraph.

---

230. In *Solomons v Magistrate, Pretoria* 1950 (3) SA 603 (T) 609H, it was said that the purpose of a private prosecution is to reduce "the temptation to an aggrieved person to take the law into his own hands."

231. Section 300 of the Criminal Procedure Act 51 of 1977. In terms of section 301 of the same Act, return of stolen property may also be ordered.

232. Section 342 of the Criminal Procedure Act of 1977.

233. Appeals are entirely regulated by provisions contained in the Criminal Procedure Act 51 of 1977, the Magistrates' Court Act 32 of 1944, the Supreme Court Act 59 of 1959 and the Constitution. See also *Sefatsa v Attorney-General, Transvaal* 1989 (1) SA 821 (A).

The prosecution has no right to appeal against an acquittal on the facts. It does, however, have a right to appeal against a court's decision on law or a court's decision to release an accused on bail. The prosecutor may appeal against a decision to exclude evidence. The prosecution furthermore has a qualified right to appeal against any sentence imposed by a lower court or High Court. This right is qualified in the sense that the appeal can only be lodged after permission to appeal has been given by a judge in chambers. Every court of appeal has the power to order the state to pay the costs incurred by an accused in opposing an appeal by the prosecution.

The Supreme Court of Appeal or the High Court may make an order concerning the constitutional validity of an Act of Parliament, a provincial Act, or any conduct of the President, but an order of constitutional validity has no force unless it is confirmed by the Constitutional Court.[234] Any person with a sufficient interest may appeal to the Constitutional Court to vary an order of constitutional invalidity.[235]

2. *High Court Reviews of Lower Court Proceedings*

The proceedings in a lower court may be brought under review before the High Court on one or more of the following grounds:[236] Absence of jurisdiction on the part of the trial court; the trial court's interest in the matter, bias, malice or corruption; a gross irregularity in the proceedings; and the admission of inadmissible evidence or the rejection of admissible evidence. An application for review may be supported by affidavits furnishing information which does not appear on the record.

South Africa also has a system of *automatic* review by the High Court of certain lower court proceedings.[237] In these instances the lower court must send the complete record of the case to the High Court where a judge is required to confirm that the proceedings "were in accordance with justice." Automatic review takes place where a magistrate of less than seven years standing imposes a sentence of imprisonment (including detention in a reformatory or rehabilitation centre) in excess of three months. If such a sentence is in excess of six months, it must also be sent on review regardless of the fact that the magistrate has been a magistrate for more than seven years. Obviously, an automatic review does not incur any costs to the accused.

3. *The "Special Review"*[238]

A magistrate who has convicted and sentenced an accused and who then afterwards doubts the correctness of his own decision, may send the case record to the High Court for a so-called "special review." There are several reported instances where this has happened.[239]

A judge may also call for a lower court case to be submitted for purposes of a review. It does not matter how such a case came to his or her attention. In *S v M*[240] a judge called for review on the basis of what was reported in a newspaper.

234. Section 172(2)(a) of the Constitution.
235. *Id* Section 172(2)(d).
236. Section 24 of the Supreme Court Act 59 of 1959.
237. Section 302 of the Criminal Procedure Act of 1977.
238. *Id* Section 304(4).
239. *S v Botha* 1978 (4) SA 543 (T).
240. 1982 (1) SA 240 (N).

4. *Review of High Court Proceedings*241

An accused who alleges that there was an irregularity[242] at his High Court trial, must apply to the trial judge concerned for a so-called special entry to take the matter to the Supreme Court of Appeal. The application must be granted unless the trial judge is of the opinion that the application is made fide or frivolous or absurd or would be an abuse of the process of the court. But even if the application is refused, the accused may still petition the Chief Justice for leave to approach the Supreme Court of Appeal.

III. Conclusion

The South African criminal justice system can be described as a system which seeks to accommodate crime control as well as due process elements. Police powers are—with a few glaring exceptions[243]—governed by legislation which upholds principles of restraint, proportionality and accountability. The exclusionary rule created by section 35(5) of the Constitution will serve as a constant check on police activities, protecting substantive and procedural rights and providing courts of law with some form of remote control over the police when they operate in the field where no immediate judicial supervision is possible.

The constitutionalization of pretrial, trial and post-trial rights of the individual has already had a marked influence on South African criminal procedure and has enhanced and reinforced its due process character. These rights are now also protected from unconstitutional parliamentary interference, ensuring that excesses of the past cannot be repeated.

It is possible that the courts have perhaps been too liberal in their interpretation of constitutional rights. One such example is the right of the defence to have virtually full access to statements obtained by the police and in possession of the prosecution, without requiring any disclosure by the defence to the prosecution.[244] On the other hand, it is equally true that the courts should not embark upon a limited interpretation of constitutional rights.

The unacceptable high incidence of crime in South Africa,[245] has put much strain on the criminal justice system. To tamper with constitutional provisions is not the answer. The answer is to improve socio-economic conditions in the country, and to ensure that prosecutors are well-trained and backed by an effective police force.

---

241. Section 317 of the Criminal Procedure Act of 1977.

242. Examples are: breach of legal professional privilege as in *S v Mushimba* 1977 (2) SA 829 (A); failure of counsel to consult his client in regard to his testifying before closing the case of the defence as in *S v Majola* 1982 (1) SA 125 (A); information conveyed to assessors and which did not form part of the evidence as in *R v Solomons* 1959 (2) SA 352 (A).

243. See the discussion of section 49 of the Criminal Procedure Act of 1977 in paragraph II,A,3,(a) above.

244. See paragraph III,A,5 above.

245. From January 1997 to September 1997 a total number of 17,709 murders were reported, a ratio of 48.8 per 100,000 of the population. During the same period 50,406 cases of robbery with aggravated circumstances were reported, a ratio of 156.1 per 100,000 of the population.

Bibliography

Dugard, *Human Rights and the South African Legal Order* (1978)

Du Toit, De Jager, Paizes, Skeen and Van der Merwe, *Commentary on the Criminal Procedure Act* (1987, as revised bi-annually)

Geldenhuys and Joubert, (eds) *Criminal Procedure Handbook* 2nd ed (1996)

Matthews, *Freedom, State Security and the Rule of Law: Dilemmas of the Apartheid Society* (1986)

Schwikkard, Skeen, and Van der Merwe, *Principles of Evidence* (1997)

Van der Merwe, Barton, and Kemp, *Plea Procedures in Summary Criminal Trials*

Chapter 11

Spain

Richard Vogler[1]

I. Introduction

A. The General Principles of the Criminal Justice System in Spain

The Spanish system of criminal justice procedure[2] is derived substantially from the French model and particularly the 1808 Napoleonic *Code d'Instruction Criminelle*. It is therefore a "mixed" type of procedure with a highly inquisitorial pre-trial and a more adversarial trial phase.[3] It is governed primarily by the codified provisions of the "Law of Criminal Procedure" (*Ley de Enjuiciamiento Criminal —LECr*) which has been in continuous operation since the original version was promulgated by Royal Decree on 14th September 1882.[4] The *LECr*, which is published annually in a variety of private editions[5], now consists of nearly 1,000 Articles, which are the subject of constant amendment.[6]

---

1. I would like to express my gratitude to the Max Planck-Institut für Ausländisches und Internationales Strafrecht in Freiburg, Germany where I was a visiting fellow in June and July 1997 while completing this section. I would also like to thank Carlos Pérez del Valle, Jon Landa Gorostiza and Manuel Diaz Martinez for their kind assistance. Responsibility for all translations and for all errors is my own.

2. There is a surprising dearth of English language academic work on the Spanish criminal justice system. Only three brief accounts are in print (Vogler, R.K. (1989). *Spain. A Guide to the Spanish Criminal Justice System.* London, Prisoners Abroad; Ruiz Vadillo, E. (1993). Spain, in Van Den Wyngaert, C.(ed.), *Criminal Procedure Systems in the European Community.* London, Butterworths, p.383-399 and Merino-Blanco, E. (1996). *The Spanish Legal System.* London, Sweet & Maxwell, p.157-191) and in comparison with sister jurisdictions in France, Germany and, since 1988, Italy, the Spanish system receives almost no attention whatsoever in the British and American literature.

3. See Hatchard, J. , Huber, B. & Vogler, R.K. (1996). *Comparative Criminal Procedure.* London, British Institute of International and Comparative Law.

4. Drafted by the distinguished jurist Don Manuel Alonso Martinez. See Esmein, A. (1968). *A History of Continental Criminal Procedure.* Augustus M. Kelley, New York, p.584.

5. Amongst the most well-known are Editorial Civitas, Editorial Aranzade and Editorial Tecnos as well as the *Boletin del Estado*. An internet edition is not yet available.

6. All references to procedural law here will be to the *LECr*, by Article number, unless otherwise indicated.

The basic procedure has changed remarkably little since 1882. However, the period since the death of the fascist dictator General Franco in 1975 has seen a remarkable liberalisation of what was originally an authoritarian and centralist system, an achievement symbolised by the enactment of the Constitution of 1978.[7] For the first time, the rule of law has been firmly established. All major constitutional provisions and protections have been incorporated directly into the *LECr*[8] and this has brought about some very significant changes to the legal order, notably in relation to the independence of the judiciary and to police powers. In addition, a number of "Organic Laws" (i.e. fundamental provisions subject only to the Constitution) have been enacted which have modernised and streamlined the procedure. Notable amongst these are the Organic Law on Judicial Authority (*LOPJ)* of 1st July 1985,[9] which reorganised the judicial structure of the courts and established single-judge courts and the Organic Law of 24th May 1984[10] which made good an undertaking in the 1978 Constitution[11] to introduce the remedy of *Habeas Corpus* on the anglo-american model to deal with unlawful detention. The Organic Law of December 28th 1988 created the so-called "abbreviated procedure" to allow speedy trial of straightforward cases[12] and the Organic Law of April 30th 1992[13] established the "abbreviated procedure with an immediate oral hearing."[14]

There have also been major changes in police organisation and powers, particularly as a result of the Organic Law of the State Security Forces and Corps (*LOFCSE*) of 13th March 1986[15] which sought to bring the police under a common disciplinary and command structure and to reinforce democratic and judicial control. However, fears of escalating crime and terrorist activity arising from the political situation in the Basque region (Euskadi) prompted the enactment of the highly contentious "Corcuera Law," the Organic Law for the Security and Protection of the Citizen (*LOPSC)* of 21st February 1992.[16] This created new powers of stop, search and detention which have been widely criticised as unconstitutional. Finally, by the Organic Law of the Jury Court (*LOTJ*) of 22nd May 1995,[17] the government made good a further constitutional undertaking to re-introduce criminal jury trial, abrogated since the period of the civil war in 1936. The introduction of the new jury procedure has been attended with enormous public controversy (see below).

---

7. Royal assent to the Constitution was given on 27th December 1978 after a national referendum held on 6th December 1978, see McGee, H.W. (1987). *Counsel for the Accused. Metamorphosis in Spanish Constitutional Rights,* 24 Coumbia Journal of Transnational Law, p.253-299, p.255-257. For a full English translation see Gloss, G.E. (1979) *The New Spanish Constitution. Comments and Full Text*, 7 Hastings Constitutional Law Quarterly, p.47-128.

8. See e.g. the Organic Laws 14/1983 of 12th December 1983 (on the treatment of detainees and prisoners) and 7/1988 of 28th December 1988 (creating the *Juzgados de lo Penal* and modifying the *LECr*). Spain ratified the European Convention on Human Rights in 1979.

9. *Ley Orgánica del Poder Judicial*, 26/1985.

10. *Ley Orgánica Reguladora del Procedimiento de «Habeas Corpus»*, 6/1984.

11. Art. 17.4.

12. *Ley Orgánica de Creación de los Juzgados de lo Penal y Modificación de Diversos Preceptos de las Leyes Orgánicas del Poder Judicial y de Enjuiciemiento Criminal*, 7/1988, now enshrined in Arts. 779-799 *LECr.* See below.

13. *Ley Orgánica de Medidas Urgentes de Reforma Procesal*, 10/1992.

14. Arts 790-2 *LECr.*

15. *Ley Orgánica de Fuerzas y Cuerpos de Seguridad del Estado*, 2/1986.

16. *Ley Orgánica de Protección de la Seguridad Ciudadana*, 1/1992.

17. *Ley Orgánica del Tribunal del Jurado*, 5/1995.

B. The Structure of the Procedure

1. Initiation of the Procedure

Criminal proceedings may be initiated in two ways:

a. *By Lodging an Information* (*Denuncia*). The *denuncia* is simply the communication to the judicial authorities, by either a private individual[18] or the police,[19] of information relating to the commission of a criminal offence. The *denuncia* can be lodged either orally or in writing at the office of the duty Judge (*juez de guardia*),[20] the prosecutor or the Police.[21] The effect of the *denuncia* is to require the Judge to initiate criminal proceedings, providing that he or she is satisfied that the facts alleged constitute an offence. The Judge is obliged to notify both the accused person[22] and the prosecutor. Thereafter, the maker of the *denuncia* plays no formal role in the proceedings except, potentially, as a witness.[23]

b. *By Lodging a Complaint* (*Querella*). Spanish criminal procedure permits a civil claim to be run alongside a criminal prosecution and to be disposed of immediately after the criminal verdict by the same trial court. The complainant (usually the victim of the offence) is entitled to certain procedural rights and to be represented throughout, although the different objectives of the prosecutor and the complainant may sometimes lead to difficulties.

The complainant has a right to initiate criminal proceedings by issuing a written *querella* alleging an offence or offences[24] to a judge having appropriate jurisdiction. It must be signed by both lawyers (*Procurador and Abogado*)[25] and give a specific account of the allegations and clearly identify the alleged offender. The *querella* will formally request the Judge to initiate proceedings and petition for the complainant to be joined in the proceedings as the Civil Party. If the Judge accepts the *querella*, he or she becomes responsible for the investigation of the case.[26] The

---

18. All citizens have a duty to report "public" offences (see below) to the authorities except, for example, minors or the mentally ill (Art. 260), the spouse or close relatives of the alleged offender (Art. 261) and others enjoying privileged communication, e.g the lawyer or a Priest taking confession (Art. 263). See Gómez Colomer, J-L (1993). *El Proceso Penal Español Para No Juristas*, Valencia, Tirant lo Blanch, p.162-165; Ramos Méndez, F. (1993) *El Proceso Penal, Tercera Lectura Constitucional*, Barcelona, Bosch, p.152-156.

19. Police reports notifying the Judge of an offence (*atestados policiales*) are defined in law as *denuncias*.

20. Arts. 259, 262 & 264.

21. Who have a duty to notify the Judge.

22. Art. 118.

23. The maker of a false or malicious *denuncia* is liable to prosecution (Art. 456, *Código Penal* (*CP*)). N.B. a new Penal Code was enacted in 1995 by the *Ley Orgánica del Código Penal*, 10/1995 of 23rd November 1995 and all references herein to the *CP* are to this text.

24. See Gómez Colomer (1993), *op cit.*, p.165-171 and Ramos Méndez *op cit.*, p.157-160. Offences are divided into three categories for this purpose. "Public offences" (*delitos perseguibles de oficio*) can be reported by anyone. In the case of "semi-public offences" (such as rape), once the victim has presented a *denuncia*, the prosecutor is obliged to prepare and present a *querella*, although the victim can do this if he or she wishes (Arts. 104-105 & 270). Only the victim can lodge a *querella* in "private criminal offences."

25. It is also necessary to include a power of attorney on their behalf.

26. Arts. 311-312.

querella procedure can be adopted by the victim of an offence in order to trigger a prosecution where, e.g. the prosecutor has decided not to proceed.

2. Choice of Court of Trial

Offences in Spain fall into two categories, namely "misdemeanours" (*faltas*) and "serious offences" (*delitos*) and the choice of trial court is determined by the nature of the offence alleged. Misdemeanours will be heard normally by the local "Instruction Court" (*Juzgado de Instrucción*)[27] or in less serious cases, by the local Justice of the Peace (*Juzgado de Paz*).[28] More serious offences (*delitos*) are divided into two categories. Middle range offences (*delitos menos graves*)[29] are tried either in the local or central *Juzgado de lo Penal*. Higher range offences (*delitos graves*) are dealt with in the "Provincial Criminal Court" (*Audiencia Provincial*) of the province in which the offence was committed.

3. Choice of Procedure Mode

The different modes of procedure available in the Spanish criminal courts are extremely complex but all are governed by the guarantees provided by the Constitution and the Constitutional Court.[30] Essentially, they are divided into "ordinary proceedings" (*juicios penales ordinarios*) and "special proceedings" (*juicios penales especiales*) i.e proceedings involving Senators, Deputies, Judges etc. As far as the ordinary proceedings are concerned, there are four basic modes of trial:

normal procedure (*juicio ordinario*), and

jury trial procedure (*tribunal del jurado*), and

abbreviated procedure (*procedimiento abreviado*), and

misdemeanour procedure (*juicio de faltas*).

The various procedures, in outline, are as follows (see chart overleaf):

a. *Normal Procedure* (*Juicio Ordinario*). In general, this procedure is adopted for all higher range serious offences (*delitos graves)* not covered by the exceptional modes of procedure set out in (b) and (c) above. It falls overall into three stages. The first, the pre-trial stage or "instruction" (*instrucción*) is quite unrecognisable to anglo-american lawyers and is conducted by the Examining Magistrate (*Juez Instructor*) who is responsible for investigating the case and for preparing a *dossier* of evidence for transmission to the trial court. Originally, this phase of the procedure was entirely secret, written and non-adversarial, although the presence of a defence lawyer and defence access to the *dossier* has been permitted since 1978. Once the Examining Magistrate concludes that the investigation has been completed, he or she will close the instruction stage and notify all the parties.

The second stage, known as the "intermediate stage" enables the parties to make written submissions about the case and the evidence and to make offers of proof for the trial. The third, trial, stage is the most familiar to anglo-american

27. Art. 14.1.
28. *Id.*
29. Offences punishable with up to six years imprisonment or a fine.
30. Ramos Méndez, *op. cit.*, p.38-40.

lawyers and is conducted in open court, on the basis of adversariality and the active participation of the parties. However, the President of the trial court will take a much more central role in calling and examining the evidence than would be acceptable in most common law systems. Also, there are no rules of evidence and the case must be decided by the trial judges on the "free evaluation" (*libre arbitrio*) principle[31] according to their "inner conviction" (*intima convicción*) of guilt or innocence. In order to facilitate appeal, the Judges are required to set out in full their written reasons for the decision. The universal right of appeal is considered essential to the procedure.

It must be understood that the roles of the participants in Spanish criminal procedure are fundamentally different to those of their anglo-american counterparts. Almost all procedural steps are initiated by the Judges themselves who have an overall responsibility for the investigation of cases, in addition to ruling on interlocutory issues and giving final judgement. Neither the police nor the prosecutors are entitled to act of their own initiative but must report the discovery of offences or the arrest of offenders immediately to the relevant judge.[32] Although the Judge may delegate acts of investigation to the police, his or her express authority is required for specific procedures such as searches or identity parades. The responsibility for investigation remains with the Examining Magistrate during the instruction stage and with the President of the trial court at the trial stage. The same Judge, however, cannot act both as Examining Magistrate and trial Judge in a single case.[33]

All references hereafter will be to the "ordinary procedure" for higher-range offences (*procedimiento penal ordinario por delitos graves*) unless otherwise indicated.

b. Jury Trial Procedure (Tribunal del Jurado). Jury trial was introduced in 1995 with the first trials taking place in 1996.[34] The requirement in Art. 125 of the Constitution to establish popular participation in the criminal justice system[35] produced considerable debate and even animosity between "*juradistas*" and "*anti-juradistas*"[36] in the press, academic and professional literature. The conflict awak-

31. Art. 741.

32. Although the police have authority to arrest and to interrogate suspects, they must report the matter to the duty Judge within 24 hours (see below).

33. *STC* 145/1988 of 12th July 1988, now enacted in Organic Law 7/1988 of 28th December 1988.

34. See e.g. Thaman, S (1998). *Spain Returns to Jury Trial*, 21(2) Hastings International and Comparative Law Review, p.241-537; Gleadow, C. (1998). *The Jury in Modern Spain: A Troubled History*. Unpub. Ph.D. Thesis, University of London.

35. According to the text of the Constitution "Citizens are allowed to intervene and to participate in the administration of justice through the institution of the jury in such a manner as accords with the penal procedure determined by the law ..."; See Gleadow, *op cit.*, and Burros, N.G. (1982). *The Spanish Jury 1888-1923*. 14 Case Western Reserve Journal of International Law, p.177-246 for previous attempts to establish jury trial in Spain.

36. See the bitter attacks launched by Fairén Guillén, a self-proclaimed "*anti-juradista*" (Fairén Guillén, V. (1979) *Los Tribunales de Jurados en la Constitución Española de 1978*, Madrid, Civitas, p.135.) and Gimeno Sendra, who has argued against the "disinterrment" of the corpse of the jury (cited in Martín Ostos, J. (1990) *Jurado y Escabinado (Participatión Popular en la Administración de Justicia)*. Madrid, Instituto Vasca de Derecho Procesal, p.9). On the other hand, authors such as Lopez-Muñoz y Larroz, G., the President of the "Pro-Jury Association" has argued strongly in favour (Lopez-Muñoz y Larroz , G. (1982). *Bases para una Nueva ley del Jurado*,252(4) *Revista de Legislacion y Jurisprudencia*, p.450-482.

ened old antagonisms between the proponents of more adversariality and adherents of the original, more inquisitorial scheme of the *LECr.* During the mid 1980's, when it was clear that the government was planning to legislate, a flurry of proposals was produced. Some favoured the mixed bench of Judges and lay participants (the "*Escabinado*") as operated in France, Germany and Portugal[37] whereas others advocated the adoption of the anglo-american model of independent jury, as the text of the Constitution seemed to imply.[38] The latter view was to prevail and in 1994 a proposal for an "Organic Law of the Jury"[39] was published and opened for comment to interested bodies. After a somewhat difficult legislative passage, complicated by the impending elections[40] the 1995 Organic Law of the Jury Court (*LOTJ*) [41] was finally enacted.

The new law envisaged a jury of nine[42] sitting with a single judge in the *Audiencia Provincial.*[43] Only certain restricted categories of offence, set out in Art.1 *LOTJ* are eligible for jury trial and these include homicide,[44] the offence of the failure to comply with the duty to give assistance,[45] threats,[46] bribery,[47] and corruption.[48] Clearly, the most important beneficiaries of the new procedure are those accused of homicide. In jury cases the instruction phase has been modified to give it more adversarial characteristics and to produce a less technical set of final submissions which will be more easily comprehensible by the lay jury. It must be emphasized that jury trials are rare—there were only about 70 in the first year—and cannot be considered "ordinary" procedure, which is discussed in section III below.

Jurors are chosen randomly from the electoral list at a public session organised by the Provincial Delegation of the Census Office, and notified publicly in advance.[49] A jury can be constituted from a minimum panel of 20[50] and the actual trial jury is selected on the day by their names being drawn from an urn by the court Clerk. Each defendant is entitled to four peremptory challenges but the complainant has none. Challenges for cause can be based upon questions to jurors

---

37. See proposals of Gimeno Sendra and Fairén Guillén, cited in Pérez-Cruz Martin, A-J. (1995). *Anotaciones a la Competencia y Composición del Tribunal del Jurado. Especial Consideracion de los Arts. 1 a 5 de la L.O. 5/1995, «In Datada»,* iii Justicia, p.63-97 at p.65. Martin Ostos has complained that the "*Escabinado*" model was not even considered during the political debates on the Constitution (*op cit.*, p.20-22) and no comparative research was undertaken (*Id.*, p.38-9).

38. See proposals of Carlos Usúa and *Parador de Chincón*, cited in *Id.*

39. *El Proyecto de Ley Orgánica del Tribunal del Jurado.*

40. Pérez-Cruz Martin *op cit.*, p.68-69. According to Fairén Guillén, "(t)he text seems to have gone from one crisis to another" (Fairén Guillén, V. (1996) *Ley del Jurado de 22 de Mayo de 1995 y modelo inquisitivo. Un apunte,* 1 *Revista de Derecho Procesal*, p.7-31, p.23). He also notes that it was necessary to enact an imediate amendment (the Law 8/1995 of 16th November 1995) before the procedure was even implemented (*Id.*).

41. See above.

42. The original 1888 jury had 12 jurors, the 1994 proposals envisaged seven, see Lorce Navarrete, A.M. (1996). *El Jurado Español. La Nueva Ley del Jurado.* Madrid, Dykinson, p.73.

43. Art.2 *LOTJ*

44. Arts.139-141, *CP.*

45. Art. 196, *CP.*

46. Arts. 169-170, *CP.*

47. Arts 421-427, *CP.*

48. Arts.430-432, *CP.*

49. Art. 13 *LOTJ* Lorca Navarette, *op cit.*, p.157-182.

50. Those under 25, politicians, military personnel on active service and those with criminal records are amongst those exempt from serving.

posed via the President of the trial court but there is no procedure as extensive as the American *voir dire*. Members of the jury are then sworn in individually. The jury follows the anglo-american independent procedure, maintaining the fact/law distinction which has proved so troubling for continental jurists.[51] It retires alone[52] to consider whether the defendant is guilty or not guilty.

A majority of seven (of nine) is necessary to establish a fact unfavourable to the defendant and five for a fact favourable to him or her. The standard of proof is the same as that adopted by the ordinary trial court.[53] However, in order to assimilate the independent jury model to the requirement of the Spanish Constitution for a right of appeal, certain innovations have been introduced which make Spanish jury practice quite unique in the world. For example, the Judge must formulate a list of questions of fact for resolution by the jury, which must then proceed to give full reasons for their answers. These reasons are susceptible to appeal. It has also been necessary to adapt some of the more technical trial and pre-trial procedures which were not designed originally to facilitate the participation of lay jurors in a fact-finding role. The main changes have included the requirement for a *prima facie* case to be made out before the start of the hearing and the reinforcement of the neutrality of the Examining Magistrate (by a corresponding increase in the powers of the prosecutor)[54] and by the requirement that another party, not the Examining Magistrate, must initiate the proceedings.

The procedure has been subjected to withering attack[55] by a range of authors including Fairén Guillén and Perez-Cruz Martin, who have argued strongly in favour of the mixed-bench alternative, pointing out the absurdity of attempting to graft elements of the anglo-american model onto the procedure, without thoroughgoing revisions to the *LECr*. In common with these authors Pedrez Penalva has argued that the anglo-american model of the jury is everywhere in retreat:

> They are trying to restore in Spain an outdated and failed concept of jury-trial in preference to the model which has evolved so successfully in countries in our region such as Germany, France, Italy, and Portugal.[56]

The press has been equally critical [57] and the Professional Association of the Magistracy has complained of "excessive haste" and "inadequate structure" as

51. See e.g. Garcia Gonzalez: "The separation between fact and law cannot be realized. It is based on a falsehood...and it is therefore clear that, constructed on this false proposition, the jury cannot either be conceived or developed" (Garcia Gonzalez (1932). *El Poder Judicial*. Madrid, p.300; See also, Pérez-Cruz Martin *op cit.*, p.86 & Martín Ostos, *op cit.*, p.11-12.

52. .In contrast to the mixed-bench procedure in France, Germany, and Portugal, where the lay participants deliberate and vote jointly with the judges.

53. See III, B, 4 below.

54. Pérez-Cruz Martin, A-J (1996). *La Instrucción en el Nuevo Proceso Penal Ante el Tribunal del Jurado*, in Pérez-Cruz Martin, A-J (*et al.*) (eds.); *Comentarios Sistemáticos a la Ley del Jurado y la Reforma de la Prisión Preventiva*. Instituto de Estudios Penales, Granada, p.127-160.

55. .See e.g. Fairén Guillén, V. (1995a). *Ensayo preliminar sobre el modelo «jurado de veredicto» en España: sobre ciertas vicisitudes de la Ley del Jurado de 1888 hasta 1936*, 3 *Revista de Derecho Procesal*, p.805-826.

56. Cited in Pérez-Cruz Martin (1995) *op cit.*, p.87.

57. See Jiménez Rodriguez, A. (1997). *Juradistas y Antijuradistas en 1995: Un Analisis a Traves de la Prensa*, ix(1) *Revista Vasca de Derecho Procesal y Arbitraje*, p.1-10.

well as dysfunction caused by a failure to consider the impact on the penal procedural code overall.[58]

c. *Abbreviated Procedure* (*Procedimiento Abreviado*)[59]. This form of procedure has been available since 1988 for more serious offences attracting penalties of up to nine years. It envisages a considerably simplified instruction phase followed by a trial in which some of the issues will have been dealt with already at the instruction stage. The normal avenues of appeal are nevertheless open.

d. *Misdemeanour Procedure* (*Juicio de Faltas*). This is available for most public order offences, minor assaults,[60] and minor property offences.[61] Essentially, the minor offence procedure dispenses with the instruction stage and allows the disposal of the case, often in the absence of the accused, at a relatively brief oral hearing.

C. The Participants

1. The Police

At the death of Franco in 1975, Spain inherited a militarized and highly authoritarian police system, which operated under the direct control of the army and which dominated criminal investigations and the courts.[62] In addition, the much-reviled para-military police, the *Guardia Civil* were engaged in a bitter and violent campaign of repression in the Basque region.[63] The Constitution of 1978 attempted to bring the police for the first time under democratic control and Article 104.1 states that their function is to "protect the free exercise of rights and liberties and to guarantee the safety of citizens." However, considerable time and political effort was necessary to break the stranglehold of the military over the police and to carry out the reorganisation of the latter along democratic lines. The situation had deteriorated so badly that in 1981 a *Guardia Civil* officer, Antonio Tejero attempted a coup against the government. However, the promises of the Constitution regarding the police were finally enacted in the 1986 *LOFCSE*.[64]

---

58. *Id*, p.6, n.18. Note also the criticisms of a Murcian judge who maintained that the jury in Spain will be a failure because it is an imported institution without any tradition and with no prospect of solving any of the structural problems of the justice system. *El Pais*, 31st October 1995, p.23.

59. See Gómez Colomer, J-L. (1992). *El nuevo proceso penal abreviado*, 26(2) Poder Judicial, p.9-24.

60. Art. 619, *CP*.

61. Arts 623-288, *CP*.

62. Macdonald, I.R.(1987), *Spain's 1986 Police Law: Transition from Dictatorship to Democracy*, 10(1) Police Studies, p.16-22 at p.19-20; Morn, F. & Toro, M. (1989). *From Dictatorship to Democracy: Crime and Policing in Contemporary Spain*, 13(1) International Journal of Comparative and Applied Criminal Justice, p.53-64.

63. Macdonald I.R.(1985). *The Police System in Spain,* in Roach, J. & Thomanseck, J. (eds); *Police and Public Order in Europe*. London, Croom Helm, p.215-254 at p.223; Morn & Toro, *op cit.*, p.246-247.

64. See above and also Greer, S. (1994). *Police Powers in Spain: the "Corcuera Law"* 43 International & Comparative Law Quarterly, p.405-416 at p.405-406; Vidal, M.T.(1995). *La Policía en la Historia Contemporanea de España (1766-1986)*. Madrid *Ministerio de Justicia e Interior*, p.233-240.

The Spanish police is divided into two national forces, the *Cuerpo Superior de Policía* numbering about 149,000 and the para-military *Guardia Civil* of about 64,000 officers. The latter operate in rural areas, territorial waters and in towns with a population of less than 20,000. Both forces are answerable to the Minister for the Interior and for State Security but the Ministry of Defence still has responsibility for the promotions and military operations of the *Guardia Civil.* In 1987 the Spanish Police were brought into conformity with most of their continental European counterparts by their assumption of the title of "judicial police," which indicates that in criminal investigations they are required to act on the instructions of judicial officers rather than on their own authority.[65] The police initially saw attempts by the judiciary to exercise this authority over them as an attack on their autonomy and there was considerable dissent. However, their subordination to the independent judiciary, already established in principle by Art. 126 of the Constitution, was secured in practice by Arts. 29-36 of the 1986 legislation which set up special units of the judicial police, seconded to the courts and answerable to them.[66] The 1986 Act also established a disciplinary and ethical code for the police and regulated union rights. As Macdonald has put it: "For the first time there is a single overall framework incorporating a set of modern and democratic basic principles placing police work fully in the context of the rule of law and the constitution ..."[67]

In 1986 the two constituent elements of the National Police, the uniformed branch (*Policía Nacional*) and the plain-clothes branch (*Cuerpo Superior de Policía*)[68] were amalgamated into a single *Cuerpo Superior de Policía.* Officers would no longer receive military training and military personnel were returned to the army. The Civil Guard is a para-military force which specialises in anti-terrorism, communications, weaponry, and explosives as well as being responsible for policing customs and frontiers, roads, airports, and outside prisons. The civil guard has a strong family and military tradition[69] and 80% of the force live in house-barracks (*casa-cuarteles*). It is subject to rigid discipline but the Director General is no longer an army Lieutenant Colonel but a civilian.

Whilst the tendency at the national level has been for the reunification of forces under a single code of conduct and chain of authority, at the local level there has been further diversification. The 1986 Act envisaged the establishment, for the first time, of autonomous police forces in the regions, initially in the Basque, Catalan, and Navarre areas but subsequently throughout Spain.[70] In 1996 the 5,500 strong Basque police *Ertzaintza,* formed in 1981 took over all policing responsibilities in Euskadi.[71] Additionally, there are now municipal police forces, totalling 15,000 of-

---

65. Fairén Guillén, V.F. (1995b). *Sobre Las Policías Judiciales Españolas, Revista de Derecho Procesal,* (1) p.7-62, (2) p.463-513.

66. See Macdonald (1987), *op cit.* p.19-20. A *comisaria general de la policia judicial* was created in 1994 (Law RD 1334, 20th June 1994).

67. (1987) *op cit.* p.21.

68. An organisation which had hitherto enjoyed a reputation for brutality (Morn & Toro, *op cit.,* p.58).

69. Morn & Toro, *op cit.,* p.60-62.

70. Greer, *op. cit.,* p.405-406, Agirreazkuenaga, I. & Greer, S. (1994). *Shoot to Kill: the Lethal Use of Firearms by the Security Forces in the Basque Country,* 45(3) Northern Ireland Legal Quarterly, p.285-293, pp.285-93, p.285.

71. *Id.*

ficers, in the local areas. Optimism after the 1986 reforms has been tempered somewhat by continuing revelations about the conduct of the anti-terrorist campaign in Euskadi. Accusations of a "shoot to kill" policy and the use of death squads, such as the *Grupo Anti-terroristas de Liberación (GAL)* with alleged connections at the highest level in the police and the former socialist government, have soured police relations with the public[72] although the deployment of *Ertzaintza* and the 1997 demonstrations against the *ETA* campaign seem to point the way towards some improvement.

2. Lawyers

The legal profession is a divided one in Spain and the relationship between the two branches, the Advocates (*Abogados*) and Solicitors (*Procuradores*), is similar to that between Solicitors and Barristers in the U.K.[73] However, in Spain, the Advocate deals with the client directly and the Solicitor merely handles the paperwork and the court timetable. A Solicitor must always be appointed by the Advocate and the selection is usually entirely in his or her discretion. Solicitors work within much more narrow geographical boundaries than Advocates (usually city-wide instead of province-wide) and so if a defendant has cases in two or more cities, different Solicitors must be appointed for each. Solicitors may act in only one jurisdiction whereas Advocates may qualify in several. Advocates are entitled to practice together in small law firms (*bufetes*) which are specialised. They also have the possibility of entering a *despacho colectivo* of up to twenty Advocates working together.[74] In theory the Solicitor is responsible for the conduct of the case and the defendant is usually asked to execute a power of attorney in his or her favour to enable the carrying out of the necessary procedural steps in the litigation. In practice, however, the defendant may have no contact with the Solicitor and it is the Advocate who effectively will be in charge of matters. The Solicitor is often referred to as the "mediator" (*mediador*) between the Advocate and the Judge.

Advocates can appear in any court in the Province in which they are enrolled in the local Bar Association (*Colegio de Abogados*).[75] They must be aged over 21, be Spanish citizens (unless they go through a process known as *dispensa de nacionalidad*), possess a *Degree of Licenciado* or Doctor of Law from a Spanish University (which generally takes five years) and be of good character with no criminal convictions. There is no further training although young Advocates usually undergo a practical course at a private law school (*escuela de práctica de jurídica*) or pupillage with a firm (*pasante*). Neither of these are obligatory. Article 13 of the General Statute of the Legal Profession (*Abogacía*) provides that Advocates must enrol in their local Bar Association. Each Association is controlled by a *Junta de Gobierno* which exercises discipline subject to a right of appeal to the National Bar Council (*Consejo General de la Abogacía*). In court, Advocates wear a black gown with a wide collar and long sleeves.

Solicitors are legal agents specialising in the preparation of documents and in representing the interests of defendants out of court. They cannot appear in court

---

72. Agirreazkuenaga & Greer, *op cit.*, pp.291-2
73. See Merino-Blanco *op cit.*, p.107-113.
74. *Id.* p.111.
75. There are 79,490 practising Advocates in Spain (Merino Blanco, *op cit.*, p.108).

as advocates but are under a professional obligation to prepare the necessary documents and to ensure that they are filed in time. Solicitors hold the same basic qualifications as Advocates. They must be of good character and hold a licence from the Ministry of Justice as well as membership of the local Solicitors' Association (*Colegio de Procuradores*) and deposit a sum by way of security. The Council of the local Solicitors' Association enforces discipline in the same way as the Bar Association.

A private lawyer (*Abogado Particular*) is entitled to charge whatever fee he or she wishes (the Bar Association lays down only minimum fees) and the Solicitor charges an "*arancel*" or fixed fee. There is no Public Defender system in Spain but state legal aid is available for lawyers in private practice representing criminal defendants in the same way as in the U.K. The free legal aid scheme, recently reformed by the law 1/1996 of 10th January 1996[76] provides a relatively high quality service, ensuring the participation of all competent lawyers who are obliged to participate (*turno de oficio*) under a rota system organised by the local Bar Association.[77] In cases which are likely to attract penalties in excess of six years, only five year qualified Advocates may appear.

3. *Prosecutors (*Fiscales*)*

The main role of the prosecutor, according to Article 124 of the Constitution is ". . . to promote the course of justice in defence of the legal order, of the rights of citizens and of the public interest ..." The prosecutor is therefore required to exercise general oversight of the proceedings and to ensure that the rights of the suspect and the victim are protected and the law applied fairly. Increasingly, however, the prosecutor is being required to adopt a more adversarial role.[78] Since prosecutors are civil servants and therefore potentially subject to political control, they have no discretion as to whether or not to prosecute where the offence appears to them to be made out.[79] They do not enjoy a monopoly of prosecutions. Prosecutors, who are known collectively as the "*ministerio fiscal*," must hold a law degree and pass a similar examination to the Judges (see below). The career structure also mirrors that of the Judges.[80]

4. *Judges (*Magistrados & Jueces*)*

Higher-ranking Judges are called "*Magistrados*" and the lower-ranking ones "*Jueces*." All Judges are functionally independent of the state and irremovable, except for misconduct.[81] Candidates for the judiciary must be over 21, of Spanish nationality, possessors of a law degree (*Licenciado* or *Doctor* of Law) from a Spanish University and be able to prove their good character to the Ministry of Justice.

76. See Gómez Colomer, J.L. (1996). *El nuevo regimen del beneficio de la asistencia juridica gratuita*, 2 La Ley, p.1579-1587.

77. See d'Armagnac, H. *et al.* (1993). *Le Système Espagnol de la Garde à Vue,* Gazette du Palais, 27-29 June , p.491-496.

78. See law 7/1988 of December 28th 1988 requiring the prosecutor to lead the investigation in the "abbreviated procedure" and law 5/1995 of 23rd May 1995 for the more active prosecutorial role in the new jury procedure.

79. Art. 105, the so-called "legality principle."

80. See Merino-Blanco *op cit.*, p.116-117; Conde-Pumpido Ferreiro, C. (1992). *El modelo post-constitucional del ministerio fiscal en España*, 27(2) Poder Judicial, p.9-21.

81. Art. 117.1 *CE.*

They sit a competitive examination for entry to the judicial college (*escuela judicial*) where they follow a one year course. If they complete this course successfully and pass the examination (*turno normal*) they are appointed either as prosecutors or Judges after a short orientation procedure. Class ranking during the course is likely to affect their appointment[82] and promotion is by seniority (except in respect of the judgeships of the Supreme Court and the Presidents of the Provincial and Territorial Criminal Courts).

There is a Judicial Council (*Consejo General del Poder Judicial*) headed by the President of the Supreme Court, which consists of the six Chamber Presidents and a Judge from each Chamber elected annually from amongst its members. This Council nominates Judges for office, whereas the Governing Chamber of the Supreme Court (*Sala de Gobierno*) proposes rules for regulating the judiciary and for disciplining Judges.

The President of the Supreme Court is also the highest Inspector of Justice. He or she receives reports from the court inspection service (*inspección de tribunales*) and from the Presidents of the Territorial Courts. Judges in the Supreme Court (Criminal Division) are appointed by the Council of Ministers on the advice of the Judicial Council. They are chosen mostly from the more senior Judges (*Magistrados de Término*) in the Provincial and Territorial Criminal Courts but a small proportion (one in five) are selected from high-ranking prosecutors and Advocates or Professors of law. Judges in the Territorial and Provincial Courts are also appointed by the Council of Ministers on the advice of the Minister of Justice, whereas Judges of the Instruction Courts are appointed directly. Justices' Court Judges are usually practising lawyers who pass a competitive examination but are not required to attend the judicial college. By Art. 117 of the Constitution, Judges cannot be involved in other public offices, political parties or unions.

D. The Courts

1. *Justices' Courts (*Juzgados de Paz*)*

These courts operate in all small communities except those which are the seats of Lower Criminal Courts (see below). The Justices' Courts sit with a single lay Judge (*Juez de Paz*) who need not be a lawyer and who is appointed on an honorary basis by the Provincial Criminal Court (see below). The Justices' Courts are supervised by the Lower Criminal Courts.

2. *Lower Criminal Courts (*Juzgados de lo Penal*)*

These courts were created following the decision of the Constitutional Court in 1988[83] that the Examining Magistrates (who had previously assumed first instance jurisdiction over lower range serious offences (*delitos menos graves*) should no longer act in both the instruction and the trial stage in the same case. In place of the former First Instance Criminal Courts (*Juzgados de Primera Instancia e Instrucción*) the Lower Criminal Courts were established with jurisdiction for lower

82. 25% of judges are selected competitively from Advocates of six years standing.

83. See above.

range serious offences[84] attracting penalties of a fine or imprisonment up to six years. This is essentially a trial and not an instruction court. In each province, and based in each provincial capital, there are one or more Lower Criminal Courts with jurisdiction throughout the province.

3. *Instruction Courts* (Juzgados de Instrucción)

These courts sit with a single professional Judge in all the more heavily populated cities in Spain. There is one court in every territorial district (*cabeza de partido*) and in provincial capitals and large cities sometimes two or more. In Madrid, for example, there is a large modern building housing 33 courts. Their work is divided into four functions.[85] The first is to prepare the evidence and to investigate cases of major offences (*delitos*) which are to be heard in the Provincial Criminal Court (see below). They cannot try these cases themselves but must prepare a preliminary report (*diligencia previa*) and, when satisfied of the existence of a *delito*, prepare a summary report known as the *sumario*. This process is known as "instruction" (*instrucción*). An Examining Magistrate (*Juez de Instrucción*) will be on duty for 24 hours on a rota system as a "Duty Magistrate" (*Juez de Guardia*) to deal with new arrests as they are brought in by the police.

The second function is to investigate and to try all misdemeanours (*faltas*) not within the jurisdiction of the Justices' Courts (see above). This is known as "*procedimiento oral.*" Appeal lies to the Provincial Criminal Court within five days. The third function is hearing applications for *Habeas Corpus* (see above) and appeals from the Justices' Courts. The Duty Magistrates also authorise exceptional procedures such as domestic searches.[86]

4. *Territorial Courts* (Audiencias Territoriales)

This court has no criminal jurisdiction except in cases of offences committed by prosecutors (*Fiscales*). It can deal with questions of jurisdiction and complaints against Judges.

5. *Provincial Criminal Courts* (Audiencias Provinciales)

Provincial Criminal Courts sit in the major centres of population in each of the 15 Spanish provinces. Each court is headed by a President and operates a Criminal Division (*Sala de Justicia*) which tries all major offences (*delitos*) not heard by the inferior courts. Trials are conducted by three professional Judges sitting alone although, since 1995, new "jury courts" have been established (see above).

The Provincial Criminal Court also hears appeals from the lower courts but there is no appeal from this court except on points of law or procedure to the Supreme Court of Justice (see below). Notice of petition for appeal must be lodged within five days of the judgement. Representation is compulsory and the prosecutor appearing in this court is the *Fiscal de la Audiencia Provincial.*

---

84. Art. 14.3.
85. *LOPJ*, Art.87.
86. *Id*, Art. 87.2.

6. *National Criminal Court (*Audiencia Nacional*)*

This sits in Madrid in a high security building containing five courts.[87] It deals with cases which relate to more than one province, treason, piracy, hijacking of aircraft and complex or serious smuggling, exchange control, or drugs cases. Proceedings are exactly the same as those in the Provincial Criminal Court[88] but because there are fewer cases, tend to be more rapid.

7. *The Supreme Court of Justice (*Tribunal Supremo de Justicia*)*

This court, which sits in Madrid, is divided into six chambers including a criminal one. Each chamber comprises 16 Judges and is headed by a President. At least five Judges must be empanelled to hear appeals and they decide on a simple majority. Appeals to this court are likely to take a year (or sometimes more). The court hears appeals on the law (*por infracción de ley*) and on procedural defects (*por quebrantamiento de forma*) from Provincial Criminal Courts. All appellants must be represented. The President of the Supreme Court of justice is selected by the King from a list of three very eminent Judges and is appointed for a three year term.

E. Due Process Rights

The primarily inquisitorial character of Spanish criminal procedure has been modified significantly (particularly in recent years) by the adoption of a number of adversarial due process rights which, although welcome, do not accord particularly well with the basic structure of the system. For example, the "presumption of innocence" is guaranteed at every stage of the procedure by Art. 24.2 of the Constitution.[89] although cases are decided ultimately on the principle of the "intimate conviction" (*intima convicción*) of the tribunal, rather than on proof beyond reasonable doubt. Notwithstanding that it is the Judges who are ultimately responsible for the collection of evidence and the conduct of the trial, the burden of proof (*carga de la prueba de la accusacion*) lies with the prosecution.[90]

The right to a fair hearing and the rights of defence are both protected by Art. 24 of the Constitution[91] whereas Art. 17 of the same sets out the important categories of rights available on arrest, including the right to be informed of the reasons for the detention, and more generally, throughout the procedure, the right to silence and the right to legal representation. Again, any exercise of the right to silence is likely to be highly disruptive of a procedure which is organised around a continuous dialogue between Judge and defendant.

87. The court has been much criticised since its establishment of the law 1/1977 of 4th January 1977.

88. *LOPJ*, arts.62-9.

89. See Vázquez Sotelo, J.L. (1984). *"Presuncion de inocencia" del imputando e "intima conviccion del tribunal."* Barcelona, Bosch; Rámos Mendez *op cit.*, p.14-16; Gómez Colomer (1993) *op cit.*, p.255.

90. *STC* 229/1988, 1st December 1988.

91. See also Art. 118 confering the right to defence and to notification of allegations.

The debate over the progressive introduction of more adversarial elements into the procedure in Spain has been intense.[92] Luciano Varela, the "notorious" adversary of the inquisitorial system of *instrucción* has written:

In no other civilised country is the person who decides when and how to conduct the investigation the same as the one who decides whether sufficient justification exists to commit the individual for trial.[93]

Fairén Guillén has responded by asserting that the introduction of more adversariality into the pre-trial would lead directly to "totalitarianism."[94]

II. Police Procedures

It is misleading to consider police procedure in Spain as a separate phase of the process. The police conduct enquiries under the authority of the judges and not independently and therefore the procedures considered in this section should properly be included under the heading of "Pre-trial Court Procedure."

A. Arrest, Search, and Seizure Law

1. Stops and Identity Checks

Art. 20 (1) of the *LOPSC* of 1992 authorises the police to require persons to produce evidence of identity and may conduct, in the public highway or wherever the production of identity is required, relevant checks to establish identity. Art. 20(2) further empowers the police to "require" anyone who fails to establish their identity to accompany them to the police station.[95] They can also exercise this power where they feel it is necessary in order to prevent an offence and a failure to comply can result in a fine of 5,000 to 25,000 pesetas. None of the normal due process requirements under Art. 520 of the *LECr* (see below) apply to such detentions and the *LOPSC* provides no guidance as to how long a detainee can be held. Surprisingly, the Constitutional Court, by a majority, has upheld this provision[96] although they stressed that a detained person had to be told the reason for the detention and could be held no longer than was necessary to establish identity and could, in any event, apply for *Habeas Corpus* (see below). The issue has again provoked considerable controversy in Spain[97] especially because the Constitutional

92. See e.g. Montero Aroca, J. (1992). *El principio acusatorio. Un intento de aclaración conceptual*, iv Justicia, p.775-788; Amanta Deu, T. (1996).*Principio acusatorio: realidad y utilización (lo que es y lo que no)*. 2 Revista Perecho Procesal, p.265-291; Fairén Guillén, (1996). *op cit.*

93. Cited in *Id*, p.18.

94. Fairén Guillén is concerned that were the prosecutor (a civil servant under the authority of the Ministry of Justice) to take on responsibility for pre-trial investigation, political pressure could be brought to bear, *Id.*, p.19.

95. López Ortega, J.J. (1992). *La Detención del Indocumentado*, 26(2) Poder Judicial, p.153-157.

96. *Sentencia de 18 Noviembre. Repertorio del Tribunal Constitucional*,1993, vol.341, p.614, see Greer *op cit.*, pp.408-411.

97. *Id.*, Gómez Colomer (1993) *op cit.*, pp.333-334; Suárez-Bárcena, *op cit.*, p.112-119.

Court has previously ruled that there were "no intermediate zones between detention and liberty."[98]

2. Frisks

The right to undertake "frisk" searches (*cacheos*),[99] although widely exercised by the police, has never been clearly articulated in Spain until relatively recently. Under Art. 786.2(a) of *LECr*, the police can take items into possession on their own authority where they suspect that they may provide evidence which may subsequently disappear. This provision gives no explicit right of search but frisks were carried out regularly on this doubtful authority[100] until the enactment of the controversial "Corcuera Law" *LOPSC* in 1992.[101] Art. 19.2 of this Act permits police officers to establish control points (*controles*) in public places in order to check the identity of persons, search vehicles and to carry out "frisk" searches (*control superficial de efectos personales*) in order to identify and to arrest offenders involved in crimes causing "public alarm" and to recover instruments, proceeds or evidence relating to such crimes. No distinct level of individual suspicion is required. For example, the search of a person disembarking from a bus which had come from an area well-known for drug dealing would not be considered to be in breach of constitutional protections.[102] Art. 19.2 has caused considerable concern in Spain but has not been overturned by the Constitutional Court. However, the power must be exercised in a way which does not contravene the constitutional right of bodily integrity [103] and so only superficial "pat down" searches are permitted in the absence of express judicial authority. Equally, searches which amount to degrading or inhuman conduct would clearly offend against Art. 18 of the Constitution.

3. Arrest

Freedom from unlawful arrest is guaranteed by Art. 17.1 of the Spanish Constitution and Art. 489 of the *LECr* confirms that noone may be arrested except in circumstances prescribed by the law. Private citizens are authorised by Art. 490 of the same to effect an arrest (*detención*) of an offender immediately before, during, or immediately after the commission of an offence. Police officers, on the other hand, have an obligation to arrest not only persons mentioned in Art. 490 above but also those that they believe to have committed a serious offence (*delito*) carrying a penalty in excess of six months.[104] Even when the offence carries a lesser penalty, an arrest can be made where the officer believes, on the basis of the criminal record and background of the offender, that he or she will not answer a summons. There is, on the other hand, no right of arrest for misdemeanours (*faltas*).[105]

98. 98/1986, see López Ortega *op cit.*, p.154.

99. See Suárez-Bárcena. E. de L. (1993). *La Policía Judicial y la Seguridad Ciudadana*, 31(2) Poder Judicial, pp.107-122, pp.120-1; Alegre Avia, J.M. (1993). *El art.21 de la Ley de Protección de la Seguridad Ciudadana*, 30(2) Poder Judicial, pp.27-42.

100. And on the authority of similar provisions such as Art. 104 of the *LOFCSE* (see above).

101. See above.

102. *Tribunal Supremo* (*TS*), 21st October 1994, *Revista General de Derecho* (*RGD*) 1995, p.3512.

103. Art. 18 of the Constitution.

104. Art. 492.

105. Art. 495.

The police are not obliged to carry out any notification procedures or other formalities at the point of arrest but the officer must ascertain the name and other details of the arrestee for communication to the Judge.[106]

a. *Detention at a Police Station.* As a result of reforms enacted in 1978 and 1983,[107] a regime of rights at the police station has now been established, although abuses of these procedures are still evident. For some years, for example, the police operated a system of classifying some arrestees as "*retenido*" (helping with enquiries) and these did not enjoy the benefit of the rights set out below. This type of custody was held to be illegal by the Constitutional Court[108] and any prisoner so treated can apply for *Habeas Corpus* (see below). The only legal status for a prisoner in police custody is "*detenido*" (arrested).[109]

On arrival, the arrestee must be notified immediately and in clear and precise terms, so as to be easily understood,[110] the reasons for the arrest and the rights set out in Art. 520 of the *LECr.* Arrestees are normally also given a written statement of these rights and asked to sign to show that it has been received. The rights include:

- The right to remain silent and to refuse to answer questions,[111] or to insist on answering only to the Examining Magistrate, and
- a privilege against self-incrimination, and
- the right to choose a lawyer and for his or her attendance at the place of custody. The lawyer may also be present during interrogations and identification procedures such as the line up. If the suspect is unable to nominate a lawyer, a duty lawyer will be appointed by the local Bar, and
- the right to notify a relative or other specified person of the facts of the arrest and the place of detention. Foreigners are entitled to notify their consular authorities, and
- the right of a person who cannot understand or speak Spanish to be assisted free of charge by an interpreter, and
- the right to a physical examination by a police doctor.

Under Art. 520.3, juveniles or disabled arrestees are entitled to have the usual details of arrest notified to a parent or legal guardian. The prosecutor (and in the case of a foreigner) the relevant consular authorities, must be notified at once.

The different police forces will take arrested persons to their own base police stations. In the case of the National Police (*Policía Nacional*) this will be the local police station (*comisaría*) although Inspectors may take prisoners back to the Group H.Q. of the judicial police (in Madrid this is the D.S.E.—*Dirección de la Seguridad del Estado*). The Civil Guard (*Guardia Civil*) will take prisoners back to the nearest barracks (*cuartelillo*) or Command H.Q. There is nothing sinister in the arrestee being taken to a barracks and all the legal protections still apply.

---

106. Art. 493.

107. See McGee *op cit.*, p.262-273 for the role of the Spanish Bar in the creation of a regime of rights in the police station.

108. *Sentencia del Tribunal Constitucional* No. 28/1986 *BOE* 23rd July 1986. See Greer *op cit.*, p.409-410.

109. But see the provisions of the "Corcuera Law" *LOPSC* 1992, above.

110. Art. 17.3 of the Constitution, Art 520.2 *LECr.*

111. .Velayos Martinez, I. (1995). *El derecho del imputado al silencio*, 1 Justicia, p.59-93.

There is usually a search and short medical inspection. Before the arrestee is put in the cells (*calabozos*) personal possessions (including belt and shoelaces) will be removed and signed for. Arrestees should be held separately,[112] although this is rarely possible in practice. At the very least, arrestees of different sex must be separated and younger persons held apart from older ones. Exceptional measures of restraint are permitted on a temporary basis only against arrestees who are violent, disruptive, rebellious, or are likely to attempt escape.[113] Provided it is not likely to interfere with the course of justice, the arrestee is entitled to receive visits from a Minister of Religion and unimpeded access to legal advice.[114] Detention facilities must be visited weekly by an Examining Magistrate[115] who is obliged to take steps to remedy any abuses which come to light.

The assistance of a lawyer at the police station is mandatory, even if positively renounced by the arrestee.[116] The Madrid Bar, for example, operates a 24 hour call-out rota system involving some 3,000 voluntary participating lawyers who are paid a flat fee of 10,000 Pesetas for each call-out. Only a request for a private lawyer will displace the duty lawyer, who will otherwise retain responsibility for the case throughout the procedure. The lawyer is entitled to be present at the interrogation (which cannot commence until either the lawyer arrives or eight hours have elapsed since the call-out)[117] and to consult privately with his or her client.[118] A failure to observe any of the above formalities will result in nullification (i.e. the removal of the offending documents from the file and non-use at trial) only where there is a "deprivation or a significant diminution of defence rights"[119] such as a failure to allow a consultation before a crucial interrogation is recorded for the *dossier*,[120] rather than, for example, merely the substitution of a duty lawyer for a nominated one.[121] Where a suspect has been told of his right to a lawyer but insists on making an immediate voluntary declaration without one, there is no infringement of constitutional rights.[122]

In principle, the arrestee must be released or produced before a Judge within 72 hours of the arrest[123] but this period can be prolonged up to a maximum of a further 48 hours where notice has been given by the Police 48 hours before the expiry of the initial period. A decision by the Judge to prolong the police interrogation phase beyond the initial period must set out the reasons in full.[124] Periodic reports on the progress of the investigation must be sent to the Judge every 24 hours.[125] In the case of an arrest for a terrorist offence, all the above rights are restricted and detention can last, with the consent of the Examining Magistrate, for

112. Art. 521.
113. Art. 525.
114. Art. 523.
115. Art. 526.
116. See McGee *op cit.*, on the role of mandatory counsel.
117. Art. 520.4.
118. See d'Armagnac, H. *et al.* (1993). *op cit.*
119. *TS*, 31st March 1997, *RGD* 1997, p.12429.
120. *Audiencia Provincial* (*AP*) de Avila, 11th October 1996, *RGD* 1997, p.10034.
121. *TS*, 20th February 1996, *RGD*, 1996, p.10049.
122. *TS* 4th March 1996, *RGD*, 1996, p.10050.
123. Art. 520.1.
124. Art. 520 bis 1.
125. Art. 295.

up to five days. All arrestees have an absolute right to make written representations to the judicial authorities.[126]

4. Searches

a. *Domiciliary Searches.* Article 18.2 of the Spanish Constitution establishes the principle that the "home is inviolable." It goes on: "No-one may enter or search a domicile without the consent of the owner or a judicial warrant, except in cases of *flagrante delito.* An unlawful entry by the police or other official constitutes an offence under Arts. 534-6 of the *CP.*" However, Arts. 545-72 of the *LECr* lay down the conditions under which lawful entries and searches may be conducted.[127] These exceptions to the general principle of inviolability include:

- Where entry and search are conducted with the consent of the owner or of a person who reasonably appears to be the owner. This consent can be either express or implied, or
- where the search has been authorised by the written warrant (*auto de entrada y registro*) of a competent Judge acting on information supplied by the Police or the prosecutor leading the investigation. The warrant must set out the justifications for issue[128] and all the relevant details (unless these are confidential[129]), or
- where entry is necessary to effect the arrest of a person unlawfully at large and facing a prison sentence of more than six months and in respect of whom a valid arrest warrant exists, or
- where a suspected offender being pursued by the police hides or seeks refuge in the premises, or
- where the police need to enter to arrest members of an armed gang, terrorists or rebels, or
- where the police need to enter to effect an arrest in circumstances of *delito flagrante*, e.g. where the police see a burglar actually inside the premises or notice the occupants of a house hiding drugs when they knock on the door.[130] A situation of *delito flagrante* arises only when the officers directly perceive the alleged wrongdoing and not when, for example, information received leads them to a particular premises.[131]

The type of premises protected by Arts. 545-72 are listed in Art.554 and include all enclosed premises or parts of the same where they are used primarily as the dwelling place of a Spanish citizen or foreign resident or their family. Protection extends to tents, caravans,[132] and hotels,[133] and to any occupied premises even when the owner is absent. Searches of public buildings, including shops and

---

126. Art. 524.

127. See Angosto Agudo, R.M. (1996). *La diligencia de entrada y registro como acto documentado, su introducción en el juicio oral*, 4 La Ley, p.1159-1164.

128. *TS* 17th June 1994, *RGD* 1994, p.12748.

129. *TS*, 22nd March 1994, *RGD* 1994, p.6785.

130. *TS* 13th July 1994, *RGD* 1995, p.1967; 3rd October 1994, *RGD*, 1995, p.3528.

131. *TS* 22nd July 1994, *RGD* 1995, p.435.

132. Queralt, J.J. & Jiminez Quintana, J. (1989). *Manual de Policía Judicial*, Madrid, Ministerio de Justicia, p.111.

133. *TS* 5th October 1992, *RGD* 1993, p.1595.

garages,[134], bars and video clubs[135] can be made at any time[136] but, except in cases of emergency, searches of private domiciles should take place during daylight hours. According to Art. 569, the Judge's Clerk and (if possible) the owner of the premises (or his or her representative) must be present for the entry and search. All items seized must be taken into the custody of the Judge in the case. The Clerk must make a formal record, signed by all present, noting the date and time of the search, how it was conducted and the outcome.[137] Items seized in breach of these provisions cannot be used in evidence.[138] Property not mentioned in the warrant (such as drugs discovered during a search for stolen goods) may be seized only where their discovery triggers the *flagrante delicto* procedure[139] or there is time to issue a new search warrant.[140]

The Spanish Constitutional Court, in contrast to its vacillation on the issue of police station detention under Art. 20 of the "Corcuera Law" 1992,[141] above, has adopted an admirably robust approach to domiciliary searches. In the face of considerable police frustration and anger, the court, in a series of widely reported cases, has insisted on a vigorous interpretation of the constitutional protections.[142] Moreover, under one of the most controversial sections—Art 21.2—of the *LOPSC* 1992 the police were empowered to enter and search a private dwelling without a warrant when they had "firm evidence to believe" that a drug-related offence was being committed there. The provision provoked a widespread constitutional debate in Spain but its effectiveness was thrown into serious doubt by the decision of the court in the *Sumare* case[143] which held that Art.21.2 could not extend the *flagrante delicto* rule enshrined in Art. 18.2 of the Constitution (above) and that the police powers purported to be created under Art 21.2 had to be exercised consistently with the constitutional provisions. On 18th November 1993 the Constitutional Court dispelled any lingering doubt by abrogating Article 21.2 entirely, thereby prompting the resignation of the Justice Minister.[144]

b. *Interception of Postal and Telephone Communications*. The privacy of communications is guaranteed by Art. 18.3 of the Spanish Constitution which refers specifically to postal, telegraph and telephone communications. However, Art. 579 of the *LECr* authorises a Judge to order that the private correspondence of a suspect be intercepted where there is evidence to suggest that it may reveal an offence or facts material to an existing offence.

Equally, under Art. 579.3, a Judge can issue a written order authorising the surveillance of a Suspect's correspondence for up to three months (renewable). The order must set out fully the reasons for the decision. In urgent cases, the Minister

134. *TS*, 6th October 1994, *RGD*, 1995, p.3524.
135. *TS*, 8th July 1994, *RGD* 1995, p.1959; *AP* de Barcelona, 24th February 1997, *RGD* 1997, p.8160.
136. Art. 546.
137. Art. 572.
138. *TS*, 28th October 1992, *RGD* 1993, p.3134.
139. *TS*, 28th April 1995, *RGD* 1995, p.10135.
140. *TS*, 28th October 1992, *RGD* 1993, p.3134.
141. *LOPSC*, See above.
142. Greer, *op cit.*, p.411-414.
143. See *El Pais* 24 & 29th July 1992.
144. *STC* 341/1993, 18th November 1993 p.614 and see Greer *op cit.*, p.411-416, Merino-Blanco *op cit.*, p.177, Queralt & Jiminez Quintana, (1989) *op cit.* p.111.

of the Interior can proceed with interception on his or her own initiative, providing that the order is confirmed by a Judge within three days.[145] Special provisions are available to authorise the government to carry out widespread interceptions of communications during states of emergency.

5. *Enforcement of Rules*

a. *Habeas Corpus*. The Organic Law 6 of 24th May 1984 introduced the remedy of *Habeas Corpus*[146] in cases of illegal detention or of detention in excess of the authorised time limits or of the infringement of an arrestee's rights. The last category would include allegations of torture and other miss-treatment, including interviews held in the enforced absence of a lawyer. An application in writing is made to the duty Examining Magistrate by the arrestee, his or her family or lawyer, or even the prosecutor. The Examining Magistrate in the case may also proceed of his or her own motion. The application may be heard at any hour of the day or night and the Examining Magistrate may order the production of the arrestee, or visit the police station to take statements. The immediate transfer or release of the arrestee may be ordered and also an inquiry into the case, which might result in disciplinary action against the officers involved.[147]

b. *Admissibility of Illegally Obtained Evidence*. This area of the law has undergone radical changes over the last two decades under the influence of anglo-american law and the need to restrict the hitherto unregulated powers of the police.[148] Article 11 of the *LOPJ* lays down the principle that "evidence obtained either directly or indirectly in contravention of fundamental rights and liberties will be of no effect." This provision has been held to apply to the guarantees set out in Art. 24.2 of the Constitution. Evidence obtained unlawfully will therefore be declared a nullity, references to it will be removed from the *dossier* and it cannot be referred to in the proceedings. The police officers or others involved may face disciplinary or penal sanctions.

A means of proof is unlawful when it is obtained in breach of a fundamental right, for example, a search without a warrant or other justification, a telephone tap carried out without authority or the use of physical or psychological torture during an interrogation.[149] Thus, the denial of medical assistance to a suspect who was released immediately after giving a statement did not result in nullification of the statement.[150] On the other hand, the failure to give an unrepresented defendant the opportunity to prepare *calificaciones* (legal submissions) or to sum up in his own defence,[151] or the taking of a statement from an [152]unrepresented defendant by an Examining Magistrate in breach of the adversariality principle,[153] clearly nulli-

145. Gómez Colomer (1993) *op cit.*, p.200.

146. See above.

147. See Ramos Méndez, *op cit.*, p.298-301, Gómez Colomer, (1993) *op cit.*, p.332-333.

148. Ortega Pinto, L-T. (1996). *Tratamiento de la ilicitud probatoria en el proceso penal*, 1 Revista de Derecho Procesal, p.171-176.

149. Ruiz Vadillo, E. (1992). *La Actividad Probatoria en el Proceso Penal Español y las Consecuencias de Violarse en ella algun Principio Constitucional de Producirse Algunas Determinadas Irregularidades Procesuales*, in *Consejo General del Poder Judicial*, La Prueba en el Proceso Penal. Madrid, Pinto, p.49-279, p.81.

150. *AP* de Segovia, 9th October 1996, *RGD* 1996, p.14098.

151. *AP* de Teruel, 1st December 1995, *RGD* 1996, p.4865.

152. *AP* de Bareclona, 13 June 1997, *RGD*, 1997, p.13517.

153. *AP* de Barcelona, 13th June 1997, *RGD*, 1997, p.13517.

fied that part of the procedure. It is fair to say, however, that the courts have not been entirely consistent in their application of the nullity rule.[154] In one set of cases it was held that the items discovered in searches going beyond the express terms of a warrant were not admissible in evidence[155] whereas in another line of cases the view was taken that such items would be admissible in evidence, provided that the search itself was not in violation of Art. 18.2 of the Constitution.[156]

B. Lineups and Other Identification Procedures

An identity parade (*reconocimiento en rueda*) may be held in cases of doubtful identification at the instigation of the Examining Magistrate, the complainant or even the suspect.[157] Although the *LECr* envisages that the procedure should be carried out under the supervision of the Examining Magistrate and a judicial order is necessary. It is usually conducted by the police alone.[158]

The suspect is usually placed behind a glass screen with at least two other persons to whom he or she bears some external resemblance.[159] The inclusion of a number of Moroccans in an identification of a blond-haired suspect[160] would, for example, vitiate the procedure but not, apparently, the presence of a bald person[161] or the previous identification by the witness from photographic or video sources.[162] The suspect's lawyer (if there is one) is entitled to be present and to sign the record and this is particularly important in the case of line-ups carried out by the Police alone. Attempts by the suspect to alter his or her appearance are prohibited by Art. 371 and the original clothes of a defendant in custody must be preserved by the prison or cell-block authorities for use in line-ups.[163] Witnesses are asked to make any identification in a "clear and determined" manner and where two witnesses are involved, they are not permitted to confer.[164] Once the line-up has been completed, it is the responsibility of the Examining Magistrate or senior Police Officer, to record all details, including the numbers of participants and the record must be signed by all present. The mere fact of producing five suspects to a complainant doesn't constitute a line-up and, in the absence of other evidence, a defendant in those circumstances must be acquitted.[165] A formal line-up is, however, not necessary when a witness spontaneously recognises a suspect, even if the latter is accompanied by police officers.[166]

---

154. Ortega Pinto, *op cit.*, see also Greer, *op cit.*,and discussion above.
155. 1706/1993 2nd July 1993 & 91/1994 21st January 1994.
156. 1309/1993, 7th June 1993.
157. Art. 368.
158. Queralt & Jiminez Quintana *op cit.*, p.100-106.
159. Art. 369.
160. *TS* 25th October *1995*, RGD 1995, p.3715.
161. *TS*, 3rd October 1991, *RGD* 1992, p.274.
162. . *TS*, 19th December 1994, *RGD*, 1995, p.6819; *AP* de Madrid, 31st January 1996, *RGD*, 1996, p.5756.
163. Art. 372.
164. Art. 370.
165. *TS* 4th March 1992, *RGD* 1992, p.5434.
166. *AP* de Valencia, 3rd February 1997, *RGD* 1997, p.6525.

C. Interrogations

(See Section II, A, 3 "Arrests" above).

III. Court Procedures

A. Pretrial

1. The Instruction Procedure

In the case of more serious offences *(delitos)* a pre-trial examination of the evidence, known as the *instrucción* or *sumario* will be conducted by an Examining Magistrate *(Juez Instructor)*. This is a procedure unique to the remaining countries which have preserved the Napoleonic pre-trial model (e.g. France, Belgium and Spain) and was abolished in Germany (1974) and Italy (1988). Proceedings are inquisitorial in the sense that they are secret and conducted in writing and lawyers or others who reveal details of the proceedings face a fine.[167] The procedure is largely conducted in the Examining Magistrates' office and its purpose is to collect all the available evidence, both exculpatory and inculpatory, in the court file *(dossier)*. To this end, the Examining Magistrate may first visit the scene of the alleged offence, examine any physical evidence, commission any expert evidence and interview the defendant and the witnesses as many times as it is necessary in order to obtain a complete written record of the surrounding circumstances. Once this investigation has been completed it will be possible to identify the exact legal description *(calificación)* of the alleged offence(s).

The *dossier* does not, of itself, constitute evidence except in certain restricted cases (e.g where evidence is no longer accessible) but is a guide to assist the judges in the conduct of the trial. The Examining Magistrate can also collect certain kinds of evidence, for example, by the judicial inspection of buildings or other locations, which it is not practical to undertake at the trial. The Examining Magistrate compiles the *dossier* under the nominal supervision of the prosecutor and must notify him or her of all actions taken.[168] The defendant will participate in the instruction only to the extent that he or she is called by the examining Magistrate to give evidence or to confront witnesses. This is clearly not an adversarial procedure, but since 1978 the defendant has been allowed to be accompanied by counsel and, if necessary, an interpreter. Both the prosecution and the defence have the right to copies of the documents in the *dossier*[169] and the right to "intervene" (e.g by suggesting potential lines of inquiry) in all stages of the instruction.[170] There is also a right of appeal against the refusal of the Examining Magistrate to comply with a request for a particular investigatory action.[171]

---

167. Art. 301.
168. Art. 306.
169. Art. 302.
170. *Id.*
171. Art. 311.

Nevertheless, the main responsibility of the Examining Magistrate is to observe the important "duty of official investigation" (*principio de investigación oficial*) which requires him or her to carry out exhaustive investigations and to explore with an open mind, all the relevant avenues of inquiry, whether or not requested by the parties.[172] Every large city will have a Duty Magistrate's Court (*Juzgado de Guardia*) where the various Examining Magistrates sit in rotation as Duty Magistrates (*Jueces de Oficio*). The Examining Magistrate works together with a Clerk (*Secretario Judicial*) who will take a note of all interviews and other investigations, usually at the dictation of the Examining Magistrate. All present on each occasion will be invited to sign the record.

a. *Visits to the Scene.* Although the *LECr* envisages an immediate visit to the scene of the alleged offence by the Examining Magistrate,[173] the collection of evidence *in situ* is of course increasingly left to the technical agencies of the police. However, a judicial description of the scene is receivable in evidence and the examining Magistrate may wish to interview witnesses at the site or even arrange a reconstruction of events.[174]

b. *Preservation of Physical Evidence.* The preservation of physical evidence (*cuerpo del delicto*) is regulated by Arts 334 to 367 of the *LE*Cr which requires the judge, in the case of a fatality, to describe the body and effect an identification.[175] In cases of violent or suspicious death, an autopsy must be ordered.[176] In fraud cases, the Examining Magistrate must collect and describe all relevant documents.[177]

c. *Interviewing the Defendant.* One of the primary and indispensable tasks of the Examining Magistrate is to interview the defendant.[178] and, where the latter is in custody, this must be done within 24 hours of the receipt of the file or of notification of the case. The period can be extended by 48 hours in exceptional circumstances.[179] At the first hearing, the Examining Magistrate will establish the identity and other basic details about the defendant and then go on to invite him or her to make any declaration which he or she may wish, before addressing the question of bail or custody.

The defendant may be called back on numerous occasions by the Examining Magistrate to complete the statement, or at his or her own request or at the request of the parties, or to be confronted with witnesses. The statements given may cover a wide range of topics including the facts of the alleged offence, the background of the defendant, including educational, occupational, sexual or personal history. Defendants can be asked about their morals or their previous conduct[180] or prior convictions. defendants can either dictate their own statement or ask the judge to compile it for them, using their own words so far as is possible.[181] Defendants are not examined under oath at any stage and cannot be prosecuted for perjury.[182] The

172. Art. 315. See Gómez Colomar (1993) *op cit.*, p.149.
173. Arts 326-333.
174. Arts 329 and 331 respectively.
175. Arts. 355 & 340-342.
176. Art. 353.
177. Art. 335.
178. Arts. 385-409.
179. Art. 386.
180. Art. 377-378.
181. Art. 397.
182. Art. 387.

constitutional rights of silence and the assistance of counsel apply at all stages in the proceedings and the use of all forms of coercion and trick questioning by the Examining Magistrate are strictly forbidden.[183] defendants are entitled to give as many statements as they wish[184] or may simply confirm the contents of a statement already given to the police.

d. *Expert Evidence.* Experts (usually at least two) are always appointed from amongst persons holding qualifications approved by the Government. All parties have a right to challenge the competence or impartiality of expert witnesses. Also the complainant and the defendant both have the right to appoint their own expert. the points under inquiry will be set out clearly by the Examining Magistrate and the experts will be expected to file written reports within a certain time. They must then attend before the examining Magistrate for questioning in the same way as the other witnesses. If two experts cannot agree, another will be appointed.

e. *Other Witnesses.* Other witnesses can be summoned by the Examining Magistrate and they can be fined if they do not attend. Close relatives up to the second degree of consanguinity are not obliged to give evidence but they can if they wish. Evidence of witnesses is taken on oath and again the Examining Magistrate will allow them to say what they wish before they are questioned. The statements will be recorded and signed by all present after having been corrected by the maker. The Examining Magistrate has the power to bring two or more witnesses together for a confrontation (*careo*) where their evidence is contradictory.

All the parties (prosecutor, defendant, and complainant) can examine the file and propose further enquiries. The Examining Magistrate must follow up these enquiries unless he or she considers them useless or prejudicial. Where such a proposal is refused, then the matter can be appealed to the Provincial Criminal Court (*Audiencia Provincial*) or even raised at the trial.[185]

On the other hand, the Examining Magistrate has the power to decide that the proceedings will be kept either partially or completely secret from the defendant or the complainant for any period up to 1 month. This period cannot include the last 10 days before the close of the instruction stage when supplementary enquiries can be made by the parties and they are entitled to be present when they are carried out.[186]

2. Intermediate Proceedings

The "intermediate procedure" is a relatively elaborate and bureaucratic means of ensuring that all the parties have notice of the contents of the dossier, have the opportunity to file submissions regarding it and to propose directions for trial.[187] The aim is to ensure that all parties are fairly treated and that the trial itself is not unnecessarily prolonged. In this phase of the procedure and in the trial, there is a much greater commitment to the principal of adversariality and, for the first time the *LECr* begins to refer to the "parties" without distinction.[188]

183. Art. 15 Constitution and Art. 389 *LECr.*
184. Art. 400.
185. Art. 311.
186. Art. 302.
187. See Gómez Colomer (1993), *op cit.*, p.213-243 and Ramos Méndez *op cit.*, p.327-340.
188. See Gómez Colomar 1993, *op cit.*, p.214-217 and Art. 24 of the Constitution.

Once the Examining Magistrate considers that the instruction stage has been completed, he or she must pass the *dossier* to the trial court, usually the Provincial Criminal Court (*Audiencia Provincial*) [189] and give notice to that effect to the prosecutor.[190] A *Rapporteur* (*Magistrado Ponente*) is selected from the Judges who will try the case and this Judge is responsible for the final preparations for trial. The first requirement is for a copy of the *dossier* (together with its associated writs, judicial orders etc.) to be sent to the prosecutor and the complainant (if there is one) in turn. They each have three to ten days in which to file submissions regarding the work of the Examining Magistrate or to ask for the case to be returned for further investigation or for the matter to be set down for trial .[191] These recommendations will be returned to the Provincial Criminal Court and the *Rapporteur* will have a further three days to decide on what action to take next.

The range of options open to the trial court at this stage includes a dismissal of the case[192] (*sobreseimiento libre*) which amounts in effect to a complete acquittal[193] or a "provisional dismissal" which is effectively an adjournment of the matter *sine die* pending the discovery of further evidence.[194] Art. 641 specifies that a provisional dismissal will be made where either doubts exist as to the facts (e.g. where the body in an alleged homicide cannot be located and the victim may be still alive) or there is insufficient proof to support the allegation. A complete dismissal, on the other hand, may be ordered on the grounds set out in Art.637 where a) there is insufficient evidence indicating that the defendant committed the offence, or b) where the facts alleged do not amount to an offence, or c) where the defendant lacks criminal responsibility. A decision on Art. 637(3) grounds, for example in the case of mental incapacity, is usually deferred until oral evidence can be heard at the trial.[195] A wrongfully accused defendant receiving a *sobreseimiento libre* may be entitled to damages in the event that the court decides that there has been a "judicial error."[196] Alternatively, the court may decide to requalify the offence as a misdemeanour *(falta)* and return it to the lower court (as above) or to remit the dossier back to the Examining Magistrate for further investigations[197] Normally, however, the case will be set down for trial and the copy *dossier* returned to the prosecutor.

At this point, the parties are entitled to prepare detailed pre-trial pleadings (*calificaciones*) in order to narrow down the issues for trial. This process is known as the "*calificación del delito.*" The prosecutor has five days in which to prepare a submission, before the complainant (if there is one) and the defendant (*Accusado*), do the same. Each party has the same time limit and is entitled to consider the *dossier* and previous *calificaciones*. The *calificaciones* are or enormous importance in setting the trial agenda and in making clear the intentions of the prosecutor and

---

189. Art.622. In the event that the Examining Magistrate concludes that on the facts disclosed, the conduct amounts only to a minor offence (*falta*), the file will be sent, instead,to a Judge of the lower courts (*juez de lo penal*).

190. Art. 623.

191. Art. 627.

192. Arts 634-645.

193. Art. 634.

194. Gómez Colomar 1993, *op cit.*, p.219-221.

195. *Id.*, p.217-219.

196. Constitution, Art. 121.

197. Art. 631.

the complainant with regard to the sentence and civil award respectively. They should indicate:

- Whether or not a crime has been committed and, if so, what kind of crime, and
- the classification of such acts within the Penal Code, and
- the level of participation of the defendant(s), and
- any mitigating or aggravating circumstances, and
- the penalties which can be imposed together with any demands by the complainant (if there is one) for civil damages.[198]

Each party is permitted to set out different conclusions just as they wish.[199] They will also prepare:

- an offer of proof, and
- a list of witnesses which they need to establish that proof, and
- a request for any pre-trial proceedings if any matter falls to be decided before trial.[200]

None of the parties are allowed to call evidence at the trial or to suggest any conclusions which they have not first mentioned in their *calificaciones*, unless it relates to the credibility of a witness or to any such unforeseeable matter.[201] When the court has received all the *calificaciones*, the *Rapporteur* studies them and, on the basis of the conclusions that he or she reaches, the court decides which offers of proof will be accepted and which will be denied as irrelevant or insufficiently specific. The court also decides which of the witnesses will be called and which rejected[202] and declares the hearing date and the place of trial. All this information is then set out in an Order and served on the defendant. The *dossier* is then lodged with the Clerk to the court where it can be consulted by the defendant and his lawyer, provided that it is not being used by the prosecutor, complainant or *Rapporteur*.

Evidence from witnesses who cannot attend the trial in person must be in writing and notarised either by a Notary Public or by Spanish Consular authorities if the individual is abroad. Written evidence obviously carries much less weight than evidence given in person at court.

B. Trial

1. The Nature of the Trial

The typical (non-jury) Spanish criminal trial is not a full hearing of all the evidence in the anglo-american sense. The purpose of the oral hearing is for the Judges to clear up any points of doubt, to hear the main issues in evidence and for the Advocates to make their final submissions.[203] The Judges, who must determine issues

198. Art. 650.
199. Art. 653.
200. Arts. 656-657.
201. Arts.728-729.
202. Art. 659.
203. See, Gómez Colomer (1993) *op cit.*, p.268-277; Ramos Méndez *op cit.*, p.367-406, Merino-Blanco *op cit.*, p.179-186.

of both fact and law, will already have familiarised themselves with the contents of the *dossier* and, although it is strictly forbidden by the jurisprudence, it will have been very hard for them not to have already developed a view about the case. It should be stressed, however, that only evidence called at the oral hearing is considered probative. The President of the court is in complete control of the trial[204] and he or she must open the proceedings, question the defendant and call the witnesses and experts and supervise the questioning.[205] It is his or her duty to ensure that the defendant has the opportunity to comment fully on the evidence and the case as a whole[206] and to close the trial[207] before considering sentence. He or she is responsible also for maintaining order in the court[208] and deciding on the order in which evidence is given, although this will normally be in the sequence proposed by the parties in their submissions *(calificaciones)*. The President also has a duty to prevent unfair questioning or attempts to entrap a witness. The trial must continue to its conclusion even if this takes several days, since an interruption may give a right to a retrial.[209]

Arts. 688 to 740 of the *LECr* guarantee the right of the defendant and his or her lawyer to be present at the trial unless they cause a disturbance.[210] The hearing of the evidence and legal argument in the Provincial Criminal Court is open to the public and to the press unless the case involves public morality or public order or is likely to cause distress to the victim or the family.[211]

Having identified the defendant, the Clerk of the court begins the trial (*in camera*) with a detailed account of the case and the previous proceedings. He or she will give the dates on which the instruction stage (*sumario*) was opened, announce whether the defendant is on bail or in custody, read out the submissions (*calificaciones*) by all the parties, together with the lists of the witnesses who have been accepted and the decision of the court with regard to the offers of proof.[212] The public is then admitted by the Usher (*Ujier*) calling out "*¡Audiencia Publica!*" and the hearing proper will begin.

a. *Guilty Pleas*. Whether or not a formal plea is taken will depend on the nature of the offence charged. A defendant is asked to plead only in cases where he or she faces a sentence of no more than 6 years in prison. It is the duty of the court to put the question in clear and precise terms and to request a categorical answer. The most serious charge is put first and the defendant must also be asked about civil liability if this is in question.[213] There are, however, a number of safeguards. If the defendant makes an admission, the lawyer will be asked to confirm that he or she is happy for the matter to proceed on a guilty plea. If the lawyer refuses to consent, then the trial will go ahead irrespective of what the defendant has said. Even if both

204. Art. 683.

205. Arts. 705-706.

206. Art. 739.

207. Art. 740.

208. Art. 684.

209. Art. 744, unless the suspension is for the reasons set out in Art. 746 (see Ramos Méndez *op cit.*, p.382-386.

210. If this happens, a warning must be given but if this has no effect, an unanimous decision of the three judges will remove the defendant or lawyer for all or part of the proceedings (Art. 687).

211. Art. 680.

212. Art. 701.

213. Arts. 688-689.

the defendant and the lawyer agree, the court still has a duty to satisfy itself that the offence is made out before proceeding to sentence.[214] Where the defendant denies the offence (either clearly or by implication), or remains silent, or the lawyer asks for a trial, the court must proceed to hear the case.[215] Similarly, where the defendant admits guilt but denies civil liability or questions the amount of civil damages due, the court will order the trial to proceed.[216] If the defendant has pleaded guilty and refused to answer questions about the civil debt, this is considered an admission of civil liability.[217]

In the case of offences carrying penalties of more than 6 years imprisonment, the case will proceed automatically to trial without a plea.

2. *Lawyers*

(For a description of the role of the lawyers see section I, C,2 above.)

3. *Witnesses*

The witnesses are called in the order given in the list attached to the parties' submissions (*calificaciones*). The prosecution witnesses are called first, then those on behalf of the complainant (if any) and finally the defence witnesses. However, the President always has the power to challenge the order of witnesses if he or she wishes.[218] Noone can be called to give evidence unless they have been named on the lists accepted by the court from the *calificaciones*. All witnesses must be heard in person and the statement compiled by the Examining Magistrate is not admissible in evidence unless the maker cannot attend as the result of circumstances beyond his or her control.[219] After the President has dealt with the formalities, the lawyer of the party calling each witness will invite him or her to give their evidence. All the parties in the case, including the defendant, have the right to cross-examine the witness and the President can intervene at any stage to clarify matters.[220] The President has a duty to prevent leading questions and those which are impertinent or intended to entrap the witness.[221] In the event that the evidence of a witness turns out to differ significantly from the version given to the Police or to the Examining Magistrate, the original version can be read out and he or she challenged. A witness who refuses to answer questions (other than those which might tend to incriminate him or her[222] or deliberately lies to the court, may be liable to criminal proceedings.[223] All evidence (except evidence given by the defendant) is heard under oath.

There is no hearsay rule and the court must weigh up the value of the evidence in each case. However, evidence obtained illegally or in violation of basic

214. Arts. 694-700.
215. Art. 695.
216. *Id.*
217. *Id.* & 700.
218. Art. 701.
219. Art. 730.
220. Art. 708.
221. Art. 709.
222. Art. 418.
223. Arts.714-716.

human rights cannot be admitted.[224] A witness may refer to documentary or other real evidence where previously authorised by the court.[225] If the President decides to proceed with a confrontation (*careo*)[226] between the defendant and the witness to help decide between contradictory testimony, he or she has a duty to protect each party from threats or insults.[227] The court also has the power to examine all real evidence including documents, articles and the site of the alleged offence.[228] Expert evidence can be heard in exactly the same way as during the instruction stage.

4. Judges

(For a description of the nature of the judicial system and the role of the judge, see section I, C, 4 above.)

5. Conclusion of the Trial

After all the evidence has been heard, the parties have the right to modify any parts of their submissions (*calificaciones*) which they made before trial. Confirmation of the original submissions can be made orally in court, but modifications must be made in writing, since it is they which will form the basis of the verdict and sentence. This is because, under the *principio de congruencia* the verdict and sentence must resolve all the issues raised by the *calificaciones* and no others. If the prosecution decides that the evidence heard during the trial requires them to lay additional or fresh charges, all parties are entitled to file new submissions and an adjournment will probably be necessary. The court has an exceptional power to raise issues on the *calificaciones* themselves when it feels that an evident mistake has been made as to the specification of the charge. This power must be used in moderation and not to the disadvantage of the defendant.[229] The lawyers for the parties will make their final submissions in the following order: prosecutor, complainant (if there is one) and finally, defendant. They will state the facts which they consider to have been proved and which not and also indicate their views on criminal and civil liability.[230] The prosecutor will usually ask for a particular sentence but the court is not bound by this in any way and will usually impose a lower one. Indeed, the court is not bound by the oral submissions of any party and is entitled to acquit even if the defence have not asked for this.

Finally, the President will ask the defendant if he or she has anything to say and will then announce that the trial is closed[231] by calling out, "*¡Listo para sentencia;*

---

224. See Merino-Blanco *op cit.*, p.183 and Article 11 of the Organic Law of the Judicial Authority, 1st July 1985.

225. Art. 712.

226. .An exceptional procedure at trial. The Supreme Court has repeatedly held that this is a mode of instruction, not proof (Ramos Méndez, *op cit.*, p.352).

227. Art. 713.

228. Arts. 726-727.

229. This is known as *La Tesis de Desvinculación,* see Gómez Colomar (1993) *op cit.*, pp.240-243, Merino-Blanco, *op cit.*, p.184.

230. Art. 734.

231. Art. 740.

despejen la sala!" This is the signal for the public to withdraw, before all parties sign the court record[232] and the court retires to consider its judgement.

6. Verdict

Officially, the judgement must be given within 5 days but because of pressure of work, the deadlines are often exceeded. Discussions are held in secret[233] and will begin immediately after the trial or, if not, at the beginning of the next business day. The philosophy of the whole trial process is based on the idea that the defendant must be given notice of the allegations in order to exercise the full rights of defence. The sentence given by the court must therefore be linked inextricably to the terms of the calificaciones.[234] The President declares the deliberations open and the *Rapporteur* summarises the case and gives his or her opinion on the outcome. After further discussion, each issue is put to the vote. The *Rapporteur* votes first, followed by the least senior Judge and the President votes last.[235] They vote separately on all the issues including guilt or innocence, civil liability and sentence. Any deadlock in the discussions must be resolved in favour of the defendant.

The Judges must reach a final decision on guilt or innocence, and cannot (at this stage) plead lack of jurisdiction. They must also rule on the civil liability. [236] No further civil or criminal proceedings can be based on the same facts. The Judges work on the basis of a presumption of the defendant's innocence (*in dubio pro reo*) but their familiarity with the case file before the hearing must in practice qualify this presumption. There is no provision regarding "reasonable doubt" but each judge must decide in his own conscience on "rational criteria" whether he or she is persuaded of the defendant's guilt or innocence. In serious drugs cases the presumption of innocence no longer applies.

The *Rapporteur* (or another Judge if the former voted against it) then writes out the decision (*sentencia*), setting out clearly and in detail the reasons justifying the conclusions. This document must be signed by all the Judges, read out by the *Rapporteur* in open court[237] and sent to all the parties (or their lawyers) either on the same or on the following day. Once written, the judgement cannot be amended except to correct obvious technical mistakes.

The written judgement is in several parts.[238] The first section or heading (*encabezamiento*) states the full details of the proceedings, with dates and the names of the parties and the Judges etc. The second part contains a summary of the facts "*antecentes de hecho*" with a clear indication of which have been proved. The third part "*fundamentos de derecho*" addresses the appropriate law, explaining the participation of the defendant and the existence of any aggravating or mitigating factors, the implications for civil liability and costs. The verdict "*el fallo*" constitutes the final part and indicates whether the defendant is guilty or innocent and the penalty and/or civil liability which is imposed. These elements are set out in numbered paragraphs.

232. Art. 743.
233. Art. 150.
234. See Ramos Méndez *op cit.*, p.390-393.
235. Art 151.
236. Art. 741-742.
237. Art. 147.
238. Art. 142.

C. Appeals

1. Appeal for Retrial

Appeal for retrial is not available from the Provincial or National Criminal Courts[239] but is possible from the Justices' Courts (to the Instruction Courts) and from the Lower Criminal Court (to the Provincial Criminal Court).[240] Notice of appeal must be given within ten days of the judgement complained of and the appeal tribunal will usually make a decision on the papers. An oral hearing will be held only in more difficult cases or where fresh evidence is to be admitted.[241]

2. "Cassation" Appeal[242]

However, all parties have the right to appeal from the Provincial or National Courts to the Supreme Court, on one of the two following grounds:

- misapplication of the law (*por infracción de ley*, e.g. substantive law or the law of proof)[243], or
- an error in procedure (*por quebrantamiento de forma*).[244]

Leave to appeal must be granted by the trial court before the appeal can proceed. To obtain leave a petition signed by both lawyers must be filed with the trial court within five days of the notification of the original judgement.[245] The petition will request a certified copy of the judgement and set out the grounds for the appeal. The court then has three days to consider the petition and, if it agrees that a ground for appeal exists, it will remit the file, within a further three days, to the Supreme Court. The file will also contain the certified copy of the judgement. At the same time all the parties will be summoned to appear at the court within 15 days. If the trial court refuses leave to appeal then the Appellant has two days to lodge a complaint (*queja*). The trial court will then proceed as if leave to appeal had been provisionally granted and remit the whole question of leave to the Supreme Court for decision.

All parties will then have the opportunity in turn to file submissions in support (or otherwise) of the complaint. The *Rapporteur* appointed by the Supreme Court will study the files and the submissions and report to the full court which will decide the matter without a hearing. If leave to continue is again refused there is no further remedy and costs will be awarded against the Appellant. If it is accepted then the trial court will be ordered to grant the necessary leave to appeal and the parties will be summoned.

Once leave has been granted (either immediately or as a result of a complaint) all parties must file submissions setting out the legal arguments on which they intend to rely. The Appellant's failure to file submissions in time will result in the dis-

239. This has been the subject of considerable criticism, since these courts deal with the more serious offences.

240. See Gómez Colomer (1993) *op cit.* , p.285-286, Ramos Méndez *op cit.*, p.422-424.

241. Art. 795.

242. See Gómez Colomer (1993) *op cit.*, p.286-290, Ramos Méndez *op cit.*, p.424-444.

243. Art. 849.

244. Under the conditions set out in arts 850-851.

245. Art. 856. In practice this deadline can be extended.

missal of the appeal with costs. The *Rapporteur* appointed by the court will have ten days in which to prepare his summary of the case and the arguments. The full court must then decide if they will admit or deny admission of the petition to the court. A petition can only be denied by the unanimous decision of the five Judges allocated to the case. Equally, unanimity is required for the court to admit the petition without a hearing. The more usual procedure is for the court to admit the matter to a hearing before a full court. This will be in public and all parties are expected to attend. Oral submissions are made by the advocates and no evidence is called. The judgement is reached and delivered in exactly the same way as in the Provincial Criminal Court (see above). Costs can be awarded against any party except the Prosecution. The options open to the court are:

- to reject the petition with costs, or
- to admit the petition on the grounds of procedural error by the trial court and remit the case back to the same court with a direction for the mistake to be remedied and for the proceedings to continue from the point at which the error was made, or
- to admit the petition on the grounds of error of law and to give a new judgement itself. The court cannot increase an Appellant's sentence.

3. Revision Proceedings

In the event that new evidence is discovered casting doubt on the conviction, "revision" (*revisión*) proceedings may be opened.[246] A petition for revision can be filed with the Ministry of Justice at any time, by the prosecutor, the prisoner or members of his or her close family or even after death in order to clear his or her name.[247] If the Ministry decides that there is a case to be argued, it will instruct the prosecutor to bring the petition before the Supreme Court for a decision. The discovery of new evidence cannot affect an existing acquittal and this procedure is not available for misdemeanours (*faltas*).

246. Art. 954.
247. Art. 961.

Chapter 12

United States

Craig Bradley

I. Introduction

In the United States, most of the law of criminal procedure comes from the United States Supreme Court's interpretation of the Constitution, in particular the Fourth, Fifth and Sixth Amendments. Though these amendments on their face apply only to the federal government, during the 1960's, the Supreme Court, in a series of cases founded on the "Due Process" clause of the post-Civil War Fourteenth Amendment, applied virtually every aspect of these amendments to the States as well. Of particular importance, however, is not just the formal application of constitutional rights against state police officials. This began in 1949 when the Fourth Amendment was applied to the States in *Wolf v. Colorado*,[1] but for the next dozen years, the States generally ignored the Fourth Amendment rules declared by the Supreme Court. Finally, in 1961, in *Mapp v. Ohio*[2] the Supreme Court required the State courts to *exclude* all evidence seized in violation of the Fourth Amendment. This was soon followed by application of the Fifth Amendment (the right against self-incrimination)[3] and the Sixth Amendment (granting the defendant various trial rights including trial by jury)[4] to the States, with concomitant exclusionary rules. These rulings, plus the highly controversial decision in *Miranda v. Arizona* (1966),[5] (requiring police to warn arrestees as to their constitutional rights prior to interrogation) placed criminal procedure in the forefront of the Supreme Court's docket for the next 25 years, with the Court deciding 20-30 cases in this area out of a total of about 150 cases every year.[6]

It is these decisions that are the source of criminal procedure law in the United States. Congress does not consider itself to have, or doesn't want to assume, juris-

1. 338 U.S. 25 (1949).
2. 367 U.S. 643 (1961).
3. *Malloy v. Hogan* , 378 U.S. 1 (1964).
4. Eg. *Duncan v. Louisiana*, 391 U.S. 145 (1968) applying jury trial right to States.
5. 384 U.S. 436 (1966).
6. Eg. "Between 1985 and 1990, the Court decided 43 Fourth Amendment cases (alone)." Phyllis Bookspan, quoted in Craig Bradley, *The Failure of the Criminal Procedure Revolution* (1993), p. 49.

diction over the ordinary activities of state and local police such that it could produce a code of criminal procedure that could be uniformly followed nationwide.[7] State law can only grant criminal defendants *more* rights than the United States Supreme Court, not fewer. Since states are generally unwilling to grant further rights beyond those guaranteed by the federal Constitution, (though there are exceptions) state court decisions and state statutes are also not a significant source of criminal procedure law. What is left is a series of, often lengthy, Supreme Court decisions written by many different Justices over the last 40 years. As a source of clear rules for police to follow, these complex lawyerly pronouncements leave much to be desired. While they have undoubtedly advanced the cause of civil rights, they are frequently unclear and sometimes inconsistent. Nevertheless, these decisions are the law, and it is upon them that the discussion in this chapter will focus.

II. Police Procedures

A. Arrest, Search, and Seizure Law (Fourth Amendment)[8]

1. *Stops*

In *Terry v. Ohio* (1968)[9] Supreme Court held that detention of a person on the street by police for the purposes of brief questioning is a "seizure" to which the Fourth Amendment applies. However, it need not be justified by probable cause, the constitutional standard for search warrants, but only by the lesser standard of "reasonable suspicion." That is, by "specific and articulable facts which taken together with rational inferences from those facts, reasonably warrant" a conclusion that "criminal activity is afoot." The Court has subsequently made it clear that reasonable suspicion of past criminal behavior also justifies such a seizure, which the Court refers to as a "Stop."[10] The key point is that such stops may not be based on mere suspicion or hunches.

a. *What is a "Stop?"* Not all police-citizen contacts are seizures. For example, approaching a person in a public place and putting a few questions to him has been held not to be a seizure and therefore, such an approach need not be justified by any particular level of suspicion. If the suspect is "free to leave" without answering police questions, no stop has occurred.[11] In *Florida v. Bostick,* (1991)[12] the

7. For an argument that Congress does have power to legislate criminal procedure rules applicable nationwide, and that it should do so, see Bradley, Id.

8. The Fourth Amendment to the United States Constitution provides: "The right of the people to be secure in their persons, houses, papers, and effects, against unreasonable searches and seizures, shall not be violated, and no Warrants shall issue, but upon probable cause, supported by oath or affirmation, particularly describing the place to be searched, and the person or things to be seized."

9. 392 U.S. 1.

10. *United States v. Hensley*, 469 U.S. 221 (1985).

11. *Michigan v. Chesternut*, 486 U.S. 567 (1988).

12. 501 U.S. 429.

Court went further, holding that police (who lacked "reasonable suspicion") approaching a passenger on a bus and asking him if he would consent to a search of his luggage was not necessarily a stop. It was true that Bostick did not feel "free to leave." But this lack of freedom was occasioned not by the police, who were not detaining Bostick, but by the fact that if he exited the bus it would leave him behind. In such a case, the Court held that the issue is "whether a reasonable person would feel free to decline the officers' request or otherwise terminate the encounter." Having found that Bostick was not "stopped," the Court went on to find that his consent to search his luggage was valid. (See, §4(c) "Consent Searches"). Thus, a stop requires detention by police where it is apparent to the person stopped that he is not free to leave.

Similarly, in *California v. Hodari D* (1991)[13] the Court held that merely chasing a suspect was also not a stop (or seizure) under the Fourth Amendment. Rather, there must be either physical force used by police *or* submission to authority by the suspect. Consequently, narcotics thrown away by the suspect during the chase were usable in evidence because, despite the lack of probable cause or reasonable suspicion by police, there had been no seizure at the time the suspect discarded the drugs.

b. *When does a "Stop" become an "Arrest?"* A seizure of the person for more than brief questioning is no longer a stop but is considered an "arrest" which must be justified by the higher standard of "probable cause." In *Florida v. Royer* (1983)[14], when narcotics agents at an airport, noting that a passenger fit the "drug courier profile," asked to see his ticket and driver's license, and questioned him for several minutes, this was a stop, justified by reasonable suspicion. But when the agents told Royer that he was suspected of smuggling narcotics, and asked him to accompany them to a police room, while retaining his ticket and driver's license, an arrest had occurred. While the suspicions of the agents, based on the drug courier profile, were sufficient to satisfy the reasonable suspicion standard of *Terry*, they did not amount to probable cause. The fifteen minute detention of Royer in the police room was an invalid arrest. Consequently, his consent to search his luggage was also invalid. Even where a suspect was free to go, detention of his luggage for an extended period by police was held to constitute an arrest in *United States v. Place.*[15]

However, in *United States v. Sharpe,*[16] an auto stop lasted twenty minutes due to the efforts of a co-suspect in a separate vehicle to avoid apprehension. The Court held that it had not turned into an arrest simply by virtue of the passage of time. The test, essentially, is whether a reasonable person would feel that he was being subjected to a brief, investigatory detention, or whether he would feel that he is being subjected to extended custody. (See also §C1a, below where the same issue is presented in regard to whether police must warn a suspect of his rights before questioning him.) The Court felt that, since the police "diligently pursued a means of investigation that was likely to confirm or dispel suspicions quickly," the stop had not turned into an arrest. (The police believed that the two vehicles were traveling in tandem, with the fleeing vehicle transporting a large quantity of marijuana

13. 499 U.S. 621.
14. 460 U.S. 491.
15. 462 U.S. 696 (1983).
16. 470 U.S.675.

and the stopped vehicle acting as an escort. When the fleeing vehicle was stopped, large quantities of marijuana were found.)

c. *Stops of Vehicles.* In *Delaware v. Prouse*[17](1990), the Court held that police may not stop an individual automobile at random, but only if they have reasonable suspicion that an offense, traffic or otherwise, is being committed. However, roadblocks that briefly detain all passing motorists to check, for example, for drunken driving, may stop cars without any particularized suspicion.[18] If a vehicle is appropriately stopped, the police may order both the driver and the passengers out of the car as a safety precaution. It is not necessary for the police to have particularized suspicion to do this.[19] (For searches of cars, see §B4b below.)

2. Frisks

If the police have reasonable suspicion that someone is "armed and dangerous" they may also conduct a patdown of his outer clothing for weapons. This is allowed during a Stop (above) but also allowed even if there has not been a stop.[20] This "frisk" is more limited than a "search,"(described below). In *Minnesota v. Dickerson* (1993)[21] the Court discouraged the use of a frisk as a means of obtaining evidence (as opposed to protecting police) by invalidating a frisk in which the officer felt a small lump in the suspect's clothing and only after manipulating it was able to conclude that it was likely a lump of crack cocaine. While non-threatening contraband may be seized if discovered during a frisk, such a seizure is only appropriate if the criminal nature of the object felt is "immediately apparent" to police.

Another important limitation on frisks can be found in *Ybarra v. Illinois* (1979)[22]. In that case, police, executing a search warrant for a bar at which drugs were sold, *searched* the patrons of the bar, finding heroin on Ybarra. The Court held that the search was inappropriate since there was no probable cause to suspect Ybarra of possessing heroin. The Court then held that a frisk of Ybarra was also inappropriate. There must be *individualized* suspicion that a person is armed and dangerous—the only legitimate basis for a frisk. Mere presence in the bar, despite information that narcotics were sold there, was not enough.

The Court did not address the issue of how the police should proceed in such a potentially dangerous situation. Presumably it would be permissible to order the patrons out of the bar, or, possibly, to make them stand with their hands against the wall while the search of the bar proceeded. The uncertainty on this point illustrates another problem with the American system of court-made "rules." Since the two techniques mentioned would not lead to the discovery of evidence, the appropriateness of either of these actions is likely never to be tested. Most criminal procedure law is developed by criminal defendants litigating to exclude improperly seized evidence. If no evidence is seized, the only way to challenge the police action

17. 440 U.S. 648.

18. *Michigan Dep't of State Police v. Sitz*, 496 U.S. 444 (1990).

19. *Maryland v. Wilson*, 117 S.Ct. 882 (1997).

20. In *Adams v. Williams*, 407 U.S. 143 (1972), a policeman was informed that a certain individual, whom the police had not "stopped" was armed. The Court upheld the policeman's reaching into a car to seize a gun from the suspect's waistband.

21. 113 S.Ct. 2130.

22. 444 U.S. 85.

is by civil suit, not something that the usual criminal suspect is likely to pursue successfully. The Supreme Court, limited by the Constitution,[23] cannot give advisory opinions on such matters (though it frequently does include detailed advice when deciding an actual case). Consequently, there are a number of areas, especially pertaining to interrogations and general treatment of arrestees, where most countries have detailed provisions in their Codes but as to which the United States Supreme Court has been silent.

3. *Arrests (Seizures of the Person)*

An arrest is also a "seizure" of the person, governed by the Fourth Amendment. It must always be justified by probable cause both that a crime has been committed and that the arrestee has committed it. An arrest occurs whenever a reasonable person would not feel that he is "free to go" within perhaps 15-20 minutes after he is detained, depending on the circumstances. (The detention prior to that point would be a stop, as described above.). However, handcuffing him, or putting him into a police car without indicating that it was for some very limited purpose, or otherwise making the suspect feel that he is "in custody", would generally turn a stop into an arrest immediately. If a suspect is told he is being returned to the crime scene to see if the victim can identify him as a thief or robber, this is not an arrest. Taking a suspect to the police station "for questioning" is an arrest, regardless of what police call it.[24] As discussed above, pulling the suspect's car over for the purpose of giving him a traffic ticket, and/or asking him some questions, is a stop that must be justified by reasonable suspicion, *not* an arrest.[25] (And also not "custody" which would require *Miranda* warnings as well, see §C1a, below). As noted above, in *Hodari* the Court held that chasing a suspect is not a stop or an arrest, but once the police catch a chased suspect, a seizure (stop or arrest depending on the circumstances) occurs.

While an invalid arrest will not prevent the defendant from being tried, it will result in exclusion of any evidence found in a search incident to that arrest or due to a consent to search, as well as exclusion of any statements made by the defendant subsequent to the arrest. Consequently, this issue is very important and often litigated.

a. *Arrest Warrants.* An arrest of an individual in a public place must be based on probable cause, but need not be authorized by a written warrant.[26] Only if the police seek to arrest a suspect at his home or the home of another need they obtain a warrant, which must be issued by a judicial officer. If the arrest is to be at the suspect's home, the warrant must demonstrate that the police have probable cause as above, plus the police must have "reason to believe the suspect is within,"[27] though this need not appear on the warrant. If he is sought at the home of another, the *warrant itself* must set forth both probable cause that the individual has committed a crime *and* that he is to be found at the place specified in the warrant.[28] As

23. Article III §2 of the Constitution limits the judicial power to certain specified "Cases" and "Controversies."

24. *Dunaway v. New York*, 442 U.S. 200 (1979).

25. *Berkemer v. McCarty*, 468 U.S. 420 (1984).

26. *United States v. Watson*, 423 U.S. 411 (1976).

27. *Payton v. New York*, 445 U.S. 1371 (1980).

28. *Steagald v. United States*, 451 U.S. 204 (1981).

noted, violation of this rule will not prevent the arrestee from being tried, but may cause much evidence to be excluded, including evidence that may inculpate the homeowner where the suspect is found, since the warrant requirement is also for the non-suspect homeowner's protection.

b. *Searches Incident to Arrest.* If a suspect is placed under arrest, his clothing, and any parcels or handbags he may be carrying are subject to a "full search" which is more extensive than a frisk (above). He can be forced to empty his pockets, to open containers he is carrying, to remove a jacket, etc. This may occur either at the scene of the arrest or at the police station, or both. Such a search is appropriate for any "custodial arrest" regardless of the seriousness of the crime or the likelihood that the search will produce evidence or weapons.[29] After his arrival at the police station, the arrestee may also be compelled to give fingerprints, blood samples, hair samples, etc., though, except for fingerprints and "breathalyzer" (i.e. alcohol) tests, this is usually done pursuant to a judicial order. Some states limit the search incident to arrest to a patdown for weapons.

(i) *Arrests in Buildings.* If a person is arrested in a building, the search incident to arrest may be extended to include the "area within his immediate control."[30] While one might suppose that this is a very limited area if the suspect is in handcuffs, the courts have construed this to mean areas into which he might have reached to grab a weapon or to destroy evidence, *before* the police gained control of him. The police may also perform a "protective sweep" to make sure that no one is waiting in adjacent rooms who might harm them. However, a full search of such rooms (e.g. looking in drawers) is not justified.[31] Contraband or evidence spotted in "plain view" during a search or sweep incident to arrest may be seized by the police and used as evidence. It need not be evidence of the crime for which the suspect is being arrested. However, as in a frisk (above), the police must have probable cause that the item found is evidence when it is discovered. They may not obtain probable cause by picking up the item and examining it, testing it, etc.[32]

(ii) *Arrests in Vehicles.* If a suspect is arrested while a driver or a passenger in a vehicle, including a recreational vehicle, then the *passenger compartment*, but not the trunk, can be fully searched. It doesn't matter if the suspect has been removed from the vehicle prior to the search. This is so regardless of whether the police have any reason to believe that additional evidence will be found in the vehicle and even though the crime may be one, such as driving with a suspended license, for which there is no evidence to be found. Moreover, the search may also extend to *containers* found within the passenger compartment.[33] The Supreme Court has, however, recognized that if a trailer or recreational vehicle is rendered immobile, such as one that is up on blocks and attached to utilities in a trailer park, it should be treated as a "home" for the purposes of arrest and search, not as a "vehicle."[34]

29. *United States v. Robinson* 414 U.S. 218 (1973). In *Robinson*, the defendant was arrested for driving with a suspended license, for which offense there was no evidence to find. Nevertheless, he was convicted of narcotics possession after the search incident to arrest disclosed narcotics in a cigarette package in his shirt pocket.

30. *Chimel v. California*, 395 U.S. 752 (1969).

31. *Maryland v. Buie*, 494 U.S. 325 (1990).

32. *Arizona v. Hicks*, 480 U.S. 321 (1987).

33. *New York v. Belton*, 453 U.S. 454 (1981).

34. *California v. Carney* 471 U.S. 386 (1985).

(iii) *Dealing With Other People.* As in the *Ybarra* case, discussed above, if a suspect is arrested in a place where others are present, the police may not routinely frisk such people for weapons or search them. Rather they must have *individualized suspicion* that each person they frisk is "armed and dangerous." If they wish to perform a full search, they must have probable cause that the person possesses evidence of a crime. This rule may be more honored in the breach than the observance, for reasons that will be described in "Enforcing the Rules,"§A5 below.

c. *Arrests Pursuant to a Statute That is Later Declared Unconstitutional.* In *Illinois v. Krull* (1987)[35] the Supreme Court held that if the police arrest someone pursuant to a statute that is later declared unconstitutional, the search incident to arrest is still valid, and any evidence seized during the arrest may be used against the defendant at trial of a charge that developed as a result of the search. (Of course, a conviction on the original, invalid, charge may not stand).

d. *Use of Force in Arrests.* In *Tennessee v. Garner* (1985)[36] police shot and killed a teenager who fled from an apparent burglary. In a civil suit brought by his parents, the Court held that deadly force may not be used to apprehend a fleeing felon unless "the officer has probable cause to believe that the suspect poses a threat of serious physical harm either to the officer or to others." This is one of very few cases where criminal procedure rules have been developed as a result of a civil suit.

e. *Appearance Before a Judicial Officer.* This matter, long specified in codes of most countries, has only fairly recently been clarified by the Supreme Court. In *County of Riverside v. McLaughlin* (1991)[37] the Court held that the police determination of probable cause must ordinarily be reviewed by a judicial officer within 48 hours of arrest, though if the defendant can establish that a delay of 48 hours or less was "unreasonable" he may show a violation. A delay of more than 48 hours is presumptively unreasonable unless the government can establish that the delay was due to "a bona fide emergency or other extraordinary circumstance." However, if the defendant has been arrested pursuant to a warrant (which must be issued by a judge) no such hearing need be held. If a delay has been found to be "unreasonable," then any evidence obtained due to that delay, including incriminating statements, may not be used at trial, though the trial itself will not be barred. Ordinarily, this appearance, usually called "arraignment," occurs within 24 hours of arrest, (except on Saturday night/Sunday morning), and legal counsel is either appointed, or appears, for the defendant at that time.

4. Searches

Up to this point, most of the discussion has focused on the "seizure" language of the Fourth Amendment. The Amendment also forbids unreasonable searches, but not all activity that might be considered "searching" in ordinary parlance falls within the protections of the Fourth Amendment. Rather, the Court has defined a "search" as an intrusion by police into an area as to which an individual has a "reasonable expectation of privacy."[38] Thus, if the police are walking down the

35. 480 U.S. 340.
36. 471 U.S. 1.
37. 500 U.S. 44.
38. *Katz v. United States*, 389 U.S. 507 (1967).

street and see what they think may be a stolen car through the door of an open garage attached to the house, this is not a "search" because no one has an expectation of privacy as to something that can be observed by the public. If they then go onto the property for a closer look, this is a "search" since one is thought to have an expectation of privacy as to his house and the area immediately surrounding it (known as the "curtilage").

By contrast, if police trespass on an "open field" (i.e. all land except the curtilage) to find evidence, the Supreme Court has held that neither a warrant nor probable cause is required. This is not a "search," because a person does not have a reasonable expectation of privacy in an open field"[39] By "reasonable" the Court means, what *it* considers reasonable, regardless of what the suspect's actual expectations may be. Even putting a fence around the field and posting "No Trespassing" signs will not render such a field subject to Fourth Amenment protection. By contrast, attaching a listening device to a phone booth is a "search" because, in the Court's view, a person has a reasonable expectation that his phone conversations will not be overheard by police.[40] But entering a phone booth to search for contraband that the suspect may have put there is not a "search" because any expectations of physical privacy he may have in such a public place are not "reasonable." Hard questions arise when the police enter semi-public areas, like the hallway of a large apartment building, and these have not been resolved by the Court.

The following activities by police have been held *not* to be "searches" by the Supreme Court: flying over a suspect's land in a helicopter in order to see if he was growing marijuana in a greenhouse;[41] searching trash that had been left at the curb to be picked up;[42] using an electronic "beeper" to more easily track a car's location on the highway.[43] While defendants might have had a subjective expectation of privacy in these cases, it was not one that the Court was willing to recognize as "reasonable." However, in *United States v. Karo*[44], the Court held that using an electronic "beeper" concealed in a drum of chemicals to determine if the drum was still located in the suspect's house was a search because it gave information about what was going on *inside* the house that would not have been available to a passerby.

If certain police action is deemed a "search," it must generally be justified by probable cause, although, as noted, searches incident to arrest can be based on the probable cause to arrest, even if the police had no particular expectation of finding evidence in the possession of the arrestee. There is no emergency exception to the probable cause requirement. Moreover, if it is a "search" inside a *structure*, it must be done, absent an emergency, pursuant to a written *search warrant* issued by a judicial officer, and probable cause must appear on the face of the warrant application. The failure of the police in *Karo* to obtain a warrant to *use* the beeper led to the suppression of the evidence, even though they had obtained a warrant to search the house based on the information supplied by the beeper. However, as discussed

39. *Oliver v. United States*, 466 U.S. 170 (1984). The Court insisted that this was so even though the field was fenced and posted with "No Trespassing" signs.

40. *Katz*, supra, n. 28.

41. *Florida v. Riley*, 488 U.S. 445 (1989).

42. *California v. Greenwood*, 486 U.S. 35 (1988).

43. *United States v. Knotts*, 460 U.S. 276 (1983).

44. 468 U.S. 705 (1984).

above, if a police activity is not considered a "search," then it need not be justified by either probable cause *or* a warrant.

a. *Search Warrants.* As noted, although the Supreme Court has never specifically held this, the gravamen of recent cases is that searches of structures (and the cortilage of houses) must be accompanied by a warrant, whereas outdoor searches, including searches of vehicles and of an arrestee's person and possessions, may be performed on probable cause alone.[45]

Moreover, the probable cause must not be "stale." Thus, it is not sufficient that an informant saw X selling narcotics from his house two weeks ago, because it is no longer probable that the narcotics are still there. The warrant must specify a particular address, including an apartment number if applicable, and the police may not search anyplace else. The warrant must further specify what they are searching for. Thus, if the warrant is for stolen 27 inch television sets, police may not look in drawers. If it is for narcotics, they may. The warrant requirement applies to business premises, garages, hotel rooms, and other structures, but is not required for searches of vehicles, for visual or electronic surveillance of outdoor activities, etc. (See discussion under "warrantless searches" §4b below.)

(i) *Plain View Doctrine.* The plain view doctrine applies in the search warrant context, as well as in non-warrant situations.. If the police find something incriminating while executing a search warrant or when performing any other legitimate activity, they may seize it as long as they were looking in a place where they were allowed to look and they had probable cause that the item was evidence of a crime. The obtainment of the plain view is not itself a search, but the seizure of the object is a "seizure" under the Fourth Amendment and must be based upon probable cause. Thus, if the police see marijuana growing in the window of a house, they must obtain a warrant in order to enter the house and seize it, unless they can establish that it was likely to be destroyed during the delay.

Moreover, as the Supreme Court made clear in *Arizona v, Hicks* (1987),[46] the police may not create a "plain view." In *Hicks*, the police legitimately entered an apartment because they heard a gunshot from within. When they arrived, the apartment was deserted, but they noticed expensive stereo equipment, inconsistent with the squalid surroundings. They picked up the equipment to see the serial numbers, called them in, and found out that the equipment was stolen. The Supreme Court excluded this evidence. While the police had a legitimate "plain view" of the equipment, they lacked probable cause to seize it. When they picked it up, that was a search which was not justified. (Had they been able to see the serial numbers without moving the equipment, that would have been OK.)

The plain view doctrine has been extended to sounds and smells, including dog-sniffs that reveal narcotics.[47] It also applies when the police enhance their abil-

45. For a discussion of this position, see, Craig Bradley, *The Court's "Two Model" Approach to the Fourth Amendment:* Carpe Diem!, 84 Journal of Crim. Law and Criminology 429 (1993). "Structures" includes warehouses, barns, hotel rooms, phone booths and anything else that is not mobile and has a roof, including, as discussed, trailers and RVs that are rendered non-mobile. The only exception is a narrow one: If police have probable cause to believe that a container (purse, briefcase, etc.) contains evidence but lack probable cause to arrest, they must get a search warrant to open the container.

46. 480 U.S. 321 (1987).

47. *United States v. Place*, 462 U.S. 696 (1983).

ity to observe by use of a flashlight or binoculars. The Court's reasoning is that people don't have a reasonable expectation of privacy as to matters that can be so easily observed by the public and therefore, the police obtainment of plain view in such a case is not a search. This reasoning is not wholly consistent with the dog sniff case, but the limited and "low tech" nature of the intrusion led to the Court's conclusion that this is not a search as well. If the police obtain their plain view by means of sophisticated electronic devices, by contrast, this does intrude on a citizen's reasonable expectations of privacy and must be justified by probable cause.

(ii) *Exigent Circumstances.* The main exception to the warrant requirement for structures is that the police are not required to obtain a warrant in case of "exigent circumstances" (i.e. an emergency), but they must still have probable cause.

(iii) *Execution of Warrants.* As discussed, the police are not allowed to exceed the scope of the warrant. Thus, if executing a warrant for stolen television sets, they may not look in drawers; they may only look in places where a television might be concealed. However, the mere fact that they don't find what they came for, but do find something else, will not invalidate the search, as long as the trial court determines that probable cause was adequately set forth in the warrant.

In *Wilson v. Arkansas*[48] (1995) the Supreme Court held that, ordinarily, the police should "knock and announce" prior to executing a search warrant, but failure to do so will not automatically render the search invalid. There is no uniform rule as to whether search warrants may be executed at night. Also, unlike many countries, there is no requirement that anyone else, such as a prosecutor, judicial officer or representative of the suspect, must be present when the warrant is executed. However, if the police desire, they can compel the occupant of the premises searched to remain during the search either to assist them, or to be subject to arrest if they find what they are looking for.[49]

(iv) *Wiretaps.* These are governed by federal statute, 18 U.S.C. §§2510, *et seq.* They are allowed by federal agents only if application is made to a judge through certain high level officials at the Department of Justice, and only for certain, specified, crimes. This statute governs state officials as well, however, they must gain approval from certain high level state law enforcement officials. There are, however, exceptions to this warrant requirement for "emergencies" involving: "conspiratorial activities threatening to national security," "conspiratorial activities characteristic of organized crime" and "immediate danger of death or serious bodily injury to any person."[50]

b. Warrantless searches. As discussed, warrants are generally required only for searches of structures. Full searches of automobiles, including the trunk, and containers found therein, may be made on probable cause alone, with no warrant.[51] Searches of the passenger compartment incident to the valid arrest of the driver are also permitted without either a warrant or any particular probable cause to search. Searches incident to arrest on the street may be founded on the probable cause to arrest and include a full search of the person and any containers he is carrying.

If a person is arrested inside his home, or the home of another, a warrant is required for the arrest, but it need not specify grounds to search the person of the ar-

---

48. 514 U.S. 927.
49. *Michigan v. Summers*, 452 U.S. 692 (1981).
50. 18 U.S.C. §2518(7).
51. *California v. Acevedo*, 500 U.S. 585 (1991).

restee or the "area within his immediate control" incident to arrest, nor need such grounds exist. The arrest itself justifies the search incident. As noted above, §3(b)(i), a "protective sweep" of the adjoining portions of the house is also allowed to look for people who may pose a threat to police. However, a full search of any part of the house not in the arrestee's immediate control may only be performed with a search warrant, absent exigent circumstances.

The only exception to the *de facto* "rule" that warrants (either search or arrest) are required for indoor searches or arrests but not outdoor ones is in the unusual case where the police see someone with a suitcase, purse, or other container which they have probable cause to believe contains evidence, but they lack probable cause to arrest him. The Supreme Court still holds to the view that, though the suspect may be stopped and questioned, a warrant is required to search the container. However, a warrant would *not* be required if the person had put the container in a car, or had been arrested.[52] It seems unlikely that this narrow and rather tortured exception will long be retained.

c. *Consent Searches*. If the police can get a suspect to consent to a search, including one of his home, none of the above rules apply. The leading case is *Schneckloth v. Bustamonte* (1973).[53] In this case the police stopped a car for a traffic violation and then asked one of the passengers, who claimed to be the owner's brother, if they could search it. He consented and some stolen checks were found. The Court rejected the argument that the police must inform the suspect of his right to withhold consent. Rather, the only criterion that must be met is "voluntariness." Furthermore, in *Florida v. Bostick* (1991),[54] discussed above, the Court held that the test for "voluntariness" was whether a reasonable *innocent* "person would feel free to decline the officers' requests or otherwise terminate the encounter." Thus, even though the suspect *knew* that acceding to the request would result in finding incriminating evidence, and therefore he *must* have felt that he had no choice but to allow the search, it will still be allowed as long as a person with nothing to hide would have felt free to refuse.

Consents are widely used as a method of avoiding search requirements. In her concurring opinion *Ohio v. Robinette* (1996),[55] Justice Ginsburg reported that the policeman in that case had requested consent to search cars in 768 traffic stops in one year. It does not matter that the police motive in making an automobile stop was primarily to obtain consent to search, as long as the stop was for a true traffic, or other violation. In other words, "pretext searches" are allowed.[56] There is, however, an assumed limit on consents: if the police have illegally stopped or arrested the suspect, any consent is deemed invalid, even though it may not have been "involuntary" in the sense that threats or coercion were employed.

5. *Enforcing the Rules*

In the United States, unlike other countries, the exclusionary rule is *mandatory*, not subject to the discretion of the trial judge. That is, once it has been deter-

52. See, Id. and cases cited therein.
53. 412 U.S. 218.
54. 501 U.S. 429.
55. 117 S.Ct. 417, 421.
56. *Whren v. United States*, 116 S.Ct. (1996).

mined that the police conduct in question broke the "rules," as set forth in the cases discussed, then the evidence that was obtained as a result of that violation (including indirect "fruits of the poisonous tree") may not be used in court, at least in the prosecution's case-in-chief. This rule has applied to both federal and state authorities since 1961. The reason for the mandatory rule stems from the fact that the "rules" the police are to follow come, via the Supreme Court, from the Constitution, rather than from a legislative body, and the Court has found it difficult to say that certain constitutional violations are less important than others. This creates problems because it encourages the courts, including the Supreme Court, to deem police behavior in a given case acceptable to avoid the exclusion of important evidence, even though it seemed, based on previous cases, to be unacceptable. Subject to the exceptions below, there is no such thing as an illegal or improper search by police where evidence obtained may nevertheless be used in the prosecution's case-in-chief.

In *United States v. Leon*,(1984) the Court established the only significant exception to the exclusionary rule.[57] *Leon* held that if the police obtain a *search warrant* (which must be issued by a judge), then, even if the warrant is later found defective, the evidence will not be excluded as long as the police relied on it in "reasonable, good faith." The Court reasoned that, ordinarily, the police have satisfied their constitutional obligation by seeking a warrant. If the warrant proves defective because it doesn't adequately set forth probable cause, or for some other reason, the mistake is that of the judge who issued the warrant, not that of the police. Since the exclusionary rule was designed to deter police misconduct, and since the only mistake here was of the judge, not the police, there was no cause to exclude the evidence.

Even though *Leon* has been criticized as an intrusion on personal liberties, it does have the salutary effect of encouraging the police to get search warrants . Moreover, *Leon* does not mean that anytime a warrant was obtained, the evidence will not be suppressed. In particular, if the police gave the issuing judge *false information*, even unintentionally, the mistake is nevertheless that of the police, and the evidence must be excluded. Also, if the warrant application was obviously deficient, then the police could not have had a reasonable belief in the validity of the warrant. Finally, improper *execution* of the warrant, such as extending the search beyond the limits authorized, could also lead to exclusion.

The Court's adherence to the notion that the purpose of the exclusionary rule is to deter police misconduct has led to some other limitations of its use, though these are not considered "exceptions." For example, the Court has held that both illegally obtained physical evidence and confessions (but not coerced confessions), may be used as rebuttal evidence if the defendant testifies in a way that is inconsistent with the excluded evidence.[58] The Court felt that excluding the evidence

57. 468 U.S. 897 (1984). See also, *Illinois v. Krull*, 480 U.S. 340 (1987), discussed above (reliance by police on invalid statute) and *Arizona v. Evans* 514 U.S. (1995) (reliance by police on erroneous computer entry by court clerks). Evidence also not suppressed.

58. For example, in *United States v. Havens*, 446 U.S. 620 (1980), customs officers had illegally searched the defendant's suitcase after he had cleared customs. They seized a T-shirt from which swatches had been cut that matched pockets sewn into a co-defendant's T-shirt in which the co-defendant had concealed cocaine. The T-shirt was not admissible against the defendant until he took the stand and denied any involvement in the co-defendant's smuggling activities. At this point, the Court held that the prosecution could impeach that claim by using the T-shirt found in the defendant's luggage.

from the prosecution's case-in-chief was sufficient to determine police misdeeds. Similarly, illegally obtained evidence may be used by the grand jury in deciding whether to indict the defendant.[59]

Somewhat inconsistent with the deterrence rationale for the exclusionary rule is the Court's insistence that a defendant must have "standing" to press an exclusionary rule claim. Thus if the police illegally interrogate A, or illegally search his house, any evidence they acquire that incriminates B may be used at B's trial (but not at A's). Since B's rights were not violated, the Court reasons, he has no right to exclude the evidence. Arguably, though, since the police engaged in wrongdoing, *any* affected party ought to be able to exclude the evidence if the purpose of exclusion is to deter police misconduct. "Standing" doctrine illustrates the Court's general distaste for the exclusionary rule, and it's consistent efforts in recent years, to cabin its use, while still retaining it where it seems likely to have a meaningful deterrent impact on police.

As noted above, the exclusionary rule applies not only to real evidence or statements obtained by violating the rules, but also to the "fruit of the poisonous tree." Thus, if the police, illegally searching A's house, find a map that shows where stolen money is hidden, the money must also be excluded from the prosecution's case. It is a "fruit" of the illegal search. Similarly, consents to search, and incriminating statements, obtained after illegal stops and/or arrests are not usable.

However, if the later evidence is "sufficiently attenuated" from the illegality it may be used. For example, if an illegally arrested defendant has been released, and the police later go to his home and get him to voluntarily consent to a search of his yard, this would be proper. The Court has further held that a live witness, even though he may have been located by means of an illegal search, will not oridinarily be considered a "fruit of the poisonous tree."[60] But merely informing a suspect of his *Miranda* rights after an illegal arrest will not "purge the taint" of the illegal arrest. Thus, any incriminating statements of such a defendant, even though voluntary and with full knowledge of rights, must be excluded.[61] This exclusionary rule also applies to the "fruits" of coerced confessions. However, a *Miranda* violation by the police does not have "fruit of the poisonous tree" consequences. Thus a confession obtained in violation of *Miranda* must be suppressed, but either subsequent, warned, statements, or real evidence obtained by means of the original inadmissible statement may be used in the government's case-in-chief.[62]

Also, if the evidence would have been "inevitably discovered" by legal actions of the police or others, the fact that it came to light through illegal behavior may not force its exclusion. Thus, in *Nix v. Williams*,(1984)[63] the police, through improper (but not coercive) interrogation ascertained where the defendant had left the victim's body. However, search parties were already abroad in the area and, the Court found, would have *inevitably discovered* the body. Therefore the body, but

59. See, *United States v. Calandra*, 414 U.S. 338 (1074) and cases cited therein.

60. *United States v. Ceccolini*, 435 U.S. 268 (1978).

61. *Brown v. Illinois*, 422 U.S. 590 (1975).

62. *Oregon v. Elstad*, 470 U.S. 298 (1985). The Court reasoned that the *Miranda* warnings are not required by the Constitution, but are a "prophylactic" device to promote compliance with the Fifth Amendment. As such, a *Miranda* violation does not have "fruit of the poisonous tree" consequences.

63. 467 U.S. 431 (1984).

not the defendant's statements to the police, could be used in the prosecution's case. Similarly, if a policeman illegally enters a warehouse and finds marijuana, while other police, with no knowledge of this illegality, are on their way to the warehouse with a search warrant, then the marijuana will be admissible on the ground that it was discovered by a source *independent* of the illegal entry (i.e. the second, warrant-authorized, entry).[64]

B. Lineups and Other Identification Procedures

1. Lineups (Identification Parades)

After a person has been arrested, he can, without any further showing or judicial authorization, be required to stand in a lineup. A lineup must not be "unnecessarily suggestive (or) conducive to irreparable misidentification."[65] Ordinarily, police will photograph or videotape a lineup so that the jury can see that it was fair, but this is not required by federal law. After "formal proceedings have begun" (e.g. indictment or arraignment), a defendant is entitled to have counsel at a lineup, but in the early stages of investigation, which is when lineups usually occur, counsel is not required.[66] A non-arrested suspect can be compelled to appear in a lineup by court order. Photo "showups," where a witness is shown a group of photographs, are also admissible in court, subject to the "unnecessarily suggestive" limitation that applies to lineups. "Alley confrontations" between a victim and a suspect, immediately after a crime, are also admissible, despite the fact that only one person has been presented to the victim.

2. Other Identification Procedures

Fingerprinting of arrestees is routinely allowed without any judicial approval. Other identification procedures, such as taking hair samples, voice printing, etc. are usually done on court order, or pursuant to a subpoena issued by the prosecutor. However, the bodily intrusion required by taking a blood sample requires a judicial warrant based on probable cause.[67] Moreover, in the case of *Winston v. Lee*,(1985)[68] the Court excluded from evidence a bullet obtained from the defendant's body after court-ordered surgery on the ground that the government had not demonstrated a "compelling need" for the evidence given the intrusiveness of the procedure. Short of surgery, however, a court order, without any particular showing of cause or need by the government, will suffice to justify such evidence gathering.

---

64. *Murray v. United States*, 487 U.S. 533 (1988). *Murray* goes even further than the principle stated above in that the agents who made the illegal entry were the *same* agents that obtained the search warrant, they just didn't mention the fact that they had already found the marijuana in the warrant application. See, Craig Bradley, *Murray v. United States, The Bell Tolls for the Search Warrant Requirement*, 64 Ind. L. J. 907 (1989) criticizing this result.

65. *Stovall v. Denno*, 388 U.S. 293 (1967).

66. *Kirby v. Illinois*, 406 U.S. 682 (1972).

67. *Schmerber v. California*, 384 U.S. 757 (1966).

68. 470 U.S. 753 (1985).

C. Interrogation

1. Before Formal Charge in Court

In the United States, the Supreme Court has required, per the Fifth Amendment to the Constitution,[69] that the well-known *Miranda*[70] warnings must be given to every criminal suspect prior to "custodial interrogation." The warnings need not be given in any particular form as long as they reasonably inform the suspect of his rights.[71] Those rights are: that the suspect has a right to remain silent, that anything he does say may be used against him, that he has a right to counsel and, if he cannot afford to hire one, a lawyer will be appointed to represent him. The Supreme Court has refused to extend the warnings requirement beyond the warnings enumerated. For example, a suspect does *not* have a right to be informed of the subject matter under investigation[72] or, if a consent to search is being sought, that he has a right to refuse consent.[73]

a. *What is "custody?"* Note that the warnings are only required in case of "custodial interrogation." Since the Supreme Court of the last two decades has been, at best, unenthusiastic about the warnings, but reluctant to overrule such a well known case, it has carefully refused to extend *Miranda*, or even, according to many, to give the case its full weight. One way to limit *Miranda* has been to closely define the terms "custody" and "interrogation." The thrust of the Court's cases in recent years, though they have not directly stated this, is that "custody," in Fifth Amendment terms means the same thing as "arrest" under the Fourth Amendment. That is, that a reasonable person would feel that he will be held by the police for a substantial period of time. The Court has refused to extend the *Miranda* requirement to a "stop."[74] On the other hand, although most of the discussion in *Miranda* focused on stationhouse interrogations, the Court has made it clear that the warnings requirement applies even to a low-key conversation in the living room of an arrested suspect's home,[75] but not to an interview in the police station which the suspect attended voluntarily.[76] (Unless the circumstances of that interview became such that a reasonable person would have felt "arrested.")[77] Thus, there are many police-citizen encounters, including most importantly "stops," of both pedestrians and motorists, where the police are not required to give the warnings.

b. *What is "interrogation?"* The Court has also limited *Miranda* in its definition of "interrogation." In *Rhode Island v. Innis*, (1980)[78] the Court defined the term rather broadly to include not only express questioning, but "any words or actions on the part of the police (other than those normally attendant to arrest and

69. The Fifth Amendment provides in pertinent part: "No person shall...be compelled in any criminal case to be a witness against himself...."
70. *Mirandev v. Arizona*, 384 U.S. 436 (1966).
71. *Duckworth v. Eagan*, 442 U.S. 195 (1989).
72. *Colorado v. Spring*, 479 U.S. 564 (1987).
73. *Schneckloth v. Bustamonte*, 412 U.S. 218 (1973).
74. *Berkemer v. McCarty*, 468 U.S. 420 (1984).
75. *Oregon v. Elstad*, 470 U.S. 298 (1985).
76. *Oregon v. Mathiason*, 429 U.S. 492 (1977).
77. *Stansbury v. California*, 511 U.S. 318 (1994).
78. 446 U.S. 291 (1980).

custody) that the police should know are reasonably likely to elicit an incriminating response." In that case, police transporting an arrested suspect discussed among themselves their concern that a missing murder weapon might be found by a child from a nearby school. The suspect then volunteered the location of the shotgun. This, strangely, was held *not* to be interrogation on the ground that "the record in no way suggests that the officers' remarks were *designed* to elicit a response."[79] Yet any reasonable reading of the police remarks suggests that this is exactly what the police sought to do. This is an example of the Court's being unwilling to declare police conduct unacceptable, even when it seems to violate the "rules"[80] because to do so would mean that important evidence would have to be excluded. This narrow application of the rule suggests that unless the police are directing their statements or actions at the suspect, "interrogation" will not be found to have occurred. This is consistent with *Miranda's* primary concern: direct pressure being put on suspects during incommunicado questioning at the police station.

(i) *Surreptitious Questioning*. In *Illinois v. Perkins(*1990)[81] the Court held that it was not interrogation under *Miranda* for the police to plant an informer in an arrestee's jail cell to pump him for an admission of guilt or other details of the crime, so long as the admissions are not coerced. The Court reasoned that a suspect who was unaware that he was being "interrogated" was not subject to the sort of official pressure that *Miranda* was designed to guard against.

c. *Exception*. There is only one exception to the rule that the warnings must precede any "custodial interrogation." In *New York v. Quarles*,(1984)[82] a rape suspect, who was believed to be armed, was chased into a supermarket. He was caught and arrested at the rear of the store and, after he was handcuffed, was asked where the gun was. He told the police and the gun was found. Both his statement and the gun were admissible despite the fact that no warnings had been given. The Court, while agreeing that this was a "custodial interrogation," held that there was a "public safety" exception to *Miranda* , presumably limited to weapons or destructive devices. The Court has never decided whether location of a dangerous co-felon would fall under the public safety exception, but assuming it does not, only the original arrestee's *statement* would be excluded at his trial. The co-felon would lack standing to protest the breach of the original arrestee's rights. Moreover, because "fruit of the poisonous tree" rules do not apply to *Miranda* violations, any statements or evidence that came to light as a result of the co-felon's arrest, would not be excluded from the original arrestee's trial. Similarly, in *Quarles* itself, the gun would have been admissible. The dispute in that case, resolved in the prosecution's favor, was whether the *statement* could also be used.

d. *Waiver.* The Court has made it easy for the police to establish that a suspect has waived his rights to silence and counsel after he has been informed of them. He need not sign a written waiver nor even specifically state that he wishes to waive. Merely answering police questions after having been warned is sufficient.[83] Also, unless the suspect specifically states that he wishes to remain silent or have a lawyer

---

79. Id. at fn. 9.

80. *Innis* is unusual, however, in that the police conduct seemed to violate the rule in that very case.

81. 496 U.S. 496 U.S. 292, (1990).

82. 467 U.S. 649.

83. *North Carolina v. Butler*, 441 U.S. 369 (1979)

he will not be considered to have "invoked" his *Miranda* protections. Thus, where the suspect asked to see his probation officer, this was held *not* to be an invocation of his *Miranda* rights and questioning was allowed to continue.[84] Similarly, saying "maybe I should talk to a lawyer" was not an invocation of rights when, upon request for clarification by the officers, the suspect concluded that he didn't want a lawyer.[85] However, once he has actually requested counsel, his "post-request responses to further interrogation may not be used to cast retrospective doubt on the clarity of the initial request itself."[86]

e. *Invocation of Right to Silence.* According to *Miranda*, if the suspect indicates that he wishes to remain silent, "questioning must cease." While this seems clear enough, the Supreme Court subsequently cast some doubt on this command. In *Michigan v. Mosley(*1975),[87]the Court held that, where a suspect who had asserted his right to remain silent was questioned two hours later about a different case by different police who again advised him of his rights, the interrogation was lawful. The Court was unclear about which of these factors governed its conclusion in *Mosley*. However, it is generally agreed that at least three factors must obtain before a suspect who asserts his right to silence may be questioned further: 1) immediately ceasing the interrogation, 2) suspending questioning entirely for a significant period of time, and 3) giving another set of warnings at the outset of the second interrogation.[88]

f. *Invocation of Right to Counsel.* In contrast to the Court's equivocal approach to assertion of the right to silence in *Mosley*, it has treated invocation of the right to counsel much more strictly. In *Edwards v. Arizona*,(1981)[89] the Court distinguished between the two rights, reasoning that, whereas assertion of the right to silence showed that the suspect felt in control of the situation, assertion of the right to counsel was a kind of cry for help. Consequently, once a suspect asserts his right to counsel, questioning must cease "until an attorney is present." This was so despite the fact that the interrogation had ceased and was not resumed until the next day after the suspect had been rewarned. Moreover, the Court has held that such an "*Edwards* defendant" cannot even be questioned about another crime[90] and that, even after the suspect has consulted a lawyer, questioning cannot resume unless the lawyer is present.[91] However, the Court has never required that a suspect who requests a lawyer need actually be provided with one, but only that *interrogation* must cease.[92] It is thus not unusual for an arrestee to request a lawyer but not to receive one until his appearance in court, usually the day after his arrest. This is so regardless of whether the lawyer is court appointed or privately retained, even if he has been retained immediately after the arrest.

---

84. *Fare v. Michael C.*, 442 U.S. 707 (1979).
85. *Davis v. United States*, 114 S.Ct. 2350 (1994).
86. *Smith v. Illinois*, 469 U.S. 91 (1984).
87. 423 U.S. 96
88. Kamisar, LaFave and Israel, *Modern Criminal Procedure* (8th ed. 1994) at p. 547.
89. 451 U.S. 477.
90. *Arizona v. Roberson*, 486 U.S. 675.
91. *Minnick v. Mississippi*, 498 U.S. 146 (1990).
92. Indeed, in *Moran v. Burbine*, 475 U.S. 412 (1986), the Court approved a confession, even though the defense attorney had asked to see the suspect, and had been incorrectly informed that interrogation of the suspect had ceased. Since the *suspect* had not invoked his right to counsel, he did not qualify as an "*Edwards* defendant."

Qualifications: There are still several ways that the police can obtain information from a suspect who has asserted his *Miranda* rights. They can engage in non-interrogative conversation among themselves as in *Innis*, above, hoping that the suspect will volunteer information. They can plant an informant in the arrestee's cell whose questions are not "interrogation," as in *Perkins*, above. Or, according to *Oregon v. Bradshaw*, they can wait to see if the arrestee himself "initiates" further conversation about the case. Then, at least if he is rewarned before questioning resumes,[93] they can question him further. This exception is evidently quite broad since the "initiation" relied upon by the Court in *Bradshaw* was simply the defendant asking, "What is going to happen to me now?" Finally, they can continue to question the suspect, realizing that though his statements will not be admissible against him, evidence that his statements lead them to will not be excluded and that the statements may be used to impeach the defendant's testimony if he testifies at trial.[94] In addition to these legal loopholes, since interrogations and confessions, as well as *Miranda* waivers, need not be recorded or in writing, (at least as far as the federal Constitution is concerned—some states may have different rules) the police can simply deny that the suspect ever asserted his rights.

(g) *Threats and Promises*. The police may not commit or threaten, directly or indirectly, physical harm to a suspect if he does not confess. In *Arizona v. Fulminante*,[95] a child molestation case, the Court excluded the testimony of a prison informant who offered the suspect protection from other inmates (who tend to treat child molesters harshly) if he "told the truth" about the alleged murder of his stepdaughter. However, although not settled by the Supreme Court, it is probably OK for the police to tell a suspect that they will drop the charges against another person if the suspect confesses, that they will "put in a good word" to the prosecutor on the suspect's behalf, etc. It is also proper for the prosecutor to become involved and to make binding promises to the suspect, though such bargaining is usually done through counsel.

(h) *Police Deception*. It is clear that the police may not deceive a suspect as to his rights or the legal consequences of waiving them.[96] Thus, they could not assure a suspect that his confession was "off the record" and then attempt to use it in court or tell him that assertion of his constitutional rights could be used against him in court (which it can't). However, deception of a suspect as to the course of the investigation, such as "we found the murder weapon" or "your co-defendant says you pulled the trigger," while never specifically endorsed by the Court, is widely considered an acceptable interrogation technique. But this only applies to suspects who have been warned but have *not* asserted their rights to silence or counsel. Neither deception, nor any other technique, may be used to encourage a suspect to talk once he has invoked his right to counsel or, usually, his right to silence. However, it is undoubtedly the case that police sometimes violate this principle by suggesting to the suspect that such non-cooperation makes him "look bad" in their eyes.

93. 462 U.S. 1039 (1983).
94. *New York v. Harris*, 495 U.S. 14 (1990); *Oregon v. Elstad*, 470 U.S. 298 (1985)..
95. 499 U.S. 279 (1991).
96. *Moran v. Burbine*, 475 U.S. 412 (1986).

2. *After Defendant Is Formally Charged*

After a defendant has been formally charged with a crime, by grand jury indictment, prosecutorial "information," or, in the usual case, his first formal appearance in court following arrest (arraignment), the rules change. Now he is, formally a "defendant," no longer a "suspect," and his Sixth Amendment right to counsel "in all criminal prosecutions" has attached. (Prior to this time, his constitutional protections, including the *Miranda* requirements, stemmed only from his Fifth Amendment right against self-incrimination.) Such a defendant need not assert his right to counsel for it attaches automatically.[97] However, it is unclear whether, and how, police may seek a waiver of counsel's presence from such a "Sixth Amendment" defendant.

For example, in *Patterson v. Illinois*,[98] where such a defendant initiated conversation about the crime, giving him the *Miranda* warnings and obtaining further voluntary statements from him was held sufficient to establish waiver of the right to counsel. Lower courts have considered such points as whether the defendant had asserted his right to counsel, and whether the police tried to talk him out of consulting with counsel in assessing the validity of a waiver.[99] The Supreme Court has indicated that a failure to inform a defendant that he had an attorney who was trying to reach him during questioning would invalidate a Sixth, but not a Fifth, Amendment waiver.[100] A "Sixth Amendment" defendant also may not be questioned by an informant, though it has been held acceptable to plant an electronic "bug" in his cell to overhear conversations among inmates, and even to use a human informant who didn't question the defendant or urge him to talk, but did say that his initial story "didn't sound too good."[101]

3. *Enforcing the Rules*

As previously discussed, coerced confessions cannot be used at all, even to develop leads, or to impeach a defendant's testimony in court. By contrast, confessions or statements obtained in violation of the rules developed in *Miranda* and its related cases also may not be used in the government's case-in-chief, but may be used for these ancillary purposes since "fruit of the poisonous tree" strictures do not apply to *Miranda* violations.[102] Statements obtained through violation of a formally charged defendant's Sixth Amendment rights, however, cannot be used directly or indirectly.

III. Court Procedures

In the United States, most criminal trials occur in state courts. Only defendants whose conduct has violated specific federal statutes and whom the United States

97. .*Brewer v. Williams*, 430 U.S. 387 (1977).
98. 487 U.S. 285 (1988).
99. LaFave and Israel, *Criminal Procedure* (2d ed., 1992) p. 309.
100. *Patterson*, supra n. 79 at fn. 9, referring to *Moran*, supra n. 77.
101. *Kuhlmann v. Wilson*, 477 U.S. 436 (1986).
102. *Oregon v. Elstad*, supra, n. 95.

Department of Justice chooses to prosecute are tried in federal courts. Most "ordinary" criminal cases, including murders, rapes, burglaries, and robberies are tried in state court, though if such crimes occur on military bases, on Indian reservations or within the District of Columbia, they may be tried by the appropriate federal authority. As a consequence of this diversified system, there is no national code of court procedures, just as there is not one for police procedures. Moreover, while, as discussed, most police procedures have become somewhat standardized because of Supreme Court case law, there is less case law on the structure of the court system. What follows then, is a description of how a criminal case usually proceeds through the system. Individual state practices may vary. The extent to which federal constitutional law has standardized procedures will be noted where applicable.[103]

A. Pretrial

1. Initial Court Appearance

In the usual case, an arrested suspect is brought before a judicial officer[104] within 24 hours of his arrest, and, in any case, no longer than 48 hours after arrest (unless he has been released by the police pending further proceedings).[105] Prior to, or at, this appearance, the magistrate or judge must make a determination that there is probable cause to hold the defendant. This may be an *ex parte*, rather than an adversarial determination, based on the material in the police report, and can be supplemented by additional information provided by the prosecutor if required. If a defendant has been arrested pursuant to a warrant, which was itself based on a judicial determination of probable cause, no such decision is required.[106] In the rare case that the magistrate finds no probable cause, the defendant must be released, but this is not a bar to subsequent arrest if more information is developed. This appearance is most commonly called an "arraignment."

At this appearance, the defendant will be informed of the charges against him and of his constitutional rights to silence, jury trial, counsel, etc. If the defendant does not have counsel, one will be appointed. Only if no incarceration is possible (or the defendant insists on proceeding without counsel)[107] may the case continue without the defendant being represented by counsel.[108] About half

---

103. For a detailed discussion of the various steps in the judicial process, as well as the structure of the system see, Kamisar, *et al.* supra, n. 88 at p 2-35.

104. In some states and in the federal system, there are "magistrates" who handle preliminary matters such as the issuance of search warrants, arraignments, etc. and, in some jurisdictions, misdemeanor trials. They are "judicial officers" who are independent from the prosecution.

105. The Constitution requires that an arrestee has a right to a "prompt" judicial determination of probable cause to arrest. This right is presumptively satisfied by an appearance in court within 48 hours of arrest, though the defendant has the right to show that even that period constituted an "unreasonable delay." *County of Riverside v. McLaughlin*, 500 U.S. 44 (1991).

106. *Gerstein v. Pugh*, 420 U.S. 103 (1975).

107. The defendant has a constitutional right to proceed without counsel, *Faretta v. California*, 422 U.S. 806 (1975), but the judge may appoint a "standby counsel," even over the defendant's objection, to advise the defendant as to courtroom procedure and other matters. However, this counsel may not take over the trial of the case without the defendant's consent. *McKaskle v. Wiggins*, 465 U.S. 168 (1984). Such trials are very rare.

108. *Scott v. Illinois*, 440 U.S. 367 (1979).

of all criminal defendants are "indigent" and receive free counsel, provided by either a public defender service (available in more heavily populated areas), or a private attorney appointed by the court. Indigent defendants are entitled to appointed counsel through the trial and the first appeal, which is mandatory in all states. However, this right does not extend to subsequent, discretionary review (which is usually in the state, and United States, Supreme Courts).[109] Following appearance of counsel, the defendant will be asked to enter a plea. This is usually "Not Guilty" though sometimes a defendant, after consultation with his counsel (if it has one) and with the prosecutor may enter a "Guilty" plea at this time.

Finally, the defendant's custody status pending trial must be established. If he has already been released from custody, that status will usually continue pending trial. If he has been incarcerated since his arrest, bail must be set, subject to the Eighth Amendment's prohibition of "excessive bail." In general, the judge/magistrate is required to impose only such conditions on the defendant as will ensure his return for trial, though some jurisdictions allow for "preventive detention" based on dangerousness and regardless of the likelihood of return.[110] The defendant may be released on cash bond supplied by a private bail bondsman (who will forfeit the bond if the defendant doesn't return for trial), by a cash bond arranged directly with the court, or on his "own recognizance" (i.e. just a promise to appear). In addition, conditions, such as remaining employed, staying away from the victim, etc. may be imposed and the defendant incarcerated if they are not met. If the court feels that no set of conditions will ensure his return, he may be held without bail. Failure to reappear as ordered is an additional criminal offense.

2. *Charging Instrument*

The Fifth Amendment provides that, "No person shall be held to answer for a capital, or otherwise infamous crime, unless upon a presentment or indictment of a Grand Jury...." The grand jury is a group of ordinary citizens (twenty three is a common number) who sit for an extended period of time—frequently about six months. However, they need not all be present at any one session. Unlike the trial jury, unanimity is never required.

This is the only criminal provision of the Constitution's Bill of Rights that has *not* been made applicable to the states by the Supreme Court. Consequently, about half the states initiate criminal prosecutions through an "information" issued by the prosecutor (though prosecutors in these states may convene grand juries for investigative purposes). The other states and the federal government (as it must), proceed by indictment issued by the grand jury. However, this does not provide any meaningful protection against prosecutorial abuse since the grand jury rarely refuses to abide by the prosecutor's will, and if they do, the prosecutor may convene another grand jury. On the other hand, the grand jury may choose to indict a de-

109. *Ross v. Moffitt*, 417 U.S. 600 (1974).Of course, the uncounselled indigent defendant petitioning for further review will have the benefit of the brief, and the free trial transcript provided for the first appeal. Moreover, it is customary for appointed counsel to file a petition for review by a higher court, and to represent the defendant should review be granted.

110. Such detention has been approved by the Supreme Court in *United States v. Salerno*, 481 U.S. 739 (1987). In 1985, about 29% of federal criminal defendants were held either without bail or because they could not meet the bail set. Kamisar, supra, n.88 at p. 877.

fendant *against* the prosecutor's recommendation. In this event, the prosecutor can dismiss such a case immediately after the indictment is issued.

Sometimes, usually in complex cases, a prosecutorial investigation, using the grand jury to subpoena witnesses, who must testify, under oath without counsel (but who retain their Fifth Amendment right against self-incrimination) will precede arrest. In these cases, "formal criminal proceedings" for the purpose of interrogation law, begin when the grand jury issues an indictment or the prosecutor issues an information. (There is no necessary difference in form between an indictment and an information other than that the grand jury foreman's signature will appear at the bottom of an indictment.) However, the defendant is then arrested and arraigned as described above.

3. *Preliminary Hearing*

In the usual case where the arrest and arraignment have marked the beginning of formal proceedings, the next step for the incarcerated defendant is the preliminary hearing. This is an adversarial proceeding with counsel[111] before a judge or magistrate in which the government must establish probable cause to continue to incarcerate the defendant while awaiting action by the grand jury. Hearsay information is allowed at this hearing which is ordinarily brief and informal. Many defendants waive the preliminary hearing, but this is usually because a guilty plea is contemplated. Otherwise, it is a good opportunity for the defense to gain information about the prosecution's case (different levels of discovery are provided in different states) and to put prosecution witnesses on the record. The prosecution thus tries to use as few witnesses as possible, usually just the chief investigating officer who will summarize what other witnesses have told him. If the judge finds probable cause, the government may continue to hold the defendant, either in jail or on bail, pending action of the grand jury in an "indictment state," or pending trial in an "information" state. If no probable cause is found, the case is dismissed. However, the government can then take the case to the grand jury and reinstate proceedings, or, avoid the preliminary hearing altogether by getting an indictment first. "Information states" differ on the use of preliminary hearings. It is unclear whether any such further judicial/grand jury determination of probable cause is constitutionally required as long as there has been at least one since arrest.

4. *Pretrial Motions*

Most jurisdictions require the defense to file pretrial motions to suppress evidence due to the operation of the various exclusionary rules discussed above. This is both to make the trial run more smoothly and to give the prosecution the opportunity to appeal an adverse ruling. Otherwise, if an erroneous adverse ruling *during* trial leads to the defendant's acquittal, double jeopardy principles would forbid prosecutorial appeal. Some states allow an interlocutory appeal by the government of adverse rulings during trial (but never after acquittal) to avoid this problem.

Another issue to be dealt with by pretrial motion is discovery of the other side's case. States vary greatly on this, with increasing numbers requiring advance dis-

---

111. Counsel is required. *Coleman v. Alabama*, 399 U.S. 1 (1970).

closure by both sides of all witnesses and evidence to be used at trial. Virtually all jurisdictions require disclosure of any statements of the defendant in the government's possession, as well as the results of scientific tests.[112] The prosecution also has a constitutional duty to disclose all "material" (i.e. possibly outcome determinative) exculpatory evidence to the defense, including evidence which, while it does not directly cast doubt upon the defendant's guilt, tends to impeach the credibility of a government witness.[113] Other matters dealt with by pretrial motion include various other arguments by the defense as to constitutional objections to the trial such as violation of the defendant's Sixth Amendment right to a speedy trial (see below), of his Fifth Amendment right against being tried twice for the same offense, claims that the trial should be moved because of local prejudice against the defendant, etc.

B. Trial

1. Nature of the Trial. The Sixth Amendment provides that "In all criminal prosecutions, the accused shall enjoy the right to a speedy and public trial by an impartial jury of the State and district wherein the crime shall have been committed." All of these provisions have been applied to the states.

a. *Speedy Trial.* All criminal codes contain statutes of limitation that provide that charges must be brought within a certain period after the crime has been committed. Five years is typical. This is not a constitutional right and certain crimes, such as murder, can be excepted from the statute of limitations. The speedy trial right, by contrast, applies *after* formal proceedings have begun, whether by indictment, information or arrest/arraignment.[114] It is not a specific time limit, and each case must be assessed on its own facts. Factors to consider include whether the defendant has demanded a trial, the length of the delay, the reason for the delay and prejudice to the defendant caused by the delay.[115] In *Doggett v. United States*[116] a delay due to government negligence in locating the defendant, who had been jailed in Panama but had returned to the United States six years before his arrest and lived openly under his own name, was held to violate the Speedy Trial right, requiring that the case be dismissed. In general, the courts have considered a delay of about a year "presumptively prejudicial," requiring the government to justify it.[117]

b. *Public Trial.* The defendant has a right to a trial open to the public and the media. This also extends to pretrial proceedings, sentencing, etc. Parts of a trial may be closed if the party seeking closure can cite an "overriding interest." Thus, it may be possible to close a hearing on a motion to suppress evidence on the ground that, if the evidence is suppressed, public knowledge of the excluded evidence would make it impossible to secure an unbiased jury. Similarly, it is not un-

---

112. LaFave and Israel, supra n. 99, §20.3.

113. .Eg. The fact that the witness was an alcoholic and thus may have been impaired in his observations of the crime. See, *United States v. Bagly*, 473 U.S. 667 (1985).

114. *United States v. Marion*, 404 U.S. 307 (1971).

115. *Barker v. Wingo*, 407 U.S. 514 (1972).

116. 505 U.S. 647 (1992).

117. Id. at n.1 p. 652.

common to exclude the public from a sex crime trial during the testimony of the victim, particularly if the victim is a child, where public presence would likely adversely affect the victim's ability to relate the details of the crime.[118] An improper exclusion of the public from the trial is grounds, *per se*, for a new trial with no showing of prejudice by the defendant.[119] The defendant may not, however, compel a private trial since the public and the press have an independent First Amendment right to attend.[120]

c. *Location of the Prosecution.* As the Sixth Amendment provides, the defendant has a right to be tried in the state and district (usually county) where the crime was committed. However, as long as a crime has an impact on a state, or partially occurs there, that state may try it, even if another state also has such a right. Indeed, double jeopardy does not prohibit a state's retrying a defendant who has already been tried, whether convicted or acquitted, in another state.[121] The defendant may move to change the location (venue) if he would be prejudiced by holding the trial in the district where the crime was committed.

d. *Trial by Jury.* The defendant has a right to a jury trial for all but "petty" offenses.[122] This is another right that the defendant does not have an absolute right to waive, but may waive only if the prosecution agrees (though the shorter non-jury trial is ordinarily to the prosecutor's liking). A jury may contain as few as six members and need not render a unanimous verdict. However, a guilty verdict by a 5-1 vote was struck down. Considering the various cases, the minimum size/ margin for a guilty verdict is probably 6-2.[123] The jury *venire* (i.e. the group of potential jurors) must be a "representative cross-section of the community." Thus, in *Taylor v. Louisiana* [124] a male defendant's conviction was reversed because women were not selected for jury service unless they had filed a written declaration stating their desire to serve. There were no women in the defendant's venire.

This representative cross-section requirement has not been extended beyond race and gender and does not apply to the petit jury that actually hears the defendant's case, for it would be too difficult to ensure that every jury contained a representative cross-section of the community as to gender and race. However, neither the prosecution nor the defense can attempt to "cook" the petit jury by using

---

118. LaFave and Israel, supra n.99, §24.1(b).

119. Id. §24.1(a).

120. *Gannett Co. v. DePasquale*, 443 U.S. 368 (1979).

121. *Heath v. Alabama*, 474 U.S. 82 (1985). In *Heath*, the defendant was convicted of murder in Georgia, where part of the crime was committed, but did not receive the death penalty. Then he was tried in Alabama for the same murder and sentenced to death. The Supreme Court upheld the two trials/sentences on the ground that the states are "separate sovereigns" whereas double jeopardy only prohibits dual prosecution by the "same sovereign." The same rule allows subsequent prosecution by the federal government after a state court acquittal, assuming a federal statute was also violated by the defendant's acts.

122. In *Baldwin v. New York*, 399 U.S. 66 (1970), the Court defined as presumptively "petty" a crime for which a sentence of no more than six months is authorized by statute, regardless of whether the defendant is actually imprisoned or not. Note that this differs from the right to counsel, where a defendant can be tried without counsel for a crime with an authorized penalty of more than six months, but cannot then receive any actual jail time.

123. See discussion in LaFave and Israel, supra n.99, §22.1(d) and (e)

124. 419 U.S. 522 (1975).

peremptory challenges[125] to exclude potential jurors on account of their race or gender.[126]

e. *Guilty Pleas.* At any time, the defendant can interrupt the proceedings and offer to plead guilty to the entire indictment/information. However, this is rarely done. Rather, the guilty plea is ordinarily given in exchange for a promise by the prosecution to drop some of the charges, to recommend a lower sentence or at least not to ask for any particular sentence, to drop a separate case pending against the defendant, etc. The prosecution is not required to engage in any bargaining. In some jurisdictions, the judge participates in plea bargaining and a specific sentence can be agreed upon. Ordinarily, the plea bargain is reached before the trial so that the prosecution can avoid the expense and difficulty of preparing its case for trial. The initial decision as to what bargain, if any, to offer is for the prosecutor, but in many jurisdictions, the judge must approve the dropping of any charges, as well as participating in sentence bargaining where that is allowed.

Before the court can accept a guilty plea it must address the defendant personally, on the record, and ascertain that the plea is knowing and voluntary. That is, the defendant must understand at least the "critical" elements of the charge to which he is pleading guilty and that he is giving up his constitutional rights to a jury trial, to confront witnesses, etc.[127] He must also understand the sentencing consequences of the plea. Furthermore, the judge must ascertain that the plea is not the result of any threats or promises beyond those spelled out in the plea bargain, the terms of which must appear on the record. Finally, in federal courts, and in most states, the judge must determine that there is a factual basis for the plea. (In states not requiring this, it suffices for the defendant to knowingly and voluntarily agree that he is guilty, without the facts being discussed.) This can be done either by the judge asking the defendant what he did, or the prosecutor stating what the government would prove if the case went to trial.[128] It is *not* constitutionally necessary that the defendant actually admit to the deeds constituting the crime. Rather, he can plead guilty in order to take advantage of the plea bargain, without admitting culpability.[129] In such a case it is required that the factual basis for the plea be fully set forth by the prosecutor. A similar plea of *nolo contendere* is allowed in federal courts and those of many states in which the defendant simply agrees not to "contend" the prosecution's case, but this is not strictly a "guilty" plea, and may not have the same collateral consequences (such as civil liability, or enhanced sentence following subsequent convictions) as a plea of guilty.

---

125. "Peremptory challenges" cause a juror to be removed from the panel with no reason being given by the attorney for doing so. These are to be distinguished from "challenges for cause" for which the attorney can give a legally acceptable reason. Obviously, challenges for cause based on the argument that members of a certain race or gender are more or less likely to be sympathetic to the defendant are also not allowed.

126. The first case on this subject forbade the prosecution's use of peremptories to exclude black jurors from the trial of a black defendant. *Batson v. Kentucky*, 476 U.S. 79 (1986). Subsequent cases have extended this rule to apply to defense use of peremptories, to use of peremptories to exclude black jurors from the trial of a white defendant, and to the use of peremptories to exclude men from a man's trial. See, Kamisar, supra, n.88 at p.1420 *et seq.*

127. *Henderson v. Morgan*, 426 U.S. 637 (1976).

128. See LaFave and Israel, supra, n.99 at §21.4.

129. *Alford v. North Carolina*, 400 U.S. 25 (1970).

2. *Defendant's Rights at the Trial*

The defendant has a constitutional right to testify under oath,[130] though this is not expressly provided in the Constitution. The Fifth Amendment does specify that he may not "be compelled...to be a witness against himself." This encompasses not only the right not to testify, but to be free from adverse prosecutorial comment for the exercise of that right,[131] and to demand a jury instruction that the defendant's failure to testify may not be held against him.[132] The defendant is not required to refuse to testify in open court.

The Sixth Amendment provides that the defendant has a right "to be confronted by the witnesses against him" and "to have compulsory process for obtaining witnesses in his favor." The confrontation clause further implies the right of the defendant to be present at "every stage of the trial," including pretrial hearings, though this can be abridged if the defendant is disruptive.[133] Also, the defendant can give up this right if he absents himself during the trial.[134] These rights also imply a duty on the state to preserve evidence for the use of the defense, but this will lead to the reversal of a conviction only if the defendant can establish bad faith on the part of the government.[135] Finally, the confrontation right includes a principal of orality—witnesses must appear in court and testify in person. Hearsay statements may not generally be used against the defendant, subject to several exceptions. Preliminary hearing testimony, which was subject to cross-examination, may be used at trial, but only if the witness is unavailable.[136]

3. *Lawyers' Role*

As noted earlier, the defendant has a constitutional right to be represented by counsel anytime "actual imprisonment" is to be imposed.[137] If imprisonment is a possible penalty for the defendant's crime, then he must be represented unless the prosecution has determined in advance that, if he is convicted, he will not be imprisoned. The right to counsel includes the right to "effective assistance" of counsel. If a defendant appeals on the ground of ineffective assistance of counsel, the burden is on him to establish both that "counsel's performance was deficient" and that "counsel's errors were so serious as to deprive the defendant of a fair trial, a trial whose result is reliable."[138] These are referred to as the "performance"prong and the "prejudice" prong. Under this test it is possible that a defendant could show that his lawyer's performance was deficient, but not succeed on his appeal because the prosecution's case was sufficiently strong that he failed to show "preju-

---

130. *Rock v. Arkansas*, 483 U.S. 44 (1987). At common law, the defendant was allowed to speak in his own defense, but not under oath.

131. *Griffin v. California*, 380 U.S. 609 (1965).

132. *Carter v. Kentucky*, 450 U.S. 288 (1981). However, the defendant may not prevent the court from giving such an instruction should the court so desire. *Lakeside v. Oregon*, 435 U.S. 333 (1978).

133. *Illinois v. Allen*, 397 U.S. 337 (1970).

134. *Taylor v. United States*, 414 U.S. 17 (1973).

135. *Arizona v. Youngblood*, 488 U.S. 51 (1988).

136. *California v. Green*, 399 U.S. 149 (1970).

137. *Scott v. Illinois*, 440 U.S. 367 (1979).

138. *Strickland v. Washington*, 466 U.S. 668 (1984). The defendant must show a "reasonable probability that, but for counsel's unprofessional conduct, the result of the proceeding would have different." Id.

dice." This "effective assistance" requirement applies equally to trials and capital(death) sentencing proceedings (which, unlike ordinary sentencing proceedings, can be very elaborate—in some states a virtual second jury trial.)

There are limited circumstances under which the defendant will be excused from establishing the "prejudice" prong. One of these is state interference with counsel's performance. For example, In *Davis v. Alaska*, (1974)[139] the trial judge prohibited the defense counsel from questioning a witness about the latter's juvenile record because of a state statute rendering this information confidential. This waas a violation of Davis' confrontation right. Davis was not required to prove "prejudice" on appeal—it was presumed. A conflict of interest by counsel, such as representing two defendants whose defenses are inconsistent, will also excuse the defendant from having to show prejudice.

4. *Witnesses*

As noted, both the defendant and the prosecution have the right to compel witnesses to appear at trial. However, the witness may refuse to testify on the ground that his testimony would tend to incriminate him, in violation of the witness' Fifth Amendment rights. The prosecution can compel such a witness to testify by granting "immunity" from any prosecution based on the testimony (but not necessarily from any prosecution at all). The defense does not have a comparable power to compel a witness to testify since immunity decisions are within the prosecutor's sole discretion.

a. *Expert Witnesses.* Expert witnesses are chosen by the parties. This means that the experts who testify may be chosen more for their ability to testify strongly in one party's favor than for their actual expertise. An indigent defendant has the right to have certain expert witnesses, such as a psychiatrist to establish an insanity defense or a ballistics expert to establish that the bullet in the victim did not come from the defendant's gun, paid for by the government.[140] However, if, as is usually the case, the government has already obtained an expert opinion on the issue, the defendant would have to make an additional showing as to why another expert opinion was necessary. This right is founded on the "due process" clause of the Fifth and Fourteenth Amendments, which generally entitles the defendant to a fair trial, rather than on any of the more specific constitutional guarantees.

5. *Judges*

In the United States, the trial is conducted by the attorneys. The judge functions as a referee, ruling on evidentiary admissions, objections by counsel, etc. as well as instructing the jury. It is, however, within the judge's power to put questions to witnesses, especially if he feels that an attorney is not properly developing an important point, but this will likely hapen only once or twice during a typical trial. Federal judges, including the Supreme Court, are appointed for life by the President, subject to approval by the Senate. State judges may be appointed by the Governor or elected. There is considerable difference among the states as to the procedures for choosing judges, however, a judge is generally a practitioner who has had

139. 415 U.S. 308.

140. *Ake v. Oklahoma*, 470 U.S. 68 (1985).

a fairly extensive legal career prior to his ascension to the bench, rather than a career judge, as is common in some other countries.

6. *Victims*

There is no generally applicable law as to the rights of victims. However, Congress has enacted a law applicable in federal trials which gives victims certain rights,[141] and a number of states have adopted similar requirements. The federal law requires prosecutors to consult the victim or his family as to the disposition of the case, including plea bargains, diversionary narcotic treatment programs, etc. Victims may also be heard as to the appropriate sentence, but, this is only a right of consultation. Victims cannot formally block, or force, action by the prosecutor. However, a victim who suffers from "memory loss" can, if effect, render a case unprosecutable.

C. Appeals

Although it has never been constitutionally required, the defendant in every state and federal trial has a right to at least one appeal of his conviction. He also has a constitutionally guaranteed right to effective assistance of counsel, and to a free transcript and government-paid counsel if he is indigent.[142] However, these rights do not extend to subsequent appeals that may be allowed by the state.[143] Only the defendant can appeal from an adverse trial verdict. Even if the defendant was acquitted because an erroneous ruling by the trial judge excluded critical evidence from the government's case, principles of Double Jeopardy forbid the defendant's retrial. (Double Jeopardy would also prevent the retrial of a defendant who was convicted or acquitted only of a lesser included offense because the government had failed to charge him with the greater offense.)[144]

The appellate court may reverse convictions because of lack of evidence, ineffective assistance of counsel, failure of the trial court to suppress evidence that was unconstitutionally obtained, improper prosecutorial argument, improper instructions to the jury, and many other legal grounds. In general, the thrust of recent cases is that the defendant will only succeed on appeal if he can establish not only that there was error, but that that error "so infected the trial with unfairness as to make the resulting conviction a denial of due process."[145]

In *Darden v. Wainwright*,[146] for example, the Supreme Court disapproved of the prosecutor's repeated references to the defendant in closing argument as a "vi-

---

141. The Victim and Witness Protection Act of 1982, 18 U.S.C. §1512.

142. See *Ross v. Moffitt*, supra n.109, and cases cited therein.

143. Id. The Court's reasoning was that subsequent appeals, usually to the state supreme court, are discretionary with the court, and are more for the purpose of resolving questions of law than for providing the defendant with a second chance to reverse his conviction. Of course, the defendant in such discretionary review already has the benefit of a transcript and a brief from his first appeal. Moreover, if discretionary review is granted, states invariably appoint a counsel to fully brief and argue the case in the higher court.

144. *Brown v. Ohio*, 432 U.S. 161 (1977). But see, *United States v. Dixon*, 509 U.S. 688 (1993) limiting this doctrine in certain circumstances.

145. *Darden v. Wainwright*, 477 U.S. 168 (1986).

146. Id.

cious animal." However, given the strength of the government's case and the viciousness of the murder in question, the Court concluded that this did not render the trial unfair. In earlier cases, however, the Court was more inclined to reverse the conviction due to constitutional error, without requiring the defendant to establish the unfairness of the trial taken as a whole, and many of these cases are still good law.[147]

In federal courts, appeals were successful about eight percent of the time in 1990, with successful appeals in state courts ranging from five to ten percent.[148] However, a "successful" appeal usually only wins the defendant a new trial, and not a complete dismissal of the charges, and it is not uncommon for such a defendant to be retried. Only if the appellate court reverses the conviction for insufficient evidence is the defendant likely to be acquitted outright by the appellate court. The theory here is that, under Double Jeopardy principles, the government should only have one chance to present its evidence against the defendant.

IV. Conclusion

The most fundamental aspects of the American criminal justice system stem from English common law. These include an adversarial trial with counsel presenting the evidence to a jury drawn from the state and locality in which the crime was committed.

However, close governance of police procedures leading up to an arrest was not a part of the common law heritage, and, until the 1960's, even constitutional limits on police conduct did not apply to the States. In interpreting the Constitution to set rather detailed rules for the police to follow, the United States Supreme Court was in the vanguard, in international terms. Since the "criminal procedure revolution" in the United States, many other countries have adopted rules that more formally restrict police powers, and advance the rights of defendants, than had been the case.

There are, however, two significant aspects of the American system that have not, and likely will not, be adopted by many other countries. These are the "mandatory" exclusionary rule and the declaration of criminal rules by the courts, rather than in a legislatively promulgated code of procedure.

There is no doubt that the current international trend is toward using exclusionary rules to enforce police compliance with procedural rules. However, with the (universal) exception that coerced confessions must always be excluded, most countries leave the exclusionary decision to the discretion of the trial judge. Moreover, all of the other countries, make use of a nationally applicable code of criminal procedure to regulate police conduct. In the United States, this is done, at the national level, exclusively by Supreme Court decisions.[149] (Some states have at-

147. Eg. *Griffin v. California*, 380 U.S. 609 (1965). (Prosecutorial comment on the failure of the defendant to testify at trial is reversible error *per se.*) See also *Mapp v. Ohio*, 367 U.S. 643 (1961). (Admission of illegally seized evidence at trial is reversible error *per se.*)

148. Kamisar, *et al.*, supra n.88 at p. 35.

149. For an argument that Congress could, and should, expand the Federal Rules of Criminal Procedure to apply to police conduct and in state courts, see, Craig Bradley, *The Failure of the Criminal Procedure Revolution* (1993).

tempted to embody these restrictions, plus others imposed by the state courts, in a code). Even as to crimes tried in the federal counts, the Federal Rules of Criminal Procedure govern the conduct of the trials, but not of law enforcement authorities.

Chapter 13

General Comments

Hans Lensing[1]

Introduction

The previous chapters present a wealth of information on many aspects of the law and practice of the criminal procedure of the systems discussed. In this chapter some general concluding remarks are made, inspired from two perspectives. The first relates to the way the discussion of the systems in the previous chapters has been organized. Are there any differences and similarities between the legal systems on the points discussed that merit attention? The second perspective relates to a more or less supranational measure to which the various systems of criminal procedure may be held: Human rights' treaties. Although most countries are parties to the International Convention on civil rights and political rights (New York 1966), another treaty is to be preferred for the purpose of this analysis. A still increasing number of countries—now more than 40—has become a party to the European Convention on human rights and fundamental freedoms (Rome 1950). The Convention has proved to be very influential on the law and practice of criminal procedure in many countries. This is mainly the result of the case law of the European Convention on human rights, that has derived detailed rules from the rather broad provisions of the Convention. Does criminal procedure in the countries under discussion satisfy the requirements—perceived as minimum requirements—of this Convention?

Noteworthy Differences and Similarities

It is important to note that the discussions of the procedural systems of the selected countries in the preceding chapters imply some restrictions for analytical purposes. First, the systems are discussed with different degrees of detailedness. This is, evidently, largely the result of the chapters having been written by various authors, with differences in backgrounds and styles. One of the consequences has

1. Judge at the district court Arnhem, the Netherlands.

been that some aspects explicitly discussed by the author of one chapter are not discussed—or in less detail—by the author of another chapter (e.g., notifications upon arrest). This implies that the analysis in this chapter should focus on more or less general aspects discussed.[2]

Second, the procedural systems are discussed in the preceding chapters on the basis of a an outline based on the American system. As a result of this approach, the outline of the chapters dealing with the other systems reflect the structure of—the selection of aspects of—U.S. law. Some concepts familiar to U.S. lawyers (e.g., "stop and frisk") are strange to lawyers in other systems, either common law or civil law systems. Similarly, typical common law features of procedure do not or may not have an equivalent in civil law systems (*e.g.*, "arraignment," "guilty plea"). This may have led to, *inter alia*, underexposure of certain features of some civil law systems, such as certain aspects of the pretrial judicial investigation and its relationship with police procedures.[3]

Given these limitations, there follows a brief discussion, following the outline of the other chapters, of some of the noteworthy differences and similarities among the countries discussed.

I. Sources[4]

In most systems the main sources of law in criminal procedure are constitution, legislation, and case law. The Constitution of South Africa is very noteworthy because of its extensive and detailed list of principles and rules. This is a marked contrast with a system as in the U.S., where the wordings in the Amendments to the Constitution are rather vague and broad, the consequence being an extensive case law of the U.S. Supreme Court containing detailed rules. In some systems (England, Israel) there is no constitution with a higher status than regular legislation.

II. Police Procedures

A.1. Stop and 2. Frisk

Most systems do not have something identical or similar to stop and frisk in U.S. criminal procedure. In some systems in which persons may be stopped or arrested for purposes of checking identity (France, Germany), the police have powers that may be termed similar to the powers of stop-and-frisk.

---

2. This may be a general problem in books in which systems are discussed by various authers. See, *e.g.*, also Ch. van den Wyngaert, *Criminal Procedure Systems in EC Countries*, London 1993.

3. Systems with a pretrial judicial investigation in this book are Argentina and France. At first sight, the problem seems to have been solved adequately in the chapters on these systems.

4. Several—according to the outline apparently minor—subjects are not discussed separately, inter alia the problem of arrest under a law later held to be unconstitutional, the permissible use of violence in arresting a suspect, identification procedures, wiretapping and discovery. Mostly, the reason is that as to those subjects for only a few systems enough information has been provided. Suffice it here to say that these examples are known in all systems discussed.

A.3. Arrest

In most systems a distinction is made between arrest with a warrant and arrest without a warrant. Inasfar as the information provided goes, a judge or magistrate is the competent authority for issuance of a warrant. In Russia and China the prosecution service has an important position.[5] It might be argued that this provides less guarantees for the citizen.

In some systems not only suspects—as defined in the system discussed—may be arrested but also witnesses.

In most systems a search is possible where the suspect can be arrested, its scope at the least extending to the person of the arrestee and her immediate surroundings.

In most systems a suspect arrested has to be brought before a judge or magistrate within 24 or 48 hours after arrest. It seems that in China a suspect has to be brought (only) before a member of the prosecution service.[6]

A.4. Searches

In contradistinction with civil law systems and some common law systems, in a number of common law systems a rather broad definition is given of the concept "search" (*inter alia*, Canada, U.S.). This includes not only the search of a place or person but also other invasions of privacy (*e.g.*, wiretapping).

In most systems a distinction is drawn between situations in which a warrant of the competent authority is required for a search and situations in which no warrant is required. The line between those instances is not the same in every system. In some systems the competent authority to issue a warrant may be a member of the prosecution service or the police (China, Italy, South Africa).

As to most frequently discussed specific aspects of the manner in which searches must be held, some points merit attention. In a number of systems the presence of witnesses of some kind during a search of a dwelling is required (Argentina, China, France, Israel, Russia). Also, in a number of systems searches may —absent special circumstances—not be held at night (Argentina, England, France; see also, Italy).

In probably all countries, searches may be held when the person concerned consents. In many systems criteria obtain as to the voluntariness of the consent or waiver. In France, the consent has to be given in writing.

C. Interrogation

In contradistinction with civil law countries and several common law countries, in some common law systems a distinction is drawn between interrogation before and interrogation after charge (England, South Africa, U.S.A.). In England and Wales the charge has the most farreaching consequence, since—absent exceptional circumstances—questioning by the police must stop. In some respects this

5. In South Africa warrants may be issued by commissioned police officers as justices of the peace.

6. The situation in Russia has not become clear to me; it may be more or less similar.

may be compared to France, where the accused cannot be examined by the police after being charged by the investigating judge.

It seems that the suspect has the same or similar rights in most systems, most notably the right to silence and the right to see a lawyer. As to the right to silence, China seems to be the only exception. As to the right to see a lawyer, some differences in scope exist. From the perspective of the accused the right seems to be strongest in the U.S.A., South Africa, England, Italy and Germany. There are some differences in the moment at which—apart from the rights as such—notifications about his rights have to be given to the suspect.

Although in all systems police tactics are forbidden as a result of which a statement of the suspect is held to be involuntarily made, not all systems require that the voluntariness of a confession be affirmatively proved, as is required in England and Wales. Interestingly, in Canada the police may legitimately lie and engage in deception, even though the voluntariness of the statement must be proved.

Argentine law is noteworthy, because formally it is the investigating magistrate who is competent to interrogate the suspect, although practice seems at variance with theory. Also, in Italy special rectrictions apply to interrogation and questioning by the police and the use in evidence of statements obtained.

Exclusion of Evidence (Sections II A. 5 and II C. 3)

In most systems procedural sanctions, most notably exclusion of evidence or something similar ("nullité") may apply where the police or other agencies have obtained evidence in an unlawful manner, either related to searches and seizures or interrogation. In many of those systems the rationale is not deterrence of the police of unlawful conduct—as it is in the U.S.A.—but fairness of the proceedings, the safeguarding of the integrity in the administration of justice and the like (*inter alia* Argentina, Canada, England and Wales, France, Germany, Italy, South Africa and —but less clear—Russia). However, in some systems (China, Israel) only considerations of reliability determine whether evidence is admissible.

The U.S. system seems the most rigid system inasfar as unlawfully obtained evidence must be excluded, and the court does not have a discretion whether to admit the evidence. However, it should be noted that this does not mean that balancing of interests is absent: The exclusionary rule does not apply to all kinds of police misconduct nor does it apply in all kinds of proceedings. For example, the American exclusionary rule does not apply in the grand jury or in deportation proceedings.

In other systems, the court has some discretion whether or not to admit illegally obtained evidence, depending on the rules violated (France, Germany) or on considerations of fairness and integrity (Canada, England and Wales, South Africa).

Inasfar as informaton is provided in the chapters on the topic of exclusion of "fruits of the poisonous tree," the systems differ considerably. In Argentina, Canada and the U.S. secondary evidence ("fruits") is excluded in the same manner as primary evidence. In South Africa the result depends on the nature of the illegality, whereas in Germany in principle secondary evidence is not excluded.

More or less the same applies to the problem whether evidence can only be excluded when it has been obtained in violation of a right of the accused ("standing"). Whereas this is relevant in Canada, the U.S. and (in principle) Argentina, it is not (at least generally not) in France and Germany.

III. Court Procedures

A. *Pretrial*

Although in (nearly) all systems the suspect must be presented to a judge or magistrate (as a requirement for continued detention) and the court may be required to decide on certain matters before trial, most systems do not have a preliminary hearing or grand jury proceedings on the same footing as the U.S. system has. Pretrial motions also seem to be a phenomenon, largely reserved to the U.S. system. In addition, they are mentioned on a relatively modest scale in the chapters on Canada and Russia. However, certain subjects may be raised in court proceedings aimed at other purposes (*e.g.*, the committal proceedings in England and Wales).

As to the charging instruments, their form is determined by the particularities of each system. In some systems the prosecutor does not have a discretion whether or not to prosecute, at least for certain categories of offences (see, *inter alia*, Argentina, Germany, Italy).

B. *Trial*

As discussed in Chapter 1, it is increasingly difficult to describe any country's entire criminal justice system as "accusatorial" or "inquisitorial."[7] However, at the trial stage, the distinction can be fairly clearly made. Too briefly sketched: The adversarial trial is more or less seen as a contest between two equal parties, whereas the inquisitorial (or non-adversary) "trial" is dominated by the idea of an official inquiry into the objective truth. In general, the features of the adversarial trial are, on the one hand, clear in the systems of Canada, England and Wales, Israel, the U.S.A. and South Africa: the judge as a neutral arbiter while parties adduce evi-

7. Much progress in the theory of comparative analysis of systems of criminal procedure has been made thanks to publications of M.R. Damaska. See, *inter alia*, *Evidentiary Barriers to Convictions and Two Models of Criminal Procedure*, 121 U. Pa. L. Rev. 506 (1973), *Structures of Authority and Comparative Criminal Procedure*, 84 Yale L.J. 480 (1975), *The Faces of Justice and State Authority* (New Haven 1986). The distinction between co-ordinate and hierarchical models concentrates on the structures of authority. The main advantage of the distinction between hierarchical and co-ordinate over the traditional adversarial-inquisitorial dichotomy is that it furnishes more and better explanations of differences in systems. Whereas the adversarial-inquisitorial distinction focuses on the trial stage, in the co-ordinate-hierarchical distinction the whole criminal process, including the pretrial stage and sentencing, is covered. In my opinion, this distinction may be very illuminating—and encouraging—to readers not very familiar with comparative criminal procedure trying to come to grips with similarities and differences between legal systems. However, the problem in analyzing the systems discussed in this book against the background of that distinction is that there is not enough relevant information for this purpose included in the chapters. Some relevant points are discussed in, *e.g.*, the chapters on England and Wales, France, and Russia. Obviously, this is a consequence of the outline of the chapters, discussed earlier, that is not, aimed at eliciting that kind of information. Because, in my opinion, the distinction between the reactive state and the activist state is not very useful here, this distinction is also not discussed.

dence, the guilty plea making the taking of evidence redundant, the defendant who may be examined only at his will and, if so, only as a witness. A rare deviation from the model can be seen in South Africa, where the accused may be examined by the court after a plea of not guilty as to the basis of his defence in order to establish the issues. In addition, in contradistinction with many other common law systems, lays do not form a separate jury but—together with the professional judge—a mixed bench.[8]

On the other hand, typical civil law, inquisitorial features can be discerned in the trial procedures of Argentina, France Germany and Russia: The court searching for the objective truth, not restricted by a guilty plea of the defendant, generally examining witnesses extensively, having the power to order additional inquiries on its own motion, while the defendant may be interrogated as such. However, he is not sworn in as a witness nor is he required to answer the questions of the court or others. However, here too, some deviations from the model, mainly related to agreements between prosecution and defence, merit attention. In Argentina, the defendant may agree to summary adjudication of the case in exchange for a reduced sentence. In Germany, something has developed that is termed a German equivalent of plea bargaining (for some situations). In France, some proceedings have developed which save time, energy and costs and, to this extent, may be compared to plea bargaining. Most notably, in Italy the Code of Criminal Procedure 1989 introduced adversarial elements into a historically inquisitorial system, such as a form of plea bargaining and the taking of evidence at trial by the parties. That includes "bargaining as to the punishment."

Some other, partly related points merit attention. In only a few systems lays do not participate as members of the court in criminal cases. Of the systems discussed, courts in Argentina and Israel do not include lays.[9] Further, broadly speaking, the rights of the defendant at trial in all systems are similar. However, in several respects the Chinese system differs. Most notably, many criminal defendants are not represented by counsel. Israel also does not require counsel in all cases, including some with high sentences. However, it may be the case that, in practice, such defendants receive counsel as a matter of judicial discretion.

In many systems the victim may commence a prosecution (Argentina, China, England, France, Germany, Israel, South Africa). In some systems this power is restricted to certain categories of offences or subject to other restrictions. Where the victim has the right to participate in the proceedings, her role and position may differ.

C. Appeals

In general, the defendant has the power to appeal against adverse decisions by a court of first instance to a higher court. There are differences in the scope of the review by the appellate court — even within one system differences obtain — ranging from an appeal on legal points to a completely new trial. In several systems, after a negative decision of the appellate court further appeal may be open, mostly on narrower grounds.

---

8. It should be noted that courts in Israel do not have lays. In Russia, the recently introduced jury seems to have a position similar to the jury in common law systems.

9. As to the question whether there is a separate jury or a mixed bench see *infra*, par. 3.1.

In a number of systems, particularly common law systems, no appeal may be made by the prosecutor against an acquittal.

The South Africa system has a remarkable particularity: It provides for automatic review of decisions of less experienced judges.

The European Convention on Human Rights: A Sketch and a Tentative Comparison.[10]

Since it became effective in the '50ties the European Convention has substantially increased in importance as a source of law in criminal procedure. After a "slow start" the European Commission and European Court of human rights (ECHR)[11] took on the policy of deriving more and more detailed rules from the rather vague and broad provisions of the Convention, e.g., in a number of cases the European Court held member states to be in violation of the accused's right to be tried within a reasonable time; *inter alia*, unjustiable periods of inactivity of the authorities of 15 months and more in a case may lead to that conclusion.[12] Another example is the case law of the ECHR on art. 6(3)(d) of the Convention on the instances in which the accused has the right to be given an adequate opportunity to have witnesses examined against him. This case law has had major consequences for systems in which reports of the police including witness statements are used as an important source of evidence at trial.[13] The effects of the increasing importance of the European Convention are most strongly felt in legal systems in which the provisions of the Convention do not have to be transformed into national law but are directly applicable. This is true of the Netherlands and, of the systems discussed in this book, France.[14]

It would go beyond the aim and scope of this book to give a complete overview of the case law of the ECHR relevant to criminal procedure.[15] Moreover, inasfar as the procedural norms of the systems discussed are in conformity with the provisions of the Convention, that exercise would not be fruitful. And it would seem that at the abstract level criminal procedure has been discussed in the preceding chapters, that, generally speaking, the law of those systems conforms to the Convention. However, it should be noted that the ECHR does not review the national provisions of the member states in the abstract but assesses whether the way they were applied in individual cases conforms to the provisions of the Convention. For

10. To prevent misunderstandings it should be noted that the Convention is a product of the Council of Europe, not the European Union.

11. A recent protocol to the Convention provides for the merger of the Commission into the Court.

12. See, *e.g.*, ECHR 26 May 1993, A 248 (*Bunkate*). Until a few years ago the decisions of the ECHR were published separately as part of the Publications of the European Court of human rights, series A (cited as: A). The compilation of the decisions in *ECHR Reports*, to be published annually, proceeds only very slowly. Since May 1997 judgments of the ECHR have been published on internet (also try www.dhcour.coe.fr/eng/recent.htm), going back to October 1996. At that moment, publication in series A stopped.

13. See, extensively, the chapter on France.

14. Dutch courts are even much more prone to follow and apply decisions of the European Court than French courts.

15. See for recent handbooks, *inter alia*, J.A. Frowein, W. Peukert, Europäische MenschenRechtsKonvention, 2nd ed., Kehl 1996, D.J. Harris, M. O'Boyle, C. Warbrick, Law of the European Convention on Human Rights, London.

these reasons, it seems best to make some general remarks on the most important provisions of the Convention for the aspects of criminal procedure discussed in this book as construed by the ECHR and, inasfar as possible, to identify some points that may be more or less problematic from the perspective of the European Convention.

Art. 5 of the European Convention reads as follows:

1. Everyone has the right to liberty and security of person.
2. No one shall be deprived of his liberty save in the following cases and in accordance with a procedure prescribed by law:
   a. The lawful detention of a person after conviction by a competent court;
   b. the lawful arrest or detention of a person for noncompliance with the lawful order of a court or in order to secure the fulfilment of any obligation prescribed by law;
   c. the lawful arrest or detention of a person effected for the purpose of bringing him before the competent legal authority on reasonable suspicion of having committed an offence or when it is reasonably considered necessary to prevent his committing an offence or fleeing after having done so;
   d. the detention of a minor by lawful order for the purpose of educational supervision or his lawful detention for the purpose of bringing him before the competent legal authority;
   e. the lawful detention of persons for the prevention of the spreading of infectious diseases, of persons of unsound mind, alcoholics or drugs addicts, or vagrants;
   f. the lawful arrest or detention of a person to prevent his effecting an unauthorised entry into the country or of a person against whom action is being taken with a view to deportation or extradition.
2. Everyone who is arrested shall be informed promptly in a language which he understands, of the reasons for his arrest and of any charge against him.
3. Everyone arrested or detained in accordance with the provisions of paragraph 1c of this Article shall be brought promptly before a judge or other officer authorised by law to exercise judicial power and shall be entitled to trial within a reasonable time or to release pending trial.
4. Everyone who is deprived of his liberty by arrest or detention shall be entitled to take proceedings by which the lawfulness of his detention shall be decided speedily by a court and his release ordered if the detention is not lawful.
5. Everyone who has been the victim of arrest or detention in contravention of the provisions of this Article shall have an enforceable right to compensation.

The most important consequence of art. 5 for the aspects of criminal procedure discussed in this book is that a suspect[16] arrested must be brought promptly be-

---

16. As to the requirement of "reasonable suspicion" see, *inter alia*, ECHR 30 August 1990, A 182 (*Fox, Campbell, Hartley*), 28 October 1994, A 300 (*Murray*).

fore a judge or other officer authorised by law to exercise judicial power (art. 5(1)(c) and (3)). In a number of judgments the ECHR has defined "reasonable suspicion":

> [F]or there to be a reasonable suspicion there must be facts or information which would satisfy an objective observer that the person concerned may have committed a criminal offence. "At the very least the honesty and bona fides of a suspicion constitute one indispensable element of its reasonableness."[17]

It has not been exactly defined what "promptly" means. A suspect is in any case not brought before a judge "promptly," where the period since arrest amounts to four days and six hours.[18] For another officer than a judge to be termed "authorised by law to exercise judicial power" the officer has to meet certain requirements. *Inter alia*, he has to be competent to order the release of the defendant and hear the suspect personally, whereas he also has to be independent from the parties and from the executive.

> [T]he "officer" is not identical with the "judge" but must nevertheless have some of the latter's attributes, that is to say he must satisfy certain conditions each of which constitutes a guarantee for the person arrested.

The first of such conditions is independance of the executive and of the parties. ... This does not mean that the "officer" may not be to some extent subordinate to other judges or officers provided that they themselves enjoy similar independence.

In addition, under Art. 5 para. 3, there is both a procedural and a substantive requirement. The procedural requirement places the "officer" under the obligation of hearing himself the individual brought before him...; the substantive requirement imposes on him the obligation of reviewing the circumstances militating for or agianst detention, of deciding, by reference to legal criteria, whether there are reasons to justify detention and of ordering release if there are no such reasons..."[19]

The combination of requirements of art. 5(3) might present some problems in at least one system discussed, if the Convention would be used as a measure.

Art. 6 of the European Convention reads as follows:

1. In the determination of his civil rights and obligations or of any criminal charge against him, everyone is entitled to a fair and public hearing within a reasonable time by an independent and impartial tribunal established by law. Judgment shall be pronounced publicly but the press and public may be excluded from all or part of the trial in the interests of morals, public order or national security in a democratic society, when the interests of juveniles or the protection of the private life of the parties so require, or to the extent strictly necessary in the opinion of the court in special circumstances where publicity would prejudice the interests of justice.
2. Everyone charged with a criminal offence shall be presumed innocent until proved guilty according to law.

---

17. *Inter alia*, ECHR 28 October 1994, A 300 (*Murray*). See also ECHR 22 October 1997 (*Erdagoz*), 27 November 1997 (*K.F.*).
18. ECHR 29 November 1988, A 145 (*Brogan*).
19. ECHR 4 December 1979, A 34 (*Schiesser*). See also, *inter alia*, ECHR 22 May 1984, A 77–79 (*De Jong e.a.*).

3. Everyone charged with a criminal offence has the following minimum rights:
    a. To be informed promptly, in a language which he understands and in detail, of the nature and cause of the accusation against him;
    b. to have adequate time and facilities for the preparation of his defence; to defend himself in person or through legal assistance of his own choosing or, if he has not sufficient means to pay for legal assistance, to be given it free when the interests of justice so require;
    d. to examine or have examined witnesses against him and to obtain the attendance and examination of witnesses on his behalf under the same conditions as witnesses against him;
    e. to have the free assistance of an interpreter if he cannot understand or speak the language used in court.

From the notion of "fair trial" included in subsection (1) the ECHR has derived several rights in addition to the rights mentioned in subsections (2) and (3): *inter alia*, the right to equality of arms, the right to adversarial proceedings,[20] the right to consult one's lawyer privately[21], the right to attend one's trial.[22] The right to equality of arms and the right to adversarial proceedings imply, *inter alia*, that the defence and the prosecution must have the opportunity to gain knowledge of the materials adduced by the other party and to comment thereon.[23] The right to be tried in one's presence is in the opinion of the ECHR presupposed by the right to free assistance of an interpreter and the right to defend oneself in person. A trial *in absentia* may not be held without the accused having knowledge thereof, unless the accused waives his right in an unequivocal manner. According to the ECHR the right to a fair trial includes the privilege against compelled self-incrimination, in the terminology of the Court: "the right ... to remain silent and not to contribute to incriminating oneself."[24] In *Saunders*[25] the Court held:

> [T]he right to silence and the right not to incriminate oneself, are generally recognised international standards which lie at the heart of the notion of a fair procedure under Article 6. Their rationale lies, *inter alia*, in the protection of the accused against improper compulsion by the authorities thereby contributing to the avoidance of miscarriages of justice and to the fulfilment of the aims of Article 6 ... The right not to incriminate oneself, in particular, presupposes that the prosecution in a criminal case seeks to prove their case against the accused without resort to evidence obtained through methods of coercion or oppression in defiance of the will of the accused. In this sense the right is closely linked to the presumption of innocence contained in Article 6 para 2 of the Convention.

---

20. See, *e.g.*, ECHR 30 October 1991, A 214 (*Borgers*), 19 December 1989, A 168 (*Kamasinski*), 28 August 1991, A 211 (*Brandstetter*).

21. ECHR 28 November 1991, A 220 (*S. v. Switzerland*). This does need any clarification.

22. ECHR 12 February 1985 (*Colozza*).

23. In its judgment of 27 March 1998 (*K.D.B.*) the Court said that the right to adversarial proceedings means "in principle the opportunity for the parties to a criminal or civil trial to have knowledge of and comment on all evidence adduced or observations filed, even by an independent member of the national legal service, with a view to influencing the court's decision."

24. ECHR 25 February 1993, A 256 (*Funke*).

25. ECHR 17 December 1996.

This applies from the moment the suspect is charged in the sense of Art. 6 of the Convention (see *infra*). As to situations before the suspect is charged the privilege may imply that answers given as a result of a duty to provide information cannot be used as evidence in the ensuing criminal case against the suspect.[26] In one of the systems discussed the suspect seems to be obliged to speak. This would seem to contravene art. 6 of the Convention.

The privilege does not extend, the Court held in 1996 in *Saunders*, to the use in criminal proceedings of material which may be obtained from the accused through the use of compulsory powers but which has an existence independent of the will of the suspect. Examples are documents acquired pusuant to a warrant, breath, blood and urine samples, and bodily tissue for the purpose of DNA testing. However, this seems at variance with the holding in *Funke* that the accused's conviction in France for refusing to disclose documents asked for by the customs in that case contravened art. 6, even though the customs secured the conviction in order to obtain certain documents which they believed must exist, although they were not certain of the fact.[27]

In addition, the notion of a fair trial has a residual meaning: Even if no specific right is violated, it may be possible that the circumstances of the case are such that the trial cannot be regarded as fair. However, the notion of a fair trial does not imply detailed rules of evidence. According to the ECHR the assessment of the evidence is a matter for the national courts of the member states, except where the right to a fair trial is violated.[28] *E.g.*, the Court is of the opinion that "t]he public interest cannot justify the use of evidence obtained as a result of police incitement" (of persons not predisposed).[29] For this reason, there is no detailed body of European Convention law on the exclusion of unlawfully obtained evidence.

Of the other rights mentioned in art. 6(1) one has been mentioned before: The right to be tried within a reasonable time.[30] The period starts to run at the moment of the "charge." This general requirement for the applicability of art. 6(1) has been construed by the ECHR in extensive case law. It has been defined as "the official notification given to an individual by the competent authority of an allegation that he has committed a criminal offence," a definition that also corresponds to the test whether the situation of the suspect has been substantially affected.[31]It may be the day of the official notification, but also the date of arrest or the date of the first interrogation by the police. Some institutional delays in a number of countries may contribute—if added to possible other, more incidental delays—to a violation of this right (*e.g.* Russia).

---

26. ECHR 17 December 1996 (*Saunders*). See also the chapter on England and Wales.

27. ECHR 25 February 1993, A 256.

28. See, *inter alia*, ECHR 12 July 1988, A 140 (*Schenk*).

29. ECHR 9 June 1998 (*Teixeira de Castro*).

30. Other parts of art. 6(1) have lead to extensive case law as well. The requirement of impartiality has presented problems where the same persons have more or less different functions in criminal proceedings against the same defendant. See, *e.g.*, ECHR 24 May 1989, A 154 (*Hauschildt*).

31. See recently, *e.g.*, ECHR 22 May 1998 (*Hozee*). "Criminal" in "criminal charge" has been given by the Court an autonomous construction as well. Thus, the requirements of art. 6 may apply to proceedings which according to domestic law are regarded as disciplinary or administrative. e.g., sanctions imposed by administrative authorities may be termed to have a "criminal" nature in the sense of art. 6. See for the tests, *inter alia*, ECHR 24 February 1994, A 284 (*Bendenoun*), 24 September 1997 (*Garyfallou*), 21 October 1997 (*Bloch*).

The presumption of innocence (art. 6(2)), *inter alia*, means that an accused must not be treated as a convicted person before conviction. From this, the view of the author of the chapter on Russia may be supported; the accused during trial is kept in a cage contravenes the presumption. The ECHR distinguishes several (other) aspects of the presumption. An important aspect is that the burden of proof may not be shifted to the accused. However that does not mean that presumptions of fact in penal provisions are completely forbidden.

Art. 6 para. 2 does not ... regard presumptions of fact or of law provided for in the criminal law with indifference. It requires States to confine them within reasonable limits which take into account the importance of what is at stake and maintain the rights of the defence.[32]

Although, obviously, this formula needs further clarification, it has been argued that it would imply that strict liability offences are not compatible with art. 6(2) as construed by the Court.

Another aspect of the presumption of innocence is that it must not appear from a judicial decision that the accused is considered to be guilty of the offence charged, if the accused has not been convicted. Thus, the Court held that someone whose guilt had not been proved by the domestic court, could not be condemned to pay the costs.[33]

As to the rights mentioned in art. 6(3) the right to counsel is of particular interest. In combination with the right to a fair trial it applies not only at trial but also at the pretrial stage. In *Murray* the ECHR held that the suspect must be afforded the opportunity to consult his lawyer in the initial stages of police interrogation, where adverse inferences may be drawn at trial to silence the suspect during interrogation.[34] Depending on the evidential consequences of the position of the suspect during police questioning, this might mean that the Convention poses more stringent requirements for provision of counsel at the investigatory stage than many of the systems discussed.

Another interesting aspect of the case law of the ECHR on the right to counsel is that it includes a right to effective assistance of counsel. This means, *inter alia*, "that the competent national authorities are required ... to intervene .. if a failure by legal aid counsel to provide effective representation is manifest or sufficiently brought to their attention in some other way."[35] Accordingly, within these limits ineffective assistance of counsel may be a grounds for an appellate court to quash a decision.

Of particular interest in art. 6(3) are also the right of the accused to examine witnesses against him[36] and the right to free assistance of an interpreter. In *Kamasinski*[37] the Court made some important remarks on this right, which is rapidly

32. ECHR 7 October 1988, A 141 (*Salabiaku*).

33. ECHR 25 March 1983, A 62 (*Minelli*). See also, *inter alia*, ECHR 25 August 1987, A 123 (*Lutz*), 25 August 1993, A 266 (*Sekanina*).

34. ECHR 8 February 1996 (*Murray*). "To deny access to a lawyer for the first 48 hours of police questioning, in a situation where the rights of the defence may well be irretrievably prejudiced, is—whatever the justification for such denial—incompatible with the rights of the accused under Article 6."

35. See, *e.g.*, ECHR 19 December 1989, A 168 (*Kamasinski*), 21 April 1998 (*Daud*).

36. Mentioned *supra* and discussed extensively in the chapter on French criminal procedure.

37. ECHR 19 December 1989, A 168.

increasing in importance since more and more defendants do not speak the official language of countries in which they are prosecuted.

> The right ... to free assistance of an interpreter applies not only to oral statements made at the trial hearing but also to documentary material and the pretrial proceedings. Para. 3(e) signifies that a person "charged with a criminal offence" who cannot understands or speak the language used in court has the right to the free assistance of an interpreter for the translation or interpretation of all documents or statements in the proceedings instituted against him which it is necessary for him to understand or to have rendered into the court's language in order to have the benefit of a fair trial.

However, para. 3(e) does not go so far as to require a written translation of all items of written evidence or official documents in the procedure. The interpretation assistance provided should be such as to enable the defendant to have knowledge of the case against him and to defend himself, notably by being able to put before the court his version of the events."

Art. 8 of the European Convention reads as follows:

1. Everyone has the right to respect for his private and family life, his home and his correspondence.
2. There shall be no interference by a public authority with the exercise of this right except such as is in accordance with the law and is necessary in a democratic society in the interests of national security, public safety or the economic well-being of the country, for the prevention of disorder or crime, for the protection of health or morals, or for the protection of the rights and freedoms of others.

In the context of criminal procedure this article has proved to be relevant for all kinds of invasions of privacy. Until now, it has not lead to an extensive and detailed case law of the ECHR.[38] However, some general points have become clear.

The concept of "private life" includes not only searches of places[39] and wiretapping.[40] The ECHR supports a very broad notion of private life, that includes not only evidently private matters but also certain aspects of business activities.

> Respect for private life must also comprise to a certain degree the right to establish and develop relationships with other human beings. There appears, furthermore, to be no reason of principle why this understanding of the notion of 'private life' should be taken to exclude activities of a professional or business nature since it is, after all, in the course of their working lives that the majority of people have a significant, if not the greatest, opportunity of developing relationships with the outside world.[41]

This position lead the ECHR to the conclusion in the case at hand that a search in the office of a lawyer amounted to a violation of the right comprised by art. 8(1) of the Convention.

---

38. This is partly caused by the margin of appreciation left to the member states, discussed *infra*.
39. See, *e.g.*, ECHR 16 December 1992, A 251 (*Niemietz*).
40. See, *e.g.*, ECHR 24 April 1990, A 176 (*Kruslin, Huvig*). The Court also held that telephone calls made from business premises may be covered by the notion of private life; ECHR 25 June 1997 (*Halford*). See also the chapters on France and England and Wales.
41. See ECHR 16 December 1992, A 251 (*Niemietz*).

Although the concept of privacy is given a broad interpretation, there are certain limits to it. In the context of criminal procedure this becomes clear where undercover operations of the police are concerned. In *Ludi*[42] the Court said:

> The aim of the operation was to arrest the dealers when the drugs were handed over. Toni thereupon contacted the applicant, who said he was prepared to sell him 2 kg of cocaine .... Mr. Ludi must therefore have been aware from then on that he was engaged in a criminal act punishable under ... and that consequently he was running the risk of encountering an undercover police officer whose task would in fact be to expose him.

Obviously, this reasoning does not apply literally to searches and seizures, for otherwise art. 8 would lose its meaning for coercive powers completely.

The approach followed by the ECHR where it is submitted that there was a violation of art. 8 in an individual case, merits some attention. First, it has to established whether there has been an interference with the right included in subsection (1). Second, if so, the question arises whether the violation is justified on the basis of subsection (2). This question is answered on the basis of several more specific questions. First, it is to be determined whether the interference was in accordance with the law. This means not only that the interference must have some basis in domestic law but also that the law in question should be "accessible to the person concerned, who must moreover be able to foresee its consequences for him, and compatible with the rule of law." That implies that the domestic law should indicate with sufficient clarity the scope and manner of exercise of the authorities' discretion in the manner. This condition is not met, when, *e.g.*, a wiretap is based on a general provision empowering the investigating judge to do everything he deems necessary.[43] Second, it is to be determined whether there was a legitimate aim as mentioned in art. 8(2) of the Convention, for the interference. The investigation and prosecution of offences are included by the aims mentioned in art. 8(2). Third, the interference must have been necessary in a democratic society. This means that there should be a pressing social need for the interference and, in particular, that it is proportionate to the legitimate aim pursued. In the context of criminal procedure, this means that searches and seizures must be proportionate to the aim pursued.[44] Although on the one hand the Court leaves to the member states a certain margin of appreciation in assessing the need for an interference, on the other hand it emphasizes "European supervision" and it adds that the restrictions of art. 8(2) are interpreted narrowly. Whereas the national legislators may legitimately deem searches and seizures necessary in the investigation of offences, the Court stresses that the relevant legislation and practice must afford adequate and effective safeguards against abuse.[45] Some examples of cases in which the Court held interferences with privacy not proportionate may illustrate how this is applied.

> In *Niemietz, supra*, the Court reasoned: "It is true that the offence in connection with which the search was effected, involving as it did not only an insult to but also an atempt to bring pressure on a judge, cannot be classified as more than minor. On the other hand, the warrant was drawn in broad terms, in that

42. ECHR 15 June 1992, A 238.

43. See, *e.g.*, ECHR 24 April 1990, A 176 (*Kruslin, Huvig*). See also, *e.g.*, ECHR 25 June 1997 (*Halford*), 25 March 1998 (*Kopp*).

44. See, *e.g.*, ECHR 16 December 1992, A 251 (*Niemietz*).

45. See, *e.g.*, ECHR 25 February 1993, A 256 (*Funke*).

it ordered a search for and seizure of "documents," without any limitation, revealing the identity of the author of the offensive letter; this point is of special significance where, as in Germany, the search of a lawyer's office is not accompanied by any special procedural safeguards, such as the presence of an independent observer. More importantly, having regard to the materials that were in fact inspected, the search impinged on professional secrecy to an extent that appears disproportionate in the circumstances; it has, in this connection, to be recalled that, where a lawyer is involved, an encroachment on professional secrecy may have repercussions on the proper administration of justice and hence on the rights guaranteed by Art. 6 of the Convention. In addition, the attendant publicity must have been capable of affecting adversely the applicant's professional reputation, in the eyes both of his existing clients and of the public at large."

In *Funke*, *supra*, the ECHR, *inter alia*, said: "the custom authorities had very wide powers; in particular, they had exclusive competence to assess the expediency, number, length and scale of inspections. Above all, in the absence of any requirement of a judicial warrant the restrictions and conditions provided for in law ... appear too lax and full of loopholes for the interferences with the applicant's rights to have been strictly proportionate to the legitimate aim pursued."[46]

On the basis of the availabe information it is hard to assess whether search and seizure law as applied in the systems discussed in this book would in all respects conform to the measure of art. 8 of the Convention.[47]

Conclusion

In spite of certain limitations discussed above, this book is a valuable contribution to comparative criminal procedure. It provides a wealth of information on a large number of systems for readers interested in the law and practice of criminal procedure of the systems discussed.[48]

A final remark as to the influences of some systems on others. It would seem that—probably partly due to the common language—the similarities among common law systems are stronger than those among civil law systems. In some respects certain common law systems may have influenced changes in civil law systems rather than the reverse. Also, the European Convention on human rights and the case law of the ECHR have contributed to an increase in the level of adversariality in some civil law systems.[49]

46. See for further examples, *inter alia*, ECHR 6 September 1978, A 28 (*Klass*), 16 December 1997 (*Camenzind*).

47. *E.g.*, it seems that the United States does not impose a proportionality principle.

48. For a recent book covering fewer systems, *e.g.*, J. Hatchard e.a. (eds.), *Comparative Criminal Procedure*, London 1996.

49. More in general, it seems that partly due the influence of human rights treaties there may be some convergence of systems with different models. See, *e.g.*, C. Harding e.a. (eds.), *Criminal Justice in Europe: A Comparative Study*, Oxford 1995.

Contributors

Craig M. Bradley (United States and Editor), James Louis Calamaras Professor at Indiana University School of Law—Bloomington. A.B. 1967, University of North Carolina; J.D., 1970, University of Virginia. Attorney Criminal Appellate Section, U.S. Department of Justice, D.C., 1970–72; Assistant U.S. Attorney, D.C., 1972–75; Clerk, Justice William Rehnquist, U.S. Supreme Court, D.C., 1975–76; Sr. Trial Attorney Public Integrity Section, Criminal Division, U.S. Department of Justice, D.C. 1976–78; Visiting Associate Professor, University of North Carolina, 1978–79; Associate Professor, Indiana University School of Law—Bloomington, 1979–85, Professor since 1985; Alexander von Humboldt Fellow, Max Planck Institute for Criminal Law, Freiburg, Germany, 1982; Institute for International Law, Kiel Germany 1992; Fulbright Senior Scholar, Australian National University, Canberra, Australia, 1989. He is the author of *The Failure of the Criminal Procedure Revolution* (1993) as well as numerous articles on American and comparative criminal procedure.

Alejandro D. Carrió (Argentina), Professor of Law, University of Buenos Aires; LL.B., Buenes Aires University, 1976, Master of Law, Louisiana State University Law School, 1982; Advisor to the *Consejo de la Consolidación de la Democracia*, a committee created by Presidential appointment, in order to propose a major reform of the Argentine Consitution, 1986; Practicing member of the Bar in Buenos Aires since 1977.

David J. Feldman (England and Wales), Barber Professor of Jurisprudence in the University of Birmingham since 1992, and is Head of the School of Law since 1997. Previously he was lecturer, then Reader, in Law at the University of Bristol (1976–92), and Visiting Fellow at the Faculty of Law, Australian National University for two semesters in 1989. Working mainly in the fields of public law (including comparative constitutional law), civil liberties, and criminal procedure, his main published works include *The Law Relating to Entry, Search and Seizure* (London, 1986); *Criminal Confiscation Orders* (London, 1986; new edition forthcoming, 1997); *Civil Liberties and Human Rights in England and Wales* (Oxford, 1993); and (ed., with Frank Meisel) *Corporate and Commercial Law: Modern Developments* (London, 1996).

Richard S. Frase (France), Benjamin N. Berger Professor of Criminal Law, at the University of Minnesota Law School. He has also taught four times in French and German law schools, under Minnesota's international exchange program. Professor Frase is the author of five books and over twenty-five articles on criminal justice topics, and is a frequent contributor to local and national news stories and programs related to issues of contemporary criminal justice. His principal current research interests are sentencing reform (especially sentencing guidelines in Minnesota and in other states) and comparative criminal justice (especially the French and German systems).

Alejandro M. Garro (Argentina), Adjunct Professor o f Law at Columbia University and Senior Research Scholar of the Parker School of Foreign and Comparative Law. He was educated in Argentina, where he received his law degree and practiced civil and commercial law. He received his LL.M. from Louisiana State University of Law and his J.S.D. from Columbia University. He was Assistant Professor at Louisiana State University, then joined Columbia Law School in 1981. Garro was a Collaborateur Scientifique at the Swiss Insititute of Comparative Law from 1983–1985. He is admitted to practice in Buenos Aires, Madrid, and New York.

Eliahu Harnon (Israel), Sylvan M. Cohen Professor of Law, Hebrew University of Jerusalem; Dr. Jur. (1963). Member of the Law Commission for the Reform of the Law of Criminal Procedure, The Israeli Ministry of Justice (as of 1969). Formerly: Director of the Institute of Criminology (1975–77); Director of the Harry Sacher Institute for Legislative Research and Comparative Law, Hebrew University of Jerusalem (1987–90); Fulbright Scholar and Bicentennial Fellow in Criminal Law and Administration at University of Pennsylvania School of Law (1965–66); Visiting Professor, New York University School of Law (1978–79); Visiting Professor at Chuo University in Japan (1987). Authored a two-volume treatise on the Israeli Law of Evidence, co-authored a book on Plea Bargaining, and published numerous articles in the area of evidence and criminal procedure.

Johannes A.W. Lensing (General Comments), Judge, district court at Arnhem in the Netherlands. Previously, senior lecturer in criminal law and procedure at the Catholic University of Nijmegen, teaching, inter alia, international criminal law, comparative criminal law and procedure and English/American criminal law. Between 1981 and 1992 he was senior lecturer at the State University of Limburg in the Netherlands and part-time judge at the district court in Maastricht. He has been the (co-)author of several books in Dutch, inter alia, concerning the interrogation of the accused (1988), on the influence of the European Convention on human rights on Dutch criminal procedure (1988), on pre-trial investigation in several foreign countries (1990), on principles of criminal procedure (1993), on punitive damages (1994), on American substantive criminal law (1996). In addition, he published many articles, some of which in English, on various subjects of criminal law and procedure. In most of his publications a comparative law approach is followed.

Catherine Newcombe (Russia), LLB (McGill), BA (Amherst). Attorney with the American Bar Associations's Central and East European Law Initiative (ABA/CEELI) where she works on the DOJ/CEELI Criminal Law Reform Project, a partnership between the U.S. Department fo Justice and ABA/CEELI focused on crime and Corruption in Central/Eastern Europe and the former Soviet Union.

Kent W. Roach (Canada), Professor of Law, University of Toronto. Formerly, Associate Professor of Law and Criminology at the University of Toronto. He received an LL.M. from Yale University and served as Law Clerk to Madam Justice Bertha Wilson of the Supreme Court of Canada. He is the author of two books,

Constitutional Remedies in Canada and *Criminal Law*, as well as the co-editor of *Cases and Materials on Criminal Law and Procedure* and *Canadian Criminal Cases*. He has also published numerous articles on various issues concerning criminal justice, criminal law and constitutional law.

Pamela J. Schwikkard (South Africa), BA (Witswatergrand) LLB, LL.M. (Natal), is a Senior Lecturer at the University of Natal, Pietermaritzburg in South Africa where she lectures courses on evidence and conflict resolution. She is a co-author of *Principles of Evidence* (Juta 1997) and *Woman and the Law* (HSRC 1994). She has contributed to a number of books and journals mainly in the area of criminal procedure, evidence and popular justice. She is an editor of the *South African Journal of Criminal Justice*. Ms Schwikkard is also an attorney of the Supreme Court of South Africa.

Alex Stein (Israel), LL.B. (1983); LL.M. (1987) (Hebrew University of Jerusalem); Ph.D. (1990) (University of London); Senior Lecturer, Faculty of Law, Hebrew University of Jerusalem (as of 1991). Visiting Professor of Law, Benjamin N. Cardozo School of Law (Spring, 1995–96); Visiting Professor of Law, University of Miami School of Law (1994–95). Member of the Advisory Board, *International Journal of Evidence & Proof* (Blackstone Press, London) (as of 1996). Member of the Law Commission for the Reform of the Law of Criminal Procedure, The Israeli Ministry of Justice (as of 1992). Edited *Evidence & Proof*, Vol. XI in the *International Library of Essays in Legal Theory* (New York University Press, 1992).

Rachel A. Van Cleave (Italy), Assistant Professor at Texas Tech. B.A., 1986 (Stanford), J.D., 1989 (Cal Hastings), J.S.M., 1994 (Stanford). Associate Managing Editor, Hastings L.J. *Admitted*: CA, 1989. Clerk, Honorable Sam D. Johnson, U.S.C.A., 5th Cir., Austin, TX 1989–90; Teaching Fellow, Stanford, 1992–94; Visiting Assistant Professor, Richmond, 1994–95; Assistant Professor, Texas Tech since 1995. Fulbright Resident Scholar, Italian Constitutional Court, Rome, fall 1996.

Stephan E. van der Merwe (South Africa), Obtained the B Juris degree from the University of Port Elizabeth in 1973, the LL B degree from the University of South Africa in 1975 and the LL D degree from the University of Cape Town in 1988. In 1989 he was appointed professor of law in the Department of Public Law, Faculty of Law, University of Stellenbosch, where he lectures on criminal procedure, law of evidence, common law crimes and aspects of legal professional ethics. He co-authored *Plea Procedures in Summary Criminal Trials* (Butterworths, 1983); *Privilegies in die Bewysreg* (Butterworths, 1984); *Commentary on the Criminal Procedure Act* (Juta & Co, 1987) and *Principles of Evidence* (Juta & Co, 1997). Prof van der Merwe has also contributed to books on social welfare law and criminal law and serves on the editorial board of the *South African Journal of Criminal Justice*.

Richard Vogler (Spain), Senior Lecturer in Law, Centre for Legal Studies, University of Sussex, U.K., where he has taught since 1987. He worked as a Solicitor in criminal practice since 1977 and obtained a Doctorate from the Institute of Criminology at the University of Cambridge in 1984. He has worked as a legal adviser for the charity "Prisoners Abroad" and has published in the areas of public order, the magistracy and continental criminal justice systems.

Liling Yue (China), Professor at the China University of Political Science and Law, Beijing and also serves as Deputy Director of the Criminal Aid Center of the Ministry of Justice. She was an Alexander von Humboldt scholar at the Max Planck Institute for Criminal Law in Freiburg, Germany, 1995–96.

Index

Please note: This index is based on the original chapter outline presented to each author. Each chapter will have the same main headings (e.g., §II A3 "Arrests"), but due to differences in the law of the various countries, not all chapters will contain the same subheadings (e.g., §II A3a "Arrest Warrants").